T0190171

Communications
in Computer and Information Science   1035

Commenced Publication in 2007
Founding and Former Series Editors:
Phoebe Chen, Alfredo Cuzzocrea, Xiaoyong Du, Orhun Kara, Ting Liu,
Krishna M. Sivalingam, Dominik Ślęzak, Takashi Washio, and Xiaokang Yang

More information about this series at http://www.springer.com/series/7899

K. C. Santosh · Ravindra S. Hegadi (Eds.)

Recent Trends in Image Processing and Pattern Recognition

Second International Conference, RTIP2R 2018
Solapur, India, December 21–22, 2018
Revised Selected Papers, Part I

 Springer

Editors
K. C. Santosh
Department of Computer Science
University of South Dakota
Vermillion, SD, USA

Ravindra S. Hegadi
Solapur University
Solapur, India

ISSN 1865-0929   ISSN 1865-0937 (electronic)
Communications in Computer and Information Science
ISBN 978-981-13-9180-4   ISBN 978-981-13-9181-1 (eBook)
https://doi.org/10.1007/978-981-13-9181-1

This Springer imprint is published by the registered company Springer Nature Singapore Pte Ltd.
The registered company address is: 152 Beach Road, #21-01/04 Gateway East, Singapore 189721, Singapore

Preface

It is our great pleasure to introduce the collection of research papers in the *Communication in Computer and Information Science* (CCIS) Springer series from the second Biennial International Conference on Recent Trends in Image Processing and Pattern Recognition (RTIP2R). The RTIP2R conference event took place at the Solapur University, Maharastra, India, during December 21–22, 2018, in collaboration with the Department of Computer Science, University of South Dakota (USA) and Universidade de Evora (Portugal). Further, the conference had a very successful workshop titled Pattern Analysis and Machine Intelligence (PAMI): Document Engineering to Healthcare, with more than 70 participants.

As announced in the Call For Paper, RTIP2R attracted current and/or recent research on image processing, pattern recognition, and computer vision with several different applications, such as document understanding, biometrics, medical imaging, and image analysis in agriculture. Altogether, we received 371 submissions and accepted 173 papers based on our thorough review reports. We followed a double-blind submission policy and therefore the review process was extremely solid. On average, there were at least three reviews per paper except the few that had desk rejections, and therefore we had 859 review reports. We also made the authors aware of plagiarism, and rejected a few of them even after making review reports.

During the event, we hosted more than 200 participants from more than 29 different countries, such as USA, Vietnam, Australia, Russia and Sri Lanka (not just limited to India). In brief, the event was found to be a great platform bringing together research scientists, academics, and industry practitioners throughout the world. We categorized the papers into five different tracks: (a) computer vision and applications; (b) machine learning and applications; (c) document analysis; (d) healthcare and medical imaging; (e) biometrics and applications; (f) data mining, information retrieval and applications; (g) image processing; and (h) image analysis in agriculture.

We also selected the best papers based on the review reports, review scores, and presentations at the conference, and provided authors an opportunity to publish their extended works in the following journals: (a) *Multimedia Tools and Applications* (Springer); (b) *International Journal of Ambient Computing and Intelligence* (IGI Global); and (c) *Journal of Healthcare Informatics Research* (Springer).

The conference event was full of new ideas, including keynote speeches that were from (a) Sameer Antani, National Institutes of Health; (b) Mohan Gundeti, University of Chicago Medicine; and (c) Ernest Cachia, University of Malta.

April 2019

K. C. Santosh
Ravindra S. Hegadi

Organization

Patron

M. M. Fadnavis

Organizing Chairs

V. B. Ghute
V. B. Patil
B. C. Shewale

Honorary Chairs

P. Nagabhushan   IIIT, Allahabad, India
P. S. Hiremath   KLE University, Hubballi, India
B. V. Dhandra   Symbiosis University, India

General Chairs

Jean-Marc Ogier   University of la Rochelle, France
Laurent Wendling   University of Paris Descartes, France
Sameer Antani   US National Library of Medicine, USA
D. S. Guru   University of Mysore, India

Conference Chairs

Ravindra Hegadi   Solapur University, India
Teresa Goncalves   Universidade de Evora, Portugal
K. C. Santosh   University of South Dakota, USA

Area Chairs

Szilard Vajda   Central Washington University, USA
Mickael Coustaty   University of La Rochelle, France
Nibaran Das   Jadavpur University, India
Nilanjan Dey   Techno India College of Technology, India
Jude Hemanth   Karunya University, India

Publicity Chairs

Hubert Cecotti	California State University, USA
Odemir Martinez Bruno	University of Sao Paulo, Brazil
Alba Garcia Seco de Herrera	University of Essex, UK
Sheng-Lung Peng	National Dong Hwa University, Taiwan
Do T. Ha	VNU University of Science, Vietnam
B. Uyyanonvara	Thammasat University, Thailand
Sk Md. Obaidullah	University of Evora, Portugal
V. Bevilacqua	Polytechnic of Bari, Italy
R. S. Mente	Solapur University, India
Pratim P. Roy	Indian Institute of Technology (IIT), India
Manjunath T. N.	BMSIT, Bangalore, India
Nadra Ben Romdhane	University of Sfax, Tunisia
M. A. Jabbar	Vardhaman College of Engineering, India

Finance Chairs

A. R. Shinde	Solapur University, Solapur, India
S. D. Raut	Solapur University, Solapur, India

Advisory Committee

Daniel P. Lopresti	Lehigh University, USA
Rangachar Kasturi	University of South Florida, USA
Sargur N. Srihari	CEDAR, USA
K. R. Rao	University of Texas at Arlington, USA
Ishwar K. Sethi	Oakland University, USA
G. K. Ravikumar	CVS Health/Wipro, Texas, USA
Jose Flores	University of South Dakota, USA
Rajkumar Buyya	University of Melbourne, Australia
Arcot Sowmya	UNSW, Sydney, Australia
Antanas Verikas	Halmstad University, Sweden
Diego Liberati	Politecnico di Milano, Italy
B. B. Chaudhuri	Indian Statistical Institute, Kolkata, India
Atul Negi	University of Hyderabad, India
Arun Agarwal	University of Hyderabad, India
Hemanth Kumar	University of Mysore, India
K. V. Kale	Dr. BAMU, Aurangabad, India
B. V. Pawar	NMU, Jalgaon, India
R. R. Deshmukh	Dr. BAMU, Aurangabad, India
Karunakar A. K.	MIT, Manipal, India
Suryakanth Gangashetty	IIIT Hyderabad, India
Kaushik Roy	West Bengal University, India
Mallikajrun Hangarge	KASCC, Bidar, India
T. Devi	Bharathiar University, Coimbatore, India

G. R. Sinha	IIIT, Bangalore, India
U. P. Kulkarni	SDMCE, Dharwad, India
Rajendra Hegadi	IIIT, Dharwad, India
S. Basavarajappa	IIIT, Dharwad, India
B. P. Ronge	SVERI'S College of Engineering, India

Technical Program Committee (Country-Wise)

Randy C. Hoover	South Dakota School of Mines and Technology, USA
Sivarama Krishnan Rajaraman	US National Library of Medicine, NIH, USA
Yao-Yi Chiang	University of Southern California - LA, USA
Ullas Bagci	University of Central Florida, USA
Yuhlong Lio	University of South Dakota, USA
Eugene Borovikov	Intelligent Automation Inc., USA
Szilard Vajda	Central Washington University, USA
Hubert Cecotti	California State University, USA
Sema Candemir	US National Library of Medicine, NIH, USA
Md Mahmudur Rahman	Morgan State University, USA
Gabriel Picioroaga	University of South Dakota, USA
Peter Dolan	University of Minnesota Morris, USA
Michael Clement	York University, Canada
Alba Garca Seco de Herrera	University of Essex, UK
Nico Hochgeschwender	University of Luxembourg, Luxembourg
Benoit Naegel	University of Strasbourg, France
Vincent Bombardier	CRAN, University of Lorraine, France
Isabelle Debled-Rennesson	LORIA, University of Lorraine, France
Camille Krutz	University Institutes of Technology (IUT de Paris), France
Jean Cousty	University Paris-Est, France
Jonathan Weber	University of Haute-Alsace, France
Sabine Barrat	University of Tours, France
Muhammad Muzzamil Luqman	University of La Rochelle, France
Mickael Coustaty	University of La Rochelle, France
Jean-Pierre Salmon	University of Bordeaux Montaigne, France
Victor Codocedo	University de Lyon, CNRS, INSA-Lyyon, France
Diego Liberati	Politecnico di Milano, Italy
Vitoantonio Bevilacqua	Polytechnic of Bari, Italy
Salim Jouili	Euro Nova, Belgium
Paulo Quaresma	University of Evora, Portugal
Luis Rato	University of Evora, Portugal
Joao Barroso	University of Tras-os-Montes e Alto Douro, Portugal
Vitor M Filipe	University of Tras-os-Montes e Alto Douro, Portugal
Mohamed-Rafik Bouguelia	Halmstad University, Sweden
Marcal Rusinol	Universitat Autonoma de Barcelona, Spain

Margit Antal	Sapientia University, Romania
Laszlo Szilagyi	Sapientia University, Romania
Srikanta Pal	Griffith University, Australia
Alireza Alaei	Griffith University, Australia
M. Cerda Villablanca	University of Chile, Chile
B. Uyyanonvara	SIIT, Thammasat University, Thailand
V. Sornlertlamvanich	Thammasat University, Thailand
S. Marukatat	Thammasat University, Thailand
I. Methasate	NECTEC, Thailand
C. Pisarn	Rangsit University, Thailand
Makoto Hasegawa	Tokyo Denki University, Japan
P. Shivakumara	University of Malaya, Malaysia
Sophea Prum	National R&D Center in ICT, Malaysia
Lalit Garg	University of Malta, Malta
Nadra Ben Romdhane	University of Sfax, Tunisia
Nafaa Nacereddine	Centre de Recherche en Techno. Industrielles (CRTI), Algeria
Aicha Baya Goumeidane	Centre de Recherche en Techno. Industrielles (CRTI), Algeria
Ameni Boumaiza	Qatar foundation, Qatar
Nguyen Thi Oanh	Hanoi University of Science Technology, Vietnam
Do Thanh Ha	VNU University of Science, Vietnam
Tien-Dat Nguyen	FPT Corp., Vietnam
T. Kartheeswaran	University of Jaffna, Sri Lanka
Shaikh A. Fattah	Bangladesh University of Engineering and Technology, Bangladesh
Pratim P. Roy	Indian Institute of Techno (IIT), India
Surekha Borra	KS Institute of Technology, (KSIT), India
Ajit Danti	JNN College of Engineering, Shimoga, India
Lalita Rangarajan	University of Mysore, Mysore, India
Manjaiah D. H.	Mangalore University, Mangalore, India
V. S. Malemath	KLE Engineering College, Belagavi, India
B. H. Shekar	Mangalore University, Mangalore, India
G. Tippeswamy	BMSIT, Bangalore, India
Aziz Makandar	Akkamahadevi Women's University Karnataka, Vijayapura, India
Mallikarjun Holi	BDT College of Engineering, Davangere, India
S. S. Patil	Agriculture University, Bangalore, India
H. S. Nagendraswamy	University of Mysore, Mysore, India
Shivanand Gornale	Ranichannamma University, Belagavi, India
S. Shivashankar	Karnatak University, Dharwad, India
Ramesh K.	Akkamahadevi Women's University Karnataka, Vijayapura, India
H. L. Shashirekha	Mangalore University, Mangalore, India
Dayanand Savakar	Ranichannamma University, Belagavi, India
S. B. Kulkarni	SDM College of Engineering, Dharwad, India

M. T. Somashekhar	Bangalore University, Bangalore, India
Manjunath Hiremath	Christ University, Bangalore, India
Sridevi Soma	PDA College of Engineering, Gulbarga, India
V. M. Thakare	SGB Amravati University, Amaravati, India
G. V. Chaudhari	SRTM University, Nanded, India
R. K. Kamat	Shivaji University, Kolhapur, India
Ambuja Salgaonkar	University of Mumbai, India
Praveen Yannavar	Dr. BAM University, India
R. R. Manza	Dr. BAM University, Aurangabad, India
A. S. Abhyankar	SP Pune University, India
V. T. Humbe	SRTMU Sub-Centre, Latur, India
P. B. Khanale	SRTMU, Nanded, India
M. B. Kokre	GGSIET, Nanded, India
Gururaj Mukrambi	Symbiosis International University, Pune, India
S. R. Kolhe	North Maharashtra University, Jalgaon, India
M. Sundaresan	Bharathiar University, Coimbatore, India
C. P. Sumathi	SDNBV College for Women, Chennai, India
J. Satheeshkumar	Bharathiar University, Coimbatore, India
Britto Ramesh Kumar	St. Joseph's College, Tiruchirappalli, India
Neeta Nain	Malaviya National Institute of Technology (MNIT), Jaipur, India
A. A. Desai	Veer Narmad South Gujarat University, Gujarat, India
Chandra Mouli P. V. S. S. R.	VIT University, Vellore, India
Nagartna Hegde	Vasavi Eng. College, Hyderabad, India
B. Gawali	Dr. BAM University, Aurangabad, India
K. T. Deepak	IIIT, Dharwad, India
P. M. Pawar	SVERI'S College of Eng., India
S. R. Gengaje	Walchand Inst. of Technology, Solapur, India
B. Ramadoss	National Inst. of Technology, Tamil Nadu, India

Local Organizers

P. Prabhakar	C. G. Gardi
S. S. Suryavanshi	P. M. Kamble
V. B. Ghute	D. D. Sawat
R. B. Bhosale	A. B. Jagtap
B. J. Lokhande	D. D. Ruikar
G. S. Kamble	P. P. Gaikwad
J. D. Mashale	

Additional Reviewers

Abdullah Mohammed Kaleem
Abhinav Muley
Addepalli Krishna
Adithya Pediredla
Aditya Patil
Ajay Nagne
Ajeet A. Chikkamannur
Ajit Danti
Ajju Gadicha
Akbaruddin Shaikh
Alba García Seco De Herrera
Alessia Saggese
Alexandr Ezhov
Almas Siddiqui
Ambika Annavarapu
Amol Vibhute
Amruta Jagtap
Anagha Markandey
Anderson Santos
Andrés Rosso-Mateus
Aniket Muley
Anita Dixit
Anita Khandizod
Anitha H.
Anitha J.
Anitha N.
Ankita Dhar
Anupriya Kamble
Archana Nandibewoor
Arjun Mane
Arunkumar K. L.
Ashish Mourya
Atish Patel
Aznul Qalid Md Sabri
Balachandran K.
Balaji Sontakke
Balamurugan Karnan
Basavaprasad B.
Basavaraj Dhandra
Bb Patil
Benoit Naegel
Bharath Bhushan
Bharathi Pilar

Bharatratna Gaikwad
Bhausaheb Pawar
Bindu V. R.
Brian Keith
C. Namrata Mahender
C. P. Sumathi
Camille Kurtz
Chandrashekhara K. T.
Chetan Pattebahadur
Daneshwari Mulimani
Daniel Caballero
Darshan Ruikar
Dattatray Sawat
Dericks Shukla
Diego Bertolini
Diego Liberati
Dnyaneshwari Patil
E. Naganathan
Ebenezer Jangam
Evgeny Kostyuchenko
G. P. Hegde
G. R. Sinha
G. S. Mamatha
Ganesh Janvale
Ganesh Magar
Ganga Holi
Gireesh Babu
Girish Chowdhary
Gururaj Mukarambi
H. L. Shashirekha
Hajar As-Suhbani
Hanumant Gite
Haripriya V.
Harshavardhana Doddamani
Hayath Tm
Hemavathy R.
Himadri Mukherjee
Hubert Cecotti
Ignazio Gallo
Jayendra Kumar
João Cardia
Jonathan Weber
Joseph Abraham Sundar K.

Jude Hemanth
Jyoti Patil
K. K. Chaturvedi
K. C. Santosh
Kalman Palagyi
Kalpana Thakare
Kapil Mehrotra
Kartheeswaran Thangathurai
Kasturi Dewi Varathan
Kaushik Roy
Kavita S. Oza
Kiran Phalke
Kwankamon Dittakan
Laszlo Szilagyi
Latchoumi Thamarai
Lingdong Kong
Lorenzo Putzu
Lp Deshmukh
Lucas Alexandre Ramos
Luis Rato
M. T. Somashekhar
Madhu B.
Mahesh Solankar
Mahmudur Rahman
Mainak Sen
Maizatul Akmar Ismail
Mallikarjun Hangarge
Mallikarjun Holi
Manasi Baheti
Manisha Saini
Manjunath Hiremath
Manjunath T. N.
Manohar Madgi
Manoj Patil
Mansi Subhedar
Manza Ramesh
Marçal Rusiñol
Margit Antal
Masud Rana Rashel
Md Obaiduallh Sk
Md. Ferdouse Ahmed Foysal
Md. Rafiqul Islam
Michael Clement
Midhula Vijayan
Miguel Alberto Becerra Botero
Mikhail Tarkov

Minakshi Vharkate
Minal Moharir
Mohammad Idrees Bhat Bhat
Mohammad Shakirul Islam
Mohan Vasudevan
Mohd. Saifuzzaman
Monali Khachane
Muhammad Muzzamil Luqman
Mukti Jadhav
Nadra Ben Romdhane
Nafis Neehal
Nagaraj Cholli
Nagaratna Hegde
Nagsen Bansod
Nalini Iyer
Nico Hochgeschwender
Nita Patil
Nitin Darkunde
Nitta Gnaneswara Rao
P. P. Patavardhan
Pankaj Agrawal
Parag Bhalchndra
Parag Kaveri
Parag Tamhankar
Parashuram Bannigidad
Parashuram Kamble
Parminder Kaur
Paulo Quaresma
Peter Dolan
Pooja Janse
Poonam Ghuli
Poornima Patil
Prabhakar C. J.
Pradeep Udupa
Prajakta Dhamdhere
Prakash Hiremath
Prakash Khanale
Prakash Unki
Praneet Saurabh
Prasanna Vajaya
Prasanth Vaidya
Pratima Manhas
Praveen K.
Pravin Metkewar
Pravin Yannawar
Prema T. Akkasaligar

Priti Singh
Pushpa Patil
Pushpa S. K.
Qazi Fasihuddin
Rafaela Alcântara
Rajendra Hegadi
Rajesh Dhumal
Rajivkumar Mente
Rajkumar Soundrapandiyan
Rajkumar Yesuraj
Rakesh K.
Ramya D.
Rashmi Somshekhar
Ratnadeep Deshmukh
Ratnakar Ghorpade
Ravi Hosur
Ravi M.
Ravindra Babu Tallamraju
Ravindra Hegadi
Rim Somai
Ritu Prasad
Rodrigo Nava
Rohini Bhusnurmath
Rosana Matuk Herrera
Rupali Surase
S. Basavarajappa
S. Ramegowda
S. B. Kulkarni
Sachin Naik
Sahana Das
Sameer Antani
Sanasam Inunganbi
Sangeeta Kakarwal
Sanjay Jain
Santosh S. Chowhan
Sarika Sharma
Satish Kolhe
Sema Candemir
Shajee Mohan
Shankru Guggari
Shanmugapriya Padmanabhan
Shanthi D. L.
Sharath Kumar
Shaveta Thakral
Sheikh Abujar
Shilpa Bhalerao
Shiva Murthy Govindaswamy

Shivani Saluja
Shivashankar S.
Shridevi Soma
Shrikant Mapari
Siddanagouda Patil
Siddharth Dabhade
Sivarama Krishnan Rajaraman
Slimane Larabi
Smriti Bhandari
Srikanta Pal
Sudha Arvind
Suhas Sapate
Sunanda Biradar
Suneeta Budihal
Sunil Nimbhore
Swapnil Waghmare
Szilard Vajda
Tejaswi Potluri
Thanh Ha Do
Ujwala Suryawanshi
Ulavappa B. Angadi
Umakant Kulkarni
Urmila Pol
Usha B. A.
Vaibhav Kamble
Veerappa Pagi
Víctor Codocedo
Vidyagouri Hemadri
Vijay Bhaskar Semwal
Vijaya Arumugam
Vikas Humbe
Vilas Naik
Vilas Thakare
Vinay T. R.
Vincent Bombardier
Virendra Malemath
Vishal Waghmare
Vishweshwarayya Hallur
Yao-Yi Chiang
Yaru Niu
Yoanna Martínez-Díaz
Yogesh Gajmal
Yogesh Rajput
Yogish H. K.
Yuhlong Lio
Zati Hakim Azizul Hasan

Contents – Part I

Machine Learning and Applications

Image Processing

Contents – Part II

Biometrics and Applications

Contents – Part III

Document Image Analysis

Image Analysis in Agriculture

Data Mining, Information Retrieval and Applications

Computer Vision and Pattern Recognition

Classification of Graphical User Interfaces Through Gaze-Based Features

Rishabh Sharma and Hubert Cecotti[(✉)]

Department of Computer Science, College of Science and Mathematics,
Fresno State, Fresno, CA, USA
hcecotti@csufresno.edu

Abstract. Graphical User Interfaces (GUIs) represent a key part for building interactive applications, and they act as a direct interface between users and software. The complexity of the GUIs increases in relation to the number of users interacting with software and performing multiple complex tasks, resulting in software that are mazes of functionalities. The impact of such a GUI system is adverse on the software quality and may result in non-robust software. To measure software quality, one has to measure attributes such as usability, efficiency, and learnability. There is no general approach for measuring software validity subjectively in a non-invasive way, i.e., without directly asking the users to evaluate directly the software through predefined use cases or through questionnaires. In this paper, we investigate this issue by detecting the presence of potential errors in GUIs by using the users gaze information collected during user interactions. Users gaze is analyzed to generate thirteen unique features based on statistical moments based on the time spent on each control, gaze path, and transitions between controls on the different GUI components present on the screen. The performance is evaluated with five state of the art classifiers. The results support the conclusion that incongruent GUI states can be reliably detected at the single trial level through gaze-based features with an accuracy of 76% (one-versus-rest classification) and 73.66 (one-versus-one classification) using a Gaussian Naïve Bayes classifier. These results suggest the possibility of co-development approaches between early stage users and developers through eyetracking.

Keywords: Eye-tracking · Graphical User Interface · Classification

1 Introduction

Software usability is one of the most important factor for the design and development of modern GUI (Graphical User Interface) based interactive software, websites, and mobile applications. Unusable user interfaces are probably the single largest reason why encompassing interactive systems – computers and users, fail in actual use, or are the source of potential errors. With the rapid development of technology and the presence of easy frameworks for creating GUIs,

© Springer Nature Singapore Pte Ltd. 2019
K. C. Santosh and R. S. Hegadi (Eds.): RTIP2R 2018, CCIS 1035, pp. 3–16, 2019.
https://doi.org/10.1007/978-981-13-9181-1_1

developers have started designing software with more complex GUI implementations, allowing users to execute multiple tasks with a single click making software more robust and efficient. However, this advancement in the technology allures both users and developers from different knowledge backgrounds, thus maintaining the continuous usability level for all the users remains a challenging task. The majority of software testing approaches assume the availability of an oracle, which is a mechanism against which testers can verify the correctness of the outcomes of test case executions [11]. However, in some cases, an oracle is unavailable or its availability is too expensive to be considered: it is the oracle problem that is a key issue for software testing [20].

Previous research studies have shown that software usability and graphical user interface validation is critical for the development of robust GUI applications that can be used by a large number of users [2,3,5,17]. In Software Industries (SI), Quality Assurance (QA) testers work closely with both programmers and designers in order to make software more efficient and user friendly. Quality assurance testers make efforts to ensure the correct implementation of the GUI application, with the former following the design specification, which was drawn by the latter. Without such an effort, there is no definite promise that a desired usability will be achieved after the complete implementation of the chosen design [5]. However, the task of the QA tester is tedious as it requires manual effort and a constant attention to perform optimally. Despite these efforts, the software usability is not guaranteed for all the users. To the majority of users, usability can be summarized in three distinct aspects: effectiveness, efficiency, and satisfaction [6].

Software effectiveness and efficiency are affected by their implementation and can be improved by using software testing techniques or appropriate software development life cycle model. Satisfaction is more an abstract quantity to measure, as it is fathomed by the user's interaction with the GUI of the underlying software and can be measured relatively by analyzing the user behavior during interactions. In the academic research, two main methods are present for analyzing the user behavior for predicting software usability. First, in the survey method, the numbers of users are provided with a survey form to complete after using the software for a certain amount of time [3,17,19]. The second approach for assessing software usability is based on computer vision technology, where QA tester are supposed to write a script to automate the GUI interaction and analyze if the automation works according to the provided requirement document [5]. The two methods have limitations: the survey-based method is time consuming and based on the subjective assessment of the subjects testing the software [9], whereas the computer vision-based method increases the task of QA tester and is dependent on the visual properties of the display. In addition, computer-vision approaches require labeled data for training the models, which is time consuming if the test phase will be limited in time.

For the improvement over time of software testing with the addition of functionalities, a modern approach is to directly gather information from the users, without asking them explicitly to perform a testing task. Currently, a large number of software are released in non-final versions to users (e.g., early access software), where users who have already paid for the software participate for the enhancement of the application by helping developers in finding bugs. In such a context, the end-users are both users and testers of the application. By considering this paradigm of dynamic enhancement and correction of an application, we propose to investigate the extent to which it is possible to detect possible issues in an existing application, without asking directly the user to participate to the testing phase, i.e., the testing phase is invisible to the user. In order to test such an approach, we propose an eye-tracking based approach for predicting the usability of the software. As eye-tracking is a free from the subjective assessment of the person using the software and is independent of the screen resolution, it overcomes the limitation of the existing methods for analyzing the user behavior for predicting the software usability. Moreover, the eye-tracking technology has been undergoing a rapid development with some improvements in accuracy, stability and sampling rate, making devices more reliable to use [8, 10]. Eye-tracking has a long history in human-computer interaction with multiple applications for people with severe disabilities [12, 13, 15]. Moreover, it has been observed that eye tracking can help people to do scientific research by recording and analyzing visual behaviors. We propose in this study an eye-tracking approach to analyze the recorded user gaze for classifying GUIs with low usability. To validate this approach, we consider a GUI where users have to verify a series of pairs, as it is common after the validation of a form where users have to check its validity, e.g., if the entered last name corresponds to the last name field. The key contributions of this paper are the creation of a set of features and its evaluation for estimating the presence of an incongruent element in the GUI, i.e., the presence of an error. Because errors can happen at any control, some control invariant detection should happen. It is not as a traditional heat map where the most salient element is highlighted, in the present case, the relevant control or set of controls can change between trials or between GUIs. The problem becomes a pattern recognition problem where features based on the gaze information acquired across the multiple controls should be extracted to determine if the GUI contains an incongruent element or not. The remainder of this paper is organized as follows: Sect. 2 details the feature extraction process and the experimental protocol to record the gaze data. Section 4 presents the classification results achieved. The impact of the results are then discussed in Sect. 5. Finally, the paper is concluded with potential prospective evolutions in Sect. 6.

2 Methods

2.1 Features Extraction

Contrary to problems where the location of a salient element is located to a specific location, or where multiple trials are combined to determine the saliency of an object in a scene, it is not possible to rely on the same approaches for the detection of an incongruent state in a GUI because the potential user will not spend a large amount of time on the different elements on the screen, and it will correspond to a single event during the software use. For these reasons, the feature extraction procedure must be robust and invariant to the position of the displayed control or controls that represent an incongruent state in the GUI, and therefore a potential source of error.

For performing the classification of the different types of GUIs, the collected raw data is not enough as it only represents the pixel information, which is too noisy and variable across trials. We define the notion of trial as a screen of the GUI that contains a set of controls that must be analyzed by the user. We propose to extract high-level features from the raw data by performing statistical computation to obtain potential discriminative features. As the information is relevant in both time and distance, we compute moments (up to the fourth moment) on transition between the components, and the time spent on each component, calculating moments (mean, standard deviation, skewness, and kurtosis), and the maximum viewed components. Furthermore, we calculate the distance traveled by the gaze using the Euclidean distance along with the total distance traveled in either direction, i.e., horizontal and vertical. The distance travel-based calculation is performed from the centroid of the component (key and value) in the GUI.

We denote by $\mathbf{x}_i$, $\mathbf{y}_i$, and $\mathbf{t}_i$ the recorded (x, y) coordinates and T timestamps of the user's gaze for the ith trial and the total number of gaze points recorded in ith trial are denoted as Ng_i. The values of Ng_i are different for each trial, as it depends on the time taken by the participant for completing each trial. In the subsequent sections, we consider the calculation for a single trial.

2.2   Distance-Based Features

For the calculation of the distance based feature, we considered a distance vector $\mathbf{d}$ containing the component number such that there exists a transition between the k_1^{th} component and k_2^{th} component, with $k_1! = k_2$ as shown in Algorithm 1 and a 2D distance Matrix M of size $N_c \times N_c$ for the ith trial of the experiment as in Algorithm 2 showing the number of transitions between two components during a trial. The transition is estimated from the component number in a row (source) to the component number in a column (destination). The threshold α corresponds to the minimum number of time points corresponding to the minimum duration (in second) spent by a user gazing to a component (label or image). compID is a function that returns the component identifier based on the coordinates of the gaze point, i.e., it checks if the coordinates are inside the bounding box corresponding to the control.

Centroid Based Feature. For the calculation of the centroid based features, we calculate a centroid vector CV such that, for the cth component of the GUI, the centroid value is represented by the coordinate $CV_c = (x_c, y_c)$

$$CV = \{CV_0, CV_1, \ldots, CV_{N_c}\} \tag{1}$$

In the present system, the elements on the screen represent couples of controls (label, image). CV_1 to CV_{N_p} represent the centroids of the labels (from top to

---

Algorithm 1. Distance Vector Computation.

1: Ng total number of recorded gaze reading in the ith trial
2: $\mathbf{x}_i$ recorded gaze x-coordinate
3: $\mathbf{y}_i$ recorded gaze y-coordinate
4: $\mathbf{t}_i$ recorded timestamp
5: $d = []$ {list of the component numbers between which the transition exists}
6: **for** k **to** Ng **do**
7:     final=k+α
8:     comp=compID(x_k,y_k)
9:     **if** (final $\geq$ k) **then**
10:         final=Ng
11:     **end if**
12:     **while** (k<final) and (compID(x_k,y_k)==comp **do**
13:         k=k+1
14:     **end while**
15:     **if** (final==k) **then**
16:         $d = [d; comp]$
17:     **end if**
18: **end for**

Algorithm 2. Transition Matrix.

1: $N_c \leftarrow$ Total number of components in a trial
2: **for** k **to** d.length-1 **do**
3:     $M(d[k], d[k+1]) = M(d[k], d[k+1]) + 1$
4: **end for**

---

bottom) and CV_{N_p+1} to CV_{N_c} represent the centroids of the images (from top to bottom). The labels and the images can be replaced by other types of control. The goal is to detect incongruent couples. All the centroid based statistical measurements are calculated using the centroid vector and the distance vector CV for $\mathbf{d}$ for each trial of the experiment, respectively.

Time-Based Features. For the calculation of the time-based feature, we create a vector $\mathbf{h}$ that represents the total amount of time (in ms) spent by the participant gazing at each component:

$$h = \{h_1, h_2, h_3, \ldots, h_{N_c}\} \tag{2}$$

Here, h_1 to h_{N_p} represent the time spent by the user gazing on the labels (top to bottom), and $h_{N_{(p+1)}}$ to h_{N_c} represent the time spent by the user gazing at the images (top to bottom). $\mathbf{h}$ represents a discretized version of a heat map.

The mean of the transition matrix represents the average number of times the user gaze performs a transition from one component to another. Similarly, the mean of the $\mathbf{h}$ represents the average duration (in ms) spent by the user during a trial.

$$\mu_M = \frac{\sum\limits_{j=1}^{N_c} \sum\limits_{k=1}^{N_c} M_{jk}}{N_c \cdot N_c} \qquad \mu_h = \frac{\sum\limits_{j=1}^{N_c} h_j}{N_c} \qquad (3)$$

For the standard deviation of the transition matrix, we calculated the amount of dispersion in a transition matrix for the ith trial, i.e., standard deviation in the gaze transition performed from each component (label and image) in the GUI. Similarly, for the standard deviation of the heat map vector, we calculate the standard deviation of the time spent by the participant in the ith trial of the experiment gazing the component (image and label) in the GUI, i.e., the variation in the time spent by the user gazing each component in the GUI.

$$\sigma_M = \sqrt{\frac{\sum\limits_{j=1}^{N_c} \sum\limits_{k=1}^{N_c} (M_{jk} - \mu_M)^2}{(N_c \cdot N_c) - 1}} \qquad \sigma_h = \sqrt{\frac{\sum\limits_{j=1}^{N_c} (h_j - \mu_h)^2}{N_c - 1}} \qquad (4)$$

For the skewness in the transition matrix, we calculate the skewness of the total number of transition performed in the ith trial, i.e., the symmetry in the number of gaze transitions between each component (label or image) in the GUI. Similarly, for the skewness in the heat map vector, we calculate the skewness in the time spend by the participant in the ith trial of the experiment. If the gaze transitions and time distribution belong to a normal distribution, then the value of skewness is close to 0. It referred to the third standardized central moment.

$$\gamma_M = \frac{1}{(N_c \cdot N_c) - 1} \sum_{j=1}^{N_c} \sum_{k=1}^{N_c} \frac{(M_{jk} - \mu_M)^3}{\sigma_N^3} \qquad (5)$$

$$\gamma_h = \frac{1}{N_c - 1} \sum_{j=1}^{N_c} \frac{(h_j - \mu_h)^3}{\sigma_h^3} \qquad (6)$$

The same way, we evaluate the kurtosis of the transition matrix. For the kurtosis if the heat map vector we calculated the kurtosis of the time spend by the participant in the ith trial of the experiment, i.e., a measure of the combined weight of the tails relative to the rest of the gaze time spend distribution vector (heat map vector) on each component (image and label) in the GUI. If the gaze transitions and time distribution belong to a normal distribution, then the value of kurtosis is 3.

$$\kappa_M = \frac{1}{(N_c \cdot N_c) - 1} \sum_{j=1}^{N_c} \sum_{k=1}^{N_c} \frac{(M_{jk} - \mu_M)^4}{\sigma_M^4} \qquad (7)$$

$$\kappa_h = \frac{1}{N_c - 1} \sum_{k=1}^{N_c} \frac{(h_j - \mu_h)^4}{\sigma_h^4} \qquad (8)$$

The maximum number of transitions is defined by:

$$MT = \underset{j}{\operatorname{argmax}} \sum_{k=0}^{N_c} M_{jk} \tag{9}$$

The total distance traveled by the gaze during the ith trial is defined as the Euclidean distance on the centroid vector using distance vector:

$$T_{Dist} = \sum_{j=1}^{N_d-1} \sqrt{(CV[\mathbf{d}_j].x - CV[\mathbf{d}_{j+1}].x)^2}$$
$$+ (CV[\mathbf{d}_j].y - CV[\mathbf{d}_{j+1}].y)^2 \tag{10}$$

Total gaze distance - X direction (T_{Dist}^X) an Y direction (T_{Dist}^Y) We calculated the linear distance travel in horizontal (or vertical) direction i.e., in x (or y) axis using the x (or y) coordinate of the centroid vector on the distance vector:

$$T_{Dist}^X = \sum_{j=1}^{N_d-1} |CV[\mathbf{d}_j].x - CV[\mathbf{d}_{j+1}].x|$$
$$T_{Dist}^Y = \sum_{j=1}^{N_d-1} |CV[\mathbf{d}_j].y - CV[\mathbf{d}_{j+1}].y| \tag{11}$$

The total duration (T_{Dura}) (in ms) spent by the participant during a trial is obtained by:

$$T_{Dura} = \sum_{j=1}^{N_c} h_j \tag{12}$$

The total set of features is therefore represented by: the average value of the transition matrix (F1) and the heat map vector (F9), the standard deviation of the transition matrix (F2) and the heat map vector (F10), the skewness of the transition matrix (F3) and heat map vector (F11), the kurtosis of the transition matrix (F4) and heat map vector (F12), the maximum number of transitions (F5), the total distance with the Euclidean distance (F6), the distance only in the x-axis (F7) and the y-axis (F8), and the total duration of the trial (F13).

3 Experimental Protocol

3.1 Participants

Twenty-five healthy adult students and faculties from California State University, Fresno, USA, participated to this study (mean age = 23 (3.5), 5 females). Participants were verbally informed about the experimental procedure and purpose prior to the experiment. The experimental procedures involving human subjects described in this study were approved by the Institutional Review Board.

3.2   Design

Participants were asked to be the part of experiment, which lasted about 5 min to complete all the N_t trials of the experiment. For each trial, participants had to gaze through the GUI for a maximum of 4 seconds and predict the type of GUI as congruent (i.e., GUI with high usability and low learning time - Type 1) or incongruent (i.e., GUI with low usability and high learning time - Type 2, 3, and 4). The different GUIs are depicted in Fig. 1. The distribution of the GUI trials in the dataset is as follow 50, 15, 15, and 20% for Type 1, 2, 3, and 4, respectively. The gaze coordinates of the participants were recorded during the experiment using a portable eye-tracker mounted under the screen. The eye-tracker was a Tobii Eye tracker 4C (frequency of 90 Hz) [1]. The experiment consists of N_t trials with $N_t = 40$.

3.3   Classification

As the recorded data was classified into four different types of GUI, two types of binary classification tasks are performed: one-vs-rest and one-vs-one. Hence, we can classify the given data in four one-vs-rest and six one-vs-one binary comparison for training a binary classifier. We define the following binary classification tasks: the pairwise classifications $C_p(i,j)$ with $1 \leq i \leq j \leq 4$ corresponding to the classification of Ti vs. Tj and the one vs. all classifications $C_a(i)$ with $1 \leq i \leq 4$ corresponding the classification of Ti vs. the other conditions, where Ti represents GUI type Type i. The distribution of the GUI information in the dataset is as follow 50% Type 1 GUI, 15% Type 2 GUI, 15% Type 3 GUI, and 20% Type 4 GUI.

Five classifiers are selected from four different categories for evaluating the ten binary classification mentioned, i.e., a density-based classifier - K Nearest Neighbor (K-NN) with $K = 5$, a Support Vector Machine (SVM) with radial basis function and penalty parameter 1.0, and Linear Discriminant Analysis (LDA) with singular value decomposition, tree-based classifier - Random Forest classifier (RFT) with the maximum number of allowed tree is set to 10, and Naïve Bayes classifier [16,18] - Gaussian Naïve Bayes (GNB) by calculating the probability distribution on Gaussian distribution curve. The performance of each classifier is assessed through the Area Under the ROC (receiver operating characteristic) Curve (AUC) [7].

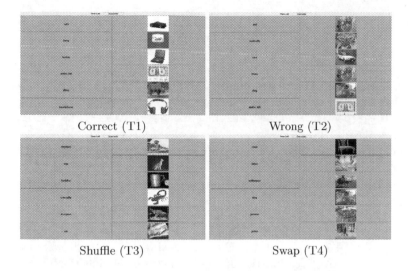

Correct (T1)   Wrong (T2)

Shuffle (T3)   Swap (T4)

Fig. 1. The four different types of GUIs.

4 Results

4.1 Behavioral Analysis

Behavior analysis was performed after calculating the human precision level for classification of the GUIs as congruent or incongruent. The recorded human performance level for the classification across all the participants is 92.5%. Furthermore, we derive the confusion matrix from the prediction values to obtain the true positive (TP), true negative (TN), false positive (FP), and false negative (FN) values in the prediction (see Table 1). The value in each cell corresponds to the mean and standard deviation across participants.

Table 1. Performance evaluation with the behavioral response.

	TN	FP	FN	TP
GUI T1	10.72 ± 2.27	4.40 ± 1.67	3.12 ± 1.24	1.76 ± 1.10
GUI T2	3.36 ± 1.52	1.08 ± 1.12	1.20 ± 1.26	0.36 ± 0.48
GUI T3	3.00 ± 1.01	1.40 ± 0.98	0.84 ± 0.61	0.76 ± 0.90
GUI T4	4.32 ± 1.12	1.72 ± 1.56	0.84 ± 0.61	1.12 ± 0.86

4.2 Gaze Detection Analysis

The performance of the all the five classifiers is evaluated by calculating the AUC of the ROC curve plotted after calculating the extracted features for each classification C1 to C10 respectively. Furthermore, the AUC is calculated by removing the trials that are wrongly classified by the participants. As all the classification are performed on the binary labels, AUC for each label in ROC curves is calculated. Furthermore, due to the class imbalance in the data, we used the average AUC of both the classes for analyzing the precision level of the classifiers to classify the GUI accurately. Figure 2 depicts the average AUC of the classes for each of one versus rest and one versus one classification case (i.e., C1 to C10) respectively for each classifier where the AUC represents the AUC without removing the incorrect prediction of the users, and the AUC-Correct represents the AUC of the ROC curve after removing the incorrect prediction of the users.

From the obtained results, the classification C3 (Type 3 GUI vs. all the other types of GUI) is the most difficult to predict accurately compared to all other classifications in one versus rest classification (i.e., C1, C2, and C4). Moreover, for the one versus one classification tasks, we can conclude that classification C10 (Type 3 GUI vs Type 4 GUI) is the most difficult to predict accurately as compared to all other classification in one versus one classification (i.e., C5, C6, C7, C8, and C9) and for both the classifications (C3 and C10) Gaussian Naïve Bayes classifier results the maximum average AUC 57% and 70% respectively, when calculated without removing the wrongly predicted data item from the dataset. Similarly, Gaussian Naïve Bayes results the maximum average AUC in classifying congruent GUI versus all the incongruent (C1 classification) GUIs with or without removing the wrongly predicted data item from the dataset, i.e., 71% and 76% respectively. Moreover, the average AUC score for the classification C5, C6, and C7 (one versus one classification of Type 1 vs. Type 2, Type 1 vs. Type 3, and Type 1 vs. Type 4) with and without the wrongly predicted values is $66 \pm 17.34\%$ and $73.66 \pm 9.81\%$, respectively.

4.3   Feature Selection

Feature selection is performed using a modified backward elimination technique algorithm for the classification of C1 to C10. The algorithm starts with the whole feature set and the feature with the less influence on the AUC is discarded at each step until there is a single feature left in the feature set. The modified feature selection algorithm returns the feature set containing the type of feature and feature influence ratio in term of AUC value. From the feature selection algorithm, we conclude that the distance-based feature has more influence on the classification than centroid-based feature and time-based feature respectively. Features F1, F2, F4, and F7 are the most influential features, while features F3, F8, F9, and F11 are the least influential features for classifying the GUI types, as depicted in Fig. 3.

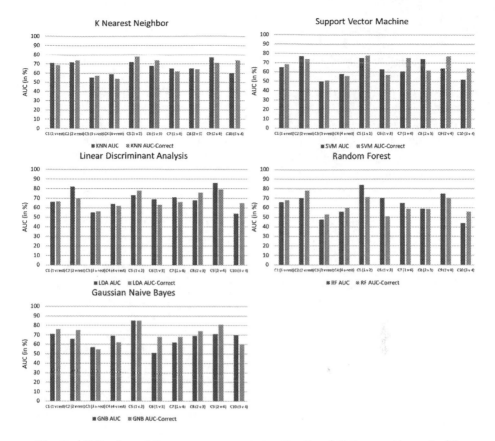

Fig. 2. AUC value of the one versus rest classification (all the results are in %).

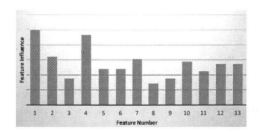

Fig. 3. Feature selection.

5 Discussion

Eyetracking is typically used for control in human-computer interface applications, e.g., virtual keyboards [4,14], in marketing and medical research, or in vision sciences to better understand cognitive and visual processes. The proposed work aims at going beyond known applications of eye-tracking to detect, within a short period, incongruent states on a screen in relation to the relationships between displayed elements. The goal of this approach is to detect potential issues in a graphical user interface that can have an impact on software quality and robustness. By using gaze based features, we have proposed a set of features and their ranking through a feature selection procedure. In this paper, we proposed a set of features for the detection of incongruent states in series of pairs of elements through eye-tracking. The increasing importance of software usability with the rise in the number of users is a key motivation for the Survey approach and a Computer Vision approaches that are used in the software industry for developing user-friendly software. Moreover, these approaches have limitations, i.e., the first approach is time consuming and highly dependent on the subjective assessment of the user, resulting in a bias judgment of the GUIs while the second approach for GUI testing increases the workload of the quality assurance tester. Furthermore, it requires a certain human effort for writing efficient testing scripts. We proposed an alternative approach inspired from the widely used concept of the early access software in the game industry, i.e., performing the software testing with the help of the users without informing them. We proposed an eye tracking technology as it is independent of the user's judgment resulting in bias free observation and is not dependent on the resolution of the system on which the software is used. In addition, it does not require any previous knowledge for writing scripts for UI testing. Furthermore, we designed the experiment for classifying the horizontally aligned key –s value paired GUI into congruent states (corresponding to GUIs with a high usability and low learning time) versus incongruent states (corresponding to GUIs with low usability and high learning time) by recording the gaze information of the user interacting with the software. Finally, we designed thirteen statistical features and test five classifiers. The analysis of the result suggests that Gaussian Naïve Bayes classifier is a suitable classifier for identifying the congruent GUIs based on the proposed feature sets.

6   Conclusion

In this study, we demonstrated the need of better techniques for measuring the software usability and classifying the GUI with high usability to GUI with low usability. Moreover, we exhibited the efficiency of eye tracking technology when it is combined with machine learning techniques for the detection of the anomalies in the GUI with high precision with only information relative to the position of the controls in the layout. By using the proposed machine learning and eye-tracking approach, we achieved an average AUC of 76% for classifying congruent vs. incongruent GUI states (C1 classification) using a Gaussian Naïve Bayes classifier under one versus rest classification, after removing the falsely identified values by the users. Furthermore, after removing the falsely identified data items from the dataset, the AUC for one versus one classification for identifying congruent GUI states vs. incongruent GUI states, i.e., C5, C6, and C7 using Gaussian Naïve Bayes gives the maximum score with an average AUC of

>73.66 (±9.81%) concluding that the Naïve Bayes classifier was more accurate than decision tree based classifier, linear classifier, or density-based classifier for performing eye-tracking classification problem for GUI classification. The following three improvements can make the classifier more reliable. First, to gather more training data, which can improve the performance of the classifiers. More data can be acquired for more participants or with longer sessions. Second, more feature analysis can be performed on the recorded gaze so that the outliers in the eye tracker data can be reduced. Third, additional physiological measurements in combination to eye-tracking could be used to enhance the reliability of the decisions, e.g., heart rate, skin conductance. In particular, brain responses associated to visual attention, to the presentation of incongruent elements can be detected and used for training the classifier making it more reliable and accurate in classification. Further work will include other types of interactive controls to extend the ability of the system to detect new GUI states.

References

1. Tobii developer documentation. https://developer.tobii.com/consumer-eye-trackers/core-sdk/. Accessed 07 Nov 2018
2. Bangor, A., Kortum, P.T., Miller, J.T.: An empirical evaluation of the system usability scale. Int. J. Hum.-Comput. Interact. **24**(6), 574–594 (2008)
3. Bevan, N.: Usability. In: Liu, L., Özsu, M.T. (eds.) Encyclopedia of Database Systems, pp. 3247–3251. Springer, Boston (2009)
4. Cecotti, H.: A multimodal gaze-controlled virtual keyboard. IEEE Trans. Hum.-Mach. Syst. **46**(4), 601–606 (2016)
5. Chang, T.H., Yeh, T., Miller, R.C.: GUI testing using computer vision. In: Proceedings of the ACM SIGCHI Conference on Human Factors in Computing Systems (2010)
6. Dix, A.: Human-computer interaction. In: Liu, L., Özsu, M.T. (eds.) Encyclopedia of Database Systems, pp. 1327–1331. Springer, Boston (2009)
7. Fawcett, T.: An introduction to ROC analysis. Pattern Recogn. Lett. **27**(8), 861–874 (2006)
8. Fu, H., Wei, Y., Camastra, F., Arico, P., Sheng, H.: Computational intelligence and neuroscience. In: Advances in Eye Tracking Technology: Theory, Algorithms, and Applications. Hindawi Publishing Corporation (2016)
9. Fu, J.: Usability evaluation of software store based on eye-tracking technology. In: Proceedings of the IEEE Information Technology, Networking, Electronic and Automation Control Conference, pp. 1116–1119 (2016)
10. Hansen, D.W., Ji, Q.: In the eye of the beholder: a survey of models for eyes and gaze. IEEE Trans. Pattern Anal. Mach. Intell. **32**(3), 478–500 (2010)
11. Hierons, R.M.: Oracles for distributed testing. IEEE Trans. Softw. Eng. **38**(3), 629–641 (2012)
12. Jacob, R.J.K.: The use of eye movements in human-computer interaction techniques: what you look at is what you get. ACM Trans. Inf. Syst. **9**(3), 152–169 (1991)
13. Lupu, R., Bozomitu, R., Ungureanu, F., Cehan, V.: Eye tracking based communication system for patient with major neuro-locomotor disabilities. In: Proceedigs of IEEE 15th ICSTCC, pp. 1–5, October 2011

14. Meena, Y.K., Cecotti, H., Wong-Lin, K., Prasad, G.: A novel multimodal gaze-controlled Hindi virtual keyboard for disabled users. In: Proceedings of the Annual Conference of IEEE Systems, Man, and Cybernetics, pp. 1–6 (2016)

15. Meena, Y.K., Cecotti, H., Wong-Lin, K., Dutta, A., Prasad, G.: Toward optimization of gaze-controlled human-computer interaction: application to Hindi virtual keyboard for stroke patients. IEEE Trans. Neural Syst. Rehabili. Eng. **26**(4), 911–922 (2018)

16. Ng, A.Y., Jordan, M.I.: On discriminative vs. generative classifiers: a comparison of logistic regression and Naive Bayes. In: Dietterich, T.G., Becker, S., Ghahramani, Z. (eds.) Advances in Neural Information Processing Systems, vol. 14, pp. 841–848. MIT Press, Cambridge (2002)

17. Nielsen, J.: Usability Engineering. Morgan Kaufmann, Burlington (1993)

18. Rish, I.: An empirical study of the Naive Bayes classifier. Technical report (2001)

19. Seffah, A., Donyaee, M., Kline, R.B., Padda, H.K.: Usability measurement and metrics: a consolidated model. Softw. Qual. J. **14**(2), 159–178 (2006)

20. Zhou, Z.Q., Xiang, S., Chen, T.Y.: Metamorphic testing for software quality assessment: a study of search engines. IEEE Trans. Softw. Eng. **42**(3), 264–284 (2016)

Let Vehicles Talk with Images for Smart Vehicular Communication System

K. C. Santosh$^{(\boxtimes)}$

Department of Computer Science, The University of South Dakota,
414 E Clark St., Vermillion, SD 57069, USA
santosh.kc@ieee.org

Abstract. In this paper, the need for image analysis and machine learning in the domain to develop smart/intelligent vehicular communication system is succinctly addressed. Like other domains, vehicular communication has to be addressed/cited through the use of big data for several different purposes, such as the vehicle or user authentication, safety and security. Not limited to one of them, the aim of the paper is to show how can we create a panoramic image from a set of images shared by several vehicles at any specific event in the particular vehicular network. The paper is the proof-of-concept prototype to see whether images (via the use of the image- and machine learning-based tools/techniques) can help enhance the driving experience.

Keywords: Image analysis · Machine learning ·
Smart vehicle communication system · Authentication ·
Safety and security

1 Introduction

Like humans and/or animals, vehicles are able to communicate, which we call vehicular communication; thanks to new technology. Often, exchanging and/or sharing ideas can be considered as data communication. The communication is clear and succinct if we are able to share enough data so that actions can be made expected. In vehicular communication, there are varieties of data that can be shared, such as sensor-based data (LIDAR, for instance), image data and other signals like voice data. Communicating with them can serve various purposes, such as vehicle or user authentication, security and safety. Speech signals can be verified and/or addressed by users. However, other data, such as sensor-based data and images (via camera: front and rear) are expected to be analyzed in a way we can share important information in any studied network. Image data is more crucial and can provide more information than other single-valued data (mostly, numeric). Let us recall the following statement:

"A picture is worth a thousand words."

© Springer Nature Singapore Pte Ltd. 2019
K. C. Santosh and R. S. Hegadi (Eds.): RTIP2R 2018, CCIS 1035, pp. 17–26, 2019.
https://doi.org/10.1007/978-981-13-9181-1_2

As we are agreed on the fact that a picture can tell us a complete story and is re-usable, in this paper, an idea of how can a set of images can be analyzed for a particular event/accident through image analysis and machine learning. The paper aims to provide a proof-of-concept in vehicular communication for various purposes, such as vehicle/user authentication, safety and security.

1.1 Overview

How good it will be if we have cars built/manufactured with cameras. In the US, the department of transportation has shown interests in keeping both front and backup cameras (rear) [1]. Conventionally speaking, cameras are used to avoid possible collisions. Assuming that cars have cameras, communication can happen with a lot of data exchanges among the vehicles in the particular vehicular communication network. Not limited to data exchanges, but also data storage can help communication robust for further analysis/research view point. As mentioned earlier, image data can provide a user good driving experience since one vehicle can collect images along the route/path that can be any event (accident) and other traffic issues. Note that traffic issues can be relayed through vehicular network(s) so that one can understand how detour can be made for security and safety reasons. Importantly, vehicle/user authentication can be analyzed and proved with the help of the data collected by the vehicles that are shared through the network.

Assuming that the Vehicular Adhoc Networks (VANETs) in place, the paper is focused on the proof-of-concept prototype – through the use of image analysis – to be able to continue serving several purposes, such as vehicle/user authentication, safety and security in addition to quality driving. However, researchers in the domain: vehicular communication should not be confused with what have been discussed in the literature i.e., security and safety, which is beyond the scope of the paper. Besides, the paper is not just about those data communication that mainly deals with cryptography issue that can help authenticate vehicles/users. Low-level data communication, text-based messages, for instance, is the scope of the current work; this is about high-level image data communication. In short, for any reasons, image data could provide more and complete information in addition to text- and/or key-based data sharing within the network. In Fig. 1, let us assume that vehicles can communicate with any data they like to share. But for this paper, let us limit the data sharing through a set of images. In any particular network, image data can be shared so that every vehicle can have all information for further analysis. Dealing with images (hundred of images) is not trivial since some images can provide no information i.e., a portion of them can happen fraud. At the same time, other images can be redundant. All of these issues can raise a question like how can it be possible to analyze hundred of images so that the right information can be shared. In this paper, the proof-of-concept framework is discussed that helps open the new trend in the domain.

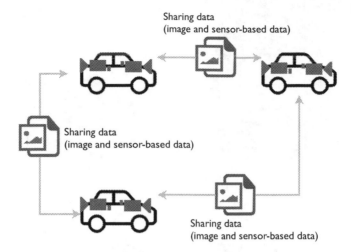

Fig. 1. An illustration about how can vehicles communicate to each other. In this illustration, all vehicles are equipped with cameras front-end and rear-end. Assuming accessible network for their communication, vehicles are supposed to communicate at the time when it is required: an event/accident, for instance.

1.2 Organization of the Paper

The remainder of the paper is organized as follows. In Sect. 2, the use of image data will be discussed, which is particularly focused on the domain: vehicular communication. Section 3 will provide high level concept on image stitching. Section 4 will focus on the problem i.e., how can we construct panoramic images from a set of images shared by several different vehicles in the particular vehicular network. Section 5 concludes the paper.

2 A Picture is Worth a Thousand Words

"A picture is worth a thousand words" is an English language-idiom that refers to the notion that a complex idea can be conveyed with just a single picture, this picture conveys its meaning or essence more effectively than a description does[1]. In a 1913 newspaper advertisement for the Piqua Auto Supply House of Piqua, Ohio, a phrase: "One Look Is Worth A Thousand Words" can help understand the importance of the picture (Piqua Leader-Dispatch. page 2. August 15, 1913). This happens mostly in all applications from healthcare (artificial intelligence and machine learning tools/techniques for medical imaging) to combating crime (biometrics), to name a few. With this background, in vehicular communication, it could be a better idea to take advantage images that can be shared in the network.

---

[1] URL: https://en.wikipedia.org/wiki/A_picture_is_worth_a_thousand_words.

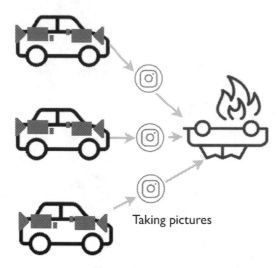

Fig. 2. An illustration of an event/accident, where pictures/images are taken by nearby vehicles. These images are shared through the network (vehicular) so that image analysis can be done at the same time. Check Fig. 1 to know how vehicles are communicated.

3 Image Stitching

In general, image stitching is the process of combining multiple images based on their common fields (overlapping fields) to produce high-resolution image. It has extremely rich state-of-the-art literature [3]. Image stitching has been widely used in several different modern applications, such as image stabilization, medical imaging, image super-resolution, video stitching (frame-by-frame image stitching) and object formation/development via insertion. In this work, images are taken by the vehicles (front- and rear-end cameras) and are shared in any particular vehicular communication network to develop panoramic image so that the complete scene can be read for further analysis/investigation (Fig. 2).

To develop a prototype, even though we have varieties of tools/techniques, the following process has been followed.

(a) Get the stable Harris points from the images (potentially used for image stitching);
(b) Based on the similarity score, find point correspondence between a pair of images using the SIFT descriptors [5,6] (VLFEAT SIFT tool box was used, URL: http://www.vlfeat.org/overview/sift.html); and
(c) Compute homography following the matched points using RANSAC (taken from RANSAC algorithm with example of finding homography: Edward Wiggin. MATLAB Central 2011).

In this study, the most stable Harris points are estimated using the scale-space maximization of the Laplacian of Gaussian (LOG) formulation [4,7,8].

Fig. 3. A set of images, collected from shared vehicles. Note that the images are not ordered since they come from different vehicles at different time.

Besides, not just limited to SIFT key points, SURF can be applied as reported in the original work [2].

In Fig. 3, four different images are shown and that are considered for image stitching (based on the significant overlapping pixels between the pairs). In Fig. 4, three pairs are shown with the matching pairs and the result is provided in Fig. 5.

Fig. 4. Three pairs of images with the matching pairs (yellow), where red circles and green plus represent the location where overlapping happens between them. (Color figure online)

For detailed information about how it has been studied in the domain: vehicular communication will be discussed in Sect. 4.

4   Panoramic Image: A Proof of Concept

To better understand the work, let us start with a scenario:

A vehicle captures an event/accident. It shares image to neighboring vehicles/users. Images can be multiple, not just limited to one. The same process holds true for other vehicles that are in the event.

In vehicular communication network, a roadside unit (RSU) is expected and it helps verify data that required RSUs higher computation power and larger storage space. These units are connected (i.e., network: wired or wireless). In the network, any data can be shared/communicated. In case we do not have RSU, one of the vehicles/users can be used for processing the data.

With the use of an image analysis techniques, based on the similarity scores (through image matching), we are able to find images in a sequence even though the images are shared at different times and in different order. For example, in Fig. 3, we have four different images that are shared by four different vehicles. It is important to note that, at the time vehicles shared images, we cannot really order them based on the time they share. In Fig. 4, the image sequence can be explored based on the similarly matching scores from all possible pair of images. For n number of images (shared in that particular vehicular network), there are $\frac{n \times (n-1)}{2}$ pairs of images to compute similarity score. For In Fig. 3, we will need to compute similarity scores from the following pairs $= \{(1,2), (1,3), (1,4), (2,3), (2,4), (3,4)\}$. It is possible to figure out the common pixels that largely happen between 2D images taken from the same event. After image matching, the resulting similarity between the images helps us determine whether the 2D images are taken from exactly the same event. This means that the machine is able to learn those images with higher similarity scores. As a result, such images are accepted/used for building panoramic image. In Fig. 4, three pairs with the image matching processes are shown. Figure 4 provides the way we locate local features and compute similarity between the possible pairs of images and check whether it is useful for building panoramic image. In this example, one can see/read the matching pairs that follow local key points (from each sample) to see how similar they are. Once the pairs are verified i.e., whether they originated from the exact same event, panoramic building process starts by stitching them. Image similarity score (via matching, see Fig. 4) helps stitch them together and makes a panoramic image. As mentioned before, panoramic images can be used for further analyzing the event (even in the future, since images care be stored and can be reused). To build a complete panoramic image, it is always good to have a set of good number of images (shared in the network). The higher the number of images, better is the quality of the panoramic image. In this prototype, the set of three images can be sufficient to build panoramic images, and at the same time, false or fraud images can be avoided.

Fig. 5. Expected panoramic image from a set of images.

Besides, possible fraud images should be eliminated from the sequence that are potentially shared by malicious vehicles/users. In this paper, fraud images are taken care of as well, which is based on the similarity score. Another way to avoid fraud images is to use the GPS location of the vehicles/users. If the GPS location of the vehicle/user is different from the real event, the images can be discarded without further image analysis processes.

As discussed above, event-related message/image can be verified through the panoramic image generated. Once the image is verified as authentic, then the vehicles on the road will use the verified information for making decision for their driving. The goal of our scheme is to prevent attacks by malicious vehicles such as message/image fabrication attack, and to provide safe and enjoyable experience to drivers by delivering only authenticated information.

It is important to note that the whole process

(a) does not just describe an event (or authenticate the event) fully
(b) but also, authenticates user.

From the set of rejected images, one can understand that they have been shared by malicious users or they are not the part of the event. How about if we still receive images from the event after the completion of the panoramic image? If it is the case, machine will learn those upcoming images that are communicated/shared for better development of the panoramic image. Once we have the panoramic image from a set of images communicated at time t, new images at time $t + i$, where $i = \{1, 2, \ldots, N\}$, will be verified to see whether they can help enrich the quality of the panoramic image. Rejection is also required. Rejection is much easier since machine can take complete panoramic image for the reference to compare based on the image matching criterion discussed above.

5   Conclusion

In this paper, the use of set of images that are shared by vehicles in any particular vehicular network, for building panoramic image has been clearly reported. The primary idea is to know how one can read/understand the complete story of what has happened about the event/accident. The focus of the study is not just to check whether images can help vehicular communication for authentication, safety and security but also improve the quality driving experience. Not to be confused, the work is not about how images are shared and improve the VANET. In a word, the paper is the proof-of-concept work, where image analysis and machine learning can help build panoramic image in vehicular communication for several different purposes.

Acknowledgements. Author would like to thank Kiho Lim, USD's computer science faculty for the discussion about the VANET and its possibility.

References

1. Federal motor vehicle safety standards; rear visibility; final rule. National Highway Traffic Safety Administration (NHTSA), Department of Transportation (DOT) **79**(66) (2014)
2. Bay, H., Tuytelaars, T., Van Gool, L.: SURF: speeded up robust features. In: Leonardis, A., Bischof, H., Pinz, A. (eds.) ECCV 2006. LNCS, vol. 3951, pp. 404–417. Springer, Heidelberg (2006). https://doi.org/10.1007/11744023_32
3. Brown, M., Lowe, D.G.: Automatic panoramic image stitching using invariant features. Int. J. Comput. Vis. **74**(1), 59–73 (2007). https://doi.org/10.1007/s11263-006-0002-3
4. Lindeberg, T.: Scale-Space Theory in Computer Vision. Kluwer Academic Publishers, Norwell (1994)
5. Lowe, D.G.: Object recognition from local scale-invariant features. In: Proceedings of the Seventh IEEE International Conference on Computer Vision, vol. 2, pp. 1150–1157, September 1999
6. Lowe, D.G.: Distinctive image features from scale-invariant keypoints. Int. J. Comput. Vis. **60**(2), 91–110 (2004). https://doi.org/10.1023/B:VISI.0000029664.99615.94
7. Mikolajczyk, K., Schmid, C.: Scale & affine invariant interest point detectors. Int. J. Comput. Vis. **60**(1), 63–86 (2004). https://doi.org/10.1023/B:VISI.0000027790.02288.f2
8. Tuytelaars, T., Mikolajczyk, K.: Local Invariant Feature Detectors: A Survey. Now Publishers Inc., Hanover (2008)

A Novel Foreground Segmentation Method Using Convolutional Neural Network

Midhula Vijayan$^{(\boxtimes)}$ and R. Mohan

National Institute of Technology, Tiruchirappalli 620015, Tamilnadu, India
midhula91@gmail.com, rmohan@nitt.edu

Abstract. Background subtraction is a commonly used approach for foreground segmentation (moving object detection). Different methods have been proposed based on this background subtraction technique. However, the algorithms give the false alarm in case of complex scenarios such as dynamic background, camera motion, shadow, illumination variation, camouflage, etc. A foreground segmentation system using convolutional neural network framework is proposed in this paper to handle these complex scenarios. In this approach, the non-handcrafted features learned from the deep neural network are used for the detection of moving objects. These non-handcrafted features are robust and efficient compared to the handcrafted features. The presented method is learned using spatial and temporal information. Additionally, a new background model is proposed to estimate the temporal information. We train the model end-to-end using input images, background images, and optical flow images. For the training purpose, we have randomly selected few images and its ground truth images from CDnet 2014. The proposed method is evaluated with benchmark datasets, and it outperforms the state-of-the-art methods in terms of qualitative and quantitative analyzes. The proposed model is capable of real-time processing because of its network architecture. Hence the model can be used in real-surveillance applications.

Keywords: Background image · Background subtraction ·
Convolutional Neural Network (CNN) · Foreground segmentation ·
Optical flow image

1 Introduction

Foreground segmentation from a video sequel is a challenging task for computer vision community. This is considered as a primary step for most of the vision-based systems such as motion tracking, activity identification, video surveillance, and robotic systems. In the recent years, different algorithms were introduced to handle the problem of "foreground segmentation". However, the methods are failed in case of real complex scenarios.

© Springer Nature Singapore Pte Ltd. 2019
K. C. Santosh and R. S. Hegadi (Eds.): RTIP2R 2018, CCIS 1035, pp. 27–40, 2019.
https://doi.org/10.1007/978-981-13-9181-1_3

Background subtraction (BGS) is one of the most known and used methods for foreground segmentation. The performance of the BGS algorithm depends on the robustness of the constructed background. The existing BGS methods are considered as unsupervised methods. However, the performance of these methods depends on different parameters in different phases such as initialization phase and background update phase. These parameters depend on the characteristics of the video sequence. Hence, the BGS methods are not purely unsupervised methods. Unfortunately, BGS methods give the false alarm in case of complex scenarios such as dynamic background, camouflage, thermal video, illumination variation, etc. Hence, these methods are not suitable for real-surveillance applications. Authors believe that training the model with labeled data is more reasonable compared to using the tuned parameters. Therefore, we propose a supervised foreground segmentation using the deep-CNN method.

The progress of deep learning in image segmentation leads to more attention to researchers in the area of foreground segmentation and in various applications [10] deep learning is used to obtain high accuracy. Most of the recent algorithms are taking either appearance information or motion information for the construction of deep-neural network model. The foreground segmentation using appearance information alone give accurate image segmentation. While the lack of motion information leads to the false alarm in video object segmentation. The presented method considers appearance and motion information for the accurate foreground segmentation. Additionally, we have used a new background model for the construction of robust segmentation model.

This paper present a novel foreground segmentation method using an end-to-end deep-CNN. The main contributions of the presented method are listed below.

- A deep-CNN is presented in this paper. The network combines the high level and low level features effectively.
- The model is created using spatial information, optical flow, and background model information. This helps the network to capture spatial and temporal information effectively.
- A new background modeling mechanism is proposed for capturing the motion information.

The outline of this paper is as follows: in Sect. 2 different algorithms for foreground segmentation are presented. Section 3 explains the proposed foreground segmentation method. This section explains the background modeling technique and CNN architecture. The qualitative and quantitative results are reported in Sect. 4. At last, Sect. 5 summarizes the entire work.

2   Related Works

Several moving object detection algorithms were proposed ,for different applications. Most of the existing methods follow BGS mechanism. The recently proposed BGS algorithms are the extended version of some basic BGS algorithms. The BGS algorithms can be divided into six different categories such as probabilistic methods [5,8,22], codebook methods [13,19], sample-based methods [3,9,20], subspace-based methods [15], vector-based models [24], and deep-learning [2,4,27] based methods.

In [22], Stauffer and Grimson have proposed a background modeling technique using probability distribution function known as Gaussian Mixture Model (GMM). This method modeled each pixel as a Gaussian mixture and then the incoming pixels are compared with the background Gaussian models. If the incoming pixel falls within any one of the Gaussian models, then the pixel is classified as background pixel otherwise classified as a foreground pixel. This method fails in complex scenarios such as illumination variation, dynamic background, camouflage, etc. Different enhanced version of GMM model [6] is also proposed in recent years.

Elgammal et al. [8] have introduced a non-parametric approach to overcome the problem of parameter tuning. In this method, kernel density estimation is used as the probability distribution function. It can handle the complex scenarios such as cluttered and dynamic backgrounds. However, the non-parametric methods are not suitable for real-time applications due to the high processing time.

In [3], Barnich et al. have introduced a sample based background construction mechanism named as ViBe. The sample-based methods use the recent past 'n' pixel values for the background modeling. The incoming pixel value is compared with these recent values for the classification of pixels. If a specified number of background pixels are similar to the incoming pixel, then the pixel is classified as background pixel otherwise marked as a foreground pixel. The similarities between the pixels are determined by a user-defined threshold value. ViBe with an adaptive background update mechanism is proposed in [9], named as pixel-based adaptive segmenter.

In contrast, Kim et al. [13] have proposed a codebook based background modeling mechanism. In this method, background pixels are modeled as codewords. Each codeword consists of color, intensity, and temporal features. The distance between the codeword and the incoming pixel information determines the classification label. If the distance is greater than a user-defined threshold value, then the pixel is labeled as foreground pixel otherwise labeled as a background pixel. This codebook method follows background updating mechanism with respect to the classification of the pixel. Temporal information is not sufficient for the construction of the robust background. Hence, St-Charles et al. [20] have used spatial and contextual information in addition to temporal information. In [21], the same authors have proposed a variant of [20] with persistence information named as PAWCS.

In real-world applications, it is difficult to construct an efficient and robust background model. With the development of deep learning, different moving object detection methods were proposed using deep-CNN [2,4,27,28]. Braham and Droogenbroeck [4] have proposed a scene-specific CNN for foreground segmentation. Here, the authors have implemented background subtraction using the neural network with block-wise processing and a fixed background model is used for background subtraction. This fixed background model and block-wise processing of images result in false detection of moving objects. Most of the recent methods use appearance information [2,27,28] for building the model. In [11], authors have used motion information and appearance information for foreground segmentation. The authors have considered two separate streams for building the model. This increases the complexity of the algorithm, and it also requires some human interventions for training the model. The presented method considers background information, optical flow information, and spatial information for the model generation. The novel foreground segmentation method is explained in the following sections.

3   Approach

The proposed method consists of two steps (1) background modeling and (2) foreground segmentation using deep-CNN. The overall view of the foreground segmentation process is depicted in Fig. 1.

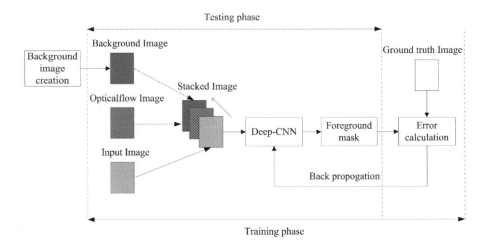

Fig. 1. Overall view of the foreground segmentation technique

We use the incoming image, optical flow image, and background image for training the model. Temporal information is an important feature in foreground segmentation. Optical flow image gives the temporal information of the current processing frame with respect to the background model. The optical flow images are not sufficient in case of camera jitter and large illumination variation. In order to overcome these difficulties, a novel background model is also used to build the foreground segmentation system. The new background modeling technique, CNN architecture, and its training procedure are explained in the following sections.

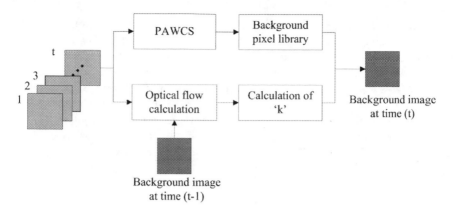

Fig. 2. Background modeling technique

3.1 Background Image Construction

This paper present a new method for the construction of background image. This background modeling technique is depicted in Fig. 2. Here, we combine the foreground mask obtained from PAWCS [21] method and optical flow image [16]. The PAWCS [21] algorithm helps to distinguish background pixels from the foreground pixels. These background pixels are used to create the background pixel library. The number of pixels used for creating the background image is varying according to the nature of processing frame. Optical flow image is used to determine this dynamically varying parameter.

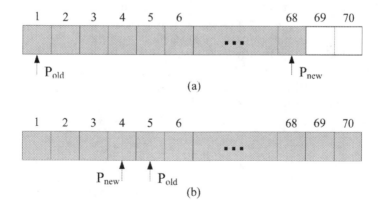

Fig. 3. Pixel bag representation with pointers

The construction of background pixel library depends on the results of PAWCS algorithm. The result of PAWCS is a binary image where the black pixel indicates the background pixel and the white pixel represents the foreground pixel. If the pixel is classified as a background pixel, then the pixel value is stored into the pixel bag corresponding to the particular pixel. The collection of pixel bag is known as pixel library. Each pixel bag keeps the recent 70 background pixel values. If the pixel bag is full, then the oldest values are replaced with new background pixel values. We maintain two indicators P_{new}, P_{old} to access the recent pixel value and the oldest pixel value from the pixel bag respectively. Figure 3 shows the pixel bag representation with pointers.

The background image is constructed using a number of recent pixel values from the background pixel bag. The number of selected pixels is determined by the nature of the optical flow image. The background pixel value of location (ϕ, ψ) at time t is computed using Eq. 1.

$$
B_t(\phi, \psi) = \begin{cases} \dfrac{\sum_{i=P_{new}-K}^{P_{new}} L_{bag}(\phi, \psi, i)}{K}, & if P_{new} > P_{old} \\ \dfrac{\sum_{i=0}^{P_{new}} L_{bag}(\phi, \psi, i) + \sum_{i=70-(K-P_{new})}^{70} L_{bag}(\phi, \psi, i)}{K}, & \text{otherwise} \end{cases}
$$

(1)

Where, K represents the number of pixels used for the construction of background image, $B_t(\phi, \psi)$ is the background pixel value of pixel (ϕ, ψ) at time t, and $L_{bag}(\phi, \psi, i)$ is the ith pixel bag entry for the pixel (ϕ, ψ). Figure 3a portrays the first case $(P_{new} > P_{old})$ of Eq. 1 and Fig. 3b portrays the second case (otherwise) of Eq. 1.

The fixed value of K will result in the outdated background image or blurred background image in case of camera jitter condition. So, the value of K should adjust according to the camera movement. In order to maintain an adaptive value for K, we should detect the nature of motion in the particular frame. If the camera jitter causes the motion, then the value of K should be less. The optical flow image determines the value of K. The non-zero pixel values in optical flow indicate the spatial or temporal motion. The large number of non-zero pixel value indicates that the camera is moving (camera jitter) or a large object starts to move. The prior is an important issue in real surveillance applications. So, we considered the high number of non-zero pixel value as a problem of camera jitter. In this case, we need to decrease the value of K. Hence, we introduced an adaptive update mechanism for K value. This adaptive update mechanism is shown in Eq. 2.

$$
K = \begin{cases} 4, & if \ N_z \geq 0.30 \\ 4 + \dfrac{0.30 - N_z}{0.30 - 0.03}, & if \ 0.03 < N_z < 0.30 \\ 70, & if \ N_z \leq 0.03 \end{cases}
$$

(2)

Where N_z represents the percentage of the foreground pixels in the current processing frame. It is defined in Eq. 3.

$$
N_z = \frac{\text{Number of non-zero pixels}}{\text{Height of the image} \times \text{Width of the image}}
$$

(3)

So the value of N_z determines the value of K. Noise is one of the main problems in video processing. In order to succeed the problem of noise in N_z, a new condition is formulated in Eq. 4.

$$N_z(t) = \varsigma \times N_z(t) + (1 - \varsigma) \times N_z(t - 1) \qquad (4)$$

Where ς is fixed as 0.75. This new background modeling mechanism helps to find the moving objects efficiently.

3.2   Deep Network Architecture and Training

The proposed CNN architecture is depicted in Fig. 4. This network follows an encoder-decoder architecture with end-to-end training. The encoder section of the proposed architecture carries thirteen convolutional layers and four pooling layers (max-pooling). It is similar to the first thirteen convolutional layers and four pooling layers of VGG 16 network. The architecture takes input image of size $(224 \times 224 \times 3)$. Current processing image, background image, and optical flow image are vertically stacked and fed in to the network. The authors followed the concept of [16] for the construction of optical flow image. In addition to this method we have considered constructed background model for finding the optical flow information. The encoder section converts the stacked 3-channel input into 512-channel feature vector using convolutional and pooling layers.

The decoder section of the architecture converts the 512-channel input into a single-channel binary image. This decoder portion of the model is composed of five transposed convolutional layers, three batch normalization (BN) layers, four PReLU layers, and one softmax layer. The PReLu function is used as the activation function in the decoder except for the last layer. The last layer of the decoder uses softmax as the activation function. The output of the model is a binary image, the black pixel denotes the background pixel and the white pixel denotes the foreground pixel.

The presented model is trained using CDnet 2014 dataset [26]. This architecture combines fine and coarse scale information using summation operation. This operation helps to extract robust non-handcrafted features. The network is trained using Adaptive moment (Adam) optimizer. Binary cross entropy (BCE) function is used as the loss function, which is defined in Eq. 5. This loss function is calculated between the output and the corresponding ground truth image.

$$BCE(s, q) = -(s \times log(q) + (1 - s) \times log(1 - q)) \qquad (5)$$

where,

   s is the actual probability.

   q is the predicted probability.

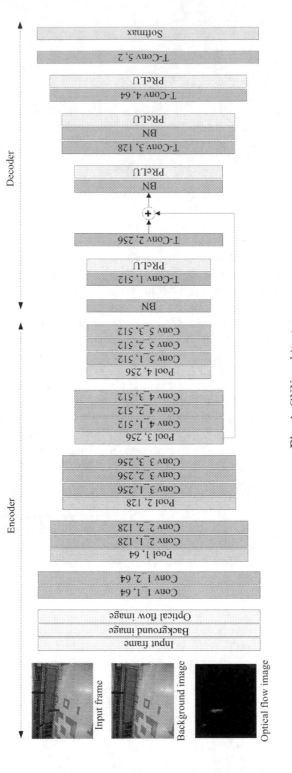

Fig. 4. CNN architecture

4   Experiments and Results

4.1   Dataset

The model is tested using changedetection.net 2014 (CDnet 2014) [26] dataset. This dataset is designed especially for the background subtraction task. CDnet 2014 [26] contains video sequences of different categories with ground truth images. It contains 53 videos under 11 different categories: bad weather (BW), thermal (TH), PTZ, night videos (NV), low frame rate (LFR), shadow (SHA), intermittent object motion (IOM), camera jitter (CJ), dynamic background (DB), baseline (BL), turbulence (TUR). PTZ contains the video shot with large camera motion. Hence, we didn't consider PTZ for the evaluation purpose. The dataset is divided into two samples training samples and testing samples for training the model. The randomly selected 50 frames from each video sequence are used for the training purpose, and the remaining frames are used to test the model.

4.2   Evaluation

A new foreground segmentation method using an effective background construction method and CNN architecture is proposed in this paper. Inorder to evaluate the performance of the presented foreground segmentation algorithm, we use FMeasure (FM). This metric is reported in CDnet 2014 [26]. FM is the harmonic mean of recall (R) and precision (P). 'R' is the ratio of correctly classified foreground pixels to the actual foreground pixels. 'P' is the ratio of correctly classified foreground pixels to all the classified foreground pixels. The FMs of presented method are compared with the FMs of recent foreground segmentation algorithms such as AAPSA [17], BMOG [14], cascadeCNN [27], CwisarDRP

Table 1. Quantitative analysis on CDnet 2014

Methods	BW	BL	CJ	DB	IOM	LFR	NV	SHA	TH	TUR
AAPSA [17]	0.7742	0.9183	0.7207	0.6706	0.5098	0.4942	0.4161	0.7953	0.7030	0.4643
BMOG [14]	0.7836	0.8301	0.7493	0.7928	0.5291	0.6102	0.4982	0.8414	0.6348	0.6932
cascadeCNN [27]	0.9431	0.9786	0.9458	0.9459	0.8505	0.8370	0.8965	0.9593	0.8958	0.9108
CwisarDRP [7]	0.8015	0.888	0.7656	0.8487	0.5626	0.6858	0.4970	0.8249	0.7619	0.7397
DeepBS [2]	0.8301	0.9580	0.8990	0.8761	0.6098	0.6002	0.5835	0.9304	0.7583	0.8455
EFIC [1]	0.7786	0.9172	0.7125	0.5779	0.5783	0.6632	0.6548	0.8202	0.8388	0.6713
M4CD V-2 [25]	0.8136	0.9322	0.8231	0.6857	0.6939	0.6275	0.4946	0.8969	0.7448	0.7978
MBS [18]	0.798	0.9287	0.8367	0.7915	0.7568	0.6279	0.5158	0.7968	0.8194	0.5858
PAWCS [19]	0.8152	0.9397	0.8137	0.8938	0.7764	0.6588	0.4152	0.8913	0.8324	0.6450
SBBS [23]	0.7403	0.9192	0.7347	0.8128	0.6795	0.5534	0.5055	0.7105	0.7499	0.6362
sharedmodel [5]	0.8480	0.9522	0.8141	0.8222	0.6727	0.7286	0.5419	0.8898	0.8319	0.7339
SuBSENSE [20]	0.8619	0.9503	0.8152	0.8177	0.6569	0.6445	0.5599	0.8986	0.8171	0.7792
WeSAMBe [12]	0.8608	0.9413	0.7976	0.7440	0.7392	0.6602	0.5929	0.8999	0.7962	0.7737
Proposed	0.959	0.9672	0.9543	0.9550	0.8813	0.8760	0.9103	0.9312	0.9120	0.8901

*The results of state-of-the-art methods are reported from CDnet 2014 findings.

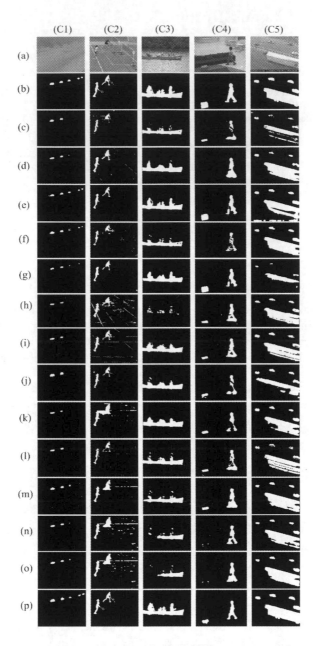

Fig. 5. Qualitative comparison of the results from different categories such as (C1) BW, (C2) CJ, (C3) DB, (C4) IOM, and (C5) LFR. The first row is the input image, the second row is the ground truth image, and the last row (p) is the result of proposed method. Rows (c)–(o) is the existing methods such as (c) AAPSA, (d) BMOG, (e) cascade CNN, (f) CwisarDRP, (g) DeepBS, (h) EFIC, (i) M4CD V-2, (j) MBS, (k) PAWCS, (l) SBBS, (m) shared model, (n) SuBSENSE, and (o) WeSAMBe

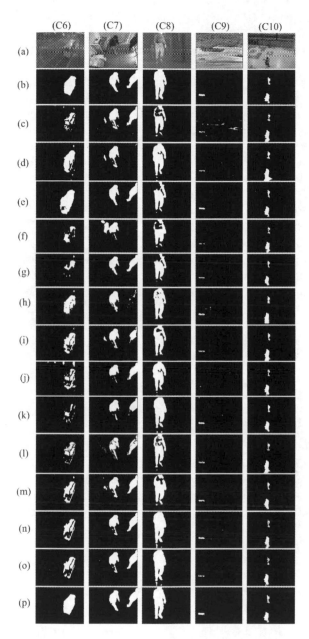

Fig. 6. Qualitative comparison of the results from different categories such as (C6) NV, (C7) SHA, (C8) TH, (C9) TUR, and (C9) BL. The first row is the input image, the second row is the ground truth image, and the last row (p) is the result of proposed method. Rows (c)–(o) is the existing methods such as (c) AAPSA, (d) BMOG, (e) cascade CNN, (f) CwisarDRP, (g) DeepBS, (h) EFIC, (i) M4CD V-2, (j) MBS, (k) PAWCS, (l) SBBS, (m) shared model, (n) SuBSENSE, and (o) WeSAMBe

[7], DeepBS [2], EFIC [1], M4CD V-2 [25], MBS [18], PAWCS [19], SBBS [23], sharedmodel [5], SuBSENSE [20], and WeSAMBe [12].

The quantitative comparisons of the presented method with the state-of-the-art methods are shown in Table 1. The proposed method gives the best results for 7 categories out of 10 categories. For the categories such as IOM, LFR, and TUR, the presented method produce average results (i.e., FM < 0.90) since the produced optical flow images are insufficient for the motion detection. However, the algorithm gives appreciable results in the case of IOM and LFR compared with the state-of-the-art methods.

Figures 5 and 6 show the qualitative results. These figures show the visual comparison between the proposed method and state-of-the-art methods such as AAPSA [17], BMOG [14], cascadeCNN [27] (supervised), CwisarDRP [7], DeepBS [2] (supervised), EFIC [1], M4CD V-2 [25], MBS [18], PAWCS [19], SBBS [23], sharedmodel [5], SuBSENSE [20], and WeSAMBe [12]. The unsupervised methods have a weak notion about the structure of the objects. This leads to the false detection of object parts. In contrast, the presented model learns to combine the motion information, appearance information, and background information. Hence, our method gives accurate results for the real challenging videos.

5   Conclusion

In this paper, we propose a foreground segmentation model using CNN. The presented method includes mainly two steps (i) background modeling and (ii) deep-CNN for learning the features. The CNN is modeled using the incoming image, optical flow image, and background image. The optical flow image gives the temporal information. Furthermore, the efficient background modeling mechanism helps to find the moving objects from the current processing frame. The presented method is robust against different challenges such as dynamic background motion, illumination variation, camera jitter, shadow etc. The qualitative and quantitative evaluation shows that our method outperforms the existing methods.

References

1. Allebosch, G., Deboeverie, F., Veelaert, P., Philips, W.: EFIC: edge based foreground background segmentation and interior classification for dynamic camera viewpoints. In: Battiato, S., Blanc-Talon, J., Gallo, G., Philips, W., Popescu, D., Scheunders, P. (eds.) ACIVS 2015. LNCS, vol. 9386, pp. 130–141. Springer, Cham (2015). https://doi.org/10.1007/978-3-319-25903-1_12
2. Babaee, M., Dinh, D.T., Rigoll, G.: A deep convolutional neural network for video sequence background subtraction. Pattern Recogn. **76**, 635–649 (2018)
3. Barnich, O., Van Droogenbroeck, M.: ViBe: a universal background subtraction algorithm for video sequences. IEEE Trans. Image Process. **20**(6), 1709–1724 (2011)

4. Braham, M., Van Droogenbroeck, M.: Deep background subtraction with scene-specific convolutional neural networks. In: 2016 International Conference on Systems, Signals and Image Processing (IWSSIP), pp. 1–4. IEEE (2016)

5. Chen, Y., Wang, J., Lu, H.: Learning sharable models for robust background subtraction. In: 2015 IEEE International Conference on Multimedia and Expo (ICME), pp. 1–6. IEEE (2015)

6. Chen, Z., Ellis, T.: A self-adaptive Gaussian mixture model. Comput. Vis. Image Underst. **122**, 35–46 (2014)

7. De Gregorio, M., Giordano, M.: WiSARDrp for change detection in video sequences. In: CVPR 2016, Google Scholar (2016, submitted)

8. Elgammal, A., Harwood, D., Davis, L.: Non-parametric model for background subtraction. In: Vernon, D. (ed.) ECCV 2000. LNCS, vol. 1843, pp. 751–767. Springer, Heidelberg (2000). https://doi.org/10.1007/3-540-45053-X_48

9. Hofmann, M., Tiefenbacher, P., Rigoll, G.: Background segmentation with feedback: the pixel-based adaptive segmenter. In: 2012 IEEE Computer Society Conference on Computer Vision and Pattern Recognition Workshops (CVPRW), pp. 38–43. IEEE (2012)

10. Jagtap, A.B., Hegadi, R.S.: Feature learning for offline handwritten signature verification using convolution neural networks. Int. J. Technol. Hum. Interact. (IJTHI) **70**, 163–176 (2017)

11. Jain, S.D., Xiong, B., Grauman, K.: FusionSeg: learning to combine motion and appearance for fully automatic segmentation of generic objects in videos. **2**(3), 6 (2017). arXiv preprint arXiv:1701.05384

12. Jiang, S., Lu, X.: WeSamBE: a weight-sample-based method for background subtraction. IEEE Trans. Circ. Syst. Video Technol. **28**, 2105 2115 (2017)

13. Kim, K., Chalidabhongse, T.H., Harwood, D., Davis, L.: Real-time foreground-background segmentation using codebook model. Real-Time Imaging **11**(3), 172–185 (2005)

14. Martins, I., Carvalho, P., Corte-Real, L., Alba-Castro, J.L.: BMOG: boosted Gaussian mixture model with controlled complexity. In: Alexandre, L.A., Salvador Sánchez, J., Rodrigues, J.M.F. (eds.) IbPRIA 2017. LNCS, vol. 10255, pp. 50–57. Springer, Cham (2017). https://doi.org/10.1007/978-3-319-58838-4_6

15. Oliver, N.M., Rosario, B., Pentland, A.P.: A Bayesian computer vision system for modeling human interactions. IEEE Trans. Pattern Anal. Mach. Intell. **22**(8), 831–843 (2000)

16. Pathak, D., Girshick, R., Dollár, P., Darrell, T., Hariharan, B.: Learning features by watching objects move. In: Computer Vision and Pattern Recognition (CVPR) (2017)

17. Ramírez-Alonso, G., Chacón-Murguía, M.I.: Auto-adaptive parallel som architecture with a modular analysis for dynamic object segmentation in videos. Neurocomputing **175**, 990–1000 (2016)

18. Sajid, H., Cheung, S.C.S.: Background subtraction for static & moving camera. In: 2015 IEEE International Conference on Image Processing (ICIP), pp. 4530–4534. IEEE (2015)

19. St-Charles, P.L., Bilodeau, G.A., Bergevin, R.: A self-adjusting approach to change detection based on background word consensus. In: 2015 IEEE Winter Conference on Applications of Computer Vision (WACV), pp. 990–997. IEEE (2015)

20. St-Charles, P.L., Bilodeau, G.A., Bergevin, R.: SuBSENSE: a universal change detection method with local adaptive sensitivity. IEEE Trans. Image Process. **24**(1), 359–373 (2015)

21. St-Charles, P.L., Bilodeau, G.A., Bergevin, R.: Universal background subtraction using word consensus models. IEEE Trans. Image Process. **25**(10), 4768–4781 (2016)
22. Stauffer, C., Grimson, W.E.L.: Adaptive background mixture models for real-time tracking. In: IEEE Computer Society Conference on Computer Vision and Pattern Recognition, vol. 2, pp. 246–252. IEEE (1999)
23. Varghese, A., Sreelekha, G.: Sample-based integrated background subtraction and shadow detection. IPSJ Trans. Comput. Vis. Appl. **9**(1), 25 (2017)
24. Vijayan, M., Ramasundaram, M.: Moving object detection using vector image model. Optik **168**, 963–973 (2018)
25. Wang, K., Gou, C., Wang, F.Y.: M4CD: a robust change detection method for intelligent visual surveillance. IEEE Access **6**, 15505–15520 (2018)
26. Wang, Y., Jodoin, P.M., Porikli, F., Konrad, J., Benezeth, Y., Ishwar, P.: CDNET 2014: an expanded change detection benchmark dataset. In: Proceedings of the IEEE Conference on Computer Vision and Pattern Recognition Workshops, pp. 387–394 (2014)
27. Wang, Y., Luo, Z., Jodoin, P.M.: Interactive deep learning method for segmenting moving objects. Pattern Recogn. Lett. **96**, 66–75 (2017)
28. Yang, L., Li, J., Luo, Y., Zhao, Y., Cheng, H., Li, J.: Deep background modeling using fully convolutional network. IEEE Trans. Intell. Transp. Syst. **19**(1), 254–262 (2018)

Classification of Vehicle Make Based on Geometric Features and Appearance-Based Attributes Under Complex Background

K. L. Arunkumar[1]([✉]), Ajit Danti[2], and H. T. Manjunatha[1]

[1] Department of MCA, Jawaharlal Nehru National College of Engineering,
Shimoga, Karnataka, India
{arunkumarkl,manjudeepa}@jnnce.ac.in
[2] Computer Science and Engineering, Christ University,
Bangalore, Karnataka, India
ajitdanti@yahoo.com

Abstract. Vehicle detection and recognition is an important task in the area of advanced infrastructure and movement administration. Many researchers are working on this area with different approaches to solve the problem since it has a many challenge. Every vehicle has its on own unique features for recognition. This paper focus on identifying the vehicle brand based on its geometrical features and diverse appearance-based attributes like colour, occlusion, shadow and illumination. These attributes will make the problem very challenging. In the proposed work, system will be trained with different samples of vehicles belongs to the different make. Classify those samples into different classes of models belongs to same make using Neural Network Classifier. Exploratory outcomes display promising possibilities efficiently.

Keywords: Auto correlogram · Color moments · Texture extraction

1 Introduction

In current trends of research recognition and classification of vehicles using the captured image has a wide area of application. Vehicle recognition is a procedure of identifying the vehicle and its make from the vehicle image captured in the rear view. However, this is a very interesting because huge number of vehicles belongs to the different models are available in the real world. This is more challenging when the images captured with occlusion, shadow and different illumination conditions. This is also an extension vehicle recognition process using traditional number-plate based vehicle recognition system. Number-plate based vehicle identification could be benefited but vehicle detection with fake number plates this will be failed. This improvised by detecting the vehicle using its

K. C. Santosh and R. S. Hegadi (Eds.): RTIP2R 2018, CCIS 1035, pp. 41–48, 2019.
https://doi.org/10.1007/978-981-13-9181-1_4

unique geometrical features which are appeared in different conditions with complex background. Vehicle recognition is performed on using different geometrical feature extracted from the vehicle image captured using digital color camera. Different machine learning algorithms are tested on the dataset of 100 rear view images of vehicles belongs to three different models. A machine learning classification is considered with broader approach for classification using the neural network algorithm: (1) geometrical featured approach and (2) appearance-based approach. The novel approach of the proposed work is to recognize the vehicle make based on the geometrical features and appearance attributes of the vehicle captured in the color image and by applying neural network algorithm vehicle make can be classified into different classes.

2   Related Researches

So many approaches have been designed for detection and classification of vehicles into different classes. Most of the approaches focused on classification into distinct classes like cars, trucks, buses etc. Based on the shape and size of the vehicles [3,4,13,14]. Wei et al. [13] developed work based on extracting the features of vehicles using topological structures and classified using a neural network. Avery et al. [11] designed an algorithm using the length-based vehicle classification algorithm. They apply this approach on video processing for vehicle classification. Based on this they are able classify the vehicles into broad categories like truck and cars.

Gupte et al. [4] also presents an algorithm on vehicle detection and classification which classified the input images into cars and non-cars. This was applied on the sequence of images captured in the traffic scenes. Petrović et al. [10] work is more related when compared all other research work. Here vehicles are identified and classified into different using the features extracted from frontal view of the vehicle. In my earlier work recognition of vehicles in the night vision using tail lights features is performed [16]. Manjunatha et al. [17] detect the sign boards using normalized correlation method to perform the red color object detection. The classification is done using nearest neighbour algorithm. They end up with the accuracy rate of 93% which was applied on 1000 images which belongs to 77 different classes.

3   Methodology

In this work a novel approach is proposed to recognise the vehicle and identification to which class it belongs to, based on the geometric features and appearance attributes of the vehicle appears in the rear-view image. In the classification task input images will be categorised into different classes of vehicle brands like Audi, BMW, Benz etc. Attainment of the proposed work is carried out in three distinguished steps.

In step one, invariant geometrical features of the vehicles are extracted to describe unique characteristics of the vehicles. Simple invariant geometrical features like length, width and height are extracted from the input image. These features are takes less computation and fairly low storage space. Detail description of extraction of these features are referred from [5].

In step two, appearance features are extracted using color correlogram. Advantages of using this technique is, spatial correlation of color is included in this, local spatial color correlations are described in the global distributions, it takes low computations cost and less storage is required.

Auto Color Correlation Algorithm. This algorithm describes computation of the mean color of all the color pixels C_j from color pixels C_i in the images with k-th distance [1]. The Auto color correlation of image I(x, y), $x = 1, 2, 3 \ldots$ M, $y = 1, 2, 3, \ldots$ N is defined as

$$ACC = (I, j, k) = MC_j \gamma_{C_i C_j}^k (I) = \{\gamma_m c_j\} \gamma_{c_i c_j}^k (I), g_m c_j \gamma_{c_i c_j}^k (I), b_m c_j \gamma_{c_i c_j}^k (I) | c_i \neq c_j \tag{1}$$

Where the quantization of primary image i(x,y) to m colors $c_1, c_2 \ldots c_m$ is performed and initially the distance between two pixels $k \varepsilon [\min M < N]$ is fixed. The RGB value of color m is treated as MC_j in an image I.

The mean colors are defined as follows:

$$\gamma_{mc_j} \gamma_{mc_j}^k (I) = \frac{\pi_{c_i \gamma c_j}^k (I)}{\pi_{c_i c_j}^k (I)} | c_i \neq c_j \tag{2}$$

$$g_{mc_j} \gamma_{mc_j}^k (I) = \frac{\pi_{c_i g c_j}^k (I)}{\pi_{c_i c_j}^k (I)} | c_i \neq c_j \tag{3}$$

$$b_{mc_j} \gamma_{mc_j}^k (I) = \frac{\pi_{c_i b c_j}^k (I)}{\pi_{c_i c_j}^k (I)} | c_i \neq c_j \tag{4}$$

The total pixels values of color C_j from any pixel of color C_i with distance k is represented in the denominator $\Pi c_i c_j (k)(I)$ when x is RGB color space and denoted $C_j \neq 0$. The number of accounting color C_j from C_i is represented by N at distance k is computed as follows:

$$N = \pi_{c_i c_j}^k (I) = \left\{ \begin{array}{l} P(x_i, x_j) \epsilon C_i | P(x_2, y_2) \epsilon C_j; \\ k = MIN\{|x_1 - x_2|, |y_1 - y_2|\}; \end{array} \right\} \tag{5}$$

In step two, color features are extracted from the two images for its comparison and indexing based on color moments. Images which are precomputed and stored in databases are used for the comparison, then the test image is matched with the database image. In image retrieval applications the first three color moments are used as features and most of the color distribution information is contained in the low-order moments [6]. Under the different lighting condition color moments can be used as a good feature because it encodes both shape and color information. Any color model can be computed using color moments and it is done in the same way as computing moments of a probability distribution.

Mean. First color moment of an image can be taken from the average color of the image. It can be computed as follows

$$E_i = \Sigma_{j=1}^{N} \frac{1}{N} \mathcal{P}_{ij} \tag{6}$$

where N is the number of pixels in the image and p_{ij} is the value of the jth pixel of the image at the ith color channel.

Standard Deviation. Standard deviation will be the second color moment, square root of the color distribution variance will give the standard deviation. It can be computed as follows:

$$\sigma_i = \sqrt{\left(\frac{1}{N}\Sigma_{j=1}^{N}(\mathcal{P}_{ij} - E_i)^2\right)} \tag{7}$$

where E_i is the first color moment or mean value, for the ith color channel of the image.

Matching. The sum of weighted difference between the moments of the two distribution is used to define the similarity function between two image distributions [7]. It can be computed as:

$$d_{moments}(H, I) = \Sigma_{i=1}^{r} w_{i1}|E_i^1 - E_i^2| + w_{i2}|\sigma_i^1 - \sigma_i^2| + w_{i3} \tag{8}$$

Where

(H, I): comparison of color distribution in two images
i: is the present channels index
r: is the number of channels
E_i^1, E_i^2: are the first moments (mean) of the two images distributions
σ_i^1, σ_i^2: are the second moments (std) of the two images distributions
W_i: are the weights for each moment.

Texture Extraction. Another important feature we extract from the appearance of the image is its texture. Texture of the image will give the unique features that can be used to match the test image with the image stored in database. Numerous techniques are available compare the texture features of two images. These methods compute image texture such as the degree of contrast, coarseness, directionality and regularity [12] or periodicity, directionality and randomness. Gabor wavelet is best technique with more efficiency for texture feature extraction from the images [2]. Hence Gabor wavelets are used to extract the texture features of images using two-dimensional filter. This is computed as follows

$$G_c[i, j] = B_e^{-\frac{(i^2+j^2)}{2\sigma^2}} cos(2\pi f(icos\theta + jsin\theta)) \tag{9}$$

$$G_s[i, j] = C_e^{-\frac{(i^2+j^2)}{2\sigma^2}} sin(2\pi f(icos\theta + jsin\theta)) \tag{10}$$

where B and C are calculated as normalizing factors. Gabor filters with 2-D can be used in image processing for more number of applications, in the above equation number 9 and 10, f denotes the frequency in feature extraction for segmentation and texture analysis. By changing the values of θ, texture orientation can be found in the particular direction and by changing the σ size of the image can be analysed.

In step three the classification is performed using feedforward neural network algorithm. This is primarily used for supervised learning. The simplest type of feedforward neural network is perceptron. The perceptron is a machine learning algorithm used to classify the input image belongs to which particular class. Proposed methodology is shown in the Fig. 1.

Proposed Method

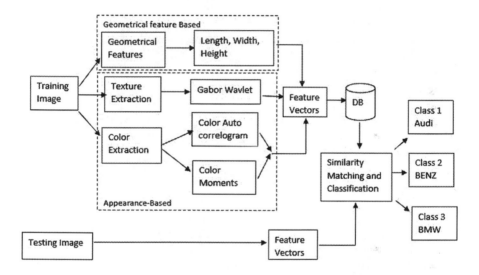

Fig. 1. Showing proposed methodology flow diagram.

4   Experimental Results

The performance analysis of our proposed work for classification of vehicles into its brands using geographical features and appearance-based features of vehicle images. We have selected 100 images randomly, containing 10 images in each category of Audi, BMW and BENZ etc., within this database. The 10 classes are used for relevance estimation, given a test image and it is assumed that the images belong to one of the trained classes.

Experiment results shows the clear classification of vehicles in the input image into different classes based on both geometrical features and appearance-based features with greater recognition rates. This approach leads to the better classification. It fetches the precious information from the input images which helps for improvement in the recognition rate in addition with the geometric attributes. In the proposed work vehicles are classified into different classes like Audi, BMW, BENZ etc. The accuracy rate of identifying the target and outlier classes is performed using feed-forward neural network classifier.

Results

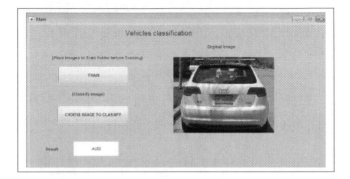

Results showing the classification of test image into AUDI class

Results showing the classification of test image into Benz class

Fig. 2. Shows results for different samples

Performance of the Proposed Work. The performance of the proposed work is evaluated using maximum number of similar images for the input image. Accuracy rate can be computed for the proposed work is shown below.

$$Accuracy = \frac{N - X}{N} * 100 \tag{11}$$

Where N is the number of similar images in the database which are trained and X is the number of dissimilar images in the database which are not trained. The input image features vectors are extracted and searched in the database and detects the matched image, also classify into the class which it belongs to. The performance is shown in the below Table 1.

Table 1. Table captions should be placed above the tables.

Target class	Trained images	Test samples	Accuracy
Audi	100 samples (Belongs to different models of same make)	20 samples	98.50%
BMW	100 samples (Belongs to different models of same make)	20 samples	95.02%
BENZ	100 samples (Belongs to different models of same make)	20 samples	98.45%
Honda	100 samples (Belongs to different models of same make)	20 samples	98.45%
Toyota	100 samples (Belongs to different models of same make)	20 samples	98.45%
Average			97.46%

5   Conclusion

Vehicle classification into its make and model is an important technology for the developing trends and technology in smart city for monitory, maintenance and security issues in the road traffic and highways. It is difficult to classify the vehicles into different class of make and model. The proposed work with the novel approach helps to classify the vehicle into the class of its make from the rear view of the vehicle. The proposed approach is very efficient in classify into different classes of vehicles make using geometrical features and appearance-based one. These extracted features are with simple computations and can be directly send to classifier to classify into different classes using these features. This approach performs well for the given samples with high accuracy rates. In the future, extension to this work to identify the intra-class classification of the models belongs to the particular make or brand of the vehicle. We would also intend to use vehicle images that do not belongs to any of the class mentioned here.

References

1. Tungkasthan, A., Intarasema, S., Premchaiswadi, W.: Spatial color indexing using ACC algorithm. In: Seventh International Conference on ICT and Knowledge Engineering (2009)
2. Manjunath, B.S., Ma, W.Y.: Texture features for browsing and retrieval of image data. IEEE Trans. Pattern Anal. Mach. Intell. **18**, 837–842 (1996)
3. Jolly, M.P., Lakshmanan, S., Jain, A.K.: Vehicle segmentation and classification using deformable templates. IEEE Trans. Pattern Anal. Mach. Intell. **18**(3), 293–308 (1996)

4. Gupte, S., Masoud, O., Martin, R.F.K., Papanikolopoulos, N.P.: Detection and classification of vehicles. IEEE Trans. Intell. Transp. Syst. **3**(1), 37–47 (2002)
5. Moussa, G., Hussain, K.: Laser intensity automatic vehicle classification system North American Travel Monitoring Exposition and Conference (NATMEC), Washington, DC, USA, 6–8 August 2008
6. Zhang, H.-J., Feng, J., Yu, H., Li, M.: Color texture moments for content-based image retrieval, pp. 929–932, September 2002
7. Hemachandran, G.K., Singh, S.M.: Content-based image retrieval using color moment and Gabor texture feature. IJCSI Int. J. Comput. Sci. **9**(5), 299 (2012). ISSN 1694-0814
8. Kato, T., Ninomiya, Y., Masaki, I.: Preceding vehicle recognition based on learning from sample images. IEEE Trans. Intell. Transp. Syst. **3**(4), 252–260 (2002)
9. Lipton, A.J., Fujiyoshi, H., Patil, R.S.: Moving target classification and tracking from real-time video. In: IEEE Workshop Applications of Computer Vision, pp. 8–14 (1998)
10. Petrović, V., Cootes, T.: Analysis of features for rigid structure vehicle type recognition. In: BMVC 2004 (1999)
11. Avery, R.P., Wang, Y., Rutherford, G.S.: Length-based vehicle classification using images from uncalibrated video cameras. In: Proceedings of the 7th International IEEE Conference on Intelligent Transportation System, pp. 737–742 (2004)
12. Niblack, W.: The QBIC project: querying images by content using color, texture and shape, vol. 1908, pp. 173–187 (1993)
13. Wei, W., Zhang, Q., Wang, M.: A method of vehicle classification using models and neural networks. In: IEEE Vehicular Technology Conference. IEEE (2001)
14. Yoshida, T., Mohottala, S., Kagesawa, M., Ikeuchi, K.: Vehicle classification systems with local-feature based algorithm using CG model images. IEICE Trans. **85**(11), 1745–1752 (2002)
15. Fisher, B., Keen, N.: Color Moment (2005)
16. Arunkumar, K.L., Danti, A.: A novel approach for vehicle recognition based on the tail lights geometrical features in the night vision. Int. J. Comput. Eng. Appl. **XII** (2018)
17. Manjunatha, H.T., Danti, A.: Indian traffic sign board recognition using normalized correlation. Int. J. Comput. Eng. Appl. **XII** (2018), ISSN 2321-3169

Material Classification Using Color and Texture Features

Shubhangi S. Sapkale$^{(\boxtimes)}$ and Manoj P. Patil

School of Computer Sciences,
Kaviyatri Bahinabai Chaudhari North Maharashtra University, Jalgaon, India
shubhangisapkale19@gmail.com, mpp145@gmail.com

Abstract. Classification of texture is a very tedious problem in computer vision and pattern recognition. In this problem, the material is assigned to particular class of texture using its properties. This paper used both color and texture features to improve the recognition performance of Flickr Material Database (FMD). Authors described method of combining Color features (RGB), Luminance and Texture features. Gray-Level Co-occurrence Matrix (GLCM) is used to extract Texture features. The classification using, K-Nearest Neighbors (KNN) classifier is discussed with the experimental results.

Keywords: Texture · Feature extraction · GLCM ·
K-Nearest Neighbors Classifier

1 Introduction

The visual content of the images can be analyzed using Textures. Texture can be found in the surface pattern of an object like fabric, glass, wood, leather etc. [1]. The main aim of texture analysis is to find the unique characteristics of texture so that it can be used for accurate classification of an object. Experiments are performed on 10 texture classes of Flickr Material Database (FMD). Figure 1 shows some samples texture images of FMD. It identifies smoothness, coarseness of the surface and gives the indication for getting significant knowledge about the texture class [2].

This material classification system builds feature vector by extracting features from input images. Further, the distance between the query image and trained data image is computed to find the similarity. This paper is organized in the following sections: Sect. 2 gives a review of the related work. Sections 3 and 4 deals with feature and feature extraction methods. In Sect. 5, K-Nearest Neighbors Classifier algorithm discussed. Result and discussions are given in Sect. 6. Conclusions are presented in Sect. 7.

© Springer Nature Singapore Pte Ltd. 2019
K. C. Santosh and R. S. Hegadi (Eds.): RTIP2R 2018, CCIS 1035, pp. 49–59, 2019.
https://doi.org/10.1007/978-981-13-9181-1_5

Fig. 1. Samples texture images of FMD dataset.

2   Literature Review

This section contains review on existing literature of material classification.

Salamati et al. [15] worked on material classification using color and NIR Images. The author used NIR images for the experiment. Luma, intensity, and color information was used to classify the images.

Chary et al. [7] worked on feature extraction techniques which used to find similarity between the color images.

Haralik et al. [10] used spatial gray tone co-occurrence texture features in the image analysis. Haralik defines fourteen texture features which were measured from the probability matrix of images. These features were used to extract the characteristics of texture statistic of an image.

Reddy et al. [16] proposed the system to classify the similarity and defect of fabric textures. The model introduced by combining two classification techniques, i.e. GLCM and the binary pattern which identifies similarity and detects defects of fabric images. Features are calculated LBP, LLBP and SLBP from GLCM and the binary pattern classification technique. PNN, K-NN and SVM classifier used for texture classification.

Mohanaiah et al. [8] worked on the Gray Level Co-occurrence Matrix (GLCM). Entropy, Angular Second Moment, Inverse Difference Moment and Correlation these four statistical texture parameters were extracted from the image using GLCM method. Same GLAM-based texture features are extracted to analyze and classify the Knee X-ray images to their corresponding class [29].

Chadha et al. [5] presented the Content-Based Image Retrieval (CBIR) system. The CBIR system retrieves images using the image descriptors i.e. texture, color, intensity, and shape. The WANG standard database used for testing.

Liu et al. [1] worked on both texture and material categorization. Proposed system based on sorted random projections (RPs). Support Vector Machine classifier combine multiple features.

Smith et al. [4] was proposed the method to extract the color regions from the images automatically.

Skaff et al. [17] worked on Material classification. For classification, the parameter includes angles spectral bands, texture features, image level features. Feature vector computed based on these parameters.

Tahir et al. [18] used FPGA (Field Programmable Gate Array) as a co-processor for the classification which speeds up the computation of GLCM and Haralik texture features.

Raheja et al. [19] proposed the comparison of Gabor filter and GLCM to detect the defect of fabric material.

Kanan et al. [20] used four types of an image descriptors and compared it with thirteen grayscale algorithms. The author demonstrates that all color-to-grayscale algorithms work same, though the illumination of image descriptors changes.

Santosh et al. [21] presented a reliable automated chest X-rays image-based screening system which used thoracic edge map to detect pulmonary abnormalities. To get focus on diseases, shape and edge feature descriptor were used.

Aafaque et al. [22] used articles from biomedical scientific research. Edge map technique used to discrete panels from composite figures. The author used an edge detection algorithm i.e. canny, Prewitt, Sobel, Robert, Zero-cross and Laplacian of Gaussian to detect the changes between the gray-level pixel.

Santosh et al. [23] presented the method for quality control using a generalized line histogram technique which computes a principal rib-orientation measure. Author used line seed filters which extract a set of lines from the posterior rib-cage. A similarity of an image pixel pairs computed using SIFT features.

Candemir et al. [24] proposed a Rotation and Scale Invariant Line based Color aware descriptor (RSILC) combines intensity, color, gradient histograms and line interpositioning to detect image key-line and their circular region. Key-line descriptor used to extract key-lines using texture, color and interline spatial information.

Santosh et al. [25] proposed a method that observes the radiological examinations using lung field for comparison. The multiscale shape, edge and texture features are used to analyze the lung region symmetry.

3   Features

3.1   Color Feature

Human mostly used the color feature for visual recognition. For example, people typically describe a sky is blue which probably implying some type of bluish hue [4]. Color image is combination of the Red, Green and Blue colors. RGB colors are called primary colors. Using different values of Red, Blue and Green other colors can be obtained. The color image gives a result as 3 two dimensional matrices viz Red, Blue, Green. Every matrix represents color features [5]. Figure 2 shows Color image and its equivalent RGB matrices.

3.2   Luminance Feature

Luminance is apparent brightness; how bright an object appears to the human eye [4]. Luminance is brightness information in an image without the color [12]. Colors with its actual brightness which captured by Light and Luminance are not perceived by the human [20] (Fig. 3).

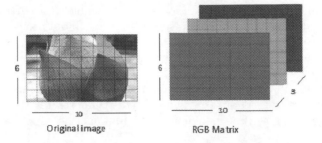

Original image   RGB Matrix

Fig. 2. Color image and RGB matrix [5]. (Color figure online)

Fig. 3. Images with different luminance spectrum. (Color figure online)

3.3   Texture Feature

Texture can be identified as rough, silky, bumpy by touching the surface. They hold a total number of repetition of two features with a particular spatial relation. The GLCM is a well-known texture analysis method. GLCM evaluates images properties using the second-order statistical method [5]. Images include repetition of patterns of local variations of pixel intensities [2]. Images can be represented by Gray Level Co-occurrence Matrices (GLCM) [5]. The GLCM calculates from the gray-scale image. The GLCM computes how frequent a pixel and its adjacent pixel occurs either horizontally, vertically and diagonally. This paper represents six statistical features as Contrast, Energy, Correlation, Homogeneity, Entropy and IDM which is extracted by the GLCM method. The feature extracting from an image using GLCM method is discussed in Feature Extraction section. Figure 4 shows two images with the same Color and different Textures. Therefore, Color features same but GLCM features are different shown in Fig. 4.

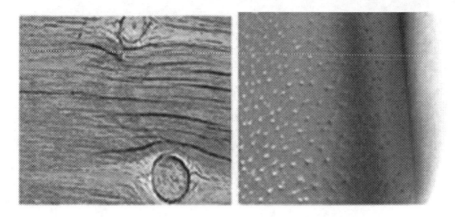

Fig. 4. Images with different Texture. (Color figure online)

4   Features Extraction

4.1   Color Feature Extraction

All colors are a mixture of three colors: Red, Green, and Blue. Variation of these colors different color can be obtained [6]. In this experiment, basic color components are used to calculate histogram based features for each color channel. These statistical values are used as one of the feature vectors to retrieve an image class [26]. Figure 5 shows Red, Green and Blue values obtained from Fabric material image.

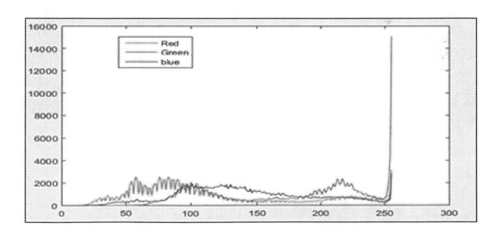

Fig. 5. Red, Green and Blue values obtained from Fabric material image. (Color figure online)

4.2   Luminance Feature Extraction

Colors with its actual brightness which captured by Light and Luminance are not perceived by the human. [20]. Luminance used a weighted combination of the RGB Channels to match human brightness perception [13].

$Y \cup V$ is to use a different representation of color information. In $Y \cup V$ system, where Y measures overall brightness or luminance of an image which is given in Eq. 1.

$$Y_{Luminance} \leftarrow 0.3R + 0.59G + 0.11B \tag{1}$$

Figure 6 shows the Luminance value of Glass image is greater than the Luminance value of Wood and Stone images.

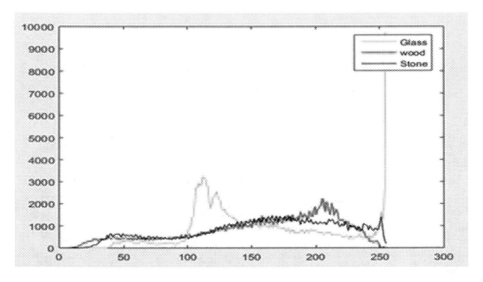

Fig. 6. Luminance values for glass, wood and stone image. (Color figure online)

4.3   GLCM Feature Extraction

Particularly in texture, features are obtained from matrix called as Co-occurrence matrix. Co-occurrence matrix can be defined as $\{Vi, j | l, \theta\}$ where l, θ can take together defined as a parameter (P) which is called as a positioned parameter. Where i and j are intensity value of two pixels, l and θ the distance and the angle between that two pixels. Co-occurrence value gives the frequency at which an intensity value at i and an intensity value at j will occur together. The position of i is defined by the position parameter P with respective intensity value j [18]. The GLCM is computed by Normalizing $V_{i,j}$ dividing it by sum of all the counts which is given in Eq. 2 [8].

$$P_{i,j} = \frac{V_{i,j}}{\sum_{i,j=0}^{G-1} V_{i,j}} \tag{2}$$

From the Normalized GLCM different kinds of feature can be extracted [8]. To identify the class of an image from Flickr Material Database (FMD), author used six different features in feature extraction as shown in Table 1.

Table 1. Feature used in extraction

Feature	Formula
Contrast	$\sum_{i,j=0}^{G-1} P(i,j)(i-j)^2$
Uniformity (also called Energy)	$\sum_{i,j=0}^{G-1} P(i,j)^2$
Correlation	$\dfrac{\sum_{i,j=0}^{G-1}(i,j)P(i,j) - \mu x \mu y}{\delta x \delta y}$
Homogeneity	$\sum_{i,j=0}^{G-1} \dfrac{P(i,j)}{1+(i-j)^2}$
Entropy	$\sum_{i,j=0}^{G-1} P(i,j)(-\ln P(i,j))$
IDM	$\dfrac{\sum_{i,j=0}^{G-1} P(i,j)}{1+(i-j)^2}$

Contrast: Contrast refers to the distinction of the gray level [8].

Uniformity (also called Energy): Energy computes repetitions of the pixel pair [11].

Correlation: Haralik defines the estimation of correlation of a pixel and its neighboring pixel from the whole image. It calculates the linear dependency of gray levels on that of the neighboring pixel [10]. Distortion, displacement, force and optic flow measured by the correlation [8].

Homogeneity: The smoothness means homogeneity can be measured using the gray level distribution of an image. It is inversely proportional with contrast. Homogeneity value is small then contrast large, whereas contrast is small then homogeneity small [11]. If big values are on the main diagonal then get the large homogeneity value.

Entropy: Entropy measures the degree of the disorder among pixel in an image. It is inversely proportional with uniformity. Entropy is large if the image contains a large number of gray level distributions [3].

IDM: If the gray levels of the pixels are the same then, the IDM value of that image is high [11].

5 K-Nearest Neighbors Classifier

K-Nearest Neighbors Classifier analyzed the number of neighbors and Euclidean distance gives the closest distance between the neighbors. The author combines both the approach and tries to find the class of an image.

Euclidean distance is measured closest distance between the neighbors which is given in Eq. 3. The distance can be calculated between two classes using distance function $d(Ts, Tr)$, where Tr, Ts are classes contains N features, such that $Ts = \{Ts_1, \ldots, Ts_N\}$, $y = \{Tr_1, \ldots, Tr_N\}$ [27,28]

$$d(Tr, Ts) = \sum_{i=0}^{N} \sqrt{Tr_i^2 - Ts_i^2} \tag{3}$$

Procedure: Find class labels.
Input: k, the number of nearest neighbors;Ts, the set of test sample; Tr, the set of training sample
Output: $Class$, the label set of test sample
1. Load DataSet (Train_Data)
2. Load DataSet (Test_Data)
3. $Class = \{\}$
4. For each ts in Ts and each tr in Tr do
5. Closest_neighbors(ts)= {}
6. If (Closest_neighbors(ts)) < k then
7. Closest_neighbors(ts)=Dist(ts,tr) $\cup$ Closest_neighbors(ts)
8. End if
9. If (Closest_neighbors(ts)= k then
10. Break
11. $Class$=Test_Class (Closest_neighbors(ts)) $\cup$ $Class$
12. End For
Notes :
Closest_neighbors(ts) return the k nearest neighbors of ts
Dist (ts, tr) return the closest elements of ts in tr
Test_Class (C) return the class label of C [29]

6   Result and Discussions

Experiments are performed on ten texture classes of Flickr Material Database (FMD). Total 1000 images are used during the experiments performed. Each class contains 100 images out of which training sample used 50 images and for testing process remaining 50 images are used. From Color feature extraction technique three feature vector extracted. Luminance of one image gives one feature. GLCM feature extraction technique gives six features. The Final feature vector consists of overall 10 features. Foliage and Glass material classified by color and luminance feature, Wood material classified by GLCM feature and combination of color, luminance and GLCM feature is classified one more material i.e. Leather. Color, Luminance and GLCM features individually classify Foliage, Glass and Wood material and the combination of these features improves the accuracy of Fabric, Leather and Wood material. Figure 7 shows Category wise classification accuracy of FMD classes using color, luminance and GLCM features (Table 2).

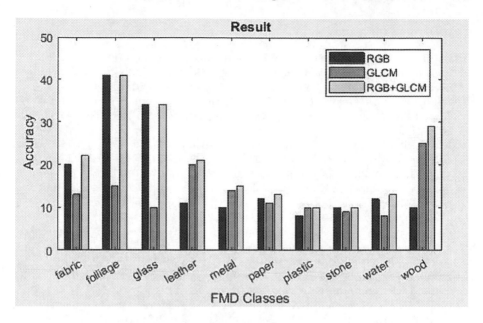

Fig. 7. Category wise classification accuracy.

Table 2. Category wise classification accuracy of FMD dataset

Class	Color descriptor (RGB+ Luminance)		Texture descriptor (GLCM)		(Color and Texture descriptor) (RGB and GLCM)	
	Out of 50	%	Out of 50	%	Out of 50	%
Fabric	20	40	13	26	22	44
Foliage	41	82	15	30	41	82
Glass	34	68	10	20	34	68
leather	11	22	20	40	21	42
metal	10	20	14	28	15	30
paper	12	24	11	22	13	26
plastic	08	16	10	20	10	20
stone	10	20	9	18	10	20
water	12	24	8	16	13	26
wood	10	20	25	50	29	58

7   Conclusions

Texture properties gives valuable clue to classify material. Combination of Color, Luminance and GLCM features classify Foliage, Glass and Wood material efficiently from other classes of Flickr Material Database (FMD). Better feature descriptor can improve the class wise classification of FMD dataset. The overall classification is implemented by using K-Nearest Neighbors (KNN) technique.

References

1. Liu, L., Fieguth, P.W., Hu, D., Wei, Y., Kuang, G.: Fusing sorted random projections for robust texture and material classification. IEEE Trans. Circ. Syst. Video Technol. **25**(3) (2015). https://doi.org/10.1109/TCSVT.2014.2359098
2. Srinivasan, G.N., Shobha, G.: Statistical texture analysis. In: Proceedings of World Academy of Science, Engineering and Technology, vol. 36, December 2008. ISSN 2070-3740
3. Kekre, H.B., Sudeep, D.T., Sarode, T.K., Suryawanshi, V.: Image retrieval using texture features extracted from GLCM, LBG and KPE. IEEE Trans. Circ. Syst. Video Technol. **25**(3) (2015). https://doi.org/10.1109/TCSVT.2014.2359098
4. Smith, J.R., Chang, S.-F.: Single color extraction and image query. In: International Conference on Image Processing (ICIP-1995), Washington, DC, October 1995. https://doi.org/10.1109/ICIP.1995.537688
5. Chadha, A., Mallik, S., Johar, R.: Comparative study and optimization of feature-extraction techniques for content based image retrieval. Int. J. Comput. Appl. **52**(20), 0978887 (2012). https://doi.org/10.5120/8320-1959
6. Lewandowski, Z., Beyenal, H.: Fundamentals of Biofilm Research, 2nd edn. CRC Press, Taylor and Francis Group, Boca Raton (2013)
7. Chary, R.V.R., Lakshmi, D.R., Sunitha, K.V.N.: Feature extraction methods for color image similarity. Adv. Comput. Int. J. (ACIJ) **3**(2) (2012)
8. Mohanaiah, P., Sathyanarayana, P., GuruKumar, L.: Image texture feature extraction using GLCM approach. Int. J. Sci. Res. Publ. **3**, 1 (2013). ISSN 2250-3153
9. Hirata, K., Kato, T.: Query by visual example content based image retrieval. In: 3rd Internal Conference on Extending Database Technology (1992). https://doi.org/10.1007/BFb0032423
10. Haralik, R.M., Shanmugam, K., Dinstein, I.: Texture features for image classification. IEEE Trans. Syst. Man Cybern. **3** (1973). https://doi.org/10.1109/TSMC.1973.4309314
11. Hall-Beyer, M.: GLCM Texture: A Tutorial, v. 3.0 March 2017 replaces v. 2.8 of August 2005 v. 3.0 incorporates all corrections up to v. 2.8
12. Park, J.-H.: Efficient luminance area based image indexing. In: International Conference on Information Science and Applications (ICISA), 16 August 2013. https://doi.org/10.1109/ICISA.2013.6579401
13. Pratt, W.: Digital Image Processing (2007)
14. Ojala, T., Pietikinen, M., Menp, T.: Multiresolution gray-scale and rotation invariant texture classification with local binary patterns. IEEE Trans. Pattern Anal. **24**(7) (2002). https://doi.org/10.1109/TPAMI.2002.1017623
15. Salamati, N., Fredembach, C., Susstrunk, S.: Material classification using color and NIR images. In: 17th Color and Imaging Conference Final Program and Proceedings, January 2009
16. Reddy, R.O.K., Reddy, B.E., Reddy, E.K.: Classifying similarity and defect fabric textures based on GLCM and binary pattern schemes. Int. J. Inf. Eng. Electron. Bus. (2013). https://doi.org/10.5815/ijieeb.2013.05.04
17. Skaff, S.: Mountain View: fusing sorted random projections for robust texture and material classification. Patent Application, Pub. No.: US 2015/0012226A1, January 2015
18. Tahir, M.A., Bouridane, A., Kurugollu, F.: An FPGA based coprocessor for GLCM and Haralick texture features and their application in prostate cancer classification. Analog Integr. Circ. Sig. Process. **43**, 205–215 (2005). © 2005 Springer, The Netherlands. https://doi.org/10.1007/s10470-005-6793-2

19. Raheja, J., Kumar, S., Chaudhary, A.: Fabric defect detection based on GLCM and Gabor filter: a comparison. Optik-Int. J. Light Electron. Opt. **124**(23), 6469–6474 (2013). https://doi.org/10.1016/ijileo.2013.05.004

20. Kanan, C., Cottrell, G.W.: Color-to-grayscale: does the method matter in image recognition? PLoS ONE **7**(1), e29740 (2012). https://doi.org/10.1371/jornal.pone. 0029740

21. Santosh, K.C., Vajda, S.: Antani, S., Thoma, G.R.: Edge map analysis in chest X-rays for automatic pulmonary abnormality screening. Int. J. Comput. Assist. Radiol. Surg. **11**, 1637 (2016). Springer. https://doi.org/10.1007/s11548-016-1359-6

22. Aafaque, A., Santosh, K.C.: Automatic compound figure separation in scientific articles: a study of edge map and its role for stitched panel boundary detection. In: Santosh, K.C., Hangarge, M., Bevilacqua, V., Negi, A. (eds.) RTIP2R 2016. CCIS, vol. 709, pp. 319–332. Springer, Singapore (2017). https://doi.org/10.1007/ 978-981-10-4859-3_29

23. Santosh, K.C., Candemir, S., Jaeger, S., Karargyris, A., Antani, S., Thoma, G.: Automatically detecting rotation in chest radiographs using principal riborientation measure for quality control. Int. J. Pattern Recogn. Artif. Intell. (IJPRAI) **29**(2) (2015). World Scientific. https://doi.org/10.1142/S0218001415570013

24. Candemir, S., Borovikov, E., Santosh, K.C., Antani, S., Thoma, G.: RSILC: rotation- and scale-invariant, line-based color aware descriptor. In: Image and Vision Computing (IVC) (2015). © 2015 Elsevier. https://doi.org/10.1016/imavis. 2015.06.010

25. Santosh, K.C., Antani, S.: Automated chest x-ray screening: can lung region symmetry help detect pulmonary abnormalities? IEEE Trans. Mcd. Imaging **37**(5) (2018). https://doi.org/10.1109/TMI.2017.2775636

26. Varish, N., Pal, A.K.: Content based image retrieval using statistical features of color histogram. In: 3rd International Conference on Signal Processing, Communication and Networking (ICSCN) (2015). https://doi.org/10.1109/ICSCN.2015. 7219922

27. Collins, J., Okada, K.: Content based image retrieval using statistical features of color histogram. In: A Comparative Study of Similarity Measures for Content-Based Medical Image Retrieval, TENCON 2003. Conference on Convergent Technologies for Asia-Pacific Region (2003). ISBN 0-7803-8162-9, TENCON.2003.1273228

28. Zhao, M., Chen, J.: Improvement and comparison of weighted k nearest neighbors classifiers for model selection. J. Softw. Eng. **10**(1), 109–118 (2016). https://doi. org/10.3923/jse.2016.109.118

29. Hegadi, R.S., Navale, D.I., Pawar, T.D., Ruikar, D.D.: Multi feature-based classification of osteoarthritis in knee joint x-ray images (Chap 5). In: Medical Imaging: Artificial Intelligence, Image Recognition, and Machine Learning Techniques. CRC Press, Boca Raton (2019). ISBN 9780367139612

LBP-Haar Cascade Based Real-Time Pedestrian Protection System Using Raspberry Pi

Mitali Mehta$^{(\boxtimes)}$ ⓘ and Rohan Gupta$^{(\boxtimes)}$ ⓘ

MPSTME, NMIMS University, Mumbai, India
mitalimkm@gmail.com, rohang.ag@gmail.com

Abstract. People detection has always posed a challenge in the image processing domain, and a lot of research has been going on to solve the problems posed due to the large number of variants present in detecting a human. In this paper, we introduce a system that integrates various components to perform pedestrian detection, safe distance calculation and a risk assessment for pedestrians, with a warning if the pedestrian is potentially in danger. The proposed system is for middle income cars, where a web camera is connected to a Raspberry Pi 3. The processor performs the calculations based on live webcam feed and gives an alert to the driver via an Android Application. This project uses a custom LBP Cascade classifier written in OpenCV, for pedestrian detection. A comparison of results between this custom classifier with the standard Haar classifier is shown here. This system is tested on an Indian dataset collected by us and on the Penn-Fudan Database for Pedestrian Detection and Segmentation dataset for comparing the results.

Keywords: Advanced driver assistance systems ·
Android Application · Collision avoidance system ·
Image Processing, LBP cascade · Object detection · OpenCV ·
Pedestrian detection · Pedestrian protection system · Raspberry Pi 3

1 Introduction

With an increase in the number of vehicles on Indian roads, and the number of fatalities due to negligent driving, a real-time system is needed to alert a driver about a possible accident. Records indicate that more than 90% of road deaths in 2016 were attributed to rash and negligent driving with the latest National Crime Research Bureau (NCRB) statistics revealing 1.5 lakh deaths in 1.35 lakh road accidents due to delinquent driving [1]. Real-time systems exist, but those are generally present in high end vehicles, not driven by the majority of the Indian population. Hence, we propose a system here that integrates various components to make a pedestrian protection system.

One of the major concerns related to building this system is that it is a real-time system. This means that we have to account for system latency and try to

ⓒ Springer Nature Singapore Pte Ltd. 2019
K. C. Santosh and R. S. Hegadi (Eds.): RTIP2R 2018, CCIS 1035, pp. 60–73, 2019.
https://doi.org/10.1007/978-981-13-9181-1_6

reduce that for accurate results. Moreover, many improvements for systems like this can still be made, since detecting humans poses a lot of complex issues. A large variability in their local and global appearance is caused by various types and styles of clothing, so that only few local regions are really characteristic for the entire category [2]. Along with the varying parameters to determine humans, a system like this must also account for bad weather or bad lighting, despite which, humans must be detected correctly, and various analysis must be performed. In our paper, we address the issue of latency as well as bad weather conditions by proposing some simple workarounds with the existing Haar cascade algorithm in combination with a LBP cascade classifier. We also further optimize that code for better results on the Pi.

The novelty of this paper lies in using a custom LBP classifier, whose comparisons are shown against pre-existing classifiers. Moreover, this system is meant for a large part of the Indian population who drive middle-income cars. High end cars already have such systems pre-installed, but people with middle income cars would not be willing to spend a high amount for such a system. Hence, to implement a system that could be sold to the masses was a major challenge, without compromising on the quality of the system. Such a system implementation is explained in this paper.

The rest of this paper is organized as follows: Sect. 2 mentions existing systems that are similar to our system. Section 3 explains our system specifications and working in detail. Section 4 shows the results from experiments we have performed on our system. Lastly, Sect. 5 concludes this paper, with some important points for future considerations and improvement.

2   Related Works

While looking to develop a system, we came across a lot of object detection methods. We have focused on Local Binary Patterns (LBP) in our research, and have also researched about pre-existing systems which work on a similar principle. Wang et al. [3] used a Histogram of Oriented gradients approach coupled with LBP, where they proposed an approach capable of handling partial occlusion, which is a challenge in pedestrian detection. They use trilinear interpolated HOG with LBP in their image framework. Satpathy et al. [4] use Discriminative Robust Local Binary Pattern (DRLBP) for human detection which they found gives better results than the original LBP classifier. Seeing that LBP in combination with another method gives good results, we have introduced a variation in what [5] has done. We have also used LBP with a Haar cascade classifier, but we have used a particular classifier to mitigate a common problem related to pedestrian detection, which is false detection of motorbike riders as pedestrians. This is explained in the coming sections.

For designing a system, we looked at various resources people have used. Cao et al. [6] developed a system using a low cost camera, instead of a sensor. They used Support Vector Machines and a coevolutionary algorithm to aid their pedestrian detection. Their system showed us a cheaper alternative could help our overall goal of a cost effective system and we have taken reference from [6] in our decision to use a camera and not a sensor. We also refer to the system developed by Kim et al. [7]. They have extracted Haar like features with an Adaboost classification algorithm to perform pedestrian detection. Their implementation was done using Verilog HDL and synthesized the gate-level circuit using 130 nm standard cell library.

3   System Overview

In this section, we introduce our system, and explain its working in detail. The system is divided into three modules, to make it clearer for the user to understand its components and how they function together. The modular design of the system is shown in Fig. 1 and its modules are explained in the following subsections.

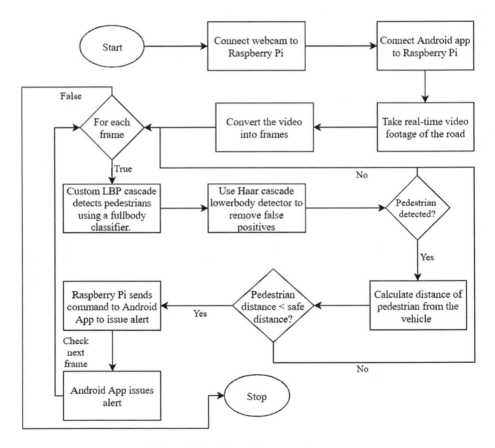

Fig. 1. Flowchart of proposed system

The webcam gets video input from the outside environment. Once the input is obtained, frames are skipped and sent for further processing. In the processing phase, pedestrian detection is performed. Then, if a pedestrian is found, the safe braking distance is used to see if the pedestrian is in danger or not. If the pedestrian is in danger, an alert is issued to the driver via the Android application. If a pedestrian is not found, or, if he is found but not in danger, then the processing module starts checking the next frame for a pedestrian.

3.1   Input Module

This is the first module of our system. The component related to the input module is the USB webcam. For our project, we have used the Logitech C270 camera. The function of this module is to take video input from the environment.

For this purpose, the webcam is attached to the back of the rear-view mirror of the car. While the system is powered on, the webcam takes input from the outside environment in the form of a real-time video footage. This video is then divided into frames, and sent to the processing module explained below, for finding out if a human is near the car or not. Two ways of interfacing the webcam to the Pi are possible. Either they should be connected with a wire, or wirelessly. Our webcam has a USB connector attached to it. Using this, the microprocessor and the webcam are connected.

To help with our goal of the system remaining unaffected by bad weather, we mount the camera inside the car, so that we do not need to offer extra protection to the equipment or complicate the connection with the Pi. Logitech C270 is a medium price-ranged camera. It was necessary for us to purchase a camera with this much clarity so that it became easier to perform object detection without spending unnecessary time and computation power in cleaning the image. In this system the video was recorded in 640×480 resolution. The frame rate is 30 fps.

3.2   Processing Module

This module forms the computational heart of our system. The processing module performs three major functions. First, it performs pedestrian detection, that is, it checks if a pedestrian is present in the frame that was sent by the webcam. Second, it performs safe distance calculation to determine if the pedestrian is at a danger of collision from the car with the installed system. Lastly, it communicates with the Android application, in case an alert is to be sent to the driver. All of these subparts are explained in detail below.

Hardware Specification. The main component used for all the processing is the Raspberry Pi 3 Model B. This is a microprocessor used to perform all computations on the image frame, and to communicate with the webcam and the Android app. The Raspberry Pi 3 Model B is the earliest model of the third-generation Raspberry Pi. It has Quad Core 1.2 GHz Broadcom BCM2837 64bit CPU, 1 GB RAM and BCM43438 wireless LAN and Bluetooth Low Energy (BLE) on board. The external ports of RPI used in this system are the USB port, for connection to the webcam, and its Ethernet port for SSH connection when viewing on a monitor.

Pedestrian Detection. For detecting pedestrians, we have used LBP cascade classifiers. Local binary patterns [8] (Local Binary Patterns, LBP) are descriptors originally used to discriminate textures. Naturally robust to changes in lighting, they were improved to be invariant to rotations and other factors, and implemented in different ways to make them useful in the detection of objects, facial recognition, temporal analysis of images, among other applications.

Basically, each pixel of an image or region of an image is analyzed, as follows: [9–11]

1. The difference between each of the surrounding pixels is evaluated (according to the implementation, immediately adjacent, to a greater radius or even interpolating values) and the central pixel of the analysis.
2. Pixels whose value is greater than or equal to the central pixel are assigned a value of 1, while those whose value is smaller receive a value of 0. Note that the difference will be maintained even if the contrast or brightness changes.
3. The values obtained are concatenated in a single binary word that represents the pixel - its original value was replaced by one that encodes the own information and that of its environment.

Other implementations analyze only non-intersected sets of pixels; that is, each pixel belongs only to one neighbourhood. There are also versions that include multi-scale information, including in the descriptor vector the values corresponding to more than one analysis radius.

Cascade classifiers are formed of stages of weak learners. During each stage of detection the classifier marks a particular region as positive (object was found) or negative (object was not found) based on the current location of the detection window. The classifier is trained to reject many negative sub-regions and successfully detecting almost all positive sub-regions. If the region is labeled as negative then the classification of that particular region is complete and the window moves to the subsequent location. In the case of positive labeling of a region, that region moves onto the next stage of classification. The final result is stated as positive if and only if the object is found in all the stages including the last stage of classification (see Fig. 2) [12].

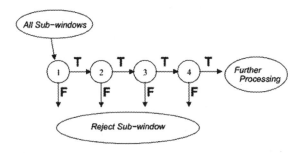

Fig. 2. Stages of the cascade classifier [12]

In this project, we have used a custom trained LBP Cascade file named 08_PEDESTRIAN_LBP_7k_10k_26x74.xml hereafter referred to as visionary_lbp classifier. It has been obtained from ARGO Vision for the purpose of integration within this system. The following cascades largely outperform the OpenCV built-in HOG detector and the HAAR cascades included in OpenCV. Full frontal/rear (with partial profiles) pedestrian detector, trained with [13]:

- Approximately 47,000 positive samples (randomly sampled)
- Approximately 1.1B of negative sub-regions containing outdoor and indoor samples (80%-20%)
- Training size w = 26 h = 74 (aspect ratio ~1:3)

Using visionary_lbp classifier in combination with the Haar Cascade lower-body classifier has helped our project improve its calculation parameters, as compared to using Haar Cascade classifiers. To further help with reducing latency, we have optimized our code. This helps in meeting one of our goals of lesser latency. While optimizing the code, we skip frames captured by the webcam, since most of the frames within a specific batch of 5 or 10 frames are repetitive. We also crop the video, which in a way works like camera calibration, so that the area of detection reduces, and the overall process speed improves.

To help with our goal of least false positives, we have used two classifier files. While performing tests, we observed that people on bikes get falsely detected as pedestrians. To avoid that, we perform classification based on the full body visionary_lbp classifier and the original Haar cascade lowerbody classifier. All these code optimizations are necessary so that we can maintain lower cost equipment without affecting accuracy of the system.

Stopping Distance Calculation. The system has to check whether the pedestrian is beyond the safe distance within which the driver needs his car to stop in order to avoid hitting him. If yes, the pedestrian is thought to be safe and the alert is not sent. If not, the pedestrian is in danger of collision, and an alert is sent via the Android App to the user, asking him to slow down.

The factors that affect the stopping distance of the car include the coefficient of friction between the car and the road, the speed of the car, the type of road and the car's braking capacity. For simplicity, we are assuming a smooth road, hence it has a constant coefficient of friction (μ) of 0.7 for dry roads and for a wet road μ is 0.4 [15]. In order to calculate the safe braking distance, the speed at which the car is travelling should be known. For the purpose of reducing computational complexity, we have taken an average speed at which cars travel on Indian roads. According to reports, the average speed of cars in Mumbai has reduced to 20 km/h as compared to earlier 45 km/h due to increase in traffic [14]. The formula for safe braking distance is as follows [16]:

$$d = \frac{v^2}{2\mu g} \tag{1}$$

where
d = braking distance
v = velocity
μ = coefficient of friction
g = acceleration due to gravity

Using Eq. 1 and the assumptions about speed and coefficient of friction, the braking distance for dry roads is 2.24 m and for wet roads is 3.92 m.

Generally, for conditions where one is not prepared, reaction time is approximately 1.0 s. The formula for calculating reaction distance is as follows [17]:

$$Reaction\ Distance = \frac{speed * reaction\ time}{3.6} \qquad (2)$$

Using Eq. 2 and the assumptions about speed and reaction time, the reaction distance is 5.55 m.

Using Eqs. 1 and 2 we calculate the total stopping distance.

$$Total\ Stopping\ Distance = Reaction\ Distance + Safe\ Braking\ Distance \quad (3)$$

Hence, using Eq. 3, for dry roads, total stopping distance is 7.79 m and for wet roads, it is 9.47 m.

In our program, we check for the current month, and depending on that, the condition for 7.79 m or 9.47 m is checked. Any person within this range is considered to be in danger, and an alert is subsequently sent.

Communication Between Processing Module and Alert Module. The message passing protocol used in this system for interfacing the Pi with the App is MQTT. MQTT stands for Message Queuing Telemetry Transport. It transports messages over a network. MQTT is used by the Pi to tell the App that the pedestrian who has just been detected is in danger, hence, the alert should be issued. In order to do this, it needs to recognize who is in the network and who has specifically asked for that message. For this purpose, MQTT uses certain terminologies as explained here.

The two entities communicating over the network are termed as the Client and Server. A client refers to a program or device that requests data over the network or sends data over the network. A client always establishes a network connection to the Server [18]. Here, the Pi and the App are both clients. A server is a program or device that acts as an intermediary between Clients which publish Application Messages and Clients which have made Subscriptions [18]. In this system, the server is the open source eclipse server, referenced as 'iot.eclipse.org'.

The first method used under MQTT in our system is the Connect method. After a Network Connection is established by a Client to a Server, the first Packet sent from the Client to the Server must be a CONNECT Packet [18]. Here, the connection happens from two different platforms. On one side, it happens from the Python program on the Pi. On the other side, it happens from the Android Application on the user's mobile phone.

The second method used by the processor is Subscription method. In order to receive and send messages over the network, MQTT needs to know which clients are interested in communicating with each other. For this reason, a SUBSCRIBE message is used, using which each client subscribes or requests access to the contents of a particular Topic [18]. In this system, the topic that both the app and Pi subscribe to is called "ppsconnect". This topic has to be used while publishing a message too, as explained below.

The third method used by the processor is the Publish method. Whenever a client wants to send data over the network, the client does so using PUBLISH message [18]. The PUBLISH message has the Topic name mentioned as one of its parameters, so that the data sent would only be sent to the people who have subscribed to that particular topic. It also contains the Payload, which is the message itself. This method is responsible for the alert request.

The last method used by the processor is the Disconnection method. At the end of the message transfer, the clients usually disconnect from the server. This is done using the DISCONNECT message [18]. In this system, once the webcam is turned off, then, before the program exits, the disconnection request is sent from the Pi to eclipse server.

3.3   Alert Module

This module's primary function is to try and prevent the accident between the driver and the pedestrian via an audio-based warning.

As a part of our system, we have developed an Android App which gets connected to the same network as the processing module, and whenever needed, sends an alert to the driver. The app, named PPS, is to be installed by the driver while installing the system, and each time he goes for a drive, he should connect to the network by pressing a connect button provided on the home page.

Some features of PPS include connection on start-up and customizations available for users. Just as the processing module must be connected to the server via MQTT, even the Android app is connected to the same network. After that, the app subscribes to the same topic as the processor, namely 'ppsconnect'. Once both the devices have subscribed to the same topic, a communication link is established with that topic name. Hence, the processor sends a message with the topic name mentioned as one of the parameters. Every device within a hearing range that has subscribed to that same topic will receive that message.

The advantage of using MQTT as the message passing protocol is that even if the passengers in the car have the app installed, and they all ask for this message, then the alert will be sounded in all their phones. Hence, the driver can get the alert even if his phone is currently not with him, provided the some other phone in the car has the app installed.

To make things more convenient for the driver, our app also allows for certain customizations for the driver. There are two options provided – alert tone and volume control. Aside from normal Android alert tones, we have provided five other tones that the driver can choose from, depending on what can give him a warning without distracting him greatly from his drive. Also, depending on his comfort level, he can adjust the volume, as in any other app on his phone. This app also works in the background when other apps are used, hence even if the driver goes back to the phone's homepage, it will not affect the app performance.

4   Results and Discussion

In this project, a dataset of humans has been collected by us, on Indian Roads. That dataset is of 26 min duration. For testing purposes, that video has been converted to image frames to compare the values with the Penn-Fudan Database for Pedestrian Detection and Segmentation dataset [19]. Two frames with detected pedestrians are shown below for each Dataset (see Figs. 3 and 4). For the sake of comparison and uniformity, the same video is used during testing on the PC as well. The results for both are shown in the tables below.

Some common parameters on which the testing is done on our dataset are:

- Total number of images: 135
- Total number of true pedestrians: 291
- The testing of this system is done during the day

Some common parameters on which the testing is done on the Penn-Fudan Database for Pedestrian Detection and Segmentation dataset are:

- Total number of images: 170
- Total number of true pedestrians: 457

(a)   (b)

Fig. 3. Pedestrians detected using proposed system in our Indian Dataset

The factors which are calculated here are:

Sensitivity: Sensitivity shows how good a test is at detecting the positives. A test can cheat and maximize this by always returning "positive" [20].

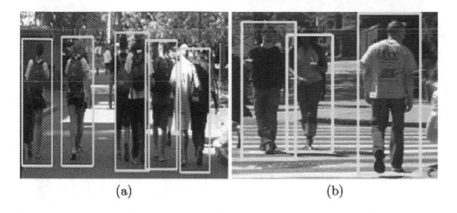

Fig. 4. Pedestrians detected using proposed system in PennFudan Dataset

Fig. 5. Proposed System mounted in the car

The formula for Sensitivity is as follows: [20]

$$Sensitivity = \frac{True\ Positive}{True\ Positive + False\ Negative} \tag{4}$$

Precision: Precision denotes how many of the positively classified were relevant. A test can cheat and maximize this by only returning positive on one result it's most confident in [20].

The formula for Precision is as follows: [20]

$$Precision = \frac{True\ Positive}{True\ Positive + False\ Positive} \tag{5}$$

Tables 1 and 2 show the test results as obtained on a 3rd Gen i7 processor and Tables 3 and 4 show the test results as obtained on a Raspberry Pi 3 Model B processor.

In all the tables, we see that the number of True Positives is the highest while using the visionary_lbp classifier alone, but it also gives the highest number of False Positives. In our proposed system, while the number of True Positives is lesser than that of the standalone visionary_lbp classifier, it is still relatively high compared to the other two classifier methods and along with that, the number of False Positives significantly decreases, hence making our proposed method viable to use.

Similarly, we can see that the Sensitivity is the highest for the visionary_lbp classifier used alone, and the Precision is the highest when Haar cascade fullbody classifier is used in combination with Haar cascade lowerbody classifier. But, using the visionary_lbp classifier file in combination with the Haar cascade lowerbody classifier gives a better balance between sensitivity and precision, since increasing the sensitivity does not drastically increase the number of false positives while keeping the precision high.

Table 1. Testing on Indian Pedestrian Dataset using 3rd Gen i7 processor.

Classifier used	True positives	False positives	False negatives	Sensitivity	Precision
Haar fullbody	29	8	157	16%	78%
Haar fullbody + lowerbody	40	5	146	22%	89%
visionary_lbp	96	21	90	52%	82%
visionary_lbp + Haar lowerbody	87	8	99	47%	92%

Table 2. Testing on Penn-Fudan Database for Pedestrian Detection and Segmentation using 3rd Gen i7 processor.

Classifier used	True positives	False positives	False negatives	Sensitivity	Precision
Haar fullbody	61	1	331	16%	98%
Haar fullbody + lowerbody	159	2	233	41%	99%
visionary_lbp	355	25	37	91%	93%
visionary_lbp + Haar lowerbody	326	13	66	83%	96%

Table 3. Testing on Indian Pedestrian Dataset using Raspberry Pi 3B processor.

Classifier used	True positives	False positives	False negatives	Sensitivity	Precision
Haar fullbody	24	5	162	13%	83%
Haar fullbody + lowerbody	36	8	150	19%	82%
visionary_lbp	91	23	95	49%	80%
visionary_lbp + Haar lowerbody	72	17	114	39%	81%

Table 4. Testing on Penn-Fudan Database for Pedestrian Detection and Segmentation using Raspberry Pi 3B processor.

Classifier used	True positives	False positives	False negatives	Sensitivity	Precision
Haar fullbody	61	0	331	16%	100%
Haar fullbody + lowerbody	158	0	234	40%	100%
visionary_lbp	359	20	33	92%	95%
visionary_lbp + Haar lowerbody	314	17	78	80%	95%

In this system, we have used a Local Binary Pattern classifier as opposed to a Haar Cascade classifier for two main reasons. Firstly, as shown by our comparison tables above, the True Positives for the custom LBP classifier in combination with the Haar lowerbody classifier are higher than either of the Haar classifiers, used alone or in combination. This indicates that the Sensitivity is higher for our proposed system, as compared to a standalone Haar classifier. Secondly, as concluded by [21], an LBP classifier gives a higher speed as compared to a Haar classifier, and is more suitable for certain detection tasks. This would help a real-time system to get faster results, hence we have chosen LBP in combination with Haar for better results.

5   Conclusion and Future Works

We presented a system that detects humans walking on the road and estimates if a possible collision can take place. To prevent that accident, we send an audio alert to the driver's phone via an application. The workarounds for latency and weather conditions are also explained in the paper, with the limited cost kept in mind.

This system can be used by most middle income cars and hence meets an important societal objective of helping mass public. Moreover, it can be used in all types of cars, since it is not car dependent, rather just phone dependent, and most recent phones have the specifications needed for the app to run. It is portable too, and does not have a lot of connection hassles from the driver's point of view. Neither does it take up much place, so as to disrupt the driver's view of the road.

While this system shows a lot of potential, in order to be commercially viable, it needs a lot more work. Some improvements that can be done on the system are its processor speed, integrating an inbuilt webcam and taking dynamic speed of the car. Since this system was made within a budget, the processor used was not of a very high speed. But, the system comparison shows that it works much faster with a higher generation of processors. If such a processor is made cheaper in the future, that can be used in place of the Pi. Also, there are IP camera applications built in the phone. To save cost, these can be used in place of the webcam. The only drawback with this includes restricted usage of the phone by the driver while driving, which could prove to be more helpful than limiting. Lastly, an optical encoder can be integrated into the project so that the speed is dynamically obtained from the car, using which a safe braking distance at that speed can be calculated, for more accurate real-time results.

Acknowledgment. We would like to thank Mr. Alessandro Ferrari and his team at ARGO Vision for sharing his LBP classifier with us for the purpose of this project. We would also like to thank them for making their resources available for students and professionals. Using this file has been crucial to our system's successful implementation.

References

1. The Times of India. https://timesofindia.indiatimes.com/india/90-deaths-on-roads-due-to-rash-driving-ncrb/articleshow/61898677.cms. Accessed 4 Nov 2017
2. Leibe, B., Seemann, E., Schiele, B.: Pedestrian detection in crowded scenes. In: 2005 IEEE Computer Society Conference on Computer Vision and Pattern Recognition (2005)
3. Wang, X., Han, T., Yan, S.: An HOG-LBP human detector with partial occlusion handling. In: 2009 IEEE 12th International Conference on Computer Vision (2009)
4. Satpathy, A., Jiang, X., Eng, H.: Human detection using discriminative and robust local binary pattern. In: 2013 IEEE International Conference on Acoustics, Speech and Signal Processing (2013)

5. Thiyagarajan, B., Mayur, A., Ravina, B., Akilesh, G.: LBP-Haar multi-feature pedestrian detection for auto-braking and steering control system. In: 2015 International Conference on Computational Intelligence and Communication Networks (2015)
6. Cao, X., Qiao, H., Keane, J.: A low-cost pedestrian-detection system with a single optical camera. In: IEEE Transactions on Intelligent Transportation Systems, vol. 9, no. 1 (2008)
7. Kim, S., Park, S., Lee, S., Park, S., Cho, K.: Design of high-performance pedestrian and vehicle detection circuit using Haar-like features. In: TENCON 2012 IEEE Region 10 Conference (2012)
8. Ojala, T., Pietikainen, M., Maenpaa, T.: Multiresolution gray-scale and rotation invariant texture classification with local binary patterns. IEEE Trans. Pattern Anal. Mach. Intell. **24**(7), 971–987 (2002)
9. Local Binary Patterns. http://bytefish.de/blog/local_binary_patterns. Accessed 25 Apr 2018
10. Local Binary Patterns with Python and OpenCV. http://www.pyimagesearch.com/2015/12/07/local-binary-patterns-with-python-opencv. Accessed 25 Apr 2018
11. Local Binary Patterns. http://www.scholarpedia.org/article/Local_Binary_Patterns. Accessed 10 Apr 2018
12. Object detection using Haar-cascade Classifier. https://pdfs.semanticscholar.org/0f1e/866c3acb8a10f96b432e86f8a61be5eb6799.pdf. Accessed 25 Dec 2017
13. BOOST THE WORLD: PEDESTRIAN DETECTION - Visionary. http://www.vision-ary.net/2015/03/boost-the-world-pedestrian/. Accessed 4 Jan 2018
14. Vehicles in Mumbai increase by more than half in seven years - Times of India. https://timesofindia.indiatimes.com/city/mumbai/Vehicles-in-Mumbai-increase-by-more-than-half-in-seven-years/articleshow/33570794.cms. Accessed 8 Jan 2018
15. Friction and Automobile Tires. http://hyperphysics.phy-astr.gsu.edu/hbase/Mechanics/frictire.html. Accessed 9 Mar 2018
16. Stopping Distance Formula. http://www.softschools.com/formulas/physics/stopping_distance_formula/89/. Accessed 10 Mar 2018
17. Stopping distance, reaction distance and braking distance. https://korkortonline.se/en/theory/reaction-braking stopping/. Accessed 10 Mar 2018
18. MQTT Version 3.1.1. http://docs.oasis-open.org/mqtt/mqtt/v3.1.1/os/mqtt-v3.1.1-os.html. Accessed 15 Jan 2018
19. Pedestrian Detection Database. https://www.cis.upenn.edu/~jshi/ped_html/. Accessed 21 Jun 2018
20. Precision, recall, sensitivity and specificity. https://uberpython.wordpress.com/2012/01/01/precision-recall-sensitivity-and-specificity/. Accessed 1 Apr 2018
21. Kadir, K., Kamaruddin, M., Nasir, H., Safie, S., Bakti, Z.: A comparative study between LBP and Haar-like features for face detection using OpenCV. In: 2014 4th International Conference on Engineering Technology and Technopreneuship (2014)

Reconstructing a 3D Room from a Kinect Carrying UAV

Eleni Mangina$^{(\boxtimes)}$, Conor Gannon, and Evan O'Keeffe

School of Computer Science, University College Dublin, Dublin, Ireland
eleni.mangina@ucd.ie
https://people.ucd.ie/eleni.mangina

Abstract. This project focuses on the creation of a portable SLAM (Simultaneous Localisation and Mapping) system, which uses an Unmanned Aerial Vehicle (UAV) as the transportation medium. The main purpose of the system is to create a 3D map of the environment, while concurrently localizing itself within the map. The real world applications of this system concentrate on search and rescue scenarios. The system uses the Microsoft Kinect as its primary sensor. Within this project we utilized Visual SLAM, which is the process of using data from the Kinect sensor to calculate position. The algorithm looked at successive frames and depth estimates from the Kinect and then matched features across the images to calculate distance and stability. The work presented in this paper is approached from a practical point of view rather than purely theoretical basis. The end result is a physical prototype which is ready to be deployed in the field for further testing.

Keywords: UAVs · Simultaneous Localisation and Mapping

1 Introduction

The aim of the project was to create a prototype capable of mapping environments in 3D for use in search and rescue operations - focusing mainly on collapsed buildings. UAVs are more versatile than traditional ground robots and they are financially affordable. A GPS is not sufficient for navigation indoors due to range and reception issues. The UAV must rely on on-board sensors to accurately gauge its state and plan trajectories.

The release of the Microsoft Kinect attracted attention among the scientific community; a module (OpenNI) was made for ROS (Robotic Operating System) [14]. The Kinect is a motion sensing device with three sensors, with an infrared laser projector, a colour camera and an infrared camera. The infrared laser projector is a depth sensor; it projects the environment in 3D with any lighting condition. The cameras have 640 × 480 resolution running at 30 frames per second. This allows the data to be transmitted in real time. The Kinect can be stripped down to a satisfactory weight of 115 grams, an easy payload for the

© Springer Nature Singapore Pte Ltd. 2019
K. C. Santosh and R. S. Hegadi (Eds.): RTIP2R 2018, CCIS 1035, pp. 74–87, 2019.
https://doi.org/10.1007/978-981-13-9181-1_7

UAV. The motion of image features from a camera can be used to create the trajectory for the UAV and also create a 3D model of the scene.

The method for calculating the trajectory uses feature matching between image frames, is Visual Odometry. If the matching is between a live map of the scene and the current image, it is Visual SLAM [18]. With Visual Slam drift does not occur. The only cost of creating and maintaining a live map is based on the computational power and the complexity needed. Visual SLAM allows a UAV in a new novel environment to gradually create an accurate map of the environment, while concurrently estimating its position within the map. Most of the current systems used for search and rescue operations are expensive and are not mass produced - making such systems financially inaccessible in impoverished regions. The idea of this project was to create a prototype that could be utilized and built in developing countries where emergency relief is slow or non-existent.

A set of underlying principles were set for the project - all of the software needed to be open source; the hardware needed to be robust and cost effective and the final prototype needed to be user friendly for non-technical operators. The objective was to create a system that would allow users to respond and react to emergency situations themselves, reducing reliance on external factors.

This paper presents the background work of the research, the design and implementation of this work. Finally the testing and evaluation of the proposed solution is presented along with the conclusions for further development.

2 Background Work

The background research focused mainly on two topics - Visual SLAM and Visual Odometry using a Kinect RGB-D camera. Although there are many different SLAM methods there is a constant principle of non existence of the environment map at the beginning. The UAV becomes the origin of the coordinate system and the measurement taken at this location is the initial measurements. Every measurement after this contains already known data and new novel data. The UAV can find an overlapping by comparing the current measurement with the data set and then calculate its new position. When the new measured data is inserted into the map, the environment can then be mapped incrementally. As GPS performs poorly within buildings, many indoor positioning methods have been developed but they have proved to be relatively expensive and require regular maintenance and calibration. The Kinect allows a novel SLAM (Simultaneous Localization And Mapping) method to be employed by providing colour images and dense depth maps. By combining the visual features and the scale information of the 3D depth sensing, a dense 3D environment can be represented. The research for this topic focused mainly on the evaluation of the RGB-D SLAM System [3] and the evaluation of SLAM Approaches for Microsoft Kinect [16].

In [3] the authors split the trajectory estimation into a front end and back end. The front end extracts spatial relations between individual observations and the back end optimizes the poses of these observations in a so-called pose graph and with respect to a non-linear error function. OpenCV [2] is used for detection and matching of the different feature types: SURF (Speeded up Robust Feature) [1], ORB [15] and SIFT (Scale invariant feature transform) [11]. The authors evaluate the accuracy and processing time for the three feature descriptors. OpenCV is essentially a library of programming functions used for real time computer vision. ORB is a key point detector and feature descriptor. The SURF key point detector keeps the number of key points stable using a self-adjusting variable. The feature locations are then projected from the image to 3D using the depth measurement at the centre of the key point. "However, no visual feature provides perfect reliability with respect to repetition and false positives", to solve the problem of noisy data the RANSAC [4] algorithm can be used. In terms of the back end, "The pairwise transformations between sensor poses, as computed by the front end, form the edges of a pose graph". This does not form a globally consistent trajectory due to inaccuracies in the estimation. To correct this, the pose graph can be optimized using the g2o framework [10]. The g2o framework is an easily extensible graph optimizer that can be applied to a wide range of problems including several variants of SLAM and bundle adjustment. Many problems in computer graphics involve the minimization of a nonlinear error function that can be represented as a graph. In graph based SLAM the state variables are the positions of the drone in the environment or the location of the landmarks in the map that can be observed with the UAV' sensors. The measurement relies on the relative location of the two state variables. If represented in a graph each node of the graph is a state variable that needs to be optimized and each edge between the variables is a pairwise observation of the nodes it connects. In summary, this approach extracts visual key points from the colour images and uses depth images to localize them in 3D. RANSAC is used to estimate the transformations between RGB-D frames and optimize the pose graph using non-linear optimization.

Corporate research in technologies, as described in [16], focuses on two different approaches, the first is based on visual key points the second one is based on point clouds. The following SLAM algorithms are evaluated in the paper: visual key points, hybrid and ICP. For visual key points, the key points have to be "detected and categorized". For example, using SURF (Speeded up Robust Feature) [1] or SIFT (Scale-invariant feature transform) [11]. The key points between two pictures that were found using the SIFT and SURF detectors can be matched with the minimal Euclidean distance technique. The key point pairs are then used to calculate the position transformation using RANSAC [4]. The goal of the RANSAC algorithm is to find a suitable model that describes the position transformation best. The authors describe the RANSAC algorithm with 4 steps in an intuitive manner. First randomly choose similar key point pairs. Define a characteristic for the model. Apply the model to all of the key points of the first picture, the key point pairs fitting the model are inliers. If the new model is better than the current model, simply replace the current model with the new. The authors allude to the main problem for SLAM methods, as the "The errors in sensor measurement accumulates over time and results in a deviation that also increases over time". To combat the errors, the TORO (Tree-based network optimizer) optimization is used [8]. The point clouds approach uses ICP (Iterative Closest Point), point clouds are inputted to then calculate position transformations. The authors use a generalized ICP approach [17]. This approach takes two point clouds which are moderately overlapping or identical and then aligns them.

2.1   Project Background Research

Research was carried out to find the best solution for path planning using SLAM. One of the objectives for the project is to allow the UAV to autonomously plan the best route for navigation. Most SLAM algorithms represent the environment using a sparse set of features. This type of representation is not sufficient for collision free path planning; it lacks information about the obstacles in the surrounding environment. The most successful path planning methods are those based on randomized sampling. Samples are stochastically drawn in the configuration space. Then neighbouring collision free samples are connected via collision-free paths forming a road map. This road map is later used to connect any two given configurations. All paths in the configuration space are equally valid. The aim is to determine the shortest path between the given start and goal configurations.

Belief Road Maps (BRM) Algorithm: In BRM the edges defining the road map include information about the uncertainty change when traversing the corresponding edge. However, the BRM technique needs an existing model of the environment. [19] technical report examines Pose SLAM graphs and their use as belief road maps (BRMs). The BRM algorithm uses a known model of the environment. It then uses probabilistic sampling to generate a roadmap. The authors employ a technique in which builds the road map on line using the Pose SLAM algorithm. The result blends BRM and Pose SLAM, "method that devises optimal navigation strategies on-line by searching for the path with lowest accumulated uncertainty for the robot pose". For Pose SLAM, only the trajectory is estimated and landmarks are used to provide relative constraints between robot poses.

Probabilistic Road Maps (PRM) Algorithm: The map for Pose SLAM only contains the collision free trajectories. Belief road maps were originally used as a variant of probabilistic road maps (PRMs). As with PRMs, BRMs are constructed by probabilistic sampling in configuration space of a given environment model. The authors argue that the set of poses defining the map in Pose SLAM can be used as the starting point for a BRM. The poses stored in the map by Pose SLAM during exploration are without obstacles, they were already traversed by the robot when the map was originally built. The result of the Pose SLAM algorithm is a directed graph, in which the nodes are poses or way points, and the edges are established through Odometry or sensor registration of the environment. The poses in the Pose SLAM map can be taken as samples for a belief road map and used for planning. An advantage of using the Pose SLAM graph versus any other delayed-state SLAM graph is that Pose SLAM has its nodes equally distributed in the information space. This allows an estimation to be made taking into account the length of the path and the uncertainty in the poses. This is in contrast with existing approaches that either take into account the path length or the path uncertainty, and combinations of both methods is usually unreliable considering they are defined in different spaces and with different units.

RGB-D Mapping: In [5] the authors introduce the idea of "using a RGB-D camera to generate dense 3D models of indoor environments". Sparse points are extracted from the RGB-D images and then matched using the RANSAC method. Iterative Closest Point matching estimates the best alignment between the frames. Alignment between successive frames can give an accurate estimation for tracking the UAV over small distances. But errors start to accumulate, most notably when the Drone is following a long path and it encounters a previously visited location. The error in frame alignment results in a map that has two representations of one location. This is the loop closure problem. The Visual Odometry approach suffers from this problem significantly - however there are many solutions to try and combat the problem. In [5] Loop closures are detected using a method of matching data frames with a collection of previously collected frames. Consistent alignments can be achieved in a multitude of ways such as sparse bundle adjustment. Further research on the loop closure problem was carried out and the research in [12] proposes a strong alternative approach of detection and correction at key frame-rate, in loops containing hundreds of key frames.

Visual SLAM and Visual Odometry: In [20] the idea of combining Visual SLAM and Visual Odometry is introduced. The Visual Odometry technique tracks hundreds of visual features per frame giving a clear and accurate estimation of relative camera motion, but drift occurs. The combination keeps the map minimal but uses more inter frame point matches leading to a more accurate pose estimate. The landmarks are not permanent therefore the computation overhead is still light. By examining the literature surrounding Visual Odometry and mapping using an RGB-D camera, there is a possibility of combing aspects of both for the project. [6] examines "the best practices in Visual Odometry using an RGB-D camera to enable the control of a micro air vehicle". These methods have become somewhat redundant with the advent of cheap structured light RGB-D cameras. However, the RGB-D cameras have limited range because of their projectors. The position and velocity can be estimated with the sensor data; the 3D motion is estimated by comparing the relative motion of the Drone "from sensor frame to sensor frame". A map can then be built with the positional data. In [6] the authors describe the algorithm they have developed for the Visual Odometry process using the following steps: image pre-processing, feature extraction, initial rotation estimation, feature matching, inlier detection and motion estimation. There are many ways to approach Visual Odometry.

2.2   Project Definition

The background research has proved that 3D maps of indoor environments can be made with inexpensive cameras such as the Kinect and autonomous flight for UAVs in indoor environments is also possible with current Visual Odometry methods. The literature proves that it is possible to create a system that is, "able to plan complex 3D paths in cluttered environments while retaining a high degree of situational awareness". However, there are still many problems that need to be addressed.

- Current mapping techniques only use "two consecutive frames to estimate the motion of the camera".
- The loop closures detected by frame to frame for visual feature matching, is not sufficient for the creation of large accurate maps.
- Most Visual Odometry techniques do not perform well in environments with few visual features.
- The Kinect performs better in small cluttered scenarios, as the Kinect's range is not sufficient for large expansive outdoor environments.

  This work is inspired by research carried out at the University of St Andrews [9], which uses the Kinect's depth sensing capabilities to aid the blind navigate novel environments. An attempt was made to allow the UAV to fly autonomously by using the Kinect's depth information alone. The UAV would essentially navigate its environment by taking turns of the least resistance. For example, if there was an object ahead it would rotate and turn; if there was no object ahead it would move forward - this process would allow the UAV to map the environment and navigate safely without colliding with objects. This form of navigation would require no operator; the UAV or multiple UAVs could be left to their own devices until they run out of power.

3   Design and Implementation

The aim of this project was to create a prototype capable of mapping environments in 3D for use in search and rescue operations – focusing mainly on collapsed buildings. Within these kind of Scenarios there is no GPS signal available for localization. From a practical point of view, operators of the prototype must be able to view the map that is being built and see the trajectory and location of the entity within the map. This will allow the operators to become spatially aware of the environment as they prepare to enter the building. A SLAM (Simultaneous Localisation and Mapping) approach was implemented. Mapping integrates all of the entities sensor information into a representation of the environment and localization is the process of estimating the pose of the entity relative to the map. In essence SLAM is the process of building a map while at the same time localizing the entity within the map.

The prototype needed to be robust and easy to use for such environments - it would have to withstand hard handling in extreme environments and have the ability to be operated by non-technical personnel. From the onset it was clear that the prototype would have to be completely wireless. This led to many technical questions - for example, how to transmit the live data and how to power the system. To bring the prototype from a loose idea into a clear design and plan, the system was broken down into various parts. The high level design is shown in Fig. 1. Transforming the Microsoft Kinect from an entertainment device into a robotic sensor proved to be rewarding and challenging. The Kinect first had to be stripped to its most minimal state due to weight restrictions imposed by the UAV's' maximum pay load. The goal was to remove as much hardware and housing as possible, as long as it did not interfere with the functionality of the two on board cameras (IR CMOS and Colour CMOS) and IR projector.

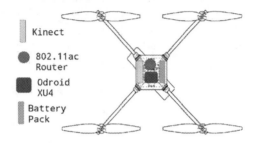

Fig. 1. High level of proposed design

As the prototype needed to be completely wireless, every component mounted on the drone had to be battery powered. The first approach taken was to build a battery box containing 8AA battery's, which gives 12 v. This solution did not align with some of the goals that were set for building the prototype - normal and rechargeable AA batteries are expensive and deteriorate quickly. Even though the experiment failed, it was concluded that the Kinect can run on a portable battery source effectively. A 12 v 6800 mAh DC rechargeable lithium ion battery was used instead. To ensure steady and correct power regulation, a RioRand adjustable boost power supply voltage converter with a digital voltmeter was used. The battery may not output 12 v 100% of the time and the RioRand acts as a booster between the Kinect and the battery source.

To utilize the data produced by the Kinect, the libfreenect driver was used, as shown in Fig. 2. The libfreenect driver, which is open source, allows access to the raw data streams produced by the Kinect- for example the depth stream, IR stream and RGB stream. OpenNI is another competing open source library, which is based on the original and official prime sense code, as shown in Fig. 3. Due to its commercial inclinations we did not utilise it for this project. The

Kinect is attached to the Odroid XU4 via USB. The Odroid runs Ubuntu 14.04 arm edition - tests were carried out with Ubuntu Mate and Arch Linux but were not compatible with ROS Indigo. ROS was manually installed on the Odroid along with the libfreenect drivers. When the Kinect is powered and connected, the libfreenect driver is launched with the aid of ROS. The data produced by the Kinect is published to various topics - for example depth stream and IR stream. The ROS master runs on the Odroid and coordinates the system from here.

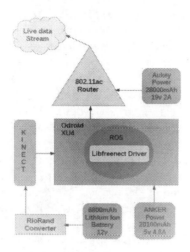

Fig. 2. Proposed solution for data transfer

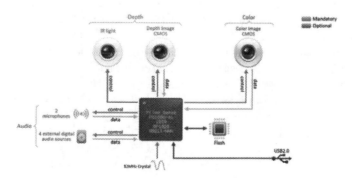

Fig. 3. PrimeSense data flow and control [13]

The Odroid is connected to a router via its Gigabit Ethernet port. ROS provides the infrastructure to create a network allowing the various nodes to contact and communicate with each other in a distributed manner. The first approach taken to power the Odroid used a 12 v lithium Ion battery and connected it to a DROK step down voltage transformer, it takes an input of 12–24 v and converts it to 5 v using 4.8 amps. This is the exact voltage and amperage needed to power the Odroid. This solution worked, but it proved to relatively delicate due to the soldering and wiring required to set it up. It would not be robust enough to survive a search and rescue environment. Instead, an Anker Power Core was used, as a portable power bank. The unit can be recharged and is very strong and robust. It proved to be a much better solution than the handmade DROK converter.

As previously mentioned it was not feasible to transmit the data from a wireless adapter connected to the Odroid. There proved to be too much latency for a SLAM solution to operate efficiently, the results were not good enough to benefit a search and rescue team on the ground. Instead the Odroid is connected to a wireless router via a gigabit Ethernet port. This gives the speed necessary for low levels of latency, the router can transmit the data much more efficiently and with higher power than any wireless adapter. The base station machine then connects to the wireless network and pulls the data stream for processing by one of the two SLAM algorithms. The wireless standard chosen was 802.11ac, this is the fastest standard and is roughly 3x times faster than 802.11n. It also has beamforming technology which is essentially a smart signal - meaning the signal is channelled in the direction of the connected devices rather than transmitting the signal in every direction. It operates on the 5Ghz band which means there is less interference. 802.11 ac is the only standard that produces satisfactory results - 802.11 a/b/g/n were tested as they are the most widely used standards. To give an idea of how much data is transmitted over the network various ROS bag files were recorded. The bag files were in the GB range for tests of less than one minute. The router is powered by an Aukey 28000 mAh multi voltage external battery. The battery can output 5,12 or 19 v at 2 amps - the battery outputs the power with a USB cable. In order to transfer the power to the router, a 3.5 mm outer DC connector was soldered to an existing USB power cable and then connected to the router.

The Robotic Operating System (ROS) coordinates the data transfer process between nodes. The wireless network is created by the on board router and the base station machine connects to the wireless network. A script is run on the base station machine and the Odroid. The script passes parameters to ROS, for example the IP address of the various devices and settings. For the libfreenect driver, parameters include the rate to throttle the images i.e. 5 Hz. On the base station one of the two algorithms packages, RGBDSLAM or RTAB-Map process the data and perform SLAM. The packages subscribe to the topics needed and the master coordinate the process, the processing is then done on the base station machine resulting in a 3D map of the environment and online SLAM.

3.1 Visual SLAM Algorithms

There are many Visual SLAM algorithms in existence, since the Kinect was being used it had to be narrowed down to algorithms that used RGB-D sensors.

RGBDSLAM: uses visual features such as SIFT (Scale Invariant Feature Transformation) and SURF (Speeded Up Robust Features) to match images and then uses RANSAC to estimate the 3D transformation between them. Objects in images contain defining points, SIFT extracts such points and turns them into a feature descriptor- the feature descriptor can then be used to identify the object in new novel images. SIFT allows recognition even if the objects are of different scale, orientation and illumination. SURF is based on SIFT and claims to be three times faster. However, these results could not be reproduced in the testing process. The deciding factor for which algorithm performed best was the ability to be used in synergy with the prototype in a real world situation. The RGBDSLAM algorithm proved to be ineffective for practical purposes. This will be explained in the testing and evaluation section.

RTAB-Map: Real Time Appearance-Based Mapping proved to be the best algorithm for practical use. It is based on an incremental appearance based loop closure detector which uses a bag of words technique to identify if an image has come from a novel location or previously visited one. Rviz and RtabmapViz are the two main visualization tools that can be used with the algorithm. As shown in the videos created, Rviz gives an excellent overview of the map building process but it is not practical for an operator to use. RtabmapViz shows the map being built in real time from the drones' perspective and also shows a clear trajectory. It also shows loop closure detection in action and other topics can be attached to the visualisation screen such as depth stream or IR stream. Rtabmapviz was modified to add a live RGBD stream in order to aid the operator navigate the transport medium - in this case a UAV.

4   Testing and Evaluation

The testing and evaluation was approached from a practical point of view. The hardware components were tested in terms of their ability to perform in harsh environments, charge capacity and general robustness. In terms of software the SLAM algorithms RGBDSLAM and RTAB-Map were tested and compared. The whole system was then tested in synergy to obtain a final result. Rather than comparing certain metrics against each other, the case of the two SLAM algorithms and their performance in a number of real world scenarios were compared -speed of map building; clarity of map building; how they react in low light environments with few features; how susceptible are they to rapid movements without losing their position within the map; level of detail within the map and practical details such as computational power needed to obtain accurate results. One had to take the position of an operator to test the system rather than approach it from a purely theoretical basis.

The first test consisted of finding the maximum run time of the system, the performance of the on-board power sources dictated this. There were three battery sources, one for each of the components in the system, all of which have different capacities and power requirements. The test consisted of letting the system run until one of the power sources failed. Five tests were carried out and the mean result was 45 min before the system had power failure. In the future, a new power source will be needed to reduce the complexity.

Three volunteers with no technical ability were given the system and asked to use it following the instruction manual. A detailed instruction manual was created to show non-technical personnel how to use the system. The end goal was to refine the system to be a complete black box; the operator would only have to perform a limited number of tasks to enable full functionality. Two of the users had little difficulty getting full functionality but the third needed further assistance. In terms of robustness, the main discoveries were weaknesses connecting the components - more specifically soldering joins and crimps. A 3D design for a case is currently being created to house the components safely, when the design is complete it can be 3D printed.

In terms of the Visual SLAM algorithms, RGBDSLAM failed a number of tests relating to practical applications of the system in a real world scenario. An early decision was made that RTAB-Map would be used for the final system. RGBDSLAM does not build a clear concise map quickly and it takes a considerable amount of time to build anything that can be utilised by the operator. RGBDSLAM also required a powerful machine. Considering this system needs to be deployed and improved upon in the developing world, a machine of average capability needs to be sufficient to process the data. However, RGBDSLAM performs well when it is connected directly to a machine as opposed to transmitting the data produced over the wireless network. Most of the applications to date have used RGBDSLAM on a ground robot connected directly to a powerful machine, which processes the data on board. In the case of a UAV, it is possible to use powerful computers to do on board processing but this comes with a cost of capital and size - which did not align with this project.

RTAB-Map allows for modifications to be made in the case of remote mapping, for example the data stream can be compressed and the rate of transmission can be changed - 10 HZ worked best in this case. RGBDSLAM does not allow for compression, other measures were taken to increase performance including using a greyscale stream instead of colour. None of these worked in terms of increasing the performance of the real time map building process. It was concluded that RGBDSLAM was not useful for any real world application using the current system. The testing of the whole system consisted of using the system in a number of locations for a fixed period of time under certain conditions, as shown in Table 1. The system performed best in enclosed environments with low UV exposure, as UV washes out the infrared pattern created by the Kinect. The best result came from a 20-minute test in an abandoned apartment complex stairwell, as shown in Fig. 4. There was an ample amount of features at the location - the trajectory and map were extremely accurate from an operator's point of view.

The system does not perform well in large expanses with few features. A test was carried out for 20 min in a car park basement. The basement had few features and was expansive, which led to a poor result. Testing for a scenario in a disaster situation was difficult - a dark and cramped attic proved to be the

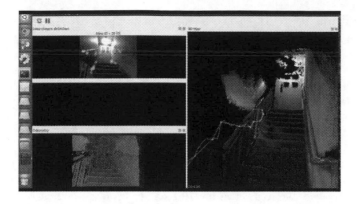

Fig. 4. 20-minute test in an abandoned apartment complex stairwell [7]

best location to do this. From an operators' point of view, the live stream was perfect and the map was coherent - artificial lighting had to be added to the environment to produce the results. This indicates that a high powered LED will most likely have to be added to the system to ensure accurate results for all scenarios.

Table 1. Testing results from a Kinect carrying UAV

Scenario	Accuracy	Speed	Latency	Map detail	Performance
Apartment complex	25 m	Real time	Unrecognizable	High	Very good
Underground car park	Inadequate	Very slow	Inadequate	Poor	Inadequate
Confined Attic	Inadequate	Very slow	Inadequate	Poor	Inadequate
Warehouse	Inadequate	Very slow	Inadequate	Poor	Inadequate
Office block	0.5 m	Real time	Unrecognizable	High	Very good

Tests were carried out with chaotic trajectories and speeds to gain an insight into how the system would react in such a scenario. As of now irregular movements sometimes cause the system to lose its position within the map, which requires the Odometry to be reset. Most of the time this reset causes the map to be destroyed, which means all previous data is lost. This is obviously an issue that needs to be resolved. At the moment possible solutions include adding a separate sensor so that the system does not rely on the Kinect's information alone. However, this may not be a major issue as the UAV's hovering abilities keep it stable, especially as it will be hovering at very lows speeds so rapid irregular movements are unlikely. In the case of computational power needed for base station processing, RTAB-Map performs much better than RGBDSLAM but still requires significant power. After 20–25 min of use, the map building and localization process start to lag and eventually become inoperable. There is a strong possibility that modifying the system will solve this issue, for example increasing RAM allocations.

5 Conclusions and Future Work

Overall the project has been successful with a prototype built for a portable SLAM system. The prototype can create a 3D map of its environment, while simultaneously localizing itself within the map that is being constructed. The system is not just a theoretical concept; it is a physical object than can be tested in the real world. The system created can be replicated easily, produced for less than 200 dollars and can be used by non-technical personnel.

There is a considerable amount of capital being invested in the robotics industry. The systems that are produced are extremely expensive and not widely available. It became apparent that robotic systems for search and rescue operations would only be available to a select few due to high commercial costs. Most of the developing world does not have the financial means to avail of such systems. Our focus was to create an open source solution that can be applied to create cost effective systems easily to be built and replicated in the developing world where emergency relief is slow. If a region had several of these systems, the inhabitants could take the rescue into their own hands. There is still a considerable amount of work to do, new issues emerge every time the prototype is tested to its limit. The testing process needs to cover as many scenarios as possible. Currently the system works in limited environments and scenarios. The aim is to make the prototype user friendly, as it needs to operate as a black box. The current manual has many steps and requirements. This needs to be refined further and rewritten in a style of language that is accessible to all. The blueprint for building the system is also being refined - the hope is that the blueprint will allow and encourage enthusiasts to improve the prototype.

Future work will also include researching further the state of the art UAV technologies. This project focused mainly on the portable SLAM system that would be mounted on the UAV. More research needs to be carried out in terms of the practicalities of using different types of UAV models.

References

1. Bay, H., Ess, A., Tuytelaars, T., Van Gool, L.: Speeded-up robust features (SURF). Comput. Vis. Image Underst. **110**(3), pp. 346–359 (2008). https://doi.org/10.1016/j.cviu.2007.09.014
2. Bradski, G., Kaehler, A.: Learning OpenCV: Computer Vision with the OpenCV Library. O'Reilly Media, Sebastopol (2008)
3. Endres, F., Hess, J., Engelhard, N., Sturm, J., Cremers, D., Burgard, W.: An evaluation of the RGB-D SLAM system. In: 2012 IEEE International Conference on Robotics and Automation, Saint Paul, MN, pp. 1691–1696 (2012). https://doi.org/10.1109/ICRA.2012.6225199
4. Fischler, M.A., Bolles, R.C.: Random sample consensus: a paradigm for model fitting with applications to image analysis and automated cartography. Commun. ACM **24**(6), 381–395 (1981). https://doi.org/10.1145/358669.358692
5. Henry, P., Krainin, M., Herbst, E., Ren, X., Fox, D.: RGB-D mapping: using kinect-style depth cameras for dense 3D modelling of indoor environments. Int. J. Robot. Res. **31**(5), 647–663 (2012). https://doi.org/10.1177/0278364911434148

6. Huang, A.S., et al.: Visual odometry and mapping for autonomous flight using an RGB-D camera. In: International Symposium of Robotics Research (ISRR) (2011). https://doi.org/10.1177/0278364912455256
7. Gannon, C.: Live test of portable SLAM prototype (2017). https://www.youtube.com/channel/UCYDCmP7B87dvna9YHEMXT3A
8. Kim, J.H., Matson, E.T., Myung, H., Xu, P.: Robot Intelligence Technology and Applications 2012, An Edition of the Presented Papers from the 1st International Conference on Robot Intelligence Technology and Applications. Springer, Heidelberg (2013). https://doi.org/10.1007/978-3-642-37374-9
9. Kristensson, O.: Supporting Blind Navigation using Depth Sensing and sonification. School of Computer Science, University of St Andrews. United Kingdom (2013). https://doi.org/10.1145/2494091.2494173
10. Kümmerle, R., Grisetti, G., Strasdat, H., Konolige, K., Burgard, W.: G2o: a general framework for graph optimization. In: Proceedings of the IEEE International Conference on Robotics and Automation (ICRA), pp. 3607–3613. https://doi.org/10.1109/ICRA.2011.5979949
11. Lowe, D.G.: Int. J. Comput. Vis. **60**, 91 (2004). https://doi.org/10.1023/B:VISI.0000029664.99615.94
12. Mur-Artal, R., Tardós, J.D.: Fast relocalisation and loop closing in keyframe-based SLAM. In: 2014 IEEE International Conference on Robotics and Automation (ICRA), Hong Kong, pp. 846–853 (2014). https://doi.org/10.1109/ICRA.2014.6906953
13. PrimeSense.org: Subsidiary of Apple Inc. (n.d). http://www.PrimeSense.org/
14. ROS.org: Powering the world's robots (n.d.). http://www.ros.org/
15. Rublee, E., Rabaud, V., Konolige, K., Bradski, G.: ORB: an efficient alternative to SIFT or SURF. In: Proceedings of the IEEE International Conference on Computer Vision, pp. 2564–2571 (2011). https://doi.org/10.1109/ICCV.2011.6126544
16. Schindhelm, C.K.: Evaluating SLAM approaches for microsoft kinect. In: ICWMC 2012: The Eighth International Conference on Wireless and Mobile Communications, Siemens AG - Corporate Research and Technologies, pp. 402–407 (2012). ISBN 978-1-61208-203-5. https://www.thinkmind.org/download.php?articleid=icwmc_2012_17_40_20438
17. Segal, A., Haehnel, D., Thrun, S.: Generalized-ICP. In: Proceedings of Robotics: Science and Systems (2009)
18. Taketomi, T., Uchiyama, H., Ikeda, S.: Visual SLAM algorithms: a survey from 2010 to 2016. IPSJ Trans. Comput. Vis. Appl. **9**, 16 (2017). https://doi.org/10.1186/s41074-017-0027-2
19. Valencia, R., Andrade-Cetto, J.: Path planning in belief space with pose SLAM. In: Mapping, Planning and Exploration with Pose SLAM. STAR, vol. 119, pp. 53–87. Springer, Cham (2018). https://doi.org/10.1007/978-3-319-60603-3_4
20. Williams, B.P., Reid, I.D.: On combining visual SLAM and visual Odometry. In: Proceedings of International Conference on Robotics and Automation, ICRA 2010, pp. 3494–3500 (2010)

Object Detection and Tracking
with Occlusion Handling in Maritime
Surveillance-A Review

Rubeena Banu$^{(\boxtimes)}$ and M. H. Sidram

Department of Electrical and Electronics Engineering,
Sri Jayachmarajendra College of Engineering, Mysuru, India
rubyms2011@gmail.com, mhsidram@gmail.com

Abstract. Video surveillance is currently proactive research theme in computer vision. It can be classified as Normal, Aerial and Maritime video surveillance. The maritime surveillance will observe all the maritime activities effectively which strengthen the security, the environment, and the economy etc. Since, maritime transportation is very important to the national security because more than 80% of world trade depends on safe maritime route. It is very essential to be conscious of every time what is happening under and on the surface of sea and coastal area to its continued safety, prosperity and environment. So the employments of maritime surveillance poses the significant challenges. This effort is on the consolidation and thorough survey of state-of-the-art of maritime surveillance methods like detection and tracking of object with occlusion handling. Occlusion takes place when distant targets are hidden by objects closer to the observer which might be full or partial. Occlusion is still a major challenge due to the dynamic nature of the ocean which will further affect the effective tracking of the maritime object. The survey work carried out has revealed that very less amount of work has been reported on maritime detection and tracking of object with occlusion handling and finally, comparison have been tabulated on state-of-the-art of the detection of object and tracking with occlusion handling techniques.

Keywords: Maritime surveillance · Video surveillance · Occlusion · Object detection · Tracking

1 Introduction

Video surveillance attempts to detect, distinguish and track objects across a sequence of images [2]. It is the tonality technology to brawl against terrorism, offence, safety of public and systematic process of traffic. In many computer vision applications object detection and tracking are significant and ambitious task. Object detection in video includes verifying the existence of an object in the image sequence and finding it exactly for recognition. Detection plays an

© Springer Nature Singapore Pte Ltd. 2019
K. C. Santosh and R. S. Hegadi (Eds.): RTIP2R 2018, CCIS 1035, pp. 88–103, 2019.
https://doi.org/10.1007/978-981-13-9181-1_8

important step for further actions like object tracking and deals with observing spatial and temporal changes of an objects in a video sequences [23,25]. Over the past decade, video surveillance have obtained more awareness from community of academic, government and industry. Surveillance system has become commercially available and now they are employed to a number of different day to day applications like crime rates, wars, terrorist attacks, security breaches, law enforcement, traffic surveillance of roads and highway accident detection and crime aversion in public places, banks, super markets and in transport systems like airport, railways, underground and maritime environment. Further, few more applications have been listed to confirm the significance of surveillance system. The list runs like covering of forest fire, pollution, animal habitats, military application, smart room and person safety etc [17]. Based on the above applications, the paper mainly highlighting on the maritime surveillance system. The maritime surveillance is utterly essential for ensuring a proper maritime safety and security. Since ocean is regularly visited by the navies of the world and sea transportation will carry out 80% of world trade and makes use of maritime transportation have become very necessary to the world economy [15]. The strike across vehicle of military marine and civilian is one wall to damage the wealth and security of a nation. Hence, this maritime surveillance interest is growing due to security and safety concern. The paper is arranged as follows: The Sect. 2 disputed about the contemporary contributions. The summary of described work has been tabulated in the Sect. 3 and at the end conclusion is outlined in the Sect. 4.

2 Contemporary Contributions

The video surveillance in the area of maritime has been analysed decade ago. Maritime surveillance can be outlined as the powerful identification of all maritime movements [14]. Many researchers have worked on this maritime surveillance such as object detection, classification and tracking. As per survey, very less amount of works have been carried out on object detection and tracking with occlusion handling. Hence, contribution in this survey paper is mainly on occlusion handling in maritime surveillance. Figure 1 shows the taxonomy of existing occlusion handling methods in maritime surveillance which is described completely in the following section.

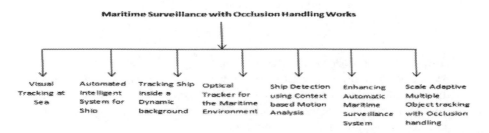

Fig. 1. Taxonomy of existing occlusion handling methods

2.1   Work1-Visual Tracking at Sea

Visual Tracking Algorithm. In different situations of interest, quality implementation of mean shift [12] tracking utilizing colour histogram becomes unsuccessful to track sufficiently. In order to recover from tracking failure in the presence of occlusion Bibby and Reid [8] employed visual tracking algorithm together with some improvements i.e. consideration of gradient information, background suppression, coping with occlusion and scaling.

-Using Gradient Information. The histogram of the magnitude of image gradient is computed, where the gradient of image is calculated employing standard finite approximation from the monochrome images.

-Background Suppression. Background suppression has been used to address issue that is, target shares some color including background which can be hard to trace accurately. Figure 2 shows construction of target and region of background.

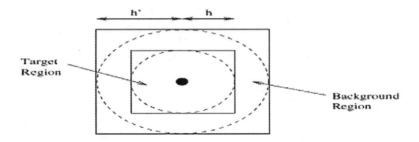

Fig. 2. Geometry of target and background model

-Coping with Occlusion. In sequence to get the capability to recuperate from failure, the Bhattacharyya surface has been sampled at distinct location on a regular grid, its size is equivalent corresponds to present scale. It gives rough estimation to the Bhattacharyya surface and later this is merged with a previous to acquire a rough posterior. Gaussian is used to weigh the Posterior centered on the prophecy and with covariance provided by the filters prediction unpredictability.

-Scaling. In this approach a Simpler method using coarse sampling of the Bhattacharyya surface in order to decide the allowance of changes. The easy measure explained as variation in between the Bhattacharya coefficients at the center and the surrounding samples mean value. The scale changes are disabled if this difference is below the threshold value.

Result

The above discussed algorithm has been completely embedded inside a robotic structure including 3 degrees of freedom, scene stabilization, and the visual tracking. In this approach, test was done on a custom constructed pan/tilt/roll and commercial pan/tilt mechanisms. To overcome some of the particular problems faced at sea, various easy but effective modifications have been proposed that enhance the robustness of tracking. It is also shown successfully tracking in many scenes that containing un-modelled ego-motion it can be reimbursed by closed loop inertia feedback control. The recovery after the occlusion is accomplished by employing the corsely Sampled Bhattacharya surface.

2.2 Work2-Automated Intelligent System for Ship

Wei et al. [30] presented Automated Intelligent Video Surveillance system for ships (AIVS3) which can be considered as boat protection problem's solution based on vision. Inside this structure, video or the image parser is created of (1) Maritime target detection module (2) Multiple target tracking module which is able to concurrently tracking high quantity of targets in cluttered scene including occlusions and (3) Hierarchical classification module.

Maritime Target Detection. Maritime environment images normally contain water and sky region. Based on area specific information, an effective and efficient detection of maritime target proposal has been developed. The approach consists of three computation steps they are

Step1: Horizon Line Detection. Initially it generates scenes binary edge map utilizing algorithm called fast edge detection and later straight line is found in the map by employing the Hough transform.

Step2: Water Model Estimation. If horizon line is not found the complete image is utilized for modelling of water. Water at low level resolution area is preferably homogeneous like waves, boat wakes and other litter in sea area are regularized. So they modelled intensity of water pixels as a regression with respect coordinates of the pixel.

$$I(m,n) = am + bn + c \tag{1}$$

where m, n represents the pixels.

Step 3: Non-water Detection of Object. If the detected horizon line cultivated into complete resolution. The residue frame is normally clamorous because it consists sea clutters at full resolution. To suppress the sea clutters employed a open-close of the morphological smoothing filter [24] with a variable size square structuring element. Particularly the B size increases from zero to a maximum size r_{max} for pixels at the horizon to pixels present at the base of the images respectively. Let r(x,y) be the size of B at pixel (x,y) then

$$r(m,n) = r_{max}\frac{n - n_h(m)}{height - n_h(m)} \tag{2}$$

where $n_h(m)$ denotes n-coordinate of the tip on the horizon which have the similar m-coordinate and height indicates the height of the image.

Multi-target Tracking (Occlusion Handling). To manage the correct identification of the target a mechanism of stitching is used to equate the current established trace with the suspended trace. For matching, Kalman filter is used that can be achieved by prophesying the location and size of every target. In addition to this an appearance data added to enhance the overall accuracy of matching. The matching score $S(T_i, R_j)$ between track T_i and connected region R_j is explained as the total of two components: the interval between the estimated posture of T_i and the position of R_j and a similitude measure between the histogram gathered over T_i of the histogram of R_j.

$$\max_{j_1,\ldots,j_n} \sum_{i=1}^{n} S(T_i, R_{ji}) \tag{3}$$

The Hungarian algorithm [20] has been used to solve the problem that number of traces may fine match to the same region. The trace that does not get right match among regions are connected, are discontinued. Further, insufficiently described connected regions examined to begin new tracks.

Hierarchical Water-Craft Classifications. A multi-class hierarchical object classifier developed over the idea of decision forest. It is a group of decision tree merged employing bagging technique [10]. The performance of decision trees notably increases by employing bagging, the reason is for every training set of bootstrap S_k, the random sampling with replacement keeps just 63% distinctive patterns from S and eliminate the remaining 37% patterns. The most well known CART methodology [11] was utilized, inside every decision tree. Every classification tree node is connected with a decision function it will categories the input samples into one of its sub node. The decision forest classification time is $O(log(N))$. It will manage data of high dimensional without reduction of dimensionality. It can be adopted to categorize classes that are not linearly divisible in the feature area.

Result

The fast and precise target detection result is achieved and also shown powerful to changes of weather, occlusion at any situation that may bring about temporary dropping of tracks. In order to measure the performance, Hierarchical multi-class classification capability compared against timely classifier i.e. Multi-class support vector machine and multi-class Naive bayes classifier. Finally, found that the present method acts consistently better than other two classifier and achieved vigorous target detection and tracking results.

2.3   Work3-Tracking Ship Inside a Dynamic Background

Szpak and Tapamo [26] presented the techniques that address the moving vessels tracking in the existence of agile background issues. The tracking system contains three main components that are described below.

Motion Clue Generation. Optical flow and background subtraction are two dominant paradigms [22]. Optical flow is computationally expensive. Hence, in presented work, the background subtraction method is used because the maritime needs real-time achievement on high resolution image. Motion clue generation follows background subtraction and its model.

-Background Subtraction. The combination of Gaussian estimation of the ocean pixels probability density function gives small advantage in trading with major problem of tracing ships on the ocean [13]. Assumptions are made that a notable quantity of ocean pixels are uni modally dispensed and background model for every pixel built employing a single Gaussian distribution. If a pixel categorized as background then the pixel of mean and variance are upgraded. If a categorized pixel is foreground, then it will not be included into the background model instantly. Rather, a average $\bar{x}$ of pixels of foreground intensities is computed for a user defined foreground monitoring delay number.

Spatial Smoothness. The motion-clue is usually produced by background subtraction. A method called fast heuristic spatial regularization has been presented to improve this model. The reason for employing Heuristic is that, they are normally computationally speedy than upstanding spatial regularization.

Tracking Using Level Set (Occlusion Handling). The spatially smoothed motion-clue image is segmented in order to track boat at the ocean. The motion-cue image segmentation is considered as advancement of level-set related active contour [1, 16]. An active contour is considered as closed curve which is positioned at frame and improved with time. The growth of the curve traced by inserting this curve in a higher dimension function and evolution of the function at a stabled Cartesian grid [1]. There is a trade off between an active contour confined in a local minimum and finding track which is new in the scene. The trade off is maintained by utilizing two active contour P and C. Where P and C represents probing and tracking active contour respectively. At every t second the contour P is again initialized to the image boundary. Therefore, it utilized to identify new target in the frame. The contour C before it is re-initialized it will utilize the topology of P. The initial location of C is f_n later, the C every time utilize its final position in frame f_{n-1}. Like this detected any new trace by prob p are moved on to curve C. It also manage the splitting as well as combining of occluded target within one framework.

Result

In order to measure the quality of various methods in these sequence, precision and recall have been employed. As quantitative result, the active contour was examined to asses the correctness of tracking and is confirmed when contour will fell within the target's minimum box. If it is fell out of the minimum boundary box then tag contour as false positives. As qualitative result, If the tracker does not miss the target then results are rated as very good or true positive and reported as false positives if the targets are not found. If the tracker sometimes loses the targets but recover it soon then the result is rated as good. The tracker is not successful, when consists huge number of false positives or the deliberated target is not localized at all. This works very good with small number of false positives except in aforementioned conditions.

2.4   Work4-Optical Tracker for the Maritime Environment

The approach consists tracking of target at high zoom on the ocean. In the presented method Bachoo et al. [3] assisted poor contrast, white cap and occlusion via the utilization of robust error function for the model of observation. The Target description, State estimation and Appearance model of the system has been described below.

Target Description. When tracker is determined, a template contains the intensity rate and its variables, which are reserved in the state model. Robust error function [32] is used to match the template to candidate patches for each frame at time t. The foremost match represents a viable position of the real target at time t.

State Estimation (Occlusion Handling). The practical filter uses the recursive Bayesian estimation to analyse a density of posterior with non-linear or non-Gaussian form. In this approach used the rectangular pixel patches instead of an ellipse structure. The dynamic state model is

$$x_t = x_{t-1} + v_{t-1} + w_{t-1} \tag{4}$$

$$s_t = s_{t-1} + \mathcal{N}(0, 0.01) \tag{5}$$

$$v_t = x_t - x_{t-1} \tag{6}$$

$$r_t = r_{t-1} + \mathcal{N}(0, 0.02) \tag{7}$$

where x, v and s denotes the component location, velocity and scale of the target respectively and t represents units of $\frac{1}{20}$ s and r represents target rotation surrounding x. Here it has analysed above mentioned equations performance good since velocity is updated all the time at each image. Preserved the Previous velocities for images and utilized to obtain the Gaussian variance in Eq. 4 to match the target motion. If occlusion is detected the variance of Gaussian in Eq. 4 is given to a large application particular value. The large difference disperse the particles and develop the detection of target. The threshold T is presently decided accurately. The y function will find the occlusion effectively if the output falls beneath of threshold or else a target is detected.

$$\rho_i(\epsilon) = \begin{cases} 1 \; if \;\; \epsilon < T \\ 0 \; otherwise \end{cases} \qquad (8)$$

where i denotes the pixel number, ϵ is $\epsilon = \frac{|x_i - y_i|}{d}$ x and y represents candidate and template pixel respectively. d is normalizing factor.

Appearance Model. The main idea is to modernize the template at time t by employing the most recent target pixels intensities. The template of candidate get to be the new one in case the error of alignment is bounded by a predetermined value. Template at the beginning $t = 0$, is regularly maintained in memory and utilized for alignment of template.

Result

In order to assess the implementation mean absolute error, standard deviation of the error, track length, number of re-initialization, track ratio are considered. Three different data sequences are used. In sequence 1, tracker is obtained 83% track length and 57% target ratio where occlusion took place by water spatter onto the boat and sea bulge. In sequence 2, tracker achieved track length and a track ratio of 83% and 73% respectively when lighthouse exists causing the long term target occlusion. Sequence 3, it is similar to sequence 1 the track error is less than the sequences which is mentioned above and 53% of track ratio. The mean error value is low when tracking is also low. The target is not tracked when the mean error is very high.

2.5   Work5-Ship Detection Using Context Based Motion Analysis

Bao et al. [5] presented an automated intelligent video surveillance system. Below Fig. 3 shows the moving ship detection flow chart, which consists a series of processing steps.

Context Modelling. The presented work focused on creating model of object centric context that gives information in advance for the motion analysis. In this scenario water is superior and therefore, described water detection approach.

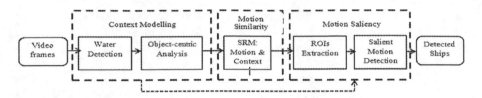

Fig. 3. Flow chart of the detection of moving ship using context and motion analysis

Once water is detected [4], context model is constructed in accordance with two considerations. The term C_{cand} is defined as a area that consists a ship and water region C_{water}. Initially, the ship in the frames are denoted by region C_{cand} that is completely or partly enclosed by water. Next, the amount of pixels in C_{cand} must be high for visualization and restricted by water region size.

$$600 < |c_{max}| < 0.5 \times \sum_{i=1}^{W} |c_{water}| \tag{9}$$

Where, $|C|$ represents the number of pixels in the corresponding area, and W denotes the amount of segments labelled as C_{water}.

Context-Based Motion Similarity and Saliency Analysis (Occlusion Handling)

1. **Motion-similarity.** In accordance with model of context non-water parts grouped into semantic areas by scrutinizing the motion resemblance to circumvent over segmentation from precursory step. First calculated the pixel wise motion employing optical flow [18] and explained combining predicate $p(c_i, c_j)$ to find wherever two regions c_i and c_j belongs to same statistical area $i \neq j$. The motion map which is produced by computing the magnitude MAG and angle ANG values for every average flow vector based on over segmentation result.

   – **Context in motion similarity analysis:** If ANG and MAG are denoted by a group of the Q individualistic random variables and whichever feasible total of that variables belong to $1, 2, ..., g$. After SRM (Statistical Region Merging) combining, the non-water segments in to regions with a specific regional motion. These combined non-water areas are potential ship region C_{cand}, then individual ship separated.

2. **Motion saliency.** The morphological operation is used to remove Region of Interest (ROI)- ships outer part C_{ship} and local background C_{bg}. It is difficult to measure the motion saliency if water considerably changes with time. So the relative motion is used in C_{ship} and C_{bg}. The water region is extracted to compute relative motions rv_{ship} of C_{ship} and rv_{bg} of C_{bg} by subtracting the

water region motion from the corresponding ROIs motion [6]. Later, analysed the motion contrast between the C_{ship} and C_{bg} to define motion saliency. The difference of the relative motion of C_{ship} and C_{bg} calculated and threshold was set to estimate the contrast.

$$\frac{|rv_{ship} - rv_{bg}|}{|rv_{ship}|} > T_1. \tag{10}$$

Subsequently, computed the variation of the motion magnitude between the C_{ship} and C_{bg} and ship motion should be adequately higher than the non-ship motion.

$$|rv_{|ship}| - |rv_{bg}| > T_2 \tag{11}$$

Result

The performance has been compared with two current algorithms i.e. the motion of ship and the cabin detector. The performance is evaluated by considering the parameter as follows, True Positive (TP), False Negative (TN), False Positive (FP), TOC and SOC. TP+FN denotes ships which is marked manually, TP+FP shows found ships, TP represents ships that is detected correctly, TOC denotes total occlusions, SOC represents occlusion condition which are solved. The presented method outperforms against other two methods and achieved 97.6% precision and 89.4% recall. The ship motion accomplished 92.8% and 75.6% in precision and recall respectively. While cabin detector achieved 82.8% precision and 79.9% recall. The presented method accomplished 169 of solved occlusions out of 203 occlusion cases.

2.6 Work6-Scale Adaptive Multiple Object Tracking with Occlusion Handling

Mou et al. [19] proposed a multiple obstacle tracking and also contributed on scale adaptive and occlusion handling issues which is very important in visual tracking. The complete process has been done by using Obstacle detection, Multiple obstacle tracking, Scale adapting and Occlusion handling which is described below.

Obstacle Detection. The obstacles are found by using plan-view-grid [29], combines data of occupancy and height. The gird map is adjusted to $600 \times 600\,\mathrm{m}$ with $1 \times 1\,\mathrm{m}$ cell size. To evaluate the prospects of the grid cell to the midway of an obstacle, the acquired occupancy and height grids are integrated using the Bayesian plan view grid map [21]. It searches for the region where the occupancy and heights value fall into the definite dispensed ranges. The measure of probability P(m,n) at position (m,n) on the grid is described as

$$P(m,n) = \frac{exp(-(\frac{(O(m,n)-\mu_0)^2}{2\sigma_0^2} + \frac{(H(m,n)-\mu_h)^2}{2\sigma_h^2}))}{2\pi\sigma_0\sigma_h} \tag{12}$$

where μ_0 and μ_h represents anticipated mean of $O(m, n)$ and $H(m, n)$ respectively, and σ_0 and σ_h denotes the corresponding standard deviation.

Multiple Obstacle Tracking. The process is composed by the spatio-temporal Context (STC) [31] relationship between the object and objects surrounding areas based on a Bayesian framework. Multiple object tracking is executed by providing every found obstacle an separate tracker. Bayesian framework is represented in equation given below

$$
\begin{aligned}
P(l) &= \sum_{c(n) \epsilon F^c} p(l, c(n)|o) \\
&= \sum_{c(n) \epsilon F^c} p(l|c(n), o) p(c(n)|o
\end{aligned}
\tag{13}
$$

Where o represents the objects exists in image and l is its position; $P(l)$ denotes object location confidence map. $c(n)$ represents context feature in the context feature part F^c. $p(l|c(n), o)$ denotes the interconnection between object position and object context. $p(c(n)|o)$ models the appearance of the local context.

Scale Adapting. The connection between $2D$ image perspective scale and the depth of $3D$ is linear in accordance with the perspective view geometry of the camera which is formulated as

$$
\frac{S_1}{S_2} = \frac{D_1}{D_2}
\tag{14}
$$

Where S_1, S_2 are the two different sizes in $2D$ image and D_1, D_2 denotes their corresponding depths. The context prior mode $p(c(n)|o)$ in equation is formulated as

$$
p(c(n)|o) = I(n) * ae^{-\frac{|n|^2}{\sigma^2}}
\tag{15}
$$

Where $I(n)$ denotes intensity of image, a represents normalization constant and σ denotes a scale parameter. The scale parameter σ is updated by

$$
\sigma_{t+1} = s_t \sigma_t = \frac{d_{t-1}}{d_0} \sigma_t,
\tag{16}
$$

Where d_0 represents tracked obstacle initial depth and $d_{(t-1)}$ denotes the tracked obstacle depth in the previous frame.

Occlusion Handling. In this approach, the depth information is used to solve the occlusion issue. The change from high to low depth and higher than T_c threshold value because only the faraway objects will be occluded. Later the occluded tracker is eliminated, meantime will save the previous depth identity numbers. Consequently, the depth change will be compared with the conserved depth information when the occlusion is below a threshold $\bar{d}$ takes place. Later, for this currently found object, set a new tracker and identity number is allocated to it has been saved, which shows that this obstacle is same as before occluded.

Result

In order to conduct test, three sequences of dataset is collected using maritime stereo vision system. Every obstacle which is tracked is allocated a unique ID and particular colours for its boundary box. Meantime, the tracked obstacle distance to the USV (Unmanned Surface Vehicle) is showed on summit of the bounding box. When the boats goes apart from the specified place and when boats move towards the specified place in both the cases the presented methods works moderately better than the compared STC. The presented method achieved the tracking result 90.5% in the presence occlusion. Here, the obstacle is get occluded and appear again only in accordance with the information of depth [28]. It may not be sufficient and weaken the performance quality of the occlusion handling.

2.7   Work7-Enhancing Automatic Maritime Surveillance System

Blosi et al. [9] described the system that is capable of fusing information from heterogeneous source and intended to improve the task of the current Vessel Traffic Service (VTS) system. This system is planed for boat detection via classification related method and tracking various ships even in the condition of occlusion. Later, fusing data from current Vessel Transfer Services (VTS) system will take place and deployable in the area of more population.

Visual Detection. Video Processing Unit (VPU) includes Visual detection which concentrates on detection of the interested object in the present frame. The building blocks of VPU are described below

- **Haar classifier:** The three kinds of Haar-like attributes [27] have been considered i.e. line, center-surrendered feature and edge. In this approach instead of a squared one a 60×30 rectangular window is employed and to smooth the image median filter is used, which decreases the presence of wakes. In order to focus on long edges the threshold of the Canny edge detector is decided.
- **Horizon line detector:** In this approach candidate line is separated and validated each line according to set of samples belonging to a rectangular area above and below it. The gray scale intensities value of points which is above the candidate lines, are compared with the value of corresponding points below the candidate line.
- **Noise filter:** Noise filter Reflection causes false observation, so a filtering is taken by calculating the number of SURF [7] key points present in every potential examination in the present image. If their is a negligible number of key points in the bounding box then the monitoring is disregarded.

Tracking (Occlusion Handling). Distributed tracking approach has been proposed which is capable to fusion of information from various heterogeneous and not synchronized sources. The input inspections have taken from the previously discussed module of the visual detection. The evaluation action is made of three main phases such as prediction, Clustering and Data association. The prediction computes the development of the estimations and given the observation issued by the sensor. The clustering groups the estimation determining the GMMs variables. In data association the track number is allocated to every object, by relating the new observation to the present tracks. Two moving traced objects examined which consists of the same directions in case the angle between their trajectories is less than 10^0. This step is later complicated by full or partial occlusion. Instead of tracking them separately considered the collapsing tracks as group when multiple tracks consists bounding boxes moving nearer to each other. The tracker store their color histogram and start consider them as group. When the occluded objects visible anew the histogram which is saved are utilized to assign it again to the right identification number, which belongs to the formerly registered tracks.

Data Fusion. The data from VTS system and camera are combined to generate an improved and dependable tracked boats. As this phase becomes difficulty and in order to manage this issue, the below algorithm is outlined. Let v_i^C denotes the boats velocity vector i in the reference frame of camera C, and V^R be the represents group of boats velocity vectors in the reference frame of VTS R. The good matching candidate in V^R to be amalgamate with the boat i in the reference frame is chosen by calculating for each $V_j^R \epsilon V^R$

$$\begin{bmatrix} v_{x_j}^R \\ v_{y_j}^R \end{bmatrix}^T \cdot \begin{bmatrix} \cos\theta & -\sin\theta \\ \sin\theta & \cos\theta \end{bmatrix} \simeq \begin{bmatrix} v_{x_i}^C \\ v_{y_i}^C \end{bmatrix}^T \tag{17}$$

θ is the rotation parameter between the VTS reference frames and camera which is computed by algorithm mentioned Policy Gradient. Later, by utilizing the initial value allotted to θ, the tracking as well as data fusion are executed. Once, the computation is over recomputed the quantitative results and analyzed in which direction the execution is enhanced.

Result

In this work, accuracy of detection is measured using two different metrics i.e. True Positive Rate (TPR) and False Alarm Rate (FAR). Electro-Optical (EO) and Infra-Red (IR) data are considered for detection. In both the detection cases, the false alarm rate reduction achieved by activating horizon line detection filter. In visual tracking result, MOTA (multiple object tracking accuracy) and MOTP (multiple object tracking precision) together with precision and recall have utilized to measure quantitatively the execution of the tracking method. By the high value of MOTA and MOTP metrics achieved a very good tracking result. Complete and partial occlusion conditions are perfectly managed by the tracking algorithm. In data fusion result, to compute the performance of this data fusion CLEAR MOTA metric MOTA and MOTP both together along with precision and recall have used including activating as well not activating horizon line filter. From the overall result noticed that the tracking execution is improved appreciably when number of data source are utilized instead of single data source.

3   Summary

Summary of above described work is tabulated which is shown in Table 1.

Table 1. Summary

Sl.No	Author	Methodology	Occlusion Type	Dataset	Results	Remarks
1	Charles and Bibby	-Meanshift -Gradient information -Background Suppression -Bhattacharya surface	Full occlusion i.e occluded by other boats	Test executed using pan/tolt/roll device and pan/tilt mechanism(Mic1-300)	Successfully tracked several scenes including in the existence of unmodelled ego-motion which is compensated by closed loop inertial feedback control	Not addressed the issue of automatic target acquisition which would be crucial for search & rescue missions
2	wei et.al.,	-Hough transform -water model estimation - Non-water object detection - Morphological open-close -smoothing filter -Hungarian Algorithm -multi-class hierarchical classifier	Full occlusion i.e occluded by other boats	Obtained Various EO and IR maritime video data with different weather conditions and sea states.	Classification performance compared against state-of-art classifier i.e. SVM and Multi-class naive Bayes classifier. Hierarchical classifier performs consistently better than the other classifier.	System not only detect, classify track various maritime targets but also helps fusing heterogeneous target information from various sources
3	Szpak et.al.,	-motion clue generation -Probability density function -Heuristic spatial regularization - spatial smoothness -Active contour - Chan-vese-energy	Full occlusion larger Sail boat passes in front of the smaller.	Captured high-resolution image of dimension 1024 × 512 at two different fields.	Results are very good, if the tracker looses the target and no false positive targets are detected.a result is good trackers occasionally looses the target but recover it shortly. And the target fails when there are too many false positive.	when contrast between the target and ocean is very poor,the background process will fail to detect motion of the target.
4	Asheer K Bachoo	-Particle filter -recursive Bayesian estimation -Gaussian covariance matrix -Gradient descent optimization	Full and Partial occlusion by water,lighthouse, camera shake and extremely low target visibility at times.	Three data sequences are used. Was captured in Simons town on the South Africa Coast	System tracks a target with an error of less than 2.5%in the presence of low contrast, white cap, camera motion and occlusion.	When not tracking the target mean errors are very high. Mean errors are relatively low when tracking the target.
5	Xinfeng Bao et.al.,	-Context based motion similarity and motion saliency analysis	Full and Partial occlusion among ship and Vegetation and two container ship overlapped	Video sequences are recorded in the harbor of Rotterdam,the Netherlands	The approach out performs against the compared ship-motion and Cabin-detector. It gives,97.6% and 89.4%Recall and Precision .respectively.	It detects each individual ship even when there are significant occlusion among ship and occlusion.
6	Xiaozheng Mou et.al.,	-Plan-view grid -Spatiotemporal model -depth of the tracked obstacle -depth information	Full occlusion occurs when two boats move towards each other along horizontal axis of the image	Dataset collected in three sequences by a pair of Point Grey CCD cameras with focal length 2800	99.3% (when two boats move from neat to far at same time no occlusion) 93.7% (when two boats move from far to near at different time no occlusion) 90.5%(when two boats move towards each other along horizontal axis and occlusion happens when they cross each other)	Here occlusion is occluded and reappear only based on depth information which may be sufficient and weaken the reliability of the occlusion handling.Searching region is set to very small,which makes the computation speed very high.
7	Domenicoet.al.,	Haar classifier -Hough transform -Noise filter -Distributed Particle Filter - -K clusterize -Colour Histogram	-Two ferry boats with complete occlusion -two sailing boat with partial occlusion -high view (boats are seen from an high view)	Used availabe MarDCT dataset (Maritime Detection Classification and Tracking dataset)	Compared visual tracking module and data Fusion module. Where in data fusion MOTP raises from 0.613 to 0.871 and the MOTA from 0.815 to 0.975.	This system requires more computation power. Tracking performance improved in case of multiple data source as compared to only camera data

4   Conclusion

The paper presented on the state-of-art methods of surveillance in a maritime environment is essential for fighting against criminal activities, pirate attacks, unlicensed fishing, and tracking of human etc. Many issues of detection and tracking occur due to the low image contrast, sea clutter, waves, camera shake, lighthouse, occlusion, vegetation, sunlight reflection, clouds, fog, different weather conditions etc. Handling occlusion is one of the major tasks which will later gives the powerful result for tracking the marine object. Hence, in order to bring out the best research works in this direction, an effective survey of contemporary works have been carried out. Finally, analyzed that the current technology still gives only a limited support to the real time situation. The issue is not fully solved because there is no much research on maritime video detection and tracking with occlusion handling issues has been reported. Hence, required enormous contributions in this direction.

References

1. Adalsteinsson, D., Sethian, J.A.: A fast level set method for propagating interfaces. J. Comput. Phys. **118**(2), 269–277 (1995)
2. Al Najjar, M., Ghantous, M., Bayoumi, M.: Video Surveillance for Sensor Platforms. Springer, Heidelberg (2014). https://doi.org/10.1007/978-1-4614-1857-3
3. Bachoo, A.K., Le Roux, F., Nicolls, F.: An optical tracker for the maritime environment. In: SPIE Defense, Security, and Sensing, p. 80501G. International Society for Optics and Photonics (2011)
4. Bao, X., Zinger, S., Wijnhoven, R., de With, P.H.N.: Water region detection supporting ship identification in port surveillance. In: Blanc-Talon, J., Philips, W., Popescu, D., Scheunders, P., Zemčík, P. (eds.) ACIVS 2012. LNCS, vol. 7517, pp. 444–454. Springer, Heidelberg (2012). https://doi.org/10.1007/978-3-642-33140-4_39
5. Bao, X., Zinger, S., Wijnhoven, R., et al.: Robust moving ship detection using context-based motion analysis and occlusion handling. In: Sixth International Conference on Machine Vision (ICMV 13), p. 90670F. International Society for Optics and Photonics (2013)
6. Bao, X., Zinger, S., Wijnhoven, R., et al.: Ship detection in port surveillance based on context and motion saliency analysis. In: IS&T/SPIE Electronic Imaging, p. 86630D. International Society for Optics and Photonics (2013)
7. Bay, H., Tuytelaars, T., Van Gool, L.: SURF: speeded up robust features. In: Leonardis, A., Bischof, H., Pinz, A. (eds.) ECCV 2006. LNCS, vol. 3951, pp. 404–417. Springer, Heidelberg (2006). https://doi.org/10.1007/11744023_32
8. Bibby, C., Reid, I.: Visual tracking at sea. In: Proceedings of the 2005 IEEE International Conference on Robotics and Automation, ICRA 2005, pp. 1841–1846. IEEE (2005)
9. Bloisi, D.D., Previtali, F., Pennisi, A., Nardi, D., Fiorini, M.: Enhancing automatic maritime surveillance systems with visual information. IEEE Trans. Intell. Transp. Syst. **18**, 824–833 (2016)
10. Breiman, L.: Bagging predictors. Mach. Learn. **24**(2), 123–140 (1996)
11. Breiman, L.: Classification and Regression Trees. Routledge, London (2017)
12. Collins, R.T.: Mean-shift blob tracking through scale space. In: Proceedings of 2003 IEEE Computer Society Conference on Computer Vision and Pattern Recognition, vol. 2, p. II-234. IEEE (2003)
13. Elgammal, A., Harwood, D., Davis, L.: Non-parametric model for background subtraction. In: Vernon, D. (ed.) ECCV 2000. LNCS, vol. 1843, pp. 751–767. Springer, Heidelberg (2000). https://doi.org/10.1007/3-540-45053-X_48
14. Fefilatyev, S.: Algorithms for visual maritime surveillance with rapidly moving camera (2012)
15. Frost, D., Tapamo, J.R.: Detection and tracking of moving objects in a maritime environment using level set with shape priors. EURASIP J. Image Video Process. **2013**(1), 42 (2013)

16. Kass, M., Witkin, A., Terzopoulos, D.: Snakes: active contour models. Int. J. Comput. Vis. **1**(4), 321–331 (1988)
17. Leira, F.S., Johansen, T.A., Fossen, T.I.: Automatic detection, classification and tracking of objects in the ocean surface from UAVs using a thermal camera. In: 2015 IEEE Aerospace Conference, pp. 1–10. IEEE (2015)
18. Liu, C., et al.: Beyond pixels: exploring new representations and applications for motion analysis. Ph.D. thesis, Massachusetts Institute of Technology (2009)
19. Mou, X., Wang, H., Lim, K.L.: Scale-adaptive multiple-obstacle tracking with occlusion handling in maritime scenes. In: 2016 12th IEEE International Conference on Control and Automation (ICCA), pp. 588–592. IEEE (2016)
20. Munkres, J.: Algorithms for the assignment and transportation problems. J. Soc. Industr. Appl. Math. **5**(1), 32–38 (1957)
21. Muñoz-Salinas, R.: A Bayesian plan-view map based approach for multiple-person detection and tracking. Pattern Recogn. **41**(12), 3665–3676 (2008)
22. Piccardi, M.: Background subtraction techniques: a review. In: IEEE International Conference on Systems, Man and Cybernetics, vol. 4, pp. 3099–3104. IEEE (2004)
23. Rout, R.K.: A survey on object detection and tracking algorithms. Ph.D. thesis (2013)
24. Serra, J., Vincent, L.: An overview of morphological filtering. Circ. Syst. Sig. Process. **11**(1), 47–108 (1992)
25. Shaikh, S.H., Saeed, K., Chaki, N.: Moving object detection using background subtraction. Moving Object Detection Using Background Subtraction. SCS, pp. 15–23. Springer, Cham (2014). https://doi.org/10.1007/978-3-319-07386-6_3
26. Szpak, Z.L., Tapamo, J.R.: Maritime surveillance: tracking ships inside a dynamic background using a fast level-set. Expert Syst. Appl. **38**(6), 6669–6680 (2011)
27. Viola, P., Jones, M.J.: Robust real-time face detection. Int. J. Comput. Vis. **57**(2), 137–154 (2004)
28. Wang, H., et al.: Vision based long range object detection and tracking for unmanned surface vehicle. In: 2015 IEEE 7th International Conference on Cybernetics and Intelligent Systems (CIS) and IEEE Conference on Robotics, Automation and Mechatronics (RAM), pp. 101–105. IEEE (2015)
29. Wang, H., Wei, Z.: Stereovision based obstacle detection system for unmanned surface vehicle. In: 2013 IEEE International Conference on Robotics and Biomimetics (ROBIO), pp. 917–921. IEEE (2013)
30. Wei, H., Nguyen, H., Ramu, P., Raju, C., Liu, X., Yadegar, J.: Automated intelligent video surveillance system for ships. In: SPIE Defense, Security, and Sensing, p. 73061N. International Society for Optics and Photonics (2009)
31. Zhang, K., Zhang, L., Liu, Q., Zhang, D., Yang, M.-H.: Fast visual tracking via dense spatio-temporal context learning. In: Fleet, D., Pajdla, T., Schiele, B., Tuytelaars, T. (eds.) ECCV 2014. LNCS, vol. 8693, pp. 127–141. Springer, Cham (2014). https://doi.org/10.1007/978-3-319-10602-1_9
32. Zhou, S.K., Chellappa, R., Moghaddam, B.: Visual tracking and recognition using appearance-adaptive models in particle filters. IEEE Trans. Image Process. **13**(11), 1491–1506 (2004)

Detection and Analysis of Video Inconsistency Based on Local Binary Pattern (LBP)

Ashok Gaikwad[1]($\boxtimes$), Vivek Mahale[2], Mouad M. H. Ali[2,3],
and Pravin L. Yannawar[4]

[1] Institute of Management Studies and Information Technology,
Aurangabad, MS, India
drashokgaikwad@gmail.com
[2] Department of CS and IT, Dr. Babasaheb Ambedkar Marathwada University,
Aurangabad 431001, MS, India
[3] Department of Computer Science and Engineering, Hodeidah University,
Al Hudaydah, Yemen
[4] Vison and Intelligent System Lab, Department of CS and IT,
Dr. Babasaheb Ambedkar Marathwada University, Aurangabad, MS, India

Abstract. In the Human life, videos popularity has increased day by day. With the help of high qualityvideo camera and video editing tools peoples easily manipulate video for malicious intent. Sonow a day, this is becoming significant topic in the recent year with more difficulties. The proposed of research work focus in texture features by using Local Binary Pattern (LBP). The object of this work is to detect video inconsistency. The work is addressing in various steps as sequentially such as preprocessing, feature extraction, matching and decision. The evaluation of propose system by using True positive Rate (TPR) and False Positive Rate (FPR). The experimental results were executives on famous dataset REWIND database, which has 20 videos which give efficiency results with evaluation parameter TPR with 0.0258%, FPR with 0.0786% and Area Under Curve (AUC) = 0.7903%.

Keywords: LBP · Video · Inconsistency · Detection · Analysis

1 Introduction

Nowadays, widely use or sharing of video in social media i.e. YouTube, Facebook, whats App and news channels [1] video increase its popularity in society and used in investigation activities it is also use as evidence. With the help of sophisticated video editing software and hardware video manipulation is also possible. Which of all the manipulation or tampering possible with in digital images may be possible with single frame or sequence of frames. In video frame sequence insertion and deletions are also done. In video editing the aim is to improve only quality of video then that editing called innocent. If video editing has done

© Springer Nature Singapore Pte Ltd. 2019
K. C. Santosh and R. S. Hegadi (Eds.): RTIP2R 2018, CCIS 1035, pp. 104–110, 2019.
https://doi.org/10.1007/978-981-13-9181-1_9

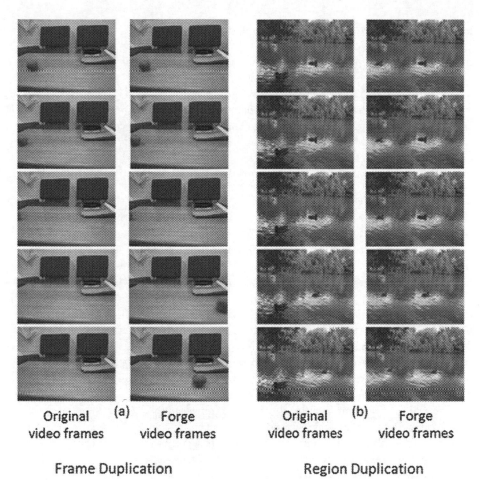

Original   (a)   Forge
video frames   video frames

Original   (b)   Forge
video frames   video frames

Frame Duplication   Region Duplication

Fig. 1. Sample video frames [4]

for adding, removing or modifying content from video that is called malicious editing. The video tempering has two approaches i.e. Intra-video forgery and Inter-video forgery. In Intra-video approach, the region or frame of video is to replace with same video sequence to hiding information. In intra-video forgery, video has replace, clipping object or frame with other video or other video frames [2]. Wang and farid [3] were exposing studies intra video forgery.

Figure 1 shows sample original and forge videos few frames from video dataset [4]. Figure 1(a) is an example of frame duplication and Fig. 1(b) is an example of region duplication. Video forgery detection method also classified in active and passive based techniques. In active approach digital video apply preprocessing like digital signature or watermark, which degrade the performance of video. Passive approach work on some basic assumptions i.e. video has naturally occurring properties and inherent fingerprint which was unique. In forge video the statistical correlations of the video is not consistent after post processing operations [1]. Video tampering attacks can be categories spatial tampering, temporal tempering attacks and spatial-temporal tampering attacks spatial tampering In spatial tampering frame content was altered. In this operation frame contents were modifying, manipulate. In this spatial tampering has involves block level and pixel level.

2   Related Work

Nowadays, researcher is focusing on detection of video inconsistencies. As per image tempering video manipulation is possible. Labartino et al. [5] they were proposed a new method that localization of forgeries in MPEG-2 video by using Group of Picture (GOP) and Double Quantization (DQ). In the video frame DQ was encoded twice. They have focus intra-frame forgery scenario. Firstly, they locate frames that have been intra-coded twice by applying DQ. Then they have used state-of-the art method in which video analysis estimating size of GOP. The DQ analysis based on proposed model specific MPEG-2. Yongjian et al. [6] they were proposed a novel method for improving fingerprinting algorithm to detecting video frame duplication. They have identified duplicate frames based on video sub-sequence fingerprints. The fingerprints were detected by employing DCT coefficients of temporally informative representative images (TIRIs). Hsu et al. [7] they were proposed a method to detect video tampering employed correlation of noise residue. In their method, they have extract block level correlation values of noise residue as a feature. They have proposed two steps approach i.e. Gaussian Mixture Model (GMM) and Bayesian Classifier is employed to find optimal threshold values.

3   Methodology

The strategy of this framework is used for distinguishing video inconsistency which is trailed by various mechanism identified with preprocessing stages, unique feature extraction. In addition to the main steps which determine the output of the system by matching and decision stages. In The preprocessing was conducted byon Reverse Engineering of Audio-Visual Content Data (REWIND) [4] dataset. Figure 2 illustrates the proposed system by graphical representation and Algorithm 1 shows the steps follow the system.

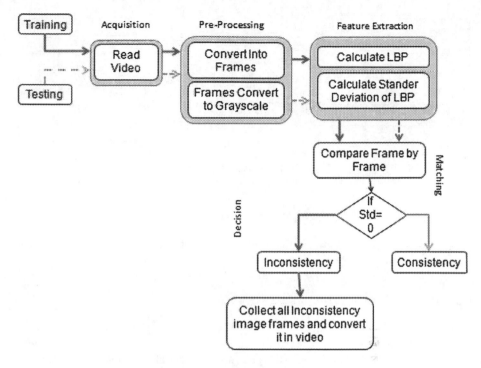

Fig. 2. The propose of study of detect Video inconsistency using LBP

Algorithm 1 describes Video Forgery detectionprocess step by step.
Algorithm 1: Automatic Video Forgery detection.

Input: video for determination of inconsistencies check
Output: classify the video into two classes (Original or Forge)
Begin:
    Step 1: Read Video as Train and test
    Step 2: Convert Color Image into Frames
    Step 3: Frames covert into Gray scale image
    Step 4: Calculate Gradient / LBP for each Frames
    Step 5: Calculate STD for each frames
    Step 6: Compare Frame by Frame
    Step 7: If (STD==0) then frames is consistence otherwise inconsistence
    Step 8: Collect all inconsistence image frames and convert it into Video
End.

3.1 Preprocessing

In preprocessing first Read train and test video from the dataset. To convert this video into frames and frames convert into grayscale image. To convert RGB (color) value into grayscale value by forming a weight sum I the R, G and B components Eq. (1);

Fig. 3. LBP calculation process

$$I = 0.298R + 0.587G + 0.114B \tag{1}$$

Here, R means red, G means Green and B mean blue of an image. Apply Gaussian filter for improve image quality.

3.2 Feature Extraction

In feature extraction we apply the LBP of each frame. The goal of LBP technique was extract the texture feature which focus on intensity value of pixel-wise on each block which makes the LBP technique is powerful to detect exact inconsistency area in videos as well as image [10]. Then we were calculating standard deviation (Std) of LBP. Local Binary pattern was introduced by Ojala et al. [8]. The idea of LBP method was based on assumption that texture has pattern and it strength aspects. The LBP operator is transform an image into array or image of integer labels, which is describing small scale visual aspect of the image [9]. The LBP is used for classification in computer vision. LBP texture analysis operator is defined as gray-scale invariant texture measure, derived from a general definition of texture in a local neighborhood. For calculating LBP value for pixel in grayscale image by comparing center pixel value with neighboring pixel by clockwise or anticlockwise order for all pixels. Suppose there are 8 neighboring pixel, then comparison for each pixel are 8. The result of comparison stored in 8th array. If current pixel value $\geq$ neighboring pixel value

Then, bit in binary array set '1'

Else if,

Current pixel value $<$ Neighboring pixel value Then, bit in binary array is '0'

Figure 3 shows process of calculating LBP value. In Fig. 3 center pixel value is '7'. We starts compare from label 0 and it is 2. The value of label 0 is less than center pixel i.e. $2 < 7$, then we reset (mean 0) in 0th bit location. The next liable 1 location has value 7 and it is equal to center pixel i.e. $7 = 7$. Then we set (1) in 1st position. So continue this process until reach the 8th neighboring pixel. Then binary pattern of 8 bit array is converting to decimal. This decimal number is stored in corresponding pixel location in LBP mask. After calculating LBP Mask, calculate LBP histogram and then normalize LBP histogram.

Table 1. TPR and FPR for video

No. of video	No. of frames	FPR	TPR
1	626	0.0985	0.0238
2	824	0.0957	0.0580
3	1018	0.0991	0.0282
4	478	0.0190	0.0997
	Mean of FPR and TPR	0.3123	0.2097

4   Matching and Decision

In matching process we have Compare Std of the train and test images, if (Std = 0) then test frame image has inconsistency otherwise consistency. If the image frame is inconsistency copy that frame in a forge image folder. Collected inconsistence frames convert into video i.e. forge part of the video.

5   Result and Discussion

In video inconsistency detection research we used 8 Videos (4 genuine and 4 copy- move forge) and addressing LBP and evaluated and compare all technique results. In evaluation, we calculate TPR (True Positive Rate) and FPR (False Positive Rate) for 4 videos shown in Table 1.

We have calculated accuracy of video inconsistency detection i.e. 79.03% .We draw ROC curve and calculate Area under the curve (AUC) shown in Fig. 4.

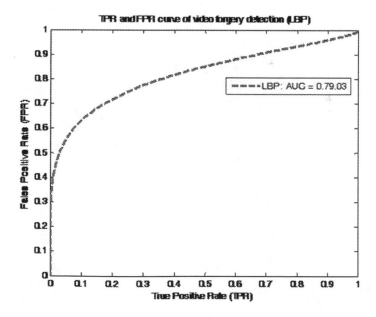

Fig. 4. Performance of the system show by ROC curve of LBP method

6   Conclusion

In this work, the video inconsistency detection with help of texture feature such as LBP was conducted successfully in this paper. The evaluation was done ona widespread dataset. And the preprocessing was done by converting color image into grayscale and covert in frames. The LBP was applied and the matching frames finally identify which the frames have forged. Efficiency of system was calculated based on TPR and FPR with the help depend on thresholds. We have achieved Accuracy reach to 79.03% and AUC of 0.7903 which show the more efficiency compare with existing system. The future work may be extend to apply on largest dataset and used different types of techniques like CNN.

References

1. Sowmya, K.N., Chennamma, H.R.: A survey on video forgery detection. Int. J. Comput. Eng. Appl. **9**(2), 17–27 (2015). http://www.ijcea.com/wp-content/uploads/2015/03/02-Sowmya-K.N.pdf
2. Kobayashi, M., Okabe, T., Sato, Y.: Detecting forgery from static-scene video based on inconsistency in noise level functions. IEEE Trans. Inf. Forensics Secur. **5**(4), 883–892 (2010). https://doi.org/10.1109/TIFS.2010.2074194
3. Wang, W., Farid, H.: Exposing digital forgeries in video by detecting duplication. In: Proceedings of Workshop on Multimedia & Security International Multimedia Conference, New York, NY, pp. 35–42 (2007). https://doi.org/10.1145/1288869.1288876
4. https://sites.google.com/site/rewindpolimi/downloads/datasets/video-copy-move -forgeries-dataset
5. Labartinoet, D., et al.: Localization of forgeries in MPEG-2 video through GOP size and DQ analysis. In: MMSP 2013, Pula (Sardinia), Italy (2013)
6. Yongjian, H.: An improved fingerprinting algorithm for detection of video frame duplication forgery. Int. J. Digit. Crime Forensics **4**(3), 20–32 (2012). https://doi.org/10.4018/jdcf.2012070102
7. Hsu, C.C., et al.: Video forgery detection using correlation of noise residue. In: IEEE International Workshop on Multimedia Signal Processing, Cairns, Australia, pp. 170–174 (2008). https://doi.org/10.1109/MMSP.2008.4665069
8. Ojala, T., Pietikäinen, M., Harwood, D.: A comparative study of texture measures with classification based on feature distributions. Pattern Recognit. **29**(1), 51–59 (1996). https://doi.org/10.1016/0031-3203(95)00067-4
9. Pietikäinen, M., Hadid, A., Zhao, G., Ahonen, T.: Local binary patterns for still images. In: Pietikäinen, M., Hadid, A., Zhao, G., Ahonen, T. (eds.) Computer Vision Using Local Binary Patterns, pp. 13–47. Springer, London (2011). https://doi.org/10.1007/978-0-85729-748-8_2
10. Mahale, V.H., Ali, M.M.H., Yannawar, P.L., Gaikwad, A.T.: Image inconsistency detection using local binary pattern (LBP). Procedia Comput. Sci. **115**, 501–508 (2017). https://doi.org/10.1016/j.procs.2017.09.097

Shot-Net: A Convolutional Neural Network for Classifying Different Cricket Shots

Md. Ferdouse Ahmed Foysal[1]([⊠]), Mohammad Shakirul Islam[1], Asif Karim[2], and Nafis Neehal[1]

[1] Department of Computer Science and Engineering,
Daffodil International University, Dhaka, Bangladesh
{ferdouse15-5274,shakirul15-311,nafis.cse}@diu.edu.bd
[2] College of Engineering and IT, Charles Darwin University, Darwin, Australia
asif.karim@cdu.edu.au

Abstract. Artificial Intelligence has become the new powerhouse of data analytics in this technological era. With advent of different Machine Learning and Computer Vision algorithms, applying them in data analytics has become a common trend. However, applying Deep Neural Networks in different sport data analyzing tasks and study the performance of these models is yet to be explored. Hence, in this paper, we have proposed a 13 layered Convolutional Neural Network referred as "Shot-Net" in order to classifying six categories of cricket shots, namely Cut Shot, Cover Drive, Straight Drive, Pull Shot, Scoop Shot and Leg Glance Shot. Our proposed model has achieved fairly high accuracy with low cross-entropy rate.

Keywords: Cricket shot classification · Convolution neural network · Deep learning

1 Introduction

Cricket is one of the most exciting games in the world, batting is the ability of hitting the cricket ball with a cricket bat, and there are different kinds of cricket shots. Batsmen have to accommodate to various conditions when playing on different cricket pitches, especially in different countries therefore, as well as having distinguished physical batting skills, top-level batsmen will have thunder reflex action, excellent decision making and be good strategists [6]. Application of computer vision and machine learning techniques in cricket for different analysis is an emerging domain now. In cricket plethora of technologies used for visualization and coaching [1–3]. From recent researches till now satisfactory results for detecting shots are not achieved.

We thought that we can do a deep convolution neural network (CNN) [2] based action detection. Therefore, we are proposing a novel approach to classify different types of cricket shots using Convolutional Neural Network and

© Springer Nature Singapore Pte Ltd. 2019
K. C. Santosh and R. S. Hegadi (Eds.): RTIP2R 2018, CCIS 1035, pp. 111–120, 2019.
https://doi.org/10.1007/978-981-13-9181-1_10

Deep Learning. An intelligent device can recognize the human corpus parts by extracting features from real data using algorithms [4]. Then all the parts of the body will be classified [5] by applying various techniques of action for the representation of model. In machine learning image processing and pattern recognition, extraction of features started from a basic set of data being measured and constructs evolved values intended to be copious and non-surplus, the following generalization moves and generalization should be facilitating. Extraction of features is related to dimensional reduction. We proposed a CNN based model where we input images in three convolution layer, three max pooling layer, four dropout layer and two dense layer.

Our goal was to classify six types of cricket shot activities by our own developed model. On our own generated and modified data-set, our CNN model recognize the activity of Cricket Shots, and moreover the similarities and difference between different shots. This task was formulated as a deep learning based real life problem, of which the difference is thought by a feature extraction approach. All other section of this paper is described as few sections, Sect. 2 elaborates the background study and related work. In Sects. 3 and 4 our model representation, train and test procedure described, result discussion is given in Sect. 5.

2   Literature Review

Several studies published on Cricket since last decade. The Hawk-Eye [1] by Collins and Evans is studied about advanced system of coaching for cricket. In 2015 a research paper was published on cricket shot classification based on motion vector by a group of Bangladeshi researcher. For action recognition, they use 3D MACH to classify the shots and to detect cricket shots they define 8 classes of angle ranges [7]. In 2016 Dixit and Balakrishnan from Stanford University published a report on Deep Learning using CNN's for Ball-by-Ball Outcome Classification in Sports [8]. They compare the performance of three different Convolutional Neural Network architectures, inspired by literature on activity recognition in videos.

In 2010 Yao and Fei-Fei published a paper on Object Interaction Activities of Human pose by using mutual context modeling [9]. In their research paper they described a new model of random field to encode poses of human in activities of human-objects. They mold the learning structure problem as a learning task of model, the summary of human activity pose, and the parts of the body are calculated using a search of structure method and new max-margin algorithm used for estimating the parameters of the model.

In another research paper, Batra, Gupta, Yadav, Gupta and Yadav proposed a multi-valued automated decision whether a ball is no-ball or wide ball [6]. Presenting game specific concept selection and event selection criteria. Another cricket shot classification using computer vision proposed by Chowdhury and Jihan divided the approach into four phases of identifying batsman's hand stroke direction, tracking, detection of a collision of bat and ball and detection of human pose and skeleton joints [10]. Another work of a semantic video analysis based on image features of high and low level knowledge for cricket video sequences [12]. Angadi and Vilas Naik worked on detection of shot boundary technique using regional color moments. They said that it can become a measurement of discovering difference among sequent video frames [11]. In [13–19], different approaches of object classification, and sports analysis works has been shown.

3   Proposed Methodology

In this canto we described our model implementation, the process of cricket shot classification. The process of training the model, testing and validation, data-set collection, data preparation, data augmentation, data resize, proposed model description and finally training procedure of the model is described in this part.

3.1   Background of CNN

Deep learning is a technique for implementing Machine Learning. It is made of artificial neural networks. Neural networks work as similar as our brain. CNN that means Convolutional Neural Network is one of the strongest networks in deep learning. It is an artificial neural network, which is also known as feed-forward ANN. In a "feed-forward" network information flows right through the networks.

Yann LeCun was the inventor of CNN. Inspired from human processes he made it. Actually CNN works like biological visual cortex. CNN is one of the most successful models in image classification. CNN's classification accuracy is better than any other traditional image classification algorithms. In CNN we don't have to do feature selection, but in other image classification algorithms, we have to do it. There are different types of layers that are used in CNN.

Convolution layer has a moving filter or kernel which passes through the image. Generally it passes through a 2D matrix (representation of image) and take a certain portion and applies dot multiplication and stores it in another matrix (Fig. 1).

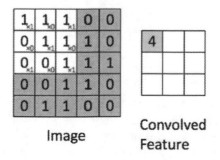

Image

Convolved Feature

Fig. 1. Convolution of a filter over 2D image

Dimension of the output matrix can be calculated by an equation. We can see an equation bellow where:

n_{out} – Output dimension
n_{in} – Input dimension
f – Window size
S – Stride

$$n_{out} = floor(\frac{n_{in} - f}{S}) + 1$$

Equation to find Output dimension

Pooling layer generally sits next to convolution layer. It mainly used to reduce memory and for fast computation. It reduces the volume. Max pooling is one of the most used layers in CNN. It sets a kernel and finds the max number from the matrix (Fig. 2).

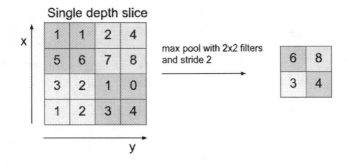

Fig. 2. Max pooling.

Fully connected layer gets 2D or 3D array as input from previous layer and converts the 2D or 3D array into 1D array.

The output layer of a convolutional neural network shows the probability of the classes. It is calculated by "Softmax" function. The equation of calculating the probability is given bellow.

$$\sigma(X_j) = \frac{e^{x_j}}{\sum_i e^{x_i}}$$

3.2   Data-Set Collection

We have made a dataset of 3600 images. The dataset have 6 classes of cricket shots, each class contains 600 images. The classes are Cut shot, Cover drive, Straight drive, Pull shot, Leg glance shot and Scoop shot. We took 80% image of the dataset that means 2880 images to train the model and 20% image of the dataset that means 720 images for testing. In the train dataset, each class contains 480 images and in the test dataset, each class contains 120 images. All the data were processed and collected by the authors (Fig. 3).

Fig. 3. The example of our dataset.

3.3 Data Augmentation

We artificially expanded the dataset to avoid overfitting. It helps to increase the amount of relevant data in the dataset. We augmented the real main data-set in 5 different way.

- Rotate $-30°$
- Rotate $+30°$
- Shear by a certain amount
- Adding Salt and Pepper noise
- Shading

3.4 Data Preperation

All the images of our dataset have different dimension such as height, width and size. Since our model requires a similar pixel size data for train and test purpose, we resized the data-set into 100×100 pixels. We have also converted the images into grayscale. Because of lower GPU in our computer, we used grayscale images to train the model.

3.5 Proposed Model

We proposed our own CNN model, which have 13 layers. There are three convolutional layers:

- First layer have 32-3 × 3 filters and 'linear' as activation function.
- Second layer have 64-3 × 3 filters and 'linear' as activation function.
- Third layer have 128-3 × 3 filters and 'linear' as activation function (Fig. 4).

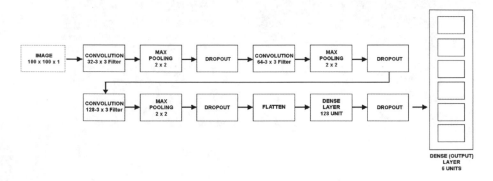

Fig. 4. Architecture of our model.

In addition, there are three max-pooling layers each of size 2 × 2. There are four dropout layer with parameter 0.20. We have a flatten layer, in the model. Lastly there are two dense layer, where in one we used 'linear' as activation function and in the other we used 'softmax' as activation function. We used softmax activation function to get the probability of each class.

3.6 Training the Model

We used Adam optimizer to compile our model. We used 80% of training dataset to train and 20% is used for validation. Training dataset has 2880 images so that we used 2304 images to train and 576 images to validate. We used a batch size of 64. We have trained the network for 40 epochs.

4 Performance Evaluation

Training accuracy is usually the accuracy when the model is applied on the training data. When the model is applied on a few selected data from random class, is known as validation accuracy. Figure 5 shows a graph which contains training and validation accuracy of our model.

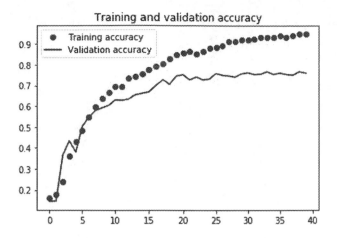

Fig. 5. Training and validation accuracy.

The error on the training data-set is called training loss. The error occurs after running the validation data-set through the trained network is known as validation loss. Figure 6 shows a graph which contains training and validation loss of our model.

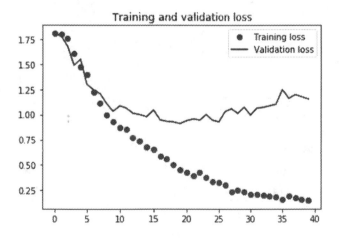

Fig. 6. Training and validation loss.

5   Result Discussion

We calculated Precision, Recall and F1-score from test dataset containing 840 images from the classification report we can see Precession average is 0.80, Recall average is 0.79 and average F1-score is 0.79. So it can be said that the performance of our classifier is pretty good, classification report given in Table 1.

From table of Classification report we can see that the classifier achieved a decent accuracy, which is 80%.

Table 1. Classification report.

Class	Precision	Recall	F-score
Cut Shot	0.69	0.76	0.72
Cover Drive	0.74	0.78	0.76
Straight Drive	0.78	0.83	0.81
Pull Shot	0.89	0.77	0.83
Leg glance Shot	0.79	0.88	0.83
Scoop Shot	0.88	0.72	0.79
Avg.	0.80	0.79	0.79

We describe the performance of our model by few figures, Fig. 7(a) Shows the confusion matrix without normalization and Fig. 7(b) Show the normalized confusion matrix.

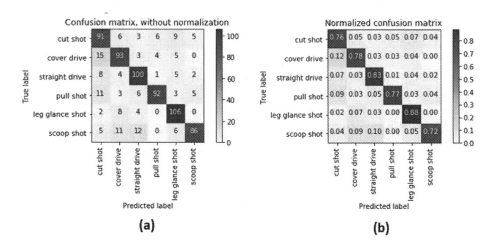

Fig. 7. (a) Confusion matrix, (b) Normalized confusion matrix.

6   Future Work

In our proposed method we can classify different kinds of cricket shots, we have used convolution neural networks to build a model for our Shot-Net data. Our future goal is to make a better neural network to get a better accuracy. We have a plan to do a 3D depth image based classification by deep learning. Where we will use MS Kinect or Intel RealSense, We will use different types of algorithm and that will select the efficient one.

7   Conclusion

In this paper, we provide an approach of cricket shot classification approach by our CNN model. We used three convolution layer, three max polling layer, four dropout layer, one flatten and two dense layer. We use dropout layers to reduce overfitting. The final achieved result we've found is so promising. We hope that this method will be developed as a real application in future for the welfare of cricket game. It will be effective for coaching system also, to improve bowling skill as-well as batting skill too.

References

1. Collins, H., Evans, R.: Hawkeye second edition public understanding revised 07 clean (2008)
2. Krizhevsky, A., Sutskever, I., Hinton, G.E.: ImageNet Classification with Deep Convolutional Neural Networks (2012)
3. Collins, H., Evans, R.: Hawkeye-final-submission (2012)
4. Shotton, J., Sharp, T., Kipman, A.: Real-time human pose recognition in parts from single depth images. Commun. ACM (2013). http://dl.acm.org/citation.cfm?id=2398381
5. Andriluka, M., Roth, S., Schiele, B.: Pictorial structures revisited: people detection and articulated pose estimation. In: Computer Vision and Pattern, pp. 1014–1021 (2009)
6. Batra, N., Gupta, H., Yadav, N., Gupta, A., Yadav, A.: Implementation of augmented reality in cricket for ball tracking and automated decision making for no ball, pp. 316–321 (2014). https://doi.org/10.1109/ICACCI.2014.6968378
7. Wikipedia, Different Cricket Shots. https://en.wikipedia.org/wiki/Batting (cricket)
8. Dixit, K., Balakrishnan, A.: Deep learning using CNN's for ball-by-ball outcome classification in sports, report submission on the course of Convolutional Neural Networks for Visual Recognition, Stanford University (2016)
9. Yao, B., Fei-Fei, L.: Modeling Mutual Context of Object and Human Pose in Human-Object Interaction Activities. IEEE (2010). 978-1-4244-6985 7/10/26.00
10. Chowdhury, A.Z.M.E., Jihan, A.U.: Classification of Cricket Shots Using Computer Vision (2014)
11. Angadi, S.A., Naik, V.: A shot boundary detection technique based on local color moments in YCbCr color space. In: CS and IT-CSCP 2012 (2012)
12. Kolekar, M.H., Palaniappan, K., Sengupta, S.: Semantic event detection and classification in cricket video sequence. In: 2008 Sixth Indian Conference on Computer Vision, Graphics and Image Processing, Bhubaneswar, pp. 382–389 (2008)
13. Islam, M.S., Foysal, F.A., Neehal, N., Karim, E., Hossain, S.A.: InceptB: a CNN based classification approach for recognizing traditional bengali games. In: ICACC-2018 (2018)
14. Patel, H.A., Thakore, D.G.: Moving object tracking using Kalman filter. IJCSMC 2(4), 326–332 (2013)
15. Zhu, G., Huang, Q., Xu, C., Xing, L., Gao, W., Yao, H.: Human behavior analysis for highlight ranking in broadcast racket sports video. IEEE Trans. Multimedia 9(6), 1167–1182 (2007)

16. Simonyan, A., Zisserman, K.: Very deep convolutional networks for large-scale image recognition (2014)
17. Rock, R.A., Gibbs, A., Carlos, P.H.: The 5 the Umpire: Cricket"s Edge Detection System (2012)
18. Forsyth, D.A., Brien, V.O.: Computer Vision: A Modern Approach, 2 edn, pp. 88–101 (2003)
19. Lowe, D.G.: Distinctive image features from scale invariant keypoints. Int. J. Comput. Vis. **60**(2), 91–110 (2004)

Execution and Performance Evaluation of Cognitive and Expressive Event on a robotic Arm

Shashibala Tarigopula[✉], Bharti Gawali, and Pravin Yannawar

Department of Computer Science and IT, Dr. Babasaheb Ambedkar
Marathwada University, Aurangabad, India
shashibala.rao@gmail.com, drbhartirokade@gmail.com,
pravinyannawar@gmail.com

Abstract. Based on specific attributes of the brain activity the Brain
Computer Interface (BCI) systems convert the brain signals into actions
for controlling the external devices which enables people suffering from
severe disabilities to lead a quality life. Interfacing the directional movements with a Robotic arm with cognitive thoughts and expressions is
attempted with wireless EEG equipment. Out of the mental state detection suits provided by Emotiv EPOC the cognitiv and expressiv suite
have been considered in this study. The following movements will be
detected (Arm up, Arm down and stop action) based on the cognitive
event selected. A performance evaluation of the system based on True–
False difference for all the events is made. Sensitivity, specificity and the
accuracy values for the subjects were calculated.

Keywords: Robotic arm · Emotiv EPOC · Cognitive event ·
Performance evaluation

1 Introduction

The signals from human brain are taken as input in the BCI systems. Depending
on the brain activity, certain features of the brain signals are taken into consideration to be transformed into actions for controlling external devices. This can
be beneficial to the disabled people who are totally paralyzed or locked in by
neuromuscular disorders to carry on their day to day tasks [1,2]. Significant
attention has been given to the BCI, which comprises of the hardware and software framework. The system provides a direct interaction human brain and the
computer. Though there have been speculations about a person being directly
able to control the electrical devices with the help of human brain, thus bypassing
the normal method of the working of peripheral nerves and muscles [3] in coor-
dination of the brain, breakthroughs are found in the past few years [4]. There
is a comprehensive use of BCI technology as a consequence of the use of modern
machine learning and signal processing methods, which has provided a means of
lessening the burden of training from the subject to statistical learning machines

© Springer Nature Singapore Pte Ltd. 2019
K. C. Santosh and R. S. Hegadi (Eds.): RTIP2R 2018, CCIS 1035, pp. 121–131, 2019.
https://doi.org/10.1007/978-981-13-9181-1_11

and thus making the BCI communication simplified for a novice user. Thus the functional, communication and entertainment applications can be ascertained for the purpose for which they are developed. Some of the important research areas consist of the study of motor reestablishment or motor commutation where the important applications are hand grasping and wheelchair control. For the normal end-users, BCI systems having multimodal approaches like Electroencephalography (EEG), Electromyography (EMG) which can be used in gaming and for standard control [5].

1.1   BCI Based Tasks Are Classified as

Visual-Evoked Potentials (VEPs): are electrical signals generated at the visual cortex region, based on direction of eye movements. It is one of the BCI methods to identify the information executed by the general functioning of the brain's normal output pathways [6].

P300-Based BCI: When there is no dependency on any muscular activity the BCI systems are defined to be independent. The example, where the subject waits for the occurrence of a unique stimulus on the background of a series of other stimuli is considered. A positive peak over parietal cortex about 300 ms (P300) is observed in P300 based BCI after appearance of stimulus [7].

BCI Based on Motor Imagery: In the motor imaginery BCI system, the user controls the cursor in the systems with the help of oscillatory brain activity in one to four possible targets. Here the subject imagines some kind of motor activity, which are then related to adapted methods [8].

ERD and ERS: Both ERD and ERS occur in response to event instead of a stimulus. The ERD and ERS are desynchronization and synchronization events, respectively, which occur in response to a motor imaginery event. ERD occurs 1 s prior to response in the mu (8–14 Hz) and beta bands (14–25 Hz). But ERS is noticed in the beta band and is observed in the 1 to 2 s after a response [9].

Slow Cortical Potentials: Slow cortical potentials are current shifts in EEG which occur in cortex for 0.5–10 s. The negative shifts are seen as a result of cortical activation, like, evoked because of implementation of a movement or take place as a result of a mental task, similarly the positive shifts imply absence of mental activation in cortical region [10].

1.2   BCI Systems

Generally, the BCI systems are controlled by people in a monitored environment, like a powered wheelchair in a house [11]. Herein the user generated brain signals would operate the BCI system. The systems are then monitored by the users to check the results of their control inputs. Few systems help users to view the control displays generated by their brain activity. The brain activity would be recorded by the electrodes placed on the scalp of the user from the surface of the scalp, which are generated as a result of the neural activation in the brain. Then the brain activity is converted into electrical signals. The feature extraction methods are applied to remove the artifacts from the electrical signal. Resultant signals are classified into feature values that correlates to the related neurological condition adopted by the user for control. The execution of motor control in the body is planned, processed and memorized in the brain. The Focus of BCI is on improving resolution and speed besides reducing health risks and also user training times [12].

The alpha rhythms of the EEG signals were first observed and stated in the year 1929 by Hans Berger. Mostly the EEG signals were used for the purpose of diagnosis of neurological problems and observation of the functioning of the brain. Since it involved analysis of large amount of data, there has been focus on serious scientific direction for research only since the last decade. One of the most convenient ways of working in BCI involves studying the EEG signals and therefore the BCI is based on detecting the EEG signals associated with certain brain activity [13]. Electrodes are usually placed along the scalp based on 10–20 system as shown in Fig. 1 to measure brainwaves of different frequencies [14]. Five major brain waves are identified with respect to their frequency ranges. These frequencies are called delta having range of 0.5–4 Hz, theta with range of 4–7 Hz, alpha in the range of 8–13 Hz, beta having range of 13–30 Hz and gamma the range is higher than 30 Hz [15].

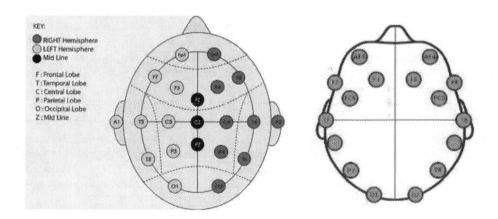

Fig. 1. 10–20 system of Electrode placement

Based on the kind of connection between the electrodes, analog circuit, digital system and computing devices, the BCI systems can be classified into two kinds, wired and wireless BCI systems. In this study the wireless BCI system Emotiv

EPOC has been selected. Emotiv EPOC integrates the largest number of sensors amongst commercially available EEG systems at the highest sampling rate among all portable [16] low-cost BCI headsets available in the market [17,18].

2   Materials and Methods

The EEG signals were captured through Emotiv EPOC, a wireless EEG system which consists of 14 channels. It provides the utilities in the form of suites. They are Expressiv, Affectiv and Cognitiv. The placement of electrodes is according to 10–20 system. The presented work is focused on cognitiv suite of Emotiv. The Technology Uncorked Octa Motion Robotic (TUOM) arm with degree of freedom three was considered for experimental purpose. The parts used in the assembly include screwdriver, spanner, high torque DC motor and a few assembled mechanical parts The robotic arm can perform the movements in the following directions namely upward, downward and the gripper is able to perform open and close actions. Atmega 16 microcontroller was used for interfacing the arm with EEG signals.

2.1   Implementation of the System

The implementation of the system can be observed in steps A to H seen in Fig. 2. (A) and (B) are the steps where amplified EEG signals are collected with a sampling frequency of 128 Hz. Wherein the subjects are shown the 3 events of the cognitiv suite and made to imagine one of the events. In the step (C), FIR, filtering technique is applied to get the data with frequency between 8–30 where mu and Beta band frequency data, required for the task can be considered and in step (D) based on the event selection by the subject the specific feature is selected. This is then matched with the stored trained data set (E). After selecting the specific matched event (F), the specific action is recognized (G) and performed by the robotic arm (H).

The designed system was implemented using Emotiv Epoc neuroheadset, Robotic arm, DB9 pin male female straight through RS 232 serial cable, laptop with processor 2.20 GHz, 4 GB RAM and 64 bit windows 10 operating system. The code was written and compiled using AVR studio 8. The .hex file that was generated was loaded into the flash buffer. This was then written on Atmega 16 microcontroller to control the robotic arm. Finally the l293D motor driver and Atmega 16 pins were interfaced to get the directional movement of the robotic arm.

The occurrence of cognitive events and their related action are shown in Table 1.

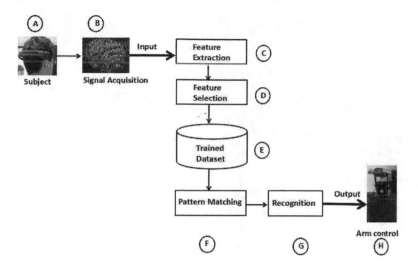

Fig. 2. Implementation of designed system

Table 1. Event Action table

Event of EPOC	Action of arm
Push	Arm down
Pull	Arm up
Neutral	Stop

2.2   Experiment

For experiment purpose five participants were considered. Out of which two were and three were female. The participants were in the age group of 25–41 years. They were normal adults having normal or corrected to normal vision. The data was collected after getting the consent of the participant.

The participants did not have any known neurological disorders. Before each experiment they were briefed about the experiment paradigm. The developed application relies on the connectivity between the laptop and with Emotiv EPOC's USB dongle, therefore establishing a connection between both devices is necessary. Data acquisition setup and the System flow of the interface can be seen in Fig. 3.

2.3   Database Creation

A database for the 3 events as database of cognitive suite events combined with expressiv events for training and testing are not available. The subjects had to

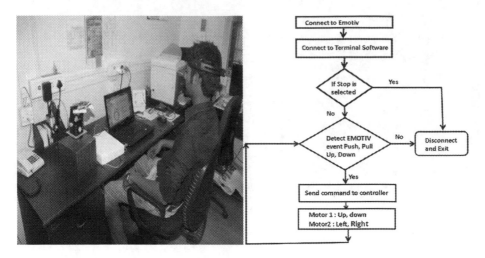

Fig. 3. Data acquisition system and system flow

undergo 5 training sessions and 5 testing sessions. The data of training session of subject 1 are shown in Table 2 for ready reference. As one training session would involve 30 trials or events, so during training and testing 300 events data is collected for every subject. For 5 subjects we had a collection of 1500 events database.

Size of database = 5 subjects × 5 training sessions + 5 subjects × 5 testing
    =50 × 30 trials (10-Push, 10-Pull, 10-Neutral events) per session
    =1500

Table 2. Entries for one training session of subject1

Event	Occurrence	Hits (TP)	Miss (FN)	TN	FP
Push	10	9	1	19/20	1/20
Pull	10	8	2	18/20	2/20
Neutral	10	8	2	20/20	0/20

BCI robotic arm was tested on five subjects and the results were collected to compute the accuracy or performance of the system. To determine the system accuracy, first the outcomes were defined: true positive, false negative, true negative and false positive of the result.

3   Performance Analysis

3.1   Results

Each subject was asked to try each action ten times, so the total number of trials will be thirty. Correct input means the correct expression that is required to make the robotic arm to do the desired move. The event by event data analysis was made to check with the intention of defining the number of true-positive classified events (TPE) and false-positive classified events (FPE) [19]. To find out the value of true positive or false negative of an action, we need to refer to the result when the subject doing a correct action for ten times. The log entries with respect to response time is seen in Table 3. On the other hand, to find out the value of true negative and false positive of an action, we refer to the results generated by other two actions which results from the rest twenty trials.

Table 3. Log table entries

Sr. No	Event	Result	Response time
1	Push	Push	6.08
2	Push	Push	5.23
3	Push	Push	3.12
4	Pull	Pull	4.00
5	Pull	Pull	3.37
6	Pull	Neutral	3.32

Parameters like sensitivity, specificity, and accuracy were also calculated based on the event outcomes. The sensitivity is also known as true positive rate, it refers to the measure of the proportion of positives that are defined correctly while the specificity, also known as true negative rate refers to the measure of the proportion of negatives that are defined correctly. Overall the accuracy is determined by the proportion of true positive and true negative in all evaluated cases within the time segments.

A correct activation of an event is a True Positive (TP), when no actions are attempted and detected, it is a True Negative (TN) and False Negatives (FN) and False Positives (FP) are failures to trigger in the required period, or a trigger occurring incorrectly. Accuracy is determined by $(TP + TN)/(TP + FP + TN + FN)$ [20] and similarly sensitivity and specificity formulas are given in Table 4. Basically, the accuracy defines the performance of the BCI robotic arm of the project.

The three actions like first bending down of robotic arm i.e. down action which occurred when the Push event of the cognitive suite was imagined, second, the up action of the arm for Pull event and third, stop action for neutral event of the arm were considered. The event related synchronization after the occurrence

Table 4. Parameters and their definitions

Parameter	Definition	Formula
Sensitivity	Sensitivity is the measure of the proportion of positives that are defined correctly. It is also referred to as true positive rate	$TP/TP+FN$
Specificity	Specificity is known as true negative rate, it refers to the measure of the fined proportion of negatives that are defined correctly	$TN/TN+FP$
Accuracy	Accuracy is determined by the proportion of true positive and true negative in all evaluated cases calculated within specified time segments	$TP+TN/TP+FN+FP+TN$

of the event is also observed which normally occurs a few milliseconds after the event. The results of sensitivity, specificity and accuracy can be seen in Tables 5, 6 and 7.

Table 5. Results of Sensitivity of Training and Testing datasets

	Training data			Testing data		
Subjects	Arm down	Arm up	Stop	Arm down	Arm up	Stop
Subject1	0.78	0.78	0.88	0.62	0.66	0.8
Subject2	0.6	0.62	0.76	0.62	0.66	0.68
Subject3	0.86	0.86	0.96	0.88	0.86	0.9
Subject4	0.42	0.46	0.58	0.46	0.42	0.54
Subject5	0.38	0.42	0.42	0.42	0.4	0.4

The highest sensitivity, specificity and accuracy values were observed in subject 3 and lowest values in subject 5.

3.2 Information Transfer Rate (ITR)

The information transfer rate in bits per minute is one of the important criteria in the performance evaluation of BCI systems [21]. The amount of information passing through a device per unit time is measured using ITR. It depends on three factors i.e, no of selections, accuracy and speed. For arm directional movement, the classification accuracy was 78%. The cuing period for training was set to 6 s, which left enough time for subjects to prepare for the movement. Later it was modified it to around 4.5 s. Though a variance was observed for the

Table 6. Results of Specificity of Training and Testing datasets

Subjects	Training data			Testing data		
	Arm down	Arm up	Stop	Arm down	Arm up	Stop
Subject1	0.94	0.93	0.95	0.91	0.91	0.95
Subject2	0.88	0.86	0.95	0.89	0.9	0.94
Subject3	0.96	0.95	0.99	0.99	0.95	0.96
Subject4	0.79	0.81	0.9	0.73	0.77	0.82
Subject5	0.73	0.69	0.79	0.73	0.75	0.73

Table 7. Results of Accuracy of Training and Testing datasets

Subjects	Training data			Testing data		
	Arm down	Arm up	Stop	Arm down	Arm up	Stop
Subject1	0.87	0.88	0.92	0.81	0.82	0.89
Subject2	0.78	0.79	0.89	0.8	0.82	0.85
Subject3	0.91	0.92	0.98	0.94	0.92	0.92
Subject4	0.66	0.68	0.79	0.63	0.63	0.73
Subject5	0.62	0.59	0.67	0.62	0.63	0.61

subjects, overall a good attention level was noticed. And from the neurophysiological analysis clear ERD/ERS patterns were observed and even response delay were shorter. The duration for trial windows has been shortened to 4.5 s, i.e. 14 trials per minute. Therefore, ITR was between 18 to 42 bits per minute for arm directional movement for the subjects. The bit-rates are given in bits/symbol, and they can be converted into bits/minute according to $B = V * R$, where V is the classification speed (in symbols/minute) and R is the information carried by one symbol (in bits/symbol) [22].

4   Conclusion

BCI systems work on the principal of extracting the particular brain response which can be used as an input to the BCI system. Many different applications have been explored and modified by researchers for Emotiv EPOC. Though it was aimed for the gaming market and is not a medical device, researchers have used it for a variety of applications. We have considered the Cognitiv suite and the Expressiv suite for controlling the movement of the arm. The actions of Arm up, Arm down and Stop were considered in our study and the Pull, Push and Neutral events of cognitiv and raise eyebrow and clench of expressiv events have been taken. The overall accuracy of 76% for Arm down movement was observed, 76% for Arm up movement and 80% for stop movement of robotic arm during testing sessions. Similarly overall accuracy of 76% for Arm down, 77% for Arm up and 85% for stop movement of robotic arm during training sessions. The Cognitiv suite has 13 directional events, in future we can extend our work by considering the other events for developing interface for controlling home appliance like the fan, light or other electronic gadgets. Such assisted devices can be of great help to people with restricted movements.

References

1. Hochberg, L.R., et al.: Reach and grasp by people with tetraplegia using a neurally controlled robotic arm. Nature **485**, 372–375 (2012)
2. Mak, J.N., Wolpaw, J.R.: Clinical applications of brain-computer interfaces: current state and future prospects. IEEE Rev. Biomed. Eng. **2**, 187–199 (2009). https://doi.org/10.1109/RBME.2009.2035356
3. El-aal, S.A., et al.: Classification of EEG signals for motor Imagery based on Mutual Information and Adaptive NeuroFuzzy Inference System, Chapter 16. IGI (2017)
4. Wolpaw, J.R., et al.: Brain-computer interface technology: a review. IEEE Trans. Rehabil. Eng. **8**(2), 164–173 (2000)
5. Duvinage, M., et al.: Performance of the Emotiv Epoc headset for P300-based applications. BioMed. Eng. OnLine (2013). https://doi.org/10.1186/1475-925X-12-56
6. Li, Y., Wang, C., Zhang, H., Guan, C.: An EEG-based BCI system for 2D cursor control. In: Proceedings of IEEE International Joint Conference on Neural Network, pp. 2214–2219 (2008)
7. Pires, G., Castelo-Branco, M., Nunes, U.: Visual P300-based BCI to steer a wheelchair: a Bayesian approach. In: Proceedings of IEEE Engineering in Medicine and Biology Society, pp. 658–661 (2008)
8. Wolpaw, J.R., McFarland, D.J., Neat, G.W., Forneris, C.A.: An EEG-based brain-computer interface for cursor control. Electroencephalogr. Clin. Neurophysiol. **78**, 252–259 (1991)
9. Grummett, T.S., et al.: Measurement of neural signals from inexpensive, wireless and dry EEG systems. Physiol. Meas. **36**, 1469–1484 (2015). https://doi.org/10.1088/09673334/36/7/1469
10. Krepki, R., et al.: Berlin brain-computer interface-the HCI communication channel for discovery. Int. J. Hum.-Comput. Stud. **65**, 460–477 (2007)
11. Bashashati, A.: A survey of signal processing algorithms in brain-computer interfaces based on electrical brain signals. J. Neural Eng. (2007)
12. Bi, L., Fan, X.-A., Liu, Y.: EEG-based brain-controlled mobile robots: a survey. IEEE Trans. Hum.-Mach. Syst. **43**(2), 161–176 (2013)
13. Ahmed, K.S.: Wheelchair movement control VIA human eye blinks. Am. J. Biomed. Eng. **1**(1), 55–58 (2011). https://doi.org/10.5923/j.ajbe.20110101.09
14. Niedermeyer, E., da Silva, F.L.: Electroencephalography: Basic Principles, Clinical Applications, and Related Fields, 5th edn, p. 140. Lippincott Williams & Wilkins, Philadelphia (2005)
15. Sanei, S., Chambers, J.: EEG Signal Processing, Chapter 1. Wiley, Hoboken (2007)
16. Volosyak, I.: Brain- computer interface using water -based electrodes. J. Neural Eng. (2010)
17. Lee, S., et al.: Review of wireless brain-computer interface systems (2013). https://doi.org/10.5772/56436

18. Comparison of consumer BCI; wikipedia the free encyclopedia. Accessed 15 July 2017
19. Townsend, G., Graimann, B., Pfurtscheller, G.: Continuous EEG classification during motor imagery-simulation of an asynchronous BCI. IEEE Trans. Neural Syst. Rehabil. Eng. **12**(2) (2004). https://doi.org/10.1109/TNSRE.2004.827220
20. Rodrigues, L.M., et al.: Parallel and distributed kmeans to identify the translation initiation site of proteins. In: IEEE International Conference on Systems, Man and Cybernectics (SMC) (2012)
21. Wolpaw, J.R., Birbaumer, N., McFarland, D.J., Pfurtscheller, G., Vaughan, T.M.: Brain-computer interfaces for communication and control. Clin. Neurophysiol. **113**, 767–791 (2002)
22. Cheng, M.: Design and implementation of a brain-computer interface with high transfer rates. IEEE Trans. Biomed. Eng. (2004)

Multiple Decompositions-Based Blind Watermarking Scheme for Color Images

S. Prasanth Vaidya[(✉)]

Department of Computer Science and Engineering,
Gayatri Vidya Parishad College of Engineering (A), Visakhapatnam, AP, India
vaidya269@gmail.com

Abstract. A blind extraction watermarking method on color images is designed to protect © & identify owner of multimedia. Watermark in color is exploited to deliver universality and boundless applicability to proposed watermarking method. The host data is decomposed by applying four decomposition techniques like Discrete Wavelet Transform (DWT), QR, SVD & Schur decomposition. Arnold transformed watermark is utilized for better security. This scheme embed's color watermark into gray-scale cover image which will be out of attacker's expectation. A probabilistic neural network (PNN) is utilized in the watermark extraction. Robustness and quality of scheme are evaluated with quality measurement functions like Peak Signal to Noise Ratio (PSNR) and Normalized Correlation Coefficient (NCC).

Keywords: Color watermarking · Arnold transform ·
Wavelet domain · Singular value decomposition · Schur decomposition

1 Introduction

The evolution in the field of networking has enabled the people all around the globe in retrieving, handling & administering "multi-media" over the internet with ease. This advancement helps in production and sharing of digital data massively for sure, but some illegal exploitation such as unauthorized copying and illicit distribution of intellectual property is also possible. To overcome such problems many intellectual property protection protocols ans security schemes such as encryption, perceptual hashing, watermarking, etc., have been materializing lately. Digital watermarking (DWM) is one such method used to claim ownership of stolen data to protect the IPR of the image content. In DWM process, watermark (wm) is embedded into the data [1–3] (images, videos, text, audio). The WM can be later extracted from the watermarked multimedia to claim ownership & also to verify it's originality. The remarkable properties of a watermarking approach include imperceptibility, robustness & security. For improving security, the watermark must be imperceptible to an unaided eye where the attacks should not affect the watermark [4,5]. By maintaining watermark perceptible transparency, the watermarked data quality will be high. The

© Springer Nature Singapore Pte Ltd. 2019
K. C. Santosh and R. S. Hegadi (Eds.): RTIP2R 2018, CCIS 1035, pp. 132–143, 2019.
https://doi.org/10.1007/978-981-13-9181-1_12

robustness of the watermarking scheme suggests that it should extract the watermark even after the attacks such as filtering, addition of noise, etc., applied by the intruders [6, 7].

The differences between spatial and transform domain are given in Table 1.

Table 1. Difference between spatial and frequency domain

Spatial domain	Frequency domain
(i) The watermark is embedded directly by altering the pixel values	(i) The transform coefficients are altered while embedding the watermark
(ii) Watermarking in the spatial domain is vulnerable to attacks	(ii) Watermarking in the transform domain is robust against attacks

Nguyen et al. [8] designed a authentication reversible watermarking method in DWT domain. Randomly generated authentication code is embedded into low-level sub-band of image block. Murali et al. [9] designed a watermarking method for copyright protection using region of interest, singular value decomposition and orthogonal polynomials transformation. Ernawan et al. [10] designed an image watermarking scheme by applying redundant DWT followed by SVD with the help of human visual characteristics. Vairaprakash et al. [11] designed method of watermarking by utilizing discrete Rajan frequency and support vector machine. The watermark is encrypted by dividing the original image into four segments, then each segment individual rows are shifted. Roy et al. [12] proposed a multiple color method of watermarking by applying Discrete Cosine Transform (DCT) and repetition code. Multiple watermarks are embedded in the blue and green components of host color image. DCT is applied to the blocks of blue and green components image and then watermark is embedded using repetition code.

It is noticed from the literature that none of the watermarking methods have entirely resisted the attacks. The proposed approach has better robustness against various attacks with the help of DWT & multiple decomposition methods like QR, SVD & Schur. Embedding of watermark is done into the subbands of the host image with low and middle frequencies.

The rest of this paper is structured as follows. An overview of the proposed watermarking scheme is described in Sect. 2. The simulation results and comparisons are presented in Sect. 3. Conclusion of the paper is given in Sect. 4.

2   The Proposed Blind-Watermarking Method

Embedding and extraction of watermarking steps are discussed in this section. A probabilistic neural network (PNN) is utilized in the watermark extraction.

2.1   Process of Watermark Embedding

The embedding process representation is given in Fig. 1.

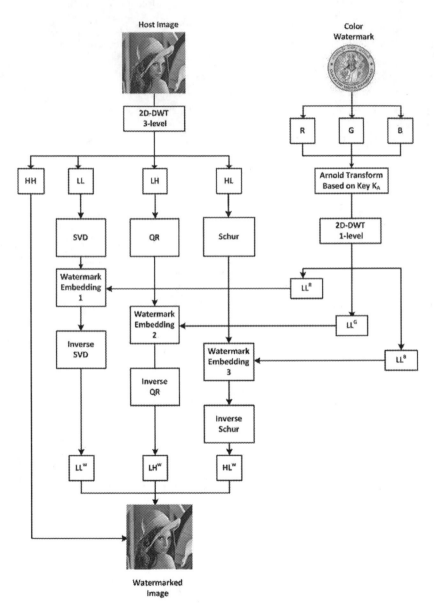

Fig. 1. Representation of watermark embedding process (Color figure online)

Watermark Pre-processing: In this scheme, color watermark is embedded into gray-scale image.

Step 1: watermark (W) is decomposed into Red-Green-Blue component watermarks (w_R, w_G, w_B).

Step 2: AT is utilized for encryption as shown in Eq. (1), in order to provide security to the watermark.

$$
\begin{aligned}
w_R^A &= AT(w_R) \\
w_G^A &= AT(w_G) \\
w_B^A &= AT(w_B)
\end{aligned}
\tag{1}
$$

Step 3: 2D-DWT for 1-level is adapted on w_R, w_G, w_B as shown in Eq. (2).

$$
\begin{aligned}
{[LLw_R, LHw_R, HLw_R, HHw_R]} &= DWT2(w_R^A) \\
{[LLw_G, LHw_G, HLw_G, HHw_G]} &= DWT2(w_G^A) \\
{[LLw_B, LHw_B, HLw_B, HHw_B]} &= DWT2(w_B^A)
\end{aligned}
\tag{2}
$$

Step 4: The host gray scale image is transformed by 2D-DWT for 3-levels.

Step 5: w_R^A (encrypted w) is embedded into transformed 3-level LL of host image. SVD is applied to LLw_R of Red component and LL3 of cover image with Eq. (3) by producing matrices of unitary and singular.

$$
\begin{aligned}
{[U, V]} &= SVD(LL3) \\
{[U_{w_R}, S_{w_R}, V_{w_R}]} &= SVD(LLw_R)
\end{aligned}
\tag{3}
$$

Step 6: Using Eq. (4), Principal components (PC) of LLw_R are generated. Equation (5), PC is embedded into S (singular matrix) of cover image with α (embedding factor).

$$
PC = U_{w_R} * S_{w_R}
\tag{4}
$$

$$
S' = S + \alpha * PC_R
\tag{5}
$$

Step 7: Watermarked LL sub-band is generate using Eq. (6) by applying inverse SVD.

$$
LL^w = U \times S' \times V^T
\tag{6}
$$

Step 8: Similarly, encrypted Green component watermark w_G^A is embedded into third-level LH sub-band of host image by applying QR decomposition to generate LH^w.

Step 9: In the same way, w_B^A is embedded into third-level HL sub-band of cover image by applying Schur to generate HL^w.

Step 10: Finally, Inverse DWT is applied to generate watermarked image H^w. Instead of LL, LH and HL, modified $LL^w, LH^w \& HL^w$ are used as shown in Eq. (7).

$$LL2^w = IDWT[LL^w, LH^w, HL^w, HH3]$$
$$LL1^w = IDWT[LL2^w, LH2, HL2, HH2] \qquad (7)$$
$$H^w = IDWT[LL1^w, LH1, HL1, HH1]$$

2.2   Neural Network Training

The base approach for classification of patterns in its learning model [13,14] is implemented by PNN, which is a supervised learning network. The learning category is selected by the PNN. Also, it estimates the probability of the sample with the help of radial basis function. PNN training is promt as it can operate in parallel & requires no feed-back for input from individual neurons. It is thus easier to learn when compared to other neural networks like back-propagation networks [15]. The PNN is made up of 4 layers of nodes which are the input, the pattern, the summation & the output layers. The distances from the input vector to the training input vectors is computed by the first layer when the input is presented. Then, it produces a vector with the elements that indicate the closeness of the input to a training input. These contributions for each class of inputs is summed-up by the summation layer to produce a net output which is a vector of probabilities. A competitive transfer function is applied finally on the previous layers output in order to select the maximum of these probabilities. It generates one for the class and zero for the other classes to obtain the watermarked binary image.

To conduct the training of PNN, a pattern node is generated, connecting it to the summation node of the target class and setting the input vector as the weight vector. The red, blue and green coefficients values are combined to from a 64×64 sized feature of the training vector. This feature is used as input to 64 PNN's for training and extraction.

2.3   Process of Blind-Watermark Extraction

The blind watermark process representation is illustrated in Fig. 2. The step by step process of extraction is as follows:

Step 1: Distorted gray-scale H^w is transformed by applying 2D-DWT for 3-levels to extract $LL', LH' \& HL'$ sub-bands.
Step 2: From the LL' sub-band, estimated PC_w is calculated using Eq. (8).

$$S'_w = LL' - LL$$
$$PC_w = \frac{U' * S'_w * V}{\alpha} \qquad (8)$$

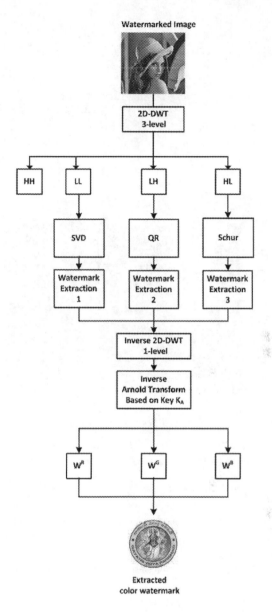

Fig. 2. Representation of watermark extraction process (Color figure online)

Step 3: With the help of V_{w1} and PC_w, LL of red component watermark is re-generated. w_R^A is produced by applying IDWT. Inverse AT is adapted by generating w_R' with Eq. (9).

$$LL'_{wR} = PC_w * V_{w1}$$
$$w_R^A = IDWT[LL_{wR}, LH_{wR}, HL_{wR}, HH_{wR}] \tag{9}$$
$$w'_R = InverseArnold(w_R^A)$$

Step 4: In the same way, reverse procedure of embedding is pursued to form watermarks w'_G & w'_B from LH and HL sub-bands by applying inverse QR, inverse Schur, IAT and IDWT.

Step 5: Finally, color watermark is generated by combining red, green and blue watermarks.

Air Plane	Boat	Bridge	Eliane	Lake
Lena	Living Room	Mandrill	Peppers	Pirate

Fig. 3. Cover images

3   Simulation Results and Comparisons

In the proposed scheme, images of size 512×512 as host images and "GVPCE (A), Copyright & Copyright symbol" color logo images of size 128×128 as watermark. Sample cover color images and watermark are demonstrated in Figs. 3 and 4. Proposed watermarking method performance is tested based on watermark invisibility, transparency & robustness. PSNR (Peak Signal to Noise Ratio) metric is utilized to measure objective closeness between cover image and WMI [16] (Fig. 5).

PSNR is determined by MSE (Mean Square Error) [17] is shown in Eq. (10) and PSNR (dB) in Eq. (11).

$$MSE = \frac{\sum_{i=0}^{m-1}\sum_{j=0}^{n-1}\left(H_{i,j} - H'_{i,j}\right)^2}{mn} \tag{10}$$

$$PSNR = 20\log_{10}\left(\frac{MAX_H}{\sqrt{MSE}}\right) \tag{11}$$

where, MAX_H is the maximum feasible pixel of image.

Table 2. PSNR & NCC values for sample images with GVPCE (A) logo

IP attacks Images	Without attack PSNR (dB)	NCC	S & P noise	Gaussian noise	Scaling	Rotation	Cropping	Mean filtering	Median filtering	Blurring	JPEG compression
Airplane	37.83	1.00	0.9898	0.9331	0.9998	0.7399	0.7968	0.9844	0.9975	0.9646	0.9999
Boat	41.50	1.00	0.9903	0.9340	0.9997	0.7793	0.7512	0.9827	0.9963	0.9883	0.9999
Bridge	38.80	1.00	0.9893	0.9330	0.9996	0.7336	0.7975	0.9807	0.9791	0.9688	0.9997
Eliane	37.33	1.00	0.9891	0.9312	0.9994	0.7400	0.7893	0.9813	0.9713	0.9686	0.9993
Lake	36.26	1.00	0.9891	0.9336	0.9997	0.7672	0.7815	0.9838	0.9869	0.9872	0.9998
Lena	34.88	1.00	0.9893	0.9347	0.9997	0.7732	0.7475	0.9868	0.9858	0.9532	0.9998
Living room	39.74	1.00	0.9879	0.9223	0.9996	0.7395	0.8160	0.9790	0.9817	0.9632	0.9996
Mandrill	39.24	1.00	0.9899	0.9312	0.9998	0.7388	0.8222	0.9822	0.9966	0.9824	0.9999
Peppers	37.83	1.00	0.9885	0.9259	0.9998	0.7444	0.7976	0.9848	0.9977	0.9671	0.9999
Pirate	40.14	1.00	0.9882	0.9320	0.9997	0.7656	0.7575	0.9833	0.9772	0.9643	0.9997

GVPCE(A)   Copyright   Copyright Symbol

Fig. 4. Color watermarks

Fig. 5. Sample watermarked images

The Normalized correlation coefficient (NCC) among $(\hat{W}(x,y))$ and $(W(x,y))$ are calculated using Eq. (12) [19].

$$\mathrm{NCC}_{W,\hat{W}} = \frac{\sum_{x=1}^{m}\sum_{y=1}^{n} W(x,y) \times \hat{W}(x,y)}{(\sqrt{\sum_{x=1}^{m} W(x,y)^2})(\sqrt{\sum_{x=1}^{m} \hat{W}(x,y)^2})}. \tag{12}$$

Various attacks like noise addition, scaling, rotation, cropping, mean filtering, median filtering, blurring and JPEG compression are applied to test the robustness. PSNR and NCC values for the sample images with and without attacks for GVPCE(A) watermark are shown in Table 2. Retrieved watermark's from distorted WMI can be seen in Fig. 6. Salt & Pepper noise is added with 0.01 density, Gaussian noise with zero mean and variance 1. Scaling the image twice and resizing back to original. Filtering attacks are applied with window size 3×3 and JPEG compression is applied with quality factor (95). Rotation attack is applied by rotating the image with 20^0 anti-clock wise direction and cropping the central portion of the image with 25% are applied. The embedding factor value α is set to 0.15.

Vaidya et al. [2] and Su et al. [18] methods are compared with the proposed method with various attacks are given in Table 3.

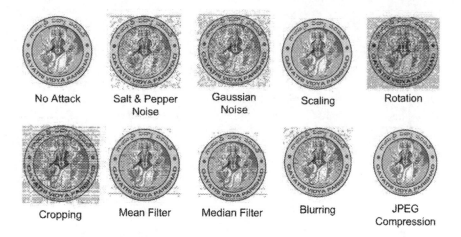

Fig. 6. Extracted GVPCE (A) watermarks from distorted watermarked images

Table 3. Correlation between proposed method and other methods with NCC values

Methods	Proposed scheme Vaidya et al. [2] Su et al. [18]		
Images/attacks	Lena	Mandrill	Peppers
WIthout attack	1.00	1.00	1.00
	1.00	1.00	1.00
	0.9966	0.9966	0.9966
Salt & Pepper noise	0.9893	0.9899	0.9885
	0.9645	0.9642	0.9665
	0.9873	0.9865	0.9875
Gaussian noise	0.9347	0.9312	0.9259
	0.8489	0.8405	0.8615
	0.8931	0.8956	0.8926
Scaling	0.9997	0.9998	0.9998
	0.9981	0.9985	0.9986
	0.9949	0.9950	0.9951
Rotation	0.7672	0.7388	0.7444
	0.4919	0.6474	0.6222
	0.7472	0.7276	0.7256
Median filtering	0.9858	0.9966	0.9977
	0.8512	0.8565	0.8543
	0.9187	0.9266	0.9311
JPEG compression	0.9998	0.9999	0.9999
	0.8121	0.8153	0.8021
	0.9355	0.9356	0.9362

4 Conclusion

In this paper, a multi-decomposition color image watermarking scheme is designed to protect IPR and calim the ownership using DWT, SVD, QR and Schur decomposition. Arnold transformation is used to provide security to the watermark logo before embedding. Stimulation results prove that the scheme is robust against attacks like noise and rotation. In comparison with related methods, better robustness results are observed.

References

1. Cox, I.J., Miller, M.L., Bloom, J.A., Honsinger, C.: Digital Watermarking, vol. 1558607145. Springer, Berlin (2002)
2. Vaidya, S.P., Mouli, P.C.: Adaptive digital watermarking for copyright protection of digital images in wavelet domain. Procedia Comput. Sci. **58**, 233–240 (2015)
3. Vaidya, S.P., Mouli, P.V.S.S.R.C., Santosh, K.C.: Imperceptible watermark for a game-theoretic watermarking system. Int. J. Mach. Learn. Cybern. (2018)
4. Cox, I.J., Kilian, J., Leighton, F.T., Shamoon, T.: Secure spread spectrum watermarking for multimedia. IEEE Trans. Image Process. **6**(12), 1673–1687 (1997)
5. Ponnisathya, S., Ramakrishnan, S., Dhinakaran, S., Ashwanth, P.S., Dhamodharan, P.: CHAOTIC map based video watermarking using DWT and SVD. In: 2017 International Conference on Inventive Communication and Computational Technologies (ICICCT), pp. 45–49. IEEE (2017)
6. Vaidya, P., Chandra Mouli, P.V.S.S.R.: Adaptive, robust and blind digital watermarking using Bhattacharyya distance and bit manipulation. Multimedia Tools Appl. 1–27 (2017)
7. Vaidya, P., Chandra Mouli, P.V.S.S.R.: A robust semi-blind watermarking for color images based on multiple decompositions. Multimedia Tools Appl. **76**(24), 25623–25656 (2017)
8. Nguyen, T.S., Chang, C.C., Yang, X.Q.: A reversible image authentication scheme based on fragile watermarking in discrete wavelet transform domain. AEU-Int. J. Electron. Commun. **70**(8), 1055–1061 (2016)
9. Murali, P., Sankaradass, V.: An efficient ROI based copyright protection scheme for digital images with SVD and orthogonal polynomials transformation. Optik **170**, 242–264 (2018)
10. Ernawan, F., Kabir, M.N.: A block-based RDWT-SVD image watermarking method using human visual system characteristics. Vis. Comput. 1–19 (2018)
11. Vairaprakash, S., Shenbagavalli, A.: A discrete Rajan transform-based robustness improvement encrypted watermark scheme backed by support vector machine. Comput. Electr. Eng. (2017)
12. Roy, S., Pal, A.K.: A blind DCT based color watermarking algorithm for embedding multiple watermarks. AEU-Int. J. Electron. Commun. **72**, 149–161 (2017)
13. Mishra, S., Bhende, C., Panigrahi, B.: Detection and classification of power quality disturbances using s-transform and probabilistic neural network. IEEE Trans. Power Deliv. **23**(1), 280–287 (2008)
14. Yu, S.N., Chen, Y.H.: Electrocardiogram beat classification based on wavelet transformation and probabilistic neural network. Pattern Recogn. Lett. **28**(10), 1142–1150 (2007)

15. Zhang, Y.: Blind watermark algorithm based on HVS and RBF neural network in DWT domain. Wseas Trans. Comput. **8**(1), 174–183 (2009)
16. Wang, Z., Bovik, A.C., Sheikh, H.R., Simoncelli, E.P.: Image quality assessment: from error visibility to structural similarity. IEEE Trans. Image Process. **13**(4), 600–612 (2004)
17. Huynh-Thu, Q., Ghanbari, M.: Scope of validity of PSNR in image/video quality assessment. Electron. Lett. **44**(13), 800–801 (2008)
18. Su, Q., Wang, G., Zhang, X., Lv, G., Chen, B.: A new algorithm of blind color image watermarking based on LU decomposition. Multidimension. Syst. Signal Process. **29**(3), 1055–1074 (2018)
19. Billings, S.A.: Nonlinear System Identification: NARMAX Methods in the Time, Frequency, and Spatio-Temporal Domains. Wiley, Hoboken (2013)

Skeleton Joint Difference Maps for 3D Action Recognition with Convolutional Neural Networks

M. Naveenkumar[✉] and S. Domnic

Department of Computer Applications,
National Institute of Technology, Trichy, India
mnaveenmtech@gmail.com, domnic@nitt.edu

Abstract. Action recognition is a leading research topic in the field of computer vision. This paper proposes an effective method for action recognition task based on the skeleton data. Four features are proposed based on the joint differences from 3D skeleton data. From the differences of 3D coordinates of corresponding joints in successive frames, three maps are extracted related to x, y and z coordinates respectively and then these maps are encoded into 2D color images, named as Joint Difference Maps (JDMs). The fourth JDM is formed by mapping the individual x, y and z difference maps into red, green and blue values. Hence, the 3D action recognition problem is converted into 2D image classification problem. It enables us to fine tune CNNs to learn informative features for 3D action recognition problem. The proposed method achieved 79.30% recognition rate on UTD MHAD dataset.

Keywords: 3D action recognition · Skeleton maps ·
Convolutional Neural Networks · Joint Difference Maps (JDMs)

1 Introduction

Action recognition is a leading research topic in the field of computer vision because it has many real time applications such as video surveillance and robotics etc. In earlier days, experiments have been conducted for action recognition using conventional RGB videos. When range sensors are available in the market, researchers have focused on the usage of RGB-D data for human action recognition in the past decade. RGB-D sensors like kinect can give two modalities: RGB and depth maps. In paper [1], Shatton et al. introduced a methodology to estimate skeleton maps from the depth data in real time. It makes the researchers to use skeleton data for action recognition and it has received much attention in the last seven years.

Deep networks are increasingly showing their superior performance in many tasks such as object detection and speech recognition etc. It is observed in the literature that deep architectures have achieved much accuracies in the past decade. In this paper, we devise a deep learning methodology for 3D action

© Springer Nature Singapore Pte Ltd. 2019
K. C. Santosh and R. S. Hegadi (Eds.): RTIP2R 2018, CCIS 1035, pp. 144–150, 2019.
https://doi.org/10.1007/978-981-13-9181-1_13

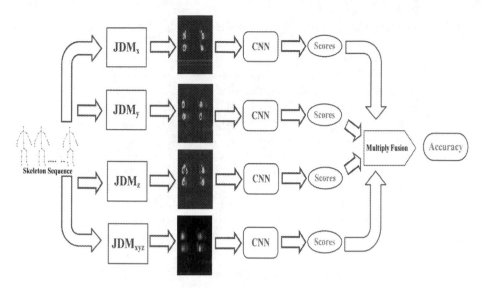

Fig. 1. Block diagram of the proposed method (Color figure online)

recognition using Convolutional Neural Networks. We employ four feature maps, referred to as Joint Difference Maps (JDMs), based on the differences between the skeleton joints. The rest of the paper is organized as follows. Section 2 discuss about related works in literature. The proposed method is presented in Sect. 3 and evaluation results are described in Sect. 4. Finally, the paper is concluded with future aspects in Sect. 5.

2   Related Work

There are two data modalities: depth maps and skeleton data. This section provides summary of various action recognition methods based on these two data modalities.

2.1   Depth Data Based Methods

In [2], each depth map is projected on to XY, YZ and XZ Cartesian planes. A bag of 3D points are generated from these projected depth maps by sampling scheme and an action graph is devised to capture the dynamics of human body motions. The action recognition system is built using action graph. Wang et al. [3] treats the depth sequence as 4D volume and the random occupancy pattern (ROP) features are constructed from depth sequence for action recognition. ROP features are robust to occlusions and noise in depth sequences. In addition, weighted sampling scheme is employed to reduce the computational time for the feature extraction as well as the training time of SVM classifier. Vieira et al. [4] devised a new methodology to encode a 3D action using Space-Time Occupancy

Patterns (STOP). In their work, time and space axes are partitioned into several segments to generate a 4D grid and the cosine distance based classifier is used for action classification.

In work [5], all 3D projections (side, top and front) are calculated for each depth frame. Then, the sum of the difference of consecutive frames is calculated for each projection view. As a result, the global descriptor called Depth Motion Map (DMM) is evolved. Histogram of Gradient (HoG) features extracted from DMM are used for 3D action recognition. Chen et al. [6] has used DMM as feature descriptor (without extracting HoG features) for real time human action recognition. In paper [7], HoG features are extracted from contourlet sub bands of DMM for the robust action recognition. Paper [8] described a methodology to estimate the skeleton maps from the depth data. It motivates the research community to work with skeleton data for action recognition. In general, the computational complexity of depth features are more than the skeleton features.

2.2   Skeleton Data Based Methods

Yang and Tian [9] proposed three features referred as posture feature, motion feature and off set feature based on pairwise joint differences rather distances. After extraction of all these features, PCA is employed on them. As a result, Eigen joints are evolved to train Naive-Bayes-Nearest-Neighbor classifier for action recognition task. Kerola et al. [10] introduced a graph based methodology for action recognition. An action sequence is encoded as spatio-temporal graph and the weights of edges in a graph are calculated based on the pair wise distances. In paper [11], the authors proposed vector quantization mechanism to convert the variable length sequence to the fixed length sequence. Pairwise distance features constructed from the vector quantized sequences is given to voting classifier for action classification task. In this work, we presents a deep learning approach for 3D action recognition based on the joint differences of the skeleton data.

3   Proposed Method

The proposed method is illustrated in Fig. 1. It has mainly three phases: (i) Feature Extraction; (ii) JDMs to color images; (iii) Action Classification.

3.1   Feature Extraction

This paper presents four features, based on the differences between skeleton joints, to capture the informative dynamics for action recognition task as depicted in Fig. 1. Let an action sequence S contains f number of frames and each frame is having n number of joints. $S = \{F_1, F_2, ..., F_f\}$, where $F_i = \{J_1^i, J_2^i, ..., J_n^i\}$ and J_n^i represents the (x, y, z) coordinates of nth joint in i^{th} frame. First three features are calculated from the individual values of x, y and z coordinate values as stated in Eqs. (1), (2) and (3). For an action sequence S, when the difference values calculated between two consecutive frames are keep in a column, three matrices are generated, each of size $(n \times f)$, named as JDM_x, JDM_y and JDM_z respectively. The fourth JDM (JDM_{xyz}) feature is formed by combining three JDMs as given in Eq. (4), and its size is $(n \times f \times 3)$.

$$JDM_x = \{(x_p^{q+1} - x_p^q)|(x,y,z) \in J_p^q; p = 1,2.., n; q = 1,2.., f\} \qquad (1)$$

$$JDM_y = \{(y_p^{q+1} - y_p^q)|(x,y,z) \in J_p^q; p = 1,2.., n; q = 1,2.., f\} \qquad (2)$$

$$JDM_z = \{(z_p^{q+1} - z_p^q)|(x,y,z) \in J_p^q; p = 1,2.., n; q = 1,2.., f\} \qquad (3)$$

$$JDM_{xyz} = [JDM_x, JDM_y, JDM_z] \qquad (4)$$

3.2   JDMs to Color Images

The four features extracted in feature extraction phase are encoded into color texture images to train the CNN. This paper uses two encoding mechanism to encode proposed JDMs to color images. They are Jet colorbar [12] and xyz to RGB mapping [13]. The 2D features JDM_x, JDM_y and JDM_z are normalized as shown in Eq. (5) to deal with variable heights of subjects. After normalization, the values in 2D JDMs are in range [0–255] and hence they look like gray images. These gray images are encoded into color images using Jet colorbar [12] whereas the fourth feature (JDM_{xyz}) uses xyz to RGB mapping.

$$NormalizedM = \frac{M}{max(M)} * 255 \qquad (5)$$

Where M is the 2D matrix to be normalized and $max(M)$ is the maximum value in matrix M.

3.3   Action Classification

For many tasks in Computer Vision, deep learning approaches have achieved promising results than classical machine learning approaches in the past decade. This paper uses popular CNN architecture "AlexNet" [14] for action classification task. The input of "AlexNet" is $227 \times 227 \times 3$. Hence, the color images of proposed JDMs are resized using bicubic interpolation and four CNNs are trained for four JDMs using the solver "Stochastic Gradient Decent with Momentum" with momentum value 0.9. The maximum number of epochs is chosen 50 for all the experiments in this work. Let $s1, s2, s3$ and $s4$ are resultant score vectors of four CNNs. They are fused as stated in Eq. (6) to find the class label for the unknown test action sequence A.

$$Label\ of\ test\ instance\ A = Index(max(s1 \circ s2 \circ s3 \circ s4)) \qquad (6)$$

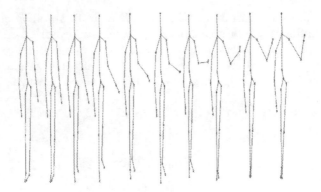

Fig. 2. Sequence of skeleton maps of wave action in UTD MHAD dataset

Table 1. Results of four features (JDMs) and their multiplication fusion on UTD MHAD

SNo	Feature	UTD MHAD dataset
1	JDM_x	52.09
2	JDM_y	66.98
3	JDM_z	63.72
4	JDM_{xyz}	69.77
5	Multiplication fusion	79.30

where $s1, s2, s3$ and $s4$ are scores of four CNNs and $\circ$ represents the element wise multiplication of scores vectors. The $max(.)$ function returns the maximum value and $Index(.)$ function returns the index (class label) of that maximum value.

Table 2. Recognition accuracy results on UTD MHAD dataset

	Accuracy(%)
EIC-KSVD [15]	76.19
Kinect and inertial, 2015 [16]	79.10
Our method	**79.30**

4   Experimental Results

4.1   UTD MHAD Dataset

UTD MHAD dataset [16] is captured using one Kinect camera and one wearable inertial sensor. The skeleton is represented using 20 joints. There are 27 actions, performed by eight persons with each one acting four times. As a result, 861 data sequences are generated in the dataset. For fair comparison, the experimental test protocol proposed in paper [16] is used to evaluate the proposed method. According to this test protocol, the odd subjects are used for training and even subjects are for testing. Hence, the data sequences in train-set and test-set are 431 and 430 respectively. The sequence of skeleton maps of wave action in this dataset is depicted in Fig. 2. The recognition accuracies of four features (JDMs) and their multiplication fusion are reported in Table 1. The proposed method is compared with other methods in the Table 2.

5   Conclusion

In this work, we devised a deep learning methodology for action recognition using skeleton data. Four features are proposed based on the differences of skeleton joints, named as Joint Difference Maps (JDMs). These JDMs are encoded into color texture images. CNNs are fine-tuned to learn informative features from color images. The experiments have been conducted on UTD MHAD dataset and the proposed method achieved 79.30% recognition rate on this dataset. In future, we would like to extend our work to incorporate an augmentation mechanism to get benefit of our proposed method.

References

1. Shotton, J., et al.: Real-time human pose recognition in parts from single depth images. In: 2011 IEEE Conference on Computer Vision and Pattern Recognition (CVPR), pp. 1297–1304. IEEE (2011).https://doi.org/10.1109/CVPR.2011.5995316
2. Li, W., Zhang, Z., Liu, Z.: Action recognition based on a bag of 3d points. In: 2010 IEEE Computer Society Conference on Computer Vision and Pattern Recognition Workshops (CVPRW), pp. 9–14. IEEE (2010).https://doi.org/10.1109/CVPRW.2010.5543273
3. Wang, J., Liu, Z., Chorowski, J., Chen, Z., Wu, Y.: Robust 3D action recognition with random occupancy patterns. In: Fitzgibbon, A., Lazebnik, S., Perona, P., Sato, Y., Schmid, C. (eds.) ECCV 2012. LNCS, pp. 872–885. Springer, Heidelberg (2012). https://doi.org/10.1007/978-3-642-33709-3_62
4. Vieira, A.W., Nascimento, E.R., Oliveira, G.L., Liu, Z., Campos, M.F.M.: STOP: space-time occupancy patterns for 3D action recognition from depth map sequences. In: Alvarez, L., Mejail, M., Gomez, L., Jacobo, J. (eds.) CIARP 2012. LNCS, vol. 7441, pp. 252–259. Springer, Heidelberg (2012). https://doi.org/10.1007/978-3-642-33275-3_31
5. Yang, X., Zhang, C., Tian, Y.: Recognizing actions using depth motion maps-based histograms of oriented gradients. In: Proceedings of the 20th ACM international conference on Multimedia, pp. 1057–1060. ACM (2012).https://doi.org/10.1145/2393347.2396382
6. Chen, C., Liu, K., Kehtarnavaz, N.: Real-time human action recognition based on depth motion maps. J. Real-Time Image Process. **12**, 155–163 (2016). https://doi.org/10.1007/s11554-013-0370-1

7. Bulbul, M.F., Jiang, Y., Ma, J.: Human action recognition based on DMMs, HOGs and Contourlet transform. In: 2015 IEEE International Conference on Multimedia Big Data (BigMM), pp. 389–394. IEEE (2015).https://doi.org/10.1109/BigMM.2015.82

8. Shotton, J., et al.: Real-time human pose recognition in parts from single depth images. Commun. ACM **56**, 116–124 (2013). https://doi.org/10.1145/2398356.2398381

9. Yang, X., Tian, Y.: Eigenjoints-based action recognition using naive-bayes-nearest-neighbor. In: 2012 IEEE Computer Society Conference on Computer Vision and Pattern Recognition Workshops (CVPRW), pp. 14–19. IEEE (2012).https://doi.org/10.1109/CVPRW.2012.6239232

10. Kerola, T., Inoue, N., Shinoda, K.: Spectral graph skeletons for 3D action recognition. In: Cremers, D., Reid, I., Saito, H., Yang, M.-H. (eds.) ACCV 2014. LNCS, vol. 9006, pp. 417–432. Springer, Cham (2015). https://doi.org/10.1007/978-3-319-16817-3_27

11. Naveenkumar, M., Domnic, S.: Vector quantization based pairwise joint distance maps (VQ-PJDM) for 3D action recognition. Procedia Comput. Sci. **133**, 27–36 (2018). https://doi.org/10.1016/j.procs.2018.07.005

12. Li, C., Hou, Y., Wang, P., Li, W.: Joint distance maps based action recognition with convolutional neural networks. IEEE Signal Process. Lett. **24**, 624–628 (2017). https://doi.org/10.1109/LSP.2017.2678539

13. Du, Y., Fu, Y., Wang, L.: Skeleton based action recognition with convolutional neural network. In: 2015 3rd IAPR Asian Conference on Pattern Recognition (ACPR), pp. 579–583. IEEE (2015).https://doi.org/10.1109/ACPR.2015.7486569

14. Krizhevsky, A., Sutskever, I., Hinton, G.E.: Imagenet classification with deep convolutional neural networks. In: Advances in Neural Information Processing Systems, pp. 1097–1105 (2012)

15. Zhou, L., Li, W., Zhang, Y., Ogunbona, P., Nguyen, D.T., Zhang, H.: Discriminative key pose extraction using extended LC-KSVD for action recognition. In: 2014 International Conference on Digital Image Computing: Techniques and Applications (DICTA), pp. 1–8. IEEE (2014). https://doi.org/10.1109/DICTA.2014.7008101

16. Chen, C., Jafari, R., Kehtarnavaz, N.: UTD-MHAD: a multimodal dataset for human action recognition utilizing a depth camera and a wearable inertial sensor. In: 2015 IEEE International Conference on Image Processing (ICIP), pp. 168–172. IEEE (2015). https://doi.org/10.1109/ICIP.2015.7350781

Novel Quality Metric for Image Super Resolution Algorithms - Super Resolution Entropy Metric (SREM)

M. S. Greeshma$^{(\boxtimes)}$ (iD) and V. R. Bindu$^{(\boxtimes)}$ (iD)

School of Computer Sciences, Mahatma Gandhi University, Kottayam, Kerala, India
greeshmams.r@gmail.com, binduvr@mgu.ac.in

Abstract. Even with the topical developments of numerous image Super Resolution (SR) algorithms, how to quantify the visual quality scores of a super resolved image is still an open research problem. Majority of SR images are evaluated by full-reference metric with the support of a reference image. There are some circumstances when a reference image is unavailable or is with degraded quality. We propose a super resolution benchmark Super Resolution Entropy Metric (SREM) which can be used to evaluate the effectiveness of pixel reconstruction and quality of the image in the absence of reference image automatically. SREM measures the experimental quality of an SR image based on the perceptions of acutance and spatial discontinuity features in the gradient domain and wavelet domain. Experimental scores illustrate that the SREM metric is competent for assessing the visual quality of super-resolved images.

Keywords: Super resolution · Image quality metric · No-reference metric · Spatial discontinuity · Acutance

1 Introduction

Image Super-Resolution (SR) mechanism is a cost-effective and feature preserving image resolution augmentation approach. It is a stimulating research area of image science to accomplish enhanced spatial resolution and quality of images. As SR technology has been advanced for more than three decades, both multi-frame and single-frame SR have key applications in our day-to-day life. SR applications comprises Generic Image Enhancement, Medical Imaging, Infrared and Ultrasonic Imaging, Satellite and Aerial Imaging, Face Hallucination, Text Image Restoration, Transforming NTSC video content to HD television, Criminal Investigation etc. A wide range of super-resolution algorithms have been introduced focused on edges [1], gradient directions [2,3], neighboring interpolation [4,5], learning-based [6], image patches [7–9] and CNN based [10]. Most of the afore-mentioned SR approaches emphasize on generating high quality HR image with

Supported by DST PURSE Phase (II), Govt. of India.

sharper edges and effective image details preservation. These key structures are generally assessed by similar features between super-resolved image and reference images via Mean Squared Error (MSE), Peak Signal-to-Noise Ratio (PSNR), Structural Similarity (SSIM) Index [11] and Feature Similarity Index (FSIM) [12] where reference image is available. In this paper, we explore a novel concept in visual quality assessment of super resolved image generated by Single Image Super Resolution (SISR) via referenceless/automatic manner.

2   Related Works and Problem Context

While performing super resolution, how much image details are preserved and what are the high quality features of SR image will determine the quality of super resolved image. The efficacy of the super resolution algorithms and the quality of the super resolved image obtained are positively correlated as illustrated by Fig. 1 and Table 1. The visual quality value of the SR images shown in Fig. 1 are compared in Table 1. According to whether the reference HR images are referred, the present metrics are (i) Full-reference (FR) metrics (ii) Semi-reference metrics and (iii) No-reference metrics. FR quality metric is simply measured as comparison between features of original image and processed image according to a reference image. FR metrics used for super resolved image quality assessment such as PSNR, SSIM [11] and FSIM [12] are experimentally proved to be constrained in effectively measuring SR performance in terms of resolution factors. In semi-reference metric, the quality of SR image is assessed based on an assessment of appropriate features extracted from SR image and reference image [13]. No-reference metric is simply defined as evaluating performance of resultant image by itself without referring to reference images. Super resolved images can be assessed by the no-reference algorithms [14–17] according to statistical features, in which quality is degraded due to distortions and this degradation can be evaluated for visual quality assessment. In the proposed approach, we evaluate the effectiveness of pixel reconstruction and quality is monitored in a dynamic manner. This category of quality assessment is known as the no-reference Image Quality Assessment (IQA). Mathematically, the metric value is calculated by features of the test image and is a challenging task. BRISQUE [16] BLIINDS [17], and DIVINE [18] are classes of no-reference metrics; these algorithms only

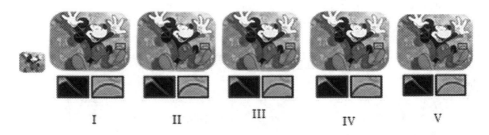

I   II   III   IV   V

Fig. 1. SR images generated from the LR image using different algorithms

Table 1. Qualitative scores of different algorithms and the correlation between SR algorithms and quality metrics.

Algorithm/metric	Bicubic (I)	BP (II)	Glanser (III)	Yang (IV)	SRCNN (V)
PSNR	24.67	26.23	29.54	30.49	32.67
SSIM	0.782	0.797	0.835	0.852	0.881
FSIM	0.883	0.901	0.926	0.922	0.956

quantify the 'naturalness' of an image. The distortion specific structures like ringing blur or blocking are not considered by these algorithms. The major problem of the SR quality assessment is the unavailability of a high-quality HR image. There are many circumstances where reference image is unavailable, such as satellite imaging, medical imaging, and criminal investigation and so on. In order to handle the aforementioned problem, we propose a novel benchmark, Super Resolution Entropy Metric (SREM) which can be used to estimate the visual quality value of super-resolved images without referring to reference images. The SR algorithms generate new intensity values/pixels and the loss of pixels or absence of intensity values causes distortions like spatial discontinuity, shagginess, blocking etc. These kinds of distortion affect the quality of an image and visual perception. However, it is important to weigh the quality of the super resolved image before using it for various applications. The SR image is evaluated in the gradient level and wavelet level which is strategic to the quality evaluation without referring to a ground truth image. The SREM metric can be used to maximize the level of quality of a super resolved image in both gradient domain and wavelet domain established on the aforementioned features. The proposed SREM metric gives quality estimation competitive to the existing image quality assessment metrics. The quality of an SR image generally characterizes the features that meet details preservation in human perception. The new paradigm of the proposed method is deliberated in Sect. 3. Section 4 discusses the experimental evaluations and analysis and the concluding remarks are given in Sect. 5.

3   Proposed Metric: Super Resolution Entropy Metric (SREM)

The dilemma of performance of the super-resolved image can be demonstrated as measuring the quality score of the SR image. The proposed SREM metric evaluates the quality of an SR image using the concepts of acutance and spatial discontinuity in the gradient domain and wavelet domain. Figure 2 illustrates the framework of the proposed SREM perceptual image quality metric. Initially, the gradient of an SR image is generated and the gradient model is constructed using efficient gradient operator. Then the key feature of the SREM metric, Fuzzy Gradient Points (FGP), is established to evaluate spatial discontinuity index. Meanwhile, acutance index of the SR image is calculated in gradient level and

Wavelet decomposition. Finally, spatial discontinuity and acutance indices which are inversely proportional are pooled to predict perceived SR image quality.

3.1   Spatial Discontinuity Index

The demanding task in image super resolution is to maintain visual quality of an image with varying enhancement factors. The quality of an SR image generally characterizes the features that meet details preservation in human perception. Numerous spatial property-based algorithms using gradient and directional changes that exploit rotation and scale invariant descriptors [19] have been proposed for vision systems and Content Based Image Retrieval systems [20]. The edge features are vital in measuring the image quality assessment. The edge is the pixel pattern at which the sharp intensity is abruptly changed and edge line is extracted from an image using gradient techniques. In state-of-the-art methods, different gradient operators are used for analyzing edge data; however it is difficult to quantify missing and discontinued edges of an image in gradient level. In proposed method, SR image is scanned in the gradient domain which on gradient-level filtering generates the information contained in the different classes of gradient points. The spatial discontinuity index IMQ_{spd} quantifies the amount of discontinued and missing edge points. The gradient points along the edges are exploited to measure the spatial discontinuity. The key part of proposed approach is a Fuzzy Gradient Point (FGP) model. Fuzzy gradient points $\mu\Delta G(x_i)$ detect different classes of pixel intensity variations and quantify spatial

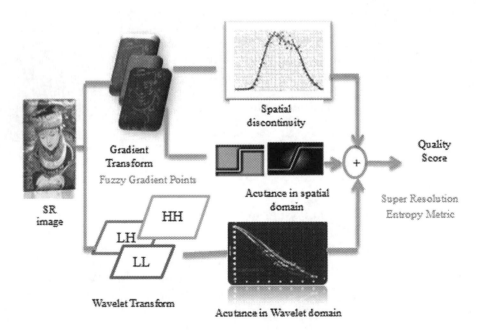

Fig. 2. Illustration of Super Resolution Entropy Metric

discontinuities. The gradient point is determined by finding image features such as edges, corners and regions. The gradient magnitude and direction are easily determined; however quantifying losing edge points is a difficult task and spatial discontinuities make it even more difficult. There exist many methods to determine gradient points using different gradient operators but involves more computational complexity, vagueness and ambiguity. Many of the algorithms more or less have the weakness of removing thin lines, distorting edges, and blurring fine details and texture in the image during edge detection. Soft-computing techniques such as fuzzy logic offer us competent tools to process human knowledge characterized as fuzzy. The influence of fuzzy systems is that they can deal with the vagueness and ambiguity efficiently, making it suitable for handling image quality assessment and image analysis [21]. Figures 3 and 5 outline the distribution of gradient points using the Fuzzy Gradient Points model (FGP) and Fig. 4 illustrates the pixel window. Normal gradient points $\Delta G(x_i)$ is generated using [22]

$$\Delta G(x_i) = \lim_{\Delta x_i \to 0} G(x, y) \tag{1}$$

$$\Delta G = ma(\Delta G) = [(\frac{\partial G}{\partial X})^2 + (\frac{\partial G}{\partial Y})^2]^1/2 \tag{2}$$

Then gradient point $\mu\Delta G(x_i)$model is established in fuzzy domain. The gradient point is determined as follows with different classes of intensity values. The directional correlation among intensity values affects gradient direction. A 3×3 localized pixel window is used to compute directional correlation. The intensity change in the edge direction is represented by $\Theta = \{45^0, 90^0, 180^0, 270^0\}$ in spatial domain.

3.1.1 Estimation of Fuzzy Gradient Value

The process of fuzzifying the gradient points is illustrated as follows; for every pixel p_i of the I_{SR} image, a 3×3 pixel window is generated. The intensity difference (Id_i) between the central pixel (c_p) and all of its eight neighbors is computed one by one. The intensity difference is calculated as follows:

$$Id_i = g_i - c_p \tag{3}$$

Where g_i is the gradient value of the pixel p_i. The membership value $\mu\Delta G$ of the eight differences (I_{di}) at a point p_i is estimated by the following equation:

$$\Delta\mu G(p_i) = \begin{cases} +[\frac{I_{di}-df_max}{df_max-df_min}], I_di \geq 0 \\ -[\frac{I_{di}-df_min}{df_max-df_min}], I_di \leq 0 \end{cases} \tag{4}$$

Where i fits to $\{1, 8\}$ signifying the eight neighbors. The df_min is min (I_{di}) and $df_max$is max (I_{di}). In positive and negative differences $[I_{di} \geq 0$ and $I_{di} \leq 0$] take $\pm$ respectively. Fuzzy gradient point decreases the gradient inconsistency problem by checking the edge orientation at the neighboring pixels. The eight difference gradient points are reflected as a fuzzy matrix of the central pixel, so

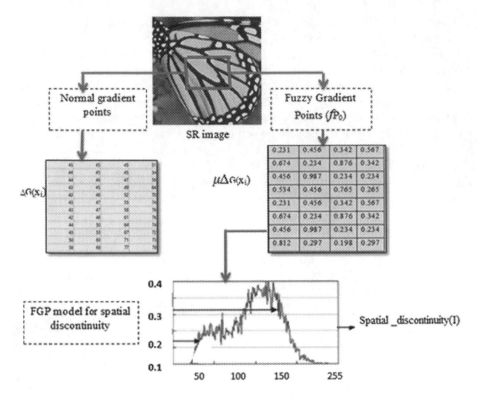

Fig. 3. Fuzzy Gradient Points (FGP) model

each and every image pixel is a fuzzy matrix of eight elements. The membership value of each element in the equivalent fuzzy matrix must express the relation between the intensity differences as in Eq. 4. Figure 5 illustrates the step-by-step fuzzy matrix construction.

3.1.2   Estimation of Spatial Discontinuity Index

Subsequently, the fuzzified gradient points are input to the spatial discontinuity estimation. In fuzzified gradient points, apply filtering on input I_{SR} image by the 3×3 Sobel operators along horizontal and vertical directions. The edge points along the horizontal and vertical direction is generated in terms of ($Isr1_{HOR}$, $ISr1_{VER}$) and ($Isr2_{HOR}$, $ISr2_{VER}$) at point (x, y) and calculates the horizontal and vertical variations are calculated at point $1 : x - 1$ and $2 : y$ of by,

$$D_{HOR} = (1 : x - 1, 2 : y)^{|} ISR1_{HOR} - ISR2_{HOR}| \tag{5}$$

$$D_{VER} = (1 : x - 1, 2 : y)^{|} ISR1_{VER} - ISR2_{VER}| \tag{6}$$

The weighted sum of the gradient points along the (WD_{HOR}, WD_{VER}) horizontal and vertical directions are computed as in Eqs. 7 and 8. The process

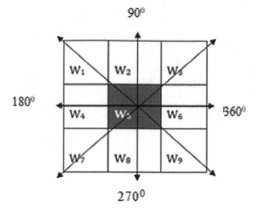

Fig. 4. 3 × 3 Pixel Window

of spatial discontinuity estimation along the horizontal and vertical directions (SP_{HOR}, SP_{VER}) respectively is done as per Eqs. 9 and 10.

$$WD_{HOR} = \sum_{2}^{x-1}(\sum_{2}^{y-1}(D_{HOR})) \tag{7}$$

$$WD_{VER} = \sum_{2}^{x-1}(\sum_{2}^{y-1}(D_{VER})) \tag{8}$$

$$SP_{HOR} = \frac{(WD_{HOR1} - WD_{HOR2})}{WD_{HOR1}} \tag{9}$$

$$SP_{VER} = \frac{(WD_{VER1} - WD_{VER2})}{WD_{VER1}} \tag{10}$$

Now, the spatial discontinuity index can be achieved via maximum rate of fuzzy gradient point changes in the horizontal and vertical directions.

$$IMQ_{spd} = argmax(SP_{HOR}, SP_{VER}) \tag{11}$$

Where IMQ_{spd} quantifies the spatial discontinuity index. The gradient points of an image are vital to provide high reliability reconstruction processes of images. The test reference SR image is not available, only the gradient points of an SR image are available. The higher the alterations, higher the deviations in the position of the gradient points in the edge map. Hence, these types of spatial discontinuities are quantified using Fuzzy Gradient Points (FGPs). The information is retained in the fuzzy gradient points that are not displaced due to distortions. As spatial discontinuity index increases the quality of SR image decreases as shown in Table 2. Table 2, tabulates spatial discontinuity index (IMQ_{spd}) of parrot SR image generated from different SR algorithms bicubic, Yang, SRCNN and fuzzy deep learning [23]. The fuzzy deep learning algorithm produces high

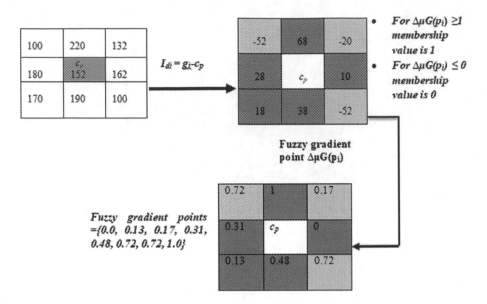

Fig. 5. Fuzzy Gradient Point depiction. A step-by-step model of the fuzzy gradient estimation on a 3×3 neighborhood window. The eight variances I_{di} of neighbors with respect to the center pixel C_p are displayed in the second matrix.

quality image as spatial discontinuity index is relatively low in comparison to other SR algorithms. The spatial discontinuity is one of the key determinants in the perception of image quality. Generally, spatial discontinuity causes stretch of edges and blot of edges, which leads to shape changes in images and quality of image is also degraded.

Table 2. Performance comparison of spatial discontinuity index IMQ_{spd} and the metric based on the butterfly SR image with different algorithms.

Algorithm (s)	Bicubic	Yang	SRCNN	Fuzzy deep learning
Spatial discontinuity index (IMQ_{spd}) of parrot SR image	0.662	0.530	0.527	0.483

3.2   Acutance Index

In the perception of SR image quality, acutance is always a key factor. The acutance index measures the amount of fine quality details of an image and the spatial discontinuity influences sharp edge points in the image altering its data structure. The SR image is evaluated in the gradient domain which on subbands decomposition constructs the information enclosed in the different blocks which are employed to illustrate the acutance of the edges in the SR image. The acutance of an SR image is essential components of the image computed by length and width in the gradient blocks. The perceived acutance is estimated from the average edge width and directional variations from each gradient chunk of the image. The acutance index in spatial domain and Wavelet domain is calculated and overall acutance index is measured by variations in both domains.

3.2.1   Calculation of Acutance in Spatial Domain

The acutance index of gradient points can be directly measured. Figure 8 illustrates the gradient points along vertical and horizontal direction at $\{90^0, 270^0\}$. The gradient decomposition of the image gives the chunks along horizontal and vertical blocks used for average width measurements: $\{GH_{BLK}, GV_{BLK}\}$. The length of the horizontal and vertical edge and directional variation of each block are calculated as;

$$Edge_{val} = \sum(sobel(I_{SR}(i))) \tag{12}$$

$$[GH_{BLK}, GV_{BLK}] = length(Edge_{val}) \tag{13}$$

In Eq. 12, Sobel operator is used to extract edge points of SR image and followed by calculation of length of edges horizontally and vertically. Then the edge width of SR image is computed as gradient points upwards and downwards at directions $\{90^0, 270^0\}$ in Fig. 6.

$$GH_{\overrightarrow{BLK}} = \frac{WD_{UP} + WD_{DN}}{cos(90)} \tag{14}$$

$$GV_{\overrightarrow{BLK}} = \frac{WD_{UP} + WD_{DN}}{cos(270)} \tag{15}$$

where $GH_{\overrightarrow{BLK}}$ and $GV_{\overrightarrow{BLK}}$ are computed by fraction of up and down deviations of edge width at 90^0 and 270^0 directions. The gradient directions are closest to the edge points. If edge width $\geq$ threshold value is computed through the following method: edge width at points $\{i, j\}$ is the difference between each horizontal/vertical points and slope of a direction, where slope is the monotonically increasing or decreasing variations up and down. Thus, the average edge width of chunks $\sum(\sum(GH_{BLK}, GV_{BLK})$ calculated by summation of the number of points along vertical and horizontal directions. The sharpest edge SH_{EDGE} from each chunk is acquired by sorting average edge widths in ascending/descending order. The acutance index of an image is given in spatial domain as:

$$IMQ_{acutance1} = \frac{count(SH_{EDGE})}{\sum_{i=1}^{j=1}(SH_{EDGE})} \tag{16}$$

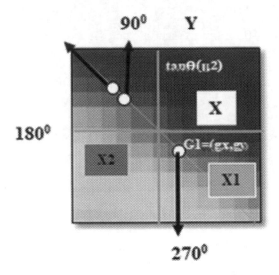

Fig. 6. Gradient points along gradient directions

3.2.2 Calculation of Acutance in Wavelet Levels

The acutance of an SR image and is represents one of the vital observed qualities of the SR image is assessed from the energy levels in the wavelet bands [24]. The perceived acutance is calculated from the spatial frequency data divided into sub-bands after performing 3 levels of decomposition LL, LH, HL, HH. The energies of each band are then calculated as:

$$Eng_x^{Ni} = log10(1 + \frac{cf(x)}{N_x^i}) \tag{17}$$

Where $cf(x)$ is a squared coefficient of sub-band x and N_x^i is the amount of coefficients of sub-scales x at level i. The acutance is assessed via weighted geometric mean of these log-energy bands computed as:

$$E_i = (\prod_{i=1} \frac{kEng_x^i}{k}) \tag{18}$$

where k is the highest constant value. The acutance index in wavelet domain is [24].

$$IMQ_{acutance2} = \sum_{i=1}^{3} 2^{3-i} Eng^i \tag{19}$$

The acutance of the super resolved image comes up as:

$$IMQ_{acutance} = \frac{(2(IMQ_{acutance2} \times IMQ_{acutance1}) + c}{(IMQ_{acutance1} \times IMQ_{acutance1}) + (IMQ_{acutance2} \times IMQ_{acutance2}) + c} \tag{20}$$

Where c can assume any lesser value to reduce the chance of denominator being zero. $IMQ_{acutance1}$ and $IMQ_{acutance2}$ are acutance in spatial domain and wavelet domain. The energy points in the wavelet bands accurately designate the points of signal acutance variations [19]. The two quality characteristics, spatial discontinuity and acutance are inexorable in the procedure of sensitive quality measurement. The predictable SR visual quality can be measured by pooling the two quality structures and thus a novel metric is generated, the Super Resolution Entropy Metric (SREM). The SREM metric can be calculated as,

$$SREM = (IMQ_{spd})^{\alpha} + (IMQ_{acutance})^{(1-\alpha)} \tag{21}$$

Where SREM is the overall prediction of perceptual image quality. The numerical weight of α has been reserved as 0.8, to attain greater numerical score to acutance and spatial discontinuity as they are the most prominent quality features.

4   Experimental Validation

The efficiency of SREM metric has been assessed experimentally by conducting several tests on a variety of super resolved (SR) test images. All the experiments are executed using MATLAB software on Intel(R) Core(TM) i5-3210M, CPU with 2.5 GHz and 4 GB memory PC. The data samples are taken from http://r0k. us/graphics/kodak/ [25], Kodak Lossless True Colour Image Suite to estimate the efficacy of the proposed metric SREM. Ten test images and 4 super resolution algorithms, few state-art-of-the no-reference IQA methods BRISQUE, BLIINDS, DIVINE and three most generally used full-reference metrics SSIM, PSNR and FSIM for SR images are used for experimental validation.

4.1   Analysis of Spatial Discontinuity Index

This section evaluates the performance of the proposed fuzzy gradient points based metric using the images from Kodak Lossless True Colour Image Suite datasets. The individual modules of spatial discontinuity index are also evaluated through three steps: (1) calculating the fuzzy gradient points $\mu\Delta G(p_i)$ using Eq. 4 and generating Fuzzy Gradient Matrix (FGM) (2) calculating the weighted average of gradient points along horizontal and vertical directions (3) calculating the maximum value of gradient point changes in the horizontal and vertical directions. The spatially discontinued edge points prevent image information from being correctly preserved and visual quality is also destroyed as shown in Fig. 7. From Fig. 7, it can be noted that spatial discontinuity index of bicubic SR image is greater than [8]. This proves that a lower spatial discontinuity index leads to better preservation of the structural information in the SR image resulting in better visual quality.

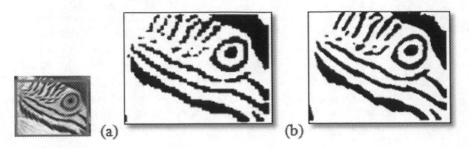

Fig. 7. Spatial discontinued edge points of parrot image, (a) bicubic $[IMQ_{spd} = 0.653]$, (b) [8] $[IMQ_{spd} = 0.417]$

4.2 Analysis of Acutance Index

The acutance is assessed from the energy levels of the improved bands of the multi-layers-decomposed sub-scales and generates the acutance of vertical, horizontal and diagonal spatial frequency. Acutance variation is graphically illustrated as Fig. 8 according to result of butterfly image in Fig. 10. From Figs. 7 and 8, it can be concluded that the spatial discontinuity and acutance metric are inversely proportional. The proposed SREM metric was used to evaluate the Bicubic, Glanser, SRCNN and Fuzzy Deep Learning algorithms [23] for super resolution techniques. Then this evaluation was compared with the evaluation of standard metrics on the same algorithms as shown in Figs. 9, 10 and Tables 3, 4 and 6. Figure 11 illustrates the evaluation of SREM on super resolved satellite image and the corresponding performance comparison of SREM is also presented in Table 5. The SREM metric is used to quantify the visual performance with image detail preservation, making it suitable for satellite SR images.

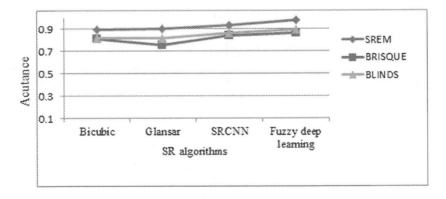

Fig. 8. Acutance variations of proposed method with state-of-the-art methods

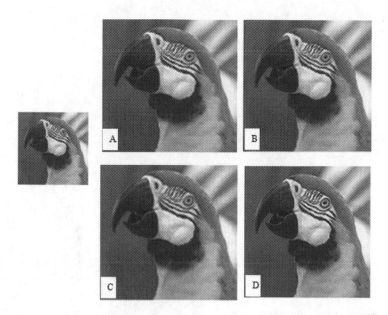

Fig. 9. SREM Parrot Results (A) Bicubic [$IMQ_{acutance} = 0.187$, $IMQ_{spd} = 0.615$, $SREM = 0.971$], (B) Glansar[$IMQ_{acutance} = 0.660$, $IMQ_{spd} = 0.136$, $SREM = 0.937$], (C) SRCNN [$IMQ_{acutance} = 0.163$, $IMQ_{spd} = 0.642$, $SREM = 0.953$], (D) Fuzzy deep learning [$IMQ_{acutance} - 0.6817$, $IMQ_{spd} = 0.128$, $SREM = 0.917$]

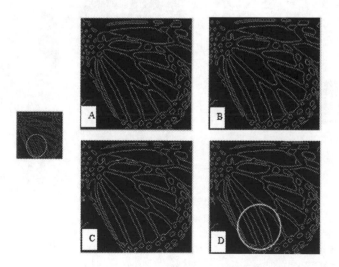

Fig. 10. SREM Butterfly Results. (A) Bicubic [$IMQ_{acutance} = 0.197$, $IMQ_{spd} = 0.625$, $SREM = 0.897$], (B) Glansar [$IMQ_{acutance} = 0.702$, $IMQ_{spd} = 0.126$, $SREM = 0.907$], (C) SRCNN [$IMQ_{acutance} = 0.163$, $IMQ_{spd} = 0.652$, $SREM = 0.953$], (D) Fuzzy deep learning [$IMQ_{acutance} = 0.721$, $IMQ_{spd} = 0.128$, $SREM = 0.989$]

Table 3. Parrot image: Performance comparison of various SR algorithms vs No-reference metrics.

SR algorithms	No-reference metric			
	SREM	BRISQUE	BLINDS	DIVINE
Bicubic	**0.917**	0.850	0.886	0.601
Glanser	**0.937**	0.738	0.862	0.525
SRCNN	**0.953**	0.843	0.843	0.625
Fuzzy deep learning	**0.971**	0.812	0.903	0.785

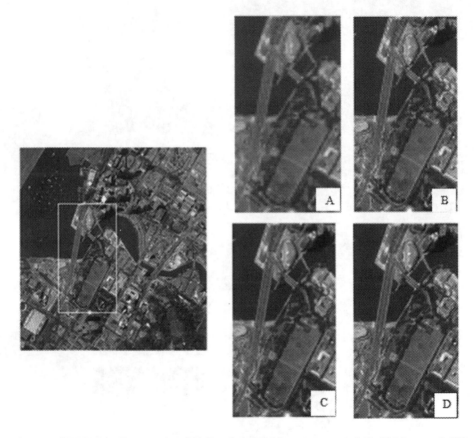

Fig. 11. SREM satellite image. (A) Bicubic [$IMQ_{acutance} = 0.478$, $IMQ_{spd} = 0.207$, $SREM = 0.827$], (B) Glansar [$IMQ_{acutance} = 0.476$, $IMQ_{spd} = 0.227$, $SREM = 0.834$], (C) SRCNN [$IMQ_{acutance} = 0.490$, $IMQ_{spd} = 0.247$, $SREM = 0.852$] (D) Fuzzy deep learning [$IMQ_{acutance} = 0.552$, $IMQ_{spd} = 0.198$, $SREM = 0.861$]

As shown in Tables 3, 4 and 5, fuzzy deep learning yields the maximum quality scores in most evaluation indices in all tests. It is clear that the SREM metric shows the good quality score. From Table 5, when reference HR images are

Table 4. Butterfly image: Performance comparison of various SR algorithms vs No-reference metrics.

SR algorithms	No-reference metric			
		SREM	BRISQUE	BLINDS	DIVINE
	Bicubic	**0.897**	0.810	0.816	0.534
	Glanser	**0.907**	0.758	0.822	0.515
	SRCNN	**0.935**	0.843	0.863	0.725
	Fuzzy deep learning	**0.989**	0.862	0.893	0.785

Table 5. Satellite image: Performance comparison of various SR algorithms vs No-reference metrics.

SR algorithms	No-reference metric			
		SREM	BRISQUE	BLINDS	DIVINE
	Bicubic	**0.827**	0.701	0.791	0.649
	Glanser	**0.834**	0.767	0.782	0.612
	SRCNN	**0.852**	0.833	0.793	0.769
	Fuzzy deep learning	**0.861**	0.848	0.813	0.799

Table 6. Parrot image: Performance comparison of SREM vs. Full-reference metrics

SR algorithms	Full-reference metric			
		SREM	PSNR	SSIM	FSIM
	Bicubic	**0.917**	24.18	0.725	0.706
	Glansar	**0.937**	27.48	0.779	0.889
	SRCNN	**0.953**	29.08	0.821	0.882
	Fuzzy deep learning	**0.971**	31.07	0.853	0.901

accessible, the SREM algorithm executes absolutely against three popularly used metrics PSNR, SSIM and FSIM. In PSNR metric, only intensity level difference is measured which does not completely yield distinction in visual discernment. The SSIM method is superior to PSNR as it targets to execute human perception and calculates similarity index among super resolved image and reference image using patches. The FSIM index is fewer powerful in assessing the super resolution execution either. Generally, the recommended metric executes certainly against the state-of-the-art algorithms. From Fig. 12, it is evident that the SREM gives high quality scores where visual quality is better.

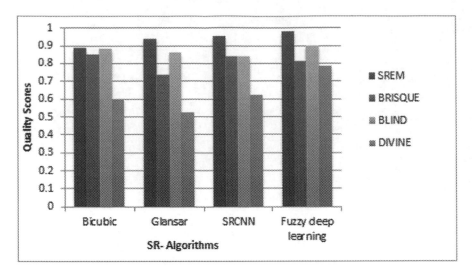

Fig. 12. Comparison of quality scores of the proposed method with state-of-the-art methods.

5 Conclusion

In this paper, we propose a novel methodology for Image visual Quality Assessment algorithm to assess the visual quality of SR images. The SREM metric is an automatic and reference less objective visual quality evaluation metric. The key features of SREM metric can be shortened as follows. First, it offers no-reference model of quality assessment, without necessitating ground truth image as reference, exploiting spatial discontinuity and acutance features to evaluate the quality. Second, it specifically models the metric for super resolution image to quantify how much details such as edges, textures are preserved. In other words, the influence of the spatial discontinuity and acutance index to the accuracy of the SR image quality prediction was measured for the finest parameters of the overall metric. Experiment results illustrate that the SREM metric executes favorably against contemporary quality assessment strategies for SR performance evaluation.

Acknowledgement. Authors acknowledge the support extended by DST-PURSE Phase II, Govt of India.

References

1. Sun, J., Xu, Z., Shum, H.: Image super-resolution using gradient profile prior. In: CVPR (2008)
2. Kim, K.I., Kwon, Y.: Single-image super-resolution using sparse regression and natural image prior. IEEE Trans. Pattern Anal. Mach. Intell **32**(6), 1127–1133 (2010). https://doi.org/10.1109/TPAMI.2010.25

3. Shan, Q., Li, Z., Jia, J., Tang, C.-K.: Fast image/video upsampling. ACM Trans. Graph **27**(5), 153 (2008). https://doi.org/10.1145/1409060.1409106
4. Rani, M., Peleg, S.: Improving resolution by image registration. CVGIP **53**(3), 231–239 (1991)
5. Timofte, R., De Smet, V., Van Gool, L.: A+: adjusted anchored neighborhood regression for fast super-resolution. In: Cremers, D., Reid, I., Saito, H., Yang, M.-H. (eds.) ACCV 2014. LNCS, vol. 9006, pp. 111–126. Springer, Cham (2015). https://doi.org/10.1007/978-3-319-16817-3_8
6. Freeman, W.T., Johnes, T.R., Pasztor, E.C.: Example-based super- resolution. IEEE Comput. Graph. Appl **27**(2), 56–65 (2002). https://doi.org/10.1109/38.988747
7. Farsiu, S., Robinson, M.D., Elad, M., Milanfar, P.: Advances and challenges in super-resolution. Int. J. Imaging Syst. Technol **14**(2), 47–57 (2004)
8. Yang, J.C., Wright, J., Huang, T., Ma, Y.: Image super-resolution via sparse representation representation. IEEE Trans. Image Process. **19**(11), 2861–2873 (2010). https://doi.org/10.1109/TIP.2010.2050625
9. Yang, J.C., Lin, Z., Cohen, S.: Fast image super-resolution based on in-place example regression. In: IEEE Conference on Computer Vision and Pattern Recognition, Portland, pp. 1059–1066 (2013). https://doi.org/10.1109/CVPR.2013.141
10. Dong, C., Loy, C.C., He, K., Tang, X.: Learning a deep convolutional network for image super-resolution. In: Fleet, D., Pajdla, T., Schiele, B., Tuytelaars, T. (eds.) ECCV 2014. LNCS, vol. 8692, pp. 184–199. Springer, Cham (2014). https://doi.org/10.1007/978-3-319-10593-2_13
11. Wang, Z., Bovik, A.C., Sheikh, H.R., Simoncelli, E.P.: Image quality assessment: from error visibility to structural similarity. IEEE Trans. Image Process. **13**(4), 600–612 (2004). https://doi.org/10.1109/TIP.2003.819861
12. Zhang, L., Mou, X., Zhang, D.: FSIM: a feature similarity index for image quality assessment. IEEE Trans. Image Process. **20**(8), 2378–2386 (2011). https://doi.org/10.1109/TIP.2011.2109730
13. Reibman, A.R., Bell, R., Gray, M.: Quality assessment for super-resolution image enhancement. In: ICIP (2006)
14. Yeganeh, H., Rostami, M., Wang, Z.: Objective quality assessment for image super-resolution: a natural scene statistics approach. In: ICIP (2012)
15. Tang, H., Joshi, N., Kapoor, A.: Blind image quality assessment using semi-supervised rectifier networks. In: CVPR (2014)
16. Mittal, A., Moorthy, A.K., Bovik, A.C.: No-reference image quality assessment in the spatial domain. IEEE Trans. Image Process. **21**(12), 4695–4708 (2012). https://doi.org/10.1109/TIP.2012.2214050
17. Saad, M.A., Bovik, A.C., Charrier, C.: Blind image quality assessment: a natural scene statistics approach in the DCT domain. IEEE Trans. Image Process. **21**(8), 3339–3352 (2012). https://doi.org/10.1109/TIP.2012.2191563
18. Moorthy, A.K., Bovik, A.C.: Blind image quality assessment: from natural scene statistics to perceptual quality. IEEE Trans. Image Process. **20**(12), 350–3364 (2011). https://doi.org/10.1109/TIP.2011.2147325
19. Candemir, S., Borovikov, E., Santosh, K.C., Antani, S., Thoma, G.: RSILC: rotation- and scale-invariant, line-based color-aware descriptor. Image Vis. Comput. **42**, 1–12 (2015). https://doi.org/10.1016/j.imavis.2015.06.010
20. Santosh, K.C., Aafaque, A., Antani, S., Thoma, G.R.: Line segment-based stitched multipanel figure separation for effective biomedical CBIR. Int. J. Pattern Recognit. Artif. Intell. **31**(5) (2017). https://doi.org/10.1142/S0218001417570038

21. Santosh, K.C., Wendling, L., Antani, S., Thoma, G.R.: Overlaid arrow detection for labeling regions of interest in biomedical images. IEEE Intell. Syst. **31**(3), 66–75 (2016). https://doi.org/10.1109/MIS.2016.24
22. Elder, J.H.: Are edges incomplete. Int. J. Comput. Vision **34**(2–3), 97–122 (1999)
23. Greeshma, M.S., Bindu, V.R.: Single image super resolution using fuzzy deep convolutional networks. In: IEEE International Conference on Technological Advancements in Power and Energy, Kollam, pp. 1–6 (2017)
24. Reenu, M., David, D., Raj, S.A., Nair, M.S.: Sharp features (WASH): an image quality assessment metric based on HVS Wavelet based. In: Second International Conference on Advanced Computing, Networking and Security, pp. 79–83 (2013)
25. Kodak Lossless True Colour Image Suite. http://r0k.us/graphics/kodak/. Accessed July 2018

Shape Descriptor Based on Centroid with Chord Lengths for Image Retrieval

Jayadevi Karur$^{(\boxtimes)}$ and Jagadeesh Pujari

S D M College of Engineering and Technology, Dharawad, India
jck1965@gmail.com, jaggudp@yahoo.com

Abstract. Shape is considered as a significant characteristic in object detection. In applications such as recognizing the shapes and classification, retrieval of shapes, extraction of shape features and their depiction plays an important role. We propose a shape descriptor which is computationally economical, compact and fast. In this work, we present three methods of feature computation based on chords. Among three, good result is obtained by the third method. Since the proposed work is based on centroid involving a global histogram, shape descriptor is invariant to all transformations. When compared to other shape signatures the proposed shape descriptor resulted in bull's eye score of 84.56% on MPEG-7 dataset.

Keywords: Computationally economical · Compact · Chords · New centroid

1 Introduction

Speedy progress in technologies of imaging and web has made it feasible for persons to refer and access an enormous number of images. Present day's applications, for example, matching and image retrieval are most natural phenomena. Retrieval of images from a huge database is the most important and thought-provoking problem in CVPR-Computer Vision and Pattern Recognition. Earlier methods of textual annotation of images are insufficient and at times, difficult in large databases due to requirement of intensive human labor. To overcome this, techniques based on CBIR (Content Based Image Retrieval), was presented. Image retrieval, in these methods, depends on visual contents instead of textual explanations. For representation and alphabetical listing of images, CBIR methods use visual fillings, for example, texture, shape and color. In object recognition, other than color and texture, shape plays an important role. Usually the shape plays a critical role in identifying regular objects [3]. Hence, in CBIR techniques, use of shape features of objects is increasing.

Two important operations of shape retrieval are shape depiction and matching. The first operation abstracts useful and perceptually significant shape features. These features are organized using data structure like string, tree, vector and so on. In the second operation, shape descriptors obtained in the first

© Springer Nature Singapore Pte Ltd. 2019
K. C. Santosh and R. S. Hegadi (Eds.): RTIP2R 2018, CCIS 1035, pp. 169–177, 2019.
https://doi.org/10.1007/978-981-13-9181-1_15

operation are used to measure closeness (or difference) among the two shapes. Numerous shape depiction and evaluation techniques have been projected all through the previous decades. Generally, the present shape depiction and portrayal techniques are divided into two categories based on contour and region. Each of these techniques is further classified into two classes as global and local.

Some renowned and latest shape descriptors based on region comprise Zernike moments, multi-scale Fourier descriptor, generic Fourier descriptor and so on. There have been many works, based on contour, for shape representation and matching. Both local and global information are contained in many contour–based shape descriptors. The descriptors belonging to this category are CSS-Curvature Scale Space, PMEM-Polygonal Multi-resolution and Elastic Matching, SC-Shape Context, IDSC-Inner Distance Shape Context, CPDH-Contour Points Distribution Histogram, HPM-Hierarchical Procrustes Matching, ST-Shape Tree, CF-Contour Flexibility and HF-Height Functions and so on. MPEG-7 community has recommended CSS [7], as one of the standards of global shape depiction. In CSS, calculation of a closeness degree is centered on the greatest potential correspondence among utmost concave/convex curvatures that are present in basic forms of the boundary outlines. In [1] PMEM three primitives of every contour section are mined at various scales. After that, the sum of absolute differences, enhanced by the elastic matching, is calculated. This is used to quantify the comparability among shapes. In SC [2], spatial dispersal of all other sample points relative to every sample point is computed. This information is represented by a histogram in log-polar space. The bins considered in histogram are uniform bins. Shape descriptor in SC is more profound to adjacent points (sample) compared to distant points (sample). Ling et al. [5] proposed a new distance named inner distance, which they defined as "length of the shortest path between two points within the shape profile". It is used as an alternative for Euclidean distance. This makes shape descriptors, based on contour, not sensitive to articulation. They have defined new shape descriptor called Inner Distance Shape Context (IDSC), which is an extension of shape context with inner distance. CPDH [13] is a global method of shape descriptor. The shape is represented by spatial dispersal of boundary points in the polar co-ordinate space. Spatial dispersals of two shapes are equated using Earth Mover's Distance. In [6] HPM, shape information is captured across different hierarchies. The ordered geometric characteristics of a shape are extracted in ST [4]. Tree matching technique is used for shape matching. The shape descriptor proposed in CF [15], defines every contour point by its deformable potential and shape matching is done using DP-Dynamic Programming. In HF [14], height function is used to define a shape descriptor. For shape matching DP-Dynamic Programming is used in HF.

In [10], to contest corresponding pairs of random features, a method, called dynamic time wrapping (DTW) is presented. The method proposed by authors in [9], DP is used for matching the random features. In this method compacting pattern into a single vector is avoided. Usually medical images are complex and contain various regions. These regions are marked using arrows in biomedical documents/publications. Simple and proficient method for recognition of arrows in images is presented in [8]. In this method, first, fuzzy binarization technique is used to convert images as binary images. Based on principle of connected component a set of candidates is calculated and convexity defect-based filtering is used to choose arrow candidates. This is followed by template matching via DTW-Dynamic Time Warping. Sequential classifier, encompassing of BLSTM-bidirectional long short-term memory classifier, trailed by convexity defect based arrowhead detection is proposed in [11]. For pattern recognition, a ranked method to extract subsets of soft output classifiers (decision rules) automatically is proposed in [12].

The above explained techniques produce outstanding retrieval precisions in the existence of diversity of distortions. These approaches utilize multifaceted distance measures, computationally complex correspondence techniques and advanced shape descriptors to attain great retrieval precisions. As a result, substantial quantity of time is spent for shape equivalent and retrieval. The existing approaches are not proper for retrieval of shapes from huge databases and online retrieval, even though they result in high retrieval accuracies. This results in dilemma to users with respect to speed-accuracy disparity. Hence we are motivated to design a new shape descriptor and matching procedure that takes into account, both accuracy and speed in its design. According to [13], a good shape depiction should be compact and should contain vital characteristics of the shape. Also it should be invariant to all types of transformations like translation, scaling and rotation, just as in the reliable human vision system. The added significant desires for favorable shape descriptor are broad-spectrum of applications, computational proficiency and compactness [14].

In this paper, we propose a new shape descriptor centered on centroid (not normal centroid) with chord lengths. It is simple and easy in computation, compact, fast retrieval rate and invariant to all transformations. MPEG-7 data set is used for experimentation purpose. The paper is organized as follows: The detailed discussion on the proposed shape descriptor is given in Sect. 2. Experimental results are presented in Sect. 3 and Sect. 4 concludes the paper.

2   Proposed Work

In this paper three methods, which are evolutionary in nature, for feature extraction and their performances are presented. The flow diagram of the work is given in Fig. 1.

MPEG-7 dataset consists of both binary and grey images. Therefore the images read from data set are binarized. The technique used in this work for determining edge pixels is called zero-crossing technique which is based on 8-neighborhood pixels only. The idea behind this technique is, all the pixels in the image are traced using 3X3 window for their 8-neighborhood connectivity. The sum of pixel values in that window is calculated. If this sum is less than 9 then it is edge pixel otherwise not edge pixel. By applying this technique over a whole image we obtained all edge pixels. The technique determines both

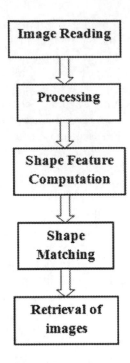

Fig. 1. Flow diagram

outer boundary pixels of the image as well as inner contour formed in the image object. Figure 2 represents result of this technique to determine edge pixels for the horse image in the dataset.

By removing the extra rows and columns that do not contain any of the object pixels we can limit the image by using minimum bounding box. The center of the bounding box is considered as a centroid (new centroid-NC) which is different from the normal definition of a centroid. NC is calculated as half of the length and breadth of minimum bounding box as shown in Fig. 3.

The circle is drawn with NC as a center and the distance of farthest edge pixel from NC as a radius using Bresenhams-circle algorithm. The algorithm returns coordinates of all points on the circle. The proposed work considers bounding box centroid rather than centroid of the image. The above procedure is followed in all three methods presented in this work as a first step. The remaining part of the work is explained below:

In the first method (M1) eight equidistance reference points on the circle are chosen. These points are set as viewing points of the object. The procedure for the same is as following:

Diameters are drawn using points on the circle. These diameters cut the edge pixels of the image. To fix first reference point on the circle, the procedure followed is given below:

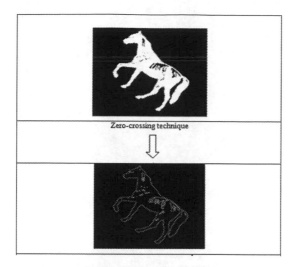

Fig. 2. Edge pixel image

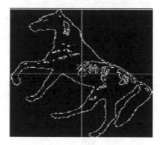

Fig. 3. Bounding box with centroid

- First distances between extreme edge pixels on every diagonal are calculated.
- The average of highest ten distances is computed. The diameter yielding the closest distance to this average establishes the first pair of reference points.

This process will choose a reference line that divides the image into symmetrical loops along its length. The remaining three pairs of reference diameters are located on the circle at offsets of $\frac{1}{8}^{th}$, $\frac{2}{8}^{th}$ and $\frac{3}{8}^{th}$ portions of the circle with reference to the first reference diameter. The eight points chosen remain relative to the structure of the shape with respect to all the transformations. Lines from each reference point (v41) to all points (like c1) in the opposite half circle are considered for feature computation as shown in Fig. 4. Each line will intersect multiple edge pixels (consider e1, e2, e3, e4 on line v41 to c1). Distances between every pair of edge pixels on every line are computed and recorded in a histogram. This is repeated for all eight points on the circle. All the features are recorded in a single histogram which serves as a transformation invariant feature vector. Closeness between two descriptors is measured by comparing feature vectors of both query image and each shape of data set using L1 norm.

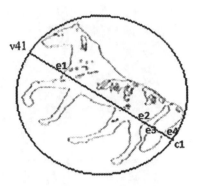

Fig. 4. Feature computation in M1

In second method (M2), feature computation involves both edge and region pixels. Fixing up reference diameter continues as explained in M1. The structure of the shape is evaluated along diameters. The diameter corresponding to this pair of reference points divides the circle into two halves. Lines from each point of one half of the circle to the corresponding point in the other half of the circle traced in the same direction are considered for feature computation (all the diameters within the half circle). These lines will intersect with edge pixels. Fraction of line lying in the original shape image is computed by counting the number of on pixels (with value 1) on a line. The ratio, named as OR (Occupancy Ratio), of this value to the length (digital length) between the extreme edge pixels on the line is calculated which represents one feature of the image as shown in Fig. 5. The Euclidean distance between extreme edge pixels, say p and q, is calculated as $distpq = \sqrt{(px - qx)^2 + (py - qy)^2}$. All the distances between extreme edge pixels are normalized by the largest distance to avoid scaling effect. All these distances and ORs are recorded in 2D histogram (64×32) where x-axis represents Euclidean distance and y axis OR values. Histograms of both query image and each shape of data set are compared using L1 norm for similarity of the two descriptors.

In third method (M3), the procedure is same as in M1, up to setting up of first pair of reference points on the circle. The diameter is drawn using these pair of points which divides the circle into two halves. Here the structure of the shape is determined in both horizontal and vertical directions of the shape along chords. All the parallel and perpendicular chords to this diameter are drawn using points on the circle and are considered for feature computation. These chords intersect with edge pixels as given in Fig. 6. Distances between extreme edge pixels on all the chords are computed. All these features are recorded in a single histogram. These distances are normalized by the largest distance in the image. The normalized histogram serves as the feature vector for the image. Closeness between two descriptors is measured by comparing feature vectors of both query image and each shape of data set using L1 norm.

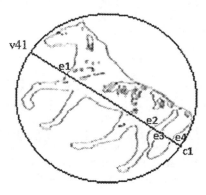

Fig. 5. Feature computation in M2 OR = on pixel(with value 1) on line e1e4/Length (digital length) of line between edge pixels e1 and e4

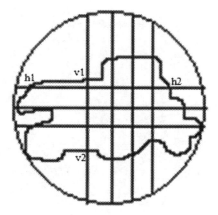

Fig. 6. Feature computation in M3

3   Experimental Results

The data set considered for the work is MPEG-7 which contains 1400 images (70 classes of objects, each class with 20 different shapes). Shapes within the same class are with some multifaceted distortions and some shapes from different classes are similar. Hence it is very challenging. The dataset is publicly available for testing.

A set of 70 arbitrarily chosen images, one from each class, forms the query set. For each query, full depth retrieval is done i.e. all 20 images of the query image class have been retrieved. To measure the retrieval performance precision and recall are used and are defined as follows:

$$precision = \frac{x}{y}$$

$$\text{recall} = \frac{x}{z}$$

where, x = number of correct images retrieved

y = total number of images retrieved

z = total number of correct images

Precisions are recorded for a standard set of eleven recall levels, in steps of 0.1 from 0 to 1 (inclusive of end values). The average precision–recall graph for the work in given in Fig. 7 and from this it is clear that method 3 of feature computation is efficient. We obtained bull's eye score of 84.56% on MPEG-7.

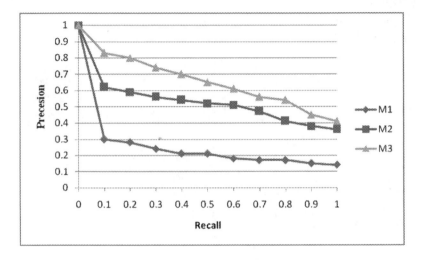

Fig. 7. Average precision – recall graph

4   Conclusion

A new shape descriptor is proposed which is centered on centroid (not normal centroid) with chord lengths. It is simple, compact, fast and computationally economical (points on circle alone are considered). Since the proposed work is based on centroid involving a global histogram, shape descriptor is invariant to all transformations.

References

1. Attalla, E., Siy, P.: Robust shape similarity retrieval based on contour segmentation polygonal multiresolution and elastic matching. Pattern Recogn. **38**(12), 2229–2241 (2005). https://doi.org/10.1016/j.patcog.2005.02.009. http://www.sciencedirect.com/science/article/pii/S0031320305000919
2. Belongie, S., Malik, J., Puzicha, J.: Shape matching and object recognition using shape contexts. IEEE Trans. Pattern Anal. Mach. Intell. **24**(4), 509–522 (2002). https://doi.org/10.1109/34.993558
3. El-ghazal, A., Basir, O., Belkasim, S.: Farthest point distance: a new shape signature for Fourier descriptors. Sig. Process.: Image Commun. **24**(7), 572–586 (2009). https://doi.org/10.1016/j.image.2009.04.001. http://www.sciencedirect.com/science/article/pii/S0923596509000393
4. Felzenszwalb, P.F., Schwartz, J.D.: Hierarchical matching of deformable shapes. In: 2007 IEEE Conference on Computer Vision and Pattern Recognition, pp. 1–8 (2007). https://doi.org/10.1109/CVPR.2007.383018
5. Ling, H., Jacobs, D.W.: Shape classification using the inner-distance. IEEE Trans. Pattern Anal. Mach. Intell. **29**(2), 286–299 (2007). https://doi.org/10.1109/TPAMI.2007.41
6. McNeill, G., Vijayakumar, S.: Hierarchical procrustes matching for shape retrieval. In: 2006 IEEE Computer Society Conference on Computer Vision and Pattern Recognition, vol. 1, pp. 885–894. IEEE (2006)
7. Mokhtarian, F., Abbasi, S., Kittler, J.: Efficient and robust retrieval by shape content through curvature scale space. In: Image Databases and Multi-Media Search, pp. 51–58. World Scientific (1997)
8. Santosh, K.C., Alam, N., Roy, P.P., Wendling, L., Antani, S., Thoma, G.R.: A simple and efficient arrowhead detection technique in biomedical images. Int. J. Pattern Recognit. Artif. Intell. **30**(05), 1657002 (2016)
9. Santosh, K.C., Lamiroy, B., Wendling, L.: DTW for matching radon features: a pattern recognition and retrieval method. In: Blanc-Talon, J., Kleihorst, R., Philips, W., Popescu, D., Scheunders, P. (eds.) ACIVS 2011. LNCS, vol. 6915, pp. 249–260. Springer, Heidelberg (2011). https://doi.org/10.1007/978-3-642-23687-7_23
10. Santosh, K.C., Lamiroy, B., Wendling, L.: DTW-radon-based shape descriptor for pattern recognition. Int. J. Pattern Recognit. Artif. Intell. **27**(03), 1350008 (2013)
11. Santosh, K.C., Roy, P.P.: Arrow detection in biomedical images using sequential classifier. Int. J. Mach. Learn. Cybern. **9**(6), 993–1006 (2018)
12. Santosh, K.C., Wendling, L.: Pattern recognition based on hierarchical description of decision rules using choquet integral. In: Santosh, K.C., Hangarge, M., Bevilacqua, V., Negi, A. (eds.) RTIP2R 2016. CCIS, vol. 709, pp. 146–158. Springer, Singapore (2017). https://doi.org/10.1007/978-981-10-4859-3_14
13. Shu, X., Wu, X.J.: A novel contour descriptor for 2D shape matching and its application to image retrieval. Image Vis. Comput. **29**(4), 286–294 (2011)
14. Wang, J., Bai, X., You, X., Liu, W., Latecki, L.J.: Shape matching and classification using height functions. Pattern Recogn. Lett. **33**(2), 134–143 (2012)
15. Xu, C., Liu, J., Tang, X.: 2D shape matching by contour flexibility. IEEE Trans. Pattern Anal. Mach. Intell. **31**(1), 180–186 (2009). https://doi.org/10.1109/TPAMI.2008.199

Learning Deep Feature Representation
for Face Spoofing

R. Srinivasa Perumal[1], K. C. Santosh[2], and P. V. S. S. R. Chandra Mouli[3(✉)]

[1] School of Information Technology and Engineering, Vellore Institute of Technology,
Vellore, Tamil Nadu, India
r.srinivasaperumal@vit.ac.in
[2] Department of Computer Science, University of South Dakota, Vermillion, USA
santosh.kc@ieee.org
[3] Department of Computer Applications, National Institute of Technology,
Jamshedpur, Jharkhand, India
chandramouli.ca@nitjsr.ac.in

Abstract. Biometrics is an emerging research area due to its easiness in identification of the person. Face Spoofing is the challenging task in face recognition systems because the human can easily trickster the system by presenting the video or photograph of the person. Many approaches are providing good results in face spoofing, but still it is challenging in intra and cross database validation. Deep learning algorithms have shown significant results in the intra and cross database. This paper used deep learning for extracting the inclusive and favorable features of the person from the face. The extracted features are used for classifying the face image as a real face or genuine face. The performance of the method is evaluated through statistical measures. The experiments were carried out NUAA and CASIA database. The method attained most promising results than other face spoofing methods.

Keywords: Feature extraction · Deep learning · Local descriptor ·
Image classification · Face spoofing

1 Introduction

Several techniques have been developed to pretend traits of the genuine users. To prevent such frauds, the spoofing detection has been developed and integrated with face recognition system [11]. Anti-spoofing techniques will determine the given input as genuine or fake user. In general, the facial features are extracted through textural and color properties. The textural properties are useful to extract the components of face such as eyes, lips, nose to identify the genuine user [16,19]. Feature extraction for face liveness detection through adaptive, global and local approaches. Adaptive approaches extract the facial information by motion analysis like movement of eyes and lips. Global approaches extract the discriminant information of the whole image and local approaches extract

© Springer Nature Singapore Pte Ltd. 2019
K. C. Santosh and R. S. Hegadi (Eds.): RTIP2R 2018, CCIS 1035, pp. 178–185, 2019.
https://doi.org/10.1007/978-981-13-9181-1_16

the information of the region. The reason for choosing color textural properties is gray level textural information is not sufficient to discriminate the fake user while image quality is poor [3]. Other than this, use of key lines and their spatial features (based on their local spatial relations) in addition to color features could potentially handle face matching/recognition [4], which is primarily based on previous concept [15].

In this paper, column local directional pattern descriptor (CLDP) is developed for extracting the favorable feature of the image and convolutional neural network is applied to classify the genuine and imposter user from the face image. CLDP texture descriptor extract the features in its first layer and later convolutional neural network will extract the high-level feature of the image. It is more robust in attack detection and detect the fake user even the pattern is complex. The general architecture of the Anti-spoofing method is shown in Fig. 1.

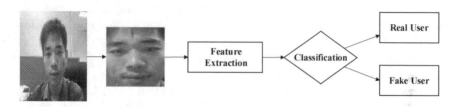

Fig. 1. General architecture for face spoofing detection

2   Related Works

Generally, texture and motion approaches are used to classify the user. Texture approaches extract the discriminant information based on shape and color for classification. Motion approaches extract the information based on the movement of eye and lip. It will take more time to capture and require the cooperation of user. Based on observation, texture approaches provide better results in face spoofing than motion approach. Many researchers developed texture model for differentiating a genuine user. A method for detecting genuine user through 2-D Fourier spectra [9]. It is simple and suitable for flat image and front pose image. It is not robust for different poses and illumination conditions. A non-intrusive method was introduced to classify the genuine user and fake user [18]. The texture information of a image was extracted and applied regression model to prevent from the fraud.

Peixoto et al. [12] extended [18] method to classify the fake user with different degrees of illumination conditions without user support. It provided better results if image is with high quality but normally, the image quality is based on the digital camera. Local descriptors provide better results even if image quality is low compared to other approaches. Local Binary Pattern (LBP) extracts the texture information from the image to define the discriminant information of the person. Maatta et al. [10] applied LBP with Gabor wavelets and Histogram of

Gradients to extract the low level features to describe the discriminant information of the face image. It is robust to various illumination condition and noise. Similarly, LBP-TOP was introduced to extract the spatio-temporal information to generate descriptor [6].

The effectiveness of LBP examined by combining SVM and other classifiers on face spoofing attacks such as face print, photo and videos [5]. Bashier et al. [2] applied local graph structure (LGS) to extract the texture information to provided a strong relationship between the image and its neighbors. It is a powerful texture descriptor and robust to monotonic gray scale changes. The image was divided into several regions and they applied LGS to each region for extracting features of the facial image to improve the results [7]. Srinivasa Perumal et al. [13] developed dimensionality reduced local descriptor (DR-LDP) to extract the complete features of the input image. It is robust to pose, illumination conditions as compared to other local descriptors. Multi-scale dynamic binarized statistical image features (MBSIF-TOP) and Multi-scale dynamic local phase quantization (MLPQ-TOP) on three orthogonal planes extract the histograms of dynamic texture for feature extraction and kernel discriminant analysis (KDA) used for classification [1]. The efficient KDA based on spectral regression used to improve the computational time and performance of the method.

Boulkenafet et al. [3] used color texture information, to detect the genuine or fake user from the chrominance and luminance channels by extracting the low-level features from various color spaces. The histogram was computed for each color channel separately and it was compared with each color channel for classification. Some of the existing approaches were not able to detect all types of attacks (photograph, video and 3D Mask). The techniques are used to extract the hand crafted texture features through Local descriptors. To extract deep features for providing more robust system the local descriptors are integrated with deep learning [17]. It motivated us to integrated CLDP with CNN to develop robust to face spoofing attacks.

3   CLDP Based Deep Learning

LDP [8] extracts the inclusive information from all the eight directions. It assigns an eight-bit binary code to each pixel in the image. It calculates the directional edge response value of a pixel by convoluting with Kirsch masks. After convoluted with Kirsch mask, LDP selects the most protuberant directions by selecting top $k(=3)$ values in a region and set the corresponding responses as 1 and the rest as 0. Column Local Directional Pattern (CLDP) is similar to LDP. In LDP, the eight directions are not treated equally due to that the some valuable information might be lost. Instead of choosing top k(=3) absolute values from the edge responses, the maximum absolute response values are selected from each column and it is represented as column local directional pattern and set the corresponding position to 1. The CLDP selects the maximum responses from each column and they are represented as C^1, C^2, C^3. The pattern is formed by selecting the C^1, C^2, C^3. The selected position is set as 1. The illustration of CLDP is shown in Fig. 2.

$$C^1 = max\{M_1, M_0, M_7\} \tag{1}$$

$$C^2 = max\{M_2, M_6\} \tag{2}$$

$$C^3 = max\{M_3, M_4, M_5\} \tag{3}$$

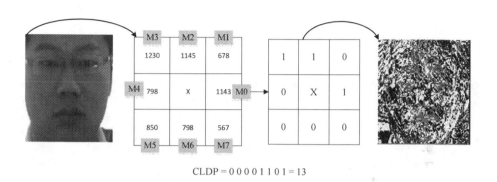

CLDP = 0 0 0 0 1 1 0 1 = 13

Fig. 2. Illustration of column LDP

Livenet network model [14] is integrated with CLDP to extract deep features for face spoofing. The network model extract the generalized feature and discriminative feature from image. It over-fitted when trained on different scale face images. In this model, the data are randomized continuously before training the network to form a small mini batches. The proposed method manage the over-fitting data in network through low amount of training data. The proposed deep learning network inherits the control of enhancing face spoofing hints from the CLDP in a deeper way. This method attained more gain in few epochs that reduce time and also it reduce the amount of over-fitting by following steps.

1. CLDP is applied as first layer in the network model.
2. The model is trained on video-frames to obtain the discriminate information from the CLDP encoded image.
3. CNN can be trained from beginning to end learning for face spoofing.
4. The indexed frame from the input can make the network deterministic and may lead to over-fitting.

The proposed network model determines whether the user is genuine or fake by using binary classification. The discriminant information of the face image is extracted to classify the genuine or fake user. The evaluation of vulnerabilities of the system is important in verification system. The FAR and FRR are the suitable metrics to compute the error rate of the system. CNN may increase the complexity, computational cost and time. The system investigated CLDP integrated with CNN with databases to prove the effectiveness of the proposed method.

4   Experimental Results

The performance of the method is analyzed with FAR and FRR that will determine the equal error rate (EER). The results show that the method performed better than other methods on CASIA and NUAA databases.

4.1   CASIA Face Anti-Spoofing Database

The database [20] consists of 50 genuine subjects and fake faces with different types of image qualities. The image qualities are categorized into low, normal and high qualities. Cut photo attack, warped photo attack and video attack were included in the database. Out of 600 images, 20 subjects are considered as training set and remaining 30 subjects considered as testing set. Figure 3 shows the normalized and cropped sample face images of CASIA database.

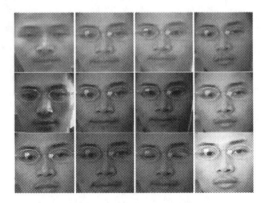

Fig. 3. Sample CASIA face spoofing database. First row: low quality images of real and attack face. Second row: Normal quality images of real and attack face. Third row: High quality images of real and attack face.

The face is localized and normalized by face detector tool, the resultant image is normalized to 112 × 112 size. The performance of the descriptors on method is presented in Table 1. It is observed from Table 1 that the CLDP with Livenet provides better performance than the other network model. The results show that our proposed method outperformed than other existing methods.

Table 1. Performance analysis on CASIA face anti-spoofing database

Descriptor	EER	FAR	FRR
LBP	12.40	13.50	11.30
LPQ	16.20	16.70	15.20
CoALBP	10.00	9.00	11.00
CoALBP+LPQ	8.70	7.30	10.10
LDP	7.50	6.50	8.50
LBPnet	5.25	5.00	5.50
n-LBPnet	4.50	4.00	5.00
CLDPnet	4.25	3.75	4.75

4.2 NUAA Database

The NUAA database [18] contains face spoofing attacks image and genuine user images. The images are gathered in 3 periods at intervals of about two weeks. The condition of the image will varied in each period based on the circumvention. It consists of 15 subjects. First 2 periods are used for training set and third period used for testing set. Figure 4 shows the normalized sample face images and photo attacks for all three periods.

Fig. 4. Sample NUAA face spoofing database. First row: First session of face images and its photo attack. Second row: Second session of face images and its photo attack. Third row: Third session of face images and its photo attack

The performance of the system is defined in terms of EER and is compared with the other method as shown in Table 2. It is observed from Table 2 that the proposed system has slightly improved the performance compared to other existing systems on face spoofing attacks. The proposed method integrating CLDP with CNN attained less error rate. This result shows that the benefit of the deep features for face spoofing. It is robust to face spoofing attacks and also it extract the discriminant information even the image contains noise.

Table 2. Performance analysis on NUAA face anti-spoofing database

Descriptor	EER	FAR	FRR
LBP	4.20	4.80	3.60
LPQ	6.70	6.20	7.20
CoALBP	8.60	9.00	8.20
CoALBP+LPQ	4.00	4.10	3.90
LDP	3.50	3.70	3.30
LBPnet	2.10	2.70	1.60
n-LBPnet	1.80	1.90	1.70
CLDPnet	1.60	1.75	1.55

5   Conclusion

In this paper, the neural model is addressed the face spoofing attacks. CLDP introduced to extract the micro structure pattern of the face image to distinguish the genuine and fake user. The neural model is integrated with CLDP to extract the deep features to improve the accuracy for face spoofing detection. It is fast and robust to illumination condition, noise, pose and facial expression than the existing methods. The experiments are carried out on CASIA and NUAA database. This system has attained better performance rate compared with the other methods. Further, it can be extended for all face spoof detection databases.

References

1. Arashloo, S.R., Kittler, J., Christmas, W.: Face spoofing detection based on multiple descriptor fusion using multiscale dynamic binarized statistical image features. IEEE Trans. Inf. Forensics Secur. **10**(11), 2396–2407 (2015)
2. Bashier, H.K., Lau, S.H., Han, P.Y., Ping, L.Y., Li, C.M.: Face spoofing detection using local graph structure. In: International Conference on Computer, Communications and Information Technology (2014)
3. Boulkenafet, Z., Komulainen, J., Hadid, A.: Face spoofing detection using colour texture analysis. IEEE Trans. Inf. Forensics Secur. **11**(8), 1818–1830 (2016)
4. Candemir, S., Borovikov, E., Santosh, K.C., Antani, S.K., Thoma, G.R.: RSILC: rotation- and scale-invariant, line-based color-aware descriptor. Image Vis. Comput. **42**, 1–12 (2015). https://doi.org/10.1016/j.imavis.2015.06.010
5. Chingovska, I., Anjos, A., Marcel, S.: On the effectiveness of local binary patterns in face anti-spoofing. In: International Conference of the Biometrics Special Interest Group, pp. 1–7 (2012)
6. de Freitas Pereira, T., Anjos, A., De Martino, J.M., Marcel, S.: *LBP - TOP* based countermeasure against face spoofing attacks. In: Park, J.-I., Kim, J. (eds.) ACCV 2012. LNCS, vol. 7728, pp. 121–132. Springer, Heidelberg (2013). https://doi.org/10.1007/978-3-642-37410-4_11

7. Housam, K.B., Lau, S.H., Pang, Y.H., Liew, Y.P., Chiang, M.L.: Face spoofing detection based on improved local graph structure. In: International Conference on Information Science & Applications, pp. 1–4 (2014)
8. Jabid, T., Kabir, M.H., Chae, O.: Local directional pattern (LDP) for face recognition. In: IEEE International Conference on Consumer Electronics, pp. 329–330 (2010)
9. Li, J., Wang, Y., Tan, T., Jain, A.K.: Live face detection based on the analysis of fourier spectra. In: Defense and Security, pp. 296–303 (2004)
10. Maatta, J., Hadid, A., Pietikainen, M.: Face spoofing detection from single images using texture and local shape analysis. IET Biom. 1(1), 3–10 (2012)
11. Menotti, D., et al.: Deep representations for iris, face, and fingerprint spoofing detection. IEEE Trans. Inf. Forensics Secur. 10(4), 864–879 (2015)
12. Peixoto, B., Michelassi, C., Rocha, A.: Face liveness detection under bad illumination conditions. In: 18th IEEE International Conference on Image Processing, pp. 3557–3560 (2011)
13. Srinivasa Perumal, R., Chandra Mouli, P.V.S.S.R.: Dimensionality reduced local directional pattern (DR-LDP) for face recognition. Expert Syst. Appl. 63, 66–73 (2016)
14. Rehman, Y.A.U., Po, L.M., Liu, M.: Livenet: improving features generalization for face liveness detection using convolution neural networks. Expert Syst. Appl. 108, 159–169 (2018)
15. Santosh, K.C., Lamiroy, B., Wendling, L.: Integrating vocabulary clustering with spatial relations for symbol recognition. IJDAR 17(1), 61–78 (2014). https://doi.org/10.1007/s10032-013-0205-4
16. Sawat, D.D., Hegadi, R.S.: Lower facial curves extraction for unconstrained face detection in video. In: Bera, R., Sarkar, S.K., Chakraborty, S. (eds.) Advances in Communication, Devices and Networking. LNEE, vol. 462, pp. 689–700. Springer, Singapore (2018). https://doi.org/10.1007/978-981-10-7901-6_75
17. de Souza, G.B., da Silva Santos, D.F., Pires, R.G., Marana, A.N., Papa, J.P.: Deep texture features for robust face spoofing detection. IEEE Trans. Circuits Syst. II Express Briefs 64(12), 1397–1401 (2017)
18. Tan, X., Li, Y., Liu, J., Jiang, L.: Face liveness detection from a single image with sparse low rank bilinear discriminative model. In: Daniilidis, K., Maragos, P., Paragios, N. (eds.) ECCV 2010. LNCS, vol. 6316, pp. 504–517. Springer, Heidelberg (2010). https://doi.org/10.1007/978-3-642-15567-3_37
19. Wen, D., Han, H., Jain, A.K.: Face spoof detection with image distortion analysis. IEEE Trans. Inf. Forensics Secur. 10(4), 746–761 (2015)
20. Zhang, Z., Yan, J., Liu, S., Lei, Z., Yi, D., Li, S.Z.: A face antispoofing database with diverse attacks. In: 5th IAPR International Conference on Biometrics (ICB), pp. 26–31 (2012)

ExNET: Deep Neural Network for Exercise Pose Detection

Sadeka Haque[✉], AKM Shahariar Azad Rabby[✉], Monira Akter Laboni,
Nafis Neehal, and Syed Akhter Hossain

Department of Computer Science and Engineering,
Daffodil International University, Dhaka, Bangladesh
{sadeka15-5210,azad15-5424,akter15-5044,nafis.cse}@diu.edu.bd
aktarhossain@daffodilvarsity.edu.bd

Abstract. Pose detection estimate human activity in images or video
frames using computer vision technique. Pose detection has many applications, such as body to augmented reality, fitness, animation etc.
ExNET represents a way to detect human pose from 2D human exercises image using Convolutional Neural Network. In recent time Deep
Learning based systems are making it possible to detect human exercise
poses from images. We refer to the model we have built for this task
as ExNET: Deep Neural Network for Exercise Pose Detection. We have
evaluated our proposed model on our own dataset that contains a total
of 2000 images. And those images are distributed into 5 classes as well as
images are divided into training and test dataset, and obtained improved
performance. We have conducted various experiments with our model on
the test dataset, and finally got the best accuracy of 82.68%.

Keywords: Human pose detection · Object detection ·
Deep learning · Exercise Pose Detection

1 Introduction

Human pose classification problem includes the recognition of different exercise
poses using the image in the computer vision community. Human pose analysis
is one of the interesting issues and a challenge to understand within automated
images. It detect human figures in images, so that one could determine, for
example, where someone's elbow shows up in an image. Pose classification has
many uses, from interactive installations that react to the body to augmented
reality, animation, fitness uses, and more.

Automatically detecting the presence of a human is an impossible task
depending on the image because it has a variety of conditions that have to do
with scale and resolution, pose etc. Most of the algorithms proposed can detect
a human pose from the image that occupies a significant portion of the image
sports a familiar and benign pose, and wears clothing that contrasts with the
background.

© Springer Nature Singapore Pte Ltd. 2019
K. C. Santosh and R. S. Hegadi (Eds.): RTIP2R 2018, CCIS 1035, pp. 186–193, 2019.
https://doi.org/10.1007/978-981-13-9181-1_17

While the use of neural networks has been successful in pose detection, because of the significant pose variation exhibited by the human body, and the impossibility of training for all possible variants. CNN's are appealing for human pose classification because there's no compelling reason to unequivocally configuration highlight portrayals and identifiers for parts in light of the fact that a model and highlights are found out from the information. The presence of profound learning has diminished the measure of hand-designed handling required for PC vision by performing numerous tasks, for example, max-pooling, cluster standardization, and resampling inside Convolutional Neural Networks (CNN). Convolutional neural systems (CNN) have made exceptional progress as of late on picture grouping and item confinement issues. They are fundamentally the same as conventional neural systems as far as that they are comprised of neurons with learnable loads and predispositions. Be that as it may, neural systems don't scale well to bigger picture sets. Every neuron in a layer is completely associated with every one of the neurons in the past layer, so we rapidly produce countless and wind up overfitting on the preparation set. CNN's exploit the way that the info comprises of pictures, so they oblige the design in an increasingly sensible manner which immensely diminishes the quantity of parameters.

In this task, we investigate one single designs for demonstrating human posture identify and action grouping. This model having 5 classes of different kind of human pose images they are swiss ball hamstring curl, pull up, push Up, walking and cycling showing in Fig. 1.

Fig. 1. Different kind of human poses

2   Literature Review

CNN's have been utilized for characterization undertakings or classification, yet they are progressively being connected towards location issues. Sermanet et al. propose an incorporated way to deal with article discovery, acknowledgment, and confinement with a solitary CNN [1]. At the abnormal state, human exercises can frequently be precisely portrayed regarding body posture, movement, and communication with scene objects [2]. However, because of the testing idea of this issue, most current movement acknowledgment models depend on all encompassing portrayals that extricate appearance and movement highlights from the video from which the pictures are pulled. Recently, Toshev et al. [3] demonstrated that applying profound CNN's to act estimation like a relapse issue has the benefit of thinking about posture in a basic however all encompassing style. This methodology accomplished (0.61) and was less complex than past strategies dependent on unequivocally planned element portrayals and graphical models. One of the initial phases toward this path has been the utilization of organized expectation over semantic division, e.g. by combining image-based DenseCRF [4] inference with CNN's for semantic segmentation [5], training both systems jointly [6], or more recently learning CNN-based pairwise terms in structured prediction modules [7]. All of these works involve coupling decisions so as to reach some consistency in the labeling of global structures, typically coming in the form of smoothness constraints.

3 Proposed Methodology

3.1 Dataset

The dataset we used for this model is collected from the publicly available sources. This dataset contains 2000 images of human exercise poses divided into five class labeled as pull up, push up, walking, swiss ball hamstring curl, cycling. Each class contains 400 images. Initially, the images had different dimension and different color and background. Figure 2 showing some example of human exercise pose.

(a) Cycling   (b) Pull up   (c) Push up   (d) Swiss ball hamstring curl   (e) Walking

Fig. 2. Exercise pose dataset

3.2 Dataset Preparation

The pose dataset contains images with various size and shape. While CNN required the fix input size. Also, the image has lots of unnecessary information. So, at first, we manually cropped all the images to reduce all the unnecessary information. Later resized all images into 32×32 pixel to get highest accuracy within lowest computation cost.

Deep learning system performs better in the event that it discovers more information. Consequently, information increase creates more data artificially. To augment the data, we choose 6 methods. First, we randomly $40°$ rotate the images, then width and height shift the images. Later normalize the images, zoom and shear the images with a horizontal flip.

When the data augmentation done, the Leeds dataset consists of about 2000 images and then it was split 80% training and 20% validation images.

3.3 Architecture of the Model

Our proposed model ExNet is a multilayer convolutional network begins with the input size of 64×64 grayscale image connected with a convolutional layer which has 32 filters, 5×5 kernel size, and swish (1) activation [10]. The next layer is also a convolutional layer with 32 filter size and 3×3 kernel. A max pool layer added followed by this two-layer with a pool size of 2. Also, we added a 25% dropout [9] layer to avoid overfitting. We also added batch normalization [8] to avoid overfitting after a dropout and a convolutional layer.

$$\sigma(z) = (1 + \exp(-z)) - 1 \tag{1}$$

Later we added three convolutional layers one after another with the same parameters of a 3×3 kernel, 64 filters with swish activation. The output is connected with a max pool layer with 25% dropout. After that we conquered the layer and connected it to a fully connected dense layer with 512 hidden units with 50% dropout. The final output layer has 5 output node. Final output unites usage the softmax (2) activation to predict the output of the model.

$$\sigma(z)_j = \frac{e^{z_j}}{\sum_{k=1}^{k} e^{z_k}} \, for \, j = 1, ...k \tag{2}$$

Figure 3 Showing the proposed model architecture.

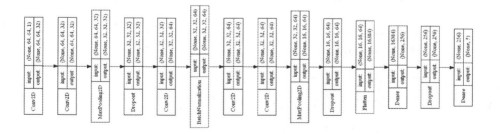

Fig. 3. Model architecture

3.4   Optimizer and Learning Rate

Optimizer plays an important role in the deep neural network. Optimizer algorithm helps us to minimize or maximize the error function of the model which depends on the model hyper-parameter which is used to compute the class label base on the model input. The hyper-parameter of a model is important to efficiently and effectively train the model and produce the accurate result. For ExNET we used the Adam optimizer. Adam stands for Adaptive Moment Estimation which computes adaptive learning rates for hyper-parameter. The Adam optimization algorithm is easy when to implement and it is computationally efficient. It requires little memory which is why it is used in most of the computer vision and NLP applications. Our given model ExNET used ADAM (3) Optimizer [11] with a learning rate of 0.001.

$$\theta_{t+1} = \theta_t - \frac{\eta}{\sqrt[1]{\widehat{v}} + \epsilon} \widehat{m} \qquad (3)$$

When we use a neural network for performing classification and prediction tasks we have to calculate the error rate to find the model performance. One of the recent studies show that the cross entropy function gives better performance than classification error and mean square error [12]. Proposed method used categorical cross entropy (4) as loss function.

$$L_i = - \sum_j t_{i,j} \log(p_{i,j}) \qquad (4)$$

To make the optimizer converge faster and closer to the global, we used an automatic Learning Rate reduction method [13]. Through the minimum loss, learning rate is the step size of walks. When the learning rate is low, it takes much time to get the global minima. On the other hand when the learning rate is high, the training can not get converged or even diverged. To get the fast computation time we set a maximum learning rate that can be automatically decreased with the monitoring of validation accuracy.

4   Training the Model

The ExNET is trained on human exercise pose dataset where 80% used as a training set and other 20% in validation set. After 50 epochs model performed accurately on classifying human exercise pose. The automatic learning rate reduction formula helps the Adam optimizer to converge faster by monitoring the validation accuracy and reduced the learning rate from 0.001 to 0.000001.

5   Evaluating the Model

The ExNET is trained on human exercise pose images and give a promising result on train and validation set.

5.1 Train Validation Split

To examine how the model performs, train and validation set has been created. The training data set is used to train the model with known output and validation data used to check how the model performs during training time and help to measure its performance and tune the hyper meters.

The human exercise pose dataset has a total of 2000 images in five class, while each class contains 400 images each. To create the train set we use 1600 images (80%) and 400 images (20%) on the validation set.

5.2 Model Performance

After 50 epochs proposed ExNET got 82.68% accuracy on classifying 2D human exercise pose from the dataset.

Analyzing the result and confusion matrix, we found that the proposed model performs so well in classifying the human exercise pose.

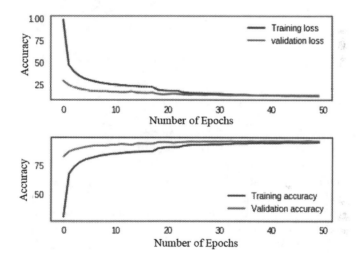

Fig. 4. Accuracy and loss for ExNet

Many exercise images were looking so similar for exercise equipment, lighting condition, and similar human pose. For those case model also did pretty good. Figure 4 showing the loss and accuracy of ExNET and Fig. 5 shows the confusion matrix for the proposed ExNET.

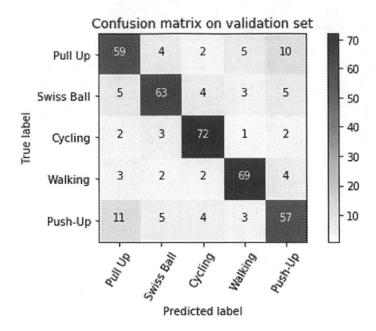

Fig. 5. Confusion matrix for ExNet

6   Conclusion and Future Work

This proposed model presenting a better performance of classification of human poses exercise. The dataset for both train and validation set for lesser epochs and less computation time compared to the other CNN model and achieve 82% accuracy on our dataset. As a result, we are able to achieve state-of-art results on several challenging exercise pose datasets.

Sometimes the proposed model confused to understand some pose due to overfitting. Future work increasing the dataset size will help to perform the model better. To diminish the gap among training and validation execution further tweak the hyper parameters of our model.

References

1. Sermanet, P., Eigen, D., Zhang, X., Mathieu, M., Fergus, R., LeCun, Y.: OverFeat: integrated recognition, localization, and detection using convolutional networks. arXiv preprint arXiv:1312.6229
2. Pishchulin, L., Andriluka, M., Gehler, P., Schiele, B.: Poselet conditioned pictorial structures. In: 2013 IEEE Conference on Computer Vision and Pattern Recognition (CVPR), pp. 588–595, Berlin, Heidelberg, June 2012, 2013
3. Toshev, A., Szegedy, C.: DeepPose: human pose estimation via deep neural networks, pp. 1653–1660 (2014)
4. Krähenbühl, P., Koltun, V.: Parameter learning and convergent inference for dense random fields. In: ICML (2013)

5. Chen, L., Papandreou, G., Kokkinos, I., Murphy, K., Yuille, A.L.: Semantic image segmentation with deep convolutional nets and fully connected CRFs. In: ICLR (2015)

6. Zheng, S., et al.: Conditional random fields as recurrent neural networks. In: ICCV (2015)

7. Chandra, S., Kokkinos, I.: Fast, exact and multi-scale inference for semantic image segmentation with deep Gaussian CRFs. In: Leibe, B., Matas, J., Sebe, N., Welling, M. (eds.) ECCV 2016. LNCS, vol. 9911, pp. 402–418. Springer, Cham (2016). https://doi.org/10.1007/978-3-319-46478-7_25

8. Ioffe, S., Szegedy, C.: Batch normalization: accelerating deep network training by reducing internal covariate shift. arXiv:1502.03167 [cs]

9. Srivastava, N., Hinton, G., Krizhevsky, A., Sutskever, I., Salakhutdinov, R.: Dropout: a simple way to prevent neural networks from overfitting. J. Mach. Learn. Res. **15**, 1929–1958 (2014)

10. Neural and Evolutionary Computing (cs.NE): Computer Vision and Pattern Recognition (cs.CV); Learning (cs.LG) arXiv:1710.05941 [cs.NE]

11. Kingma, D.P., Ba, J.: Adam: a method for stochastic optimization. arXiv:1412.6980 [cs.LG], December 2014

12. Janocha, K., Czarnecki, W.M.: On loss functions for deep neural networks in classification. ArXiv, abs/1702.05659 (2017)

13. Schaul, T., Zhang, S., LeCun, Y.: No more pesky learning rates. arXiv preprint arXiv:1206.1106 (2012)

Background Subtraction and Kalman Filter Algorithm for Object Tracking

Shridevi S. Vasekar[1]([⊠]) and Sanjivani K. Shah[2]

[1] Sinhgad College of Engineering, Savitribai Phule Pune University, Pune, India
shree.raut@rediffmail.com
[2] Smt. Kashibai Navale College of Engineering, Savitribai Phule Pune University,
Pune, India
san_shah@rediffmail.com

Abstract. Today's world is confronting real issue regarding open security for which visual surveillance framework is required. Object tracking increases loads of enthusiasm for dynamic research in applications, for example, video surveillance, vehicle navigation, video compression and so on. Distinctive strategies are produced for object tracking purpose however that experiences corruption in execution because of occlusion, complex shapes and enlightenments. In this proposed work, discovery of the moving item has been finished utilizing straightforward background subtraction and a Kalman filter algorithm. Following calculation has been completed and attempted on MATLAB 2013a with working system windows. Strategy contrasts and examines different execution measures and different calculations.

Keywords: Kalman filter · Video surveillance · Object tracking · Occlusion

1 Introduction

The present world is stacked with automated and of altered structure in which Object acknowledgment and item following are fundamental parts of visual following systems. Object acknowledgment is first basic advance for any video reconnaissance. Following is required in bigger sum applications. Right now utilized techniques for recognizable proof are optical stream framework, foundation subtraction system, outline differencing procedure. In foundation subtraction strategy capability between two back to back edges is taken to discover the closeness of an area. In optical stream strategy, gathering process is performed. This system gives finish data about the moving thing. In foundation subtraction strategy, the multifaceted nature between current casing and the foundation picture is utilized to pick test position.

The Kalman Filter algorithm includes the state space approach for class of following. It depends on the state space condition and the estimation condition for tackling following issue. Kalman Filter measures the speed, position, and

© Springer Nature Singapore Pte Ltd. 2019
K. C. Santosh and R. S. Hegadi (Eds.): RTIP2R 2018, CCIS 1035, pp. 194–202, 2019.
https://doi.org/10.1007/978-981-13-9181-1_18

increasing speed of the objective in casing arrangement. It will anticipate speed, area and quickening of moving focus in the wake of figuring its focal point. The state vector and estimation vector are the parameters of the Kalman filter.

For point following, portion following and outline following those are sorts of article following have various approaches. The principle issues looked amid item following are impediment and complex shapes. The issue of impediment is happens while following single or various items and it is significant reason for loss of data. Impediment is the one which obstructs our view. Treatment of complex shape is additionally testing undertaking. This paper looks at past systems for item following in segment II. The article following structure layout, stream of framework and programming need delineated in segment III. Kalman channel calculation and its logical conditions are in like manner cleared up in segment 3. Result and dialog of structure are given in area 4. Finally work is done up in area 5.

2   Related Work

Various methods for object tracking are described below.

Presents novel approach for unsupervised video following after by examining the advantages of neighborhood unsavoury sets. A territory harsh filter is illustrated in this methodology for beginning stamping of endless moving object(s) even inside seeing a couple of assortments in various spaces. The territories and shading of subject models are surveyed using their approximations in spatio-shading neighborhood granular space [1].

Proposes a following technique that has been particularly intended to track the different street clients that might be experienced in a urban domain. Since street clients have exceptionally differing appearances and shapes, proposed technique begins from background subtraction to remove the potential from the earlier obscure street clients. Every one of these street clients is then followed utilizing an accumulation of key points inside the recognized frontal area districts, which permits the addition of protest areas not withstanding amid objects unions or occlusions [2].

Detailed a novel system for following moving objects in view of a composite structure and a reporter mechanism. The composite system tracks moving objects utilizing distinctive trackers and produces sets of forward/in reverse tracklets. A robustness score is then computed for every tracker utilizing its forward/in reverse tracklet combine to locate the most dependable moving object direction. The reporter fills in as the recuperation component to correct the moving article direction when the strength score is low, mostly utilizing a mix of molecule channel and layout coordinating. The proposed system can deal with halfway and substantial impediments; in addition, the structure of the system empowers reconciliation of other client particular trackers. Broad investigations on ongoing benchmarks demonstrate that the proposed structure beats other current best in class trackers because of its intense direction examination and recuperation system [3].

Propose an estimation those uses Kalman Filter and Mean move for following the item. Furthermore strategy uses Histogram for impediment dealing with. Immediately, use Mean Shift estimation to get point of convergence of needed item. Regardless, the solid of following isn't, so use Kalman Filter to upgrade the effect of following. Bhattacharyya coefficient and Edge Histogram are used for finding impediments. Following of article is increasingly exact with this methodology. The results show that the powerful of following is great [4].

Automatic video observation frameworks are exceptionally valuable for security reason. The framework will follow the distinguished item. Identification of item is finished by basic foundation subtraction and following by Kalman channel. The standard datasets CAVIAR and PETS are utilized [5].

The Proposed algorithm is mainly based on background subtraction and Kalman filter for tracking. For software requirement MATLAB R2013a with operating system windows used for system implementation.

A Input video

Camera which is associated with the PC catches the video and send it to PC. Video is changed over into no. of frames are used by MATLAB as an information picture.

B Background Subtraction

After transformation from video to frames, Background subtraction is connected in which two frames are viewed as, one is reference image and other is present image. The pixel to pixel contrast is figured keeping in mind the end goal to recognize moving object. Thresholding is then connected. The principle assignment of thresholding is to change over grayscale picture to binary image. The aftereffects of background subtraction are upgraded, tasks, for example, enlargement and disintegration, morphological open and close are performed. Morphological activities are done to expel noise content. After that blob analysis is utilized to identify gatherings of associated pixels. object with largest area is chosen.

C Bubble sorting algorithm

In case more than one items are accessible in the video by then perform bubble sorting calculation which will sort objects from broad to minimal dependent upon the object area. Find the point of convergence of mass and scope of the greatest object.

D Object tracking: Kalman filter algorithm

The Kalman Filter calculation has a place with the state space approach class of tracking calculations. It takes care of the tracking issue in light of the state space condition and estimation condition. Kalman Filter partitions to two stages: prediction condition and correction condition. Kalman Filter gauges the speed, position, and increasing speed of the object in each edge of the succession yet it has been assumed that the changes in speed of the object are in restriction.

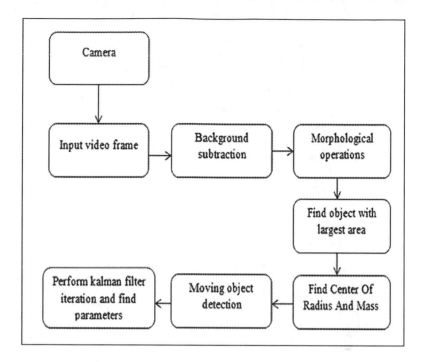

Fig. 1. Overview of system

Overall system architecture of proposed system used for object tracking is as shown in Fig. 1. Algorithm

1. To begin with instate camera.
2. Get input video frames from camera.
3. Perform background subtraction by subtracting each frame from background image.
4. Perform morphological activity, for example, disintegration.
5. After that select object with biggest area.
6. Apply bubble sorting calculation.
7. Discover center of mass and radius of biggest object.
8. Apply kalman filter cycle.
9. object identification and tracking.

Kalman filter design consists of mathematical equations of two types:

1. Time Update Equations
   Time update equations obtain the preliminary estimation for the next state and stated covariance depending upon the current state and state covariance. Kalman filter consists of estimation of newer state by linear equations.

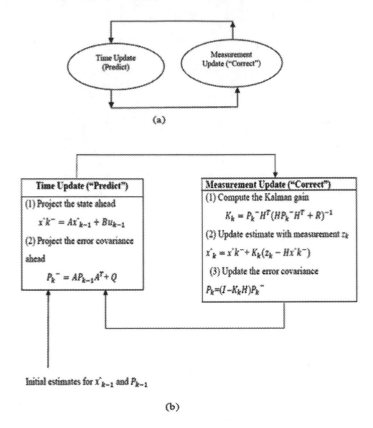

Fig. 2. Discrete kalman filter. (a) Discrete kalman filter cycle (b)Prediction and correction equations.

2. Measurement Update Equations
   Second type is measurement update. These update equations obtains the succeeding estimation for next state and error covariance. Kalman filter uses linear combination of measurement and prior estimation. Kalman filter corrects the prior estimations by measurement updates.

E Parameter measurement
   Measurement of parameters such as correct rate, precision, recall and F-measure are done after tracking objects of interest (Fig. 2).

3   System Analysis

The proposed object tracking system is implemented based on background subtraction and kalman filter algorithm by using MATLAB. Experimental results and graphs are shown in Figs. 3, 4, 5, 6 and 7. Proposed method is tested using

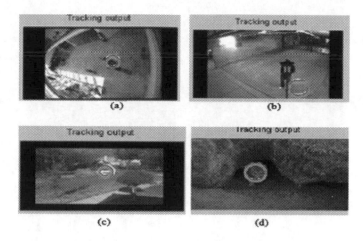

Fig. 3. Tracking output for different datasets (a) Pet walk (b) Mot walk (c) Car turn and (d) Pet animal

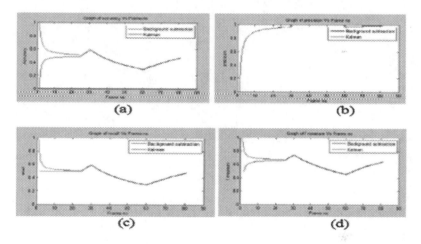

Fig. 4. Performance parameters for Pet walk (a) Accuracy (b) Precision (c) Recall and (d) F-measure

four standard databases. Occlusion handling is tested using Pet walk and Mot walk database. For complex shape handling Car turn and Pet animal database is used. Performance parameters like precision, recall, accuracy, F-measure are also calculated for these four databases. In this work object motion is tracked. Kalman filter and Background subtraction tracking is implemented. As shown in Fig. 3 standard databases taken as input video. Features of interested object are segmented. The object is tracked smoothly even though occlusion is present (Table 1).

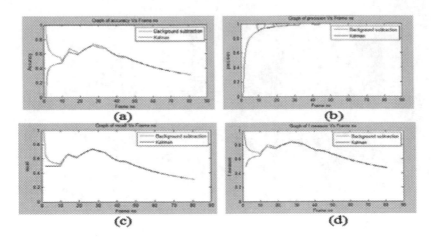

Fig. 5. Performance parameters for Mot walk (a) Accuracy (b) Precision (c) Recall and (d) F-measure

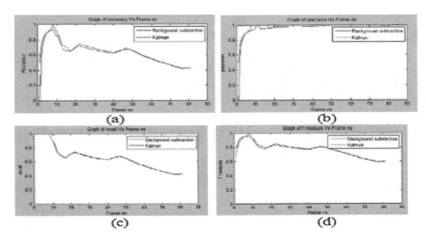

Fig. 6. Performance parameters for Car turn (a) Accuracy (b) Precision (c) Recall and (d) F-measure

Graphical representation of various performance parameters for background subtraction and kalman filter algorithm are shown in Figs. 4, 5, 6 and 7. Accuracy and Precision values of Kalman filter are good than the Background subtraction tracking method. Recall and F-Measure values of Kalman filter are improved than the Background subtraction tracking method.

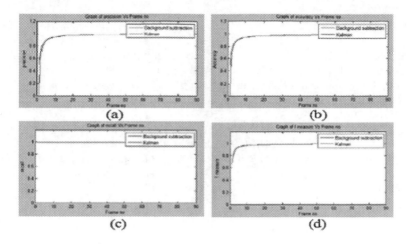

Fig. 7. Performance parameters for Pet animal (a) Accuracy (b) Precision (c) Recall and (d) F-measure

Table 1. Comparison of various performance parameters

Parameters	Mot walk		Pet walk		Car turn		Pet animal	
	Kalman filter	Back. Sub	Kalman filter	Back. Sub	Kalman filter	Back. Sub	Kalman filter	Back. Sub
Accuracy	0.74	0.7	0.61	0.6	1	0.96	0.99	0.97
Precision	1	0.97	1	0.98	1	0.98	1	0.98
Recall	0.77	0.77	0.6	0.6	0.72	0.71	1	1
F-Measure	0.83	0.82	0.77	0.76	1	0.91	1	1

4   Conclusion

This paper demonstrates the novel technique for object tracking which utilizes kalman filter algorithm and background subtraction for tracking. The framework comprises of static camera and moving item with settled foundation. The entire framework is actualized utilizing MATLAB R 2013a programming. The method efficiently handles occlusion and complex shapes for that system is tested using four standard datasets. Various performance measures are compared and analyzed between Kalman filter and Background subtraction method.

Acknowledgment. The creator might want to express her earnest on account of her cherished and regarded Guide Dr. S. K. Shah for her significant references and steady consolation. Creator appreciatively recognizes her for granting significant fundamental learning of image processing.

References

1. Chakraborty, D.B., Pal, S.K.: Neighborhood rough filter and intuitionistic entropy in unsupervised tracking. IEEE Trans. Fuzzy Syst. **26**, 2188–2200 (2017)
2. Jodoin, J.-P., Bilodeau, G.-A., Saunier, N.: Tracking all road users at multimodal urban traffic intersections. IEEE Trans. Intell. Transp. Syst. **17**(11), 3241–3251 (2016)
3. Abdelpakey, M.H., Shehata, M.S., Mohamed, M.M., Gong, M.: Adaptive framework for robust visual tracking. IEEE (2018) https://doi.org/10.1109/ACCESS.2871659
4. Iraei, I., Faez, K.: Object tracking with occlusion handling using mean shift, Kalman filter and edge histogram. In: 2nd International Conference on Pattern Recognition and Image Analysis (IPRIA 2015), 11–12 March 2015
5. Dhulekar, P.A., Hire, V.D., Agnihotri, M.S.: Moving object tracking using Kalman filter. Int. J. Adv. Found. Res. Comput.(IJAFRC) **2**(1) (2015)

A Blind Color Image Watermarking Using BRISK Features and Contourlet Transform

S. Prasanth Vaidya$^{(\boxtimes)}$

Department of Computer Science and Engineering,
Gayatri Vidya Parishad College of Engineering (A), Visakhapatnam, AP, India
vaidya269@gmail.com

Abstract. A digital blind-watermarking scheme on color images is designed using Contourlet Transform (CT) and QR-decomposition to provide authentication and Intellectual Property Rights protection. Firstly, cover color image is transformed to Luminance, Chroma blue and red components (YCbCr). Secondly, the luminance component of cover image is transformed by CT and divide the low-level sub-band to 4×4 blocks (non-overlapping). Thirdly, the blocks are decomposed using QR decomposition. Finally, watermark encrypted using Arnold transform is embedded into cover image with adaptively calculated embedding factor values using Binary Robust Invariant Scalable Key-points features. In blind-watermarking extraction, the watermark is extracted without cover image from distorted watermarked images. Simulation results demonstrate that the designed digital blind-watermarking method has high invisibility and strong robustness from different attacks (image and signal processing). The proposed scheme has good results in comparison with related methods.

Keywords: Digital watermarking ·
Binary Robust Invariant Scalable Key-points features ·
Arnold transform · Contourlet transform · QR decomposition

1 Introduction

In recent times, digital data is being transferred with ease. Digital devices provide lot of applications to share, capture and store the digital data. Protection of digital data from intruders is the most challenging task. To safeguard authority and authenticity, watermarking is the best approach where significant information is incorporated within the data. Digital watermarking is done on digital multimedia data (text, audio, image & video) [1]. Image watermarking plays a vital role in protecting intellectual property rights (IPR). Watermark is embedded imperceptibly into digital image without affecting image quality by considering copyright data as watermark. To verify rightful owner of the content, the

© Springer Nature Singapore Pte Ltd. 2019
K. C. Santosh and R. S. Hegadi (Eds.): RTIP2R 2018, CCIS 1035, pp. 203–215, 2019.
https://doi.org/10.1007/978-981-13-9181-1_19

embedded watermark is extracted [2]. The watermarking system should exhibit robustness, imperceptibility, security and fidelity properties.

Digital watermarking methods are roughly divided into spatial and frequency domains where watermarking scheme is carried out. Least-significant-bit substitution and additive watermarking are the techniques in spatial domain. Discrete Fourier Transform (DFT), Discrete Wavelet Transform (DWT) and CT are examples of transformation methods. The adversaries try to destroy the watermark with different attacks of image processing like noise attacks, cropping, JPEG compression, filtering attacks, rotation and scaling [3]. In protecting the watermark from adversaries, robust digital watermarking schemes are designed and are utilized for authenticity and copyright protection [4,5].

In [6], permuted binary watermark is embedded using hybrid-fuzzy back-propagation network. In this scheme, basic characteristics of the HVS model are utilized. In [7], watermarking scheme is implemented in wavelet domain. Amiri et al. [8] designed a visual cryptography based watermarking approach by applying DWT, singular value decomposition and Scale Invariant Feature Transform (SIFT). Amsaveni et al. [9] proposed a data hiding scheme which is reversible on images using error expansion of Gaussian weight. Using singular values of every band in IWT domain, watermark is embedded. Optimization of embedding strength is done using Artificial Bee Colony [10]. Cedillo-Hernandez et al. [11] designed an object-based system in watermarking by embedding watermark into middle-frequency band of DFT. The embedding region is selected with speeded-up robust features. Ishtiaq et al. [12] considered both strength of watermark and selection of region as optimization issues, and solved them by utilizing particle swarm optimization and genetic algorithm. Nikolaidis et al. [13] proposed a method for region-based watermarking system. After performing normalization using image moments, a set of features is extracted from normalized image which acts as a center for embedding the watermark. SIFT feature detection is used while extracting. Embedding is processed by changing singular characters of implication image utilizing singular characters of watermark. Shen et al. [14] embedded dual watermarks with pseudo-random sequence based bit substitution method. In [15], utilizing Bhattacharyya distance metric and exponential function, a robust blind watermarking scheme is designed. In [16], semi-blind watermarking system is designed with multiple decompositions. The host image is subjected to DWT-CT-Schur-SVD in series to embed the watermark. Prasanth Vaidya et al. [17] proposed an adaptive invisible watermarking system in wavelet domain using Bhattacharyya distance and kurtosis.

Several watermarking schemes are designed in protecting copyright and identifying the owner using image features and transformation techniques where the robustness is limited, and also calculation of embedding factor is non-adaptive in nature. To overcome the limitations of the aforementioned watermarking schemes, an adaptive blind watermarking method is proposed to protect copyright of digital images. Compared to [17] and other methods in literature, the proposed method is blind in nature where cover image is not required during watermark extraction. The cover image is transferred to a suitable color space and good features are considered for calculating embedding factor. The optimal factor values are calculated with the help of BRISK features for each image separately. For embedding watermark, all the 4×4 non-overlapping blocks of low-level sub-band are selected to provide imperceptibility. For embedding watermark bits, relation between the elements of Q matrix are considered. To provide security to digital watermark, Arnold transform is applied to scramble the image. Efficacy of proposed method can be observed from the performance evaluation results and comparison results.

The rest of the paper is organized as follows. The preliminaries of the related methods were discussed in Sect. 2. In Sect. 3, the process of proposed embedding and extraction of watermark schemes are discussed. Simulation results and comparative analysis is presented in Sect. 4. Finally, Sect. 5 concludes the paper.

2   Preliminaries

2.1   Contourlet Transform

Minh Do and Martin Vetterli introduced contourlet transform [18]. It is an efficient multi-resolution directional transform used to represent 2D signals and produce curves and smooth contours efficiently. Construction of CT is done in two stages. In the first stage, image in multi-scale is decomposed using Laplacian Pyramid (LP) to capture point singularity. In the second stage, Directional Filter Bank (DFB) is utilized by gathering singular points that are scattered in uniform direction [19].

2.2   Binary Robust Invariant Scalable Key-points (BRISK)

BRISK is a new scheme in detecting, description and coordinating key-points. In the state of art algorithms, BRISK attains adaptivity, high performance and also low computational cost [20]. The steps involved in extracting BRISK features are

- Detection of scale-space key-point
- Description of Key-point.

Brisk Points=5   Brisk Points=10   Brisk Points=20   Total Brisk Points

Fig. 1. Brisk key-points detection for luminance Lena image.

Detection of Scale-Space Key-Point. The scale space pyramid has n octaves and intra-octaves (c_i, d_i) respectively, where i $= [0 \ldots n - 1]$. In a typical framework, the number of octaves $= 4$. The original image is progressively half-sampled to form octaves. The original image is taken as first octave and labeled as c_0. The intra-octaves are formed between two consecutive octaves. The first intra-octave is formed by down sampling c_0 by a factor of 1.5 and the rest of the intra-octaves are formed by successive half sampling. Formation of octaves and intra-octaves is followed by computation of features from accelerated segment test score. The score is computed for every pixel such that it represents maximum threshold by considering each image point as a corner.

Description of Key-Point. Detection of key-points are done in octave and intra-octave layers of image pyramid. The location and scale values are obtained using quadratic function fitting in continuous domain. The key points detected are described in scaled concentric circles. The pixel pairs are classified as short & long distance pairs. A local gradient is computed for long-distance pair of pixels. The gradients obtained are summed to determine the orientation. The short distance pair of pixels are rotated using acquired orientation. Finally, BRISK descriptor is obtained from short distance pair of pixels [21]. The strongest or topmost $5, 10, 20$ and total BRISK feature points for luminance Lena image are shown in Fig. 1.

2.3   QR Decomposition

QR decomposition is an orthogonal-triangular decomposition [22,23], and its decomposition for a matrix A is given as follows.

$$[D]_{i \times j} = [Q]_{i \times i}[R]_{i \times j} \tag{1}$$

where Q $=$ unitary matrix and the matrix column space for D is formed using columns of Q and R is right triangular matrix. Gram-Schmidt orthogonalization procedure is utilized in obtaining Q columns [24]. The computational complexity of QR decomposition is less than SVD by $\mathcal{O}(2n^3/3)$.

From the decomposition, special feature of orthogonal matrix Q can be observed where all the values in Q matrix first column are closer. To improve imperceptibility of watermark, it is embedded in Q matrix first column. The elements of first column are chosen based on the correlation between them.

3   The Proposed Blind-Watermarking Method

Watermark embedding and watermark extraction steps are discussed in this section.

3.1   Key Estimation

Using the strongest BRISK features, an underlying bounding box is created. The region obtained by BRISK features for luminance component of host images is considered as saliency map. Using Eigen values of the saliency map, threshold value (α) is computed to minimize the intra-class variance using Eq. (2).

$$\alpha = \mu\,(M) + \sigma\,(M) \tag{2}$$

where M is Eigen value matrix of the saliency map, μ & σ are mean and variance.

3.2   Process of Watermark Embedding

The process of watermark embedding method is explained in the following steps. The watermark embedding process shown in Fig. 2

Step 1: Binary watermark W is scrambled to W^A by using Arnold transform (AT)/Cat Face transfer for k_A times. Using Eq. (3), AT is applied on W by producing scrambled watermark image.

$$\begin{pmatrix} p' \\ q' \end{pmatrix} = \begin{pmatrix} 1 & 1 \\ 1 & 2 \end{pmatrix} \begin{pmatrix} p \\ q \end{pmatrix} (modO) \tag{3}$$

where (p, q) and (p', q') are pixels of original watermark and per-mutated watermark images, O is order of the watermark. From the periodic nature of Arnold transform, the number of permutations is consider as key k_A (A = 16) to enhance the security.

Step 2: The RGB host image I is converted into YCbCr.

Step 3: Y (luminance component) is transformed by one-level using CT.

Step 4: Low-frequency sub-band is selected and decomposed into 4×4 blocks(non-overlapping). By embedding watermark in low-frequency sub-band, designed watermarking method robustness can be improved.

Step 5: All the non-overlapping blocks are considered for embedding watermark in order to improve imperceptibility. All the divided blocked are decomposed using Eq. (1) to obtain orthogonal Q matrix.

Step 6: By using Eq. (4), watermark is embedded into the blocks. The $\{q_5, q_9\}$ elements of Q (orthogonal matrix) is modified as $\{q_5', q_9'\}$.

$$\left. \begin{array}{l} \text{If } W^A = 1, \\ \qquad q_5' = sign(q_5) \times (Q_{avg} + \alpha) \\ \qquad q_9' = sign(q_9) \times (Q_{avg} - \alpha) \\ \text{else} \\ \text{If } W^A = 0, \\ \qquad q_5' = sign(q_5) \times (Q_{avg} - \alpha) \\ \qquad q_9' = sign(q_9) \times (Q_{avg} + \alpha) \end{array} \right\} \tag{4}$$

where W^A is scrambled watermark bit and $Q_{avg} = \frac{|q_5| + |q_9|}{2}$.

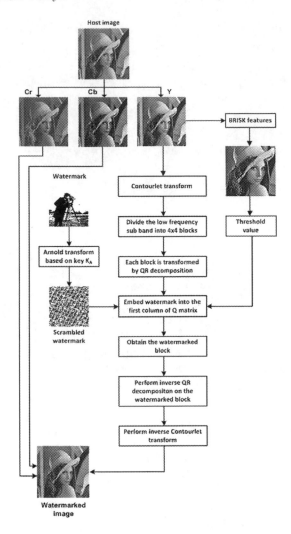

Fig. 2. Watermark embedding using CT, QR & BRISK features

From this step, it can be observed that only q_5 and q_9 elements are modified since the correlation between q_5 and q_9 is high when compared to other elements [15, 25].

Step 7: Using Eq. (5), inverse QR decomposition is applied to obtain watermarked image block (A^*).

$$[D^*]_{i\times j} = [Q^*]_{i\times j}[R]_{i\times j} \tag{5}$$

Step 8: Apply one-level inverse CT on A^*, to obtain luminance watermarked image (Y^*).

Step 9: Y^* is combined with CbCr by producing watermarked color image (I^*).

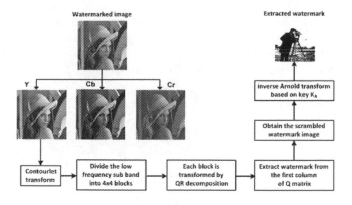

Fig. 3. Blind watermark extraction using CT, QR & BRISK features

3.3   Process of Blind-Watermark Extraction

Blind watermark extraction procedure is shown in Fig. 3. The cover image & W are not required since the extraction process is blind. The step by step process of extraction is as follows:

Step 1: The distorted watermarked image I^{**} is decomposed into YCbCr components.

Step 2: Y^{**} (luminance component) of I^{**} is transformed by one-level CT.

Fig. 4. Sample cover images: (a) bridge, (b) boat, (c) girl, (d) lake, (e) couple, (f) Lena, (g) mandrill, (h) peppers, (i) airplane, (j) monarch, (k) woman and watermark

Step 3: As the watermark is embedded in low-frequency sub-band, it is selected and decomposed into 4×4 blocks (non-overlapping).

Step 4: All the non-overlapping blocks are considered for watermark extraction. All the blocks are decomposed by QR using Eq. (1) to get watermarked orthogonal Q matrix.

Step 5: Using Eq. (6), scrambled watermark W^{A*} is extracted from orthogonal Q matrix.

$$w^{A*} = \begin{cases} 0, & if(q_5' > q_9') \\ 1, & if(q_5' \leq q_9') \end{cases} \tag{6}$$

Step 6: The extracted scrambled watermark W^{A*} is inversely scrambled by using inverse AT to obtain final watermark W^*.

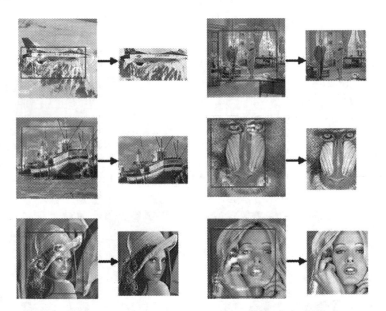

Fig. 5. Sample images with BRISK-key points selection and its saliency map

Fig. 6. Sample watermarked images

4 Simulation Results and Analysis

Proposed watermarking method performance is tested based on watermark invisibility & robustness. In the proposed scheme, images (color) of size $512 \times 512 \times 3$ are used as host images and "cameraman" (watermark) of size 64×64. Sample cover color images and watermark are demonstrated in Fig. 4 respectively. For calculating embedding factor value adaptively, BRISK features of host luminance image are utilized. The strongest or topmost 20 feature points are considered to form a polygon region/saliency map. The BRISK-key points and saliency map for sample luminance component images are demonstrated in Fig. 5, watermarked color images in Fig. 6. Proposed watermarking method performance is analyzed based on PSNR (Peak Signal to Noise Ratio) and NCC (Normalized Correlation Coefficient) values.

Table 1. Correlation between cover image and watermarked image with PSNR values on varied attacks

Images/ Attacks	Without attack	S&P noise	Gaussian noise	Cropping	Rotation	Scaling	Translation	Mean filtering	Median filtering	Blurring	JPEG compression
Bridge	35.63	18.08	13.73	33.25	32.03	29.73	32.31	27.29	24.12	24.47	22.55
Boat	38.20	17.78	14.09	36.32	34.55	34.04	34.78	25.21	29.75	32.16	25.80
Girl	39.41	18.34	13.56	36.00	34.79	32.26	35.00	27.40	26.54	27.09	23.63
Lake	39.04	18.37	13.60	38.69	37.37	33.59	37.60	27.53	28.05	28.26	27.30
Couple	35.95	17.92	13.97	34.21	33.34	32.45	33.67	26.95	28.39	29.38	24.41
Lena	41.35	18.37	13.64	39.63	37.69	34.44	37.93	28.12	28.49	28.89	25.60
Mandrill	35.79	18.39	13.55	34.89	34.15	31.72	34.38	27.72	25.97	26.60	23.91
Peppers	34.62	18.32	13.47	31.02	31.02	28.80	31.44	26.39	22.81	23.20	21.73
Airplane	39.49	18.19	13.73	37.63	36.85	35.47	37.36	28.07	30.78	33.40	27.40
Monarch	39.18	18.24	13.66	36.21	35.55	32.78	35.82	28.44	27.06	27.52	24.68
Woman	40.89	18.44	13.55	37.37	36.26	32.93	36.48	27.45	26.88	27.34	24.86

Table 2. Correlation between watermark and extracted watermark with NCC values on varied attacks

Images/ Attacks	Without attack	S&P noise	Gaussian noise	Cropping	Rotation	Scaling	Translation	Mean filtering	Median filtering	Blurring	JPEG compression
Bridge	1.00	0.9772	0.9585	0.9243	0.7573	0.9939	0.8206	0.9896	0.9736	0.9576	0.9969
Boat	1.00	0.9995	0.9995	0.9296	0.7945	0.9918	0.8571	0.9877	0.9700	0.9589	0.9957
Girl	1.00	0.9875	0.9846	0.9294	0.7119	0.9993	0.8620	0.9895	0.9772	0.9557	0.9989
Lake	1.00	0.9989	0.9961	0.9296	0.7019	0.9941	0.8502	0.9895	0.9725	0.9595	0.9997
Couple	1.00	0.9857	0.9659	0.9284	0.7502	0.9982	0.8240	0.9874	0.9744	0.9533	0.9989
Lena	1.00	0.9920	0.9804	0.9296	0.7002	0.9991	0.8559	0.9893	0.9782	0.9580	0.9993
Mandril	1.00	0.9890	0.9800	0.9263	0.7211	0.9967	0.8801	0.9863	0.9733	0.9503	0.9978
Peppers	1.00	0.9954	0.9918	0.9273	0.7402	0.9980	0.8064	0.9876	0.9769	0.9572	0.9995
Airplane	1.00	0.9837	0.9727	0.9284	0.7121	0.9984	0.8683	0.9889	0.9765	0.9574	0.9982
Monarch	1.00	0.9866	0.9692	0.9280	0.7189	0.9987	0.8664	0.9884	0.9759	0.9535	0.9980
Woman	1.00	0.9976	0.9952	0.9280	0.7977	0.9978	0.8586	0.9876	0.9761	0.9569	0.9991

PSNR metric is utilized to measure objective closeness between I^* & I. PSNR is determined by MSE (Mean Square Error) [26], is shown in Eqs. (7) and (8).

$$MeanSquareError = \frac{\sum_{i=0}^{m-1}\sum_{j=0}^{n-1}\left(I_{i,j} - I_{i,j}^*\right)^2}{mn} \tag{7}$$

$$PeakSignaltoNoiseRatio = 20\log_{10}\left(\frac{MAX_I}{\sqrt{MSE}}\right) \tag{8}$$

where $I_{i,j}$, $I_{i,j}^*$ symbolize pixel values (i, j) of I^* & I, and m, n denote width and height of the images. MAX_I is maximum feasible pixel value.

NCC metric is used to measure robustness of watermark and is estimated between W (original watermark) & W^* (extracted watermark), and is given in Eq. (9). The NCC values adjacent to 1 implies that W^* is similar to W i.e., $W = W^*$ [27].

$$NCC = \frac{\sum_{i=1}^{m}\sum_{j=1}^{n}W(i,j)\times W^*(i,j)}{(\sqrt{\sum_{i=1}^{m}W(i,j)^2})(\sqrt{\sum_{i=1}^{m}W^*(i,j)^2})} \tag{9}$$

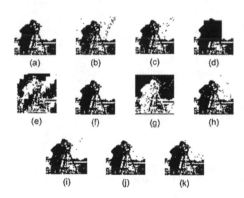

Fig. 7. Watermarks extracted (a) Without attack, (b) Salt and Pepper noise, (c) Gaussian noise, (d) Cropping, (e) Rotation, (f) Scaling, (g) Translate, (h) Mean filter, (i) Median filter, (j) Blurring, and (k) JPEG compression

4.1 Imperceptibility

In this scheme, watermark (binary) is embedded into color images with adaptively calculated embedding factor values. PSNR is utilized to analyze image imperceptibility and quality. Table 1 lists the PSNR values of sample watermarked images with different attacks.

Table 3. Correlation between proposed method and other methods with PSNR values in no attacks

Cover images	Lena	Mandrill	Peppers
Schemes	Prasanth Vaidya et al. [17]	Prasanth Vaidya et al. [17]	Prasanth Vaidya et al. [17]
	Agoyi et al. [7]	Agoyi et al. [7]	Agoyi et al. [7]
	Proposed method	Proposed method	Proposed method
PSNR	35.11	33.67	22.73
	29.41	28.97	34.25
	41.35	35.79	34.62

Table 4. Correlation between proposed method and other methods with NCC values

Cover images	Methods\Attacks	No attack	S&P noise	Gaussian noise	Cropping	Scaling	Blurring	JPEG (90)
Lena	Prasanth Vaidya et al. [17]	1.00	0.8458	0.8489	0.8944	0.9827	0.8732	0.9053
	Agoyi et al. [7]	0.8694	-	0.7955	-	0.9263	0.5471	0.8469
	Proposed Method	1.00	0.9920	0.9804	0.9296	0.9991	0.9580	0.9993
Mandrill	Prasanth Vaidya et al. [17]	1.00	0.7156	0.8053	0.8946	0.9956	0.8625	0.8983
	Agoyi et al. [7]	0.8837	-	0.7796	-	0.7675	0.3535	0.8469
	Proposed Method	1.00	0.9890	0.9800	0.9263	0.9967	0.9503	0.9978
Peppers	Prasanth Vaidya et al. [17]	1.00	0.9465	0.9279	0.8942	0.9980	0.8738	0.8818
	Agoyi et al. [7]	0.9030	-	0.8083	-	0.9644	0.7666	0.8901
	Proposed Method	1.00	0.9800	0.9918	0.9273	0.9980	0.9572	0.9978

4.2 Proposed Method Robustness

In watermarking, images are generally attacked by noising, cropping, rotating, scaling, translating, filtering and compressing. Table 2 provides correlation between watermark and extracted watermark with various attacks. Salt & Pepper noise is added with 0.01 density, Gaussian noise with zero mean and variance 1. Cropping by 30%, scaling to 0.25 and translate (5.3, 10.1) XY-direction. The mean and median filters are used on watermarked images with window size 3×3 and compression (JPEG-90).

The scheme is correlated with watermarking methods Prasanth Vaidya et al. [17] and Agoyi et al. [7] respectively. Tables 3 and 4 gives the comparison results & Fig. 7 shows the extracted watermarks after different attacks.

4.3 Imperceptibility and Robustness Analysis

Proposed method PSNR values are high in Table 1 because only two elements of orthogonal Q matrix are modified. Correlation between proposed method and other methods are given in Table 3 with different attacks. From the NCC values of Tables 2 and 4, the proposed watermarking scheme has high robustness. The proposed scheme is having better robustness for various attacks since embedding of watermark is done in lower sub-band of CT adaptively.

5   Conclusion

A robust, blind-color image watermarking method with contourlet transform and QR decomposition is designed to protect IPR and ownership identification. Watermark encrypted with Arnold transform is embedded in orthogonal Q matrix. For calculating embedding factor adaptively, BRISK features are utilized. Simulation results prove that the proposed blind watermarking scheme achieves robustness, imperceptibility and security, and has overcome attacks of image and signal processing. In correlation with other watermarking schemes, the proposed scheme is highly robust with good imperceptibility.

References

1. Tsougenis, E., Papakostas, G.A., Koulouriotis, D.E., Karakasis, E.G.: Adaptive color image watermarking by the use of quaternion image moments. Expert Syst. Appl. **41**(14), 6408–6418 (2014)
2. Wang, X., Liu, Y., Li, S., Yang, H., Niu, P.: Robust image watermarking approach using polar harmonic transforms based geometric correction. Neurocomputing **174**, 627–642 (2016)
3. Wang, S., Lou, D., Jeng, D., Yeh, C.: Rotation, scaling and translation resilient digital image watermarking using log-polar mapping. Imaging Sci. J. **57**(4), 177–190 (2009)
4. Liaoa, K., Leea, W., Liaob, C.: Security of fragile watermarking scheme for image authentication. Imaging Sci. J. **54**(3), 129–133 (2006)
5. Prasanth Vaidya, S., Chandra Mouli, P.V.S.S.R., Santosh, K.C.: Imperceptible watermark for a game-theoretic watermarking system. Int. J. Mach. Learn. Cybern. **10**, 1323–1339 (2018)
6. Agarwal, C., Mishra, A., Sharma, A.: A novel gray-scale image watermarking using hybrid Fuzzy-BPN architecture. Egypt. Inf. J. **16**(1), 83–102 (2015)
7. Agoyi, M., Çelebi, E., Anbarjafari, G.: A watermarking algorithm based on chirp z-transform, discrete wavelet transform, and singular value decomposition. Signal Image Video Process. **9**(3), 735–745 (2015)
8. Amiri, T., Moghaddam, M.E.: A new visual cryptography based watermarking scheme using DWT and SIFT for multiple cover images. Multimedia Tools Appl. **75**(14), 8527–8543 (2016)
9. Amsaveni, A., Vanathi, P.: An efficient reversible data hiding approach for colour images based on Gaussian weighted prediction error expansion and genetic algorithm. Int. J. Adv. Intell. Paradig. **7**(2), 156–171 (2015)
10. Ansari, I.A., Pant, M., Ahn, C.W.: Secured and optimized robust image watermarking scheme. Arab. J. Sci. Eng. 1–20 (2017)
11. Cedillo-Hernandez, M., Garcia-Ugalde, F., Nakano-Miyatake, M., Perez-Meana, H.: Robust object-based watermarking using SURF feature matching and DFT domain. Radioengineering **22**(4), 1057–1071 (2013)
12. Ishtiaq, M., Jaffar, M., Choi, T.S.: Optimal sub-band and strength selection for blind watermarking in wavelet domain. Imaging Sci. J. **62**(3), 171–177 (2014)
13. Nikolaidis, A.: Local distortion resistant image watermarking relying on salient feature extraction. EURASIP J. Adv. Signal Process. **2012**(1), 97 (2012)
14. Shen, H., Chen, B.: From single watermark to dual watermark: a new approach for image watermarking. Comput. Electr. Eng. **38**(5), 1310–1324 (2012)

15. Prasanth Vaidya, S., Chandra Mouli, P.V.S.S.R.: Adaptive, robust and blind digital watermarking using Bhattacharyya distance and bit manipulation. Multimedia Tools Appl. 1–27 (2017)

16. Prasanth Vaidya, S., Chandra Mouli, P.V.S.S.R.: A robust semi-blind watermarking for color images based on multiple decompositions. Multimedia Tools Appl. 1–34 (2017)

17. Prasanth Vaidya, S., Chandra Mouli, P.V.S.S.R.: Adaptive digital watermarking for copyright protection of digital images in wavelet domain. Procedia Comput. Sci. 58, 233–240 (2015)

18. Do, M.N., Vetterli, M.: The contourlet transform: an efficient directional multiresolution image representation. IEEE Trans. Image Process. 14(12), 2091–2106 (2005)

19. Su, Q., Wang, G., Lv, G., Zhang, X., Deng, G., Chen, B.: A novel blind color image watermarking based on Contourlet transform and Hessenberg decomposition. Multimedia Tools Appl. 76(6), 8781–8801 (2017)

20. Leutenegger, S., Chli, M., Siegwart, R.Y.: BRISK: binary robust invariant scalable keypoints. In: 2011 IEEE International Conference on Computer Vision (ICCV), pp. 2548–2555. IEEE (2011)

21. Calonder, M., Lepetit, V., Strecha, C., Fua, P.: BRIEF: binary robust independent elementary features. In: Daniilidis, K., Maragos, P., Paragios, N. (eds.) ECCV 2010. LNCS, vol. 6314, pp. 778–792. Springer, Heidelberg (2010). https://doi.org/10.1007/978-3-642-15561-1_56

22. De Moor, B., Van Dooren, P.: Generalizations of the singular value and QR-decompositions. SIAM J. Matrix Anal. Appl. 13(4), 993–1014 (1992)

23. Su, Q., Niu, Y., Wang, G., Jia, S., Yue, J.: Color image blind watermarking scheme based on QR decomposition. Signal Process. 94, 219–235 (2014)

24. Mehta, R., Rajpal, N., Vishwakarma, V.P.: LWT-QR decomposition based robust and efficient image watermarking scheme using lagrangian SVR. Multimedia Tools Appl. 75(7), 4129–4150 (2016)

25. Su, Q., Niu, Y., Zhao, Y., Pang, S., Liu, X.: A dual color images watermarking scheme based on the optimized compensation of singular value decomposition. AEU-Int. J. Electron. Commun. 67(8), 652–664 (2013)

26. Huynh-Thu, Q., Ghanbari, M.: Scope of validity of PSNR in image/video quality assessment. Electron. Lett. 44(13), 800–801 (2008)

27. Campbell, J.Y., Lo, A.W.C., MacKinlay, A.C., et al.: The Econometrics of Financial Markets, vol. 2. Princeton University Press, Princeton (1997)

Gray Level Face Recognition Using Spatial Features

Md. Fawwad Hussain, Haidong Wang, and K. C. Santosh[✉]

Department of Computer Science, The University of South Dakota,
414 E Clark St., Vermillion, SD 57069, USA
santosh.kc@ieee.org

Abstract. Face recognition has always been an active research area with several applications, such as security access control, human-machine interface and gender classification. More often, in real world, grayscale images have been used: video surveillance, for instance. Further, difficulties in face recognition could be due to face poses, orientation, lighting, aging etc. Faces, either in color or grayscale and are having any difficulties (as mentioned earlier) can be learned through edge map and texture, where spatial properties could be learned. Inspired from the fact that face can be considered as line-rich pattern/object, we propose novel face recognition framework that helps learn/recognize via spatial arrangements of edges (and textures as complement). To exploit edge map, we use shape context (SC) and pyramid histogram of orientated gradient (PHOG), and similarly GIST as texture features. Experimental tests (on four different publicly available datasets, such as Caltech, ColorFERET, IndianFaces and ORL) conforms that spatial features are crucial in face representation and recognition.

Keywords: Gray level images · Spatial features · Shape context ·
Pyramid histogram of oriented gradients · Gist · Biometrics ·
Face recognition

1 Introduction

Automated face recognition system turns out to be one of the most successful applications in image processing, pattern recognition, and computer vision. There are many reasons for the growing demand in face recognition system that include rising concerns for public security, identity verification in high-security areas, face analysis and modeling techniques in digital entertainment. Research for face recognition started in 1960, and there has been a remarkable success in this area. Many face detection and recognition systems have been developed and a number of algorithms have been designed so far by various research scientists in different domains but still, there is a number of challenges present in making an accurate and a robust face detection and recognition system in real-world environments. For many applications, the performance of face recognition systems in controlled environments has now reached a satisfactory level, but there

K. C. Santosh and R. S. Hegadi (Eds.): RTIP2R 2018, CCIS 1035, pp. 216–229, 2019.
https://doi.org/10.1007/978-981-13-9181-1_20

are still many challenges presents when dealing with uncontrolled environments. Some of the challenges are caused by variations in illumination, face pose, expression, and etc. It's a true challenge to build an automated system which equals the human ability to recognize faces. Humans can recognize faces, but too many faces sometimes being hard to get. Now, machine learning is now being improved a lot to do this crucial task. The ability to make the machine thinks like humans and recognize faces in a limited amount of time and memory is the must.

1.1   Problems

Face pose is a specifically difficult problem in this aspect simply because all faces seem similar; specifically, all faces consist of two eyes, mouth, nose, and other features that are in the same location. As human face is a dynamic object having the high degree of variability in its appearance. Most face images captured by surveillance systems are non-ideal because they are often affected by many factors such as pose, illumination, expression, occlusion, distance, weather and so on. The human face is not a unique rigid object and each of the faces have a variety of deformations. Human face varies from person to person. The gender, age, emotions, expressions and other physical characteristics have to be taken into account thereby creating a challenge for the research scientist in computer vision.

1.2   Goal

The primary goal of our research is to build an automated face recognition systems that are fast, robust, accurate, with less computational overheads, relatively simple algorithms and techniques that would be easy to understand and to implement it on a large programmable system. To achieve higher efficiency in terms of storage and computation, grayscale images are used. The primary reasons behind the use of grayscale images can be summarized as follows:

(a) Many commercial applications used to process grayscale images because of its low computational complexities and overheads.
(b) Many Cameras in high-alert zones used grayscale images for different identification and verification. It is relatively easier to deal with (in terms of storage) a single color channel (shades of white/black) than color channels.
(c) An application like object detection would barely require information at the edges of an image, which can as well be obtained in gray scale images (also can be obtained in color images, at an expense of complexity).

1.3   Contributions

Following the importance of the spatial features, three different features are used.

(a) We start with the hape context (SC) is used to compute the shape similarity based on the features points extracted from internal or external contours of face image [5]. The technique is based on the low level (edge-based) representation of an image. Edge map can give us a better understanding of the human face features and covers all aspects of human face recognition. The approach is invariant to rotation and scale and consumes very low memory requirement.

(b) We also employ an extremely rich global shape descriptor which has information from all over the shape in terms of histogram of edge orientations and spatial distribution of edges [6]. The approach is insensitive to small deformations and consumes low memory requirements as well.

(c) Another idea based on the spatial layout is given by Oliva and Torralba [19]. The approach is based on the low level representation of the shape called the spatial envelope. The descriptor encodes the information based on the spatial frequencies and orientations that contains enough information to identify the shape.

2   Related Works

2.1   Context

Many different approaches and techniques have been developed so far in the field of face matching and recognition for the reliable and efficient system. These techniques use different methods such as the appearance based method and model-based methods. Recent work in face matching uses appearance-based approach for fast and robust face recognition system where the image is considered as a high-dimensional vector. Modern appearance-based recognition system needs a rich descriptor for shape matching. Some descriptors use all image information as a fact that all pixels in the image are equally important which leads to high computational complexities and requires a high degree of correlation between the probe and gallery images. Such descriptors contain high inconsistencies and variations in pose, scale, and illuminations.

2.2   Relevant Publications

Some descriptors use non-dense image information such as edges or various key spots for feature matching. They can handle small deformations and variations in pose, scale, orientation as well. Recent work by Candemir et al. [8] (inspired from previous work [20]) which uses a hybrid technique by processing descriptors that includes features from both categories. They present a rotation-and-scale-invariant, line-based color-aware (RSILC) descriptor which allows matching of objects in terms of their key-lines, line-region properties, and line spatial arrangements. This general purpose descriptor is color-aware, invariant to rotation/scale and is robust to illumination changes.

Another well known local key point descriptor scale invariant feature transform (SIFT) [18] is one of the most robust key-points descriptors among local feature descriptor. It first detects a number of key points in the images and then computes a local descriptor for each point. Recognition can be performed by matching each key point descriptor in the test image against the descriptor extracted from all images in the database. SIFT key point detector and descriptor have shown remarkable success in a number of applications including object recognition, face recognition, image stitching etc. But it contains a huge computational burden for real-time systems. Later, they introduced a new variant of SIFT that is color SIFT (CSIFT) [1] which also takes color information into the account. The color invariant SIFT is more robust as compared to conventional SIFT but still, it is not rotation and scale invariant. Based on the SIFT algorithm, Liu et al. [17] propose a novel method SIFT flow to align an image to its nearest neighbors in a database. The SIFT flow algorithm consists of matching densely sampled, pixel-wise SIFT features between two images, while preserving spatial discontinuities. Another well-known interest point detector and descriptor is speeded up robust features (SURF) [4] which outperforms another state of the art descriptor due to its robustness and distinctiveness. The computed descriptor is also rotation and scale invariant and provides a quicker way to detect key points. It has been successfully used in many object and shape matching application including face matching. Analyzing the importance of SURF as a local descriptor, Dreuw et al. [12] proposed an approach of using SURF algorithm to face recognition problem.

Local binary pattern (LBP) [2], which is originally introduced for texture representation, has proved to be a powerful descriptor for face recognition. This new approach considered both shape and texture information of face image. The face area is first divided into small regions from which Local Binary Pattern (LBP) histograms are extracted and concatenated into a single feature histogram, spatially enhanced feature histogram efficiently representing the face image. The similarity of images can be compared by measuring the distance between their histograms. Research shows that face recognition using the LBP method provides remarkable results, both in terms of speed and discrimination performance. This technique seems to be quite robust against face images with different facial expressions, different lighting conditions, image rotation and aging of persons.

As the human recognize line drawings well, the machine can also. Gao et al. [14] describe a novel descriptor for face recognition using line edge map (LEM) which extracts features line segment from a face edge map. This approach is robust and efficient in retrieval capability as compared to Eigenface [21]. Deboeverie et al. [10] proposed an approach in which faces are represented as curve edge maps. CEM describes polynomial segments with a convex region in an edge map. With these concepts in mind, in this paper, for gray level face verification we follow the works by Belongie [5], Bosch et al. [6] and Oliva and Torralba [19]. Serge Belongie [5] presents a novel approach for measuring the similarity between shapes for object recognition. The key-points descriptor also contains global spatial relationship of other key-point descriptors relative to it. The shape context descriptor is tolerant to all common shape deformations. This novel approach is widely used in many shape matching applications. Besides, the work by Bosch et al. [6] who proposed a novel descriptor based on histogram of oriented gradients

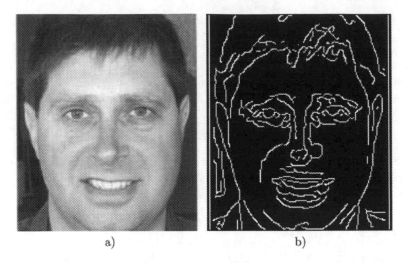

a)   b)

Fig. 1. Output images from edge detection algorithm: (a) Input Image; and (b) Edge based representation using Canny.

called the pyramid histogram of orientation gradients (PHOG). This descriptor represents an image by its local shape and the spatial layout of shape information. The local shape is represented by a histogram of edge orientations. The spatial layout is represented by tiling the image into regions at multiple resolutions. These are designed so that the shape correspondence between two images can be measured by the distance between their descriptor. The descriptor is rotation dependent and color blind. Oliva and Torralba [19] proposed a method that represents an image in a low dimension space that contains enough information to identify the scene, which also bypasses the segmentation and processing of individual objects or regions. That low-level representation of the scene is called spatial envelope. They define the features that separate a scene from the rest. It was mainly used for scene recognition.

3   Spatial Features for Face Representation and Recognition

3.1   Shape Context (SC)

The central idea behind this approach came from the point of how to compute shape similarity and find the difference between two shapes so that category-level recognition is possible.

The SC [5] has been useful in measuring the similarity between the studied shapes by recovering from point correspondences and exploiting it for shape-based object recognition. In general, the shape context at a point captures the distribution over relative positions of other shape points and thus summarizes global shape information in a rich local descriptor. Inspired from the work [8],

Fig. 2. Example of the original sampled points (that was set to 400) from two face shapes belonging to the same person with varying light and expression. Feature points representing in blue and red refer to two different faces. (Color figure online)

where line-rich object, i.e. face has been used, in this study, we used Canny edge detection algorithm (an industrial standard tool) to produce possible edge map (as shown in Fig. 1). With the edge map, the shape now can be sampled into a set of N feature points. To reduce the computational complexity, we have roughly uniform spacing to 400 feature points (see Fig. 2).

The shape context descriptor is now computed for each sample point (follow Fig. 2) that will describe the coarse arrangement of the rest of the shape with respect to the point. For any point p_i on the shape, the coarse histogram of the relative coordinates of the remaining $n - 1$ points,

$$h_i(k) = \#\{q \neq p_i \quad : \quad (q - p_i) \in bin(k)\}.$$

The above equation is considered to be the shape context of p_i. We used a log-polar coordinate system that has 12 equally spaced angle bins and 5 equally placed log-radius bins. Figure 3 shows an example of it. For matching two different face shapes, we follow the exact same procedure as mentioned in the original work [5].

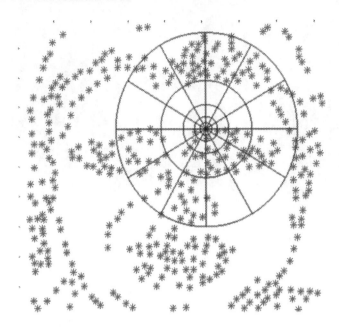

Fig. 3. Computing shape context and store them in log-polar bins.

3.2   Pyramid Histogram of Oriented Gradients (PHOG)

Bosch et al. [6] proposed a descriptor that not only works on the local image shape but it also takes spatial relationship into account. It captures the spatial distribution of edges and stored them as 1D vector representation. With the 1D feature vector, the similarity between two images can easily be computed (just bu using distance metrics).

PHOG is an excellent image global shape descriptor inspired by the two sources: the image pyramid representation of Lazebink et al. [16] and the Histogram of Gradient Orientation (HOG) of Dalal and Triggs [9]. It consists of a histogram of orientation gradients over each image subregion at each resolution level. An image is represented by its local shape (distribution over edge orientations within a region) and its spatial layout (tiling the image into regions at multiple resolutions). It has two major aspects: (a) local appearance and (b) spatial layout.

Local appearance can be described by a histogram of edge orientations (quantized into K bins) within an image subregion. The edge orientations are quantized into K bins, each of which represents the number of edges which have a certain angular range orientations. The spatial layout of the shape is based on the concept of spatial pyramid matching [15]. Each image is divided into a sequence of increasingly finer spatial grids by doubling the number of grids in each axes direction. The number of points in each grid cell is then recorded. Figure 4 illustrates an idea about PHOG computation.

Fig. 4. Computing PHOG with level 2.

In general, the PHOG descriptor of the entire image is a vector with dimensionality $K \times \sum_{l \in L} 4^l$. For example, for level L = 1 and K = 20 bins, the size of the PHOG feature vector is of $(20 \times 4^0 + 20 \times 4^1)$ 100.

3.3   Gist: Spatial Envelope

Object recognition tool that can bypass the segmentation process is always interesting. Gist descriptor, proposed by Oliva and Torralba [19] is one of such techniques. Such technique produces a very low dimensional representation of the image, which we call spatial envelope.

Spatial envelope, for image recognition, is considered as a set of global properties. At the image level, each scene property, or the whole image, can be represented by a low-dimensional vector that encodes the distribution of orientations and scales in the image along with a coarse description of the spatial layout. The spatial envelope representation that has semantic attributes about the image provides a way of computing high-level image and space similarities between 2D sequences/images. Such representation of an image is a proof that object shape or identity may not be required for image segmentation/categorization.

In our study, for an input face image, a gist descriptor is computed by:

– Convolve the image with 32 Gabor filters at 4 scales, 8 orientations, producing 32 feature maps of the same size of the input image.
– Divide each feature map into 16 regions (by a 4 × 4 grid), and then average the feature values within each region.
– Concatenate the 16 averaged values of all 32 feature maps, resulting in a $16 \times 32 = 512$ gist descriptor.

In Fig. 5, an illustration about how can we compute the gist feature is provided.

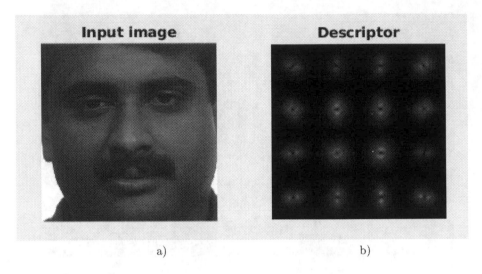

Fig. 5. Computing the gist descriptor of a face image.

4   Experiments

4.1   Datasets and Evaluation Metric

Datasets. For a through test, it is highly recommended to use standard datasets (publicly available) so that fair comparison is possible. In our study, the following datasets (see Table 1 for additional information) are used:

(a) Caltech dataset;
(b) AR face dataset;
(c) Color FERET dataset;
(d) ORL dataset; and
(e) Indian face dataset.

The California Institute of Technology (Caltech) is a world-renowned science and engineering research and education institution. It has an important part in discovering new knowledge and innovations. For face recognition system, the dataset provided by Caltech contains 450 frontal face images of 27 distinct subjects with varying conditions.

The AR Face dataset was developed by Aleix Martinez and Robert Benavente in the Computer Vision Center (CVC) at the U.A.B. The rich dataset contains over 3000 face images corresponding to 126 subject which includes 70 men and 56 women.

The FERET database was developed under the supervision of Face Recognition Technology (FERET) program to develop new techniques, technology, and algorithms for the automatic recognition of human faces. For FR system, the dataset consists of 500 frontal face images of 105 distinct subjects with varying conditions. In our study, we ignore color pixels.

Table 1. Datasets used in our experiments.

Datasets	Dimension	Images/subject	Total
Caltech	190×232	27	450
AR Face	120×165	11	550
ColorFERET	346×351	4 (min.)	500
ORL	92×112	10	400
Indian faces	232×232	11	675

The ORL database of faces was developed under the supervision of Cambridge University Laboratory. The database consists of 400 frontal face images of 40 distinct subjects with varying lighting conditions, poses and facial expressions.

The Indian Face database was developed by IIT Kanpur. There are eleven different face images of each of 40 distinct subjects. Different orientations of the face are included for example looking front, looking left, looking right, looking up, looking up looking down along with different facial emotions.

Evaluation Metric. The various testing protocols have been designed so that algorithm performance can be computed. A common approach of testing the tool is to provide two sets of images to the algorithm, the probe image which is considered to be an unknown individual and training image which consist of known individuals from the gallery. The images in the testing set are the unknown facial images that have to be identified by the tool (proposed tool, let us say). The decision is made on the basis of similarity score computed by the algorithm. To test the performance of our tool, the *hit rate* is used.

The *hit rate* counts the successful top-k matches using the query set of size $|q|$. The higher the recognition rate, the greater the hit rate. We define the hit rate for top-k matches as

$$Hit\ rate\ (k) = \frac{Hit\ count(k,\ q)}{|q|}.$$

The system is capable of accepting or rejecting the claim.

Like most of the face recognition tools (in the literature), we follow leave one out validation protocol, where each image act as a query knows as the testing data and processed with the remaining set of images known as training data.

4.2   Results, Analysis and Comparison

In Table 2, our tool with SC features shows encouraging results in all the major face image databases except the Indian faces. This shows that shape context can achieve more in the field of face recognition.

Table 2. Hit rate (in %) using the SC features for different datasets.

Datasets	Top-1	Top-3	Top-5
Caltech	0.92	0.95	0.95
ColorFERET	0.79	0.89	0.91
ORL	0.94	0.96	0.98
Indian faces	0.53	0.62	0.66

Table 3. Hit rate (in %) using the PHOG features for different datasets.

Datasets	Top-1	Top-3	Top-5
Caltech	0.92	0.95	0.96
ColorFERET	0.97	0.98	0.99
ORL	0.99	0.99	1.00
Indian faces	0.61	0.66	0.70

The results using the PHOG features produce better scores (see Table 3) than the ones that uses the SC features. It is also important to note that the PHOG descriptor can outperform major state-of-the-art descriptors (follow comparison Table 5 at the end).

In Table 4, the gist features shows similar trends like previous results (Tables 2 and 3). Comparatively, all features produce better score on ORL dataset. The difficulty for all of them lies on Indian faces dataset, which is primarily due to the fact that face poses have been widely varied from the same person.

For a quick comparative study, in Table 5, we have taken baseline results reported in the literature. These are primarily based on 2D principal component analysis (2D PCA) [22], histogram of gradients (HOG) [11], PCA with linear discriminant analysis (LDA) [23], rotation- and scale-invariant, line-based color-aware descriptor (RSILC) [8], scale-invariant feature transform (SIFT) [3], local binary pattern (LBP) [2] and speeded up robust features (SURF) [13]. In this comparison table (Table 5), we observe that spatial features are worth-taking for face recognition. More importantly, the proposed method does not take color images into account to ease the process, i.e. time complexity.

Table 4. Hit rate (in %) using the gist features for different datasets.

Datasets	Top-1	Top-3	Top-5
Caltech	0.97	0.98	0.98
ColorFERET	0.93	0.96	0.97
ORL	0.98	0.99	0.99
Indian faces	0.59	0.67	0.70

Table 5. Comparison: hit rates (in %) of different approaches. [T1: Top 1, T3: Top 3, T5: Top 5]

Datasets	2D-PCA [22]	HOG [11]	PCA, LDA [23]	RSILC [8]	SIFT [3]	LBP [2]	SURF [13]	Method 1 (SC)	Method 2 (PHOG)	Method 3 (gist)
ORL	0.98	0.95	—	—	—	—	—	T1: 0.94 T3: 0.96 T5: 0.98	T1: 0.99 T3: 0.99 T5: 1.00	T1: 0.98 T3: 0.99 T5: 0.99
ColorFERET	—	—	0.95	0.98	—	0.95	0.95	T1: 0.79 T3: 0.89 T5: 0.91	T1: 0.97 T3: 0.98 T5: 0.99	T1: 0.93 T3: 0.96 T5: 0.97
Caltech	—	—	—	0.96	—	—	—	T1: 0.92 T3: 0.95 T5: 0.95	T1: 0.92 T3: 0.95 T5: 0.96	T1: 0.97 T3: 0.98 T5: 0.98
Indian faces	—	—	—	0.80	—	—	—	T1: 0.53 T3: 0.62 T5: 0.66	T1: 0.61 T3: 0.66 T5: 0.70	T1: 0.59 T3: 0.67 T5: 0.70

5   Conclusion and Future Works

In this paper, we have studied the usefulness of spatial features for gray level face image representation and recognition. The reason behind the use of gray level images is public video surveillances, for instance, are always in gray tone format due to limited storage capacity. The study has not been inspired from the real-world data but also has been attempted to take advantage of computational complexity (since no color information has been used), i.e. processing time without missing information about the face images. We have observed that faces can be learned/recognized by the use of spatial arrangements of edges and textures. We have used shape context (SC) and pyramid histogram of orientated gradient (PHOG), and similarly GIST as texture features. Comparative study (on four different publicly available datasets, such as Caltech, ColorFERET, IndianFaces and ORL) shows that spatial features are worth-taking for face recognition.

Since spatial features can be compared with the state-of-the-art works, our immediate plan is to integrate/combine them so that gray level face recognition can be possible with no color information it. Another idea is to work on machine learning classifier-based idea, such as active learning [7] at the time when we need real data or live data.

References

1. Abdel-Hakim, A.E., Farag, A.A.: CSIFT: a SIFT descriptor with color invariant characteristics. In: 2006 IEEE Computer Society Conference on Computer Vision and Pattern Recognition, vol. 2, pp. 1978–1983. IEEE (2006)
2. Ahonen, T., Hadid, A., Pietikainen, M.: Face description with local binary patterns: application to face recognition. IEEE Trans. Pattern Anal. Mach. Intell. **28**(12), 2037–2041 (2006)
3. Aly, M.: Face recognition using sift features. CNS/Bi/EE report 186 (2006)
4. Bay, H., Ess, A., Tuytelaars, T., Van Gool, L.: Speeded-up robust features (SURF). Comput. Vis. Image Underst. **110**(3), 346–359 (2008)
5. Belongie, S., Malik, J., Puzicha, J.: Shape context: a new descriptor for shape matching and object recognition. In: Advances in Neural Information Processing Systems, pp. 831–837 (2001)
6. Bosch, A., Zisserman, A., Munoz, X.: Representing shape with a spatial pyramid kernel. In: Proceedings of the 6th ACM International Conference on Image and Video Retrieval, pp. 401–408. ACM (2007)
7. Bouguelia, M., Nowaczyk, S., Santosh, K.C., Verikas, A.: Agreeing to disagree: active learning with noisy labels without crowdsourcing. Int. J. Mach. Learn. Cybern. **9**(8), 1307–1319 (2018)
8. Candemir, S., Borovikov, E., Santosh, K., Antani, S., Thoma, G.: RSILC: rotation- and scale-invariant, line-based color-aware descriptor. Image Vis. Comput. **42**, 1–12 (2015)
9. Dalal, N., Triggs, B.: Histograms of oriented gradients for human detection. In: IEEE Computer Society Conference on Computer Vision and Pattern Recognition 2005, CVPR 2005, vol. 1, pp. 886–893. IEEE (2005)

10. Deboeverie, F., Veelaert, P., Philips, W.: Face analysis using curve edge maps. In: Maino, G., Foresti, G.L. (eds.) ICIAP 2011. LNCS, vol. 6979, pp. 109–118. Springer, Heidelberg (2011). https://doi.org/10.1007/978-3-642-24088-1_12

11. Do, T.T., Kijak, E.: Face recognition using co-occurrence histograms of oriented gradients. In: 2012 IEEE International Conference on Acoustics, Speech and Signal Processing (ICASSP), pp. 1301–1304. IEEE (2012)

12. Dreuw, P., Steingrube, P., Hanselmann, H., Ney, H., Aachen, G.: SURF-face: face recognition under viewpoint consistency constraints. In: BMVC, pp. 1–11 (2009)

13. Du, G., Su, F., Cai, A.: Face recognition using SURF features. Proc. SPIE **7496**, 749628-1 (2009)

14. Gao, Y., Leung, M.K.: Face recognition using line edge map. IEEE Trans. Pattern Anal. Mach. Intell. **24**(6), 764–779 (2002)

15. Grauman, K., Darrell, T.: The pyramid match kernel: discriminative classification with sets of image features. In: Tenth IEEE International Conference on Computer Vision 2005, ICCV 2005, vol. 2, pp. 1458–1465. IEEE (2005)

16. Lazebnik, S., Schmid, C., Ponce, J.: Beyond bags of features: spatial pyramid matching for recognizing natural scene categories. In: 2006 IEEE Computer Society Conference on Computer Vision and Pattern Recognition, vol. 2, pp. 2169–2178. IEEE (2006)

17. Liu, C., Yuen, J., Torralba, A., Sivic, J., Freeman, W.T.: SIFT flow: dense correspondence across different scenes. In: Forsyth, D., Torr, P., Zisserman, A. (eds.) ECCV 2008. LNCS, vol. 5304, pp. 28–42. Springer, Heidelberg (2008). https://doi.org/10.1007/978-3-540-88690-7_3

18. Lowe, D.G.: Object recognition from local scale-invariant features. In: The Proceedings of the Seventh IEEE International Conference on Computer Vision 1999, vol. 2, pp. 1150–1157. IEEE (1999)

19. Oliva, A., Torralba, A.: Modeling the shape of the scene: a holistic representation of the spatial envelope. Int. J. Comput. Vis. **42**(3), 145–175 (2001)

20. Santosh, K.C., Lamiroy, B., Wendling, L.: Integrating vocabulary clustering with spatial relations for symbol recognition. Int. J. Doc. Anal. Recogn. **17**(1), 61–78 (2014)

21. Turk, M.A., Pentland, A.P.: Face recognition using eigenfaces. In: Proceedings of the IEEE Computer Society Conference on Computer Vision and Pattern Recognition 1991, CVPR 1991, pp. 586–591. IEEE (1991)

22. Yang, J., Zhang, D., Frangi, A.F., Yang, J.: Two-dimensional PCA: a new approach to appearance-based face representation and recognition. IEEE Trans. Pattern Anal. Mach. Intell. **26**(1), 131–137 (2004)

23. Zhao, W., Chellappa, R., Krishnaswamy, A.: Discriminant analysis of principal components for face recognition. In: Proceedings of the Third IEEE International Conference on Automatic Face and Gesture Recognition 1998, pp. 336–341. IEEE (1998)

Application of Gabor Filter for Monitoring Wear of Single Point Cutting Tool

Prashant Ambadekar[1,2(✉)] and Chandrashekhar Choudhari[3]

[1] SIES Graduate School of Technology, Mumbai, India
prashantambadekar@gmail.com
[2] Father Conceicao Rodrigues Institute of Technology, Mumbai, India
[3] Terna Engineering College, Mumbai, India

Abstract. Tremendous use of sophisticated computer aided manufacturing systems necessitates monitoring of tools. Monitoring of tools facilitates to reduce machine tool downtime, increases quality of the product, provide better surface finish and reduces cost. Sophisticated digital image processing algorithms and availability of high resolution cameras has enabled automated monitoring of tools. To exactly predict the tool wear is a challenging task due to its complexity involved in the algorithm that facilitates extraction of features. In this paper, tool wear monitoring through texture feature extraction using Gabor filter is presented. Gabor filter has demonstrated better multi resolution properties that facilitate texture feature extraction. Statistical parameters such mean, standard deviation, variance, skew and kurtosis are calculated to measure the tool wear. Experimental results demonstrate better tool wear prediction as compared to other algorithms.

Keywords: Gabor filter · Tool wear monitoring ·
Statistical parameters

1 Introduction

Most of the manufacturing operations involve use of processes like turning, milling, drilling and grinding. Each of these manufacturing operations uses "cutting tool" as a component that needs periodic replacement. In conventional machining processes, the cutting tool is considered as one of the important element considering the following facts: (i) it produces the desired surface on the component (ii) it is responsible to provide the desired dimension in the given tolerance zone (iii) the flow, quality, quantity, thickness and type of chip is affected by the tool geometry and orientation (iv) parameters like current, power and vibration are affected by the status of cutting tool (v) tool replacement consume about 20% of the production time reported Zhang [1] which can delay the rate of production. The replacement of cutting tools due to wear or breakage

© Springer Nature Singapore Pte Ltd. 2019
K. C. Santosh and R. S. Hegadi (Eds.): RTIP2R 2018, CCIS 1035, pp. 230–239, 2019.
https://doi.org/10.1007/978-981-13-9181-1_21

upsets the economics of the total production. It is thus important to keep regular update on the status of cutting tool to prevent the average flank wear reaches to 0.3 mm. In regards to this the cutting tool should be replaced exactly when it is worn out and should not be underused or overused as both causes unnecessary downtime. Whereas in the latter case the tool itself would get machined Loizou et al. [2] that may not be identified in real time, the former is not advisable from economic point of view. Unmanned production system is possible only if a proper tool condition monitoring system (TCM) is available. It is even possible to increase the cutting speed and reduce the downtime if a proper TCM technique is implemented and can also result in savings between 10% and 40% [3]. Tool wear can be monitored by direct or indirect method. Direct method are traditionally used but are time consuming as compared to indirect method which uses either sensors or work piece images to monitor tool wear and needs no interruption in machining operation. The following paragraphs provide use of indirect methods such as acoustic emission (AE), cutting force, sound, vibration and image processing based.

Gomez et al. [4] recorded AE signal from drilling of steel samples and correlated with torque and degree of tool wear and found that torque has best relation with moving average of mean power as compared to RMS. Hase et al. [5] examined the features of AE signals generated during wear to recognize the wear mechanism as abrasive or adhesive. A frequency analysis of these signal wave-forms was performed which showed the difference in peak formed in various frequency region. Papacharalampopoulos et al. [6] studied wave propagation in cutting tool to understand how the propagated AE signals are affected by the material and the geometry of the tool. Authors applied a two dimensional Boundary Element method for simulation and commented how excitation, clamping, microstructure and wear affect the AE signal. Neslusan et al. [7] presented the analysis of chip formation with the use of AE sensors which is not possible with conventional processing of AE signals. Two sensors with different frequency range were used in the study with some selected AE parameters related to different processes in the cutting zone during chip separation. Authors stated that techniques are very sensitive systems for the monitoring of specific processes like formation of segmented chips, cracking process in the shear zone, in the cutting zone.

Ravindra et al. [8] commented that even though force ratios can be used to monitor tool wear, modelling of tool wear is required. Lee et al. [9] studied the effect of dynamic components of cutting force to detect the flank wear which showed a monotonically increasing behaviour of dynamic force and in correlation to flank wear. Choudhury and Kishore [10] developed a mathematical model correlating the force ratio to flank wear height to predict flank wear in turning. A strain gauge dynamometer measured the values of feed force and cutting force that formed the force ratio. Sound recorded by a sensor involves noise due to operation of components of the machine itself, vibration or nearby operating machines, but this being mostly in the range of 0 to 2 kHz frequency. Mannan et al. [11] used a digital audio system was that record the sound generated during turning process and then decomposed using wavelet. The power spectral density of sound signals shows that the sound energy increases as the tool becomes dull and is more prominent in the frequency range above 5 kHz. As the tool wears out due to adhesion, the asperity height is reduced as proved by Lu [12]. They measured sound signals using microscope that are generated as the system gets excited due to interaction between asperities and as the tool wear increases, the power spectrum shows a shift to higher frequency range. Tekiner and Yesilyart [13] performed experimentation using sound as a basis on AISI 304 austenitic stainless steel and concluded that cutting sound pressure level can be used as a method for TCM as they got parallel results to that of the conventional methods. Authors also suggested the ideal cutting parameters to be used for any further work in the said condition wherein the researcher only need to add sound pressure level that is caused by the machine used by them to perform the experiments.

Dimla Snr [14] performed time and frequency analysis of the signal obtained from turning of two different material components and correlated with direct measurement. Authors commented that the vibration signals can be used effectively to monitor the wear of cutting tool. Alonso and Salgado [15] studied the applicability of the SSA method and cluster analysis to automatic signal processing in the area of on-line TCMS. The vibration signals obtained from the turning processes was processed to extract statistical features that are well correlated with tool condition. It was found that only the RMS and standard deviation of the medium and high frequency signals of the longitudinal vibration and the RMS and standard deviation of the high-frequency components of the transverse vibration showed a monotonic behavior with the tool wear.

A study on fractal dimension (FD) analysis of surface machined by milling was performed by Kang et al. [16]. Authors found that as the cutting length increases, the tool wear and surface roughness values also increases and the FD also increases as well. This result could be used for TCM using fractal dimension. Kassim et al. [17] used fractals on milled components to classify tool wear into sharp, semi dull or dull states using Hidden Markov Model (HMM). The features of fractals and HMM can be used for monitoring of tool wear. Grzesik and Brol [18] determined the surface profile of different material components machined by turning operation. Further they applied DWT to calculate energy parameter. This parameter was used to find the Fractal dimensions. Gadelmawla et al. [19] introduced a new method, called the best grey level histogram for assessment of surface texture. To get the most accurate image of a surface a program was written in C++ software that displays the grey level histogram and selects the best values from brightness, contrast, saturation and hue for any grey image. The histogram could also compare roughness of different surfaces and comment on the quality of surface.

Gadelmawla [20] used GLCM texture features to correlate with cutting conditions in milling. Images of components were captured and GLCM textural features were found using GLCM software. The result provided correlation of GLCM features in descending order with feed, speed and depth of cut respectively. Priya and Ramamoorthy [21] using GLCM technique to study the effect of inclination on surface roughness measurement and concluded that the surface should be kept flat during measurement of surface roughness to get the optimum value. Though fewer details about the use of co-occurrence matrix were provided, the surface whose image is to be captured should be perpendicular to camera. Dutta et al. [22] studied GLCM technique to investigate the wear of cutting tool by capturing images of machined surface and commented that contrast and homogeneity were the two best features suitable for TCM. Though authors used different values for pixel pair spacing, but did not present as to how optimum spacing of pixel pair is to be obtained. Thus the focus of TCM is now shifted to indirect online methods using machine vision as these are advantageous over direct methods.

The use of digital image processing for tool wear monitoring can provide online real time solution for tool wear problem. In general a proper TCM system consists of three stages: Monitoring, Signal Processing (Feature Extraction) and Classification. In this paper, a new approach to acquire tool wear monitoring through texture feature extraction using Gabor filter is presented. Gabor filter facilitates better texture feature extraction than wavelet transform. Statistical parameters such mean, standard deviation, variance, skew, kurtosis and entropy are calculated to measure the tool wear. The paper is organized as follows, the Sect. 2 illustrates the application of Gabor filter in feature extraction. Measurement of statistical parameters and results are discussed in Sect. 3 and concluding remarks are given in Sect. 4.

2   Gabor Filter

Dennis Gabor in 1946, introduced Gabor filter which is used for texture examination in spatial as well as transform domain. It provides a multi-channel analysis by allowing variation in scale and orientation owing to which it has demonstrated better performance than other multi resolution approaches [23]. Because of their optimal localization properties, these filters are suitably applied for edge detection and texture analysis. Gabor filters resembles the simple cells in the mammalian visual system [24] which makes it more popular for texture analysis.

A one-dimensional Gabor function is defined as the complex sinusoidal wave modulated by a Gaussian envelop. It's one-dimensional representation is given in Eq. (1).

$$g(x) = \frac{1}{\sqrt{2\pi\sigma}} \exp^{\left(\frac{-x^2}{2\sigma_x^2}\right)} + \exp^{2\pi j w_x} \tag{1}$$

where, σ represents the bandwidth of Gabor filter.

A two-dimensional Gabor filter can be obtained by extending these functions to two dimensions. The 2-D Gabor filter is obtained by convolution of a sinusoid wave with a particular frequency by a Gaussian function. A Gabor filter in 2-D form has a general form given by Eq. (2).

$$g(x,y) = \frac{1}{2\pi\sigma_x\sigma_y} \exp^{\left(-\frac{1}{2}\left(\frac{x^2}{\sigma_x^2} + \frac{y^2}{\sigma_y^2}\right) + 2\pi jw_x\right)} \tag{2}$$

where, σx and σy represent standard deviation

Gabor functions are linear, bandpass filters that forms a complete though non-orthogonal basis set. The non-orthogonality infers that the filtered image contains redundant information which is to be reduced. In order to do so, let us define two constants, $f_h = 1$ and $f_l = 0.75$ as upper and lower center frequencies of interest, to ensure that the half-peak magnitude support of the filter responses in the frequency spectrum touch each other.

The Gabor filter image representation obtained after convolution of Gabor kernel g_{mn} on the image I (x, y) with is given in Eq. (3)

$$G_{mn}(x,y) = \sum s \sum t I(x-s, y-t)g*_{mn}(s,t) \tag{3}$$

where, s and t are the kernel size variables, $g^*{}_{mn}$ is the complex conjugate of the mother Gabor function g_{mn} and G_{mn} is the output after convolution of image with the kernel.

The textural features of the images in the form of statistical parameters are represented by mean μ, standard deviation σ, variance v, skew α and kurtosis γ. Their mathematical equations are given in Eqs. (4) to (8) and a feature vector F is created as given in Eq. (9).

$$E_{mn} = \sum x \sum y |G_{mn}(x,y)| \tag{4}$$

$$\mu_{mn} = \frac{E_{mn}}{P*Q} \tag{5}$$

$$\sigma_{mn} = \frac{\sqrt{\sum x \sum y(|G_{mn}(x,y)| - \mu_{mn})^2}}{P*Q} \tag{6}$$

$$\alpha_{mn} = \frac{\left(\sum x \sum y(|G_{mn}(x,y)| - \mu_{mn})^3\right)^{\frac{1}{3}}}{P*Q} \tag{7}$$

$$\gamma_{mn} = \frac{\left(\sum x \sum y(|G_{mn}(x,y)| - \mu_{mn})^4\right)^{\frac{1}{4}}}{P*Q} \tag{8}$$

$$F = (\mu, \sigma, v, \alpha, \gamma) \tag{9}$$

3   Result and Discussion

MTAB manufactured CNC lathe was used for experimentation as shown in Fig. 1. The turning operation was performed in dry cutting conditions by a single point cutting tool to ensure that sufficient wear takes place and also the cutting parameters were kept fixed so as to have uniformity in obtaining the results.

Fig. 1. CNC lathe machine

3.1   Machining Conditions and Setup

Aluminum was selected as the work piece material as it can be easily machined without the use of coolant. A number of work pieces were machined and each work piece was machined to reduce the diameter to 16 mm as per the program using Fanuc controller. The experimental conditions are shown in Table 1.

Table 1. Experimental conditions

S.N.	Parameter	Value	Unit
1	Spindle rpm	1800	rpm
2	Feed	100	mm/min
3	Depth of cut	0.5	mm

3.2   Algorithm

In this work, an image analysis of surface texture of images of work piece obtained through camera is demonstrated using statistical parameters such as mean, standard deviation, variations, skew and kurtosis. Continuous operations using cutting tool increases its dullness that can be captured through machined surface morphology. It is reflected in an image through non-uniform intensity and surface roughness. Thus the statistical parameters capture the surface morphology through Gabor filter that represents the tool wear. The algorithm in the form of flow chart is represented in Fig. 2. The images were cropped to 300 × 300 pixel and all the processing was done in MATLAB (R 2013b) environment.

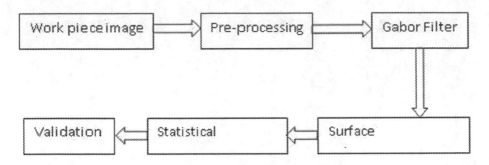

Fig. 2. Tool wear detection algorithm

The work piece images obtained as per conditioned illustrated in Table 1 are shown in Fig. 3. Initially the obtained images were pre-processed by standard histogram equalization process to enhance the contrast for better surface measurements as shown in Fig. 4. Gabor filter is applied on the resultant pre-processed image to enhance surface roughness that assist in accurate measurement of statistical parameters. Resultant images through Gabor filter are shown in Fig. 5 that clearly indicates the surface roughness. Finally to extract edges and enhance roughness, Laplacian operator was applied on the filtered image which clearly indicates tool wear.

Fig. 3. Pre-processed images of work piece

The results obtained through image processing algorithm described was verified through statistical parameters such mean, standard deviation, variance, skew and kurtosis. These parameters have been applied in various algorithms for analysis of the texture/surface of the images. It completely captures the surface morphology and assist in experimental verification. The statistical parameters obtained from the processed images are illustrated in Table 2. Results clearly demonstrate that kurtosis captures surface roughness whereas other statistical parameters such as mean, standard deviation and variance support the claim.

Fig. 4. Filtered images of work piece

Fig. 5. Processed images of work piece clearly indicating tool wear

Table 2. Statistical parameters

Images	1	2	3	4	5	6
Mean	1.11	1.16	1.23	1.33	1.36	1.45
Standard Deviation	2.84	2.95	3.06	3.18	3.20	3.42
Variance	8.06	8.8	9.37	10.11	10.22	11.69
Skew	0.0030	0.0030	0.0031	0.0031	0.0031	0.0032
Kurtosis	1.96	2.00	2.06	2.13	2.14	2.20

The experimental measurement of surface roughness is given in Table 3. The values of kurtosis show a strong correlation with the measured values of surface roughness.

Table 3. Comparison of surface roughness with Kurtosis

Images	Surface roughness (Ra)	Kurtosis
1	1.78	1.96
2	1.89	2.00
3	2.04	2.06
4	2.45	2.13
5	2.66	2.14
6	2.88	2.88

4   Conclusion

The experimental results clearly indicate that contrast is the most useful parameter for analysis and measurement of the tool wear through image processing algorithms. The proposed algorithm through three step of process histogram equalization, Gabor filter and Laplacian operator provides complete surface morphology of the tool wear. Statistical parameters further assist in providing quantitative analysis of the tool wear that can be further applied for the classification through neural network. Further the algorithm can be verified on low resolution and noisy images. Also a good imaging and illumination system is must in acquiring images.

References

1. Zhang, C., Zhang, J.: On-line tool wear measurement for ball-end milling cutter based on machine vision. Comput. Ind. **64**(6), 708–719 (2013)
2. Loizou, J., Tian, W., Robertson, J., Camelio, J.: Automated wear characterization for broaching tools based on machine vision systems. J. Manuf. Syst. **37**, 558–563 (2015)
3. Rehorn, A.G., Jiang, J., Orban, P.E.: State-of-the-art methods and results in tool condition monitoring: a review. Int. J. Adv. Manuf. Technol. **26**(7–8), 693–710 (2005)
4. Gómez, M.P., Hey, A.M., Ruzzante, J.E., D'Attellis, C.E.: Tool wear evaluation in drilling by acoustic emission. Phys. Procedia **3**(1), 819–825 (2010)
5. Hase, A., Mishina, H., Wada, M.: Correlation between features of acoustic emission signals and mechanical wear mechanisms. Wear **292**, 144–150 (2012)
6. Papacharalampopoulos, A., Stavropoulos, P., Doukas, C., Foteinopoulos, P., Chryssolouris, G.: Acoustic emission signal through turning tools: a computational study. Proc. CIRP **8**, 426–431 (2013)
7. Neslušan, M., Mičieta, B., Mičietová, A., Čilliková, M., Mrkvica, I.: Detection of tool breakage during hard turning through acoustic emission at low removal rates. Measurement **70**, 1–13 (2015)
8. Ravindra, H.V., Srinivasa, Y.G., Krishnamurthy, R.: Modelling of tool wear based on cutting forces in turning. Wear **169**(1), 25–32 (1993)
9. Lee, J.H., Kim, D.E., Lee, S.J.: Statistical analysis of cutting force ratios for flank-wear monitoring. J. Mat. Process. Technol. **74**(1–3), 104–114 (1998)
10. Choudhury, S.K., Kishore, K.K.: Tool wear measurement in turning using force ratio. Int. J. Mach. Tools Manuf. **40**(6), 899–909 (2000)
11. Mannan, M.A., Kassim, A.A., Jing, M.: Application of image and sound analysis techniques to monitor the condition of cutting tools. Pattern Recogn. Lett. **21**(11), 969–979 (2000)
12. Ming-Chyuan, L., Kannatey-Asibu, E.: Analysis of sound signal generation due to flank wear in turning. J. Manuf. Sci. Eng. **124**(4), 799–808 (2002)
13. Tekıner, Z., Yeşılyurt, S.: Investigation of the cutting parameters depending on process sound during turning of AISI 304 austenitic stainless steel. Mater. Des. **25**(6), 507–513 (2004)
14. Dimla, D.E., et al.: The correlation of vibration signal features to cutting tool wear in a metal turning operation. Int. J. Adv. Manuf. Technol. **19**(10), 705–713 (2002)

15. Alonso, F.J., Salgado, D.R.: Analysis of the structure of vibration signals for tool wear detection. Mech. Syst. Sig. Process. **22**(3), 735–748 (2008)

16. Kang, M.C., Kim, J.S., Kim, K.H.: Fractal dimension analysis of machined surface depending on coated tool wear. Surf. Coat. Technol. **193**(1–3), 259–265 (2005)

17. Kassim, A.A., Mian, Z., Mannan, M.A.: Tool condition classification using hidden Markov model based on fractal analysis of machined surface textures. Mach. Vis. Appl. **17**(5), 327–336 (2006)

18. Grzesik, W., Brol, S.: Wavelet and fractal approach to surface roughness characterization after finish turning of different workpiece materials. J. Mater. Process. Technol. **209**(5), 2522–2531 (2009)

19. Gadelmawla, E.S., Koura, M.M., Maksoud, T.M.A., Elewa, I.M., Soliman, H.H.: Using the grey level histogram to distinguish between roughness of surfaces. Proc. Inst. Mech. Eng. Part B: J. Eng. Manuf. **215**(4), 545–553 (2001)

20. Gadelmawla, E.S., Eladawi, A.E., Abouelatta, O.B., Elewa, I.M.: Investigation of the cutting conditions in milling operations using image texture features. Proc. Inst. Mech. Eng. Part B: J. Eng. Manuf. **222**(11), 1395–1404 (2008)

21. Priya, P., Ramamoorthy, B.: Machine vision for surface roughness assessment of inclined components. In: Key Engineering Materials, vol. 437, pp. 141–144. Trans Tech Publ (2010)

22. Datta, A., Dutta, S., Pal, S.K., Sen, R., Mukhopadhyay, S.: Texture analysis of turned surface images using grey level co-occurrence technique. In: Advanced Materials Research, vol. 365, pp. 38–43. Trans Tech Publ (2012)

23. Ali Younesi and Mehdi Chehel Amirani: Gabor filter and texture based features for palmprint recognition. Proc. Comput. Sci. **108**, 2488–2495 (2017)

24. Daugman, J.G.: Uncertainty relation for resolution in space, spatial frequency, and orientation optimized by two-dimensional visual cortical filters. JOSA A **2**(7), 1160–1169 (1985)

Performance Analysis of Log-Gabor Based Multimodal Systems and Its Fusion Techniques

H. D. Supreetha Gowda[1]([⊠]), Mohammad Imran[2]([⊠]),
and G. Hemantha Kumar[1]([⊠])

[1] Department of Computer Science, University of Mysore, Mysore 560 007, India
supreethad3832@gmail.com, ghlk2007@gmail.com
[2] #125 & 126, 1st Floor, Brigade Arcade, Brigade Metropolis, Mahadevapura Post,
Garudacharpalya, Bengaluru 560048, India
emraangi@gmail.com

Abstract. Single biometric modality may not be enough to achieve the best performance in real time applications. Multimodal biometric system provides high degree of recognition and more population coverage by combining different source of biometric modalities which in turn enhances the performance superiority and error rate shrinking properties. This work addresses the performance comparison in terms of verification rate of the unimodal and bimodal biometric systems holding face trait as the primary modality and Fingerprint, Iris, Palmprint and Handvein as secondary modality. The potential of the proposed verification system is judged by conducting empirical analysis on both the types of fusion strategies- pre and post classification. Overall gist of the paper summarizes few issues, (a) Which secondary physiological modality would be the optimal combination that gives the complimentary information along with the face trait, (b) impact and adoptability of fusion strategies at various levels of fusion to be adhered, (c) finally a brief overview that addresses face centric bimodal systems developed at all levels of fusion on both clean and noisy data.

Keywords: Face Recognition · Multimodal · Fusion strategies · Log-Gabor · Robustness

1 Introduction

Achieving the three primary security constituents such as authentication, authorization, and accountability is of major concern in preventing privacy breaches, as we know usage of digital imagery from different sources is now ubiquitous. Identity verification is a perfectly natural process practiced by humans in everyday activities in a non-automated manner. We humans employ several identity verification techniques, e.g., appearance and color, body language, and so on. As getting closer to each other, we can identify based on features such as voice, gait.

© Springer Nature Singapore Pte Ltd. 2019
K. C. Santosh and R. S. Hegadi (Eds.): RTIP2R 2018, CCIS 1035, pp. 240–254, 2019.
https://doi.org/10.1007/978-981-13-9181-1_22

We practice identity verification techniques withoutknowing specific parameters, but still we identify him/her accurately. However, automation of same kind of identity verification through machine is not an easy job. Hence, Biometric technology has emerged very significantly, which is a science of identifying an individual based on physiological and/or behavior characteristics. Biometric system is basically pattern recognition which makes use of individual's modality to identify him/her, face, fingerprint, iris, palmprint, hand geometry, handvein, finger knuckle print are physiological modalities and modalities under behavioral are, voice, gait, signature and key stroke.

However, most of the biometric systems employed in real world application are unimodal—it means that they rely on single source of modality, as it is simple and easily adoptable. These unimodal systems struggle with number of challenges to face such as noise in the sensed data, intra-class variations, inter-class similarities, non-universality, spoof attacks etc. These limitations of unimodal biometric systems can be overcome by adopting the Multibiometric system. A multibiometric system relies on multiple source of information by multi-sensor, multi-algorithmic, multi-sample and multi-instance ways. Primary concern in any multibiometric system is to determine the viability of fusing multiple information to achieve desired level of accuracy. Based on the type of information available, different type of fusion can be performed. Fusion strategies at various levels are sensor level, feature level, score level and decision level.

It is well known that real time data is always prone to noisy conditions, hence building the system with the classifiers that is capable of handling imprecision to a certain degree is a prerequisite for any robust biometric model. Giving a meaningful conclusion to any robust model in a positive aspect needs to be diagnosed by inducing artificial noise and checking its threshold of noise tolerance [27] Attaining unified measures performance and robustness simultaneously in a biometric model that is essentially designed in addressing real time noisy issues is disregarded in literature so far. Generally there are two types of noises, class noise (Ex: labelling errors) and attribute noise (Ex: attribute instance corruption) that hinders the noise model which in turn reduces system's performance. Noise affects the performance of the system and when compared to the accuracy of the model without noise, generally there would be a difference. Building a generalized model that takes care of real time noises and proving itself insensitive to such noises is a challenging work.

In this paper, we have designed face centric multimodal biometric system by fusing face biometric data with other modalities such as Fingerprint, Iris, Palmprint and Handvein. Prominent contribution of this paper are:

1. Different combination of physiological traits employed along with the face considering it has *facecentric* bimodal systems are proposed and their evaluation at all levels of fusion is carried out. The proposed multimodal systems are evaluated using all conventional fusion strategies.
2. We also have proposed rotation invariant segmentation technique to extract ROI from Palm print images. In case of Handvein images, to reduce storage

and computational burden, we have proposed a method to extract sufficient ROI required for discrimination.

3. Log-Gabor filter is a generalized feature extraction for most of the 2D data modality as against 1D data modality (such as speech, online signature etc). We have exploited Log-Gabor features in this study which helps us to know potential benefits/limits of employing this feature set on different modalities.
4. Extensive experiments are conducted to ascertain behavior of various multimodal systems. Results are substantiated with appropriate analysis.

Face modality has several advantages that makes it preferable in many biometric applications such as non-intrusiveness in nature, availability of strong feature extraction algorithms (subspace, active shape models) under different levels of controlled environment (Face Recognition Grand Challenge, Face Recognition Vendor Test, Face Recognition Technology (FERET)) data sets. On the other hand, there are several studies in literature that showed fusion of face with other modalities such as palmprint, fingerprint etc. However, these papers address only a particular fusion technique but did not provide a complete knowledge considering all pre and post classification fusion schemes. Hence, it is evident that there are plenty of reasons to carry out this type of study. We have listed below some important reasons that instigated us to do this work:

- To the best of our knowledge, there is no single paper in the literature that addresses face centric bimodal systems developed at all levels of fusion.
- In general, results obtained from this study helps us to determine: (a) the optimal modality combination for face trait. (b) the robust level of fusion of face trait with particular secondary modality against Gaussian noise and (c) impact of fusion strategies at various levels of fusion.
- Facial feature extraction algorithms are tried at various capacities for enhanced recognition rate: such as developing multi-algorithmic approach, multi-sensor face recognition system, multi-level fusion algorithms, multiple classifiers etc. This paper works on similar lines to know the optimal combination of other biometric modality with face.
- The type of fusion carried out has great impact on verification accuracy. This itself can be motivating to evaluate the fusion at all four levels.

The organization of paper is as follows: Sect. 2 presents a brief review of literature related to multimodal approach. Section 3 presents the proposed segmentation method of Palmprint and Handvein images. Section 4 discusses the tools and techniques employed in this paper. Experimental setup, results and subsequent analysis are presented in Sect. 5. Section sec6 presents concluding remarks followed by future avenues based on this study.

2   Review of Literature

Over the last two decades, numerous multimodal biometric systems have been proposed. Geng et al. [4] proposed context-aware multi-biometric fusion, which can dynamically adapt the fusion rules to the real-time context. As a typical application, the context-aware fusion of gait and face for human identification in video are investigated. Two significant context factors that may affect the relationship between gait and face in the fusion are considered i.e. view angle and subject-to camera distance. Fusion methods adaptable to these two factors based on either prior knowledge or machine learning are proposed and tested.

Chhabria et al. [21] proposed multimodal gesture biometric recognition system, authors have discussed pre classification and post classification techniques and also explored various statistical and normalization rules. Finally they have concluded with few inferences: score level fusion is most prevalent and easier to conduct. Score level fusion gives good results when the samples are of good quality for investigation, as a result weights could be assigned to individual scores based on quality issues. Hezil et al. [6] developed biometric identification system under the feature level fusion by fusing two modalities- ear and palm print, which is a unique combination in literature. They have performed extensive experimentation on benchmark databases such as IIT Delhi-2 ear and IIT Delhi palmprint, local texture descriptors were adopted to extract discriminating features. Separation of original signal from noise can be done in one of the ways: homogeneous area pre classification which estimates the noise variance image filtering techniques, Local variance estimation [6]. By adopting Discrete cosine transform, image structure can be preserved by high frequency coefficients and noise variance in the image can be computed by low frequency coefficients, such that it helps in separation of noise from the original image. They proposed noise variance estimation in two steps, in first step noise variance is estimated with the linear combination of normalized moments and learned coefficients and in the next step the look up table is generated by analyzing the Cumulative distribution function values of the training images. For a new image noise variance is computed by its CDF looking in to the look up table.

Pyatykh et al. [25] proposed noise level estimation adopting Principal component analysis blocks and the contributions of their work are as follows: efficient in performance issues, though the image is non homogeneous processing is done and also attained the good performance when compared with the state-of-art methods. Kearns M proposed a statistical approach for noise tolerance where a learning algorithm is restricted from identifying individual samples of the unknown target function [10]. Nadheen and Poornima [18] developed a multimodal biometric system adopting iris and ear extracting PCA features and fused these features at the score level using the statistical sum rule.

Youssef et al. [7] proposed a multimodal system employing on face and ear modalities, authors extracted block-based LBP features from these two traits and then fused them using the score level fusion. Eskandari et al. [3] proposed multimodal biometric system by fusing the match scores of face and iris that are obtained from several standard classifiers, authors have extracted features using several local and global feature extraction methods. Transformation based score level fusion and classifier based score level fusion is done in to classifying the concatenated matching scores.

Zhu et al. [20] proposed a multimodal biometric identification system based on finger geometry, knuckle print and palm print features. First preprocessing is done to get the finger and palm ROI (Region of Interest). Finger geometry features and knuckle print features of index, middle, ring and little fingers were extracted from the finger ROI, palmprint features represented with key points and their local descriptors were extracted from palm ROI. A coarse-to-fine hierarchical method was employed to match multiple features for efficient recognition in a large database. In the decision level AND rule fusion was adopted which has shown improvement in perfromance.

Tao et al. [26] proposed an optimal fusion scheme at decision level by the AND or OR rule, based on optimizing matching score thresholds. Both the theoretical analysis and the experimental results have been presented. In theory, the proposed decision fusion will always bring improvements over the original classifiers that are fused, and in practice, it also improves the system performance effectively, in away comparable or even better than the conventional matching score fusion. Marcialis et al. [16] proposed a novel mathematical model to perform serial fusion, which is simple and able to predict the performance of two serially combined matchers. The proposed model helps the designer in finding the processing chain allowing a trade-off between performance and matching time. Experiments carried out on well-known bench mark datasets made up of face and fingerprint images supports the use fullness of the proposed methodology when compare it with standard parallel fusion.

Separation of original signal from noise can be done in one of the ways: homogeneous area pre classification which estimates the noise variance [14,15] image filtering techniques [1], Local variance estimation [2]. By adopting Discrete cosine transform, image structure can be preserved by high frequency co-effiecients and noise variance in the image can be computed by low frequency co-efficients, such that it helps in separation of noise from the original image [17]. They proposed noise variance estimation in two steps, in first step noise variance is estimated with the linear combination of normalized moments and learned coefficients and in the next step the look up table is generated by analyzing the Cumulative distribution function values of the training images. For a new image noise variance is computed by its CDF looking in to the look up table. Pyatykh et al. proposed noise level estimation adopting Principal component analysis blocks and the contributions of their work are as follows: efficient in performance issues, though the image is non homogeneous processing is done and also attained the good performance when compared with the state-of-art methods [22]. Kearns proposed a statistical approach for noise tolerance where a learning algorithm is restricted from identifying individual samples of the unknown target function [13].

3 Preprocessing

In this section, we propose Region of Interest (ROI) extraction from Palmprint and Handvein images.

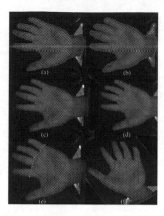

Fig. 1. Region of Interest extraction of Palmprint: (a) and (b) Automatic contour detection (c) and (d) locating key points, these Points will be used to select the ROI (e) and (f) Final ROI is rectangular shape that forms 4 green points (Color figure online)

3.1 Rotation Invariant ROI Extraction from Palmprint Image

The algorithm that we are proposing here extracts essential palm region which is invariant to rotation. The main steps for obtaining the rectangular area ROI called central part sub-image of a Palmprint are summarized as in Fig. 1 and steps are as follows:

- Anisotropic filter is applied to improve edge detection and also to find the contours of the palmprint image
- Trace the boundary of the holes between the fingers. Calculate the center of gravity of the holes and decide the key points k_1, k_2, k_3 respectively.
- Line up k_1 and k_3 to get the Y-axis of the Palmprint coordinate system and then make a line through k_2 perpendicular to the Y-axis to determine the origin of the palmprint coordinate system.
- Once the coordinate system is decideda fixed size sub-image of the central part of a Palmprint is extracted.
- Calculate rotation angle in using above key points and crop exact ROI.

3.2 ROI Extraction from Handvein Images

There are essentially two reasons for us to propose ROI extraction from Handvein images:

1. The discriminative information in an Handvein image is located in central region. There is very less or almost no useful features along the four sides.
2. To reduce the storage and computational burden.

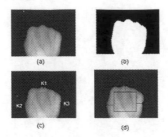

Fig. 2. Region of Interest extraction of Handvein

As the essential region of interest in Handvein image. To increase the verification accuracy we have to extract the Region of Interest of handvein modality. Given raw handvein image, the process of extracting the ROI follows.

- Convert gray scale image to binary by selecting suitable threshold.
- Scan the image contour from left to right (profiling).
- Select Knuckle tip (K1) as control point, then locate other key points K2 and K3 by scanning
- Move some appropriate number of pixels from key points, that give reliable ROI.

Our algorithm of ROI extraction are shown in Fig. 2(a)–(d).

4   Proposed Multimodal System

The multimodal biometric system exhibits number of advantages as compared to that of unimodal biometric system and are listed below [23]

- Multimodal biometric system works with more than one modality, hence it offers a substantial improvement in the accuracy as compared to other approaches of multibiometric system.
- Multimodal biometric solves non-universality issues by covering a large population of users. If user cannot possess a single valid biometric trait still they can be enrolled into a system by using another valid biometric trait. However, it gives certain degree of flexibility to the user.
- Multimodal biometric systems are less sensitive to imposter attacks. It is very difficult to spoof the legitimate user enrolled in multimodal biometric system.
- Multimodal biometric systems are robust to the noise on the sensed data i.e. when information acquired from the single biometric trait is corrupted by noise we can use another trait of the same user.
- These systems also help in continuous monitoring or tracking the person in situation when a single biometric trait is not enough. For example tracking a person using face and gait simultaneously.

Multimodal biometric systems are gaining popularity as it provides very high degree of performance and also high universality [12]. Since multimodal biometric system combine the information from different biometric traits, the core of the multimodal biometric system involves in performing the fusion of these information from different biometric trait. Fusion can be carried out at four different levels such as sensor level, feature level, match score level and decision level [19].

4.1 Sensor Level Fusion

At sensor level fusion, raw images acquired by different sensors or multiple snapshots are combined. The aim of sensor level fusion is to obtain the detailed information from both the images subjected to fusion [11]. In our experiments, we have adopted wavelet based image fusion. In wavelet based image fusion, decomposition is done with a high resolution image as it decomposes an image into a set of low resolution images with wavelet coefficients at each level. Then, it replaces a low resolution image with an MS band at the same spatial resolution level and finally, performs a inverse wavelet transformation to convert the decomposed image and replaced set back to the original resolution level. Further, features extraction and matching is performed on fused image.

4.2 Feature Level Fusion

In feature level fusion each individual modality process outputs a collection of features. The fusion process fuses these collections of features into a single feature set or vector. Feature level fusion performs well, if the features are homogenous (i.e. of same nature). However, if the features are heterogeneous, then it requires normalization to convert them into a range that makes them more similar. We used four well-known normalization methods [24].

1. **Min-Max (MM)** method: This method maps the raw scores (s) to the [0, 1] range. The quantities max(s) and min(s) specify the end points of the score range:

$$n = \frac{s_i - min(s)}{max(s) - min(s)} \tag{1}$$

2. **Z-score:** This method transforms the scores to a distribution with mean of 0 and standard deviation of 1. The operators mean() and std() denote the arithmetic mean and standard deviation operators, respectively:

$$n = \frac{s_i - mean(s)}{std(s)} \tag{2}$$

3. **Tanh:** This method is among the so-called robust statistical techniques. It maps the raw scores to the (0, 1) range:

$$n = \frac{1}{2} \left[tanh \left\{ 0.01 \cdot \frac{s_i - mean(s)}{std(s)} \right\} + 1 \right] \tag{3}$$

4.3   Score Level Fusion

In this fusion, the matching scores of multiple palmprint spectral images are fused into a single score using different rules, such as sum rule, min rule and max rule; later scores are compared with the system acceptable threshold. The n_i^m represents the normalized score for matcher m ($m = 1, 2, \cdots, M$, where M is the number of matchers) applied to user i ($i = 1, 2, \cdots, I$, where I is the number samples in the database). The fused score for user i is denoted as f_i. Popular rules used in score level fusion are [5]:

- Sum Rule: $f_i = \sum_{m=1}^{M} n_i^M \forall i$
- Min Rule: $f_i = min(n_i^1, n_i^2, \cdots, n_i^M) \forall i$
- Max Rule: $f_i = max(n_i^1, n_i^2, \cdots, n_i^M) \forall i$

4.4   Decision Level Fusion

Fusion at decision level can be done by adopting appropriate threshold, but only a small amount of information is available in taking decisions [5]. Hence, it is not very accurate, here only Boolean decisions exists like, *accept* or *reject*. The output of each matcher can be merged into one single decision using logical *AND* and *OR* rule which finally gives single decision.

4.5   Log-Gabor Based Feature Extraction

We have adopted Log Gabor as feature extraction algorithm for all the modalities which we have selected to effectively represent biometric samples. Log Gabor transform have consistently achieved high recognition rates in all traditional unimodal biometric system. The Log Gabor transform has a response that is Gaussian when viewed on a logarithmic frequency scale instead of linear one. Because of their Gaussian profile, Log Gabor filter provide an optimal joint space-frequency localization whose shape is smooth, symmetric, infinitely differentiable [9]. Hence Log Gabor transform allows one to capture more information in high frequency areas and also possess high pass characteristics and there by reflecting the frequency response of image more realistically. On the linear frequency scale, the transfer function of the Log Gabor transform has the form [8]

$$G(\omega) = exp \left\{ \frac{-\log(\omega/\omega_o)^2}{2 \times \log(k/\omega_o)^2} \right\} \tag{4}$$

where w_0 is the filter's center frequency. To obtain constant shape ratio filters, the term k/w_0 must also be held constant for varying w_0. In our experimentation, we have selected effecitve parameter such as filter has a bandwidth of approximately 2 octaves and filter bank is constructed with 8 orientations and 4 different scales.

5   Experimental Results and Discussion

5.1   Experimental Setup

In this section, we on the experimental setup made in our study. For face samples, we have considered AR database, we used PolyU databases for Palmprint and High resolution fingerprint. Iris and Handvein databases of CASIA and Bosphorus respectively. In all the experiments, training was performed by considering three views of each user and two views were used for subsequent testing. Since, Handvein database consists of maximum five samples of each user. The performance was studied under both clean and noise conditions, for unimodal as well as different face centric multimodal approaches.

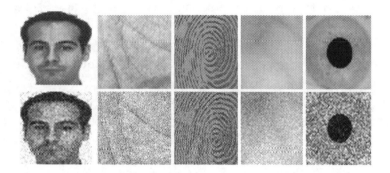

Fig. 3. Few example images of face, palmprint, fingerprint, handvein and iris modalities: clean images (Top) and corrupted by noise (Bottom)

We have used real time noise in our experiments such as Gaussian noise, to validate the robustness of both unimodal and multimodal systems. For training we have used clean three samples of individual modality and while testing have considered the two noise corrupted samples. The clean and noise corrupted images are shown in Fig. 3.

5.2   Results on Clean vs Noisy Unimodal Biometric Systems

The main objective of our experimentation is to provide consequences of level of fusion under different strategies of face centric multimodal system. We have chosen Face, Palmprint (Pp), Iris, Handvein (Hv) and Fingerprint (FP) modalities and log gabor as feature extraction algorithm which is assumed in yielding good performance to all the above modalities. In all of our experiments, performance of levels of fusion is measured in terms of False Acceptance Rate (FAR) at values 0.01%, 0.1% and 1% and its related values of Genuine Acceptance Rate (GAR in %) is tabulated.

Initially, we have conducted experiments on each single modality; the performance is measured for each modality and results are tabulated $Clean^{(Noise)}$.

Table 1. Performance analysis of unimodal system

FAR (%)	GAR (%)				
	Face	Fingerprint	Palmprint	Handvein	Iris
0.01	$33.5^{(24.5)}$	$-^{(27)}$	$51.0^{(3.5)}$	$32.5^{(10)}$	$3.0^{(6.5)}$
0.1	$80.5^{(74.5)}$	$54.5^{(44.5)}$	$59.0^{(20.5)}$	$38.0^{(19.3)}$	$25.5^{(17)}$
1	$92.0^{(92)}$	$65.5^{(60.8)}$	$72.5^{(73.5)}$	$55.0^{(39)}$	$50.5^{(45)}$

Table 1 indicates that clean and noisy face modality GAR is higher at 0.1% and 1% value of FAR. Compared to other modalities fingerprint, palmprint, Handvein and iris. However, the at 0.01% FAR clean palmprint biometric outperform the better than considered biometrics. The lowest performance is observed in table for iris unimodal system on clean and corrupted by noise condition.

5.3   Results on Clean vs Noisy Multimodal Biometric Systems

In this section, we have presented empirical results on comparative analysis at different levels of fusion under various rules in developing multimodal approach. Different bio-modal biometric systems are proposed preserving facial feature has common modality in fusing with other employed modalities.

Table 2. Face and palmprint fusion at various levels

Fusion	Rules	GAR for face and palm		
		0.01% FAR	0.1% FAR	1% FAR
Sensor level	Wavelet	$67.5^{(50.5)}$	$82.0^{(81.5)}$	$94.5^{(92.5)}$
Feature level	Min-Max	$85.5^{(53.5)}$	$92.0^{(86.5)}$	$96.0^{(94.0)}$
	Z-Score	$81.5^{(42)}$	$89.5^{(60)}$	$95.0^{(83)}$
	Tanh	$81.5^{(43.5)}$	$90.0^{(61)}$	$94.0^{(83.5)}$
Score level	Min	$80.5^{(77)}$	$89.9^{(88.5)}$	$94.0^{(92)}$
	Max	$47.5^{(33)}$	$89.5^{(65)}$	$97.5^{(88)}$
	Sum	$87.5^{(86.5)}$	$93.0^{(91.5)}$	$97.5^{(96)}$
Decision level	OR	$47.5^{(32)}$	$89.5^{(71)}$	$97.5^{(88.5)}$
	AND	$63.0^{(54)}$	$75.0^{(66)}$	$83.0^{(76.5)}$

Table 2, shows the evaluation of face and palmprint modalities being fused and comparison is done on sensor, feature, score and decision level fusion with their relevant fusion rules. On fusion of face with palmprint modality, the bimodal verification system has yielded results: at sensor level fusion (94.5%, 92.5%), feature level-Min-Max rule (96%, 94%), score level-Sum rule (97.5%, 96%), decision level-Or rule (97.5%, 88.5%) of GAR at 1% FAR on clean and noisy database respectively. We can observe that sum rule of score level fusion gives highest values of GAR% at different values of FAR% compared to other fusion levels and its rules. Definitely these results proves performance is high when compared to the earlier experimented unimodal case.

Table 3. Face and fingerprint fusion at various levels

Fusion	Rules	GAR for face and fingerprint		
		0.01% FAR	0.1% FAR	1% FAR
Sensor level	Wavelet	$68.0^{(-)}$	$80.5^{(65)}$	$93.5^{(89.5)}$
Feature level	Min-Max	$54.0^{(51.5)}$	$57.5^{(56.5)}$	$69.5^{(68)}$
	Z-Score	$44.5^{(39.5)}$	$61.0^{(58)}$	$74.0^{(71)}$
	Tanh	$44.5^{(39)}$	$61.0^{(57.5)}$	$76.5^{(72)}$
Score level	Min	$53.0^{(44)}$	$61.0^{(58.5)}$	$70.5^{(69)}$
	Max	$34.0^{(29.5)}$	$80.5^{(79)}$	$92.0^{(90)}$
	Sum	$78.5^{(70)}$	$91.5^{(80)}$	$96.5^{(92)}$
Decision level	OR	$34.0^{(30)}$	$80.5^{(58.5)}$	$92.0^{(73.5)}$
	AND	$44.0^{(29.5)}$	$56.5^{(54)}$	$69.0^{(65)}$

Table 4. Face and Handvein fusion at various levels

Fusion	Rules	GAR for face and Handvein		
		0.01% FAR	0.1% FAR	1% FAR
Sensor level	Wavelet	$46.0^{(34)}$	$81.5^{(72.5)}$	$91.5^{(89)}$
Feature level	Min-Max	$45.0^{(24.5)}$	$80.5^{(79.5)}$	$92.5^{(90)}$
	Z-Score	$42.5^{(33)}$	$78.0^{(50)}$	$94.5^{(75)}$
	Tanh	$42.5^{(34)}$	$78.0^{(54)}$	$94.5^{(80)}$
Score level	Min	$45.0^{(22.5)}$	$78.5^{(73.5)}$	$91.5^{(90)}$
	Max	$30.5^{(10.5)}$	$41.5^{(21)}$	$58.5^{(39.5)}$
	Sum	$75.5^{(54)}$	$88.0^{(83)}$	$95.0^{(92.5)}$
Decision level	OR	$45^{(22.5)}$	$78.5^{(73.5)}$	$90.5^{(89)}$
	AND	$30.5^{(10.5)}$	$41.5^{(22)}$	$58.5^{(41)}$

Results on fusion of face and fingerprint is tabulated in Table 3, Sensor level fusion (93.5%, 89.5%), feature level-Tanh rule (76.5%, 72%), score level –sum rule (96.5%, 92%), decision level (92%, 73.5%) has obtained GAR at 1% FAR for clean and noisy database respectively. Again here also score level fusion sum rule is performing better than other levels of fusion. Even the sensor level fusion performance is healthier. The lowest performance is found on decision level AND rule.

Table 4 infers the multimodal approach of face and Handvein. Even though, score level fusion-Sum rule gives (95%, 92.5%) highest performance on both clean and noisy data respectively, the feature level fusions normalization schemes Min-Max, Z-score and Tanh perform equally well with GAR% with different values of FAR.

Table 5. Face and Iris fusion at various levels

Fusion	Rules	GAR for face and Iris		
		0.01% FAR	0.1% FAR	1% FAR
Sensor level	Wavelet	$61.0^{(53.5)}$	$78.5^{(74.5)}$	$92.5^{(89.5)}$
Feature level	Min-Max	$78.0^{(70)}$	$89.0^{(82.5)}$	$96.0^{(94)}$
	Z-Score	$74.5^{(40)}$	$86.5^{(60.5)}$	$95.0^{(84)}$
	Tanh	$78.0^{(42)}$	$92.0^{(65)}$	$96.0^{(87)}$
Score level	Min	$41.5^{(36)}$	$57.0^{(52)}$	$75.5^{(70)}$
	Max	$35.0^{(21.5)}$	$82.0^{(64.5)}$	$93.5^{(89.5)}$
	Sum	$71.0^{(70)}$	$83.0^{(80)}$	$94.0^{(90)}$
Decision level	OR	$34.0^{(30)}$	$82.0^{(74.5)}$	$93.5^{(87)}$
	AND	$41.5^{(24)}$	$57.0^{(52)}$	$75.5^{(65)}$

Finally, we have fused Face with Iris, at different levels of fusion. Results from Table 5 states that, all the normalization schemes of feature level outperform other level of fusion and has given highest level of accuracy. In all the set of experiments score level fusion is performing consistently.

6   Conclusions

This paper presents an overview of unimodal and multimodal biometric verification systems and comparative study on levels of fusion. Multimodal biometric systems will solve the drawbacks faced by unimodal systems more elegantly as seen from our results. From the experimental results obtained we arrive at the following inference: (a) all biometric modalities performance is always dependent on feature extraction in our case we have used a generalized feature extraction Log gabor which gives better performance results. (b) A new modality introduced to any biometric system gives complementary information. Hence, one can find significant improvement in accuracy. (c) In Score level fusion, sum rule always gives better performance compared to other levels of fusion. (d) While improved performance is available with increasing additional modalities, judging the right combination is very critical. (e) The proposed model gathers the results collectively on both the clean and noisy data experimented on all levels of fusion under the adopted rules gives the robustness analysis, we can see from the results obtained that the system is performing consistently on both kinds of data on most of the evaluation sets exhibited on the tables. In general multimodal always yields better results than any other approaches. However developing a generalized framework that governs the dynamic selection of Modality/Fusion/Feature extraction algorithms implies higher cost, more processing and difficult to deploy and maintain, our future work would be intended working on this idea.

References

1. Yang, S., Shin, D., Park, R., Jung, J.: Block-based noise estimation using adaptive Gaussian filtering. IEEE Trans. Consum. Electr. **51**, 218–226 (2005)
2. Capobianco, L., Moretti, S., Chiarantini, L., Alparone, D.L., Selva, M., Butera, F.: Quality assessment of data products from a new generation airborne imaging spectrometer. In: Proceedings of IEEE International Geoscience and Remote Sensing Symposium, vol. 4, pp. 422–425 (2009)
3. Eskandari, M., Toygar, Ö., Hasan, D.: A new approach for face-iris multimodal biometric recognition using score fusion. Int. J. Pattern Recogn. Artif. Intell. **27**(03), 1356004 (2013)
4. Geng, X., Smith-Miles, K., Wang, L., Li, M., Qiang, W.: Context-aware fusion: a case study on fusion of gait and face for human identification in video. Pattern Recogn. **43**(10), 3660–3673 (2010)
5. He, M., et al.: Performance evaluation of score level fusion in multimodal biometric systems. Pattern Recogn. **43**(5), 1789–1800 (2010)
6. Hezil, N., Boukrouche, A.: Multimodal biometric recognition using human ear and palmprint. **6**, 351–359 (2017)
7. Rasmy, M.E., Badawi, A.M., Youssef, I.S., Abaza, A.A.: Multimodal biometrics system based on face profile and ear (2014)
8. Jain, A.K., Chen, Y., Demirkus, M.: Pores and ridges: high-resolution fingerprint matching using level 3 features. IEEE Trans. Pattern Anal. Mach. Intell. **29**(1), 15–27 (2007)
9. Kahlil, A.T., Abou-Chadi, F.E.M.: Generation of iris codes using 1D log-gabor filter. In: 2010 International Conference on Computer Engineering and Systems (ICCES), pp. 329–336 (2010)
10. Kisku, D.R., Rattani, A., Gupta, P., Sing, J.K.: Biometric sensor image fusion for identity verification: a case study with wavelet-based fusion rules graph matching. In: 2009 IEEE Conference on Technologies for Homeland Security, pp. 433–439, May 2009
11. Kisku, D.R., Rattani, A., Gupta, P., Sing, J.K.: Biometric sensor image fusion for identity verification: a case study with wavelet-based fusion rules graph matching. In: 2009 IEEE Conference on Technologies for Homeland Security, HST 2009, pp. 433–439, May 2009
12. Li, S.Z., Jain, A.K. (eds.): Handbook of Face Recognition, 2nd edn. Springer, Heidelberg (2011)
13. Kearns, M.: Efficient noise-tolerant learning from statistical queries. **45**(6), 983–1006 (1998)
14. Luthon, F., Liévin, M., Keeve, E.: Entropic estimation of noise for medical volume restoration. **3**, 871–874 (2002)

15. Ricci, E., Salmeri, M., Mencattini, A., Salsano, A.: Noise estimation in digital images using fuzzy processing. In: Proceedings of International Conference on Image Processing, vol. 1, pp. 517–520 (2001)
16. Marcialis, G.L., Roli, F., Didaci, L.: Personal identity verification by serial fusion of fingerprint and face matchers. Pattern Recogn. **42**(11), 2807–2817 (2009)
17. Zriakhov, M., Kaarna, A., Ponomarenko, N., Lukin, V., Astola, J.: An automatic approach to lossy compression of AVIRIS images. In: Proceedings of IEEE International Geoscience and Remote Sensing Symposium, vol. 4, pp. 472–475 (2007)
18. Nadheen, M.F., Poornima, S.: Fusion in multimodal biometric using iris and ear. In: 2013 IEEE Conference on Information Communication Technologies, pp. 83–87, April 2013
19. Poh, N., et al.: Benchmarking quality-dependent and cost-sensitive score-level multimodal biometric fusion algorithms. IEEE Trans. Inf. Forensics Secur. **4**(4), 849–866 (2009)
20. Zhu, L., Zhang, S.: Multimodal biometric identification system based on finger geometry, knuckle print and palm print. Pattern Recogn. Lett. **31**(12), 1641–1649 (2010)
21. Dharaskar, R.V., Chhabria, S.A., Thakare, V.M.: Survey of fusion techniques for design of efficient multimodal systems. In: 2013 International Conference on Machine Intelligence and Research Advancement, pp. 486–492 (2013)
22. Hesser, J., Pyatykh, S., Zheng, L.: Image noise level estimation by principal component analysis. **22**(2), 687–699 (2013)
23. Sim, T., Zhang, S., Janakiraman, R., Kumar, S.: Continuous verification using multimodal biometrics. IEEE Trans. Pattern Anal. Mach. Intell. **29**(4), 687–700 (2007)
24. Snelick, R., Uludag, U., Mink, A., Indovina, M., Jain, A.: Large-scale evaluation of multimodal biometric authentication using state-of-the-art systems. IEEE Trans. Pattern Anal. Mach. Intell. **27**(3), 450–455 (2005)
25. Pyatykh, S., Hesser, J., Zheng, L.: Image noise level estimation by principal component analysis. **22**, 687–699 (2013)
26. Verlinde, P., Chollet, G., Acheroy, M.: Multi-modal identity verification using expert fusion. Inf. Fusion **1**(1), 17–33 (2000)
27. Wu, X., Zhu, X.: Class noise vs. attribute noise: a quantitative study. **22**, 177–210 (2004)

Temporal Super-Pixel Based Convolutional Neural Network (TS-CNN) for Human Activity Recognition in Unconstrained Videos

G. G. Lakshmi Priya[1], Mrinal Jain[1], K. C. Santosh[2],
and P. V. S. S. R. Chandra Mouli[3](✉)

[1] School of Information Technology and Engineering, Vellore Institute of Technology, Vellore, Tamilnadu, India
lakshmipriya.gg@vit.ac.in
[2] Department of Computer Science, University of South Dakota, Vermillion, USA
santosh.kc@ieee.org
[3] Department of Computer Applications, National Institute of Technology, Jamshedpur, Jharkhand, India
chandramouli.ca@nitjsr.ac.in

Abstract. Human activity recognition and video analysis is quite an interesting field and is relevant to a number of research areas. A plethora of applications like (active) video surveillance systems, human-computer interaction, medical analysis, sports (video) interpretation, and video retrieval for content-based search engines depend on extensive video understanding. To determine human actions in highly controlled environments is quite simple and solved; however, this task still remains to be a challenge in an unconstrained environment. In this paper, a temporal super-pixel based convolutional neural network (TS-CNN) is proposed to recognize human activity for enabling real-time monitoring of patients, children, and elderly persons in an unconstrained environment. For every video segment, temporal super-pixels are extracted and output of these pathways are combined with CNN architecture to correctly recognize the human activity. The performance of the proposed method (measured by metrics like accuracy and confusion matrix) is compared with the existing model.

Keywords: Human activity recognition · Temporal super-pixel · Convolutional neural network

1 Introduction

Due to advancement in the field of multimedia and internet technologies, a large number of video data sets are made available online. Currently, a lot of research is being conducted on understanding human activities and behaviors from these

K. C. Santosh and R. S. Hegadi (Eds.): RTIP2R 2018, CCIS 1035, pp. 255–264, 2019.
https://doi.org/10.1007/978-981-13-9181-1_23

videos. Such automated systems, that can analyze and interpret the content of these videos are in great demand. Recognition of human activities (and later, their localization) is the major component of such a system, and of paramount importance, as it determines the performance of the entire system. Researchers have devised a number of methods to interpret human actions in highly controlled and/or simulated environments. However, extrapolating these techniques to the real world remains a challenge, accounting to several erratic factors such as camera motion, cluttered (and perhaps irrelevant) background, occlusion, and variations in scale/viewpoint/perspective. Furthermore, the same action can be performed by two persons in a different manner. Occlusion of objects may occur frequently in the unconstrained environments. This dissimilarity can be further exacerbated by other factors like clothing, illumination in frames and unexpected background changes.

In supervised learning, it is extremely tedious to collect sufficient training data for the events occurring in an unusual environment. In this case, algorithms which used large training data for constructing the unusual event model become unsuitable. There is a need for a method that learns from a minimum number of sample data and yields better accuracy in recognizing the human actions.

The complexity of human activity recognition arises due to the difficulty in understanding the variety of problems, ranging from gestures recognition to the identification (and possible segmentation) of physical activities like running or climbing up the stairs. Recent breakthroughs state that deep learning is a substitute for hand-crafted feature extraction and classification techniques. Convolutional Neural Networks (CNN) are producing state-of-the-art results in both speech and image domains [3,4]. However, this end-to-end deep learning concept can not only benefit image and speech, but can also be used for video domains (including, but not limited to human activity recognition).

In this paper, a temporal super-pixel based convolutional neural network (TS-CNN) is proposed to recognize human activity for enabling real-time monitoring of patients, children, and elderly persons in an unconstrained environment. For every video segment, temporal super-pixels are extracted and output of these pathways are combined with CNN architecture to correctly recognize the human activity.

2   Related Work

Various research works have been carried out on this topic where few of the researchers' works are highlighted in this discussion:

Chang et al. [1]extracted local space-time features and for recognition, integrate such video representations of the features with SVM classification schemes. Ibrahim et al. [2] proposed a deep model to capture dynamics based on LSTM (long short-term memory) models. Not surprisingly, in other domains, such as biomedical and healthcare, bi-directional LSTM has been addressed [7,8].

Wang et al. [12] proposed a robust and efficient video representation for action recognition which improves dense trajectory video features by explicit camera motion estimation and illustrated the efficiency of the proposed action recognition on a number of video benchmarks.

EXMOVES: Mid-level Features for Efficient Action Recognition and Video Analysis by Tran and Torresani [11]utilizes a scalable mid-level representation for video analysis based on exemplary movement classifiers. MoFAP: A Multi-Level Representation for Action Recognition by Wang et al. [13] introduces a multi-level video representation consisting of local motion, atomic actions and composites, illustrating results on activity understanding.

Ryoo and Matthies [6] examine interaction-level human activities from a first-person viewpoint and considers temporal patterns generated by various types of interactions. Zhao et al. [14] describe latent-variable models that learn mid-level representations of activities defined by multiple group members.

Li et al. [5] presents a graphical model for learning and recognizing human actions. Authors also presented a novel approach for automatic recognition of human activities for video surveillance applications. Thakkar et al. [10] present a 3-D Convolutional neural networks (3-D CNN) based hierarchical approach for human action classification. In general, human actions refer to positioning and movement of hands and legs and hence can be classified based on those actions performed by hands or by legs or, in some cases, both.

3   Proposed Method

In this paper, a temporal super-pixel based convolutional neural network (TS-CNN) is proposed to recognize human activity. For every video segment, temporal super-pixels are extracted and output of these pathways are combined with CNN architecture to correctly recognize the human activity.

3.1   Data Pre-processing

The videos were captured at a frame rate of 25 fps. It is known that within a second, a human body does not perform the very significant movement. This implies that most of the frames (per second) in the video will be redundant. Therefore, only a subset of all the frames in a video can be extracted which will reduce the size of the input data and in turn help the model train faster and can also prevent over-fitting. Frame skipping is performed which extracts the frames sparsely and uniformly from the entire video. However, frames are extracted irrespective of its visual content. Instead of using a frame skipping concept, frames can be selected based on temporal super-pixels [5]. Grouping of pixels into a meaningful homogeneous region within the frame are referred to as super-pixels and the temporal relationship between the super-pixels of the same object across the frames are extracted as temporal super-pixels. Based on the temporal coherence super-pixels, a frame for the video segment is selected which acts as the input image for the model.

3.2   Model Description

The image is divided into regions, and each region is then assigned to different hidden nodes. Each hidden node finds a pattern in only one of the regions in the image. This region is determined by a kernel (also called a filter/window). A filter is convolved over both x-axis and y-axis. Multiple filters are used in order to extract different patterns from the image. The output of one filter when convolved throughout the entire image generates a 2-d layer of neurons called a feature map. Each filter is responsible for one feature map. These feature maps can be stacked into a 3-d array, which can then be used as the input to the layers further. This is performed by the layer known as the convolutional layer in a CNN. These layers are followed by the pooling layers, that reduce the spatial dimensions of the output (obtained from the convolutional layers).

In short, a window is slid in both the axes and the max value in that filter/window is taken (Max-Pooling layer). Sometimes average pooling layer is also used where the only difference is to take the average value within the window instead of the maximum value. Therefore, the convolutional layers increase the depth of the input image, whereas the pooling layers decrease the spatial dimensions (height and width).

The importance of such an architecture is that it encodes the content of an image that can be flattened into a 1-dimensional array. It's 2-dimensional because the filter is convolved along the x-axis and y-axis of the image. But in the case of a video, we have an additional temporal axis – z-axis. So, a 3-d convolutional layer is used – where the filter (also 3-dimensional) is convolved across all the three axes. Multiple convolutional and pooling layers are stacked together. These are followed by some fully-connected layers, where the last layer is the output layer. The output layer contains 6 neurons (one for each category). The network shown in Fig. 1 gives a probability of an input to belong to each category/class.

Model Parameters: For each convolutional layer:

- filters - the number of feature maps required as the output of that convolutional layer.
- kernel_size - the size of the window that will get convolved along all the axes of the input data to produce a single feature map.
- strides - the number of pixels by which the convolutional window should shift by.
- padding - To decide what happens on the edges - either the input gets cropped (valid) or the input is padded with zeros to maintain the same dimensionality (same).
- activation - activation function to be used for that layer – ReLU

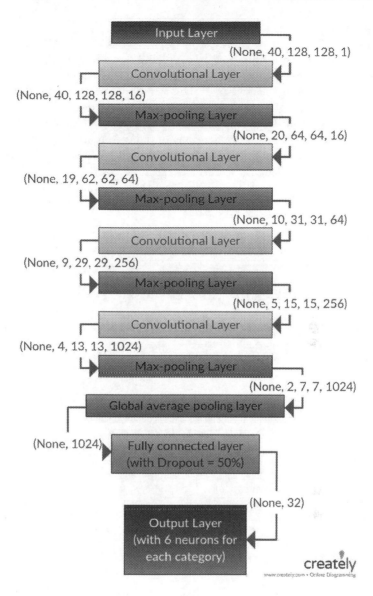

Fig. 1. Model architecture

For each pooling layer:

– pool_size - the size of the window.
– strides - the number of pixels by which the pooling window should shift by.
– padding - To decide what happens on the edges - either the input gets cropped (valid) or the input is padded with zeros to maintain the same dimensionality (same).

Following are some of the important specifications of the model:

- The depth of the vector obtained by the last convolutional layer is 1024.
- A Global Average Pooling layer (GAP) then takes the average value from each of these 1024 dimensions and gives a 1-dimensional vector representing the entire video.
- The GAP is followed by a fully-connected layer containing 32 neurons. This fully-connected layer also has a dropout of 0.5, meaning that for each epoch, 50% of the neurons of this layer will be deactivated. This is what helps the model prevent overfitting.
- Finally, there is the output layer with 6 neurons (one for each category). The network gives a probability for the input video to belong to each of the 6 categories.
- All the convolutional layers have 'ReLU' as the activation function. It gives the best performance out of a CNN.

4   Experimental Results and Discussions

The proposed method is evaluated using the KTH dataset [9] containing 600 video files, 100 videos for each of the 6 categories. Table 1 depicts the class labels of the human activity in the dataset.

Table 1. Class label of human activity in the videos

Class label	Mapped integer
Boxing	0
Handclapping	1
Handwaving	2
Jogging	3
Running	4
Walking	5

The proposed model results in an accuracy of 64.5% and Fig. 2 below, depicts the learning curve of the model over 40 epochs.

Benchmark: The existing models [11] use the local features in space-time extracted to capture and describe local occurrence of events in a video. The general idea is to describe the nature of events that defines several types of image descriptors over local spatio-temporal neighborhoods and evaluate these descriptors in the context of recognizing human activities. These feature points have stable locations in space-time and provide a potential basis for part-based representations of complex motions in the video.

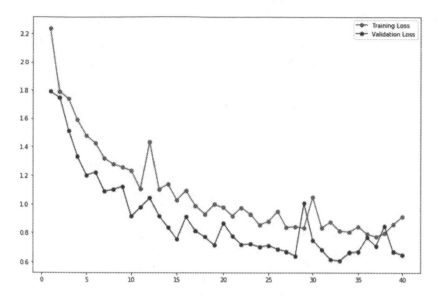

Fig. 2. Learning curve for model evaluation

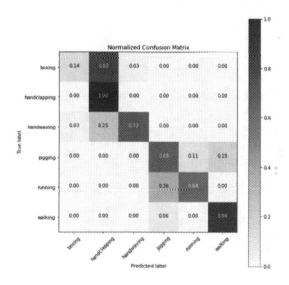

Fig. 3. Proposed model confusion matrix (normalized)

Comparison of Proposed Model with the Benchmark

In case of 'Walking', when the actual label was 'walking' – the benchmark predicted the label as 'walking' 84% of the time, whereas the proposed model predicted 'walking' 94% of the time (Figs. 3 and 4).

This suggests that the proposed model was better (or at par) at predicting these actions than the benchmark model (Table 2).

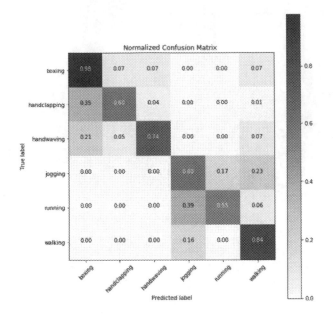

Fig. 4. Benchmark model confusion matrix (normalized)

Table 2. Overall results

Action	Benchmark model	Proposed model
Walking	0.84	0.94
Jogging	0.60	0.69
Handwaving	0.74	0.72
Handclapping	0.60	1.00
Running	0.55	0.64
Boxing	0.98	0.14

Some observations:

- For 'handclapping' the proposed model gave 100% accurate results (i.e., the model successfully distinguished handclapping from all other activities and had "no confusion" when giving a prediction about handclapping).
- Videos in which the action being performed was 'Boxing' was predicted by the benchmark model with a better recognition rate than that of the proposed model. Our model confused 'Boxing' with 'Handclapping' 83% of the time.

In the case of 'walking', since the movement of the person is slow, he is captured in most of the frames. As the speed of movement of the person is increased, more and more frames captured are empty – they do not describe any action. It can be observed in the case of 'running', only a handful of frames show a person running, rest all the frames are empty. This is one major problem

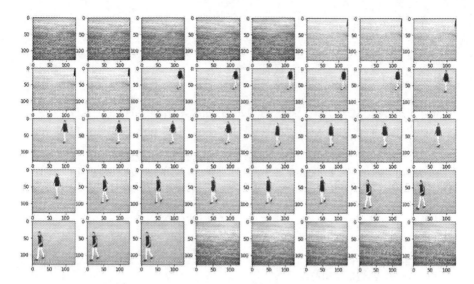

Fig. 5. Video frames of the action 'Walking'

with the dataset used. Suppose, if for the proposed model, a video that has all empty frames (no human performing any action) is given as input then still the model will predict it as 'running', as the frames of the video resemble that of 'running' with a high probability. This is also the reason why the proposed model gave a lower false positive rate for the actions involving the hands (boxing, handclapping, and handwaving) than those involving the legs (or movement of the entire body). One possible way to solve the problem could be to calculate the average intensity of frames (with and without a human in the frame). Then, while selecting the frames, discard those with the average intensity similar to the average intensity of frame without any human (Fig. 5).

5   Conclusion

In this paper, a new temporal super-pixel based convolutional neural network (TS-CNN) is proposed to recognize human activity in unconstrained videos. Based on the temporal coherence super-pixels, a frame for the video segment is selected which acts as the input image for the model. Constructing the model with different structure and hyperparameters and choosing the best was the most challenging task. The proposed model, as seen in the learning curve, overfitted to the training data after a certain number of epochs. This suggests that there is a lot of tuning that can be on the model in order to prevent overfitting and hence improving the results. Also, in the future, there is the possibility of constructing a potential model that can give a much better performance than our current model.

Acknowledgment. The first author thank VIT University for providing 'VIT SEED GRANT' for carrying out this research work.

References

1. Chang, J., Wei, D., Fisher, J.W.: A video representation using temporal superpixels. In: Proceedings of the IEEE Conference on Computer Vision and Pattern Recognition, pp. 2051–2058 (2013)
2. Ibrahim, M.S., Muralidharan, S., Deng, Z., Vahdat, A., Mori, G.: A hierarchical deep temporal model for group activity recognition. In: Proceedings of the IEEE Conference on Computer Vision and Pattern Recognition, pp. 1971–1980 (2016)
3. Hafemann, L.G., Sabourin, R., Oliveira, L.S.: Learning features for offline handwritten signature verification using deep convolutional neural networks. Pattern Recogn. **70**, 163–176 (2017)
4. Krizhevsky, A., Sutskever, I., Hinton, G.E.: Imagenet classification with deep convolutional neural networks. In: Advances in Neural Information Processing Systems, pp. 1097–1105 (2012)
5. Li, W., Zhang, Z., Liu, Z.: Expandable data-driven graphical modeling of human actions based on salient postures. IEEE Trans. Circ. Syst. Video Technol. **18**(11), 1499–1510 (2008)
6. Ryoo, M.S., Matthies, L.: First-person activity recognition: feature, temporal structure, and prediction. Int. J. Comput. Vis. **119**(3), 307–328 (2016)
7. Saini, R., Kumar, P., Kaur, B., Roy, P.P., Dogra, D.P., Santosh, K.: Kinect sensor-based interaction monitoring system using the BLSTM neural network in healthcare. Int. J. Mach. Learn. Cybern. (2018). https://doi.org/10.1007/s13042-018-0887-5
8. Santosh, K.C., Roy, P.P.: Arrow detection in biomedical images using sequential classifier. Int. J. Mach. Learn. Cybern. **9**(6), 993–1006 (2018). https://doi.org/10.1007/s13042-016-0623-y
9. Schuldt, C., Laptev, I., Caputo, B.: Recognizing human actions: a local SVM approach. In: 2004 Proceedings of the 17th International Conference on Pattern Recognition, ICPR 2004, vol. 3, pp. 32–36. IEEE (2004)
10. Thakkar, S., Joshi, M.V.: Classification of human actions using 3-D convolutional neural networks: a hierarchical approach. In: Rameshan, R., Arora, C., Dutta Roy, S. (eds.) NCVPRIPG 2017. CCIS, vol. 841, pp. 14–23. Springer, Singapore (2018). https://doi.org/10.1007/978-981-13-0020-2_2
11. Tran, D., Torresani, L.: Exmoves: mid-level features for efficient action recognition and video analysis. Int. J. Comput. Vis. **119**(3), 239–253 (2016)
12. Wang, H., Oneata, D., Verbeek, J., Schmid, C.: A robust and efficient video representation for action recognition. Int. J. Comput. Vis. **119**(3), 219–238 (2016)
13. Wang, L., Qiao, Y., Tang, X.: MoFAP: a multi-level representation for action recognition. Int. J. Comput. Vis. **119**(3), 254–271 (2016)
14. Zhao, F., Huang, Y., Wang, L., Xiang, T., Tan, T.: Learning relevance restricted boltzmann machine for unstructured group activity and event understanding. Int. J. Comput. Vis. **119**(3), 329–345 (2016)

Content Based Video Retrieval Using SURF, BRISK and HARRIS Features for Query-by-image

Tejaswi Potluri[1(✉)] and Nitta Gnaneswara Rao[2]

[1] VNR Vignana Jyothi Institute of Engineering and Technology,
Hyderabad, India
tejaswi_p@vnrvjiet.in
[2] VFSTR, Guntur, India
gnani.nitta@gmail.com
http://www.vnrvjiet.ac.in/csedept/faculty/39.pdfl

Abstract. Content Based Video Retrieval (CBVR) is an approach for retrieving most relevant videos from the video database. Applications of CBVR are increasing day by day. This paper uses Speeded up Robust Feature (SURF), Binary Robust Invariant Scalable Key Points (BRISK) and HARRIS corner Detector to retrieve the similar videos. Our proposed system firstly identifies the key frames from the video using color Histogram method. In this method the color component is used to identify the key Frame. Next, above said three features are derived from all the videos in database. The three features are also calculated for the query image. By using similarity matching techniques, all the features are jointly used to assign rankings to the videos in the database based on the features of query image. The videos having ranks below threshold can be retrieved as most relevant videos to the query image given.

Keywords: CBVR · SURF · BRISK · HARRIS · Color histogram · Key frame

1 Introduction

In our day to day life, it is observed that, entire world keeps on browsing for some information. Most of the world prefers with the data which is visualised effectively. That is the reason where videos are playing a vital role in providing the information. This increases the scope for the research in Video Processing.

Due to the advancement in the latest trends, challenging task is to retrieve the most relevant videos from the large datasets. Content based Video retrieval is the method where most relevant videos to the query are retrieved from the datasets based on the features (content of the video) extracted from the video and the query. The query can be given in two ways i.e., Query-by-image and Query-by-video. Proposed system uses Query-by-image. In Query-by-image input is taken as a image for which most relevant videos will be retrieved.

© Springer Nature Singapore Pte Ltd. 2019
K. C. Santosh and R. S. Hegadi (Eds.): RTIP2R 2018, CCIS 1035, pp. 265–276, 2019.
https://doi.org/10.1007/978-981-13-9181-1_24

The organization of paper is described as below: Sect. 3 explains about the flow of the proposed system SHB Features for retrieval, Sect. 3.1 explains the key frame selection and storage of key frames. Section 3.2 describes the three feature extraction where Sect. 3.3 explains how the similarity matching is performed. Section 4 shows the results and comparison of the results of existing system with proposed system.

2   Literature Survey

Due to the advancement in the technology, most of the people are depending upon the videos of the data. As most of the data is in the format of videos, there is need of retrieving videos from the dataset. There are several ways to retrieve most relevant videos from the database. The basic method is retrieving the videos by text annotation. In this method, the text keywords given to the title of the video are used to retrieve the most relevant videos. The context differs from person to person which doesn't give better results using text annotation.

Due to this limitation the retrieval of videos from database is done by using content of the video. The content is the features of the video. There is lot of content in the video. The content is like color, shape, texture, motion analysis etc.

The key factor of video retrieval depends upon the Key Frame selection. In some of the existing systems [4,5], the key frame selection is not done by efficient algorithms. The applications where key frame selection is done by efficient algorithms can retrieve the most relevant videos.

Existing system explained in [22] uses texture features for retrieval. But, this feature works efficiently for medical images. As medical images are not used here, texture feature is not considered.

As explained in [21], region based image retrieval is used which can also be used for video retrieval. This has more complexity which is not suitable for our dataset.

As explained in [9], the color feature is used for similarity based retrieval where, color indexing and color clustering are implemented. These are implemented on two datasets i.e., trademark images and flag images. The time complexity increases logarithmically with the database size.

Some of the existing systems [4,5] use only the color feature to extract the most relevant videos. But only color feature doesn't give better results as videos of different con-texts may have same color combination. Some of the existing systems [7,8,10,12–17] use only shape feature, texture feature or combination of both to retrieve most relevant videos from the database.

The system proposed in [1] uses the SURF descriptor to match the input to the videos in the database and retrieves the most relevant videos. The only SURF descriptor uses huge storage for video indexing. Stochastic dimensionality reduction is also implemented in this paper. Minimum distance classifiers are used in retrieval stage. The performance of the system is 78% as mentioned in [1]. To improve the efficiency, all three features like SURF, HARRIS, BRISK are combined in our proposed system.

3 SHB (SURF, HARRIS, BRISK) Model for Retrieval

Here, SHB Features stands for SURF, Harris, and Brisk Features. In our proposed system, all the videos of our database are pre-processed. In pre-processing, for all the videos in the database, key frames are generated and stored in the database. The key frames are generated using color histograms. For all the key frames, the mean values of three features like SURF, HARRIS, BRISK are extracted. These mean values are stored in the database.

In our proposed system, the query is given as an image. When query is given to our system, mean values of all three features are calculated. These mean values of query image are compared with the mean values of database. Based on the ranks obtained, most relevant videos can be retrieved. This process can be observed in the Fig. 1:

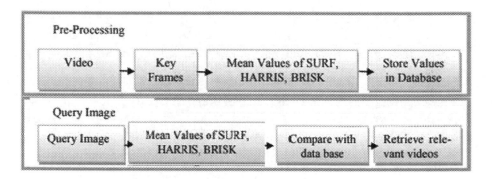

Fig. 1. Proposed system data flow

3.1 Key Frame Selection

Generally, Video is a collection of frames which are in turn images. In general, a video can have a rate of 20 frames per second to 30 frames per second. It is observed that not all the frames have the useful content or information which can be used for retrieval or processing. The complexity of the system increases if all the frames are processed. So, the frames which are having meaningful and useful content or features are considered. These selected frames are termed as Key Frames.

From the Fig. 2, it is observed that Video can be divided into shots. The shot is nothing but the scene change. It is not preferred to select the key frames [11] on time basis as key frame selection based on time does not result the frames based on content. The number of shots differs from video to video. In the next step, shots are divided in to frames. In the next step, key frames are selected from the set of frames by using color histograms.

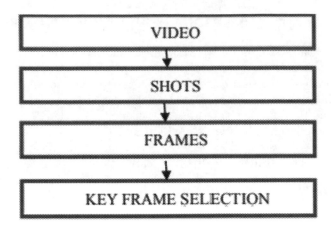

Fig. 2. Categorising video into key Frames

There are several ways to find out the key frames from a video based on the application. In our system, color histograms are used to find out the key frames of videos.

There are different color models for an image like RGB, HSV etc. Color histogram [2] can be constructed for any model. When these two models are compared, HSV model is considered as a better color model than RGB. This is because HSV model has more linear scalability and more acceptable.

RGB model is converted in to HSV Model. After converting, if all the colors are considered, it results in 16 million dimensional vectors. So color quantization is performed. Color quantisation means to designate a group of colors to represent the image color space and then map the color space to colors selected. The color quantisation of an image is done by the method used in [2]. Color quantisation results in one dimensional vector. Color histogram is the estimation of pixel probability. Probability of all the color pixels can be calculated through color histogram.

Color histograms for frames are constructed. Euclidean Distance is used for comparing two color histograms. Key Frame is selected based on the threshold value.

From the Fig. 3 you can understand that, in the first step, color histograms are constructed for all the frames. In the next step comparison of the color histograms of two frames is done. The frame for which the Euclidean distance value is less than the threshold value is considered as key frame.

The same process is repeated for all the frames in the video and then the key frames are identified. The number of key frames identified for each video will differ from video to video. It depends upon the scene change. The key Frames identified are stored in our database, so that the next processing is done only for the key frames.

Figure 4, is the screenshot about the key frame selection. In the left side corner, you can identify the key frame selected for that video. The size of key

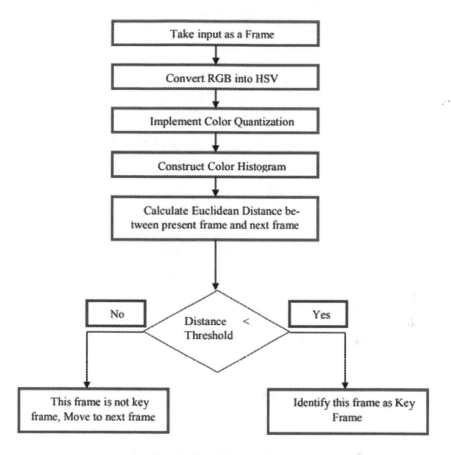

Fig. 3. Key frame selection

Fig. 4. Key frame

frame is 320 by 240. Observe the key frames generated for a video in Fig. 5. All these key frames are saved in a database. The same process is implemented for all the videos in our database. The Key Frames of all the videos are stored in the data-base. In the Fig. 5 you can identify the various key frames of videos in the database. The various key frames are stored with different naming conventions.

3.2   Feature Extraction

Key frames are only processed for the feature extraction. Features like SURF, BRISK, HARRIS are extracted for all the key frames. The comparison of these features and their performance can be analysed from [19]. The detailed explanation of all the feature extraction is given below. Instead of using single feature alone for comparison, all the three features are combined for implementing similarity matching. The similarity matching is also detailed below.

SURF Feature. SURF stands for Speeded up Robust Features [6,18]. It is a local feature descriptor and locator which is calculated based on the intensity distribution over the neighbourhood. Rotational invariance can be achieved by calculating orientation incircular manner. SURF's feature descriptor calculation is based upon the sum of the Haar wavelet responses which are calculated in the both x and y directions around the local point of interest. This can be computed by the help of integral image as below.

$$S(x,y) = \sum_{i=0}^{x} \sum_{j=0}^{y} I(i,j) \tag{1}$$

Firstly, the square region centred on the feature point is constructed which in turn is divided into 4×4 sub regions. For each region haar wavelet response is calculated by weighing using guassian. Thus, each sub region is associated with four dimensional vectors as below.

$$V = \left(\sum dx, \sum dy, \sum |dx|, \sum |dy| \right) \tag{2}$$

HARRIS Feature. One of the famous computer vision algorithms is the Harris Corner Detector. It is used to extract corners and inter features of an image [20]. It is widely used in image applications as it works efficiently under changing illumination and rotation.

Harris corner detection algorithm works on gray scale images. So, color image is firstly converted into gray scale image. Spatial derivative Ix (x, y), Iy(x, y) is constructed over gray scale image. Now Structure tensor M is calculated. Harris response can be found as below

$$\lambda_{min} \approx \frac{\lambda_1 \lambda_2}{\lambda_1 + \lambda_2} = \frac{det(M)}{trace(M)} \tag{3}$$

Fig. 5. Key Frames of all videos

BRISK Feature. BRISK stands for Binary Robust Invariant Scalable Key points. This feature helps in reducing the computation time [3]. In this key points are detected in octave layers of the image pyramid and as well as in layers in–between. This feature results in uniform sampling point density at given radius around the keypoint.Pairwise brightness comparison results are also included in the BRISK descriptor. The implementation of BRISK can be obtained from [3].

3.3   Similarity Matching

All the three features are calculated for key frames. These features are retrieved as an array. Match metric is the distance between features. Match-metric is extracted considering these features as input. Match metric is the distance between features. To find this match-metric, either 'Exhaustive' or 'Approximate' search method is used. Exhaustive method, computes the pairwise distance between different feature vectors. Approximate method, nearest neighbor search method is used. Unique matching of features is only considered to get unique matching between the frames. Match metric is calculated for all the three features. Find the mean for these match metric values. When query is given as an image, the same process is repeated for query image and features array is extracted. The mean array of query is compared with the mean array of a key frame.

From this match-metric, identify the most similar frames to our query image. Hamming Distance is used to find out the distance between matching features. SSD (Sum of Squared Differences) or SAD (Sum of Absolute Differences) can also be used. For a perfect match, match metric results in the value zero. If the frame is not a perfect match, it results in non-zero values which is considered as rank. On the rank basis, most relevant videos to our query images can be selected.

From Figs. 6 and 7 it is observed that most relevant videos are retrieved without any deviations.

4   Results and Comparison

In this section, the results are explained in detail. In the Figs. 6 and 7, observe the query image in the left down corner.

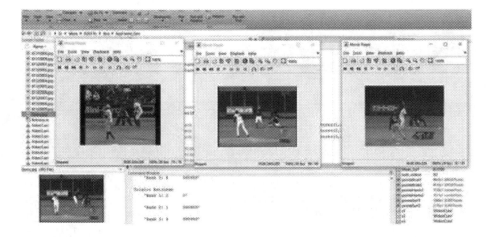

Fig. 6. Relevant videos related to cricket

UCF 11 dataset is used in this paper. This data set consists of action Categories like Basketball shooting, biking/cycling, Diving, golf swinging, horseback riding, soccer juggling, swinging, tennis swinging, trampoline jumping, volleyball spiking, and walking with a dog. These are of MPEG-4 format. Each category has 25 groups with more than 4 clips in each. Our proposed approach is implemented on these data sets. While comparing our results with the existing approach you can observe that performance is improved than existing methodologies. In the existing system, they have used only SURF descriptor. But in our proposed system, three descriptors in combination are used.

From the Figs. 8 and 9 you can observe that our proposed system has better performance compared to the existing system. The same can be observed from the below tables.

It is observed from Fig. 8 that proposed system have high precision in most of the cases when compared to other methodologies. At one point, it is observed that system which identifies brisk features performs well than our proposed system. It is observed from Fig. 9 that our proposed system has good precision

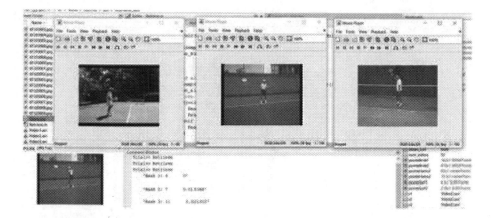

Fig. 7. Relevant videos related to Badminton

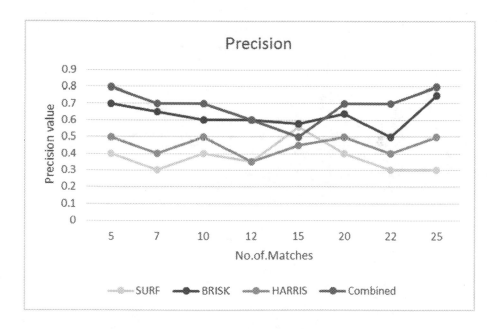

Fig. 8. Precision values for comparison

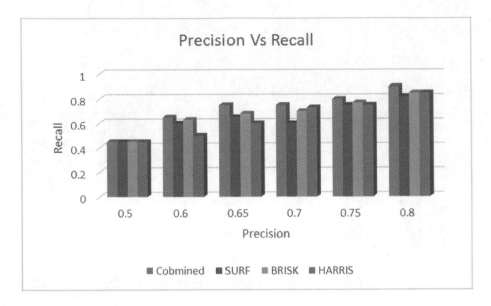

Fig. 9. Precision vs Recall

recall ratio when compared to other existing systems. At one point, proposed system performs same as the other systems, where it performs well in other cases. Although there is minor improvement in the performance in terms of precision and recall, the time complexity of proposed system is better than the existing systems (Tables 1 and 2).

Table 1. Precision values for comparison

No. of matches	SURF	BRISK	HARRIS	Combined
5	0.4	0.7	0.5	0.8
7	0.3	0.65	0.4	0.7
10	0.4	0.6	0.5	0.7
12	0.35	0.6	0.35	0.6
15	0.56	0.58	0.45	0.5
20	0.4	0.64	0.5	0.7
22	0.3	0.5	0.4	0.7
25	0.3	0.75	0.5	0.8

Table 2. Precision vs Recall

Precision	Combined	SURF	BRISK	HARRIS
0.5	0.45	0.45	0.45	0.45
0.6	0.65	0.6	0.63	0.5
0.65	0.75	0.65	0.68	0.6
0.7	0.75	0.6	0.7	0.73
0.75	0.8	0.75	0.77	0.75
0.8	0.9	0.82	0.85	0.85

5 Conclusion and Future Work

This paper have developed an efficient Content based Video Retrieval system using three features like SURF, HARRIS and BRISK. Key frames are found by using color histograms on HSV model along with color quantisation which reduces the computation time. The mean values of all the features are calculated. The combination of features better works in change of illumination and rotation. The match-metric is used to extract the exact matches and to retrieve the videos on the rank basis. This paper have implemented this system by taking input an image. This system can be extended for retrieving most relevant videos when input is given as video.

References

1. Asha, S., Sreeraj, M.: Content based video retrieval using SURF descriptor. In: Third International Conference on Advances in Computing and Communications (ICACC), pp. 1399–1408. IEEE (2013)
2. Zhang, H.J., et al.: An integrated system for content-based video retrieval and browsing. Pattern Recogn. **30**(4), 643–658 (1997)
3. Leutenegger, S., Chli, M., Siegwart, R.Y.: BRISK: binary robust invariant scalable keypoints. In: 2011 IEEE International Conference on Computer Vision (ICCV). IEEE (2011)
4. Potluri, T., Sravani, T., Ramakrishna, B., Nitta, G.R.: Content-based video retrieval using dominant color and shape feature. In: Satapathy, S.C., Prasad, V.K., Rani, B.P., Udgata, S.K., Raju, K.S. (eds.) Proceedings of the First International Conference on Computational Intelligence and Informatics. AISC, vol. 507, pp. 373–380. Springer, Singapore (2017). https://doi.org/10.1007/978-981-10-2471-9_36
5. Potluri, T., Nitta, G.: Content based video retrieval using dominant color of the truncated blocks of frame. J. Theor. Appl. Inf. Technol. **85**(2), 165 (2016)
6. Bay, H., et al.: Speeded-up robust features (SURF). Comput. Vis. Image Underst. **110**(3), 346–359 (2008)
7. Grundmann, M., et al.: Efficient hierarchical graph-based video segmentation. In: 2010 IEEE Conference on Computer Vision and Pattern Recognition (CVPR). IEEE (2010)

8. Fundamentals of Digital image and video processing by North Western University. https://www.coursera.org/course/digital

9. Babu, G.P., Babu, M.M., Mohan, S.K.: Color indexing for efficient image retrieval. Multimed. Tools Appl. **1**(4), 327–348 (1995)

10. Ansari, A., Mohammed, M.H.: Content based video retrieval systems - methods, techniques, trends and challenges. Int. J. Comput. Appl. **112**(7) (2015)

11. Girgensohn, A., Boreczky, J.: Time-constrained key frame selection technique, pp. 756–761 (1999)

12. Delp, E.J., Saenz, M., Salama, P.: Block truncation coding (BTC). In: Bovik, A.C. (ed.) Handbook of Image and Video Processing, pp. 176–181. Academic Press, Cambridge (2000)

13. Hu, W., Xie, N., Li, L., Zeng, X., Maybank, S.: A survey on visual content-based video indexing and retrieval. IEEE Trans. Syst. Man Cybern. Part C (Appl. Rev.) **41**(6), 797–819 (2011)

14. Chen, L.-H., Chin, K.-H., Liao, H.-Y.: An integrated approach to video retrieval. In: Proceedings of the Nineteenth Conference on Australasian Database, vol. 75, pp. 49–55 (2008)

15. Liu, Y., Zhang, D., Guojun, L., Ma, W.-Y.: A survey of content-based image retrieval with high-level semantics. Pattern Recogn. **40**(1), 262–282 (2007)

16. Roth, V.: Content-based retrieval from digital video. Image Vis. Comput. **17**(7), 531–540 (1999)

17. Yang, Z., Shen, D., Yap, P.-T.: Image mosaicking using SURF features of line segments. PloS ONE **12**(3), e0173627 (2017)

18. Chatoux, H., Lecellier, F., Fernandez-Maloigne, C.: Comparative study of descriptors with dense key points. In: 2016 23rd International Conference on Pattern Recognition (ICPR). IEEE (2016)

19. Hassaballah, M., Abdelmgeid, A.A., Alshazly, H.A.: Image features detection, description and matching. In: Awad, A.I., Hassaballah, M. (eds.) Image Feature Detectors and Descriptors. SCI, vol. 630, pp. 11–45. Springer, Cham (2016). https://doi.org/10.1007/978-3-319-28854-3_2

20. Wang, X.G., Fuchao C.W., Wang, Z.H.: Harris feature vector descriptor (HFVD). In: 19th International Conference on Pattern Recognition, ICPR 2008. IEEE (2008)

21. Rao, N.G., Sravani, T., Vijaya Kumar, V.: OCRM: optimal cost region matching similarity measure for region based image retrieval. Int. J. Multimed. Ubiquitous Eng. **9**(4), 327 (2014)

22. Rao, N.G., Vijaya Kumar, V., Rao, P.S.V.S.: Novel approaches of evaluating texture based similarity features for efficient medical image retrieval system. Int. J. Comput. Appl. **20**(7), 8887 (2011). (0975–8887)

An Empirical Study:
ELM in Face Matching

Haidong Wang[1], Md. Fawwad Hussain[1], Himadri Mukherjee[2],
Sk. Md. Obaidullah[3], Ravindra S. Hegadi[4], Kaushik Roy[2],
and K. C. Santosh[1(✉)]

[1] Department of Computer Science, University of South Dakota,
Vermillion, USA
santosh.kc@ieee.org
[2] Department of Computer Science, West Bengal State University,
Kolkata, India
kaushik.mrg@gmail.com
[3] Department of Computer Science, Aliah University, Kolkata, India
sk.obaidullah@gmail.com
[4] Department of Computer Science, Solapur University,
Solapur, India
rshegadi@gmail.com

Abstract. Face data happens everywhere and face matching/
verification is the must, such as it helps track criminals; unlock your
mobile phone; and pay your bill without credit cards (e.g. Apple Pay).
More often, in real world, grayscale image data are used since the color
images require more storage. Gray level faces can be studied through two
different features: edges and texture since spatial properties could be preserved. Such features could be used to classify faces from one another.
Instead of using distance-based feature matching concept, in this paper, a
fast machine learning classifier, which we call extreme learning machine
(ELM) is used, where we have taken several different activation functions, such as *tanh, sigmoid, softlim, hardlim, gaussian, multiquadric* and
inv_multiquadric. In our tests, five different publicly available datasets,
such as Caltech, AR, ColorFERET, IndianFaces and ORL are used. For
all activation functions, we have tested with and without feature selection
techniques, and compared with the state-of-the-art results.

Keywords: Gray level images · Spatial features · Face matching ·
Extreme learning machine · Activation functions · Feature selection

1 Introduction

Face data happens everywhere and face matching/verification is the must, such
as it helps track criminals; unlock your mobile phone; and pay your bill without
credit cards (e.g. Apple Pay). Therefore, automated face recognition system
is the need. Since 60's, there has been a remarkable success in this domain

K. C. Santosh and R. S. Hegadi (Eds.): RTIP2R 2018, CCIS 1035, pp. 277–287, 2019.
https://doi.org/10.1007/978-981-13-9181-1_25

and commercial tools are available. However, we face a number of challenges in making an accurate and a robust face detection and recognition in real-world environments. More often, uncontrolled environments can be one of the primary challenges. This includes variations in illumination, face pose and expression, just to name a few.

In face recognition, aforementioned difficulties cannot be sidelined. Even though human face varies from person to person, human face is not a unique rigid object and each of the faces have a variety of deformations. Therefore, other physical properties, such as gender, age and emotions can help add more information to create a challenge for the research scientist in computer vision.

In statistical pattern recognition, face matching/recognition can be made

(a) either by feature-based matching, where similarity score (typically based on the distance function) can help decide unknown face images (test images) with the help of known ones.
(b) or by feature-based training (using known face images) via machine learning classifier(s), where decision can be made for unknown face images (test images).

The paper is the complement of the work presented earlier [13], where the idea of feature-based matching has been strictly followed. Such a technique suffers from the high time complexity issue, since test face image(s) require(s) to match with all known face images in the database. We are aware that one would be interested in recognizing unknown faces in a limited amount of time. Not only time, memory can be considered as another issue for a compact (and/or reasonable) face matching tool/technique. Therefore, in this paper, using the exact same features that are employed in [13], we basically rely on training machine learning classier for a decision making.

The primary goal of our research is to build an automated face recognition systems with the use of the fast machine learning classifier. With this idea, we employ an Extreme Learning Machine (ELM) – a well known fast machine learning classifier in the domain, so decision can quickly be made unlike the conventional feature matching-based concept (via distance function). In the ELM, we study several different activation functions, such as *tanh, sigmoid, softlim, hardlim, gaussian, multiquadric* and *inv_multiquadric* to check which one performs the best in terms of recognition rate and processing time. Besides, we employ feature selection techniques to check whether we can improve the performance of the system in terms of decision making time and memory in use. Like before [13], we also hold the similar concepts of using grayscale images instead of color ones: A few of the reasons can be summarized as follows: (a) more often, video surveillances are used to store grayscale images because of its storage issue; (b) edge information can be considered as an important feature for applications, such as line-rich object detection (face image, for instance) and such an attribute can be achieved in gray scale images; and (c) having both issues, it is always interesting to use grayscale images by realizing tools with low computational complexities and overheads.

The remainder of the paper can be organized as follows. Section 2 provides related works. In Sect. 3, we clearly explain the proposed work. Section 4, datasets, evaluation metrics and results (with analysis) are provided. Section 5 concludes the paper.

2   Related Works

Many different approaches and techniques have been developed so far in the field of face matching and recognition for the reliable and efficient system. More often, face matching uses appearance-based concept, where they consider shape descriptors are rich enough to describe its appearance. However, they depend on the complexity of the problem, and in a few cases, all pixels are equally important that leads to high computational complexities and requires a high degree of correlation between known and unknown face images. In case when face images are taken from the controlled environment, not all pixels (from the images) are required to recognize i.e., a few of them (but selected ones) are sufficient. In all respects, training machine learning classifiers can help decide unknown face images like humans do. Training can be quick and is desirable in case extracted features are compact.

As reported earlier, since this study uses the exact same features from another work [13], in this section, we particularly focused on shape-based object description. It is desirable to have a descriptor that includes non-dense image information, such as edges or various key points and/or regions so they are able to cope deformations and variations in pose, scale, orientation as well. Since a decade, line-rich objects have been described by the set of line segments i.e., edges in general. To have an idea of this, we refer to the work reported in 2015 [5], where they present a rotation-and-scale-invariant, line-based color-aware (RSILC) descriptor for face matching in terms of their key-lines, line-region properties, and line spatial arrangements. The concept was inspired from previous work reported in 2014 [17]. Authors claimed that their descriptor is color-aware, invariant to rotation/scale and is robust to illumination changes. In 2002, line edge map (LEM) was introduced that is able to extract features from the line segments of a face image [9], which is found to be robust and efficient as compared to Eigenface [18]. We also noted that curve edges collect more information [7], and it is called by the name curve edge map.

Key lines (including edges i.e. edge map) may not take texture information into account. Since texture is an important attribute, in computer vision, Local Binary Pattern (LBP) [1] proved to be a powerful descriptor for face recognition. We find that face recognition using the LBP performs better in terms of speed and recognition rate. It can also handle face images with different facial expressions, different lighting conditions, image rotation and aging.

Integrating both key line (can be edge map, see Fig. 1) with texture features could potentially produce better performance in object recognition.

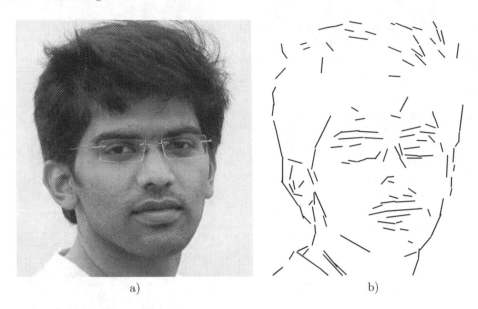

a)   b)

Fig. 1. An example of an (a) input image; and its corresponding (b) edge based representation.

3   Contributions

In Fig. 1, one can observe that edge map i.e. key line features, alone, can help identify human face. However, for comprehensive object recognition, texture-based features can complement key line-based features. This means that we would like to express the importance of spatial features in our study: face matching. Following our work [13], the following features are considered.

(a) For edge map-based features, we employ pyramid histogram of orientation gradients (PHOG) i.e., histogram of edge orientations and spatial distribution of edges [2]. More importantly, both descriptors do not suffer from memory issue. To extract texture-based features, we employ low level representation of the shape called the spatial envelope [15], which encodes spatial frequencies and orientations.

(b) Once we have features in place, we train extreme learning machine and for decision making, we use several different activation functions, such as *tanh*, *sigmoid*, *softlim*, *hardlim*, *gaussian*, *multiquadric* and *inv_multiquadric*. For all activation functions, we test the ELM with and without feature selection techniques, and compared with the state-of-the-art results.

3.1   Spatial Features

For more detailed information about spatial features for face representation and recognition, we refer to [13].

For PHOG, we worked on [2], since it captures the spatial distribution of edges and stored them as 1D vector representation. PHOG is inspired by the two sources: the image pyramid representation of Lazebink et al. [14], and the Histogram of Gradient Orientation (HOG) of Dalal and Triggs [6]. Local appearance can be described by a histogram of edge orientations (quantized into K bins) within an image subregion. The edge orientations are quantized into K bins, each of which represents the number of edges which have a certain angular range orientations. The spatial layout of the shape is based on the concept of spatial pyramid matching [10]. Each image is divided into a sequence of increasingly finer spatial grids by doubling the number of grids in each axes direction. The number of points in each grid cell is then recorded. The PHOG descriptor of the entire image is a vector with dimensionality $K \times \sum_{l \in L} 4^l$. For example, for level L = 3 and K = 20 bins, the size of the PHOG feature vector is of $(20 \times (4^0 + 4^1 + 4^2 + 4^3))$ 1700.

Regarding gist: spatial envelope, we worked on Oliva and Torralba [15] so it produces a very low dimensional representation of the image, which we call spatial envelope. Spatial envelope can be represented by a low-dimensional vector that encodes the distribution of orientations and scales in the image along with a coarse description of the spatial layout. The spatial envelope representation that has semantic attributes about the image provides a way of computing high-level image and space similarities between 2D sequences/images. In our study, for an input face image, a gist descriptor is computed by: (a) convolving the image with 32 Gabor filters at 4 scales, 8 orientations, producing 32 feature maps of the same size of the input image; (b) dividing each feature map into 16 regions (by a 4×4 grid); and (c) concatenating the 16 averaged values of all 32 feature maps. As a result, it produces a feature vector of size $16 \times 32 = 512$.

3.2 ELM and Activation Functions

Extreme learning machines [4,8,11,12] are feedforward neural networks for a variety of challenges, such as classification, regression, clustering, sparse approximation, compression and feature learning with a single layer or multiple layers of hidden nodes, where the parameters of hidden nodes (not just the weights connecting inputs to hidden nodes) need not be tuned. Note that this is not the first time, we work on ELM for face matching [19]. Compared to [19], in our study, we used spatial features. Also, as different activation function provides different results, we use the following.

(a) Tanh: It is a shifted as well as scaled variant of the logistic sigmoid transfer function. It depicts asymptotic symmetry and also leads to faster convergence. In general, it can be expressed as, $tanh(x) = \frac{e^x - e^{-x}}{e^x + e^{-x}}$.

(b) Multiquadric and inverse multiquadratic: The multiquadric function is a type of radial basis function. It is neither a positive definite nor a reproducing activation function. It is conditionally negative definite in nature and it produces a unique solution. In general, we write it as, $multiquadric(x) = \sqrt{1 + x^2}$. Therefore, we have $inv\_multiquadric(x) = \frac{1}{\sqrt{1+x^2}}$.

(c) Hardlim and softlim: It is the short form for hard limit transfer function. This function outputs 1 when the net input value reaches a threshold and 0 in the other condition. Using python package, we express hardlim as $hardlim(x) = numpy.array(x > 0)$. Inversely, we have $softlim(x) = numpy.clip(x, 0.0, 1.0)$.

(d) Sigmoid: This function derives its name from its "S" like shape and hence the name sigmoid. It is a kind of logistic function whose domain is all real numbers. It returns monotonically increasing values mostly between 0 to 1, and simply it can be expressed as, $sigmoid(x) = \frac{1}{1+e^{-x}}$.

(e) Gaussian: It is a bell shaped continuous function. Its output is interpreted in terms of class membership which depends on the closeness of a value to a threshold. In general, it can be written as, $gaussian(x) = e^{-x^2}$.

3.3 Feature Selection

Instead of relying on complete features extracted from the data, it is wise to use select them so that important and/or distinguished attributes are preserved for recognition. With this concept in mind, we employ the following technique [16].

Linear models penalized with the L1-norm have sparse solutions: many of their estimated coefficients are zero. When the goal is to reduce the dimensionality of the data to use with another classifier, they can be used along with feature selection (L1 based) to select the non-zero coefficient. In particular, sparse estimators useful for this purpose are the lasso for regression, and of Logistic regression and SVM for classification. With SVMs and logistic-regression, the parameter C controls the sparsity: the smaller C the fewer features selected. With Lasso, the higher the alpha parameter, the fewer features selected. In short, L1 regularization adds a penalty $\sum_i^n |W|$ to the loss function (L1-norm). Since each non-zero coefficient adds to the penalty, it forces weak features to have zero as coefficients. Thus L1 regularization produces sparse solutions, inherently performing feature selection. For more detailed information, please visit https://scikit-learn.org/stable/modules/feature_selection.html.

4 Results

4.1 Datasets and Evaluation Metric

For a through test, it is highly recommended to use standard datasets (publicly available) so that fair comparison is possible. In our study, the following datasets are used:

(a) Caltech dataset;
(b) AR face dataset;
(c) Color FERET dataset;
(d) ORL dataset; and
(f) Indian face dataset.

Table 1. Results on Caltech dataset: average recognition rate (in %) and time (in seconds).

Activation function	Avg.	Avg. (FS)	Time	Time (FS)
tanh	0.988064386	0.994570991	0:00:14.930470	0:00:10.031956
sigmoid	0.986382294	0.990485189	0:00:14.902907	0:00:09.932660
softlim	0.984676056	0.994560776	0:00:14.478697	0:00:09.727814
gaussian	0.988643863	0.995020429	0:00:14.832572	0:00:09.955706
multiquadric	0.988635815	0.99546476	0:00:14.440570	0:00:09.771844
inv_multiquadric	0.989199195	0.9936619	0:00:14.523050	0:00:09.720032
hardlim	0.959702213	0.971470889	0:00:15.010304	0:00:09.646865

Table 2. Results on AR dataset: average recognition rate (in %) and time (in seconds).

Activation function	Avg.	Avg. (FS)	Time	Time (FS)
tanh	0.885454545	0.927636364	0:00:19.683048	0:00:14.822395
sigmoid	0.878636364	0.940727273	0:00:19.314931	0:00:14.650711
softlim	0.830454545	0.882545455	0:00:18.740531	0:00:14.296371
gaussian	0.859090909	0.912	0:00:19.012984	0:00:14.693428
multiquadric	0.893181818	0.930909091	0:00:18.686136	0:00:14.327555
inv_multiquadric	0.872272727	0.908727273	0:00:18.743095	0:00:14.414840
hardlim	0.624090909	0.596	0:00:18.754820	0:00:14.383245

The California Institute of Technology (Caltech) is a world-renowned science and engineering research and education institution. It has an important part in discovering new knowledge and innovations. For face recognition system, the dataset provided by Caltech contains 450 frontal face images of 27 distinct subjects with varying conditions. The AR Face dataset was developed by Aleix Martinez and Robert Benavente in the Computer Vision Center (CVC) at the U.A.B. The rich dataset contains over 3000 face images corresponding to 126 subject which includes 70 men and 56 women. The FERET database was developed under the supervision of Face Recognition Technology (FERET) program to develop new techniques, technology, and algorithms for the automatic recognition of human faces. For FR system, the dataset consists of 500 frontal face images of 105 distinct subjects with varying conditions. In our study, we ignore color pixels. The ORL database of faces was developed under the supervision of Cambridge University Laboratory. The database consists of 400 frontal face images of 40 distinct subjects with varying lighting conditions, poses and facial expressions. The Indian face database was developed by IIT Kanpur. There are eleven different face images of each of 40 distinct subjects. Different orientations

Table 3. Results on ColorFERET dataset: average recognition rate (in %) and time (in seconds).

Activation function	Avg.	Avg. (FS)	Time	Time (FS)
tanh	0.957460317	0.980302521	0:00:07.979022	0:00:03.684192
sigmoid	0.955873016	0.970957983	0:00:08.009312	0:00:03.586650
softlim	0.95	0.980302521	0:00:07.924479	0:00:03.478982
gaussian	0.945767196	0.979092437	0:00:07.991454	0:00:03.575078
multiquadric	0.96031746	0.975697479	0:00:07.806041	0:00:03.457342
inv_multiquadric	0.96031746	0.981445378	0:00:07.736843	0:00:03.481617
hardlim	0.895661376	0.942857143	0:00:07.706740	0:00:03.555562

Table 4. Results on Indian faces dataset: average recognition rate (in %) and time (in seconds).

Activation function	Avg.	Avg. (FS)	Time	Time (FS)
tanh	0.667037037	0.692740741	0:00:24.481315	0:00:22.178926
sigmoid	0.654444444	0.691851852	0:00:24.500733	0:00:21.841826
softlim	0.638888889	0.655407407	0:00:23.904217	0:00:21.502019
gaussian	0.651851852	0.675555556	0:00:24.265890	0:00:21.955657
multiquadric	0.668888889	0.689481481	0:00:23.812052	0:00:21.522418
inv_multiquadric	0.657407407	0.670518519	0:00:23.836929	0:00:21.512923
hardlim	0.537037037	0.52562963	0:00:23.925644	0:00:21.694868

Table 5. Results on ORL dataset: average recognition rate (in %) and time (in seconds).

Activation function	Avg.	Avg. (FS)	Time	Time (FS)
tanh	0.964375	0.99	0:00:13.672983	0:00:09.582739
sigmoid	0.965625	0.9855	0:00:13.605367	0:00:09.427775
softlim	0.971875	0.9895	0:00:13.729829	0:00:09.161826
gaussian	0.966875	0.993	0:00:13.587183	0:00:09.431332
multiquadric	0.97375	0.99	0:00:13.402822	0:00:09.337323
inv_multiquadric	0.970625	0.9925	0:00:13.519410	0:00:09.224058
hardlim	0.951875	0.9715	0:00:13.433424	0:00:09.239333

of the face are included for example looking front, looking left, looking right, looking up, looking up looking down along with different facial emotions.

For our validation, we performed k-fold cross validation, where $k = 5$, and reported the average results (see sections below).

Table 6. Feature dimensions with and without FS.

Dataset	Features (dimension)	
	Without FS	With FS
Caltech	2212	577
AR	2212	977
ColorFeret	2212	1192
Indian	2212	1298
ORL	2212	802

4.2   Results, Analysis and Comparison

In Tables 1, 2, 3, 4, and 5, one can see the following:

(a) Tests were done separately for different datasets.
(b) For all datasets, tests were compared with and without Feature Selection
(FS). Note that for all datasets, we have a feature vector of size 2212 i.e.,
1700 (PHOG) + 512 (gist).
(c) For all activation functions, both recognition rates (in %) and processing
times (in seconds) were provided. For simplicity, note that average results
were reported (using k-fold cross validation, where k=5).

With these in hands, we observe the following:

(a) We have achieved recognition rate up to 99.50% (Caltech dataset). Indian
face dataset is found to be difficult one as compared to others. Note that
the proposed study is limited to whether (i) activation functions need to be
used correct and (ii) feature selection can help.
(b) Feature selection technique improved the performance with a maximum difference of 6.2% in accuracy and 5.632 s in processing time. The reason behind
the positive jump is due to the fact that feature dimensions were reduced
significantly, where redundancies were deleted (see Table 6).

5   Conclusion and Future Works

In this paper, we have studied different activation functions used in Extreme
Learning Machine (ELM) by considering spatial features for gray level face image
representation and recognition. Besides, we have demonstrated that the usefulness of the feature selection in both recognition rate and processing time. In
our tests, we have compared (on five different publicly available datasets, such
as Caltech, AR, ColorFERET, IndianFaces and ORL) activation functions used

in ELM in addition to feature selection. In a new future, we plan to work on machine learning classifier-based idea, such as active learning [3] at the time when we need real data or live data.

References

1. Ahonen, T., Hadid, A., Pietikainen, M.: Face description with local binary patterns: application to face recognition. IEEE Trans. Pattern Anal. Mach. Intell. **28**(12), 2037–2041 (2006)
2. Bosch, A., Zisserman, A., Munoz, X.: Representing shape with a spatial pyramid kernel. In: Proceedings of the 6th ACM International Conference on Image and Video Retrieval, pp. 401–408. ACM (2007)
3. Bouguelia, M., Nowaczyk, S., Santosh, K.C., Verikas, A.: Agreeing to disagree: active learning with noisy labels without crowdsourcing. Int. J. Mach. Learn. Cybern. **9**(8), 1307–1319 (2018)
4. Cambria, E., et al.: Extreme learning machines. IEEE Intell. Syst. **28**(6), 30–59 (2013). https://doi.org/10.1109/MIS.2013.140
5. Candemir, S., Borovikov, E., Santosh, K., Antani, S., Thoma, G.: Rsilc: rotation- and scale-invariant, line-based color-aware descriptor. Image Vis. Comput. **42**, 1–12 (2015)
6. Dalal, N., Triggs, B.: Histograms of oriented gradients for human detection. In: 2005 IEEE Computer Society Conference on Computer Vision and Pattern Recognition (CVPR'05), vol. 1, pp. 886–893. IEEE (2005)
7. Deboeverie, F., Veelaert, P., Philips, W.: Face analysis using curve edge maps. In: International Conference on Image Analysis and Processing, pp. 109–118. Springer (2011)
8. Ding, S., Zhao, H., Zhang, Y., Xu, X., Nie, R.: Extreme learning machine: algorithm, theory and applications. Artif. Intell. Rev. **44**(1), 103–115 (2015). https://doi.org/10.1007/s10462-013-9405-z
9. Gao, Y., Leung, M.K.: Face recognition using line edge map. IEEE Trans. Pattern Anal. Mach. Intell. **24**(6), 764–779 (2002)
10. Grauman, K., Darrell, T.: The pyramid match kernel: discriminative classification with sets of image features. In: Tenth IEEE International Conference on Computer Vision (ICCV'05), vol. 2, pp. 1458–1465. IEEE (2005)
11. Huang, G., Huang, G.B., Song, S., You, K.: Trends in extreme learning machines. Neural Netw. **61**(C), 32–48 (2015). https://doi.org/10.1016/j.neunet.2014.10.001
12. Huang, G., Wang, D., Lan, Y.: Extreme learning machines: a survey. Int. J. Mach. Learn. Cybern. **2**(2), 107–122 (2011). https://doi.org/10.1007/s13042-011-0019-y
13. Hussain, M.F., Wang, H., Santosh, K.C.: Gray level face recognition using spatial features. In: Santosh, K.C., Hegadi, R.S. (eds.): RTIP2R 2018. CCIS, vol. 1035, pp. 216–229 (2019)
14. Lazebnik, S., Schmid, C., Ponce, J.: Beyond bags of features: spatial pyramid matching for recognizing natural scene categories. In: 2006 IEEE Computer Society Conference on Computer Vision and Pattern Recognition (CVPR'06), vol. 2, pp. 2169–2178. IEEE (2006)
15. Oliva, A., Torralba, A.: Modeling the shape of the scene: a holistic representation of the spatial envelope. Int. J. Comput. Vis. **42**(3), 145–175 (2001)
16. Pedregosa, F., et al.: Scikit-learn: machine learning in Python. J. Mach. Learn. Res. **12**, 2825–2830 (2011)

17. Santosh, K.C., Lamiroy, B., Wendling, L.: Integrating vocabulary clustering with spatial relations for symbol recognition. Int. J. Doc. Anal. Recogn. **17**(1), 61–78 (2014)
18. Turk, M.A., Pentland, A.P.: Face recognition using eigenfaces. In: Proceedings CVPR'91, IEEE Computer Society Conference on Computer Vision and Pattern Recognition, 1991, pp. 586–591. IEEE (1991)
19. Zong, W., Huang, G.: Face recognition based on extreme learning machine. Neurocomputing **74**(16), 2541–2551 (2011). https://doi.org/10.1016/j.neucom.2010.12.041

Optimal Selection of Bands for Hyperspectral Images Using Spectral Clustering

Vanshika Gupta[1], Sharad Kumar Gupta[2], and Dericks P. Shukla[2(✉)]

[1] Department of Civil Engineering, National Institute of Technology Karnataka,
Surathkal, Mangalore 575025, Karnataka, India
[2] School of Engineering, Indian Institute of Technology Mandi,
Kamand 175005, Himachal Pradesh, India
dericks@iitmandi.ac.in

Abstract. High spectral resolution of hyperspectral images comes hand in hand with high data redundancy (i.e. multiple bands carrying similar information), which further contributes to high computational costs, complexity and data storage. Hence, in this work, we aim at performing dimensionality reduction by selection of non-redundant bands from hyperspectral image of Indian Pines using spectral clustering. We represent the dataset in the form of similarity graphs computed from metrics such as Euclidean, and Tanimoto Similarity using K-Nearest neighbor method. The optimum k for our dataset is identified using methods like Distribution Compactness (DC) algorithm, elbow plot, histogram and visual inspection of the similarity graphs. These methods give us a range for the optimum value of k. The exact value of clusters k is estimated using Silhouette, Calinski-Harbasz, Dunn's and Davies-Bouldin Index. The value indicated by majority of indices is chosen as value of k. Finally, we have selected the bands closest to the centroids of the clusters, computed by using K-means algorithm. Tanimoto similarity suggests 17 bands out of 220 bands, whereas the Euclidean metric suggests 15 bands for the same. The accuracy of classified image before band selection using support vector machine (SVM) classifier is 76.94% and after band selection is 75.21% & 75.56% for Tanimoto and Euclidean matrices respectively.

Keywords: Hyperspectral remote sensing · Band selection ·
Dimensionality reduction · Clustering · Similarity graphs

1 Introduction

Hyperspectral remote sensing, also called as Imaging Spectroscopy, is used to record data in hundreds of continuous adjoining narrow bands of the electromagnetic spectrum. This allows whole spectral curve to be recorded with individual absorption features, thus providing information related to surface material. This

K. C. Santosh and R. S. Hegadi (Eds.): RTIP2R 2018, CCIS 1035, pp. 288–304, 2019.
https://doi.org/10.1007/978-981-13-9181-1_26

information can be exploited to characterize, quantify and automatically detect the targets of interest with much better accuracy than multi-spectral or RGB image [1]. However, one of the major drawbacks of hyper-spectral imagery is it's high redundancy due to data recorded at a bandwidth as small as 5 nm. This means that the image contains multiple bands carrying almost the same information, thus resulting in high computational cost and requiring huge amount of data storage for feature extraction or any further processing of the image. It is therefore important to reduce the dimensionality of our data and make it computationally optimized without losing considerable information.

The concept of Clustering, originally a technique under Machine Learning used for grouping data [2], is used for spectral dimensionality reduction of hyper-spectral images. This is done by representing bands having high correlation, with a single band that can effectively convey the information carried by all the bands in its cluster. Various similarity measures like Cosine similarity, Pearson coefficient, etc. have been developed and used previously to depict the correlation and distance between different data-points [3–5]. Using the pairwise distances d_{ij} or pairwise similarities s_{ij}, a given set $x = x_1, \ldots, x_n$ of data points can be transformed into a graph [6]. The methods include fully connected graph using Gaussian function, K-nearest neighbor (KNN) and ϵ-neighborhood [7]. The aim behind constructing a similarity graph is to represent the local neighborhood relationships between the data points. Moreover, most of the methods lead to a sparse representation of the data, which has computational advantages [6]. Laplacian Matrix is a self defined term and is a field of ongoing research. Other than clustering, there are various other applications of graph Laplacians such as manifold reconstruction [8], semi-supervised learning [9] and in the field of machine learning. Many clustering algorithms which are often used for remotely sensed data, require a defined number of clusters k [10]. For certain cases, k can be estimated based on expert knowledge about the land covers [11]. However, for many situations, such as a complex remote sensing image, k cannot be known a priori [10], and hence it must be estimated using some methods. If the value of k is over-estimated or under-estimated, then the quality of clustering results will be severely affected. Therefore, accurate estimation of k is of utmost importance in clustering analysis.

Various methods such as [10–15] etc. aim at finding k. Some methods such as elbow method, visual assessment [12], etc. give us the approximate range whereas others such as Calinski-Harabasz Index [16], Silhouette plot [17], Davies-Bouldin index [18], etc. are used to obtain the exact value of k. For clustering, among the most popular and simplest ones is the k-means. Other methods like Hierarchical clustering [19], Fuzzy Clustering, etc. [20] are also being used recently to overcome the drawbacks of the k-means clustering algorithm which includes lack of pattern recognition, assumption of a spherical dataset, etc. The primary objective of this work, is finding the optimum no. of clusters k which leads to the best representation of the dataset, also to show the effect of band selection on classification accuracy of hyper-spectral data.

The paper is organized into five sections. In Sect. 1, we describe about clustering and band selection methods. Section 2, shows the dataset used in the study. Sections 3, describes the theoretical background of the methods used and methodology followed to achieve the objectives. The results obtained from the data are described and reported in Sect. 4. The Sect. 5, shows conclusion of the study. In the text, 'K-nearest neighbor' will be used with uppercase 'K' and 'k-means' will be used with lowercase 'k', which refers to the optimum clusters k.

2   Dataset

The dataset used is the "standard 220 Band Hyperspectral Image of Indian Pine Test Site 3 (2 × 2 mile portion of Northwest Tippecanoe County, Indiana)" as shown in Fig. 1, gathered by the AVIRIS sensor on June 12, 1992 available from the Purdue University Research Repository (PURR) [21] (https://engineering. purdue.edu). The MATLAB data files of the image were taken from Grupo de Inteligencia Computacional website ("http://www.ehu.eus/ccwintco/index.php/ Hyperspectral_Remote_Sensing_Scenes").

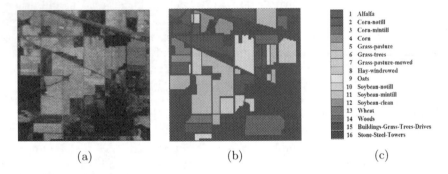

(a)   (b)   (c)

Fig. 1. (a) Gray (Mono color) image of Indian Pine data, (b) Ground truth Image used for validation and (c) Ground truth classes

This image consists of 224 spectral bands and 145 × 145 pixels spread over 0.4–2.5 μm wavelength range of electromagnetic spectrum. The Indian Pines scene comprises of two-thirds agriculture and one-third forest or other natural perennial vegetation. There is a rail line, some small roads, two major highways, few built structures as well as some low density housing. Water absorption bands (104–108; 150–163 and 220) have been eliminated to reduce the no. of bands from 224 to 200 bands.

3   Theoretical Background and Methodology

3.1   Similarity Measures

Similarity measure refers to a relative quantity used to establish a relationship between the data points. It is a real-valued function, usually an inverse of a distance metric. Most commonly used similarity measures include negative Euclidean distance, Tanimoto coefficient, Cosine Similarity, Pearson Coefficient, Mahalanobis Distance, etc. In this study, Jaccard/Tanimoto coefficient and Euclidean Distance has been used to form a similarity matrix or *Affinity* matrix.

3.1.1   Euclidean Distance

Given an N-dimensional dataset denoted by $S = \{S_1 \ldots, , S_n\} \in \mathbb{R}^{N \times D}$ such that $S_i = \{x_1 \ldots, , x_D\} \in \mathbb{R}^{D \times 1}$, where N is the no. of bands, which corresponds to the size of data points and D refers to the no. of pixels, which determines the dimensionality of high-dimensional space. The Euclidean distance (d_{ij}) between S_i and S_j is defined [22] as

$$d_{ij} = \sqrt{\sum (x_i - x_j)^2} \tag{1}$$

or

$$d_{ij} = \sqrt{\|S_i - S_j\|} \tag{2}$$

where x_i and x_j denote the corresponding elements in samples S_i and S_j respectively.

3.1.2   Tanimoto Coefficient

It is also known as extended Jaccard coefficient. It considers the "ratio of intersecting set to the union set" as the measure of similarity [5] and is defined as

$$T_{ij} = \frac{S_i.S_j}{\|S_i\|^2 + \|S_j\|^2 - S_i.S_j} \tag{3}$$

where $S_i.S_j$ represents the scalar product of the two vectors.

3.2   Similarity Graph

"A comprehensive way of representing the data is in form of a *Similarity Graphs* [23] $G = (V, E)$ where the vertices $V = \{V_1 \ldots, , V_N\}$ represent the data points and E represents the connection edge between two vertices carrying a non-negative weight $W_{ij} \geq 0$". If weight, $W_{ij} = 0$, then the vertices V_i and V_j are disconnected or are not related. The similarity matrix is attributed as a non-directional or undirected (symmetric matrix), weighted graph, where $V_{ij} \in V$ represents the edge between the pairs of datapoints S_i and S_j , and the weight

$W_{ij} \in W$ measures the similarity between the vertices (we will further be representing similarity by W_{ij}).

Since we have defined a measure of similarity W_{ij}, we now aim at splitting the data points into several groups such that points in different groups are unalike to each other and the points lying in the same group are similar, i.e. to find a partition of the graph such that the "the edges within a group have high weight and edges between different groups have low weights".

3.3   Types of Similarity Graphs

The Sect. 3.1 results in an undirected graph where all the edges have weights. Constructing a similarity graph from the similarity matrix leads to a sparse representation of the data. There are various methods for constructing a similarity graph [6].

3.3.1   Fully Connected Graph

In this type of graph, all vertices having positive weight are connected, with edges weighted by W_{ij}. This type of graph lacks the sparse structure we require, unless the similarity function can serve the purpose. The Gaussian similarity function, which is the most commonly used function, can be written as

$$W(i,j) = e^{-\frac{d_{ij}^2}{2\sigma}} \tag{4}$$

Here the parameter σ controls the width of the neighborhoods, and is regarded as a *scaling parameter* such that only bands having high similarity or small distance retain in the graph and all others become 0 (or are not connected).

3.3.2   *K*-nearest Neighbor Graph

In this type of graph, the vertex V_i and V_j are connected and weighted by W_{ij} *if* V_j is among the K nearest neighbors of V_i. However, this neighborhood relationship is not symmetric or is directed [6]. The problem can be fixed in two ways.

Mutual K-nearest (MKNN): In this, we do not take into consideration the directions of the edges, i.e. V_i and V_j are connected $\Longleftrightarrow$ V_i is among the K-nearest neighbors of V_j and V_i is also among the K-nearest neighbors of V_j. It can be regarded as the *intersection* of the directed KNN graph along the principal diagonal to obtain an undirected graph.

Normal K-Nearest: In this, we connect V_i and V_j $\Longleftrightarrow$ V_i is among the K-nearest neighbors of V_j *or* V_i is among the K-nearest neighbors of V_j. It can be regarded as the *union* of directed KNN graph along the principal diagonal to obtain an undirected graph.

3.3.3 ϵ-neighborhood Graph

Here, all points whose similarity is larger (*smaller* for distances) than a threshold ϵ are connected [6,24]. Setting the value of ϵ play a major role.

In this section, conversion of the similarity matrix to an adjacency matrix or similarity graph is carried out using the K-nearest neighbor algorithm. The Tanimoto matrix is directly acted upon by MKNN. However, the Euclidean matrix is first converted into similarity matrix by using the Gaussian similarity Function, and then MKNN is applied. The *Adjacency matrix* so formed is *Sparse, Block-Diagonal, Symmetric* and *non-negative*. MKNN has been used as it gives our graph the much needed sparse structure. However, ϵ-neighborhood method can also be used [24].

3.4   Laplacian Matrix of Graph

Study of these matrices is an important research area in the field of Spectral Clustering [23,25]. All its details and properties are beyond the scope of this paper, however we present a brief idea regarding its definition and importance. The *Degree vector*, which is the sum of rows of the adjacency matrix, is defined as

$$d_i = \sum_{j=1}^{n} W_{ij} \tag{5}$$

The *Degree Matrix* is defined as the diagonal matrix with its principal diagonal elements defined by d (degree vector).

$$D(i,j) = \begin{cases} 0 & i \neq j \\ d_i & i = j \end{cases} \tag{6}$$

3.4.1   The Un-normalized Laplacian

The un-normalized Laplacian matrix [26] is defined as

$$L \quad or \quad L_{unnormalized} = D - W \tag{7}$$

1. *L is symmetric and positive semi-definite.*
2. *L has N non-negative eigenvalues* $0 = \lambda_1 \leq \lambda_2 \ldots, \leq \lambda_n$

3.4.2   The Normalized Laplacian

The normalized Laplacian matrix [27] is defined as

$$L_{sym} = D^{-1/2} L D^{-1/2} \tag{8}$$

where L_{sym} corresponds to the symmetric normalized Laplacian and

$$L_{rw} = D^{-1} L \tag{9}$$

where L_{rw} is the *random walk* Laplacian as it resembles a random walk. Both L_{sym} and L_{rw} follow the property 2 of unnormalized Laplacian matrix [6].

There exists various forms of Laplacian matrix, as described in [7]. Each form has a unique significance in terms of optimizing the clustering problem. It is associated with the graph cut optimization (finding partition of a graph based on similarity), each presenting a different idea for finding the best partitions of the similarity graph. The use of unnormalized Laplacian for clustering maximizes only the Ratio Cut (related to number of vertices in a partition). The normalized Laplacian maximizes both, the Normalized Cut (related to the edge weights in the partition) and the Ratio Cut, thus maximizing the *within-cluster similarity*. Hence, L_{rw} or L_{sym} is preferably used.

3.5   Eigenvalue Decomposition

The eigenvalue decomposition of a square matrix can be defined as the solution to:

$$Lv = \lambda v \tag{10}$$

where L is a $N \times N$ Laplacian matrix and $v = \{v_1 \ldots, v_N\}$ corresponding to $\lambda = \{\lambda_1, \ldots, \lambda_N\}$ where v_i is an $N \times 1$ eigenvector and $\lambda_i \in \mathbb{R}$ is eigenvalue of L.

3.6   Spectral Clustering Algorithm

The Ng–Jordan–Weiss (NJW) algorithm [27,28] for spectral clustering is used and modified after [6] as follows

i Construct the required similarity matrix W. The number of clusters k are known a priori. Then we set the diagonal elements of W matrix to 0, i.e., $W_{ii} = 0$.

ii Construct the matrix L (may be or $L_{unnormalized}$ or L_{sym} or L_{rw}).

iii Perform Eigenvalue decomposition and obtain v and λ.

iv Normalize 'v', and make each of v's rows have unit length and thus obtain u.

$$u_{ij} = \frac{v_{ij}}{\sqrt{\sum_{j=1}^{N} v_{ij}^2}} \tag{11}$$

v Apply k-means algorithm or any other method to group the rows of u matrix into k clusters.

vi Assign the original training sample S_i to cluster j if and only if row i of the matrix u was assigned to cluster j.

3.7 k-means

k-means is one of the most generic and popular clustering algorithm that works on the simple principle of squared euclidean distance as a measure of dissimilarity. Centroids are assigned and change iteratively till a certain threshold is reached between the previous means and the present means. One of the drawbacks of k-means is its random assignment of initial centroids which changes at each run. To overcome this problem, mean of 30 observations of final centroids obtained by running k-means was used as the initial centroids for further processing.

3.8   Finding Optimum Value for Number of Clusters k

Any clustering algorithm requires the no. of clusters k as input. Every dataset of higher dimension N when visualized in N-dimensional space, can be observed to form groups where high probability density distribution exists. By optimum k, we mean the least number of such groups in which our data can be represented effectively.

To determine the value of k, several algorithms and methods have been proposed that present different ideas of a good clustering as discussed in Sect. 1. Here, some of the several available methods are used to determine the value of k for the given data set.

3.8.1   Distribution Compactness (DC) Algorithm

Compactness measures how close are the objects within the same cluster. The DC algorithm is based on this measure of distribution. This algorithm analyzes the distribution compactness of sparse representations of band vectors in the kernel space by using a nonparametric estimate of the probability density function of dataset [14] and then determines k. The DC computation is defined as follows

$$DC = \sum_{i=1}^{N} \lambda_i \{1_N^T v_i\}^2 \tag{12}$$

where W is the similarity or adjacency matrix, λ_i and v_i correspond to the ith eigenvalue and eigenvector of W respectively and 1_N is a $N \times 1$ vector containing all ones. The value of k is obtained by examining the plot of sorted values of $\lambda_i \{1_N^T v_i\}^2$ against i. Value of k corresponds to the *elbow* of the logarithm plot (DC plot). However, this method can only provide the range for k.

3.8.2   Distribution Compactness Percentage

The DC plot we obtain in Sect. 3.8.1 can be analyzed in yet another way by measuring the percentage contribution of $\lambda_i \{1_N^T v_i\}^2$ for every $i = \{1, .., N\}..$. The approximate range of k can be obtained by setting a threshold for the percentage contribution. The number of bands having percentage greater than this threshold is set as number of clusters. This threshold can be set by analyzing the histogram of the percentage plot or computing the variance of the distribution.

3.8.3   WSS Plot

The *within cluster sum of squares* (WSS) is defined as the sum of the squared Euclidean distance between the data points lying within the same cluster. Given that we have formed i clusters, we find the WSS corresponding to i clusters and then plot WSS for varying i. The value of i may be taken as $\{1, \ldots, 30\} \in \mathbb{N}$. The point where an elbow occurs depicts the approximate range of k. However, sometimes the sum of distance of the centroid and the data points in a cluster can also be used instead of data point and data point. It is then regarded as the *elbow method* [29]. However, this method is not very accurate and works mostly for data groups distant far apart or relatively simple datasets.

Other methods include visual inspection using the *Visual Assessment of Tendency (VAT)* algorithm [12]. When the adjacency matrix is represented in the form of an image matrix, the number of distinct blocks along the diagonal gives us a range for k value. However, the matrix may sometimes form small or at times visually unrecognizable regions.

Hence, a range of k derived from different methods is obtained. Now, methods that will provide us the exact value of k can be used. It is recommended to adopt approximate methods first, since they give us an idea of our data set and also specify the regions of the indices to look at.

3.8.4   Calinski-Harabasz Index

The Calinski-Harabasz index is based on the idea of maximizing the Between cluster sum of squares (BSS) (defined as the sum of squared euclidean distance of the points lying in different clusters) and minimizing the WSS i.e. maximizing the *Variance Ratio Criterion (VCR)* [16, 30]. The Calinski-Harabasz index (CH) is defined as

$$CH = \frac{BSS}{k-1} \Big/ \frac{WSS}{N-k} \tag{13}$$

where N and k correspond to the total data points (same as described before) and the number of clusters respectively. The Calinski-index is plotted against $k = i$ for $i \in [2, 30] \in \mathbb{N}$ and the point where the maxima occurs is the value of k. This index is said to be one of the most accurate methods for finding k.

3.8.5   Davies-Bouldin Index

The Davies-Bouldin index presents the idea of minimizing the average maximum overlap of regions defined by the clusters. [18]. The Davies-Bouldin index (DB) is defined as

$$DB = \frac{1}{N_c} \sum_{i=1}^{N_c} R_i \tag{14}$$

$$R_i = \max_{\substack{j=[1,N_c]\in\mathbb{N} \\ i\neq j}} (R_{ij}) \tag{15}$$

$$R_{ij} = \frac{S_i + S_j}{d(V_i, V_j)} \tag{16}$$

$$S_i = \frac{\sum_{x \in C_i} d(x, V_i)}{||C_i||} \tag{17}$$

where d represents the euclidean distance, V_i represents the centroid of the ith cluster and C_i is the cluster i. The Davies-Bouldin Index is plotted against $k = i$ for $i \in [1, 30] \in \mathbb{N}$ and the point where the minima occurs is the value of k. This index does not necessarily indicate the best value for k.

3.8.6 Dunn's Index

The Dunn's Index is defined as the ratio of minimum inter-cluster distance and maximum cluster size [31]. Larger inter-cluster distances indicate dissimilarity whereas small cluster sizes indicate compactness, thus leading to a higher DI value. The Dunn's index (DI) is given as

$$DI = \frac{\min_{1 \leq i \leq j \leq k} d(C_i, C_j)}{max_{1 \leq c \leq k} ||N_c||} \tag{18}$$

where $d(C_i, C_j)$ is the distance between clusters i and j and k is the number of clusters. The Dunn's-index is plotted against $k = i$ for $i \in [1, 30] \in \mathbb{N}$ and the point where the maxima occurs is the value of k.

From above three indices, we are able to find some values of k. In this final step, we take all the obtained values and analyze the silhouette plot for each value of k to get the final number of clusters.

3.8.7 Silhouette Plot

In this index, it is assumed that *good* clusters are those whose patterns are close to each other compared to the next closest cluster [17,30]. This index tells us the similarity of each point to the points in its own cluster. Silhouette index (SI) is defined as

$$SI_i = \frac{b_i - a_i}{\max(a_i, b_i)} \tag{19}$$

where b_i is the minimum (over all clusters) of the average distance from the ith point to the points in another cluster and a_i is the average distance from the ith point to the other points in its cluster.

4   Results and Discussion

In the Fig. 2a, we see dark colors clustered along the diagonal, in contrast to Fig. 2b which has light colors for the same. This is because the Euclidean distance matrix is a *Dissimilarity matrix* i.e. large distances denote poor similarity and vice versa whereas the notion of similarity is opposite. Since Euclidean distance is a dissimilarity measure, it is converted into a similarity metric using the Gaussian function as given in Eq. (4). The value of σ is set according to the variance or the range of values present in the matrix, such that all the elements of the matrix neither become 0, nor very close to 1 (value of σ neither too large, nor too small). The similarity graph is constructed using the MKNN algorithm which gives our adjacency matrix a sparse block diagonal structure.

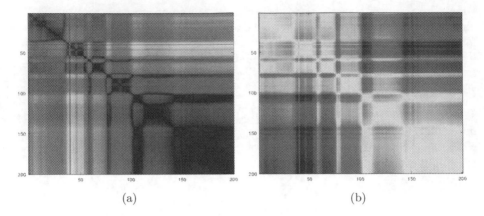

Fig. 2. (a) Euclidean distance Matrix (b) Tanimoto similarity matrix represented in the form of an image

The symmetric normalized Laplacian (L_{sym}) matrix instead of the unnormalized Laplacian is used as it gives a better convergence of eigenvalues as stated in [6] and Sect. 3.4. Further, eigenvectors and the corresponding eigenvalues of the Laplacian matrix are computed. To determine the value of k, k-means is used and the various indices are computed giving the eigenvector matrix as input. Here, k-means is not directly applied to our original adjacency matrix or similarity matrix. This is because the original data is randomized and may not consist of perfect clusters. Hence, it may not be able to deliver accurate results. The whole idea behind the given process is to bring the points very close together such that they can form perfect, distinct groups.

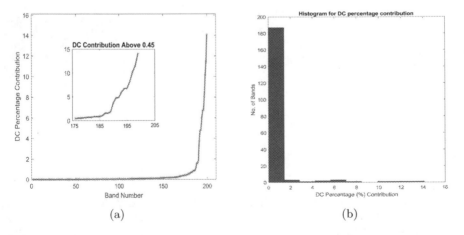

Fig. 3. (a) DC percentage sorted plot for elbow (graph inside shows a clear view of the elbow) (b) Histogram plot DC percentage contribution for Euclidean similarity matrix

In Fig. 2a or b, we can see blocks or squares along the principal diagonal forming groups. By visually analyzing the figures, count of blocks can be done to obtain an approximate idea of range of k. However, it becomes difficult to locate very small blocks in between. In Fig. 3a, the sorted DC contribution percentage is plotted as described in Sect. 3.8.2. The elbow occurs somewhere between 12–18 from right. In Fig. 3b, the histogram for DC percentage contribution is plotted and it depicts that nearly 2% can be regarded as the threshold, i.e. the number of clusters above 2% can be regarded as number of clusters. However, this is only an unsupervised method and number of cluster changes as we change the threshold.

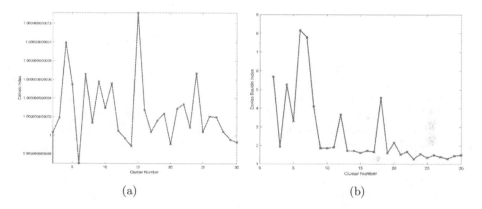

(a)   (b)

Fig. 4. (a) Calinski-Harabasz index plot, (b) Davies-Bouldin index plot for Euclidean similarity matrix

In Fig. 4a, the Calinski-index is plotted and clearly it can be seen that it reaches a maxima at $k = 15$. However, it must be noted that the Calinski-plot will change each time we run k-means, as its result is dependent on the position of the final centroids and the position of the final centroids is in turn dependent on the initial centroids position, which are chosen at random. Hence, average observation must be taken by running the clustering algorithm many times.

In the Davies-Bouldin plot as shown in Fig. 4b, a local minima is observed at $k = 15$, however, the global minima occurs at $k = 23$. In the Dunn's index plot 5a, the global maxima occurs at $k = 15$ (the starting values are set as 1 to scale the graph). In Fig. 5b, the silhouette index is plotted corresponding to each data point corresponding to $k = 15$. The Silhouette index ranges form -1 to 1. Large positive values indicate that the point is well matched with the other points in its cluster. Negative values indicate positive dissimilarity or mismatch with points in its own cluster.

The drawback of these indices is the fact that they change each time the clustering is performed and hence, sometimes a stable value cannot be obtained. After getting the value of k, clustering algorithm is applied as directed in

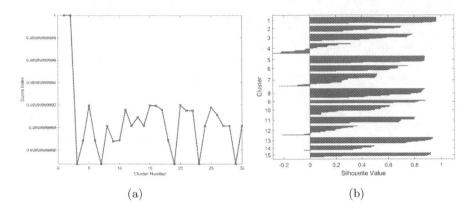

(a)   (b)

Fig. 5. (a) Dunn's index plot (b) Silhouette Plot for k = 15 for Euclidean similarity matrix

Sect. 3.6. After getting the final centroids for 15 clusters, the bands which lie closest to the centroids of the respective cluster we are sorted. In this way, the final representative bands reduced from 200 to mere 15 bands are obtained. Now after obtaining the clusters, the classification accuracy of our assigned clusters can be determined.

The Support Vector Machine (SVM) classifier is used for our classification process. However, first the background pixels in the original classified image and the classified image after doing band selection are equalized. This is required because the background contains a lot of mixed pixels and not equalizing the background pixels would decrease the classification accuracy to a very small value due to the large class size. Therefore, it is assumed that the background class is classified with 100% accuracy. SVM classifier is used to classify the image obtained after band selection as well as the original image with 200 bands. Hence, we find the accuracy of our classification irrespective of the background class i.e using 16 classes only.

After computing the statistics using confusion matrix, an accuracy of 75.56% is obtained for the image after band selection and 76.94% for the original image. The Fig. 6a shows the classification of the original image in contrast to the spectral subset Fig. 6b. It can be seen that some classes towards the top left corner show more misclassification after band selection. This is attributed to the fact that there is loss of information during the process of band selection, which may lead to errors in the classification process. The error associated determines the accuracy of the spectral clustering process. As we can see from the results, there is only 1.4% change in the accuracy, which is not so significant.

The results discussed above are for the similarity graph obtained using "Euclidean distance metric". We perform the same procedure for the Tanimoto similarity matrix and the results obtained are summarized in the given Table 1. The Tanimoto similarity measure indicates 17 clusters and an accuracy of 75.21%. It can be seen that the Davies-Bouldin Index does not give very

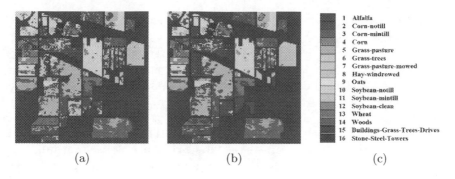

(a)   (b)   (c)

Fig. 6. (a) Classified ground truth image before band selection (b) Classified ground truth after band selection using SVM and (c) Ground truth classes

accurate results. When observed for other datasets too, this index fails to give appropriate value of k relative to other indices. This is mainly due to the notion it assumes as a good clustering. However, the same index may give much accurate results as compared to other indices on a dataset having relatively different characteristics. Therefore, it is important to do a comprehensive study of the given dataset before assuming any method as *'appropriate'* for evaluating the value of k.

Table 1. Number of bands selected from original image using Tanimoto and Euclidean matrix and Corresponding classification accuracy and computation time

Comparative results			
Methods used	Original image (200 bands)	No. of selected bands using Tanimoto Matrix	No. of selected bands using Euclidean Matrix
DC elbow plot	-	14–20	12-18
Calinski-Harabasz	-	17	15
Davies-Bouldin	-	15	23
Dunn's	-	16	15
Silhouette	-	17	15
Classifcation Accuracy	**76.94%**	**75.21%**	**75.56%**
Time required for Classification (in seconds)	**5.7**	**2.9**	**2.6**

The Silhouette index is however a better approach to any given dataset. The Silhouette plot is taken as a verification criteria for choosing the best value of k out of the different values obtained using other methods. It should be noted here that the number of clusters is a function of the similarity measure used, since the notion of similarity changes with the change in similarity measure.

This study has been performed on HP Z238 workstation with Intel Xeon CPU E3-1225 v5 @ 3.30 GHz and 24 GB primary memory and 2 GB graphics memory. Table 1 shows the elapsed computation time for classification of original as well as image after bands selection. The small computation time (in order of few seconds) is attributed to the size of study area. The computation time increases with increasing number of spectral bands as well as the size of study area. It can be inferred from the Table 1 that there is ∼2× speedup in classification after band selection with a reduction of mere ∼1.5% accuracy. The classification of image with band selection requires 45.61% and 50.88% (for Euclidean and Tanimoto matrix respectively) of the time required to classify the original image. It can be inferred from the results that band selection process is useful for classification, if the image has countably many bands as well as if the study area is quite large.

5   Conclusion

Band Selection using Spectral Clustering is an important part of hyper-spectral image processing. It allows more information to be stored in the same space, which is much needed when each image file size is in Gigabytes. We conclude through this paper that accuracy of classification or any other processing changes by a very minimal amount even after selecting only 15 or 17 bands out of the 200 bands. The whole criteria is about how to select bands and which bands to select. Here, we reviewed various methods developed to make this process more and more efficient based on the idea of a '*good*' clustering. Depending on the data set characteristics, some indices and methods have poor performance while some give more accurate results.

References

1. Dutra, L.V., Mascarenhas, N.D.: Some experiments with spatial feature extraction methods in multispectral classification. Int. J. Remote Sens. **5**(2), 303–313 (1984)
2. Fisher, D.H.: Knowledge acquisition via incremental conceptual clustering. Mach. Learn. **2**(2), 139–172 (1987)
3. Gan, S., Cosgrove, D.A., Gardiner, E.J., Gillet, V.J.: Investigation of the use of spectral clustering for the analysis of molecular data. J. Chem. Inf. Model. **54**(12), 3302–3319 (2014)
4. Weller-Fahy, D.J., Borghetti, B.J., Sodemann, A.A.: A survey of distance and similarity measures used within network intrusion anomaly detection. IEEE Commun. Surv. Tutor. **17**(1), 70–91 (2015)
5. Cha, S.H.: Comprehensive survey on distance/similarity measures between probability density functions. Int. J. Math. Model. Methods Appl. Sci. **1**, 300–307 (2007)
6. von Luxburg, U.: A tutorial on spectral clustering. Stat. Comput. **17**(4), 395–416 (2007)
7. Weiss, Y.: Segmentation using eigenvectors: a unifying view. In: Proceedings of Seventh IEEE International Conference on Computer Vision, vol. 2, pp. 975–982. IEEE (1999)

8. Belkin, M., Niyogi, P.: Laplacian eigenmaps for dimensionality reduction and data representation. Neural Comput. **15**(6), 1373–1396 (2003)
9. Chapelle, O., Scholkopf, B., Zien, A.: Semi-supervised Learning. MIT Press, Cambridge (2006)
10. Naeini, A.A., Saadatseresht, M., Homayouni, S.: Automatic estimation of number of clusters in hyperspectral imagery. Photogram. Eng. Remote Sens. **80**(7), 619–626 (2014)
11. Liang, J., Zhao, X., Li, D., Cao, F., Dang, C.: Determining the number of clusters using information entropy for mixed data. Pattern Recognit. **45**(6), 2251–2265 (2012)
12. Huband, J.M., Bezdek, J.C., Hathaway, R.J.: bigVAT: visual assessment of cluster tendency for large data sets. Pattern Recognit. **38**(11), 1875–1886 (2005)
13. Iam-on, N., Garrett, S.: LinkCluE: a MATLAB package for link-based cluster ensembles. J. Stat. Softw. **36**(9), 1–36 (2010)
14. Sun, W., Zhang, L., Du, B., Li, W., Lai, Y.M.: Band selection using improved sparse subspace clustering for hyperspectral imagery classification. IEEE J. Sel. Top. Appl. Earth Obs. Remote Sens. **8**(6), 2784–2797 (2015)
15. Kassambara, A.: Practical guide to cluster analysis in R: unsupervised machine learning. STHDA (2017)
16. Calinski, T., Harabasz, J.: A dendrite method for cluster analysis. Commun. Stat. - Theory Methods **3**(1), 1–27 (1974)
17. Rousseeuw, P.J.: Silhouettes: a graphical aid to the interpretation and validation of cluster analysis. J. Comput. Appl. Math. **20**, 53–65 (1987)
18. Davies, D.L., Bouldin, D.W.: A Cluster Separation Measure. IEEE Trans. Pattern Anal. Mach. Intell. PAMI-1(2), 224–227 (1979)
19. Navarro, J.F., Frenk, C.S., White, S.D.M.: A universal density profile from hierarchical clustering. Astrophys. J. **490**(2), 493–508 (1996)
20. Gan, G., Ma, C., Wu, J.: Fuzzy clustering algorithms. In: Data Clustering: Theory, Algorithms, and Applications, pp. 151–159. Society for Industrial and Applied Mathematics (2007)
21. Baumgardner, M.F., Biehl, L.L., Landgrebe, D.A.: 220 Band AVIRIS Hyperspectral Image Data Set: June 12, 1992 Indian Pine Test Site 3 (2015)
22. Xing, E.P., Xing, E.P., Ng, A.Y., Jordan, M.I., Russell, S.: Distance metric learning, with application to clustering with side-information. Adv. Neural Inf. Process. Syst. **15**(15), 505–512 (2003)
23. Chung, F.R.K.: Spectral graph theory. Published for the Conference Board of the Mathematical Sciences by the American Mathematical Society (1997)
24. Rosenberger, C., Brun, L.: Similarity-based matching for face authentication. In: 19th International Conference on Pattern Recognition, ICPR 2008, pp. 1–4. IEEE (2008)
25. Mohar, B.: Some applications of Laplace eigenvalues of graphs. In: Hahn, G., Sabidussi, G. (eds.) Graph Symmetry, pp. 225–275. Springer, Dordrecht (1997). https://doi.org/10.1007/978-94-015-8937-6_6
26. Perona, P., Freeman, W.: A factorization approach to grouping. In: Burkhardt, H., Neumann, B. (eds.) ECCV 1998. LNCS, vol. 1406, pp. 655–670. Springer, Heidelberg (1998). https://doi.org/10.1007/BFb0055696
27. Shi, J., Malik, J.: Normalized cuts and image segmentation. IEEE Trans. Pattern Anal. Mach. Intell. **22**(8), 888–905 (2000)
28. Ng, A.Y., Jordan, M.I., Weiss, Y.: On spectral clustering: analysis and an algorithm. Adv. Neural Inf. Process. Syst. **14**, 849–856 (2001)

29. Ketchen, D.J., Shook, C.L.: The application of cluster analysis in strategic management research: an analysis and critique. Strateg. Manag. J. **17**(6), 441–458 (1996)
30. Honarkhah, M., Caers, J.: Stochastic simulation of patterns using distance-based pattern modeling. Math. Geosci. **42**(5), 487–517 (2010)
31. Dunn, J.C.: Well-separated clusters and optimal fuzzy partitions. J. Cybern. **4**(1), 95–104 (1974)

Classification of Natural Flower Videos Through Sequential Keyframe Selection Using SIFT and DCNN

V. K. Jyothi[1(✉)], D. S. Guru[1], and Y. H. Sharath Kumar[2]

[1] Department of Studies in Computer Science, University of Mysore,
Manasagangotri, Mysore 570006, India
jyothivk.mca@gmail.com, dsg@compsci.uni-mysore.ac
[2] Department of Information Science and Engineering,
Maharaja Institute of Technology Mysore (MITM), Mandya 571438, India
sharathyhk@gmail.com

Abstract. This paper presents an algorithmic model for automatic selection of keyframes for the classification of natural flower videos. For keyframe selection Scale Invariant Feature Transform and Discrete Cosine Transform are recommended. The selected keyframes are further used for classification process. To extract the features from the selected keyframs Deep Convolutional Neural Network (DCNN) is used as a feature extractor and for classification of flower videos Multiclass Support Vector Machine (MSVM) is applied. For experimentation, we have created dataset of natural flower videos consisting of 1825 flower videos of 20 different classes. Experimental results show that the proposed keyframe selection algorithm gives good compression ratio and the proposed classification system generates good classification accuracy.

Keywords: Keyframe selection · Scale Invariant Feature Transform · Discrete Cosine Transform · Classification of flower videos

1 Introduction

Keyframe selection is one of the elementary research areas in computer vision. The complexity in terms of both time and space burden increases to process all frames of the flower video for the classification process. Therefore, the main content of the video can be represented concisely through keyframes [1]. To reduce the redundant frames of the flower video, keyframe selection process is essential. The selected keyframes can be further applied for classification of flower videos.

At the present time there is a growth in the demand of flowers, floriculture has become a marketable trade. Floriculture industry involves flower plant marketing, yielding seed, micro propagation and oils can be extracted from flowers [2,3]. To examine a flower of users interest exists in the database or not. In such cases, automation of video flower identification and classification is essential [4].

© Springer Nature Singapore Pte Ltd. 2019
K. C. Santosh and R. S. Hegadi (Eds.): RTIP2R 2018, CCIS 1035, pp. 305–318, 2019.
https://doi.org/10.1007/978-981-13-9181-1_27

Designing and developing a natural flower video keyframe selection and classification system is a challenging task. Due to the flower videos captured in different climatic conditions there exists challenges namely, lighting effect, differences in viewpoint of the flower in frames, partially occluded flowers, several instances of flowers in the video etc. The more challenging is the flowers in videos exists in the cluttered background.

2   Related Works

Keyframes can be selected in sequential order by comparing successive frames [5]. The authors in [6], suggested a new way to represent a video by selecting the first, middle and last frame of video as keyframes. In [7,8], the authors proved that the keyframes can be obtained by using thresholding to find the histogram difference between frames of a video. Based on the histogram of color and detection of edge the redundant frames are removed in [9]. In [1], the authors proposed a keyframe extraction method using Harris corner detector. Dynamic programming algorithm is used to select keyframes from saliency feature maps of the frames [10]. The authors in [11] used an efficient visual attention model to select keyframes. The first and last frames of the video are used to represent the video [12]. The combination of moments of inertia and visual features namely histogram of color and color channels are used to select keyframes [13]. The major observation from the related work is that there is no sequential comparison of consecutive frames to select keyframes from natural flower videos. In this work, a method for selecting keyframes sequentially is proposed. The method selects the distinct frames preserving contents of the video. The selected keyframes are used for classification of flower videos with deep learning approach.

Deep learning methods have been found to be suitable for classification of images and videos. DCNN is used in [14] to classify sports videos. To classify museum images in [15] DCNN is used. In [16] Neural network has been applied for the classification of videos from low and high resolution. From the literature we observe that the deep learning techniques are not applied for the classification of flower videos. Therefore, we are motivated to use DCNN instead of bundle of hand designed features.

The paper is arranged as follows, in Sect. 3 the proposed model of keyframe selection, classification and also briefly the DCNN with a classifier namely, Support Vector Machine are explained. Section 4 depicts the collected dataset of our own. Section 5 shows the experimental results. The work is concluded in Sect. 6.

3   Proposed Model

There are 4 stages in the proposed model, namely, preprocessing, extraction of features, selection of keyframes, classification using DCNN with MSVM. Figure 1 shows the proposed model of the keyframe selection and Fig. 2 shows the overall architecture of the proposed model for the classification of flower videos.

3.1   Preprocessing

A video V_i, consisting of 'n' number of frames is defined as,

$$V_i = f_1, f_2, f_3, f_4, ..., f_i, ...f_n \tag{1}$$

During preprocessing, we recommend removing noise using median filter [17] and each frame is resized into 256×256 size. We also make sure that only 30 frames are considered on an average per second.

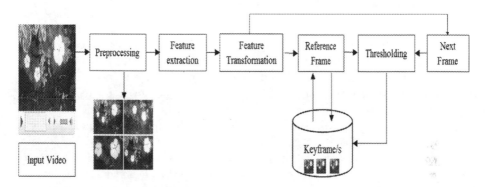

Fig. 1. Block diagram of the proposed keyframe selection model

3.2   Median Filtering

Noise arises in frames of flower videos. Sometimes flowers in frames cannot be seen clearly due to camera movement while capturing, which causes the edges of the flowers in frames look blur. Edges of flowers play an important role in its appearance. While capturing a video, due to movement of the camera a small number of blurs may occur on flower parts also. To reduce this blurness and noise, filtering is essential. Widely used filtering method is median filtering [17] because of its ability to reduce noise and preserving edge [18]. The median filter reduces each frame noise by replacing median value of the mask. We consider 3×3 mask (window)to reduce the noise of the frames.

3.3   Extraction of Feature

Features are extracted from each frame of a video for the identification of keyframes of a flower video. As our interest is to select distinct keyframes from a given flower video, we extract SIFT features to match frames sequentially and select distinguishing frames. For classification of flower videos DCNN is used to extract features from keyframes.

Scale Invariant Feature Transform (SIFT) Descriptors. SIFT is used to detect local descriptors. It gives the description of detected points which are invariant to geometric transformations namely scaling, translation, rotation. And also, which are invariant in illumination. The authors in [19] proposed SIFT feature extraction method. It consists of three phases. In the first phase, based on invariant geometric property it detects local points of the frame. In the second phase, on detected positions of the frame it assigns direction and orientation property. Descriptors are generated in the third phase with a kernel of 4×4 histogram of 8 bins [19]. The result of the histogram can be represented in the form of descriptors.

Discrete Cosine Transform (DCT). The DCT has been widely used to transfer signal from spatial domain to frequency domain. The DCT is an extensively applied method for image and video compression and also for features dimensionality reduction. The DCT expresses data points in terms of sum of cosine functions oscillating at different frequencies. Let F (x, y) be the intensity of pixel in row x and column y, F (u, v) is the DCT coefficient in row u and column v of the DCT matrix. The proposed method extracts SIFT feature descriptors from all frames of the video, these extracted descriptors vary from frame to frame, consequently it's difficult to compare frames, therefore we need to normalize the SIFT feature descriptors using DCT. We use two-dimensional discrete cosine transform (2D DCT) to normalize the features. The 2D DCT transform of an $M \times M$ frame [20, 21] is given as

$$F(u,v) = \frac{2}{M}c(u)(v) \sum_{y=0}^{M-1} f(x,y)cos[\frac{(2x+1)u\pi}{2N}]Xcos[\frac{(2y+1)v\pi}{2N}] \quad (2)$$

where u, v $= 0,1, \ldots,$ M -1 and

$$c(u) = \begin{cases} \frac{1}{\sqrt{2}}, & if \ u = 0 \\ 1, & if \ u \neq 0 \end{cases}$$

The transformation equation is defined as

$$F(u,v) = \frac{2}{M} \sum_{v=0}^{M-1}\sum_{u=0}^{M-1} c(u)c(v)f(u,v)cos[\frac{(2x+1)u\pi}{2M}]Xcos[\frac{(2y+1)v\pi}{2M}] \quad (3)$$

3.4 Classification Using Deep Convolutional Neural Network (DCNN) with Multiclass Support Vector Machine (MSVM)

Deep learning techniques learn features automatically from raw data, which is becoming an important to design and develop computer vision and machine learning applications. DCNN is one of the most widely used deep learning method as it learns features from layers to layers with abstracting features. Initially, it starts extracting features deeply from pixel wise, then it goes on layers to layers by abstracting the deep features. Therefore, the name Deep Convolutional Neural network. DCNN consists of three layers in general namely, convolutional, pooling and fully connected layers [22]. In the proposed model the AlexNet ConvNet architecture is used. The architecture AlexNet ConvNet consists of eight layers [23] and is used to extract the features from the selected keyframes, which learns features directly from keyframes without depending on hand crafted features. After the features are extracted from keyframes, to classify a flower video multi class support vector machine is used. Initially, SVM classifier is used to classify a two-class problem. It can be used to classify multiclass which can be done by comparing one class support vectors with all remaining classes support vectors [24]. The following Fig. 2. shows the ConvNet architecture for classification of flower videos using MSVM [25].

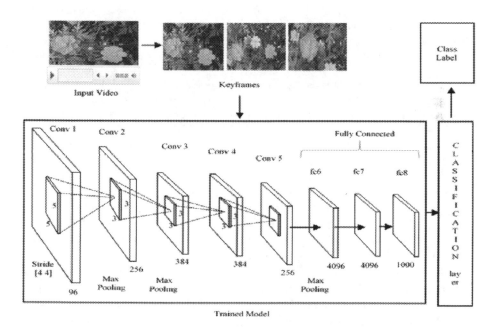

Fig. 2. Proposed ConvNet architecture for classification of flower videos

3.5 Algorithm for Proposed Keyframe Selection and Classification Model

The Algorithm 1 describes the overall summary of the proposed keyframe selection and classification system.

Algorithm 1. Algorithm for keyframe selection and classification

---

1: From the video sequence defined in equation (1), for the first trial consider the same order of sequence of frames and for next 4 trials randomly arrange the frames, select first frame, that is f_i then find $T = \mu(f_i)$ initialize f_i is the reference frame and first keyframe Kf_1 and save this frame as a keyframe

2: Extract SIFT features and normalize the extracted features with DCT, explained in section 3.3.2

3: Fix the threshold $T = \mu(f_i)$, compare T with next successive frame in equation (1) and check the following threshold criteria

$$T > \mu(f_{i+1}) \ \ or \ \ T < \mu(f_{i+1}))$$

if condition becomes true then select $f_{(i+1)}^{th}$ frame and go to step 4

4: Check the frame obtained from step 3 with the existing keyframes if the threshold value is same then ignore this frame and go to step 3. Otherwise select it as a next keyframe and save this frame as a keyframe and now $f_{(i+1)}^{th}$ frame is the new reference frame

5: With new reference frame, repeat steps 2, 3 and 4 until for all frames in the video sequence

6: Collect the keyframes obtained from step 1 and step 4

7: To classify videos Extract features from selected keyframes using Deep Convolutional Neural Network and Multiclass Support Vector Machine as a classifier

---

4   Dataset

In this section, we describe briefly the flower video dataset of our own. There is no availability of standard dataset, we have created our own flower video dataset. Collected 1825 videos of 20 classes of flowers using 8 mega pixel mobile device namely, Samsung mobile. Each class contains 42 to 159 videos with the duration of 4 to 60 s. The collected videos consists of challenges such as variations in lightning effects is called illumination, view point variations, occlusion and clutter background. Videos are captured at different environmental conditions such as sunny, cloudy and rainy. Experimentation conducted on the dataset created. Sample videos are shown in Fig. 5 and sample selected keyframes are shown in Fig. 6.

5   Experimentation

In this section, we present the details of experimental results of the proposed method. Experimentation conducted to demonstrate our proposed model on our own data set. The model gives efficient results with possible chances of keyframes exists in the video.

5.1   Experimental Results of Keyframe Selection

To evaluate the performance of the proposed keyframe selection model we computed the fidelity measure and compression ratio. The model is tested with 5 trials, initially once with a sequence of frames, choosing first frame is a reference frame and comparing with next successive frames. Next 4 trials checked on randomly arranged sequence of frames. From the experimentation it can be observed that almost similar results are obtained in all cases; therefore, the proposed method is robust. The results of average compression ratio and fidelity values with comparative study are shown in Tables 1 and 2 respectively. The robustness of the proposed keyframe selection method is graphically shown in Figs. 3 and 4.

Fidelity Measure: The fidelity measure finds the maximum of minimal distance between the set of keyframes or semi-Hausdorff distance [26]. It compares selected keyframe with the remaining frames of the video [27]. It preserves the global content of the video.

Let the sequence of video frames of ith video be

$$S_F = \{f_1, f_2, f_3...f_i...f_n\} \tag{4}$$

where S_F is the frames set

The keyframes selected from S_F be

$$S_{KF} = \{kf_1, kf_2, kf_3...f_j...f_r\} \tag{5}$$

where S_{KF} is the selected keyframes set.

The semi-Hausdroff distance between the keyframes set S_{KF} and the sequence of video frames S_F can be computed as

$$d(S_{F_i}, S_{KF_j}) = min\{dist(f_i, kf_j)\} \tag{6}$$

Where $i = 1, 2, 3...n$ and $j = 1, 2, 3...r$.

Then the semi - Hausdroff distance between is S_F and S_{KF} defined as

$$D(S_{F_i}, S_{KF_j}) = max\{d(S_{F_i}, S_{KF_j})\} \tag{7}$$

where $i = 1, 2, 3...n$ and $j = 1, 2, 3...r$

Compression Ratio: The aim of the keyframe selection is to reduce the redundant frames and select distinct frames, which describe the contents of the video. Compression ratio shows the percentage of video summary. The compression ratio of a video is defined as follows

$$Compression\ Ratio = 1 - \frac{Number\ of\ selected\ keyframes}{Total\ number\ of\ frames} \tag{8}$$

Table 1 describes that there are 20 classes of flower videos and corresponding number of videos and total number of frames exists in each class and the average compression ratio. The proposed keyframe selection model provides better compression results when compared with the work of [7]. And also, it shows that the proposed keyframe selection model is robust for selecting keyframes either randomly or sequentially comparing the video frames that is shown in the Table 1 with 5 trials. First trial with sequence of frames and next four trials on randomly arranged sequence of frames. The result analysis of all 5 trials of proposed keyframe selection model is graphically shown in Fig. 3.

Table 2 describes that the proposed keyframe selection model provides better fidelity values for selecting keyframes either randomly or sequentially comparing the video frames when compared with the work of [16]. The fidelity values of all 5 trials of proposed keyframe selection model is graphically shown in Fig. 4.

Table 1. Comparison of average compression ratio of keyframe selection methods

Classes	No. of videos	Total frames	Sheena and Narayan [7]	Proposed model				
				Trial 1	Trial 2	Trial 3	Trial 4	Trial 5
1	113	28097	0.75	0.99	0.99	0.99	0.99	0.99
2	84	17570	0.83	0.98	0.98	0.98	0.98	0.98
3	42	10011	0.76	0.99	0.99	0.99	0.99	0.99
4	122	32569	0.76	0.98	0.98	0.98	0.98	0.98
5	116	27860	0.77	0.99	0.99	0.99	0.99	0.99
6	105	25525	0.72	0.99	0.99	0.99	0.98	0.98
7	67	16691	0.74	0.99	0.99	0.99	0.99	0.99
8	107	23969	0.77	0.99	0.99	0.99	0.99	0.99
9	135	35542	0.81	0.99	0.99	0.99	0.99	0.99
10	53	13506	0.78	0.98	0.98	0.98	0.98	0.98
11	88	19182	0.81	0.99	0.98	0.99	0.99	0.99
12	159	37188	0.82	0.99	0.99	0.99	0.99	0.99
13	75	25995	0.76	0.99	0.99	0.99	0.99	0.99
14	119	30099	0.8	0.99	0.99	0.99	0.99	0.99
15	49	13404	0.75	0.99	0.99	0.99	0.99	0.99
16	85	21364	0.73	0.99	0.99	0.99	0.99	0.99
17	67	16311	0.76	0.99	0.99	0.99	0.99	0.99
18	70	19009	0.73	0.99	0.99	0.99	0.99	0.99
19	52	14389	0.78	0.99	0.99	0.99	0.98	0.99
20	117	27951	0.83	0.99	0.99	0.99	0.99	0.99

5.2   Experimental Results of Classification of Flower Videos

The performance of classification of flower videos is evaluated in this section. The keyframes selected from the proposed model are used to represent a video. Then, features are extracted using Deep Convolutional Neural Network from

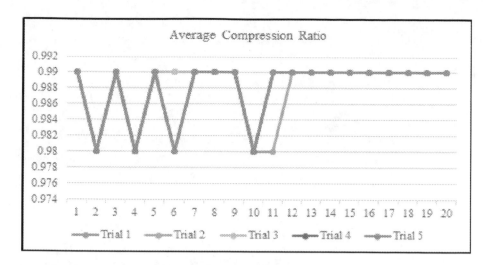

Fig. 3. Average compression ratio of proposed keyframe selection method

Table 2. Comparison of average fidelity measure of keyframe selection methods

Classes	Sheena and Narayan [7]	Proposed model				
		Trial 1	Trial 2	Trial 3	Trial 4	Trial 5
1	0.36	0.92	0.93	0.9	0.97	0.91
2	0.23	0.38	0.39	0.32	0.3	0.37
3	0.24	0.48	0.43	0.41	0.45	0.46
4	0.2	0.59	0.53	0.51	0.59	0.51
5	0.36	0.95	0.93	0.96	0.97	0.93
6	0.81	0.72	0.79	0.78	0.76	0.73
7	0.62	0.89	0.83	0.86	0.89	0.83
8	1	0.73	0.73	0.79	0.74	0.78
9	0.46	0.58	0.54	0.51	0.55	0.56
10	0.31	0.77	0.67	0.73	0.77	0.74
11	0.41	0.67	0.64	0.69	0.68	0.64
12	0.25	0.64	0.65	0.61	0.63	0.59
13	0.43	0.48	0.51	0.5	0.54	0.54
14	0.38	0.9	0.96	0.96	0.94	0.98
15	0.23	0.28	0.24	0.24	0.2	0.28
16	0.51	0.65	0.67	0.67	0.69	0.67
17	0.54	0.67	0.63	0.63	0.67	0.68
18	0.86	1	1	1	1	1
19	0.27	0.82	0.82	0.82	0.87	0.89
20	0.56	0.78	0.72	0.72	0.71	0.73

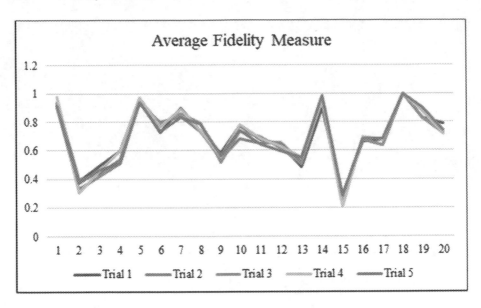

Fig. 4. Average Fidelity measure of proposed keyframe selection method

the selected keyframes. Support vectors are generated using Multiclass Support Vector Machine for classification of flower videos. For the analysis of results, the performance measures such as Precision, Recall, F-measure and Accuracy are used. The training and testing videos are varied with different intervals to analyze the performance of the proposed classification model. Table 3. Shows the classification results of our own dataset using proposed keyframe selection model.

$$Accuracy = \frac{NCCV}{TNVDB} \tag{9}$$

$$Precision = \frac{NCCV}{NCCV + NNRVC} \tag{10}$$

$$Recall = \frac{NCCV}{NCCV + NRVNC} \tag{11}$$

$$F - Measure = \frac{2 * Precision * Recall}{Precision + Recall} \tag{12}$$

Where NCCV is the Number of Correctly Classified Videos. TNVDB is the total number of videos in the database. NNRVC is the number of non-relevant videos classified. NRVNC is the number of relevant videos not classified.

Table 3 describes that the results of proposed flower videos classification system. The results computed with varied training and testing samples in percentage. Good accuracy can be obtained with 80% training and 20% testing. For 60% training and 40% testing highest Precision, Recall and F-Measure can be obtained.

Table 3. Results of classification of flower videos using proposed keyframe selection model

Train %–Test %	Accuracy	Precision	Recall	F-Measure
30–70	95.68	95.9	94.68	95.29
40–60	97.18	95.43	95	95.22
50–50	97.86	97.17	94.03	95.57
60–40	97.9	1	98.15	99.07
70–30	97.86	1	1	97.78
80–20	98.16	1	96.3	98.11

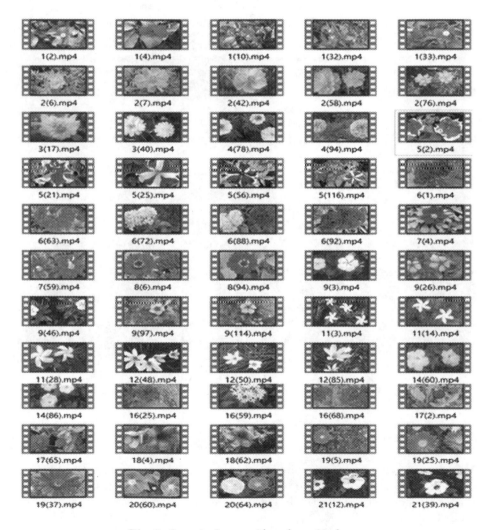

Fig. 5. Sample flower videos from 20 classes

Fig. 6. Sample keyframes selected from the proposed model

6   Conclusion

In this paper, a method for automated selection of keyframes from natural flower videos is proposed. The method is verified with 5 trials and compared with other keyframe selection method. The proposed keyframes selection method is applied for the classification of natural flower videos. For classification features are extracted using Deep Convolutional Neural Network and a classifier Multiclass Support Vector Machine is used. The selected keyframes are further useful for the retrieval of flower videos.

References

1. Lin, H., Yang, X., Pei, J.: Key frame extraction based on multi scale phase based local features. In: ICSP2008 Proceedings. IEEE (2008). (978-1-4244-2179-4/08)
2. Guru, D.S., Sharath, Y.H., Manjunath, S.: Texture features and KNN in classification of flower images. In: IJCA Special Issue on "Recent Trends in Image Processing and Pattern Recognition", RTIPPR, pp. 21–29 (2010)
3. Guru, D.S., Sharath, Y.H., Manjunath, S.: Textural features in flower classification. Math. Comput. Model. **54**, 1030–1036 (2011)
4. Das, M., Manmatha, R., Riseman, E.M.: Indexing flower patent images using domain knowledge. IEEE Intell. Syst. **14**(5), 24–33 (1999)
5. Chatzigiorgaki, M., Skodras, A.N.: Real-time keyframe extraction towards video content identification. IEEE (2009). (978-1-4244-3298)
6. Pentland, A.: Video and image semantics, advanced tools for telecommunications. IEEE Multimedia Summer **1**, 73–75 (1994)
7. Sheena, C.V., Narayanan, N.K.: Key-frame extraction by analysis of histograms of video frames using statistical methods. Procedia Comput. Sci. **70**, 36–40 (2015)
8. Thakre, K.S., Rajurkar, A.M., Manthalkar, R.R.: Video partitioning and secured keyframe extraction of MPEG video. Procedia Comput. Sci. **78**, 790–798 (2016)
9. Kumthekar, A.V., Patil, J.K.: Key frame extraction using color histogram method. IJSRET **2**(4), 207–214 (2013)
10. Ferreira, L., Cruz, L., Assuncao, P.: A generic framework for optimal 2D/3D keyframe extraction driven by aggregated saliency maps
11. Naveed, E., Mehmood, I., Baik, S.W.: Efficient visual attention based framework for extracting key frames from videos. Sig. Process.: Image Commun. **28**, 34–44 (2013)
12. Sreeraj, M., Asha, S.: Content based video retrieval using SURF descriptor, August. IEEE (2013)
13. Naveed, E., Tayyab, B.T., Sung, W.B.: Adaptive key frame extraction for video summarization using an aggregation mechanism. J. Vis. Commun. Image **R.23**, 1031–1040 (2012)
14. Joe, Y.-H.N., Matthew, H., Sudheendra, V., Oriol, V., Rajat, M., George, T.: Beyond short snippets: deep networks for video classification. In: CVPR2015, pp. 4694–4702. IEEE Xplore (2015)
15. Nanne, V.N., Eric, P.: Learning scale-variant and scale-invariant features for deep image classification. Pattern Recogn. **61**, 583–592 (2017)
16. Cheng, M.-H., Hwang, K.S., Jeng, J.H., Lin, N.W.: Classification-based video super-resolution using artificial neural networks. Sig. Process. **93**, 2612–2625 (2013)
17. Niu, Y., Zhao, Y., Ni, R.: Robust median filtering detection based on local difference descriptor. Sig. Process.: Image Commun. **53**, 65–72 (2017)
18. Zeng, H., Liu, Y.Z., Fan, Y.M., Tang, X.: An improved algorithm for impulse noise by median filter. In: 2012 AASRI Conference on Computational Intelligence and Bioinformatics, AASRI Procedia, vol. 1, pp. 68–73 (2012)
19. Lowe, D.G.: Distinctive image features from scale-invariant keypoints. Int. J. Comput. Vis. **60**, 91–110 (2004)

20. Asnath, Y., Amutha, R.: Discrete cosine transform based fusion of multi-focus images for visual sensor networks. Sig. Process. **95**, 161–170 (2014)
21. Haghighat, M.B.A., Aghagolzadeh, A., Seyedarabi, H.: Multi-focus image fusion for visual sensor networks in DCT domain. Comput. Electr. Eng. **37**(5), 789–797 (2011)
22. Guo, Y., Liu, Y., Oerlemans, A., Lao, S., Wu, S., Lew, M.S.: Deep learning for visual understanding: a review. Neurocomputing **187**, 27–48 (2016)
23. Krizhevsky, A., Sutskever, I., Hinton, G.E.: ImageNet classification with deep convolutional neural networks. In: Proceedings of the 25th International Conference on Neural Information Processing Systems, vol. 1, pp. 1097–1105 (2012)
24. Iosifidis, A., Gabbouj, M.: Multi-class support vector machine classifiers using intrinsic and penalty graphs. Pattern Recogn. **55**, 231–246 (2016)
25. Jyothi, V.K., Guru, D.S., Sharath Kumar, Y.H.: Deep learning for retrieval of natural flower videos. Procedia Comput. Sci. **132**, 1533–1542 (2018)
26. Manjnath, S.: Video archival and retrieval system. Thesis, UOM (2012)
27. Gianluigiand, C., Raimondo, S.: An innovative algorithm for key frame extraction in video summarization. J. Real-Time Image Process. **1**, 69–88 (2006)

Hyperspectral Remote Sensing Image Analysis with SMACC and PPI Algorithms for Endmember Extraction

Dhananjay B. Nalawade[1,2]($\boxtimes$), Mahesh M. Solankar[1,2],
Rupali R. Surase[1,2], Amarsinh B. Varpe[1,2], Amol D. Vibhute[3],
Rajesh K. Dhumal[3], and Karbhari Kale[2]

[1] Geospatial Technology Research Laboratory,
Dr. Babasaheb Ambedkar Marathwada University,
Aurangabad, Maharashtra, India
dhananjay.bamu@gmail.com, mmsolankar@gmail.com,
rupalisurase13@gmail.com, varpeamarsinh@gmail.com
[2] Department of Computer Science and IT,
Dr. Babasaheb Ambedkar Marathwada University,
Aurangabad, Maharashtra, India
kvkale91@gmail.com
[3] School of Computational Sciences,
Solapur University, Solapur 413255, MS, India
amolvibhute2011@gmail.com, dhumal19@gmail.com

Abstract. The hyperspectral data endmember extraction plays a prominent role. In recent years, many researchers put their efforts to develop a new approach for endmember extraction from hyperspectral data. The endmember extraction algorithms especially used to discover the purest type of each spectrally distinct component on a scene. Endmember extraction process can be influenced by type of data, number of endmembers, number of pixels being processed, and number of spectral bands in data, used algorithms and also by the type of noise present in the data. The identified endmembers can be used in the further processing of identification and classification. Comparison of endmember extraction algorithms is a challenging task due to absence of unified criteria and unavailability of a standardized dataset to validate any new algorithm. Previously comparison of endmember extraction algorithm has been carried out on Landsat 4-5 data (Multispectral), Hyperion and the airborne visible/infrared imaging spectrometer (AVIRIS) Cuprite Hyperspectral dataset. In this paper, we have analyzed two widely used methods of endmember extraction the Sequential Maximum Angle Convex Cone (SMACC) and Pixel Purity Index (PPI) on AVIRIS-Next Generation (NG) hyperspectral dataset of Jhagadiya, Gujarat, Jasper Ridge and Hyperion dataset. From the experimental results, it is concluded that SMACC performs better than PPI.

Keywords: Endmember extraction · SMACC · PPI · AVIRIS-NG

© Springer Nature Singapore Pte Ltd. 2019
K. C. Santosh and R. S. Hegadi (Eds.): RTIP2R 2018, CCIS 1035, pp. 319–328, 2019.
https://doi.org/10.1007/978-981-13-9181-1_28

1 Introduction

Hyperspectral imaging becomes a vital tool for the observation of earth with the advances of imaging spectroscopy. The information available in the form of spectral details is a key benefit of hyperspectral remote sensing (HRS). Spectral response of various surface materials and land covers varies with their spectral properties [1]. To distinguish and map these spectral responses it requires various important spectral features. The HRS applications are limited due to huge variety of materials and lack of information about their spectral properties [2]. HRS data like AVIRIS-NG which measures the wavelength range from 380 nm to 2510 nm with 5 m sampling which is capable for differentiating most of the earth surface materials. Availability of several channels along with narrow bandwidth provides much more information about the earth surface. Despite availability of numerous spectral channels it's not easy to differentiate spectral variations in spectral image due to sensors and atmosphere [3].

In the processing of hyperspectral image, a big challenge is to decompose the mixed pixel into its constituents that forms the pixel, referred as endmember. However, the spectral signatures of corresponding fraction referred as abundances. And the problem is well-known as unmixing problem. Endmember extraction is one of the basic and important step in hyperspectral data analysis. In recent years, endmember extraction gains interest of many researchers to develop algorithms for the extraction of pure pixels from the hyperspectral dataset [4]. Ultimately an endmember extraction method searches for unique composition of each spectrally different material from the data [5]. The linear mixing model is used as a typical model to carry out the endmember extraction and hyperspectral unmixing, model is shown as [6],

$$X_i = \sum_{k=1}^{P} V_{ik} e_k + e_i, \quad i = 1, \ldots, N \tag{1}$$

Where,

P is the number of endmembers, N is the number of pixels in the image, e_i is an error term, V_{ik} is the proportion of endmember k in pixel i, and e_k is the k th endmember. The above model satisfies the following constraints in,

$$\sum_{k=1}^{P} V_{ik} = 1 \tag{2}$$

$$V_{ik} \geq 0, \quad \forall_k = 1, \ldots, P$$

Generally, when linear mixing model are applied to a single set of endmembers, input pixels are considered as, linear mixture of all endmembers in the data [7].

The present study gives comparison of endmember extraction algorithm by comparing PPI and SMACC algorithms using the AVIRIS-NG dataset. The paper is organized in four sections. Section first gives the introduction of the topic. The endmember extraction methods are revealed in section two. The experimental results are discussed in section three. Section four gives the conclusion and future work.

2   Endmember Extraction Methods

According to the definition in [8], an endmember is an idealized pure signature for a class. Finding pure composition of a class in hyperspectral imagery is considered to be an important and crucial task in Hyperspectral data exploitation. The implemented methodology for the endmember extraction is drawn in Fig. 1.

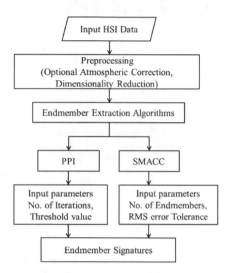

Fig. 1. Proposed methodology for endmember extraction

The following methods are commonly used in the endmember extraction process. The best methods for endmember collection are mentioned in this section.

2.1   Pixel Purity Index (PPI)

The PPI method is based on the convex sets and is commonly used for endmember extraction, in the analysis of hyperspectral image [9]. It is a supervised algorithm, developed by Boardman et al., in 1995 [10]. It uses minimum noise fraction for dimensionality reduction and noise whitening. PPI assumes spectral pixels as vectors in an N-dimensional feature space. The execution of algorithm starts by generating a huge number of random vectors from dataset, referred as skewers. Every data point pointing unique position projected onto each skewer. The data points which are having maximum values in the direction of skewers are recognized and listed out. As the number of skewers generated increases, they are placed and matched in the list. Since the pixel purity index gives count of pure pixels, the pixels with highest matches are considered as the pure one [11]. The shortcoming of PPI includes, it randomly selects skewers from the dataset and more importantly it does not recognize a list of final endmember.

The PPI executes as follows [12]:

(a) Skewer generation: Generate a set of k random unit vectors $\{skewer_j\}_{j=1}^{k}$ where k is sufficiently large positive integer.

(b) Score projection: All the data sample vectors are projected onto skewer for each $skewer_j$ to find sample vectors with extreme locations and make a set of extreme values for each $skewer_j$, denoted as, $S_{extrema}(skewer_j)$. In spite of the fact that each skewer generates $S_{extrema}(skewer_j)$ there may be chances of appearance of sample vector in multiple set. To elaborate this concept, An indicator functions of a set S, $I_s(r)$ is given:

$$I_s(r) = \{^{1,\ \ if\ r\ \in\ S}_{0,\ \ if\ r\ \notin\ S} \tag{3}$$

and

$$N_{ppi}(r) = \sum_j I_{S_{extrema}}\left(skewers_j^{(k)}\right)^{(r)} \tag{4}$$

Where, $N_{ppi}(r)$ is defined as the PPI score of sample vector.

(c) Endmember Selection: Find the pixel vectors from all sample vectors defined by (1) with scores of $N_{ppi}(r)$ above the threshold and mark them as spectral endmembers.

2.2   The Sequential Maximum Angle Convex Cone (SMACC)

Gruninger, J.H. had developed an algorithm based on convex cone model for end-member extraction. In this algorithm endmembers are automatically selected from the dataset. This algorithm works sequentially for finding endmembers, firstly it searches for extreme boundary points to find a convex cone, which is expressed as first end-member. The new endmembers are chosen on the basis of a data vector which makes the higher angle with existing cone [13]. This process continues till a projection finds an endmember which already present in the convex cone or it reaches the specified count for endmembers. The algorithm confirms the abundances of current and previous endmembers remain positive or zero by updating abundances of existing endmembers. The mathematical model of SMACC based on convex cone, is given as [14],

$$P(c,i) = \sum_k^N M(c.k)S(k,j) \tag{5}$$

Where,
i is the pixel index.
j and k are the endmember indices from 1 to the expansion length, N.
M is a matrix that contains the endmember spectra as columns.
c is the spectral channel index.
S is a matrix that contains the fractional contribution (abundance) of each endmember j each endmember k for each pixel.

3 Datasets

As per the reviewed literature, some of the datasets like a Cuprite dataset of Nevada, Hyperion data of EO-1 satellite, Hyperion image were utilized by researcher for the study [15]. For current study we have used following datasets:

3.1 AVIRIS-NG Dataset of Jhagadiya, Gujarat

The AVIRIS-NG mission was conceptualized by JPL team in 2007 on the basis of input from research community. AVIRIS-NG provides continuous access to high signal to noise ratio measurements. It has dimensions $300 \times 300 \times 372$ (BIL) format and measures the wavelength range from 380 nm to 2510 nm with 5 nm sampling [3]. False color composite (FCC) of subset of Jhagadiya, Gujarat AVIRIS-NG dataset is shown in Fig. 2(A).

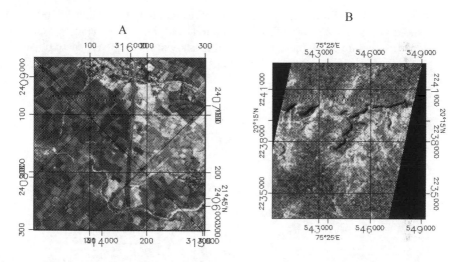

Fig. 2. (A) FCC of subset of Jhagadiya dataset (B) FCC of Hyperion dataset

3.2 Jasper Ridge Dataset

Another widely used dataset is Jasper Ridge, which contains 512×612 pixels in it. It measures the wavelength from 380 nm to 2500 nm with 224 channels. This dataset is preprocessed, some channels containing dense water vapors and atmospheric effects hence they were removed. So this dataset has 198 channels [16].

3.3 EO-1 Hyperion Dataset

The Eo-1 Satellite Launched by USGS with NASA, which uses Hyperion sensor for collecting earth surface features in continuous narrow wavebands. It has 242 spectral channels with 30 m spatial resolution and 10 nm spectral resolutions. This data is

preprocessed and in band sequential (BSQ) format with 196 channels after preprocessing. The wavelength range for this data is 355.59-2577.08 nm [17] FCC of
Hyperion dataset is shown in Fig. 2(B).

4   Experimental Results and Discussion

In this experiment the SMACC and PPI were applied for the specified dataset in
Environment for Visualizing Images (ENVI) 5.1 software developed by Research
System Inc. [12]. To extract endmembers using PPI method, we need to perform three
steps:

(a) Dimensionality reduction using minimum noise fraction (MNF) algorithm.
(b) Employing PPI to resulting images of MNF.
(c) Results of PPI visualized using the n-dimensional tool in ENVI and in the end
    selection of endmember clouds were made.

While executing PPI, we have supplied parameters as number of iterations to 1000, and
the threshold value to 1.2. It derives MNF eigenvalues plot which depicts eigenvalue
for each corresponding MNF transformed band as shown in Fig. 3(A). The plot shows
if the eigenvalue is high then its respective transformed band has higher data variance.

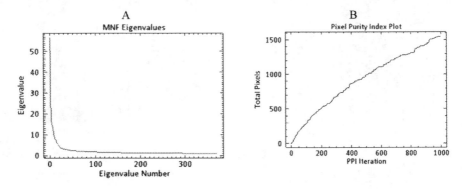

Fig. 3. (A) Plot of eigenvalues derived using MNF for PPI (B) Plot of PPI.

The PPI iteration looks for the pixels falls inside the n-dimensional cloud of data.
The data hits can be controlled with threshold values by user. Pixels which are having
higher count of hits selected as most pure ones, which can be visualized in Fig. 3(B).
The distinct pixels which fall in the corner of the scene are selected and the final
endmembers are derived from these pure signatures. In this experiment, we get 48
redundant spectral signatures of vegetation and other classes, as shown in Fig. 4(A).

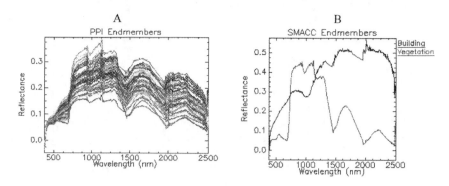

Fig. 4. Jhagadia dataset Endmember (A) using PPI (B) using SMACC

However, in case of the SMACC algorithm, we set number of endmembers as 10, RMS error tolerance to 0.1, and unmixing constraint for endmember abundance to positive only with coalesce redundant endmember to 0.1. On the basis of above parameters, we get results in the form of two purest signatures of vegetation and building or concrete or rock or barren land. Spectral signatures derived from the scene using SMACC algorithm shown in Fig. 4(B).

By using similar parameter on Jasper Ridge dataset for PPI, we get 48 redundant signatures as shown in Fig. 5(A) and two purest signature of water and vegetation using SMACC as shown in Fig. 5(B).

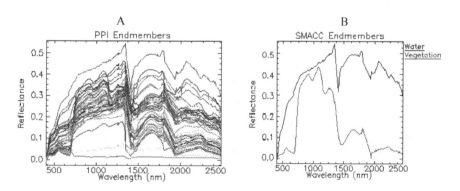

Fig. 5. Jasper Ridge dataset Endmembers (A) using PPI (B) using SMACC

After applying similar parameters on Hyperion dataset for PPI, we get same results as 48 endmember signatures as depicted in Fig. 6(A) and two purest signatures of rock and vegetation with SMACC as shown in Fig. 6(B).

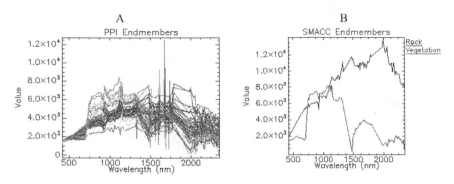

Fig. 6. Hyperion dataset Endmembers (A) using PPI (B) using SMACC

The Table 1 shows summary of PPI algorithm extracted endmembers with given parameters. The Table 1 depicts that as the threshold value increases at certain value no endmembers detected.

Table 1. Input parameters for PPI algorithm to extract the endmembers

Algorithm	Dataset	Parameters		Extracted endmembers
		No. of iterations	Threshold value	
PPI	Hyperion	1000	1.2	48
		2000	1.2	48
		4000	1.2	48
		1000	1.5	48
		1000	2.0	48
		1000	2.5	48
		1000	2.6	0
	Jhagadiya, Gujarat, AVIRIS-NG	1000	1.2	48
		1000	1.3	48
		1000	1.4	48
		1000	1.5	48
		1000	1.6	0
	Jasper Ridge, AVIRIS	1000	1.2	48
		1000	1.3	48
		1000	1.4	48
		1000	1.5	0

The Table 2 shows summary of endmembers extracted using SMACC algorithm. From this Table we can analyze that SMACC algorithm gives pure signatures of given dataset. As the RMS error tolerance value increases we get unique spectral signatures, but at certain value no endmember detected.

Table 2. Input parameters for SMACC algorithm to extract the endmembers

Algorithm	Dataset	Parameters		Extracted endmembers
		No. of endmembers	RMS error tolerance	
SMACC	Hyperion	10	0.1	2
		10	0.2	2
		10	0.3	1
		10	0.4	1
		10	0.5	1
		10	0.6	1
		10	0.7	1
		10	0.8	1
		10	0.9	0
	Jhagadiya, Gujarat, AVIRIS-NG	10	0.1	2
		10	0.2	1
		10	0.3	1
		10	0.4	1
		10	0.5	0
	Jasper Ridge, AVIRIS	10	0.1	2
		10	0.2	2
		10	0.3	1
		10	0.4	0

In this experiment, we found that unique spectral signature are derived using SMACC (setting coalesce redundant endmember to 0.1) algorithm, whereas in PPI it gives redundant spectral signatures of mixed pixels. In this scenario, we observed that SMACC gives better result than PPI because of constraint specified coalesce redundant endmember.

5   Conclusion and Future Scope

The present paper shows comparative result of endmember extraction methods SMACC and PPI. The procedure of extraction of endmember spectral signature from preprocessed AVIRIS-NG and Jasper Ridge hyperspectral dataset provides better results with exiting methods. These algorithms derive spectral signatures without prior knowledge of endmembers and do not require any assumptions. The specified algorithms are applied on the subset of Jhagadiya area, Gujarat, AVIRIS-NG, Jasper Ridge and Hyperion dataset. From the results obtained in the form spectral signature, we can derive conclusion that SMACC performs better than PPI algorithm with specified constraint. In future we will try to identify the exact feature or endmember such as road, rock, barren land or concrete with ground truth collection.

Acknowledgements. Authors would like to acknowledge DST-NISA, UGC SAP (II) DRS Phase-II and DST-FIST for providing technical support to Department of Computer Science & IT, Dr. Babasaheb Ambedkar Marathwada University, Aurangabad, Maharashtra, India and also thanks for financial assistance under DST- NISA research fellowship for this work.

References

1. Martínez, P.J., Pérez, R.M., Plaza, A., Aguilar, P.L., Cantero, M.C., Plaza, J.: Endmember extraction algorithms from hyperspectral images. Ann. Geophys. **49**(1), 93–101 (2006)
2. Plaza, A., Martínez, P., Perez, R., Plaza, J.: A comparative analysis of endmember extraction algorithms using AVIRIS hyperspectral imagery. In: Summaries of the 11th JPL Airborne Earth Science Workshop, p. 2002. JPL (2002)
3. Bhattacharya, B.K.: Overview of first phase of AVIRIS-NG Airborne hyperspectral science campaign over India. https://vedas.sac.gov.in/aviris/pdf/Overview_AVIRIS_NG_Phase_1_campaign.pdf. Accessed 15 July 2018
4. Mozaffar, M.H., Zoej, M.V., Sahebi, M.R., Rezaei, Y.: Vegetation endmember extraction in hyperion images. In: International Archives of the Photogrammetry, Remote Sensing and Spatial Information Sciences, vol. 37, Part B7. Beijing (2008)
5. Zhang, J., Rivard, B., Rogge, D.M.: The successive projection algorithm (SPA), an algorithm with a spatial constraint for the automatic search of endmembers in hyperspectral data. Sensors **8**(2), 1321–1342 (2008)
6. Graceline Jasmine, S., Pattabiraman, V.: Hyperspectral image analysis using end member extraction algorithm. Int. J. Pure Appl. Math. **101**, 809–829 (2015)
7. Keshava, N., Mustard, J.F.: Spectral unmixing. IEEE Sig. process. Mag. **19**(1), 44–57 (2002)
8. Chang, C.-I. Hyperspectral Imaging: Techniques for Spectral Detection and Classification, vol. 1. Springer (2003)
9. Ifarraguerri, A., Chang, C.I.: Multispectral and hyperspectral image analysis with convex cones. IEEE Trans. Geosci. Remote Sens. **37**(2), 756–770 (1999)
10. Boardman, J.W., Kruse, F.A., Green, R.O.: Mapping target signatures via partial unmixing of AVIRIS data. In: Summaries, Fifth JPL Airborne Earth Science Workshop, vol. 1, pp. 23–26. JPL (1995)
11. Parente, M., Plaza, A.: Survey of geometric and statistical unmixing algorithms for hyperspectral images. In: 2010 2nd Workshop on Hyperspectral Image and Signal Processing: Evolution in Remote Sensing (WHISPERS), pp. 1–4. IEEE (2010)
12. Chang, C.I., Plaza, A.: A fast iterative algorithm for implementation of pixel purity index. IEEE Geosci. Remote Sens. Lett. **3**(1), 63–67 (2006)
13. Gruninger, J.H., Ratkowski, A.J., Hoke, M.L.: The sequential maximum angle convex cone (SMACC) endmember model. In: Algorithms and technologies for multispectral, hyperspectral, and ultraspectral imagery X, vol. 5425, pp. 1–15. International Society for Optics and Photonics (2004)
14. Aggarwal, A., Garg, R.D.: Systematic approach towards extracting endmember spectra from hyperspectral image using PPI and SMACC and its evaluation using spectral library. Appl. Geomatics **7**(1), 37–48 (2015)
15. Zhu, F.: Hyperspectral unmixing: Ground truth labeling, datasets, benchmark performances and survey. arXiv preprint arXiv:1708.05125, 1–15 (2017)
16. Ahmed, A.M., Duran, O., Zweiri, Y., Smith, M.: Hybrid spectral unmixing: using artificial neural networks for linear/non-linear switching. Remote Sens. **9**(8), 775 (2017)
17. Vibhute, A.D., Kale, K.V., Dhumal, R.K., Mehrotra, S.C.: Hyperspectral imaging data atmospheric correction challenges and solutions using QUAC and FLAASH algorithms. In: International Conference on Man and Machine Interfacing (MAMI), pp. 1–6. IEEE (2015)

Real Time Hand Gesture Recognition for Differently-Abled Using Deep Learning

C. N. Gireesh Babu[1(✉)], M. Thungamani[2], K. T. Chandrashekhara[1],
and T. N. Manjunath[1]

[1] BMS Institute of Technology and Management, Bengaluru, India
{gireeshbabu,chandru,manju.tn}@bmsit.in
[2] University of Horticultural Sciences, Bagalkot, India
thungamani_k@rediffmail.com

Abstract. In the field of Computer science, Gesture recognition is an alternative user interface for providing real-time data to a computer. This paper focuses on a system which provides the communication between the vocally impaired people and the normal people of the society by translating Sign Language system into Text and Speech in English. The system can recognize one handed sign representation of the standard alphabets (A–Z) and numeric values (0–9). In this paper we used OpenCV for gesture capture through web camera and deep learning algorithms to train and recognize the gesture. The system is very efficient and consistent with respect to output.

Keywords: Hand Gesture Recognition ·
Human computer interactions · CNN · Keras · OpenCV

1 Introduction

Gesture recognition is one of the concepts in computer science and Sign language technology to interpret human gestures through different algorithms. Gestures can be obtained by any bodily motion but normally from the hand or face. Various technologies that Gesture Recognition used mostly depend on extra peripherals such as multiple sensors or wearable devices. Sign Language is an entity of natural language based Gestures and it helps in communication between the common and vocally-impaired people. There are various devices in the market for the hearing impaired, through which they can communicate easily. But sign language is the communication medium for the speech impaired people. The issue arises when speech impaired people communicate with normal people or vice-versa. Since common people does not know the language of vocally impaired, it creates communication barrier between them. To avoid this, a common person must have the knowledge of the Speech impaired standard gestures. There by the system will translate sign language from vocally impaired person to the Standard English language or speech which is easily understand by common people.

© Springer Nature Singapore Pte Ltd. 2019
K. C. Santosh and R. S. Hegadi (Eds.): RTIP2R 2018, CCIS 1035, pp. 329–335, 2019.
https://doi.org/10.1007/978-981-13-9181-1_29

The main objective of this paper is to provide a system or model that translates Sign Language to Standard English Language then to speech and thus providing the communication between the two communities. This paper deals with developing a Convolutional Neural Network model that is trained on a dataset of gestures. This can then recognize real time gestures which are obtained using openCV without refer-ring to a database. The network will output the gesture in the form of text which is converted to speech by a Google API.

2 Related Work

A paper [1] by Rung-huei liang discussed a large vocabulary sign language interpreter with real time gesture recognition using Data Glove which is expensive that is an extra peripheral needed. In deep learning only intrinsic camera is sufficient.

A paper [2] by Oyebade K. Oyedotun explained the use of CNN to recognize hand gesture but which limited to 24 letters and less accuracy.

A Paper [3] by Sunny patel describes automated speech generation for recognize gesture which is limited to basic idea which just references with gesture database.

A paper [4] by Hussain and saxsena deals with human commanding computer, which is limited to few commands. But this relates to societal backdrop were main focus is to make disjoint communities interact.

Kulloli gave an idea of effective communication solution for the hearing impaired persons [5], here they have focused mainly on machine learning approach which were KNN and PNN with different accuracies which could be enhanced using deep learning.

3 Proposed System and Methodology

We have six modules in our system architecture as shown in Fig. 1 and they are: Setting hand histogram, create and capture gestures, loading the images for training, training the dataset, recognizing the gesture and converting to text, convert the text to speech. In this process the basic concept is to capture gestures using web camera and generated images will be the input to our Neural Network to train on. The format of the hands giving the symbol, the camera starts taking 1200 images for a single symbol for our dataset. These images are used to train the Convolutional Neural Network (CNN) which is a Deep Learning architecture for image classification built using Keras API.

The Developers are provided access to the database or the storage of the gestures folder, where they can manipulate the gesture according to their wishes. On the other hand, End User are only entitled to give their gesture to obtain a letter or words speech as an output as shown in Fig. 2.

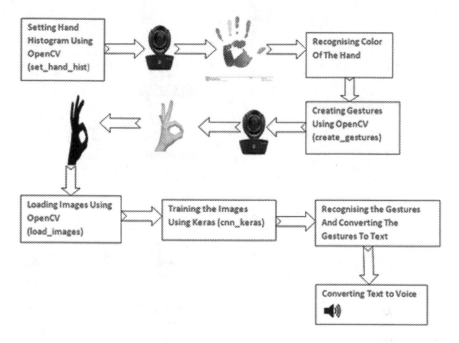

Fig. 1. System architecture

Image histograms can be useful tools for threshold in the field of computer vision. This threshold value can then be used for edge detection, co-occurrence matrices and image segmentation. The gesture can be created and captured using OpenCV, it will allow capturing 1200 gestures i.e. the training data set. The gestures that is stored in the training dataset, after loading is ready to be trained for recognition. This model uses Keras as the API for training the model. Convolution neural networks (CNNs) models are applied to the input image at multiple hierarchical layers. A cross validation method is used to train the data and predicting results. The images are passed as a tensor to the Neural network and it produces its output based on the default parameters which are set. The set parameters include optimizers, weights, biases, Convolution matrices etc. These generated outputs are compared with the expected output which yields a loss function. The loss function calculates the difference between expected and obtained output and is a measure of the efficiency of our model. During training, the network changes it's parameters to minimize the loss function hence improving efficiency. After the training is completed, the model is now ready to recognize or predict the given input gesture which is the main motivation for training. This module will predict the gesture provided as an input to the model and the gesture in the training data-set. Using the positions of fingers and palm dimensions, we model our hand. Then we compare the model with a dictionary of Gestures defined in GestureAPI.py to determine presence of gestures.

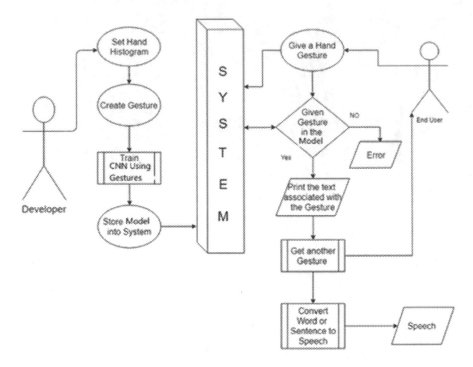

Fig. 2. Use case diagram

Import all the required keras packages as shown in Fig. 3 using which we are going to build our CNN, make sure that every package is installed properly in your machine; there is two ways of using keras, i.e. Using Tensor flow backend or by Using Theano backend. Here keras models are used to initialize our neural network model as a sequential network.

```
import keras
import numpy as np
from keras import backend as K
from keras.models import Sequential
from keras.layers.core import Dense, Flatten,Dropout
from keras.layers import Activation
from keras.optimizers import Adam,SGD
from keras.metrics import categorical_crossentropy
from keras.preprocessing.image import ImageDataGenerator
from keras.layers.normalization import BatchNormalization
from keras.layers.convolutional import *
```

Fig. 3. Importing keras layers

4   Results

We have successfully built a system that takes in gestures as an input, converts the gesture provided into text and further the text into speech. Our system consists of different modules, so we show the results for each model.

4.1   Setting Hand Histogram

This is the first module of the system. This module is to detect the colour of the hand as shown in Fig. 4. First set your hand histogram. You need to make sure the background is clear with proper lightings. Once the histogram is set you do not need to set it again unless the lighting conditions change.

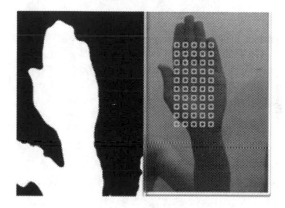

Fig. 4. Detecting hand color

4.2   Creating the Gestures

In this module, we capture images to train for the model. The recognition of gesture uses the captured 1200 photos of the gesture to compare. In Fig. 5, we have given a hand gesture to store that gesture in the system.

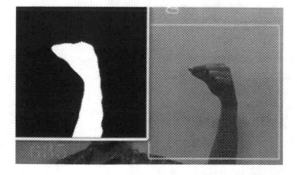

Fig. 5. Creating gestures

4.3   Recognizing Gestures

This is the gesture recognition module. This module accepts the gestures and converts the given gesture that has been captured and trained into text and text further into speech. We can see in the Table 1, how the sign has been converted to text.

Table 1. Converting gestures to text

After testing, it gives the correct results for different inputs viz individual letters to various length of words to recognize the gestures in our model.

4.4   Validating the Model

In Fig. 6, the acc: refers to the accuracy of the model achieves on the training data, while the val_acc: refers to the accuracy of model achieved on the data from a real world, i.e. validating the model. This is the end result of the Convolutional neural network. Google Text to Speech (TTS) API is used to convert text to speech and command line utility to save spoken text to mp3. Finally we design a model that takes in hand gesture as an input, convert the gesture to text and further the text to speech.

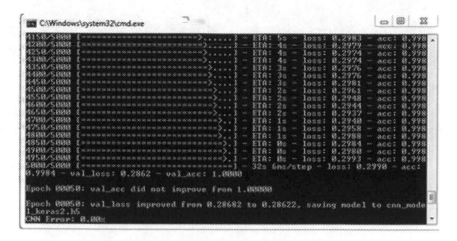

Fig. 6. Training and Validation

5   Conclusion

This paper presents the concept of sign language to speech conversion, which helps to overcome the difficulty in communication between the common people and vocally impaired people of the society. Unlike other existing system' this paper not only focuses on the gesture to letter or word display but also on various length of words or sentences and speech synthesis. This system can be adapted on various Smartphone's in the form of application, so that it is accessible to everyone. It can further be integrated with other language synthesizer instead of only English. This concept can be used to make a model for blind people too.

References

1. Liang, R.-H., Ouhyoung, M.: A real-time continuous gesture recognition system for sign language. In: Third IEEE International Conference on Automatic Face and Gesture Recognition, pp. 558–567 (1998)
2. Oyedotun, O.K., Khashman, A.: Neural Comput. Applic. **28**, 3941 (2017). https://doi.org/10.1007/s00521-016-2294-8
3. Patel, S., Dhar, U., Gangwani, S., Lad, R., Ahire, P.: Hand-gesture recognition for automated speech generation. In: IEEE International Conference on Recent Trends in Electronics Information Communication Technology, 20–21 May 2016, India, pp. 226–231. https://doi.org/10.1109/RTEICT.2016.7807817
4. Hussain, S., Saxena, R.: Hand gesture recognition using deep learning, pp. 48–49. https://doi.org/10.1109/ISOCC.2017.8368821
5. Goudar, R.H., Kulloli, S.S.: A effective communication solution for the hearing impaired persons: a novel approach using gesture and sentence formation, pp. 168–172. https://doi.org/10.1109/SmartTechCon.2017.8358363

Video Annotation and Player Classification Using Hough-Grid Transformation (HGT) Method

Aziz Makandar[1] and Daneshwari Mulimani[2(✉)]

[1] Computer Science Department, Akkamahadevi Women's University,
Vijayapur, Karnataka, India
azizkswu@gmail.com
[2] AWUV, BLDEA, S.B Arts and KCP Science College,
Vijayapur, Karnataka, India
danuam9@gmail.com

Abstract. Video processing is a most challenging research area among image processing. It has made its mark over the world by the rapid development of technology in various fields. Extending the study in the area of sports video digitization, proposed methodology initiated the novel approach on Asian game that is 'Kabaddi'. It is a team game, in which we emphasize on half of the court. This paper proposes a content analysis of kabaddi game includes both foreground and back ground annotation. Player classification, detection and tracking by dominant Color-based Feature Extraction (CFE). Blob generation for each player with consequences of team has performed using accumulation array with grid based transaction and Centroid Region Of Interest (CROI). Then by applying the grids over the play court, line detection and labeling is done by Hough Grid Transformation (HGT) method. Algorithms are implemented on MATALAB tool and tested on self developed videos having 535 frame set videos clips for privileged accuracy in the obliged aspects. By examining the results, proposed methodology can be referred in the Kabaddi tournaments for game annotation and player performance analysis.

Keywords: HGT · HLT · Player tracking · Line detection · Labeling

1 Introduction

Research in the video processing has spread over all corner of the world because of rapid development of technology and user demands in the internet broadcasting system. The immense profitable appeal to sports program has major focus in the field of entertainment. It made focus on content analysis includes video summarization, player performance analysis, game point validation, strength and weakness measures etc. These major observations insist researchers to develop large scale real time systems. Having glimpse over the existing research has majority of trained systems for tennis, badminton [3], cricket, soccer [2] and table tennis. Plenty of techniques and digital equipments are introduced by the researchers by giving more accuracy in the required aspects [4]. Where as in team games, scene extraction, condensed gain points, each

© Springer Nature Singapore Pte Ltd. 2019
K. C. Santosh and R. S. Hegadi (Eds.): RTIP2R 2018, CCIS 1035, pp. 336–344, 2019.
https://doi.org/10.1007/978-981-13-9181-1_30

player examination by occlusion handling, precise tracking with prediction are challenging issues to the area of video processing.

By diversifying the study in the field of sports and the existing literature over match analysis system, very less surveillance has found in Kabaddi game. This made us to take an initiation towards the novel approach of Asian Game. It is on the whole of an Indian game, which requires both skill and power. It combines the distinctiveness of wrestling and rugby. Kabaddi is an Asian game that includes more than sixty five Countries. It is a team game includes 7 players in each team (two). The complete court has 13×10 m for men, 11×8 m for boys and women. We have followed a line of investigation only on the half of the kabaddi court as per women's court measures. With this appendix we have developed kabaddi annotation system in MATALB tool.

The major Contributions of this paper are

1. Frame by frame analysis of object and its behaviour modelling
2. Background extraction for court line detection and ground truth measures for line labeling.
3. Foreground extraction, Player detection and tracking with accurate occlusion handling.
4. Team classification based on the dominant color based feature extraction process.
5. Player identification and labelling for individual player performance measures.

2   Literature Review

Lu [1], introduced an intelligent system that tracks and identifies players and labeling in broadcast sports videos filmed by a single pan-tilt-zoom camera. Introduce a new source of weak labels – the play-by-play text, which is widely available in sports videos. To assign a game time-stamp to every video frame, applied optical character recognition (OCR) system. Deformable Part Model (DPM) helps to automatically locate sport players in video frames. Hidden Markov Model (HMM) [30] for shot segmentation. The emission probability is modelled by a Gaussian Mixture Model (GMM) where features are RGB color histograms, and the transition probability is formulated to encourage a smooth change of shots. The DPM consists of 6 parts and 3 aspect ratios and is able to achieve a precision of 73% and a recall of 78% in the test videos.

Liu et al. [2] proposed automatic player detection, labelling and tracking in broadcast soccer video for multiple player detection, unsupervised labelling and efficient tracking. Players' position and scale are determined by a boosting based detector. Player tracking is achieved by Markov Chain Monte Carlo (MCMC) data association. Some data driven dynamics are proposed to improve the Markov chain's efficiency. This method can reach high detection and labeling precision, and reliably tracking in cases of scenes such as multiple player occlusions, moderate camera motion and pose variation.

Ghosh et al. [3], proposed an end-to-end framework for automatic attributes tagging and analysis of sport videos to analyze a large amount of badminton broadcast videos by segmenting the points played, tracking and recognizing the players in each point and annotating their respective badminton strokes. evaluate the performance on 10 Olympic matches with 20 players and achieved 95.44% point segmentation accuracy, 97.38% player detection score (mAP@0.5), 97.98% player identification accuracy, and stroke segmentation edit scores of 80.48%. Like many video processing techniques have developed for the different sports video [4].

3   Proposed Methodology

Once we state a research problem, the first most things required is the valid data base to carry out the research. This was the major issue we faced in the proposed case study. There is no appropriate data available for the research purpose that to process as per computer vision criteria's. Since, we decided to develop our own data which meet-out the ground truth measures and game conventions. We took help of Physical Education Department (PED) director and kabaddi coach to guide accordingly. The accurate ground truths are produced on the indoor 1/ 2 of the court. The game was played by 8 (one-teaser, 7-chasers) international woman kabaddi players toshoot required game points with respect to research objectives. Every scene has captured as per the instruction of the coach.

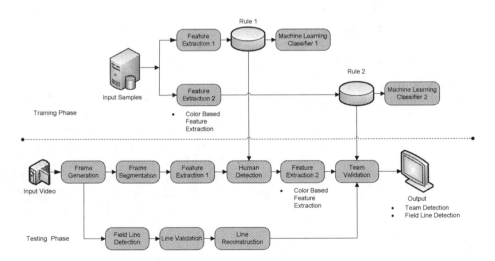

Fig. 1. Proposed system architecture

3.1   Line Segmentation and Labelling

3.1.1   Flowchart for Line Segmentation and Labelling

In Fig. 2 We stated flow chart which elaborates the work flow of line segmentation in which each frame is tested for the presence of court lines with respective constant measures. Because every sports annotation is completely depends on the boundary lines over the court [5].

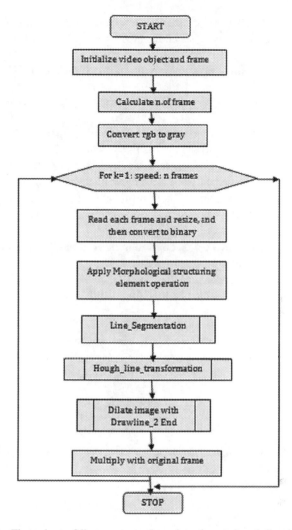

Fig. 2. Flow chart of line segmentation, detection and each line labeling

Proposed work primarily obtains the data on half of the court. In that we get one end line, one middle line, two lobby lines. Based on these circumstances we have taken the matrix measurements on the ground truth in a predetermined angle. Then we extracted the background object with foreground subtraction process. Line segmentation is done with Hough line transformation technique. We applied colour based feature extraction and morphological structuring elements to detect the line and symbolize with black color throughout the court [11, 12]. Each line labelling is done based on accurate ground measures on matrix grid analysis method. This gridding is applied on each frame then extracts the static line measure on base of pixel distribution in matrix measure. Then we apply the 2D digital film on each frame after processing with morphological operations, and then we apply HGT method for grid analysis to detect the line covariance's [5]. This process will get sphere on all the frames in the current scene. Then we named the each line with their respective significance [13] (Fig. 3).

3.1.2   Algorithm for Team Classification and Tracking Using HGT Method

Step 1. Hough Grid Transform (GHT) for detecting the straight lines in sports video.

Step 2. This algorithm uses two new techniques: a gridding method to select points to work on; a linelet processing to acquire the linelets and compute the measure function based on linelets. (we find the linelets from each block (grid). A long straight line should be cut into some linelets. In contrast these linelets will indicate the existence of the long line over the frame grids. There it finds the court line existence

Step 3. Gridding method is to draw horizontal and vertical straight lines on the each frame

Step 4. Each square is called a block and four sides of block consist of the boundary of the block.

Step 5. We ignore the block that has more than τ 1 (a threshold) points on its boundary because such block has a low signal-to-noise ratio.

Step 6. obtain a set of linelets

$$\Omega = \{K_1, K_2, \ldots, K_p\}. \text{ Let } K \in \Omega \text{ be a linelet}$$

Step 7. Voting grid function with straight line parameter

$$V(K, \rho, \theta) = \begin{cases} 1, & \text{if the parameters of K is } (\rho, \theta). \\ 0, & \text{otherwise.} \end{cases}$$

Step 8. The measure function is defined on the Hough space based on the voting function

$$M(\rho, \theta) = \sum_{i=1}^{p} V(K_i, \rho, \theta).$$

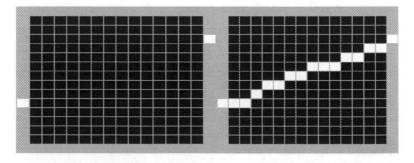

Fig. 3. An enlarged gridded block. It is a block in Fig. 1 at the 7th row and 8 is the 8th column. (a) shows two points on its boundary; (b) shows all the points between two boundary points.

4 Team Localization and Tracking

Line detection is done with background extraction. Moving on to foreground data, we consider each player inside the court boundaries. These edges have already framed by the HGT method. We apply the Color-based Feature Extraction (CFE) technique for the team tagging. Player(team) classification is done with RGB color based classification based on their track suit as represented in video. We applied the kalman filter with EGMM(Extended Gaussian Mixture Model) method for occlusion handling [6–10] in the player tracking process. thi will predict the player occlusions for accurate tracking of each player. The following work flow states the player classification, tracking process.

Algorithm:

step 1: Analyzing the frame by frame pixels, set default parameter value

step 2: Calculate No.of Frames

step 3: Measuring and building the accumulation Array

step 4: Apply the Local Maximum Filter

step 5: Segment the area of interest

step 6: Calculate the maximum No. of pixels in the group

step 7: Compute the Centroid point

step 8: Gridding and Linelet: Grid the map into the small blocks with s being the side length several times. Find linelets in each block and form the set of linelets $\Omega = \{K1, K2, ..., Kp\}$.

step 9: Computing the Measure Function: Compute the measure function $M(\rho, \theta)$ through doing statistics on the parameters of all the detected linelets.

step 10: Find Straight Line Candidate p Consider (ρ, θ) are the straight line parameters in which if $M(\rho, \theta) > \tau 2$ ($\tau 2$ is predefined threshold).

step 11: Evaluation of Straight Line Candidates and then Label the each line: line detection and labeling is done with Hough line transformation(HLT) and CROI in which each line with respect to the x and y axis will measured and detected with black line indent. Each line is labeled with their respective meaning.

step 12: Apply fill image region and holes with Morphological operation

step 13: Player classification: Calculate mean color for team 1 and team 2 max min value R, G, B region using CFE.

step 14: Measure the properties of image region.

step 15: Create Bounding Box with different color.

5 Experimental Results

Frame by frame analysis is done as shown in the above result snapshots. The Fig. 4(a), shows the current processing frame in the input video. The Fig. 4(b) shows the line detection by black color with respect to the each line labeling that indicates the identity of each line framing on half of the game court. The Fig. 4c and d, shows the processing frame 343 with player detection with unique team identification by T1 and T2. Each player is detected and tracked along with bounding box by differentiating with blue and green color with respect to the team members. Detection and tracking accuracy is as follows (Table 1).

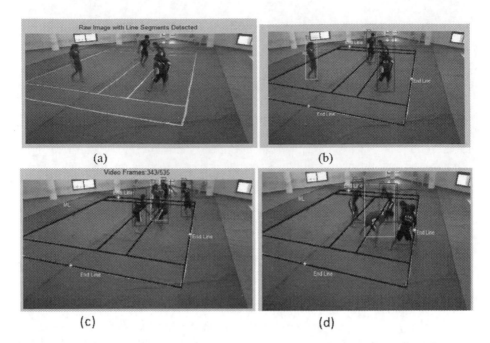

Fig. 4. Figure (a) shows the current processing frame, (b) shows line segmentation and each line labeling, c & d-player classification by labeling and tracking (Color figure online)

Table 1. Overview of result analysis with different sports videos with respect to the techniques implemented, detection and tracking accuracy is shown based on number of players and detection modes.

Si. no	Sports video	Algorithm used	No. of players	Detected/tracked players	Accuracy
1	Soccer [2]	MCMC	11	10 (no labeling)	94.8%
2	Tennis	GMM	2	2 (no labeling)	98.78%
3	Basket Ball [14]	MIM	9	8 (with labeling)	94.67%
4	Basket Ball	Linear programming relaxation	8	8 (with labeling)	89%
5	Badminton	HOG, Kalman filter	2	2 (without court line, no labeling)	97.78%
		GM-PHD (Gaussia hypothesis density)			
7	Tennis (2016) [16]	Logical AND operation	2	2 (with ball tracking)	88.33%
8	Baskel ball (2017)	Morphological operation and homograph matrix	7	7 (no label no bounding box) pixel point detection	95.6%
9	Kabaddi (current case study)	Proposed method CROI, HGT, CFE	5	5 (with player and line labeling)	100%

6 Conclusion

The proposed method proves the vigorous technique for play court detection and player classification process on innovative case study. Algorithms are tested on self developed data set. Both the approaches have given the best result as compared with the existing work, such as tennis, soccer video. Experimental results are clearly shown the detection accuracy inside the field in accordance with frame by frame evaluation. Since this paper concludes that HGT and HLT are preeminent techniques for the kabaddi video analysis process.

Acknowledgment. There is no legal data set available for the research on the kabaddi game, since have created our own data set. This was done with the guidance of Dr.Rajakumar Malipatil, (Registrar Evaluator) Director of Physical Education Department (PED), Akkamahadevi Woman's University Viajayapur (AWU), for the right ground truth examination and played by AWU-PED International Kabaddi players. Another data set was created in Mangalore University by taking official permission from the parent university and Alva's PED Director. We are grateful to both PED team for their supervision, which made possible to develop required data set on as per the required research criterions.

References

1. Lu, W.-L., et al.: Learning to track and identify players from broadcast sports videos. IEEE Trans. Pattern Anal. Mach. Intell. **35**(7), 1704–1716 (2013)
2. Liu, J., et al.: Automatic player detection, labeling and tracking in broadcast soccer video. Pattern Recogn. Lett. **30**(2), 103–113 (2009)
3. Ghosh, A., et al.: Towards structured analysis of broadcast badminton videos (2017). IETarX4:1706.00672v2 [cs.CV]
4. Shih, H.-C.: A survey on content aware video analysis for sports. In: IEEE Transactions on Circuits and Systems for Video Technology, vol. 99, no. 9. Member, IEEE (2017)
5. Yu, X., et al.: A gridding Hough transform for detecting the straight lines in sports video. In: IEEE Xplore Conference Paper, 2015. https://doi.org/10.1109/icme.2005.1521474
6. Schindler, K., et al.: Improved multi-person tracking with active occlusion handling. In: Proceedings of the IEEE ICRA Workshop on People Detection and Tracking Kobe, Japan (2009)
7. Ong, L.-Y., et al.: Performance of invariant feature descriptors with adaptive prediction in occlusion handling. In: Third International Conference on Control, Automation and Robotics. IEEE (2017). 978-1-5090-6088-7117/$31.00 ©2017
8. Bogun, I., Ribeiro, E.: Robstruck: improving occlusion handling of structured tracking-by-detection using Robust Kalman filter. IEEE (2017). 978-1-4673-9961-6/16/$31.00 ©2016
9. Raman, R., et al.: Occlusion prediction algorithms for multi-camera network. IEEE (2018). 978-1-4503-1772-6
10. Chandel, H., Vatta, S.: Occlusion detection and handling: a review. Int. J. Comput. Appl. **120**(10), (2015) (0975 – 8887)
11. Sharma1, R., Sharma, R.: Image segmentation using morphological operations for automatic region growing. Int. J. Comput. Sci. Inf. Technol. **4**(6), 844–847 (2013)

12. Resmi, H.B., Deepambika, V.A., Abdul Rahman, M.: Symmetric mask wavelet based detection and tracking of moving objects using variance method. In: Second International Symposium on Computer Vision and the Internet (VisionNet'15). ELSEVIER Procedia, Computer Science, pp. 58–65 (2015)
13. Choroś, K.: Detection of tennis court lines for sport video categorization. In: Nguyen, N.-T., Hoang, K., Jędrzejowicz, P. (eds.) ICCCI 2012. LNCS (LNAI), vol. 7654, pp. 304–314. Springer, Heidelberg (2012). https://doi.org/10.1007/978-3-642-34707-8_31
14. Wen, P.-C., Cheng, W.-C., et al.: Court reconstruction for camera calibration in broadcast basketball videos (2015)
15. Tsai, T.-Y.: Recognizing offensive tactics in broadcast basketball videos via key player detection. In: 2017 IEEE International Conference on Image Processing (ICIP), 22 February 2017
16. Archana, M., Kalaiselvi Geetha, M.: Robust player tracking in broadcast tennis video using Kalman filter. I J C T A, pp. 411–418 (2016)

Hyperspectral and Multispectral Remote Sensing Data Fusion for Classification of Complex-Mixed Land Features Using SVM

Amol D. Vibhute[1]([⊠]), Sandeep V. Gaikwad[2], Rajesh K. Dhumal[1],
Ajay D. Nagne[3], Amarsinh B. Varpe[2], Dhananjay B. Nalawade[2],
Karbhari V. Kale[2], and Suresh C. Mehrotra[2]

[1] School of Computational Sciences, Solapur University, Solapur 413255, MS, India
amolvibhute2011@gmail.com, dhumal19@gmail.com
[2] Geospatial Technology Research Laboratory, Department of Computer Science and
IT, Dr. Babasaheb Ambedkar Marathwada University, Aurangabad 431004, MS, India
sandeep.gaikwad22@gmail.com, varpeamarsinh@gmail.com,
dhananjay.bamu@gmail.com, kvkale91@gmail.com, mehrotra.suresh15j@gmail.com
[3] Dr. G.Y. Pathrikar College of Computer Science and Information Technology,
M G M, Aurangabad, MS, India
ajay.nagne@gmail.com

Abstract. In the present paper, classification and analysis of complex land features on the combined outcome of the high spectral resolution Hyperion-Hyperspectral Remote Sensing (HRS) data and high spatial resolution Resourcesat-II Linear Imaging Self-Scanning System IV (LISS-IV) multispectral data were investigated. The traditional way of satellite image fusion is based on high spatial resolution panchromatic image and low spatial-spectral resolution multispectral image. However, in the current study, a novel approach via considering HRS and LISS-IV multispectral data is proposed for classification of complex features of earth surface. The used multi-date, multi-sensor and multi-resolution satellite imagery was acquired on 20th March, 2015 and 28th February, 2014 of HRS and LISS-IV data having spatial resolution 30 m and 5.8 m respectively. Three pixel level image fusion algorithms were computed such as Gram-Schmidt Transform (GST), Principal Component Spectral Sharpening Transform (PCSST) and Color Normalized Spectral Sharpening (CNSS) for fusion of datasets. The quality of the fusion algorithms has been estimated on the classification accuracy of mixed features. Moreover, the performance of three fusion algorithms was compared with the classification results. The assessment results of fused data using all the methods were acceptable in view of spatial-spectral accuracy of data. The Support Vector Machine (SVM) approach with its Gaussian Radial Basis Function (GRBF) kernel was implemented for classification of original and fused data. In conclusion, the SVM algorithm resulted accurate with 97.65, 97.47, 96.30, 86.20 and 74.44% accuracy for CNSS fused, PCSST fused, GST fused, and original multispectral and origi-

K. C. Santosh and R. S. Hegadi (Eds.): RTIP2R 2018, CCIS 1035, pp. 345–362, 2019.
https://doi.org/10.1007/978-981-13-9181-1_31

nal hyperspectral data respectively and proved very robust method for mixed feature classification.

Keywords: Satellite image fusion · Spatial-spectral classification · Gram-Schmidt Transform ·
Principal Component Spectral Sharpening · Support vector machine · Hyperspectral data

1   Introduction

Classification of complex mixed features and its analysis is a key exercise for numerous applications like urban land cover classification, complex forest tree classification, multiple crop classification, etc. Single sensor and low spatial-spectral images does not provide the details of complex terrain surface features as well as no single technology can be constantly enough for reliable image interpretation. Fusion of remote sensing images is a promising approach to solve complex mixed feature classification for near real-time applications. Classification of heterogeneous urban land covers [1–5] and forest areas [6] are very challenging task due to complex and mixed features of earth surface. Satellite remote sensing imagery is widely acceptable by remote sensing community for several applications. In the present era, high spatial and spectral resolution remote sensing images have become available. However, the single channel panchromatic image has high spatial resolution with lower spectral information. The high spectral information is found to be more in multi-channel images, though multi-channel images have low spatial information. Nevertheless, an image has less number of bands and low spectral resolution is basically known as multispectral imagery which is tough to discriminate the similar patterns of land covers [1]. On the other hand, more spectral channels and high spectral resolution are obtainable in hyperspectral images [1] that contain a lot of information about spectral characteristics of the land cover features [4]. However, merely single sensor panchromatic, multispectral or hyperspectral images are not sufficient for classification of complex-mixed land cover objects [2,7]. The high spatial and spectral resolution images are indispensable to overcome the limitations of using only single sensor images [1,4,5]. Consequently, a new joint high spatial and spectral resolution image approach is obtained by the image fusion using high spatial resolution panchromatic or multispectral image and high spectral resolution hyperspectral image. The amalgamation of multiple images to form a new image through improved methods is named as image fusion. The image fusion can be obtained by combination of image modalities or spatial-spectral properties. In the present paper, high spatial resolution multispectral image with high spectral resolution hyperspectral image is utilized for obtaining a new joint high spatial and spectral resolution image to discriminate complex-mixed land cover patterns of the earth surface.

2   Literature Survey

Several researchers in the particular field of satellite image fusion have worked on panchromatic and multi or hyperspectral images. The ultimate objectives were development of new methods for classification of land patterns [4] or better visual interpretation of satellite images. For instance, an authors in [1] have worked on satellite image fusion for investigation of pixel-based and object-based classifications for mapping the urban land cover. The Hyperion and IRS-PAN images were used for fusion of images and obtained good classification accuracy with object and pixel based approaches [1]. The hyperspectral and LiDAR datasets were considered with unsupervised and supervised approaches and a graph-based method for the fusion of spectral, spatial, and elevation information [2] for the classification of land patterns. The comparison of image fusion methods was performed using very high resolution World View-2 panchromatic and multispectral data for classification of urban land cover area in [3]. The fusion of morphological and statistical information has been considered for classification. Mathematical morphology was used for the extraction of spatial features with decision level fusion in classification of hyperspectral data from the urban areas [8]. On the other hand, complex forest area [6], mapping biomass and stress in the Sierra Nevada [9] and urban area classification [10,11] have been carried out with the fusion of LiDAR data and hyperspectral image. Furthermore, both multispectral images were also pondered for vegetation and urban area classification with low and high resolutions. The Landsat-5 Thematic Mapper image along with World View-2 image was fused which has 30 m and 2 m spatial resolutions, respectively through linear spectral unmixing model [12]. The literature has more pointed out on multi-sensor and multi-resolution satellite images either panchromatic with multispectral or panchromatic with hyperspectral datasets. The attention on multispectral with hyperspectral image fusions were less for land cover classification. Where, the fusion of these images provides additional spectral and spatial information. In addition, multi-date satellite image fusion is critical issue due to varied properties of earth surface features. In the present research, the fusion framework is proposed using hyperspectral and multispectral satellite images with varied date for complex-mixed land pattern classification to overcome the limitations of single sensor and single date low resolution images.

3   Architecture of the Proposed Methodology

3.1   Satellite Image Pre-processing

The satellite image pre-processing is carried out through various methods. The satellite image was rectified to the Universal Transverse Mercator (UTM) zone 43 North and World Geodetic System (WGS)-84 datum. The coordinates of the study area for upper left was 200945.47 N and 752122.44 E, whereas lower right was 200514.54 N and 752624.19 E. As obtained datasets were in the raw format and these raw data is needed to be correct for further processing. The raw

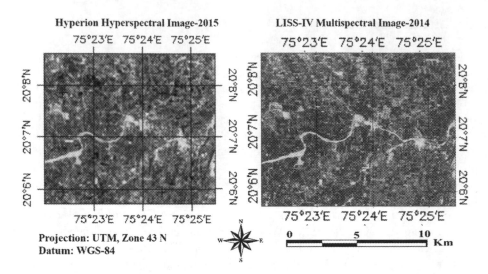

Fig. 1. The geo-location of the study area and its corresponding Hyperion and LISS-IV Data

Hyperion data which was in GeoTIFF format were converted into ENVI standard format using 'Hyperion tool' and the converted image was used for rest of the analysis. An orthorectification was done of both the converted satellite data. The multispectral data has required merely that much preprocessing to execute the fusion and classification algorithms. In other case, Hyperion image has uncalibrated water vapor and overlapping bands. Accordingly, an amount of 87 bands among the 242 were identified as a bad and water vapor bands and eliminated from the further processing. Besides, conversion to reflectance of both satellite images was done. Subsequently, the Hyperion image was atmospherically corrected by QUAC algorithm [13] and spatial subset was generated through ROIs. The images were obtained by the various sources and satellite platforms, so the images were registered to the same projection and geographic coordinate system. The data processing was carried out through ENVI 5.1 image processing package. The spectral subset of Hyperion image was generated according to the wavelength range of LISS-IV image. The multispectral image has three bands ranging from 520-860 nm. Therefore, thirty five spectral bands of Hyperion image was used for fusion and rest of the 120 bands were skipped form the further processing. Utilized bands from the Hyperion image was ranging from 518.39-864.35 nm with 35 bands. The original preprocessed Hyperspectral and multispectral images are depicted in Fig. 1.

3.2 Fusion Framework for Hyperspectral and Multispectral Imagery

Mostly, satellite image fusion can be derived by three fusion levels such as pixel-based or iconic level, feature level, and decision or knowledge level [14,15]. The

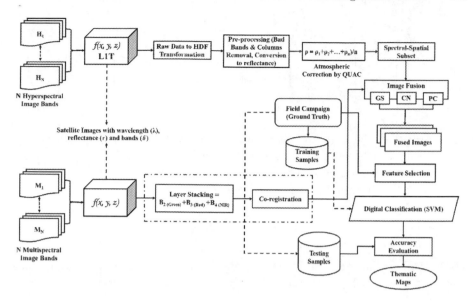

Fig. 2. Architecture of the developed fusion framework

image fusion levels may be varying according to various data types, objectives, applications of image fusion or density of the problem. Where, pixel-level fusion may be generally used to enhance the efficiency of image classification and detection algorithms [14]. In the present study, the fusion of multispectral and hyperspectral images have been carried out for land cover classification. The present section highlights the fusion framework of both the datasets along with classification approaches depicted in Fig. 2. The three fusion algorithms were implemented for fusion of satellite images to extract the spatial and spectral information from the heterogeneous objects. The hyperspectral and multispectral bands were converted with appropriate format to obtain the raw images and some preprocessing was done for both the images. The preprocessed images were used for fusion and fused images for digital classification.

Fusion Method Relay on GST. The GST algorithm uses the spectral response factor of an assumed instrument for assessing the high resolution image. The GST algorithm is used for jointly transmitting synthesized high spatial image and low resolution image. The values mean and high frequency variance of a high spatial resolution image is then extracted. Subsequently, the first factor of GST is replaced by the new high resolution image. Lastly, the obtained set is inversely transformed for generating the high resolution image [1,16,17]. The mathematical procedure of GST algorithm is given in Eq. 1.

$$\begin{pmatrix} HSRI \\ LSRI_1 \\ . \\ . \\ . \\ LSRI_N \end{pmatrix} \xRightarrow{GST} \begin{pmatrix} GS_1 \\ GS_2 \\ . \\ . \\ . \\ LSRI_{N+1} \end{pmatrix} \xRightarrow[with\,modified\,HSRI]{Replace\,GS1} \begin{pmatrix} MHSRI \\ GS_2 \\ . \\ . \\ . \\ LSRI_{N+1} \end{pmatrix} \xRightarrow[GST]{Inverse} \begin{pmatrix} X \\ F_1 \\ . \\ . \\ . \\ F_N \end{pmatrix}$$

(1)

where, HSRI is the high spatial resolution synthesized image combine transformed with LSRI low spatial resolution images, MHSPI is the modified HSRI and F is the fused images. The GST method is implemented by Eq. 2 for constructing the synthesized high resolution image.

$$HSRI = \frac{1}{N} \sum_{i=1}^{N} LSRI_{i\uparrow}$$

(2)

where, HSI is the synthesized image (high spatial resolution), $LSRI_{i\uparrow}$ is the up-scaled i^{th} low spatial resolution image bands and N is the total number of LSRI.

Fusion Method Relay on PCSST. The PCSST method was used for our study which is statistically rigorous that renovates a multivariate dataset of correlated factors into a dataset of uncorrelated linear combinations of the factors. The PC method generates an uncorrelated feature space of LSRIs while transferring the PCs according to the eigenvectors of their corresponding covariance matrices. First PCs comprises most of the data variance among all the remaining bands. The HSRI is statistically adjusted to match with the PCs. Subsequently, inverse PC transformation is executed on the obtained new set of PCs and high resolution fused images are generated [1, 16, 18]. The mathematical procedure of PCSST algorithm is given in Eq. 3.

$$\begin{pmatrix} LSRI_1 \\ LSRI_2 \\ . \\ . \\ . \\ LSRI_N \end{pmatrix} \xRightarrow{PCT} \begin{pmatrix} PC_1 \\ PC_2 \\ . \\ . \\ . \\ PC_N \end{pmatrix} \xRightarrow[with\,modified\,HSRI]{Replace\,PC1} \begin{pmatrix} MHSRI \\ PC_2 \\ . \\ . \\ . \\ PC_N \end{pmatrix} \xRightarrow[PCT]{Inverse} \begin{pmatrix} X \\ F_1 \\ F_2 \\ . \\ . \\ . \\ F_N \end{pmatrix}$$

(3)

where, LSRI is the low spatial resolution images, PC is the principal components, MHSPI is the modified HSRI and F is the fused images. The PCT method is implemented by Eq. 4 for fusion of used images.

$$F_i = LSRI_{i\uparrow} + v_i(HSRI - PC1)$$

(4)

where, F_i is the ith band in fused image, $LSRI_{i\uparrow}$ is the up-scaled i^{th} low spatial resolution image bands, v_i is the ith element of most significant eigenvector and HSRI is the high resolution image and PC1 is the first PCT of LSRI.

Fusion Method Relay on CNSS. The CNSS algorithm is an extension of CN Brovey transform [19] used in multispectral images and revised for hyperspectral data sharpening. The method can be simultaneously used to sharpen any number of bands from the data and retain the input images original data type with dynamic range. The bands of provided input images are clustered into spectral segments defined by the spectral range of the sharpening bands. The input bands (LSRI) is multiplied by the HSRI sharpening bands and then resulted values are normalized by averaged LSR data over the spectral bands in the segment (covered range of HSRI) [20,21]. The CNSS algorithm is defined by the Eq. 5.

$$F_i = \frac{LSRI_i \times HSRI}{LSRI_s} \tag{5}$$

where, F_i is the sharpened image, $(LSRI)_i$ is the LSRI band, $LSRI_s$ is the band averaged LSRI over the $HSRI$ spectral bands in the segment (covered wavelength range).

4   Data Set and Study Area

The study area (Fig. 1) selected is a complex-mixed land view with hills of Aurangabad district of Maharashtra, India located at 19°28'43.27"- 20°24'52.19" N latitude and 75°13'10.75" -75°30'14.87" E longitude [22,23]. The landscape of the study area is uneven and it extends across the region of around 32.04 Km^2.

For the present study, two datasets were used for image fusion acquired from USGS [24] and NRSC via Earth Observing-1 (EO-1) Hyperion and IRS-P6 Resourcesat-II LISS-IV sensors respectively. The hyperspectral and multispectral images (Fig. 1) were individually acquired on April 15, 2015 at 17:15 hrs and March 05, 2014 at 14:18 hrs respectively. The Hyperion data consist of 242 spectral bands ranging from 355.59–2577.08 nm with high spectral resolution of 10 nm along with 30 m spatial resolution and 7.74 km by 100 km swath per view. The Hyperion data of level 1 T was orthorectified by the provider with band sequential (BSQ) mode [13,25]. The major parameters of Hyperion data and LISS-IV data are depicted in Table 1. Alternatively, LISS-IV data has high spatial resolution of 5.8 m with 23.5 km swath per scene. In addition, the spectral bands are three which consist of 520–860 nm spectral range of Green, Red and Near Infrared (NIR). Accordingly, these three bands are essential for fusing the visible to NIR region of hyperspectral data. In our proposed approach, an amount of 38 spectral bands of Hyperion data were fused with three spectral bands of LISS-IV data.

Concurrently, the ground truth points (GTP) were collected through field visit during the tenure of February 10, 2015 to March 25, 2015 in between 0800 to 1330 h with clear environmental conditions. The GTPs were collated using near real time Global Positioning System (GPS) on Android smart phone and observed ground locations were captured via digital cameras. Discussions were done with local people and noted on digital notebooks for verifying the ground observations. The collected GTPs and proximal sensing data were digitized for

Table 1. Hyperion and LISS-IV data parameters

Spacecraft/Instrument	USGS E0-1/Hyperion	NRSC(IRS)-P6 Resourcesat-II/LISS-IV
Product type	Level 1T (GeoTIFF)	GeoTIFF
Acquisition date	21-02-2015	21/02/2014
Orbit path/target path	147/146	096
Orbit row/target row	46/46	056
Spectral range	355.59-2577.08 nm	520–860 nm
Number of visible/near infrared bands/short wave infrard bands	35/35/172	2/1/0
Spatial resolution/number of bands/swaths width	30 m/242/7.5 km	5.8 m/3/23.5 km
Spectral coverage	Continuous	Broad
Temporal resolution	200 days	5 days

further processing. All GTPs were then transformed to region of interests (ROIs) on the co-registered hyperspectral and multispectral imagery and used for the development of the training and testing sets. Additionally, Google map and Google earth were often used for verification and validation of used data. Survey of India (SOI) toposheet at 1:50,000 scales used for base map preparation.

5   Supervised Classification Based on SVM

The proposed approach has been classified with advanced classification algorithm, specifically appropriate to analyze the satellite images. The algorithm is an advance level machine learning approach relies on SVM. In the following section, we briefly recall the key properties of used classification method for our study.

5.1   Support Vector Machine

It is the advance supervised machine learning approach that overcomes the limitations of traditional methods. The SVM is developed by the Vapnik [26] in 1995 based on statistical learning theory. The SVM methods have undergone better improvement in the preceding decade and have been extensively used for several remote sensing applications [7,27]. The major cause behind the use of SVM is justified from some key characteristics such as (1) Architecture design is easy and requires less training pixels or values of data. (2) The accuracy of SVM is better than other machine learning approaches [28]. The SVM offers separation hyperplane or boundary for classification also known as support pixel vectors.

The closest pixels of the hyperplane are used for training purposes. The confusion between classes is minimized through the hyperplane while maximizing the margin between the closest training pixels those are situated at the boarder of the support vectors. Merely support vectors are considered and others are eliminated. Thus, minimum pixels are effectively used with better accuracy [28, 29]. The mathematical formulation and main concepts of SVMs are illustrated below.

Let us consider the supervised binary problem. Let us assume that the closest training set $(x_1, y_1), (x_2, y_2), (x_n, y_n), y_i \in (+1, -1)$, and is considered. where, x is the training pixels and $y_i \in (+1, -1)$ are the target classes and $+1$ and -1 denote the labels of pondered classes. The concluding inner product operation has corresponding representation. Thus, the decision function is obtained through the convex optimization problem (Eq. 6).

$$MaxA(\alpha) = \sum_{i=1}^{N} \alpha_i - 0.5 \sum_{i,j=1}^{N} \alpha_i \alpha_j y_i y_j k(x_i \bullet x_j) \qquad (6)$$

Subject to: $\sum_{i=1}^{N} \alpha_i y_i = 0$ and $\alpha_i \geq C \geq 0$, i = 1,2,...N.
where, α_i is a Lagrange multipliers, C represents the penalty value and k is the kernel function.

The SVM provides various kernels for identifying suitable hyperplane. The own implementation of SVM was used based on RBF (Eq. 7) and minimal optimization process for training and classification of used data.

Gaussian Radial Basis Function (RBF):

$$k(x_i, x_j) = exp(-\gamma \bullet ||x_i - x_j||^2), \gamma > 0 \qquad (7)$$

where,γ, g and b are the kernel constant parameters.

6   Results and Discussion

6.1   Fusion of Hyperspectral and Multispectral Data

The three fusion approaches were implemented on the said datasets and achieved better results as compared to original images for classification. The Fig. 3 illustrates the obtained results by CNSS algorithm, GST algorithm and PCSST algorithm respectively fused through hyperspectral image with high spatial resolution multispectral image.

The visual illustration of CNS sharpening and PCS sharpening was quite good than GST algorithm. The GST fused image has more color distortions with respect to the original image. However, CNSS and GST method has given the alike results besides original and PCSS image has provided near similar results.

Approximately, all the three methods have delivered good spatial and spectral information. The spectral profiles of every class have been plotted for comparison of used fusion approaches with the original one (Figs. 4, 5 and 6). The

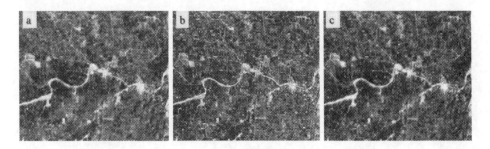

Fig. 3. (a) CNSS, (b) GST and (c) PCSST fused images

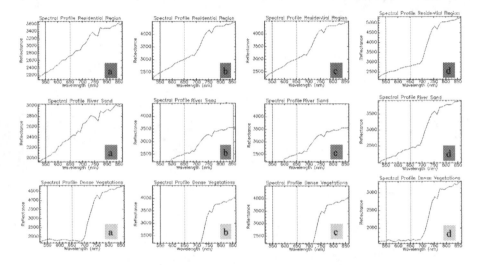

Fig. 4. Spectral profiles of (a) original hyperspectral image, (b) CNSS image, (c) GST image and (d) PCSST image for residential region, river sand and dense vegetations respectively

spectral signatures of residential class were slightly similar for original and fused images. River sand class has given similar spectra of residential region for original hyperspectral image and also for PCSST image. On the other hand, the spectral curves of dense and sparse vegetations were considerably matched with original and PCSS image as compared to CNSS and GST images. The spectra of dense vegetation are slightly increased for CNSS and GST methods.

The black soil have generated varied spectra, as these soils have physicochemical properties, soil moisture, clays and soils may vary according to geolocation. Whereas, bare soil reflected well for all the results and these soils have less amount of water.

The spectra of road class have high reflectance for original and PCSST image as compared to CNSS and GST images. PCSST method has given higher reflectance of water in visible regions, whereas original hyperspectral image has

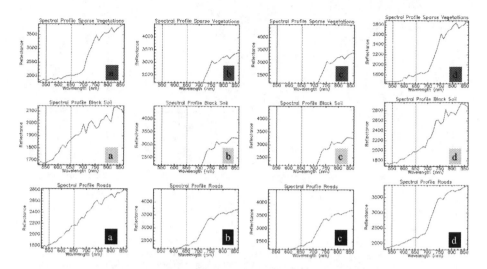

Fig. 5. Spectral profiles of (a) original hyperspectral image, (b) CNSS image, (c) GST image and (d) PCSST image for sparse vegetations, black soil and roads respectively

produced erroneous spectra due to the unavailability of water on March 2015. The experimental results were evaluated on the basis of spectral signatures and classification performances. The SVM method is implemented on original high spectral resolution hyperspectral image, high spatial resolution multispectral image, fused images using CNSS algorithm, GST algorithm and PCSST algorithm.

6.2   Classification Outcome

The statistical SVM method was computed with its GRBF kernel and evaluated the obtained results of original hyperspectral image, multispectral image and CNSS fused, GST fused and PCSST fused images. Eight major objects were identified accordingly field campaign, ground reference data and spectral signatures of individual objects (Figs. 4, 5 and 6) by the satellite images. Consequently, training and testing pixels were derived from the both original images and used for the evaluation. The training and testing pixels for multispectral image was individually used due to dissimilarity of multispectral and hyperspectral patterns. The training and testing pixels were similar for hyperspectral and fused images. Table 2 point out the identified classes, training and testing samples along with its color code of classification for all datasets.

The number of 687 samples was used for training and 1203 samples were used for testing of multispectral image. Similarly, the training of hyperspectral and fused data was carried out through 285 samples and 2734 random samples were successfully utilized for testing the data with good accuracy. The said training pixels were given as an input to the SVM classifier with 0.333 Gamma value in kernel function. The GRBF kernel function was chosen of SVM method as it

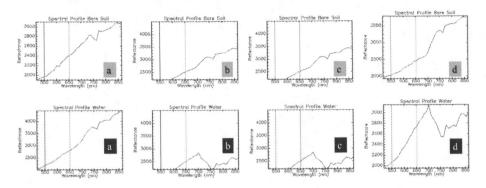

Fig. 6. Spectral profiles of (a) original hyperspectral image, (b) CNSS image, (c) GST image and (d) PCSST image for bare soil and water respectively

Table 2. Image classes, training and testing pixels for multispectral and hyperspectral image along with classification color codes of classes

Class name	Multispectral image		Hyperspectral image		Classification color of classes
	Training pixels	Testing pixels	Training pixels	Testing pixels	
Residential regions	71	176	58	414	RED
River sand	232	353	64	762	Pink
Dense vegetations	37	68	34	315	Purple
Sperse vegetation	124	182	44	57	Green
Black soil	114	239	18	633	Yellow
roads	25	48	20	209	Black
Bare soil	67	114	28	230	Faint Pink
Water	17	23	19	114	Blue

requires determining a less amount of factors and produces good results [30] as compared to other kernels of SVM, where penalty parameter was preserved as 100. First pyramid level was selected of SVM approach with 0.90 reclassification threshold of pyramid. Additionally, classification probability threshold was set as 0.20. The outcome of the original multispectral image is shown in Fig. 7 which clearly indicates that, the classification of every individual class is obtained well as per the provided training samples. The color code of classes is given in Table 2 for all classes.

Similarly, original hyperspectral image is trained through the said parameters (Table 2) and achieved the good outcomes (Fig. 8). According to the results of hyperspectral data, roads and water is not detected as these classes were misclassified with soils and vegetations as per the characteristics of objects. The accuracy of original data was near about seventy three percent which is quite unsatisfactory due to misclassification. The reason behind the misclassification is as

Fig. 7. SVM classification output layer of original multispectral image

hyperspectral data have more alike spectral characteristics. Consequently, fusion of hyperspectral image is carried out with multispectral image and achieved acceptable output with the form of classified layers and accuracies.

The misclassification was reduced while the use of fusion algorithms. CNSS and GST method produced similar spectral characteristics for all classes and every class have classified well instead of water (Fig. 9-a and b). PCSST algorithm performed very accurate results for every object (Fig. 9-c). The Fig. 9 depicts the output map of three fusion approaches CNSS, GST and PCSST generated by SVM method.

6.3 Evaluation of Classification Accuracy

The performance of classification accuracy of SVM method is measured through confusion matrix which includes producer's accuracy, user's accuracy, overall accuracy and kappa statistics. The ground control points were used to generate the confusion matrix. Besides, an overall accuracy and kappa statistic was implemented using Eqs. 8 and 9 for the evaluation of the classification results

$$Overall\ Accuracy = \frac{\sum_{x=1}^{A} C_{xx}}{N} \times 100\% \tag{8}$$

where, C_{xx} is the element at position x^{th} row and x^{th} column, N and A is the total number of pixels and classes respectively.

Fig. 8. SVM classification output layer of original hyperspectral image

Fig. 9. SVM classification output layers of fused (a) CNSS, (b) GST and (c) PCSST images respectively

$$k = \frac{\sum_{i=1}^{r} X_{ii} - \sum ci \sum ri}{N^2 - \sum_{i=1}^{r}(\sum ci \sum ri)} \tag{9}$$

where, r = number of rows and columns in the error matrix, $X_{(ii)}$= number of observations in row i and column i, $\sum ci$ = marginal total of column i, $\sum ri$ = marginal total of row i, N = total number of observations [31]. The class specific accuracy along with overall accuracy and kappa values are drawn in Table 3 for the original images. The accuracy of the SVM classification for both the original images indicates several incorrectly identified pixels of classes (Table 3), where the multispectral image produced by SVM seems more accurate results than hyperspectral. Dense vegetations (66.18%) and bare soil (63.16) generated low class specific accuracy for MS image and overall accuracy was 86.20% with 0.82 kappa statistics.

Table 3. Performance Evaluation of SVM classification for original images

	RR	RS	DV	SV	B1_S	ROADS	BARE SOIL	WATER	OA	K
MS	72.73	89.90	66.18	98.35	99.16	75.00	63.16	100	86.20	0.82
HS	32.76	85.94	94.12	100	100	50	82.14	0	74.44	0.69

It seems that, dense vegetations are misclassified with sparse vegetations and bare soil is with black soil. Whereas, hyperspectral image produced low output for residential region (32.76%), roads (50%) and water (0%). The said classes are misclassified with river sand, bare soil and roads respectively. An unavailability of the water is also one of the major causes of misclassification for hyperspectral image as the data was of March, 2015. Hyperspectral image produced 74.44% overall accuracy and 0.69 kappa statistics. The class specific confusion was diminished by the fusion mechanism as this approach produced good accuracy (Table 4) for all classes except sparse vegetations which was misclassified with roads and black soil. The overall accuracy was 96.30, 97.47 and 97.65% with kappa values of 0.95, 0.96 and 0.97 for GST fused, PCSST fused and CNSS fused images respectively (Table 4 and Fig. 10). The comparisons of obtained accuracy of original and fused images are illustrated in Fig. 10. The minimum class specific accuracy was assigned to the sparse vegetation class. The water and road class made the second lowest class specific accuracy due to the spectral confusion between roads and bare soil and water with vegetations.

Table 4. Performance Evaluation of SVM classification for fused images

	RR	RS	DV	SV	B1_S	Roads	Baren land	Water	OA	K
GS fused	96.86	96.46	100	78.95	99.21	87.08	98.70	87.72	96.30	0.95
PC fused	98.07	98.03	99.05	75.44	100	92.34	98.70	91.23	97.47	.96
CN fused	99.03	98.03	100	36.84	100	95.69	100	100	97.65	0.97

The original hyperspectral image has no water. However, multispectral image has water. When fusion was made, the water class was fused with hyperspectral image and assigned water class to all fusion approaches. The spectral signature confusion between residential regions, sands and roads is common as these class spectra are similar. Moreover, the black soil and bare soil is also have alike spectral signatures, so confusion was increased. Similarly, spectral signatures of dense and sparse vegetations are similar to each other.

Overall, the acquisition time of both the satellite data was of one year which causes the error for some classes like water, soil and vegetations as these classes vary according to time. Nevertheless, the field campaign, user knowledge of

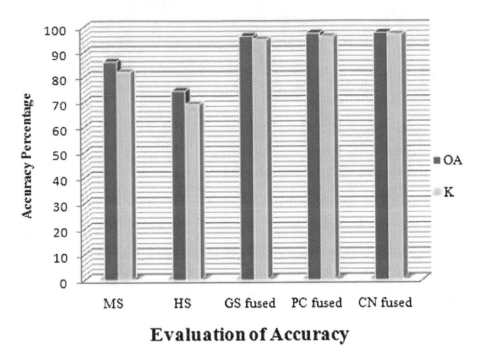

Evaluation of Accuracy

Fig. 10. Comparisons of accuracy assessment

ground objects as well as satellite data produced better training samples for the data. Furthermore, reference data was suitable and Google map and Google earth was used for validation of earth surface objects. On the other hand, the proposed methodology is novel due to followed strategy and implemented methods with accepted results. Consequently, the present work will be used by the other researchers for their work for similar type of research.

7   Conclusions

The use of fusion approaches have been pondered for classification of very heterogeneous and mixed objects on the planet surface. Three fusion algorithms were implemented to achieve the said objectives with better outcome of classification. As per our knowledge, the fusion of hyperspectral image with multispectral image is carried out first time with accepted results. The statistical supervised approach i.e. SVM with its GRBF kernel was computed on original images and also on fused images. Moreover, other three kernels of SVM method was also used and tested on original images. However, the results were not acceptable due to low classification performance and low accuracy. Subsequently, quantitative evaluation was constructed on fused images and classified images. It is concluded that, all the three fusion methods have performed well as per its spectral behavior and classification results. The hyperspectral image has highlighted its spatial features while performing fusion of it with multispectral image. As a result, we obtained combine high spatial information from the multispectral image and high spectral information through the hyperspectral image using the fusion approaches. The CNSS method has provided highest results i.e. 97.65% with 0.97 kappa statistics. The outcome of the present study will be beneficial for better land management and decision making.

Acknowledgements. The authors would like to thanks to the United States Geological Survey (USGS) for providing EO-1 Hyperion Data for this study.

References

1. Zoleikani, R., Zoej, M.V., Mokhtarzadeh, M.: Comparison of pixel and object oriented based classification of hyperspectral pansharpened images. J. Indian Soc. Remote Sens. **45**(1), 25–33 (2017)
2. Debes, C., et al.: Hyperspectral and LiDAR data fusion: outcome of the 2013 GRSS data fusion contest. IEEE J. Sel. Top. Appl. Earth Obs. Remote Sens. **7**(6), 2405–2418 (2014)
3. Rajput, U.K., Ghosh, S.K., Kumar, A.: Comparison of fusion techniques for very high resolution data for extraction of urban land-cover. J. Indian Soc. Remote Sens. **45**(4), 709–724 (2017)
4. Benediktsson, J.A., Palmason, J.A., Sveinsson, J.R.: Classification of hyperspectral data from urban areas based on extended morphological profiles. IEEE Trans. Geosci. Remote Sens. **43**(3), 480–491 (2005)
5. Benediktsson, J.A., Pesaresi, M., Amason, K.: Classification and feature extraction for remote sensing images from urban areas based on morphological transformations. IEEE Trans. Geosci. Remote Sens. **41**(9), 1940–1949 (2003)
6. Dalponte, M., Bruzzone, L., Gianelle, D.: Fusion of hyperspectral and LIDAR remote sensing data for classification of complex forest areas. IEEE Trans. Geosci. Remote Sens. **46**(5), 1416–1427 (2008)
7. Fauvel, M., Benediktsson, J.A., Chanussot, J., Sveinsson, J.R.: Spectral and spatial classification of hyperspectral data using SVMs and morphological profiles. IEEE Trans. Geosci. Remote Sens. **46**(11), 3804–3814 (2008)
8. Benediktsson, J. A., Palmason, J. A., Sveinsson, J. R., Chanussot, J.: Decision level fusion in classification of hyperspectral data from urban areas. In: 2004 Proceedings of the IEEE International Geoscience and Remote Sensing Symposium, IGARSS 2004, vol. 1. IEEE, September 2004
9. Swatantran, A., Dubayah, R., Roberts, D., Hofton, M., Blair, J.B.: Mapping biomass and stress in the Sierra Nevada using LiDAR and hyperspectral data fusion. Remote Sens. Environ. **115**(11), 2917–2930 (2011)
10. Abbasi, B., Arefi, H., Bigdeli, B., Motagh, M., Roessner, S.: Fusion of hyperspectral and LiDAR data based on dimension reduction and maximum likelihood. Int. Arch. Photogram. Remote Sens. Spat. Inf. Sci. **40**(7), 569 (2015)
11. Man, Q., Dong, P., Guo, H.: Pixel-and feature-level fusion of hyperspectral and LiDAR data for urban land-use classification. Int. J. Remote Sens. **36**(6), 1618–1644 (2015)
12. Kumar, U., Milesi, C., Nemani, R.R., Basu, S.: Multi-sensor multi-resolution image fusion for improved vegetation and urban area classification. Int. Arch. Photogram. Remote Sens. Spat. Inf. Sci. **40**(7), 51 (2015)

13. Vibhute, A.D., Kale, K.V., Dhumal, R.K., Mehrotra, S.C.: Hyperspectral imaging data atmospheric correction challenges and solutions using QUAC and FLAASH algorithms. In: 2015 Proceedings of the International Conference on Man and Machine Interfacing (MAMI), pp. 1–6. IEEE, December 2015

14. Tsagaris, V., Anastassopoulos, V.: Multispectral image fusion for improved RGB representation based on perceptual attributes. Int. J. Remote Sens. **26**(15), 3241–3254 (2005)

15. Ashraf, S., Brabyn, L., Hicks, B.J.: Image data fusion for the remote sensing of freshwater environments. Appl. Geogr. **32**(2), 619–628 (2012)

16. Basaeed, E., Bhaskar, H., Al-Mualla, M.: Comparative analysis of pan-sharpening techniques on DubaiSat-1 images. In: 2013 Proceedings of the 16th International Conference on Information Fusion (FUSION), pp. 227–234. IEEE, July 2013

17. https://www.harrisgeospatial.com/docs/gramschmidtspectralsharpening.html

18. https://www.harrisgeospatial.com/docs/pcspectralsharpening.html

19. https://www.harrisgeospatial.com/docs/cnspectralsharpening.html

20. Ehlers, M., Klonus, S., Johan Åstrand, P., Rosso, P.: Multi-sensor image fusion for pansharpening in remote sensing. Int. J. Image Data Fusion **1**(1), 25–45 (2010)

21. Hsu, S.M., Burke, H.H.: Multisensor fusion with hyperspectral imaging data: detection and classification. In: Handbook of Pattern Recognition and Computer Vision, pp. 347–364 (2005)

22. Vibhute, A.D., Kale, K.V., Mehrotra, S.C., Dhumal, R.K., Nagne, A.D.: Determination of soil physicochemical attributes in farming sites through visible, near-infrared diffuse reflectance spectroscopy and PLSR modeling. Ecol. Process. **7**(1), 26 (2018)

23. Vibhute, A.D., Dhumal, R.K., Nagne, A.D., Rajendra, Y.D., Kale, K.V., Mehrotra, S.C.: Analysis, classification, and estimation of pattern for land of Aurangabad region using high-resolution satellite image. In: Satapathy, S.C., Raju, K.S., Mandal, J.K., Bhateja, V. (eds.) Proceedings of the Second International Conference on Computer and Communication Technologies. AISC, vol. 380, pp. 413–427. Springer, New Delhi (2016). https://doi.org/10.1007/978-81-322-2523-2_40

24. http://earthexplorer.usgs.gov/

25. Beck, R.: EO-1 user guide, version 2.3. Satellite Systems Branch, USGS Earth Resources Observation Systems Data Center (EDC) (2003)

26. Vapnik, V.N.: An overview of statistical learning theory. IEEE Trans. Neural Netw. **10**(5), 988–999 (1999)

27. Heras, D.B., Argüello, F., Quesada-Barriuso, P.: Exploring ELM-based spatial-spectral classification of hyperspectral images. Int. J. Remote Sens. **35**(2), 401–423 (2014)

28. Richards, J.A., Jia, X.: Remote Sensing Digital Image Analysis, vol. 3. Springer, Heidelberg (2006)

29. Zhang, C., Wang, T., Atkinson, P.M., Pan, X., Li, H.: A novel multi-parameter support vector machine for image classification. Int. J. Remote Sens. **36**(7), 1890–1906 (2015)

30. Widjaja, E., Zheng, W., Huang, Z.: Classification of colonic tissues using near-infrared Raman spectroscopy and support vector machines. Int. J. Oncology **32**(3), 653–662 (2008)

31. Gao, J.: Digital Analysis of Remotely Sensed Imagery. McGraw-Hill Professional (2008)

Bird Species Detection and Classification Based on HOG Feature Using Convolutional Neural Network

Susanto Kumar Ghosh$^{(\boxtimes)}$ and Md. Rafiqul Islam

Computer Science and Engineering Discipline, Khulna University,
Khulna 9208, Bangladesh
susanto_bag@yahoo.com, dmri1978@gmail.com

Abstract. Bird detection and classification for real time image are complex tasks but crucial improvement can be performed by the best computer vision algorithms to solve such kinds of problems. Some challenges like lighting conditions of the images, similarities in subspecies of birds may be raised. During the last few years, CNN appeared as the state of the art with regard to the accuracy for a number of computer vision work such as image classification, object detection, and segmentation. To identify the object like bird CNN has been used in this work. Here, we have designed bird detection and classification system based on Gaussian and Gabor filters, HOG as well as Convolutional Neural Networks. HOG is one of the accepted features for object detection and it can be extracted from all portions of the image. So, Histogram of Oriented Gradients (HOG) is used to implement the CNN. We have done experiment with the standard datasets and have found better results than other methods by applying above procedures.

Keywords: Bird detection · Bird classification · Gabor filter ·
HOG feature · CNN

1 Introduction

In recent years, deep neural network has made a exceptional progress in detecting and recognizing images [1]. But this is mostly used for recognition of faces, though demand for recognition of different types of objects has been expanded. To cope up with this issue and for solving some ecological problems, detecting birds and recognizing crows and hawks is our main concern.

To resolve bird classification problem, models of fine-grained recognition have shown a tremendous success in recent years [2,3]. As for detecting birds the main challenge is determining different gesture of the birds. It is a tough task to differ birds from other flying objects and it is the main problem for eradicating accidents in the sky. For solving these types of dilemma fine-grained model is a great prevention. Besides this prevention, now-a-days image based detection

© Springer Nature Singapore Pte Ltd. 2019
K. C. Santosh and R. S. Hegadi (Eds.): RTIP2R 2018, CCIS 1035, pp. 363–373, 2019.
https://doi.org/10.1007/978-981-13-9181-1_32

manipulate camera is one of the auspicious procedure [4–7]. Large visual information can be found and higher resolution can be utilized in this system. Thus in last few decades the recognition performance has been incremented, added with availability of big data, increasing performance of computers and quiet new and developed machine learning algorithms which include deep learning algorithm, such as deep neural network, CNN, RNN etc. Besides, features like shape, size, color, HOG, Haar-like, discriminative, texture-based are used to get better results [3, 8–10]. These deep learning algorithms show improving results in different types of competitions for detecting and recognizing objects (Fig. 1).

Fig. 1. The images of birds capture a wind farm (above) [8] are extently separate from the collective image identification datasets (under) [3]

However, though the improvements of accuracy in detection and recognition of objects using deep neural network is unavoidable, in practical terms for detecting wild birds it is not so predictable. Where the only omission is some new works relating to detect wild birds and recognize them which include the work of Akito et al., Fagerlund et al., Branson et al., Aditya et al. and Kidane et al. [11–15]. Where Akito et al. designed a model to solve the difficulty of bird identification in case of enlarged scene images for utilization in the industry of wind energy [11]. On the other hand, the target of Fagerlund and Seppo was to develop an automated method for bird species identification from their sounds produced in field situation [12]. According to Branson, Steve et al., they proposed a model in order to build an architecture for ocular categorization that approaches expert human performance in case of grouping different bird species [13]. Whereas, Aditya, Ameya and Rohit proposed a complete model which would help amateur bird watchers identify bird species by capturing images [14]. Though, these works had been done earlier the accuracy of detection is not so high and the precision rate is not so stable and it is not so sure for low resolution images of birds.

To get the actual detection rate for low-resolution images of the birds, a wild bird dataset about a wind farm has been used as a standard dataset [1] and a new method has been proposed, in which the images have been filtered through Gaussian and Gabor filters and then HOG features have been found from the images. Finally, Convolutional Neural Network (CNN) has been utilized for greater accuracy in detection and classification. According to our expected method the precision rate of detection is 99.32% which is a quiet good performance in this research area.

All the other paper is well ordered as listed below; Sect. 2 explain the previous works of this research field, Sect. 3 states proposed methodology, Sect. 4 briefs experimental results and Sect. 5 concludes this paper.

2   Related Works

Akito et al. (2016) designed a model to solve the problem of bird identification in case of enlarged landscape images as applications in the industry of wind power [11]. First of all, CNN-based detector was trained and a pixel-based semantic fragmentation method was used. A successor of CNNs was used in order to detect small birds. For larger areas in the images, a fully FCNs and SuperParsing method was used for the benefit of simultaneously detecting birds and recognizing the background. Then, Linear SVMs are applied to integrate all detected results in a single module. The results of the three procedure are merged by applying support vector machines to get the high detection execution. The experimental outputs on a bird image dataset showed significant high precision and effectiveness of the expected methodology [11].

Fagerlund and Seppo (2007) proposed a method to ensure automatic identification of bird species according to the nature of their vocalization [12]. The target was to develop an automated approach for bird species identification from their sounds produced in field situation. At first, they classified the bird sounds into two specific parameters based on signal level. The SVM classification systems were applied to automated identification of bird species. A decision tree classifier method was used along with the SVM. The classifying methods performed classification between two species of birds at each node of the decision tree. Then, the performance of recognition was tried with two different sets of bird species whose identification has been before tested with a range of different methods. Their proposed methodology suggest identical better or equal achievement when compared to other present methods.

Branson, Steve et al. (2014) proposed a model in order to build an architecture for ocular classification that approaches professional human performance in case of grouping different bird species [13]. At the beginning, they found out the local image features from the images of birds. Then, the extracted features are calculated using deep convolutional network to image fragment that are located and normalized by the pose of the object in an image. A graph-based clustering algorithm is give for learning a compressed pose normalization space. The performance improvements of their proposed methodology was because of using CNN features that were modified on CUB 200–2011 dataset for each region and using various CNN layers for various types of adjustment levels. Also they used a similarity-based warping function that was calculated applying more numbers of identified key points from the image. Finally they introduced an approach for learning a set of pose regions that explicitly reduces pixel adjustment error and works for complicated pose warping functions [13].

Aditya, Ameya and Rohit proposed a complete model which would help amateur bird watchers identify bird species by capturing images [14]. The target of the research was to identify the qualitative elaboration of various bird species applying machine learning systems. Mainly three key features were used to solve this problem. They used the color, pattern and shape features of a particular part of the images. Two different machine learning algorithms were used for detecting birds in the images; the KNN and Naive Bayes classifier techniques. Various feature selection and feature reducing approaches were applied to see the improvement of the accuracy. At first, different changing beans for SVM Linear and Radial Basis operation were used. Next, feature reduction methods like PCA and then SVM, Logistic Regression and LDA were applied on the reduced features from before. Then L1 based method was used to eliminate features with low variance, univariate tree based feature selection. PCA was used for feature reduction trailed by feature selection for obtaining a new feature data. On this data, we applied LDA, Logistic Regression and SVM. This methodology boosted the precision of their proposed work [14].

A detector which is based on feature for birds was proposed by Kidane Mihreteab and Masahiro Iwahashi in 2012. This approach train to use feature extraction for crow birds detection. Here discriminative descriptor feature is applied which is produced by combining HOG and Center-Symmetric Local Binary Pattern (CS-LBP). In the case of machine learning algorithm Support Vector Machine (SVM) is implemented here. In this method HOG CS-LBP feature combination is compare with HOG-LBP based feature combination and finally HOG CS-LBP based combination outperforms HOG-LBP based combination [15].

An approach was proposed by Ryota Yoshihashi, Rei Kawakami in 2017 for bird detection applying time-lapse images about a wind firm. Mainly in this method they make a comparison between two approaches, firstly combination of a learning algorithm like AdaBoost and a feature extracting algorithm like Haar-like or HOG and the other approach is convolutional neural networks (CNN). Finally they compared the detection rate and classification rate between above two approaches [8].

3 Methodology

3.1 Training Phase

In the proposed work, some positive and negative samples have been taken for the training phase where positive samples contain bird and negative samples do not contain bird. The samples pass through the pre-processing and the feature extraction processes to form training set and validation set where the training set is utilized for training the classifier and validation set is utilized for checking the classifier accuracy. The validation set is improving the classifier by checking accuracy. Then the training set and validation set are fed into the classifier.

Pre-processing.

- The images are resized to 28×28 to send it for further processing.
- Gaussian filter is used to get clear image by removing noise for fine-grained bird detection. So we have used the Gaussian filter to preserve every useful detail in the image by reducing noise [16]. The equation of Gaussian filter is given in Eq. 1.

$$G(x, y) = \frac{1}{2\pi\sigma^2} exp^{\frac{-(x^2+y^2)}{2\sigma^2}}$$

(1)

Here, x and y are strengths of the input image, σ denotes standard deviation of the Gaussian distribution.

Feature Extraction. Feature extraction defines the relevant shape information contained in a pattern so that the task of classifying the pattern is created easy by a formal technique. Features are the machine understandable codes that illustrate the characteristics of different objects present in an image which may or may not be understandable to human every time. Before getting features, various image pre-processing methods are utilized to the sample image. After that, feature extraction techniques are applied to get features of the sample image. The whole feature extraction procedure is shown in Fig. 2.

- The pre-processed colour image is converted into grayscale image to apply the Gabor filter. The image is sent for HOG feature extraction after applying Gabor filter.
- HOG feature is assessed constructed on local histograms of image and can be extracted from all portions of the image. HOG feature extraction method, the image is separate into small connected are as called cells. within each cell a histogram of gradient instruction is composed for the pixels. HOG detects the direction when it enters from high intensity to low intensity. First, a filter of 16×16 cells is used to compute the gradient of the input image of size 28×28. The filter describes a patch of an image to provide a compact representation. The gradient of this patch contains two values such as magnitude and direction. Gradients of an image are responsive to overall lighting. We have made the image darker by splitting all pixel values by 2 to make our descriptor to be autonomous of lighting variations. In other words, we would like to regulate the histogram in such a way that they are not affected by lighting variations. Now the 16×16 cells slide through the whole image and finally return the HOG extracted image.

Fig. 2. The feature extraction process

Classifier. In the proposed methodology, the Convolutional Neural Network (CNN) has been utilized in this work. CNN showed good performance in several assignments including digit recognition, image classification, object detection and face recognition, indic handwritten script identification [17–22]. [] The main advantage of CNN is high accuracy in image recognition and detection. CNN automatically learns a complex model for extract visual features from the pixel-level content, as well as exploiting a sequence of simple process such as filtering, local contrast normalization, non-linear activation, local pooling. Convolutional Neural Networks depend on large training datasets and a training technique based on back propagation. In our convolutional neural network architecture, we have used three convolutional layers and three hidden layers. In this architecture, the input size of 28×28 is passed through the convolutional layer that has 32 filters with 3×3 filter size. We have used Rectified Linear Unit (ReLU) activation function that is the positive part of its argument. That means if any negative value wants to pass through layer it can't. It only passes the positive value or zero. The function of ReLU is given below:

$$f(x) = max(0, x) \tag{2}$$

Then it has been to another two convolutional layer that has 64 and 128 filters with 3×3 filter size. The feature map is converted into a flattened array after finishing the convolutional layer. Then it is sent to the hidden layer that is fully connected with each other. In all three hidden layers, we use 128 neurons with activation function ReLU. The output layer with a sigmoid function that is also fully connected with the previously hidden layer. The reason behind the use of sigmoid function in the output layer is that it exists with the value between 0 and 1. As the proposed model is a binary classifier and the output will be 0 or 1 like a predictive model so we use the sigmoid function here. The sigmoid function is given below:

$$S(x) = \frac{1}{1 + e^{-x}} \tag{3}$$

If the value of the output layer is 0 then it can be decided that there is no bird in the image. On the other hand, if the value of the output layer is 1 then there is one or more birds in the image. The propose model is depicted in Fig. 3.

Testing Phase. Some positive and negative samples were taken for testing phase. The pre-processing and the feature extraction method are the same as

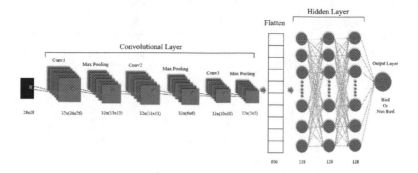

Fig. 3. Model of CNN

the training phase. Then the extracted features were sent to the classifier to predict the result. If the predicted result is 0 then there is no bird in the image. If the predicted result is 1 then the image contains at least one bird. The whole procedure of the system architecture is shown in Fig. 4.

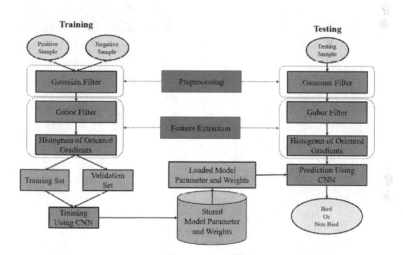

Fig. 4. System architecture

4   Experimental Result

This section demonstrates the performance of the proposed method for bird detection and classification based on HOG features using the dataset used in [8]. We utilized 6000 positive and 20000 negative samples to test the proposed

370 S. K. Ghosh and Md. R. Islam

method. Figure 5 shows some sample images of the dataset with birds and non birds. According to our proposed method, the accuracy rates of detection is 99.32% and classification is 89.2% respectively, which indicates quiet good results in this research area. The accuracy is considered by the following equation.

$$Accuracy = \frac{TP + TN}{TP + FN + FP + TN} \tag{4}$$

where, TP = True Positive, TN = True Negative, FN = False Negative and FP = False Positive.

From the Table 1, we can clearly perceive that, our proposed method have given 0.12% better results than beside methods in the case of bird detection and 2.2% better results in the case of bird classification [8]. So our proposed method has given better results than other methods in both detection and classification (Figs. 6 and 7).

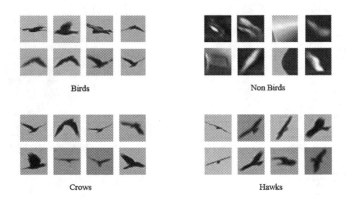

Fig. 5. Sample images of the dataset [8]

Table 1. Experimental results of accuracies

Method	Bird detection	Bird classification
Proposed method	99.32%	89.2%
RGB	99.2%	-
LeNet	99.1%	83%
ResNet	-	87%

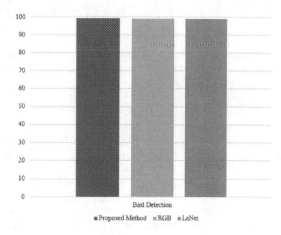

Fig. 6. Performance compare of proposed method with other methods in case of bird detection

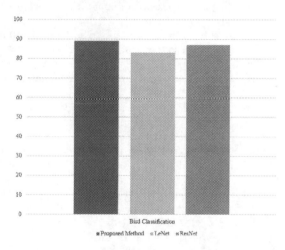

Fig. 7. Performance compare using of proposed method with other methods in case of bird classification

5   Conclusion

To solve issues on ecological problems and detect low contrast bird images the proposed procedure gives a state-of-the-art solution and utilizing this procedure, we classify hawks and crows conveniently. In computer vision, using benchmark dataset from real world, the high performance results have been provided by implementing the proposed method and we revealed the effectiveness of CNN in this particular research area. However, propose system can easily detect any bird from any region from real world, but in bird classification, this model can be refurbished and further inflation can possible in obtaining greater recognition rate.

References

1. Yoshihashi, R., Kawakami, R., Iida, M., Naemura, T.: Evaluation of bird detection using time-lapse images around a wind farm. In: European Wind Energy Association Conference (2015)
2. Krause, J., Jin, H., Yang, J., Fei-Fei, L.: Fine-grained recognition without part annotations. In: Proceedings of the IEEE Conference on Computer Vision and Pattern Recognition, pp. 5546–5555 (2015)
3. Pang, C., Yao, H., Sun, X.: Discriminative features for bird species classification. In: Proceedings of International Conference on Internet Multimedia Computing and Service, p. 256. ACM (2014)
4. Clough, S.C., McGovern, S., Campbell, D., Rehfisch, M.M.: Aerial survey techniques for assessing offshore wind farms. In: International Council for the Exploration of the Sea, Conference and Meeting (CM) Documents (2012)
5. Rioperez, A., de la Puente, M.: DTBird: a self-working system to reduce bird mortality in wind farms. In: European Wind Energy Association Conference (2010)
6. May, R., Hamre, Ø., Vang, R., Nygård, T.: Evaluation of the DTBird video-system at the smøla wind-power plant. Detection capabilities for capturing near-turbine avian behaviour. NINA Report 910 (2012)
7. Clough, S., Banks, A.: A 21st century approach to aerial bird and mammal surveys at offshore wind farm sites. In: EWEA Conference (2011)
8. Yoshihashi, R., Kawakami, R., Iida, M., Naemura, T.: Bird detection and species classification with time-lapse images around a wind farm: dataset construction and evaluation. Wind Energy 20(12), 1983–1995 (2017)
9. Santosh, K., Wendling, L., Antani, S., Thoma, G.R.: Overlaid arrow detection for labeling regions of interest in biomedical images. IEEE Intell. Syst. 31(3), 66–75 (2016)
10. Santosh, K., Antani, S.: Automated chest X-ray screening: can lung region symmetry help detect pulmonary abnormalities? IEEE Trans. Med. Imaging 37(5), 1168–1177 (2018)
11. Takeki, A., Trinh, T.T., Yoshihashi, R., Kawakami, R., Iida, M., Naemura, T.: Detection of small birds in large images by combining a deep detector with semantic segmentation. In: ICIP, pp. 3977–3981 (2016)
12. Fagerlund, S.: Bird species recognition using support vector machines. EURASIP J. Appl. Signal Process. 2007(1), 64–64 (2007)
13. Branson, S., Van Horn, G., Belongie, S., Perona, P.: Bird species categorization using pose normalized deep convolutional nets. arXiv preprint arXiv:1406.2952 (2014)
14. Bhandari, A., Joshi, A., Patki, R.: Bird species identification from an image (2014). http://cs229.stanford.edu/proj2014/Aditya%20Bhandari,%20Ameya%20Joshi,% 20Rohit%20Patki,%20Bird%20Species%20Identification%20from%20an%20Image. pdf
15. Mihreteab, K., Iwahashi, M., Yamamoto, M.: Crow birds detection using HOG and CS-LBP. In: 2012 Proceedings of the International Symposium on Intelligent Signal Processing and Communications Systems (ISPACS), pp. 406–409. IEEE (2012)
16. Deng, G., Cahill, L.: An adaptive Gaussian filter for noise reduction and edge detection. In: 1993 IEEE Conference Record Nuclear Science Symposium and Medical Imaging Conference 1993, pp. 1615–1619. IEEE (1993)
17. Cireşan, D.C., Meier, U., Gambardella, L.M., Schmidhuber, J.: Deep, big, simple neural nets for handwritten digit recognition. Neural Comput. 22(12), 3207–3220 (2010)

18. Krizhevsky, A., Sutskever, I., Hinton, G.E.: ImageNet classification with deep convolutional neural networks. In: Advances in neural information processing systems, pp. 1097–1105 (2012)
19. Szegedy, C., Toshev, A., Erhan, D.: Deep neural networks for object detection. In: Advances in Neural Information Processing Systems, pp. 2553–2561 (2013)
20. Lawrence, S., Giles, C.L., Tsoi, A.C.: Convolutional neural networks for face recognition. In: 1996 Proceedings of the IEEE Computer Society Conference on Computer Vision and Pattern Recognition 1996, CVPR 1996, pp. 217–222. IEEE (1996)
21. Sawat, D.D., Hegadi, R.S.: Unconstrained face detection: a deep learning and machine learning combined approach. CSI Trans. ICT 5(2), 195–199 (2017)
22. Ukil, S., Ghosh, S., Obaidullah, S.M., Santosh, K., Roy, K., Das, N.: Deep learning for word-level handwritten indic script identification. arXiv preprint arXiv:1801.01627 (2018)

Automated Flower Region Segmentation from Color Images

Monali Y. Khachane[✉]

Yashwantrao Chavan School of Rural Development, Shivaji University,
Kolhapur, India
monalikhachane@gmail.com

Abstract. Segmentation of flower region is one of the important parts in flower image retrieval. Flower segmentation is the challenging task because of variety in colors and different light conditions. In this paper fully automated flower segmentation method using HSV and texture features is proposed. The texture features namely contrast, correlation, Energy and Homogeneity computed from Hue and Value image. Further these features are used to decide the value for global threshold for converting the image into binary image. The proposed method is tested on flower image dataset contain 102 flower classes and also tested on Oxford-102. The experimental results shows that proposed method is effectively segment the flower regions from images.

Keywords: GLCM (Gray Level Co-occurrence Matrix) ·
HSV (Hue, Saturation and Value) · Texture features · Morphology

1 Introduction

Flower image segmentation is the challenging task because of the variety of flowers and variety in colors within a class of flowers. Also the different light conditions and different poses make the segmentation task more difficult. Due to this Intra class and Interclass variety of flowers discrimination between some classes is difficult. Though they have different color and petal structure. Many time similarities with background is also make this task difficult. Segmentation of flowers from photographs is one of the important steps for classification of flowers into its class. In this paper the attempt is made to automatically segment the flower regions from digital images. Section 2 describes the techniques proposed by the earlier researchers for segmentation and classification of flowers. Section 3 explores the proposed methodology and material used for current work. In Sect. 4, results obtained from experimental work are discussed. Conclusion presented in Sect. 5.

2 Literature Review

Segmentation plays important role in almost all image processing and computer vision-based application like object detection, recognition, visualization and simulation development. Various segmentation methods are enlisted in this session.

© Springer Nature Singapore Pte Ltd. 2019
K. C. Santosh and R. S. Hegadi (Eds.): RTIP2R 2018, CCIS 1035, pp. 374–382, 2019.
https://doi.org/10.1007/978-981-13-9181-1_33

A fuzzy rule based system was presented in [1] for plant identification using shape, texture features and amplitude of Zernike moments. Young, dry and cut leaves of Hibiscus, Tickseed, Rose, Mango, Asoka plants were taken as sample. Increase in plant categories increases the complexity of this system. In Dataset images back-ground is same and avoided the images with bright sunlight and shadows. Sharm et al. [2] used four layer Feed forward Neural Network for plant species recognition with rate 91.13%. Dataset contained 440 leaves of different 16 classes. Morphological features like major axis, minor axis length, area, convex area, eccentricity, perimeter, solidity orientation, extent, Euler number and equidimeter used. Kaur [3] reviewed the literature related to leaf classification and noted that there is no any comparative work done on leaf classification techniques. Marwa et al. [4] developed a software to retrieve the flower images by matching the shape of queried flower image. Hu moments used to compare shape of queried image. Guru et al. [5] analyzed dataset of 1250 images from 25 different classes using texture features, Gober responses and KNN classifier. Sundar et al. [6] proposed a technique to count the flowers in yield. RGB images converted into Lab color space. k-means clustering segmented image into 3 clusters from which cluster 1 further threshold to obtain flower regions. Circular Hue transform used to count flowers. Prim's Minimum spanning tree and k-means clustering is used by [7] also. A feature matrix formulated by combining texture and color features. Texture features extracted using Log Gabor filter and color features extracted by calculating mean and standard deviation of R, G and B color channels. Prims Minimum spanning tree algorithm outperform k-means clustering still the accuracy rate is 72% and need to improve. Whorl based image segmentation applied on flower images to obtain skeleton of flower. Length and angle features extracted from Delaunay triangulation. Experiment conducted on 3000 images of 30 flower classes. 94%accuracy achieved for 80% training data [8]. Tiay et al. [9] presented a method for flower recognition system using Hu's seven moment algorithm for edge features and kNN classifier produces 80% accuracy. 100 images of 10 flower species tested. Sima et al. [10] proposed maximum entropy based new clustering segmentation approach for color image segmentation. The entropy maximum estimation used to determine numbers of clusters in K-means. Gurua et al. [11] used a probabilistic neural network classifier for flower classification. Color texture moments, gray-level co-occurrence matrix and gabor responses used as features. Dataset contained 35 flower class images with different light and climatic conditions. Experimental work shown that proposed approach produced higher accuracy for less number of flower classes. Sharath Kumara et al. [12] presented a model for representation and indexing of flower images for retrieval of flower images based on sketch of flower. Shape descriptors Scale Invariant Feature Transform (SIFT), Histogram of Gradients (HOG) and Edge Orientation Histograms used. Dataset contained 127 classes of flowers, consists of 13169 flower images. 100 flower sketches collected by 20 different users. Nisar et al. [13] proposed digital image processing techniques for automation of agricultural products and prediction of yield using color, size and shape features. The average percentage error in yield prediction for Dragon fruit is 1.40% and Daisy flower is 5.52%. Sharath Kumar et al. [14] proposed skeleton based flower classification approach. Distance features extracted from skeleton endpoints and junction points. Discrete Cosine Transform used for feature normalization. Dataset contained 3000 samples of 30 flower classes. Shaparia et al. [15] presented technique to classify flower images using color moment features and GLCM texture features with neural network classifier. 95% classification accuracy produced by system. An approach to segment flower images from color photographs was proposed by [16]. Image color distribution and flower shape model used. The designed model could be used for segmentation of leaves and stalk but not suitable for field of flowers. Mukane et al. [17] extracted Gray level co-occurrence matrix (GLCM) and discrete wavelet transform (DWT) features from flower images and classified them using Artificial Neural Network (ANN). Dataset contained 50 images of 5 flower classes. 85% accuracy achieved by ANN using GLCM only. Basavaprasad et al. [18] proposed a method to enhance and segment general images using fuzzy rule and graph cut method. Fuzzy rule based system used for image enhancement. Fuzzy rule and graph cut combined to segment the image. Weighted average used to frame normalized graph cut. Proposed technique tested on Berkeley Segmentation database and evaluated by using index rand probabilistic, global consistency error, sensitivity, Dice similarity coefficient and positive predictive value. Adaptive GrowCut method segment general image into first level and then color image segmentation performed on the image using k-means clustering. User interference required for tough image segmentation [19]. Contour-Based Segmentation was proposed to detect Glomerulosclerosis in Diabetic Nephropathy by modifying the values of parameters of Chan-Vese algorithm. 86% rate of recognition produced by the technique [20]. Hegadi et al. [21] obtained Bilateral Vector Flow to enhance the edge information and to suppress noisy gradients of medical images. Fuzzy binarization applied on the medical images to detect overlaid arrows. Connected components taken from Key points of arrowheads from every level of binarization. Geometrical Convex properties symmetry and overlap of arrow were used. Comparatively Template-free method produced better results [22]. Iris data extracted by separating iris region from pupil and sclera using roipoly and inverse roipoly. Reduced pixel block algorithm used to match extracted features with database. CASIA-IrisV3-Interval dataset used for experimentation [23]. Sequential classifier was pro-posed by comprising of bidirectional long short-term memory (BLSTM) classifier followed by convexity defect to detect arrowhead. Fuzzy binarization used for segmentation [24].

3   Methodology and Material

3.1   Dataset

For experiment the OXFORD-102 class flower image dataset is used. This dataset contains flower images of 102 categories (8,189 images with variety in colors and poses). Minimum 40 images of each category. For the same dataset flower segmented image dataset is also available which are obtained by graph cut method and iterative segmentation method [25]. These segmentation results are used to evaluate proposed approach.

3.2 Proposed Methodology

HSV (Hue, Saturation and Value) Color space Model- Alvy Ray Simth introduced HSV model in 1978. HSV stands for Hue, Saturation and Value. Hue is expressed as a number from 0 to 360 degrees. Hues of red (which start at 0), yellow (starting at 60), green (starting at 120), cyan (starting at 180), blue (starting at 240) and magenta (starting at 300). Saturation is the amount of gray from zero percent to 100% in the color.

GLCM (gray level co-occurrence matrix)- GLCM is obtained by calculating how often a pixel with gray level (intensity) I occurs horizontally adjacent to a pixel with the value j. From GLCM texture measures are calculated by using following formulae.

Contrast: Returns a measure of the intensity contrast between a pixel and its neighbor over the whole image.

$$\sum_{i,j} |i-j|^2 p(i,j) \tag{1}$$

Correlation: Returns a measure of how correlated a pixel is to its neighbor over the whole image.

$$\sum_{i,j} \frac{(i-\mu i)(j-\mu j)p(i,j)}{\sigma i \sigma j} \tag{2}$$

Energy: Returns the sum of squared elements in the GLCM.

$$\sum_{i,j} p(i,j)^2 \tag{3}$$

Homogeneity: Returns a value that measures the closeness of the distribution of elements in the GLCM to GLCM diagonal.

$$\sum_{i,j} \frac{p(i,j)}{1+|i-j|} \tag{4}$$

Morphological Operations. "Mathematical morphology is a tool for extracting image component and description of region shape. Dilation grows the objects in binary image and Erosion shrinks objects in binary image. Where the thickening and shrinking is controlled by a structuring element of different shapes like disk, line, diamond, square etc." [26] Mathematical notation of dilation of image I by structuring element s is as follows

$$I \oplus S = \{z|(S)_z \cap I \neq \emptyset\} \tag{5}$$

The mathematical notation of erosion of image I by structuring element s is as follows

$$I \ominus S = \{z|(S)_z \cap I^c \neq \emptyset\} \tag{6}$$

For the proposed approach disk type structuring element of size 10 is used for erosion and dilation purpose.

Proposed Algorithm

Step 1: Convert RGB color space image into HSV Colorspace.
Step 2: Separate the H(Hue) channel and V(Value) Channel.
Step 3: Extract the Contrast, Correlation, Energy and Homogeneity of the H and V Image separately as Hstat and Vstat.
Step 4: Calculate the mean of Hstat and Vstat as Hmean and Vmean respectively.
Step 5: Determine the Thresholding Image (H or V) from above extracted features.
Step 6: Convert image into Black and White (B/W) Image.
Step 7: Apply morphological Dilation operation.
Step 8: Apply morphological Erosion operation.
Step 9: Remove noise from the image (by removing smaller objects from the Image).
Step 10: Extract Flower region from color image using resultant B/W image (Fig. 1).

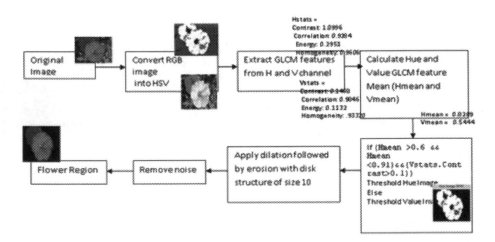

Fig. 1. Proposed methodology for automated flower image segmentation (Color figure online)

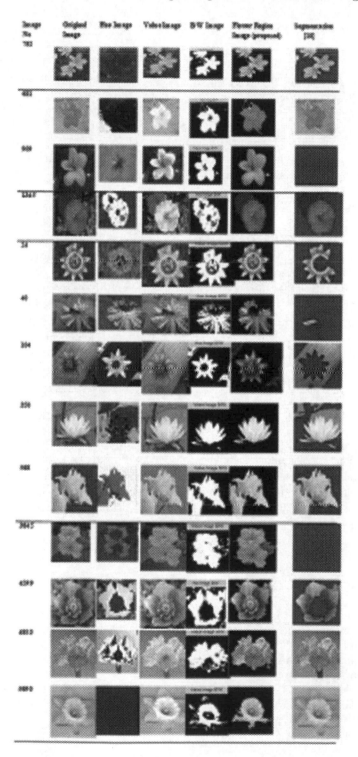

Fig. 2. Results obtained by applying proposed approach (Color figure online)

4   Results and Discussions

The HSV colorspace and Texture features of the Hue and Value channel are used for flower image segmentation. The proposed method produced promissing results for flower segmentation in different color, light conditions and poses.The segmentation results for flower images in the dataset are presented in Fig. 2. In previous work researchers used petal detection or sketch based flower segmentation approaches which are relatively complex methods. The proposed approach used simple method. The Hue or Value image selection for thresholding is needed for proper segmentation. The proposed approach is compared with the segmentation results noted in [25]. Few of the cases discussed in this section. Image 792 belongs to class frangipani is correctly segmented by proposed approach. Image 681 belongs to class corn poppy and Image 568 belong to magnolia are properly segmented by the proposed method while the method proposed by [25] unsuccessful to segment the image and resultant image is the original image.

Image 909 belongs to frangipani and Image 3645 belongs to tree poppy are not segmented by [25] while proposed approach successfully segmented the images. For Image 1345 belongs to morning glory and Image 4599 belongs to the Lenten rose the approach proposed by [25] only petals segmented while proposed approach segmented complete flower images. Complete background is segmented in Image 350 of class Lotus, Image 104 and 4855 of class hippeastrum by the proposed approach which are comparable better then segmentations in [25].

5   Conclusion

In this paper we attempt to propose a novel and simple approach for flower image segmentation. Flower image segmentation is the difficult task because of variety in flowers shape and color similarities, different light conditions and poses. The image is selected for thresholding from The Hue or Value image by using texture features. For improving the flower image classification rate the correct segmentation is necessary. The proposed segmentation method is providing promising results. Future work will be carried out for flower classification.

References

1. Rajpurohit, V.S., Bhat, S., Devurkar, S., Patil, S., Sirbi, S.: Application of image processing techniques in object shape recognition. J. Latest Trends Eng. Technol. (IJLTET) 18–25 (2013)
2. Sharma, S., Gupta, C.: Recognition of plant species based on leaf images using multilayer feed forward neural network. Int. J. Innovative Res. Adv. Eng. (IJIRAE) 6(2), 104–110 (2015)
3. Kaur, G., Monga, H.: Classification of biological species based on leaf archi-tecture- a review. IRACST - Int. J. Comput. Sci. Inf. Technol. Secur. (IJCSITS) 2(2), 332–334 (2012)

4. Marwa, G.K., Din, S.: Development of software for flower recognition using image processing technique. Int. J. Innovative Res. Comput. Commun. Eng. **3**(5), 4804–4811 (2015)
5. Guru, D.S., Sharath, Y.H., Manjunath, S.: Texture features and KNN in classification of flower images. IJCA Spec. Issue Recent Trends Image Process. Pattern Recogn. RTIPPR **1**, 21–29 (2010)
6. Sundar, V.S., Bagyamani, J.: Flower counting in yield approximation using digital image processing techniques. Int. J. Adv. Res. Sci. Eng. **4**(3), 97–106 (2015)
7. Ashwini, R., Roopa, K.: Classification of flower images using clustering algorithms. IJCTA **8**(3), 1025–1032 (2015)
8. Sharath Kumar, Y.H., Vinay Kumar, N., Guru, D.S.: Delaunay triangulation on skeleton of flowers for classification. Proc. Comput. Sci. **45**, 226–235 (2015)
9. Tiay, T., Benyaphaichit, P., Riyamongkol, P.: A flower recognition system based on image processing. In: 2014 Third ICT International Student Project Conference (ICT-ISPC 2014) (2014)
10. Sima, H., Liu, L.: Clustering color image segmentation based on maximum entropy. In: The 2nd International Conference on Computer Application and System Modeling, Paris, France, pp. 1466–1468, Atlantis Press (2012)
11. Gurua, D.S., Sharath Kumara, Y.H., Manjunath, S.: Textural features in flower classification. Math. Comput. Model. **54**(2), 1030–1036 (2011)
12. Sharath Kumara, Y.H., Gurub, D.S.: Retrieval of flower based on sketches. Proc. Comput. Sci. **46**, 1577–1584 (2015)
13. Nisar, H., Yang, H.Z., Ho, Y.K.: Predicting yield of fruit and flowers using digital image analysis. Indian J. Sci. Technol. **8**(32), 01–06 (2015)
14. Sharath Kumar, Y.H., Guru, D.S.: Classification of flowers: a symbolic approach. In: Proceedings of International Conference on Multimedia Processing, Communication and Information Technology, MPCIT, pp. 229–235 (2013)
15. Shaparia, R.H., Patel, N.M., Shah, Z.H.: Flower classification using texture and color features. Kalpa Publi. Comput. **2**, 113–118 (2017)
16. Nilsback, M.-E., Zisserman, A.: Delving deeper into the whorl of flower segmentation. Image Vis. Comput. 01–14 (2007)
17. Mukane, S.M., Kendule, J.A.: Flower classification using neural network based image processing. IOSR J. Electron. and Commun. Eng. (IOSR-JECE) **7**(3), 80–85 (2013)
18. Basavaprasad, B., Hegadi, R.S.: A fusion technique of image enhancement and segmentation using fuzzy rule and graph cut method. Asian J. Inf. Technol. **16**(2–5), 323–332 (2017)
19. Basavaprasad, B., Hegadi, R.S.: Color image segmentation using adaptive growcut method. Proc. Comput. Sci. **6**(2), 328–335 (2015). International Conference Computing Technologies and Applications(ICACTA-2015)
20. Ravi, M., Hegadi, R.S.: Detection of glomerulosclerosis in diabetic nephropathy using contour - based segmentation. Proc. Comput. Sci. **45**, 244–249 (2015). International Conference Computing Technologies and Applications(ICACTA-2015)
21. Hegadi, R.S., Pediredla, A.K., Seelamantula, C.S.: Bilateral smoothing of gradient vector field and application to image segmentation. In: ICIP 2012, vol. 6, no. 2, pp. 317–320 (2012)
22. Santosh, K.C., Wendling, L., Antani, S., Thoma, G.R.: Overlaid arrow detection for labeling regions of interest in biomedical images. IEEE Intell. Syst. **31**(3), 66–75 (2016)

23. Kulkarni, S.R.B., Hegadi, R.S., Kulkarni, U.P.: ROI based Iris segmentation and block reduction based pixel match for improved biometric applications. In: Unnikrishnan, S., Surve, S., Bhoir, D. (eds.) ICAC3 2013. CCIS, vol. 361, pp. 548–557. Springer, Heidelberg (2013). https://doi.org/10.1007/978-3-642-36321-4_52
24. Santosh, K.C., Roy, P.P.: Arrow detection in biomedical images using sequential classifier. Int. J. Mach. Learn. Cyber. **9**, 993–1006 (2018)
25. Nilsback, M.-E., Zisserman, A.: Automated flower classification over a large number of classes. In: Proceedings of the Indian Conference on Computer Vision, Graphics and Image Processing (2008)
26. Monali, K., Ramteke, R.J.: Morphology based text separation and pathological tissue segmentation from CT images. IJPRET **4**(9), 1713–1719 (2016)

Dimensionality Reduction Technique on SIFT Feature Vector for Content Based Image Retrival

Mukul Kirti Verma, Rajesh Dwivedi$^{(\boxtimes)}$, Ajay Kumar Mallick,
and Ebenezer Jangam

Indian Institute of Technology (ISM), Dhanbad, India
mukulkirtiverma@gmail.com, anubhav.dwivedi8@gmail.com,
mallickajay6@gmail.com, ebenezer.jangam@gmail.com

Abstract. Scale-Invariant Feature Transform (SIFT) descriptors plays very important role for depicting and matching the digital images between various views. There are various practical issues like keypoint localization and image retrieval that uses the SIFT descriptors for matching the image content among different views. The problem associated with these descriptors of an image is that calculation and matching of SIFT features descriptors are very cumbersome and slow process.For removing this problem the proposed method presents a technique that reduces the complexity, size and the time for matching of SIFT descriptors used in robot localization and indoor image retrieval.The proposed method reduces the number of SIFT descriptors and the complexity of every SIFT descriptor for determining an image. Our outcomes demonstrate that there is a negligible loss of exactness in feature retrieval while accomplishing a critical decrease in picture descriptor estimate and coordinating time. Proposed technique diminishes the descriptor size (number of descriptors) and furthermore speed up the searching of an image from extensive dataset. Decreasing the descriptor estimate also reduces the storage space required for storing the image descriptor.

Keywords: Image retrieval · Key points · SIFT descriptors · Reduced SIFT descriptors

1 Introduction and Related Work

Retrieval and Matching of images in view of visual substance is considered to be the major issue in computer vision. Retrieval based image matching issue are conducted in numerous frameworks from an assortment of fields including retrieval of images, keypoint localization etc.

A very basic idea for matching these images is extraction of 'interest point' or 'key point' in different images (that shares a common view) after that matching of these key points of different images [1–3]. The effective extraction of interest

© Springer Nature Singapore Pte Ltd. 2019
K. C. Santosh and R. S. Hegadi (Eds.): RTIP2R 2018, CCIS 1035, pp. 383–394, 2019.
https://doi.org/10.1007/978-981-13-9181-1_34

points is done by addition of invariant features [4]. The invariant features of an image do not change during various image transformations. Prior research on invariant features is mainly concentrated on invariance to turn and interpretation [5,6], but these method got success only with 2D Image matching. After that research extended for growing their invariance to brightening, scale and relative changes and there is also a research topic to make fully invariant features [7,8]. However full invariance has not been accomplished due somewhat unfeasible substantial computational cost.

Matching of two key points is done by matching the descriptors of these key points [8–10]. Descriptors are generated by using gradient magnitude and orientations. If 65% to 70 % descriptors of a key point are matched with the descriptors of another key point then the matching these two key points are successful.

There are various CBIR techniques to match the images that share a common view. The mixture of main features like Texture, color and Structure etc. are used in the most well known CBIR strategies to describe an image. A similarity measures is also included with these descriptors for retrieving the similar images [11]. In more advance systems images are retrieved by applying learned mapping [12] in feature space to make the groups of similar images or by linking statistically linguistic indexes and fetching the image via index association [13].

A very common approach for matching two image by using SIFT descriptors. SIFT descriptors are invariant to rotation, translation, and scale variety amongst pictures and in part invariant to illumination, noise, variance and affine distortion. The SIFT descriptors are used in various applications like keypoint localization [14], Object recognition [15], etc. But a critical disadvantage associated with SIFT descriptors is that it includes high computational cost and more amount of data is generated.

In the proposed method a reduction is performed on sift descriptors is by calculating the resultant vector for all adjacent 16×16 pixels to the key points. The objective of this reduction is to make them more practical and proficient with regards to retrieval of images without a huge decrease in discrimination and accuracy.

2   Extraction of SIFT Descriptors

The SIFT features is a technique for extracting and depicting 'interest points' or 'key points' which are relatively invariant to various image transforms. Subsequently, SIFT includes following four main stages-

1. **Scale Space extrema identification:** In this stage, a searching is performed over scale space by using difference between Gaussian function to recognize the powerful key points.
2. **Localization of key points:** In this stage, location and scale of every key point is determined and the selection of key points is done considering a measurement on stability.

3. **Assignment of orientation:** In this Stage, every key point are assigned with a one or sometime even more orientations based on the gradients of local image.
4. **Generation of Key point descriptor:** In this stage a descriptor is created for every interest point from the information of local image gradient at the scale got in second stage.

A critical part of this technique is that it produces an expensive number of corresponding features over a wide range of locations and scales. The count of features are generated using this algorithm is depends on the size and image content along with the parameters used in the algorithm. A typical image having 500×500 pixels will produce around 2000 interest point and for every interest point there exist 128 descriptors but in the proposed method just 32 descriptors are required for each keypoint.

Fig. 1. Lena image having many keypoints.

The SIFT algorithm depends on discovering locations inside the scale space of a picture that are reliably extracted as shown in Fig. 1. First stage searches for the scale space extrema locations $D(x, y)$ and the Difference of Gaussian function (DoG) , that can be calculated by taking the difference of two very nearby scaled image isolated by using a multiplicative factor k by using Eq. 1:

$$D(x, y, \sigma) = (G(x, y, k\sigma) - G(x, y, \sigma)) * I(x, y)$$
$$= L(x, y, k\sigma) - L(x, y, \sigma) \tag{1}$$

The term $L(x, y, \sigma)$ used in Eq. 1 denotes the scale space of any given image, generated by Convolving the Gaussian kernel $G(x, y, \sigma)$ and the image $I(x, y)$.

The local extrema points in the DoG function in their particular scale, one scale above and one scale below is considered as keypoints. At this stage, the extrema point generation depends on the initial smoothing σ_0 and scale space

k. After that these keypoints are correspondingly filtered out for achieving more stable keypoint matching that can be precisely localized to scale and its sub pixel image area. Prior to descriptor construction for a key point, the keypoint is allocated with an orientation to make the descriptor relatively rotation invariant. Orientation of that keypoint is computed from the orientation histogram of corresponding local gradients from the nearest smoothed picture $L(x, y, \sigma)$. For every sample of image L(x, y), the gradient magnitude $m(x, y)$ and corresponding orientation θ(x, y) is evaluated by taking the pixel differences according to Eqs. 2 and 3.

$$m(x,y) = (((L(x+1,y) - L(x-1,y))^2 \atop +(L(x,y+1) - L(x,y-1))^2)^{0.5} \tag{2}$$

$$\theta(x,y) = tan^{-1}\frac{L(x,y+1) - L(x,y-1)}{L(x+1,y) - L(x-1,y)} \tag{3}$$

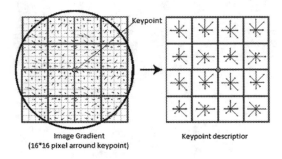

Image Gradient
(16*16 pixel arround keypoint)

Keypoint descriptior

Fig. 2. Generating keypoint descriptors form neighbouring vectors.

For covering the 360° range of orientation the corresponding orientation histogram have 36 bins. Each and every point that is added to histogram is weighted by magnitude of gradient $m(x, y)$ and a circular Gaussian having a sigma variance equal to 1.5 times of the scale of keypoint.

In the literature, keypoint descriptors uses 16 orientation histogram which are aligned in a 4×4 grid. Thus, each histogram have 8 orientation bins which are created over a 4×4 pixels. Finally, the resulting feature vectors are with 128 elements(descriptors) as shown in Fig. 2.

3   Proposed Method for Reducing the SIFT Descriptor Size

The main requirement of CBIR is the fast retrieval, but due to large descriptor size the computation cost increases because as a keypoint is detected the computational cost increases exponentially. The proposed system Architecture is described in Fig. 3.

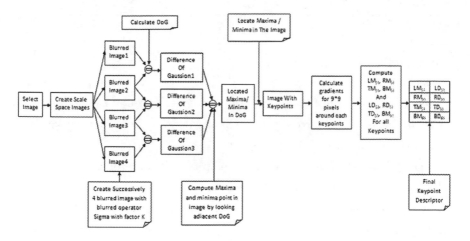

Fig. 3. Proposed method framework.

The high computational cost is the main disadvantage of SIFT features compared to other descriptor. Extraction of SIFT feature generates a huge amount of information which are redundant in most of the cases. In many cases up to 80% of key points are not matched between corresponding images which are perceptually similar so it is essential to reduce the number of key points without much change in the count of matching key points.

The critical part of SIFT is to match the two images which shares a common view by matching their descriptors. On an average, an image of size 512×512 pixels having approximate 2000 keypoints and in SIFT each keypoint is having 128 descriptors so the total number of key descriptors for this image will be $2000 \times 128 = 256000$ that is so huge. If both the images having 2000 key points then the total comparison for descriptors is equal to 256000×256000 which is too high. For searching a particular image in the large database, it is required to compare all the database images with that particular image that is extremely huge and cumbersome process.

In the proposed work only 32 descriptors are created instead of 128 descriptors discussed above. So the matching time for these 32 descriptors is very less in comparison to 128 descriptors. Instead of directly creating bins of descriptors, the vector magnitude and vector directions are calculated by taking the input of neighboring pixels magnitudes and directions. These vector magnitude and vector directions around each keypoint are denoted as descriptors of that key point. The complete algorithm for calculating these 32 descriptors is as follows:

the operation '.' used in Eqs. 5, 6, 7, and 8 is defined in Eq. 4.

$$V_1.V_2 = \sqrt{||V_1||^2 + ||V_2||^2 + 2 * ||V_1|| * ||V_2|| * cos\theta} \tag{4}$$

Algorithm 1. Propsed Algorithm for Total Descriptor Generation.

Input: Image

Output: Total Feature Descriptor

1: Select the input image.

2: Create scale space of the image of the size $\frac{1}{2}$, $\frac{1}{3}$, $\frac{1}{4}$ size of the image.

3: Create successively blurred images (Gaussians) for every scale space image.

4: Compute Difference of Gaussians.

5: Identify Maxima or minima with the help of Difference of Gaussian images.

6: Plot maxima or minima locations on the original image. These maxima or minima are denoted as keypoints for the input image.

7: For each processing key point pixel $k(x,y)$, four vectors are calculated in all four directions(Left, Right, Top, Bottom) denoted as Left information vectors (Ln), Right information vectors (Rn), Top information vectors (Tn) and Bottom information vectors (Bn), where n varies from 1 to 4.

8: The left information vectors(Ln) are calculated in form of vector magnitudes $LM1$, $LM2$, $LM3$, $LM4$ and vector directions $LD1$, $LD2$, $LD3$, $LD4$ by using Eqs. 5 and 9 and taking the input as vector magnitudes and vector directions of three adjacent pixels, next five adjacent pixels, next 7 adjacent pixels and then next nine adjacent pixels respectively in left direction.The calculation of descriptors in shown in Fig. 4.

9: Similarly Rn, Tn, and Bn are calculated by taking input in Right, top and bottom direction as discussed in *Step 2* by using the magnitude from Eqs. 6, 7, and 8 and direction from Eqs. 10, 11 and 12. The operation '.' used in Eqs. 5, 6, 7, and 8 is defined in Eq. 4. Finally, in Eqs. 5, 6, and 7, 8, 9, 10, 11, and 12 the pixel at the location(x,y) is current processing pixel and θ is the angle between two vectors.

10: These Ln, Rn, Tn, and Bn are treated as bins as shown in Fig. 5 and each bin contains 4 vectors. So the total number of vectors in proposed work is 4 bins$\times$4 vectors $= 16$ vectors, these vectors direction and vectors magnitude are treated as descriptors of that key point.

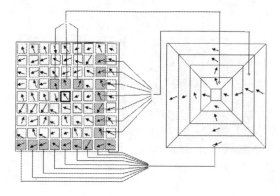

Fig. 4. Computation of descriptors from neighbouring pixels around keypoint.

$$LM_n = \sum_{i=1}^{2n} V_{(x+2n-i,y+n)} \cdot V_{(x+2n-(i+1),y+n)} \tag{5}$$

$$RM_n = \sum_{i=1}^{2n} V_{(x+2n-i,y-n)} \cdot V_{(x+2n-(i+1),y+n)} \tag{6}$$

$$BM_n = \sum_{i=1}^{2n} V_{(x+n,y-2n+i)} \cdot V_{(x+n,y-2n+(i+1))} \tag{7}$$

$$TM_n = \sum_{i=1}^{2n} V_{(x-n,y-2n+i)} \cdot V_{(x-n,y-2n+(i+1))} \tag{8}$$

$$LD_n = \sum_{i=1}^{2n} tan^{-1} \frac{||V_{(x+2n-i,y+n)}|| * sin\theta}{||V_{(x+2n+(i-1),y+n)}|| + ||V_{(x+2n+i,y+n)}|| * cos\theta} \tag{9}$$

$$RD_n = \sum_{i=1}^{2n} tan^{-1} \frac{||V_{(x+2n-i,y-n)}|| * sin\theta}{||V_{(x+2n-(i+1),y-n)}|| + ||V_{(x+2n-i,y-n)}|| * cos\theta} \tag{10}$$

$$BD_n = \sum_{i=1}^{2n} tan^{-1} \frac{||V_{(x+n,y-2n+i)}|| * sin\theta}{||V_{(x+n,y-2n+(i+1))}|| + ||V_{(x+n,y-2n+i)}|| * cos\theta} \tag{11}$$

$$TD_n = \sum_{i=1}^{2n} tan^{-1} \frac{||V_{(x-n,y-2n+i)}|| * sin\theta}{||V_{(x-n,y-2n+(i+1))}|| + ||V_{(x-n,y-2n+i)}|| * cos\theta} \tag{12}$$

where the pixel at the location (x, y) is current processing pixel and θ is the angle between two vectors.

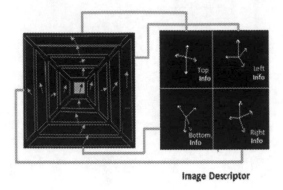

Image Descriptor

Fig. 5. Creation of bins for resultant vectors

4   Image Retrieval Using Modified SIFT Descriptors

Comparison technique for matching with modified SIFT descriptors is quite different from the traditional SIFT algorithm for CBIR. In this technique, to compare two images each key point descriptor is matched with every key point descriptors in the database image and tries to find nearest descriptor by considering magnitude and direction.

As discussed earlier each information bin have four vectors and each vector have its magnitude and direction. Descriptor matching is performed by matching these vectors magnitudes and directions, for comparing magnitudes difference is calculated if the difference between these magnitudes is less than a threshold value 0.025 then it is considered that magnitude matched successfully. If the difference between directions is less than a threshold value 0.005 then the directions matched successfully.

For reducing the comparison Time, top information bin of a key point in query image is relatively compared with all information bins of a keypoint in database image. If at least 80% of the matching is happened then the comparison is performed for all other bins between these two images otherwise that keypoint simply skipped. If the more than 70% of the keypoints of query image is matched with the keypoints of a database image then that database image will be retrieved as similar image. The three points given below shows that how the presented algorithm is invariant under rotation, illumination, resolution and full perspective. The matching of keypoints under rotation by 90 in left direction of a Lena image with original Lena image is presented in Fig. 6.

1. If magnitudes are matched for all four bins, for 65% of the key points between two images but direction are not matched then it (Database image) is considered as the rotated view of query image so this algorithm is invariant under rotation.
2. If the magnitude difference for all the four bins, for 70% of key points between two images are almost same then database image is considered as either

Fig. 6. Matching of the keypoints under rotation.

blurred copy or contrast/brightness changed copy of the query image. So this algorithm is invariant under resolution and illumination.
3. If the magnitude difference for all four bins, for 70% of the key points between two images are same but direction not matched then the database image is same image as query image but different in prospective. So this algorithm is invariant under prospective.

5   Results

The Accuracy is tested by taking a general purpose and well exploited database that comprises of 10,000 pictures of 100 classes from the Corel Image Gallery. These images with diverge and effective representation have been used by CBIR research communities. The Corel database consist of various images of various classes like "BUS", "flower", "eagle", "sunset", "horse" etc . Figure 7 display the result of search of query image of a tower using modified SIFT algorithm. Image at top of left-hand corner is the termed as query image. The result 20 images are the retrieved images based on the given query.

Accuracy of proposed work is calculated using Eq. 13

$$Accuracy = \frac{tp + tn}{tp + tn + fp + fn} \tag{13}$$

Where tp and tn are the Counts of true positives and true negatives recognized by the system respectively. fp and fn are the counts of true negatives identified as positives and true positives identified as negative identified by the system respectively. The proposed method have 40% less time complexity than traditional SIFT algorithm also their are negligible loss (3%–5%) of accuracy in image retrieval.

Fig. 7. The image retrieval result using modified SIFT algorithm having query image as a tower.

Figure 8a shows a comparison on the size of descriptors between modified SIFT and traditional SIFT algorithm [15]. This figure shows that very less number of descriptors are required in modified SIFT algorithm.

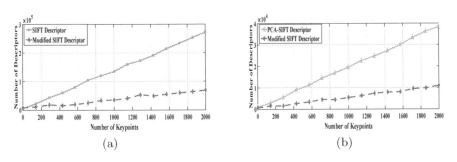

Fig. 8. Comparison of descriptor size (Number of Descriptors) between (a) SIFT [15] and Modified (Proposed) SIFT, and (b) PCA-SIFT [16] and Modified (Proposed) SIFT.

In modified SIFT, for a image having Size of 512×512 pixels and 2000 keypoints only 0.64×10^5 descriptors are created whether in traditional Sift algorithm 2.56×10^5 descriptors are created which are very large in comparison with modified SIFT algorithm.

The proposed method is also compared with Principal Component Analysis (PCA) based SIFT algorithm [16] as shown in Fig. 8b of Fig. 8, for an image of Size 512×512 with 300 keypoint. PCA-SIFT is used for the efficient image retrieval, it reduces most of the redundant keypoints by performing dimensionality reduction. Comparison shown in Fig. 8b represents that in modified SIFT only 9600 descriptors are created which are very less in comparison with 38400 descriptors calculated by PCA-SIFT.

6 Conclusion

SIFT features gives an unmistakable and precise method for matching the computerized pictures for vision based localization and image retrieval. In the proposed work a reduction on descriptors are presented to improve the time complexity of traditional SIFT features by having a negligible loss of accuracy. From the results it can be concluded that this reduction have very less effect on the retrieval rates of the images and satisfactorily reduces the time consumed for generating and matching descriptors.

References

1. Goodrum, A.A.: Image information retrieval: an overview of current research. Inf. Sci. **3**(2), 63–66 (2000)
2. Eakins, J., Graham, M.: Content-based image retrieval (1999)
3. Koskela, M., Laaksonen, J., Oja, E.: Comparison of techniques for content-based image retrieval. In: Proceedings of the Scandinavian Conference on Image Analysis, pp. 579–586, June 2001
4. Schmid, C., Mohr, R.: Local grayvalue invariants for image retrieval. IEEE Trans. Pattern Anal. Mach. Intell. **19**(5), 530–535 (1997)
5. Siggelkow, S., Feature histograms for content-based image retrieval. Doctoral dissertation, University of Freiburg, Freiburg im Breisgau, Germany (2002)
6. Schulz-Mirbach, H.: Invariant features for gray scale images. In: Sagerer, G., Posch, S., Kummert, F. (eds.) Mustererkennung 1995. Informatik aktuell, pp. 1–14. Springer, Heidelberg (1995). https://doi.org/10.1007/978-3-642-79980-8_1
7. Brown, M., Lowe, D.G.: Invariant features from interest point groups. In: BMVC, vol. 4, September 2002
8. Mikolajczyk, K., Schmid, C.: An affine invariant interest point detector. In: Heyden, A., Sparr, G., Nielsen, M., Johansen, P. (eds.) ECCV 2002. LNCS, vol. 2350, pp. 128–142. Springer, Heidelberg (2002). https://doi.org/10.1007/3-540-47969-4_9
9. Iqbal, Q., Aggarwal, J.K.: Using structure in content-based image retrieval. In: SIP, pp. 129–133, October 1999
10. Liu, F., Picard, R.W.: Periodicity, directionality, and randomness: wold features for image modeling and retrieval. IEEE Trans. Pattern Anal. Mach. Intell. **18**(7), 722–733 (1996)
11. Mirmehdi, M., Periasamy, R.: CBIR with perceptual region features. In: BMVC, pp. 1–10, September 2001
12. Laaksonen, J., Oja, E., Koskela, M., Brandt, S.: Analyzing low-level visual features using content-based image retrieval. In: Proc International Conference on Neural Information Processing, Taejon, pp. 14–18, November 2000

13. Li, J., Wang, J.Z.: Automatic linguistic indexing of pictures by a statistical modeling approach. IEEE Trans. Pattern Anal. Mach. Intell. **25**(9), 1075–1088 (2003)
14. Kosecká, J., Li, F.: Vision based topological Markov localization. In: 2004 Proceedings of the IEEE International Conference on Robotics and Automation 2004, ICRA 2004, vol. 2, pp. 1481–1486. IEEE, April 2004
15. Lowe, D.G.: Object recognition from local scale-invariant features. In: Proceedings of the seventh IEEE International Conference on Computer Vision 1999, vol. 2. IEEE (1999)
16. Ke, Y., Sukthankar, R.: PCA-SIFT: a more distinctive representation for local image descriptors. In: Proceedings of the 2004 IEEE Computer Society Conference on Computer Vision and Pattern Recognition 2004, CVPR 2004, vol. 2, pp. II. IEEE, June 2004

Scale Invariant Texture Representation Using Galois Field for Image Classification

S. Shivashankar and Medha Kudari[✉]

Karnatak University, Dharwad 580003, India
shivashankars@kud.ac.in, medha.k27@gmail.com

Abstract. This paper presents a Galois Field method to scale invariant representation of texture image. The method is based on addition of neighbours in Galois Field. Scale invariance is achieved by considering the neighbours at different levels. The texture is represented using the features extracted by transforming it into a Galois Field based addition. Then the normalized cumulative histogram (NCH) bin values are considered as textures. For scale invariance, features are extracted at different levels. Thus obtained features are used for scale invariant classification. The average classification accuracy of 80.77%, 91.74%, 98.52% and 74.08% is achieved for Mondial Marmi, Brodatz, Vectorial and Outex datasets at level 3. The features can be used for suitable applications.

Keywords: Texture classification · Scale invariance · Galois Field

1 Introduction

Texture has been playing an important role as one of the properties in identifying objects in an image. Texture representation has found many real-world applications in medical imaging [10,21], signature verification, biometrics and satellite imagery. In a digital image, texture gets distorted by occlusion, scale, angle and illumination. Texture representation in such cases becomes a challenging task. Over the years, many researchers have investigated this area and have proposed many varied methods for representing texture under different conditions.

One of the reasons for image distortion is scale. Scaling is the process of enlarging or diminishing an image and scale factor is the measure of how much scaling has been done. The objective of scale invariance texture classification is to identify either an enlarged or diminished image as the same image in its original size. Some works have been done on scale invariant feature extraction in texture classification. First among them was Lowe who extracted scale invariant features through a staged filtering approach and creating image keys for object recognition in [14]. Alignment of Radon features using dynamic time warping for pattern recognition was presented by Santosh, Lamiroy and Wendling [20]. An effective way of exploiting local organizations of scales and directions of visual patterns

© Springer Nature Singapore Pte Ltd. 2019
K. C. Santosh and R. S. Hegadi (Eds.): RTIP2R 2018, CCIS 1035, pp. 395–406, 2019.
https://doi.org/10.1007/978-981-13-9181-1_35

for iterative rotation-covariant texture learning using steerable Riesz wavelets was proposed by Depeursinge, Foncubierta-Rodriguez, Van de Ville and Muller [6]. Normalized statistical edge feature distribution was used by Yao and Sun [30] to resist the variation in scale. Statistical method modelled by the joint probability distribution of filter responses for textures was developed by Varma and Zisserman [25]. Extracting texture signatures by Harris key points and Laplacian key points was proposed by Lazebinik, Schmid and Ponce [11] and Zhang and Marszalek [31] respectively. A statistical histogram was computed by extracting a local fractal vector by Varma and Garg [24]. A scale- and rotation-invariant descriptor called SURF, based on Hessian approximations was proposed by Bay, Ess, Tuytelaars and Van Gool [1]. Joint distributions of pixel intensities in a neighbourhood were used for image patch representation by Varma and Zisserman [26]. Classification of image pixels into multiple point sets by gray intensities or local feature descriptors was implemented by Xu, Ji and Fermuller [29] and Quan, Xu and Sun [17] respectively. Instead of extracting scale invariant features, pyramid histograms with shifted matching scheme were proposed by Crosier and Griffin [5] and Zhang, Liang and Zhao [32]. A robust texture classification system based on random local features and BoW(Bag-of-Words) representation was developed by Liu, Fieguth, Kuang and Zha [13]. Random projection was applied for densely sampled image patches and histogram signature was extracted by Liu and Fieguth [12] for scale invariant images. A statistical framework combining the global multifractal spectrum statistical measurement and local feature descriptors using the gradient orientation histogram was proposed by Xu, Huang, Ji and Fermuller [28]. An alternate technique to represent texture property by taking the set of visual cues like lines, edges and high level contextual information was suggested by Candemir, Borovikov, Santosh, Antani and Thoma [4].Dominant LBP-based method in scale space to address scale variation for texture classification was proposed by Guo, Wang, Zhou and You [8]. A Fractal Weighted local binary pattern using fractals which is invariant to scale changes was used by Roy, Bhattacharya, Chanda and Chaudhuri [19].

Galois Fields have been used in computer science in fields like computer networks, satellite links or storage systems. It was first used in image processing by Reed, Truong, Kwoh and Hall [18].

In this paper, texture is represented using Galois fields. The method is based on addition of neighbours in Galois Field. Scale invariance is achieved by considering the neighbours at different levels. The texture is represented using the features extracted by transforming it into a Galois Field based addition. Then the normalized cumulative histogram (NCH) bin values are considered as features. For scale invariance, features are extracted at different levels. Thus obtained features are used for scale invariant classification. To classify texture, k-NN classifier with Euclidean distance measure is used. Mondial Marmi, Brodatz, Vectorial and Outex are the four datasets on which the experiments were performed. The observations prove that Galois Field based method achieves good classification rates for scale invariant images.

The rest of the paper is organized as follows: The Galois Field based texture representation is described in Sect. 2. Section 3 includes the classification process for scale invariance. Section 4 presents the experimental data. Section 5 presentsthe observations and discussion. Section 6 concludes the paper.

2 Galois Field (GF) Based Representation of Texture for Scale Invariant Classification

2.1 Proposed Methodology

A grayscale image I is considered with intensity values ranging from 0–255 and it is represented in 8-bit binary form. The 8-bit binary form is considered as an element in a Finite Field of 2^8 i.e. $GF(2^8)$. We propose Galois Field operator for neighbouring pixels at three different levels. The pictorial representations of neighbouring pixels considered at different levels are shown in Fig. 1.

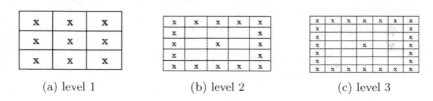

(a) level 1   (b) level 2   (c) level 3

Fig. 1. Neighbour pixels considered for level 1, 2 and 3

At level 1, the eight nearest neighbours and the pixel $I_{i,j}$ under consideration are added in $GF(2^8)$, which yields a 8-bit binary value, $I'_{i,j}$. This is repeated for all the pixels in the image I, resulting into I' at level 1 [22,23]. The procedure is repeated for level 2 and level 3 to yield GF transformed image I'_2 and I'_3 respectively. The GF transformed image at level 1, level 2 and level 3 represent the image at different scales.

2.2 Feature Computation

Construct the histogram [7] for the images I'_1, I'_2 and I'_3. A discrete function of a histogram is given below:

$$h(r_k) = n_k$$

where r_k is the kth value and n_k is the number of r_k values in I'_1.
    Further, the C_k is given by

$$C_k = \Sigma h(r_j)$$

where k represents the number of gray levels.

Then C_k is normalized Thus, the normalized cumulative histogram (NCH) is obtained and given by

$$N_1C = \frac{C_k}{\| C \|}$$

where

$$\| C \|= \sqrt{c_0^2 + c_1^2 + c_2^2 + ... + c_k^2 + ... + c_{255}^2}$$

The NCH is also constructed for I'_2 and I'_3 giving N_2C and N_3C respectively. The bin values of the NCH, N_1C , N_2C and N_3C are considered as features at different scales. This illustrates that the GF operator for level 1, level 2 and level 3 represents texture features for scale invariant classification. The feature representation of texture image using the proposed method is diagrammatically represented in Fig. 2.

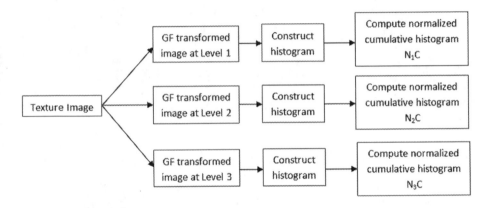

Fig. 2. Feature representation of texture image

3 Scale Invariant Classification

Texture classification is a process of assigning a category/class to the unknown sample based on the available known samples. A bipartite graph [9] of histograms for the train sample and test sample is built as shown in Fig. 3

The labeled edges in the bipartite graph indicate the distance between the histograms. A minimum cost of the graph is considered as the distance between train and test images. The minimum cost of the graph indicates the best match among the three scales. Further these distances are used for classification. The classification approach is described in detail as follows:

1. Let Nt_1C, Nt_2C and Nt_3C be the normalized cumulative histogram obtained using the proposed method for the training sample t.

2. Let TN_1C, TN_2C and TN_3C be the normalized cumulative histogram for the test sample T

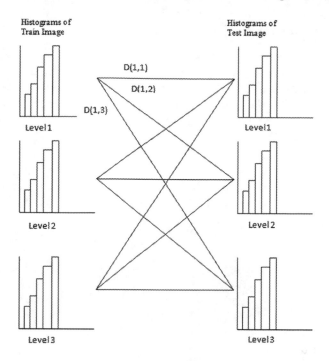

Fig. 3. Bipartite graph showing 3 histograms of train and test images

3. The minimum cost match distance between the train sample and test sample is now defined as

$$D(T, t) = min_{i,j}\{d(TN_iC, Nt_jC)\} \qquad i, j = 1, 2, 3$$

where

$$d(X, Y) = \sqrt{\Sigma_b(x_b - y_b)^2}$$

x_b and y_b are the bth bin value of histograms X and Y respectively

4. The k-NN classifier is used to classify the test sample T.

The above approach exhibits a scale invariant classification of the texture image.

4   Experimental Data

Accuracy of the proposed method is tested and evaluated by conducting the experiments on the benchmark datasets (Mondial Marmi [15], Brodatz [3], Vectorial [27] and Outex [16]). Bianconi and Fernandez [2] have considered for experimentation these four datasets of planar images. The sample images of the four datasets are presented in Figs. 4, 5, 6 and 7.

4.1   Mondial Marmi

The scaled dataset consists of images scaled from 1.0 to 3.0 in steps of 0.2 and cropped from the center of the scaled image to the original size in the dataset i.e. 272×272. The details of the dataset are given in [23]. Images are subdivided into subimages (16 non-overlapping) of size 272×272 pixels. Hence it results in 16 subsamples of each class, resulting in a dataset of 12 classes $\times$ 16 subimages $\times$ 10 scales $= 1920$ images.

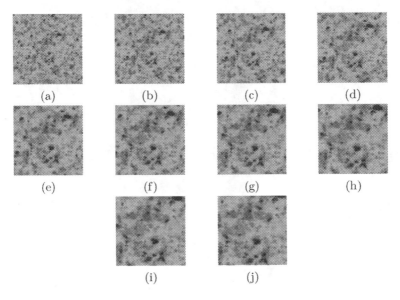

(a)   (b)   (c)   (d)

(e)   (f)   (g)   (h)

(i)   (j)

Fig. 4. BiancoCristal a texture chosen from Mondial Marmi, different scales ranging from 1.2 to 3.0 with steps of 0.2.

4.2   Brodatz

Images are subdivided into subimages (16 non-overlapping) of size 205×205 pixels. Thus it results in 16 subsamples of each class. These samples are scaled in steps of 0.2 ranging from 1.0 to 3.0, which forms the scaled dataset of 13 classes $\times$ 16 subimages $\times$ 10 scales $= 2080$ images. To retain the original size of the image, the scaled images are chosen from the center of the image. The details of the dataset are available in [23].

4.3   Vectorial

Artificial images form the Vectorial dataset which contains 20 texture classes. Details of the dataset are presented in [23]. Images are subdivided into subimages (16 non-overlapping) of size 225×225, resulting in 16 subsamples of each class.

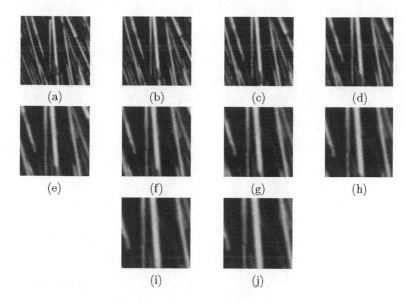

Fig. 5. D15 texture chosen from Brodatz, different scales ranging from 1.2 to 3.0 with steps of 0.2.

The images are scaled from 1.0 to 3.0 with a scale factor of 0.2 and chosen from the center of the image to the original size. Hence the number of images in the dataset is 20 classes × 16 subimages × 10 scales = 3200 images.

4.4   Outex

Outex is a popular dataset which is used for texture analysis. There are 45 different texture classes present in Outex_0045. The subimages are formed by dividing the images into 20 non-overlapping subimages of size 128 × 128. These subimages are scaled by a scale factor of 0.2 from 1.0 to 3.0 and chosen from the center of the image to the original size. The scaled dataset consists of 45 classes × 20 subimages × 10 scales = 9000 images. Further details of the dataset can be found in [23].

5   Observations and Discussion

The classification percentages using the proposed method at level 1 is presented in Table 1. The rows show the classification accuracy of Mondial Marmi, Bordatz, Vectorial and Outex datasets for different scales. For training, the sample images of scale factor 2.0 are considered. To evaluate the classification accuracy, the images of varying scales are used. From the table, it can be seen that the

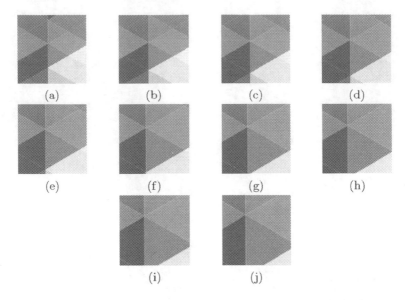

Fig. 6. Abstract3 texture chosen from Vectorial, different scales ranging from 1.2 to 3.0 in steps of 0.2.

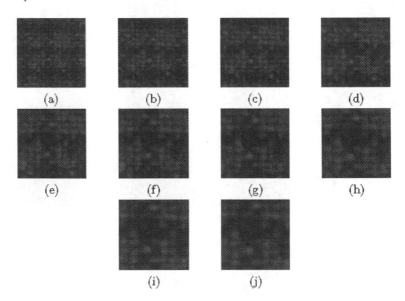

Fig. 7. canvas005 texture chosen from Outex, different scales ranging from 1.2 to 3.0 in steps of 0.2.

classification percentage goes on decreasing as the scale increases or decreases. The average classification of 83.62%, 90.51%, 97.5% and 77.90% is achieved for Mondial Marmi, Brodatz, Vectorial and Outex datasets respectively.

Table 1. Classification percentages (%) of Galois field transform at level 1

Scale	Mondial Marmi	Brodatz	Vectorial	Outex
1.0	63.02	67.31	91.56	30.55
1.2	73.44	82.69	95	59.11
1.4	82.29	89.90	95.94	75.88
1.6	87.50	91.35	99.06	86.22
1.8	95.83	97.60	100	96.33
2.0	100	100	100	100
2.2	96.35	99.04	100	96.55
2.4	86.98	95.19	99.37	87.11
2.6	80.74	93.75	99.37	80.44
2.8	78.13	90.38	97.19	75.22
3.0	75.52	88.46	95	69.44
Average	**83.61**	**90.51**	**97.5**	**77.90**

Table 2 shows the classification results of four different datasets. In this experiment, level 1 and level 2 features are used. It can be clearly seen that there is a significant increase in the classification accuracy for Brodatz and Vectorial datasets.

Table 2. Classification percentages (%) of Galois field transform at level 2

Scale	Mondial Marmi	Brodatz	Vectorial	Outex
1.0	73.96	75	94.69	51.44
1.2	72.40	82.21	96.88	54.11
1.4	78.65	87.98	99.06	68.22
1.6	84.38	92.78	99.69	82
1.8	94.27	98.08	100	94.67
2.0	100	100	100	100
2.2	95.31	99.04	100	95.67
2.4	85.94	95.67	100	84.78
2.6	80.73	93.75	100	77.22
2.8	75	91.35	98.44	71.78
3.0	72.40	89.42	97.81	65.44
Average	**83.01**	**91.39**	**98.78**	**76.85**

In the same manner, the features are obtained for level 1, level 2 and level 3. These features are further used for classification. The results of classification are shown in Table 3.

Table 3. Classification percentages (%) of Galois field transform at level 3

Scale	Mondial Marmi	Brodatz	Vectorial	Outex
1.0	69.79	78.37	92.50	39.78
1.2	70.83	83.17	97.19	53.44
1.4	77.08	89.42	98.44	64
1.6	83.85	92.31	100	78.67
1.8	93.75	97.60	100	93.67
2.0	100	100	100	100
2.2	95.31	98.56	100	94.89
2.4	83.33	96.63	100	82.11
2.6	70.83	94.23	99.34	75.56
2.8	71.35	90.87	98.44	69.44
3.0	72.40	87.98	97.81	63.33
Average	**80.77**	**91.74**	**98.52**	**74.08**

Table 4 summarizes the classification results obtained at level 1, level 2 and level 3 for all the four datasets. The results are better for level 1, it shows that the proposed method is able to classify images irrespective of changes in the scale. Hence the proposed method achieves scale invariance.

Table 4. Average classification rates (%) of Galois field transform at various levels on scaled databases

Level	Mondial Marmi	Brodatz	Vectorial	Outex
Level 1	83.61	90.51	97.5	77.89
Level 2	83.01	91.39	98.78	76.85
Level 3	80.77	91.74	98.52	74.08

6   Conclusion

In this study, a novel scale invariant classification method is proposed. An effort has been made to represent scaled texture image using Galois Field. The average classification accuracy of 80.77%, 91.74%, 98.52% and 74.08% is achieved for Mondial Marmi, Brodatz,Vectorial and Outex datasets at level 3. The classification performed at level 1 yields a comparable results at reduced time. The features can be used for the development of scale invariant applications such as offline signature verification and face recognition.

References

1. Bay, H., Ess, A., Tuytelaars, T., Van Gool, L.: Speeded-up robust features (SURF). Comput. Vis. Image Underst. **110**(3), 346–359 (2008)
2. Bianconi, F., Fernández, A.: Rotation invariant co-occurrence features based on digital circles and discrete fourier transform. Pattern Recognition Letters **48**, 34–41 (2014)
3. Brodatz, P.: Textures: A Photographic Album for Artists and Designers. Dover Publications (1966)
4. Candemir, S., Borovikov, E., Santosh, K.C., Antani, S., Thoma, G.: RSILC: rotation-and scale-invariant, line-based color-aware descriptor. Image Vis. Comput. **42**, 1–12 (2015)
5. Crosier, M., Griffin, L.D.: Using basic image features for texture classification. Int. J. Comput. Vis. **88**(3), 447–460 (2010)
6. Depeursinge, A., Foncubierta-Rodriguez, A., Van de Ville, D., Müller, H.: Rotation-covariant texture learning using steerable riesz wavelets. IEEE Trans. Image Process. **23**(2), 898–908 (2014)
7. Gonzalez, R.C., Woods, R.E.: Image processing. Digit. Image Process. **2**, 1 (2007)
8. Guo, Z., Wang, X., Zhou, J., You, J.: Robust texture image representation by scale selective local binary patterns. IEEE Trans. Image Process. **25**(2), 687–699 (2016)
9. Harary, F.: Graph theory (1969)
10. Karargyris, A., et al.: Combination of texture and shape features to detect pulmonary abnormalities in digital chest X-rays. Int. J. Comput. Assist. Radiol. Surg. **11**(1), 99 106 (2016)
11. Lazebnik, S., Schmid, C., Ponce, J.: A sparse texture representation using local affine regions. IEEE Trans. Pattern Anal. Mach. Intell. **27**(8), 1265–1278 (2005)
12. Liu, L., Fieguth, P.: Texture classification from random features. IEEE Trans. Pattern Anal. Mach. Intell. **34**(3), 574–586 (2012)
13. Liu, L., Fieguth, P., Kuang, G., Zha, H.: Sorted random projections for robust texture classification. In: 2011 IEEE International Conference on Computer Vision (ICCV), pp. 391–398. IEEE (2011)
14. Lowe, D.G.: Object recognition from local scale-invariant features. In: The Proceedings of the Seventh IEEE International Conference on Computer Vision 1999, vol. 2, pp. 1150–1157. IEEE (1999)
15. Mondialmarmi database. http://dismac.dii.unipg.it/mm/ver_1_1/index.html
16. Outex database. http://www.outex.oulu.fi/ (2002)
17. Quan, Y., Xu, Y., Sun, Y.: A distinct and compact texture descriptor. Image Vis. Comput. **32**(4), 250–259 (2014)
18. Reed, I.S., Truong, T.K., Kwoh, Y.S., Hall, E.L.: Image processing by transforms over a finite field. IEEE Trans. Comput. **C–26**(9), 874–881 (1977)
19. Roy, S.K., Bhattacharya, N., Chanda, B., Chaudhuri, B.B., Ghosh, D.K.: FWLBP: a scale invariant descriptor for texture classification. arXiv preprint arXiv:1801.03228 (2018)
20. Santosh, K.C., Lamiroy, B., Wendling, L.: DTW-Radon-based shape descriptor for pattern recognition. Int. J. Pattern Recogn. Artif. Intell. **27**(03), 1350008 (2013)
21. Santosh, K.C., Wendling, L., Antani, S., Thoma, G.R.: Overlaid arrow detection for labeling regions of interest in biomedical images. IEEE Intell. Syst. **31**(3), 66–75 (2016)

22. Shivashankar, S., Kudari, M., Hiremath, P.S.: Texture representation using Galois field for rotation invariant classification. In: 2017 13th International Conference on Signal-Image Technology and Internet-Based Systems (SITIS), pp. 237–240. IEEE (2017)

23. Shivashankar, S., Kudari, M., Hiremath, P.S.: Galois field-based approach for rotation and scale invariant texture classification. Int. J. Image, Graph. Signal Process. (IJIGSP) **10**(9), 56–64 (2018)

24. Varma, M., Garg, R.: Locally invariant fractal features for statistical texture classification. In: IEEE 11th International Conference on Computer Vision 2007, ICCV 2007, pp. 1–8. IEEE (2007)

25. Varma, M., Zisserman, A.: A statistical approach to texture classification from single images. Int. J. Comput. Vis. **62**(1–2), 61–81 (2005)

26. Varma, M., Zisserman, A.: A statistical approach to material classification using image patch exemplars. IEEE Trans. Pattern Anal. Mach. Intell. **31**(11), 2032–2047 (2009)

27. Vectorial database (2012). http://all-free-download.com

28. Xu, Y., Huang, S., Ji, H., Fermüller, C.: Scale-space texture description on sift-like textons. Comput. Vis. Image Underst. **116**(9), 999–1013 (2012)

29. Xu, Y., Ji, H., Fermüller, C.: Viewpoint invariant texture description using fractal analysis. Int. J. Comput. Vis. **83**(1), 85–100 (2009)

30. Yao, C.H., Chen, S.Y.: Retrieval of translated, rotated and scaled color textures. Pattern Recogn. **36**(4), 913–929 (2003)

31. Zhang, J., Marszałek, M., Lazebnik, S., Schmid, C.: Local features and kernels for classification of texture and object categories: a comprehensive study. Int. J. Comput. Vis. **73**(2), 213–238 (2007)

32. Zhang, J., Liang, J., Zhao, H.: Local energy pattern for texture classification using self-adaptive quantization thresholds. IEEE Trans. Image Process. **22**(1), 31–42 (2013)

A Novel Approach for Detection and Recognition of Traffic Signs for Automatic Driver Assistance System Under Cluttered Background

H. T. Manjunatha[1](✉), Ajit Danti[2], and K. L. ArunKumar[1]

[1] Department of MCA, Jawaharlal Nehru National College of Engineering, Shimoga, Karnataka, India
manjunatha.ht@gmail.com, arunkumarkl@jnnce.ac.in
[2] Computer Science and Engineering, CHRIST (Deemed to be University), Bengaluru, Karnataka, India
ajit.danti@christuniversity.in

Abstract. Traffic sign detection and recognition is a core phase of Driver Assistance and Monitoring System. This paper focuses on the development of an intelligent driver assistance system there by achieving road safty. In this paper a novel system is proposed to detect and classify traffic signs such as warning and compulsory signs even for occluded and angular tilt images using Support Vector Machines. Exhaustive experiments are performed in order to demonstrate the efficiency of proposed method.

Keywords: Driver assistance systems ·
SVM (Support Vector Machine) classifiers · YCbCr

1 Introduction

The number of vehicles increasing on the road, increasing physical and mental strain of the driver's chances of accidents are increasing by every day and sophisticated on-board systems are needed for driver assistance. Using intelligent design of hardware like camera, infrared, ultra sound, sophisticated system can be designed that can guide the drives, alert them over possible problems on the road and help minimizing the accidents. Driver guidance system is very essential in all vehicles in order to save money, save lives and to improve traffic environment. The road signs are missing most of the times. If suppose there is a system with integrated motion camera and an integrated onboard computer with the vehicle it will generate alert message to driver. The proposed method mainly focus on potential difficulties of detection and recognition of traffic sign is as follows

- Lighting conditions changeable because of cloudiness and whether conditions.
- Signs may be damaged, Angular tilt, color fades because long exposure to sun.

© Springer Nature Singapore Pte Ltd. 2019
K. C. Santosh and R. S. Hegadi (Eds.): RTIP2R 2018, CCIS 1035, pp. 407–419, 2019.
https://doi.org/10.1007/978-981-13-9181-1_36

- Road Sign deformation, appearance of road sign is not proper because so many degrees of freedom.
- Occluded road sign: Road signs are hidden by another object.

The core part of the methodology contains two stages such as detection and recognition. In detection phase image is to preprocessed and segmented based on color and shape. In recognition phase the SVM (Support Vector Machine) classifier is used to classify whether the input image is Warning sign or Compulsory signs. Road traffic signs are classified into 3 categories such as Warning, Compulsory and, Regulatory signs are shown in Fig. 1.

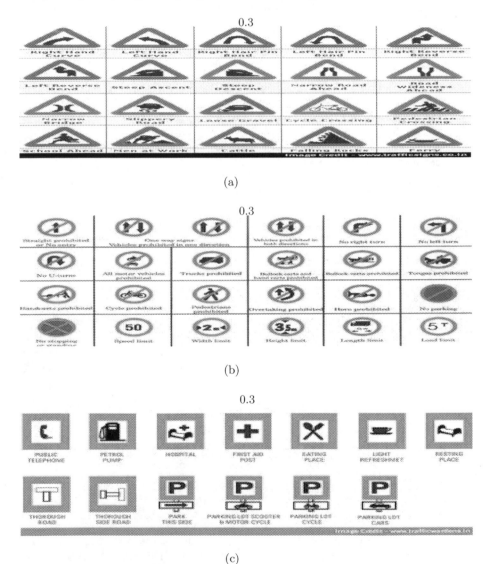

(a)

(b)

(c)

Fig. 1. (a) Compulsory signs (b) warning signs (c) informative signs

2   Literature Survey

Most of the detection and recognition algorithms focused on three stages (i) Extract ROI (Region of Interest) using segmentation techniques (ii) Feature extractions (iii) Classification technique. Most of algorithm technique focuses on a smaller number of features with less accuracy of experimental results. Our work concentrated on a greater number of features with higher accuracy rate. Danti et al. proposed the detection and recognition of Indian road signs. In this paper Haugh Transformation technique is used for image enhancement and ROI (Region of Interest) segmentation with color thresholding is implemented for detecting the road sign images and road sign is recognized by using KNN classifiers. The proposed methodology uses only the ideal images not for the images under cluttered background [2]. Siogkas et al. describes detection and classification of road signs only in night mode and rainy scenarios. The paper explains symmetry detection and center localizations are adopted for determining the shape of the road sign and classification is based on cross correlation metho [5]. Azad et al. developed a system that detect and recognized Iranian road sign images. The methodology contains angle feature extraction, transit feature extraction is implemented for SVM based classification technique and proposed system focused only the speed limit sign board [18]. Our proposed system focused on different categories of road sign images. Maldonad et al. proposes detection and recognition of road sign system using SVM classifier and methodology uses HSI color space for chromatic signs. The blobs are extracted from the segmentation that are classified using linear SVMs. The recognition processes are based on SVM with Gaussian kernels [20]. MaryReeja, et al. developed a system which detects and recognizes the traffic sign using SVM classifier. The region of interest is extracted by using Maximal Stable External Regions and Wave equations and for shape classification HOG and SVM classifiers are used [22]. Gautam et al. proposed a low contrast color image enhancement technique by using GLSE with contrast stretching, Paper explains different enhancement technique such as spatial domain methods, frequency domain methods and fuzzy domain technique [21]. Ahmed Hechri et al. presented a shape based and color-based segmentation technique in order to detect the outdoor road sign images. The paper describes template matching technique for classifying different categories of road sign images [1]. Dean et al. describes conversion of RGB color space to YCbCr space and shape-based filtering technique is used for extracting candidate object based on color. The paper explains the classification of road sign images using neural network [7]. kher et al. represents detection of road sign images from the complex background such as angular tilt, broken images, night mode images and occluded images. The paper focused the color-based segmentation technique by using YCbCr color space [8]. Kale et al gives the information on PCA (Principle Component analysis) such as mean, variance covariance and standard deviation of different dataset for detection and uses neural network for classifying variety of road sign images [3]. Feyeh et al. explains traffic sign recognition system based on using Legendre moments and uses two different SVM classifiers trained with Legendre moments [6]. Santosh et al. proposes structural symbol recognition with variety of statistical features and uses spatial organization descriptors and visual vocabulary that composes the symbol. It uses ARG based symbol descriptor that compose a symbol by using spatial organization and shape features of visual vocabulary [11]. Santosh et al. proposes overlaid arrow detection for labeling regions of interest in biomedical images. The proposed work uses fuzzy binarization technique for extracting candidate regions and candidate will be selected by using symmetry, overlap and triplet criteria, template free geometric signature method for detecting arrow annotation on bio medical images and detecting the arrow by comparing discrete and theoretical approach [12]. Santosh et al. proposes detection in biomedical images using sequential classifier. The methodology uses multilayer image segmentation technique, extracting the radon features, detecting and recognizing the arrow template by using BLSTM (Bi directional Long Short-Term Memory) [13]. Santosh et al. proposes arrowhead detection technique in biomedical images. The methodology describes template matching technique with DTW (Dynamic Time Wrapping) in order to detect the arrowhead [14]. The author Santosh proposed a methodology focusses on key issues in document image processing and graphical symbol recognition. It covers several aspects such as statistical, structural, syntactic and its merits and demerits considering the context [15]. Greenhalgh et al. proposed a novel application maximally stable external regions (MSERs) for detecting real time traffic road signs and recognition is performed with histogram-oriented gradient which are classified using linear support vector machines [9]. Arturo de la Escalera et al. describes detection of road sign by using color thresholding, optimal corner detector and corner extraction techniques. The paper explains gaussian filter for removing unwanted noise and road sign images are recognized by using neural network [4]. Arunkumar et al. propose a novel approach for vehicle recognition based on tail lights geometric features in the night vision. Proposed methodology extractes the features of an image such as centroid, eccentricity, Euler number, Solidity and Elongation. The classification done using Template Matching technique [23]. Manjunatha et al. describes the detection of sign board using normalized correlation method. The road sign is classified using nearest neighbour classification technique.

3 Methodology

The proposed methodology contains four phases (i)Image Acquisition (ii) Pre-processing (iii) Feature Extraction technique (iv) Road Sign Recognition. The main steps of proposed methodology are as follows. (i) Converting RGB to YCbCr Color space (ii) Image enhancement for cluttered background (iii) Red color segmentation (iv) Employed different feature extraction technique (v) Recognizing road sign images using SVM (Support Vector Machine) classifiers. The flow of proposed methodology has been shown in the Fig. 2.

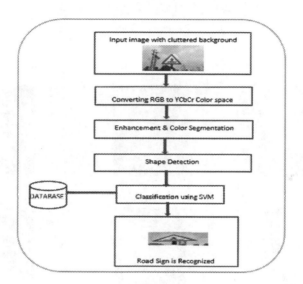

Fig. 2. The flow of proposed methodology

3.1 Image Acquisition

It is a process of retrieving Road Sign images with the cluttered background from the digital camera for further processing, Road sign had been employed for database in JPEG type file.

3.2 Image Preprocessing

The main agenda of preprocessing is removing image noise and make image sharper. One of the important aspects of the image preprocessing is color space conversion. In order to avoid the lower resolution capability of RGB color sapce the YCbCr color space is used. The first stage of proposed methodology converts captured road sign with RGB color space into YCbCr color space. Compulsory and warning signs are usually surrounded by red color. Later color threshold will be applied to extract red color in order to remove unwanted elements from the present images are shown in the Fig. 3b. The Next immediate step is removal of noise using morphological operation. The equation for RGB to YCbCr color space is shown below.

$$y = 16 + \frac{65.738R}{256} + \frac{129.057G}{256} + \frac{25.064B}{256} \qquad (1)$$

$$Cb = 128 - \frac{37.945R}{256} - \frac{74.494G}{256} + \frac{112.439B}{256} \qquad (2)$$

$$r = 128 - \frac{112.439R}{256} + \frac{94.154G}{256} - \frac{18.285B}{256} \qquad (3)$$

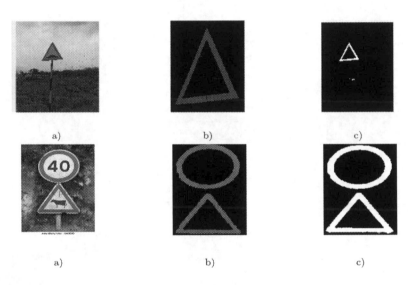

a)   b)   c)

a)   b)   c)

Fig. 3. (a) Original image (b) Red color extraction (c) Segmented image (Color figure online)

The proposed methodology uses linear contrast stretching method to enhances the input image by changing range of pixel intensity values [18, 21, 22]. Contrast stretching enhancement technique for contrast enhancement in order to detect low light road sign images and it enhances the pixel values to the desired range using the Eq. 4.

$$D(EN) = 255 * \frac{DN - DN_{min}}{DN_{max} - DN_{min}} \qquad (4)$$

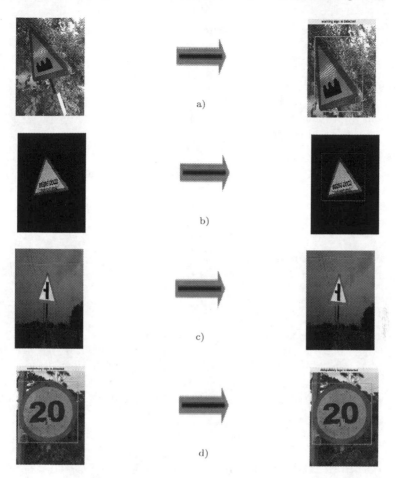

Fig. 4. Detection results of warning sign and compulsory sign. (a) angular tilt images (b) deformation images (c) night mode (d) broken images

where D(EN) is the enhanced output image and range, DNmin-DNmax are rescaled to the range 0–255 in the output image. In this section shape features are used to extract the location of the road sign. Some of the detection results of angular tilt images, deformation images, broken images night mode images are shown in the Fig. 4.

3.3   Feature Extraction

Image Features plays one of the important aspect in a detection and recognition system. It plays a vital role in order to represent the different set of classes and get the differences between different classes.

(i) Circular and Triangular Metrics

$$metric = \frac{(4*\pi*area)}{perimeter} \tag{5}$$

Circular $= 0.8 \lessgtr Metric \lessgtr 2$
Triangle $= 0.57 \lessgtr Metric \lessgtr 0.67$
Circular and Triangular metrics identifies whether the input image is in circular or triangular in shape.

(ii) Center of the image
Center of the image is obtained by the following equations

$$center(x) = \tfrac{w}{2} \quad center(y) = \tfrac{h}{2} \tag{6}$$

where w represents width of the image and h represents height of the image

(iii) Eccentricity of a triangle
Eccentricity of a triangle is obtained by using the Eq. 7 as mentioned below

$$\frac{p}{\sqrt{A}} \tag{7}$$

where P and A are the perimeter and Area of Triangle
(iv) Angle feature extraction Angle feature s plays a vital role in order to achieve high order accuracy, miss classification and for detecting the angular tilt images. Angle feature extraction is calculated by using the Eq. (8). The better accuracy invariant to scale and transition is considered [13]

$$(a_b) = \sum_{k=1}^{n_b} \tfrac{1}{n} + \theta_K^b \tag{8}$$

3.4   Road Sign Recognition and Classifications

Support Vector Machine (SVM) model associated with variety of learning algorithms for understanding and processing the data used for classification of different classes with rich set of features techniques. The SVM classifier classifies the images by using two method such as binary and multi class problem method. SVM classifier construct the maximal margin in the hyperplane among two datasets. Maximum distance between the data sets leads less error there by improving the classification accuracy. Normalization is one of the important before the data is fed into the SVM. In the proposed work all the features of warning and compulsory road sign images have been stored to knowledgebase later SVM classifier matches between stored features against the target image features, then SVM classifier classifies whether it is a compulsory sign or warning sign. The proposed methodology uses binary classification formulated for two class classification problem.

Binary Classification: In our system the SVM uses two linear classifiers such as triangle and circle which is surrounded by red color and determines lenear hyperplane with minimal classification exceptions. The equation for linear separation hyperplane is as shown below in Eq. 9.

$$F(x) = W^t * x + b \tag{9}$$

where W represents set of features or vector space and b represents the bias. F(x) represents the linear separating hyperplane function with class label x.

Proposed Algorithm.

1. To train extract all robust and invariant feature vector of warning and compulsory road sign and create a knowledge base.
2. Input the test query road sign images and segment the ROI using color thresholding
3. Compute center of the image, area, eccentricity, angle feature extraction as a regional property
4. Construct the feature vector of all features obtained in the step 2
5. The recognition model was trained on the training set and tested on the test set
6. The SVM classifier recognizes whether the input image is warning sign or compulsory sign

4   Implementation and Experimental Result

In this study for an experimental result we focused on Indian compulsory and warning road signs database for detection and recognition. Database contains around 250 images of different geometric shapes such as angular tilt, broken image occluded image and night mode images with 2 classes with 640*480 dimensions. One class is for compulsory road signs and another for Warning road signs images. Sample database road sign images are shown in the Fig. 5. The Detection and classification results are shown in Table 1. The proposed module achieves an accuracy of 95 compare to other methodologies. The comparative analysis is shown in the Table 2. Some of the warning and compulsory sign results are shown in the Fig. 6.

Table 1. Detection and classification result.

Shapes	No of road sign	Correct classified	False classified
Circle	100	85	15
Triangle	150	140	10

Table 2. Comparative analysis

Methods	No of images	Technique	Efficiency (%)
[5]	139	Normalized cross correlation	60
[20]	200	SVM (shape based)	93
[9]	300	SVM (shape based)	60
[3]	150	Neural network	60
[Our method]	250	SVM (both color and shape)	60

Road sign recognition and detection rate under cluttered background as shown in the Table 3.

Table 3. Detection and classification result

Road sign	Rate(%)
Occluded	100
Angular tilt	100
Broken	85
Night mode	85

Fig. 5. Some sample database for road signs

Fig. 6. Sample road sign recognition results

5   Conclusion and Future Work

The detection and recognition phase of road signs in a cluttered background is one of the key challenges for any researchers. The proposed methodology focussed on detection of road signs based on color and shape under complex background. The YCbCr color space is used to overcome the illumination sensitivity of RGB color space. The different Feature technique is employed in order to overcome the detection problem of images with the cluttered background. The SVM Classifier is used to classify the warning and compulsory road sign images. The prosed work shows high classification rate with less error rate. Present work is implemented only for still images. In the future We have planned to develop more robust detection techniques for video streams with different classes of road sign images.

References

1. Hechri, A., Mtibaa, A.: Lanes and road signs recognition for driver assistance system. IJCSI Int. J. Comput. Sci. Issues **8**(6), 1 (2011)
2. Danti, A., Kulkarni, J.Y., Hiremath, P.S.: Processing approach to detect lanes, pot holes and recognize road signs in Indian roads. Int. J. Model. Optim. **2**(6), 658–662 (2012)
3. Kale, A.J., Mahajan, R.C.: Detection and classification of vehicles, a road sign detection and the recognition for driver assistance systems, 30 October 1–November 2015. IEEE (2015)
4. de la Escalera, A., Moreno, L.E.: Road traffic sign detection and classification. IEEE Trans. Ind. Electron. **44**(6), 848–859 (1997)
5. Siogkas, G.k., Dermatas, E.S.: Detection tracking and classification of road signs in adverse conditions. In: IEEE MELECON, Spain (2006)

6. Feyeh, H., Doghrty, M.: SVM based traffic sign classification using legendre moments. Computer Science Department, Dalarna University, Sweden (2007)
7. Dean, H.N., Jabir, K.V.T.: Preceding vehicle recognition based on learning from sample images real time detection and recognition of Indian traffic sign using Matlab. IJCSI Int. J. Comput. Sci. Issues **4**(1), 1 (2015)
8. kher, H.R., Nagarkar, P.D.: Algorithem for road sign detection for driver assistance from complex background. Int. J. Eng. Res. Technol. (IJERT) **4**(01) (2015). ISSN 2278–0181
9. Greenhalgh, J., Mirmehdi, M.: Real-time detection and recognition of road traffic signs. In: Manuscript received, 14–15 January (2014)
10. Santosh, K.C., Wendling, L., Antani, S., Thoma, G.R.: Integrating vocabulary clustering with spatial relations for symbol recognition. Int. J. Doc. Anal. Recogn. **17**(1), 61–78 (2013)
11. Santosh, K.C., Wendling, L., Antani, S., Thoma, G.R.: Overlaid arrow detection for labeling regions of interest in biomedical images. IEEE-IS **31**(3), 66–75 (2015). Accepted manuscript, special issue: Pattern Recognition
12. Santosh, K.C., Roy, P.P.: Vehicle classification systems with local-feature based algorithm using CG model images. In: Arrow Detection in Biomedical Images Using Sequential Classifier. Springer, Heidelberg (2016)
13. Santosh, K.C., Alam, N., Roy, P.P., Wendling, L.: A simple and efficient arrowhead detection technique in biomedical images. Int. J. Pattern Recogn. Artif. Intell. **30**(5), 1657002 (2016)
14. Santosh, K.C.: Document image analysis: road traffic sign detection and classification. In: Current Trends and Challenges in Graphics Recognition, 29 November 2018. ISBN 978-981-13-2339-3
15. Azad, R., Azad, B., Kazerooni, I.T.: Optimized method for Iranian road signs detection and recognition system. Int. J. Res. Comput. Sci. **4**(1), 19–26 (2014). ISSN 2249-8265
16. Maldonad, S., Lafuente, S., Gil-Jimenez, P.: Road-sign detection and recognition based on support vector machines. IEEE Trans. Intell. Transp. Syst. **8**(2), 264–278 (2007)
17. Gautam, S., Saxena, T., Trived, V.: Low contrast color image enhancement by using GLCE with contrast stretching. Int. J. Res. Sci. Innovation (IJRSI), **5**(2) (2018). ISSN 2321–2705
18. MaryReeja, Y., Latha, T., MaryAnsalinShalini, A.: Traffic sign detection and recognition in driver support system for safety precaution ARPN. J. Eng. Appl. Sci. **10**(5) (2015). ISSN 1819–6608
19. Arunkumar, K.L., Danti, A.: A novel approach for vehcle recognition based on tail lights geometric features in the night vision. Int. J. Comput. Eng. Appl. **44**(6) (2018). ISSN 2321–3169
20. Manjunatha, H.T., Danti, A.: Indian traffic sign board recognition using normalized correlation. Int. J. Comput. Eng. Appl. **XII** (2018). ISSN 2321-3169
21. Ruikar, D.D., Santosh, K.C., Hegadi, R.S.: Automated fractured bone segmentation and labeling from CT images. J. Med. Syst. (2019). https://doi.org/10.1007/s10916-019-1176-x

22. Ruikar, D.D., Santosh, K.C., Hegadi, R.S.: Segmentation and analysis of CT images for bone fracture detection and labeling, chap. 7. In: Medical Imaging: Artificial Intelligence, Image Recognition, and Machine Learning Techniques. CRC Press (2019). ISBN: 9780367139612

23. Hegadi, R.S., Navale, D.I., Pawar, T.D., Ruikar, D.D.: Multi feature-based classification of osteoarthritis in knee joint X-ray images, chap. 5. In: Medical Imaging: Artificial Intelligence, Image Recognition, and Machine Learning Techniques. CRC Press (2019). ISBN: 9780367139612

Ishara-Bochon: The First Multipurpose Open Access Dataset for Bangla Sign Language Isolated Digits

Md. Sanzidul Islam$^{(\boxtimes)}$, Sadia Sultana Sharmin Mousumi, Nazmul A. Jessan, AKM Shahariar Azad Rabby, Sheikh Abujar, and Syed Akhter Hossain

Department of Computer Science and Engineering, Daffodil International University, Dhaka, Bangladesh
{sanzidul15-5223,sadia15-5191,nazmul15-4668,azad15-5424, sheikh.cse}@diu.edu.bd, aktarhossain@daffodilvarsity.edu.bd

Abstract. Ishara-Bochon, the first multipurpose comprehensive open access isolated digits dataset for Bangladeshi Sign Language (BdSL) is introduced in this article. Sign language digits is a major part of communication for deaf and hearing impaired people. It is important in their everyday stuff, such as – in routine accounting and to interact with general people. Ishara-Bachon dataset contains 100 sets of 10 Bangla basic sign digits (0, 1, 2 . . . 9), collected from different deaf and general volunteers from different institutes. After discarding maximum errors and performing different preprocessing methods, 1000 images of Bangla sign language isolated digits were included in the first dataset. After collectiong raw data, some effective preprocessing methods were performed for making those data useable for computer vision model and any other application development purposes.

Keywords: Bangla Sign Language · NLP · Computer vision · Machine Learning · Image processing · Sign language digits · BdSL · Open source data · Pattern recognition

1 Introduction

Conducting communication with deaf and hearing impaired people is more challenging to ordinary people. In Bangladesh, there are 2.6 million [1] deaf and hearing impaired persons who use different signs for regular communication purpose. The only way of improving communication with them is to let them understand their mother language (Bengali Language) thorough teaching Bangladeshi Sign Language (BdSL). Which may help a lot. General people have a mother language learned from the environment, through what they communicate with others more easily. But by birth hearing impaired people, they can't hear something from surroundings that's why became deaf ultimately.

Sometimes Bangladeshi deaf communities use their own local signs because of not having proper concern of maintaining a fixed standard of Bangla sign

K. C. Santosh and R. S. Hegadi (Eds.): RTIP2R 2018, CCIS 1035, pp. 420–428, 2019.
https://doi.org/10.1007/978-981-13-9181-1_37

language. To solve this dissonance still, now it was trying to develop a standard platform of BdSL. There are two common form of BdSL, one was made through following British pattern and another was in American pattern. A book named "Bangla Ishara Bhasa Obhidhan" was written at the time of 1994 and reprinted in 1997, which follows British sign pattern. Now, another book is now more popular for BdSL, named "Ishara Bhasy Jogajog" by CDD (Centre for Disability in Development). Now the most used signs among the Bangladeshi deaf community is CDD standard Sign Language.

A very few research was successfully held on Bangladeshi Sign Language (BdSL) but no dataset is available in web repository to work further for this impaired community. In this mindset, it is going to introduce the first open access Bangla sign language digits dataset for BdSL. This dataset was collected from different aged group students of different deaf schools at Dhaka.

Ishara-Bochon contains sign images of Bangla Sign Language Digits from zero to nine (0–9), total ten (10) classes (Fig. 1).

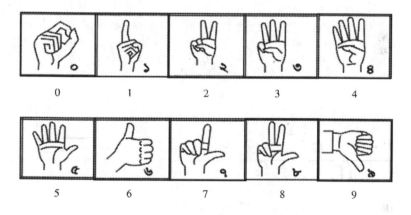

Fig. 1. Bangla sign language digits sample.

It became very necessary to solve the problem of deaf and hearing impaired people, Purpose of dealing with daily stuffs requires proper communication. So, general people need to interact with deaf and impaired people through sign language, but most of the people don't know how to use different signs. This proposed dataset will help to build a system for reducing the limitations and/or gaps between deaf and general people. Which will act as an interpreter as well will help to understand Bangla sign language digits easily.

2   Literature Review

Many researchers did research on Bangla Sign Language and wrote about dataset but no dataset for BdSL is not open access for further research and development work. In recent decades researchers are thinking about new and newer approaches and algorithms for getting better output from hand gesture related works like - Convolution Neural Network, Support Vector Machine, Hidden Markov Model etc. But effective works and resources for Bangla Sign Language is not going well parallel to modern time.

In 2014, Rahaman, Jasim, Ali and Hasanuzzaman did a Computer Vision-Based Real-Time Bangla Sign Language Recognizer [2] where they proposed Bengali Hand gesture recognition system focusing on Computer Vision.

In September 2017 Hasan, Khaliluzzaman, Himel, and Chowdhury proposed a sign language recognizer framework [3] for various Bangla characters using Artificial Neural Network (ANN) and they attained a good recognition rate.

In [4], they used scale invariant feature transform (SIFT) for feature extraction in Bangla sign expressions and then applied k-means clustering. They also introduced the bag of words model to their hybrid approach.

Shahriar, Zaman, Ahmed, Khan and Maruf proposed a communication platform between Bangla and Sign language in 2017 [5]. They worked with Bangla speech which converts speech to sign and show to impaired persons. They mainly focused on speech recognition algorithms.

Datta, Sarkar, Datta et al. proposed a framework for Bangla text to Bangla sign language based on translation system [6]. In that approach, the input text arranges the words in the correct order for Bangla sign language, and show the correct video file related to each word given.

3   Data Collection and Preprocessing

The entire data collection process has been divided into five different states. All those states are described in Fig. 2.

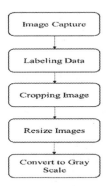

Fig. 2. Flow of working procedures.

3.1   Capturing Image

The white background was choose as background color and then captured images one by one from deaf and general volunteers. DSLR camera was used for taking hand signs images. White spaces were removed from hands edge as much as possible while capturing images. Figure 3 shows few samples captures.

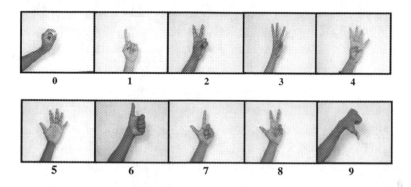

Fig. 3. Captured raw images.

3.2   Labeling Data

A script was developed to label the data after data collection. Initially, ten Different directories (named - 0, 1, 2, 3, 4, 5, 6, 7, 8, 9) was built and then stored those images into individual classes to make more organized.

3.3   Cropping Images Manually

Sign images were cropped manually for making those more noise free. The image area of actual hands from captured images was extracted and stored. White spaces are removed as efficiently as possible by cropping.

3.4   Resizing Image and Convert to Gray Scale

All images are resized by 128 * 128 pixels square area, the purpose of preparing all images into a standard form and ensuring same pixels in height and width. As well, for ensuring better performance from the dataset while using in computer vision or in system development (Fig. 4).

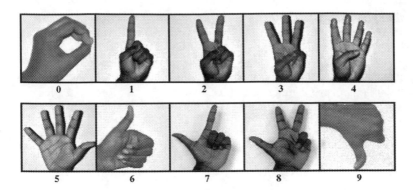

Fig. 4. Converted images into gray-scale.

4 Dataset Properties

Development through Data science requires a useable dataset, where data properties hold a major factor. Such as - data label, quantity, image size, and quality will increase the usability through Machine Learning or Deep Learning algorithms. Further development of this research will introduce the most useable dataset. Some basic properties are mentioned below. Ishara-Bochon contains sign images of total 10 classes of Bangla sign digits (0, 1, 2, 3 . . . 9).

- Every class has 100 different images of different people's hand.
- Ishara-Bochon Dataset has total 1000 (10 * 100 = 1000) images.
- All sign images is cropped and resized by 128 * 128 pixels.
- Dataset images is formatted in .jpg format.

5 Possible Usage of Ishara-Bochon Dataset

- Ishara-Bachon dataset will help NLP and Data Science researchers to work with Bangla Sign Language.
- System development for deaf and hearing impaired people.
- Making Sign Language interpreter to decrease the distance between Deaf and General people.
- Bangla sign language resources are increased, it would be a virtual standard for BdSL.

6 Naming Convention and Data Repository

The dataset name is "Ishara-Bochon", where Ishara is a Bangla word which means signs and Bochon means number. The dataset holds different folders for each Bangla sign digits. As we have 10 individual classes for digits.

In short, 10 folders naming by the digit value, like - 0, 1, 2, 3, 4, 5, 6, 7, 8, 9. Every folder contains 100 different images of that digit naming in .jpg extension of file type, like - 0_001.jpg, 0_002.jpg. 1_001.jpg, 1_002.jpg and so on. Here before underscore ('_') mean the digit and after underscore mean the serial number of data.

7   Model Construction

We aims at constructing a model in deep learning approach for recognition of sign digit for Bangla Sign Language (BSL). We used CNN to train particular signs with a respective training dataset for acquire our aim. Our model gained 92.87% accuracy.

The model used to recognize these digits here used multi-layer convolution neural networks which are connected each other. The model is represented by total eight layers (Fig. 5).

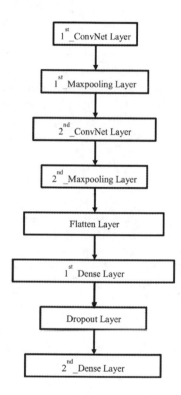

Fig. 5. Model architecture.

7.1   Model Optimization and Learning Rate

The choice of optimization algorithm can make a sufficient change for the result in Deep Learning and computer vision work. The Adam optimizer [7] says, "...many objective functions are composed of a sum of subfunctions evaluated at different subsamples of data; in this case, optimization can be made more efficient by taking gradient steps w.r.t. individual sub-functions ...". The Adam optimization algorithm is an extension to stochastic gradient descent that recently adopting most of the computer vision and natural language processing application. The method computes individual adaptive learning rates for different parameters from estimates of first and second moments of the gradients.

Proposed method used ADAM Optimizer with learning rate = 0.001. When using a neural network to perform classification and prediction task. A recent study shows that cross entropy function performs better than classification error and mean square error. Cross-entropy error, the weight changes don't get smaller and smaller and so training isn't s likely to stall out. Proposed method used categorical cross entropy (1) as loss function.

$$L_i = \sum_j t_{i,j} \log(p_{i,j}) \tag{1}$$

To make the optimizer converge faster and closer to the global minimum of the loss function, using an automatic Learning Rate reduction method. Learning rate is the step by which walks through the minimum loss. If higher learning rate use it will quickly converge and stuck in a local minimum instead of global minima. To keep the advantage of the fast computation time with a high Learning Rate, after each epoch model dynamically decreases the learning rate by monitoring the validation accuracy.

7.2   Model Evaluation

The dataset was divided into two portions - training data and test data. The model was trained with the training data and then validated with the validation data. The model developed with Ishara-Bochon dataset performed 92.87% validation accuracy and 96.52% training accuracy. As occurred the training loss and validation loss is also shown below in graphical representation (Figs. 6 and 7).

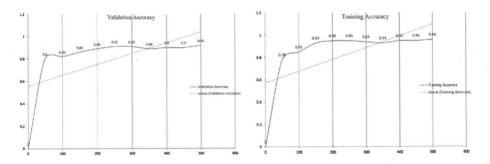

Fig. 6. Accuracy graph.

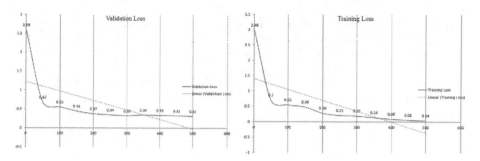

Fig. 7. Occurred loss graph.

8   Conclusion and Future Work

In Bangladesh, opportunities and resources for working on disable communities are too much difficult in perspective of other countries. Because of less availability of digital dataset on a specific domain, as well more importantly in a standard format. Ishara-Bochon dataset will help other researchers to work further for deaf and hearing impaired people in future. The dataset now contains Bangla sign digits only. Signs of other Bangla characters and words is not included yet. In purpose of doing something helpful for disabled people, dataset size needs to increase further. In future, all Bangla characters and other signs will be included in Ishara-Bochon dataset.

Acknowledgement. I would like to express my heartiest appreciation to all those who provided us the possibility to complete this research under the Daffodil International University. A special gratitude we give to Daffodil International University NLP and Machine Learning Research LAB for their instructions and support. Furthermore, I would also like to acknowledge that, this research partially supported by Bijaynagar Deaf School, Mirpur Deaf School, Mymensing Deaf School and all of the volunteers team who gave permission to collect valuable data. Any errors are our own and should not tarnish the reputations of these esteemed persons.

References

1. Hasan, S.M.K., Ahmad, M.: A new approach of sign language recognition system for bilingual users. In: 2015 International Conference on Electrical & Electronic Engineering (ICEEE). IEEE (2015)
2. Rahaman, M.A.: Real-time computer vision-based Bengali Sign Language recognition. In: 2014 17th International Conference on Computer and Information Technology (ICCIT). IEEE (2014)
3. Hasan, M.M.: Hand sign language recognition for Bangla alphabet based on Freeman Chain Code and ANN. In: 2017 4th International Conference on Advances in Electrical Engineering (ICAEE). IEEE (2017)
4. Yasir, F.: Sift based approach on Bangla sign language recognition. In: 2015 IEEE 8th International Workshop on Computational Intelligence and Applications (IWCIA). IEEE (2015)

5. Shahriar, R.: A communication platform between Bangla and sign language. In: 2017 IEEE Region 10 Humanitarian Technology Conference (R10-HTC). IEEE (2017)
6. Sarkar, B.: A translator for Bangla text to sign language. In: 2009 Annual IEEE India Conference (INDICON). IEEE (2009)
7. Kingma, D.P., Ba, J.: Adam: a method for stochastic optimization. arXiv:1412.6980 [cs.LG], December 2014

A Simple and Mighty Arrowhead Detection Technique of Bangla Sign Language Characters with CNN

Md. Sanzidul Islam[✉], Sadia Sultana Sharmin Mousumi,
AKM Shahariar Azad Rabby, and Syed Akhter Hossain

Department of Computer Science and Engineering, Daffodil International University,
Dhaka, Bangladesh
{sanzidul15-5223,sadia15-5191,azad15-5424}@diu.edu.bd,
aktarhossain@daffodilvarsity.edu.bd

Abstract. Sign Language is argued as the first Language for hearing impaired people. It is the most physical and obvious way for the deaf and dumb people who have speech and hearing problems to convey themselves and general people. So, an interpreter is wanted whereas a general people needs to communicate with a deaf and dumb person. In respect to Bangladesh, 2.4 million people uses sign language but the works are extremely few for Bangladeshi Sign Language (BdSL). In this paper, we attempt to represent a BdSL recognition model which are constructed using of 50 sets of hand sign images. Bangla Sign alphabets are identified by resolving its shape and assimilating its structures that abstract each sign. In proposed model, we used multi-layered Convolutional Neural Network (CNN). CNNs are able to automate the method of structure formulation. Finally the model gained 92% accuracy on our dataset.

Keywords: Bangla Sign Language · NLP · Computer vision ·
Machine learning · Image processing · Sign language characters ·
BdSL · BSL · CNN · Pattern recognition

1 Introduction

Deaf is an incapability that emasculate their hearing and establish them disable to listen [1], while mute is an incapability that emasculate their speaking and establish them disable to talk [2]. Both of them can't just speak and hear but can do much all other things. One thing that has separated them from ordinary people is communications. The hearing impaired people live like a normal people if there was any way to communicate. Sign Language is the only way for deaf and mute to communicate.

A sign Language is a language which is represented by alliance of gesture or movement of the hands. Sign Language is the visual language because of these sign language and spoken language both is different. In real world, people face

© Springer Nature Singapore Pte Ltd. 2019
K. C. Santosh and R. S. Hegadi (Eds.): RTIP2R 2018, CCIS 1035, pp. 429–437, 2019.
https://doi.org/10.1007/978-981-13-9181-1_38

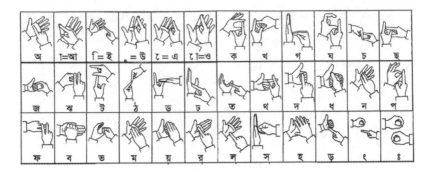

Fig. 1. Bangla sign language characters sign.

different gestures, Fig. 1 has some example. Different country has different sign languages rely on their alphabets and native expression. There are various sign language for example American, Arabic, French, Spanish, Chinese, and Indian etc.

In Bangladesh where around 2.4 million people use Bengali Sign Language. But normal people are not accustomed with their sign. For effective communication speech and hearing impaired people and normal people must have the similar set of knowledge for an individual gesture. It is difficult for the deaf and mute people to learn their sign as there is no appropriate model that work as a communication method. For this, a distance has been created in the society. Bangla Sign Language that creates sign more difficult to realize. So it is essential for construct a model which is convert the sign language to text that supported the mute people to communicate with general people and each other. Now a days, Bangladeshi Sign Language Recognition (BdSL) becomes one of the challenging topics in the area of machine learning and computer vision.

In this paper, a CNN based Sign Language Recognition is offer to acquire highest recognition rate. Here we have focused on static hand gesture in Bangla Sign Language (BSL) which is still challenging because of it visually same yet several sign. So we receive advantage of convolutional neural networks to fulfil a real time and appropriate sign language recognition system. It is mentioning that we can eliminate the obstacle of moving hands from background for hands because CNNs have the ability to learn structures automatically from raw data without any prior knowledge [3].

2   Literature Review

Convolutional Neural Networks have been really effective in image recognition and classification problems, and have been effectively executed for human sign recognition in recent years [4]. Automatic Sign Language Finger Spelling uses CNN architecture from Kinect Depth images. The system trained CNNs for the classification of 24 alphabets and 0–9 numbers using 33000 images and trained the classifier with different parameter configurations [5].

Kang et al. take the extremely well-organized primary step of automatic fingerspelling recognition system using convolutional neural networks (CNNs) from depth maps. In this work, they consider comparatively larger number of classes related with the forgoing literature. They train CNNs for the classification of 31 alphabets and numbers using a subset of collected depth data from multiple subjects [6]. In Deep Convolutional Neural Networks for Sign Language Recognition paper they proposed a CNN architecture for classifying selfie sign language gestures. A stochastic pooling method is applied which pools the benefits of both max and mean pooling techniques. They generates the selfie sign language database of 200 ISL sign with 5 signers in 5 user dependent viewing angles for 2 sec each at 30 fps generating a total of 300000 sign video frames [7].

Hosoe et al. demonstrated a structure for recognition of static finger spellings on images. This recognition of hand gestures is done using a convolutional neural network, which has been trained using physical images. They recorded 5000 images with static finger spellings from Japanese Sign Language [8]. Huang et al. developed a 3D CNN model for sign language recognition that acquires and removes temporal features by performing 3D convolutions. They use multilayer perceptron classifier to classify these feature demonstrations [9]. A voice/text format architecture is being proposed using the neural networks identification to translate the sign language and introduce the Point of Interest (POI) and trajectory idea delivers originality and cuts the storage memory condition in Real-time Sign Language Recognition based on Neural Network Architecture paper [10].

Pigou(B) et al. contribute a recognition system using the Microsoft Kinect, convolutional neural networks (CNNs) and GPU acceleration and making complex handcrafted features. They were able to recognize 20 Italian gestures with 91.7% accuracy [11]

Tsai and Huang use Support Vector Machine (SVM) to recognize the static sign and put on HMM model to classify the dynamic signs and they expended the finite state machine to confirm the correctness of the grammar of the recognized TSL sentence [12].

Yasir et al. measured leap motion controller to take the continuous frame and preprocessed structure and they take out the vital features from hand and fingers using LMC. They presented segmented HMM to discrete sign of expression from the constant frame by transition states. Next fetching the expression, they executed all the features as an input layer and accepted all of them as the limit to the convolutional layer [13].

In this paper, we develop CNN based recognition system which is significant algorithm for object recognition.

3   Proposed Methodology

A neural net is used in this system to recognize hand signs which is Convolution Neural Network. The neural net layer explanation, dataset properties, data process, model training and many other methodology is discussed in this section.

3.1 Dataset Properties

The Eshara-Lipi dataset which was collected for this project we used to train the model. Eshara-Lipi dataset contains Bangla Sign Language characters from 0 to 35 (0, 1, 2 . . 36) (Fig. 2).

The dataset has following properties.

- Every class has 50 different images of different people's hand.
- Ishara-Lipi Dataset has total 1800 (36 * 50 = 1800) images.
- All sign images is cropped and resized by 128 * 128 pixels.
- Dataset images is formatted in .JPG format.

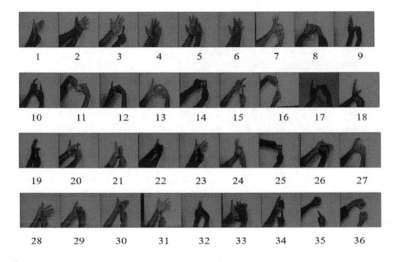

Fig. 2. Bangla sign language characters dataset samples.

3.2 Data Preprocessing

The Eshara-Lipi dataset provides 128 * 128 pixels grayscale images. For making this model did some reprocessing works like - convert grayscale image to binary and threshold. The method we used determines the threshold automatically from the image using Otsu's method.

3.3 Model Preparation

Algorithm 1:

1: Convolution 1 (Filter, Kernel Size, Stride, Padding, Activation)
2: Convolution 2 (Filter, Kernel Size, Stride, Padding, Activation)
3: Convolution 3 (Filter, Kernel Size, Stride, Padding, Activation)
4: Convolution 4 (Filter, Kernel Size, Stride, Padding, Activation)

5: Convolution 5 (Filter, Kernel Size, Stride, Padding, Activation)
6: Convolution 6 (Filter, Kernel Size, Stride, Padding, Activation)
7: Convolution 7 (Filter, Kernel Size, Stride, Padding, Activation)
8: Convolution 8 (Filter, Kernel Size, Stride, Padding, Activation)
9: Convolution 9 (Filter, Kernel Size, Stride, Padding, Activation)
10: Convolution 10 (Filter, Kernel Size, Stride, Padding, Activation)
11: Flatten (data format)
12: Dense (Units, Activation, Kernel initializer, Bias Initializer)
13: Dropout (Rate)
14: Dense (Units, Activation, Kernel initializer, Bias Initializer)
15: Dropout (Rate)
16: Dense (Units, Activation, Kernel initializer, Bias Initializer)
17: end for

Proposed Model in this paper use ADAM optimizer with a learning rate of 0.001. The model has multi layered CNN. For convolution 1 and 2, where filter size is 30, kernel size is (3×3), Stride is (1×1), "same" padding with ReLU (1) activation. Followed 20, 60 filter size and 3, 5, 7 kernel size in other conv layers. Then used 25% dropout to reduce overfitting.

$$ReLu(x) = Max(0, x) \tag{1}$$

For convolution 3, 4 and 5, the filter is 20, kernel size is (3×3), (5×5) and (7×7), Stride is (1×1), "same" padding with ReLU activation. Then used 25% dropout. Then flatten the layer and use a Dense layer with 2560 units with ReLU activation and 50 % dropout. At final output layer, used 36 units with SoftMax (2) activation.

$$S(y_i) = \frac{e^{y_i}}{\sum_j e^{y_i}} \tag{2}$$

Densed layer is actually the linear operation on the layer's input vector. It works as below (Fig. 3).

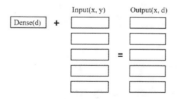

Fig. 3. Densed layer working method.

The flattening step is needed so that we can make use of fully connected layers after some convolutional layers (Fig. 4).

Fig. 4. Flattening layer working method.

Then finally the whole model architecture could be shown in a picture. Figure 5 is showing the neural network architecture.

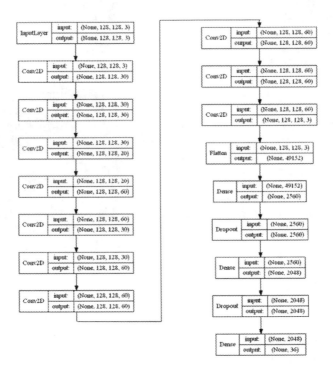

Fig. 5. The whole model architecture.

3.4   Model Optimization and Learning Rate

The choice of optimization algorithm can make a sufficient change for the result in Deep Learning and computer vision work. The Adam paper says, "...many objective functions are composed of a sum of subfunctions evaluated at different subsamples of data; in this case, optimization can be made more efficient by taking gradient steps w.r.t. individual sub-functions ...". The Adam optimization algorithm is an extension to stochastic gradient descent that recently adopting most of the computer vision and natural language processing application. The method computes individual adaptive learning rates for different parameters from estimates of first and second moments of the gradients. Proposed method used ADAM Optimizer with learning rate $= 0.001$.

When using a neural network to perform classification and prediction task. A recent study shows that cross entropy function performs better than classification error and mean square error. Cross-entropy error, the weight changes don't get smaller and smaller and so training isn't s likely to stall out. Proposed method used categorical cross entropy (3) as loss function.

$$L_i = \sum_j t_{i,j} \log(p_{i,j}) \tag{3}$$

To make the optimizer converge faster and closer to the global minimum of the loss function, using an automatic Learning Rate reduction method. Learning rate is the step by which walks through the minimum loss. If higher learning rate use it will quickly converge and stuck in a local minimum instead of global minima. To keep the advantage of the fast computation time with a high Learning Rate, after each epoch model dynamically decreases the learning rate by monitoring the validation accuracy.

4   Model Evaluation

The dataset was divided into two portions - training data and test data. The model was tarined with the training data and then validated with the validation data. For Ishara-Lipi sign character database, after 30 epoch model gets 92.65% accuracy on the training set and 92.74% accuracy on the validation set. Figure 6 shows the loss value and accuracy of the training set and the validation.

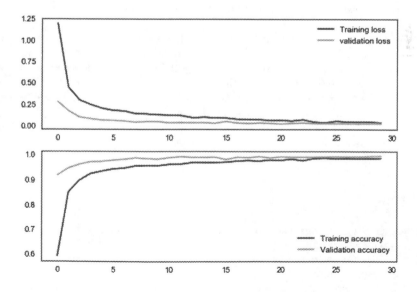

Fig. 6. Model evaluation graph.

5   Conclusion

Developing models that recognize sign from images is a challenging task. The capability of automatically recognize sign language could have a great impression on the lives of hearing impaired people. This will help them in their daily life communication.

In this paper, we represented a convolutional neural network (CNN) approach for a classification algorithm of Bangla Sign Language. The CNN have four convolutional layer which increases the speed and accurateness in recognition. CNN can create outcome in real-time manner and able to recognizing static sign language gesture. Here, we introduced a self-made large dataset that includes 1800 images of 36 alphabets for the Bangla Sign Language. This dataset is open for all researcher. We were capable of get an accuracy of 88% for our CNN classifier. By contributing to the arena of automatic sign language recognition the goal of our model is to reduce the difficulty of communication between hearing impaired people and normal people.

6   Future Work

Studying the boundary of this completed method like structure classification, a more exact sign recognition system can be exhibited. We will try to establish our model more efficient in future. We experiment for 36 Bengali alphabets and we will extent the accuracy for all the Bengali alphabets. In future, additional feature like body movements and facial expressions will proposed in BdSL. Enhance the vocabulary can also be computed as a future work. Our final destination, to build model for identify sign of the BdSL and to interpret them to Bangla text. We would like to conduct this model as a standard platform.

Acknowledgement. I would like to express my heartiest appreciation to all those who provided us the possibility to complete this research under the Daffodil International University. A special gratitude we give to Daffodil International University NLP and Machine Learning Research LAB for their instructions and support. Furthermore, I would also like to acknowledge that, this research partially supported by Bijaynagar Deaf School, Mirpur Deaf School, Mymensing Deaf School, CDD (Centre for Disability in Development) and all of the volunteers team who gave permission to collect valuable data. Any errors are our own and should not tarnish the reputations of these esteemed persons.

References

1. Press CU. Cambridge Dictionary (2017). https://dictionary.cambridge.org/dictionary/english/deaf
2. Press CU. Cambridge Dictionary (2017). https://dictionary.cambridge.org/dictionary/english/mute
3. LeCun, Y., Bottou, L., Bengio, Y., Haffner, P.: Gradient-based learning applied to document recognition. Proc. IEEE **86**(11), 2278–2324 (1998)

4. Agarwal, A., Thakur, M.: Sign language recognition using Microsoft Kinect. In: IEEE International Conference on Contemporary Computing (2013)
5. Beena, M.V., Namboodiri, M.N.A.: Automatic sign language finger spelling using convolutional neural network: analysis. Int. J. Pure Appl. Math. **177**(20), 9–15 (2017)
6. Kang, B., Tripathi, S., Nguyen, T.Q.: Real time sign language finger-spelling recognition using convolutional neural network from depth map. In: 3rd IAPR Asian Conference on Pattern Recognition (2015)
7. Rao, G.A., Syamala, K., Kishore, P.V.V., Sastry, A.S.C.S.: Deep Convolutional Neural Networks for Sign Language Recognition, Department of ECE, KL Deemed to be UNIVERSITY, SPACES-2018 (2018)
8. Hosoe, H., Sako, S., Kwolek, B.: Recognition of JSL finger spelling using convolutional neural networks. In: 15th IAPR International Conference on Machine Vision Application (MVA). Nagoya University, Nagoya, 8–12 May 2017
9. Huang, J., Zhou, W., Li, H., Li, W.: Sign language recognition using 3D convolutional neural networks, University of Science and Technology of China, Hefei, China (2015)
10. Mekala, P., Gao, Y., Fan, J., Davari, A.: Real-time sign language recognition based on neural network architecture. IEEE Conference, April 2011
11. Pigou, L., Dieleman, S., Kindermans, P.-J., Schrauwen, B.: Sign language recognition using convolutional neural networks. In: Agapito, L., Bronstein, M.M., Rother, C. (eds.) ECCV 2014. LNCS, vol. 8925, pp. 572–578. Springer, Cham (2015). https://doi.org/10.1007/978-3-319-16178-5_40
12. Tsai, B.-L., Huang, C.-L.: A vision-based Taiwanese sign language recognition system. In: International Conference of Pattern Recognition (2010)
13. Yasir, F., Prasad, P.W.C., Alsadoon, A., Elchouemi, A.: Bangla sign language recognition using convolutional neural network. In: International Conference on Intelligent Computing, Instrumentation and Control Technologies (ICICICT) (2017)

SISU - A Speaker Identification System from Short Utterances

Himadri Mukherjee[1]([✉]), Moumita Dutta[1], Sk Md. Obaidullah[2],
K. C. Santosh[3], Santanu Phadikar[4], and Kaushik Roy[1]

[1] Department of Computer Science, West Bengal State University, Kolkata, India
himadrim027@gmail.com, moumitadutta.email@gmail.com, kaushik.mrg@gmail.com
[2] Department of Computer Science and Engineering, Aliah University, Kolkata, India
sk.obaidullah@gmail.com
[3] Department of Computer Science, The University of South Dakota,
Vermillion, SD, USA
santosh.kc@ieee.org
[4] Department of Computer Science and Engineering,
Maulana Abul Kalam Azad University of Technology, Kolkata, India
sphadikar@yahoo.com

Abstract. Technology has made a paramount impact in our daily life over the last decade by assisting us in ways more than we could have imagined of in the last century. Safeguarding our identity in the digital world has been one of the primary concerns in this era and scientists have devoted their attention to biometric security for the same due to its array of advantages. Humans can be identified using a lot of biometrics and voice is one of them. SISU (Speaker Identification from Short Utterances) is a system proposed towards identification of humans from voice clips of very short length. The system works by Mel Frequency Cepstral Coefficient (MFCC) based features. The system was tested on a short utterance phoneme database of 3290 clips and a highest accuracy of 96.66% was obtained using Random Forest amidst different classifiers for the system.

Keywords: Speaker identification · Biometric · Phoneme · MFCC

1 Introduction

There was once a time when every task or the other was manually completed by humans from scratch. Such times now lay peacefully amidst the pages of History books due to the dedicated work of researchers from across the globe. Researchers have revolutionized technology to such an extent that we now have assistance for almost everything in our day to day life. The digital world has integrated beautifully with our daily life and we share a bond with the same which is stronger than ever. Such technological advancements have also brought along more sophisticated crimes, one of them being in the form of a threat to our identity in the digital world. To cope up with such problems, researchers

K. C. Santosh and R. S. Hegadi (Eds.): RTIP2R 2018, CCIS 1035, pp. 438–448, 2019.
https://doi.org/10.1007/978-981-13-9181-1_39

have come up with various means of making technology more secure. They have always attended to the fact of keeping everything simple and at the same time provide maximum security. Such thoughts have pointed them towards biometric based security which is harder to fool [1] and easier to handle. Speech is one of such biometrics which can be used to identify people with ease as it is very easy to obtain. Moreover in multifarious cases, like telephonic transactions, speech is the only biometric which can be used by a system to identify the caller. Another reason of using speech for security is because people use their voice all the time to communicate and they do not find it awkward or threatening to provide their voice for such purpose as compared to fingerprints, iris, etc. One of the goals of designing such systems is perhaps incorporating speaker identification capability in scenarios where minute fragments of speech samples are available. SISU is a system aimed towards performing this task. The working methodology of the proposed system is presented in Fig. 1.

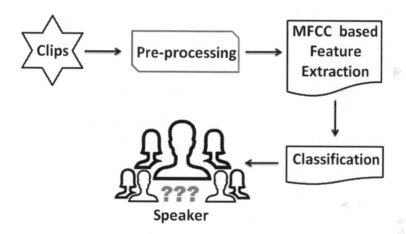

Fig. 1. Working methodology of the proposed methodology

In the rest of the paper, the related works are presented in Sect. 2, followed by the details of the database in Sect. 3. The proposed methodology encompassing pre-processing, development of feature set and classification is detailed in Sect. 4. Section 5 presents the result and discussion and finally the conclusion and future scope of work is presented in Sect. 6.

2 Related Works

Chakroun et al. [2] designed a speaker identification system using Support Vector machine for 80 speakers from the TIMIT database. The feature set comprised of 12 MFCC features along with log energy for 10 ms frames as well as deltas and double deltas ultimately leading to a 39 dimensional vector. The use of a RBF kernel produced a lowest equal error rate of 3.12% for the system. Chaudhari et al. [3] designed a speaker identification system using MFCC, log of energy, delta and double delta features. Vector quantization technique was used to generate speaker specific models and a highest accuracy of 96% was obtained for 75 speakers with the help of 30 MFCC filters and 32 quantization centroids. A Speaker Recognition system for smart TVs was designed by Tsai et al. [4] using spectral subtraction technique. The dataset consisted of 8 Mandarin commands, which were uttered 10 times each by 15 speakers. In order to test the system in real world scenario, noise was artificially added to the data. A highest accuracy of 89.1% was obtained for the system by modelling the speakers using GMMs. Indumathi et al. [5] employed Coiflet wavelet and singular value decomposition for feature extraction and selection respectively in order to identify 83 speakers. A highest accuracy of 94.29% was obtained for the system by applying Reptree classifier along with bagging technique. Chakroun et al. [6] used a hybrid approach to identify 64 speakers from the TIMIT database using both SVM and GMM. An accuracy of 100% was obtained for the system using 15 dimensional MFCC features. Lei et al. [7] proposed a Shannon's Entropy and Wavelet based feature to recognize speakers which was used along with Probabilistic Neural Networks. A highest accuracy of 89.9% was obtained for 40 speakers from the TIMIT database. Sardar et al. [8] adopted a Vector Quantization based approach coupled with MFCC features for speaker recognition from normal as well as whispered speech. The system produced accuracies of 91.40% and 68.56% for normal and whispered speech for 35 speakers and Euclidean distance was used to identify the unknown speakers. Ma et al. [9] designed a speaker identification system by adding MFCC values of 3 neighbouring frames into a single unit. They used a probability based model for capturing the characteristics of the speakers. A Histogram Transform Technique was used to estimate Probability Density Function of the features. The system produced an accuracy of 99.52% when evaluated on the TIMIT. Lin [10] used GMM based clustering technique for speaker identification in order to avoid the choice of a random initial cluster as in the case of K-means. 13 MFCC features along with their deltas and double deltas were used to characterize 67 speakers. 70% of the data was used for training and the remaining was used for testing and baseline accuracies of 99.87% and 93.87% were obtained for clustering and recognition. Biagetti et al. [11] designed a speaker identification system using truncated discrete Karhunen - Loé ve transform of speech signals. The system produed a highest accuracy of 100% for 30 speakers and a lowest of 91.86% for 100 speakers while the accuracy was 99.11% for 50 speakers. Shafee et al. [12] designed a system to recognize speakers in noisy environment. The use of Grammatone Frequency Cepstral Coefficient features coupled with Radial basis Neural Network yielded an accuracy of 84.25%. The system was tested using 8 Telugu commands, spoken 10 times each by 10 speakers. The command list comprised of upwards, downwards, start, stop, forward, reverse left and right in Telugu. Al-Kaltakchi et al. [13] designed a speaker identification system for 120 speakers from the TIMIT database with the help of MFCC and Power Normal Cepstral Coefficient which produced a highest accuracy of 95%. AboElenein et al. [14] designed a speaker identification system to work in real time using MFCC features and GMM. The system detected gender prior feature extraction of the voice signals. The feature dimension was reduced by applying vector quantization and a test case was matched in the gender separated datasets after determining its gender. The system produced a highest accuracy of 91% with a testing time of 0.1051 s on the CHAINS corpus.

3 Dataset

One of the most important aspects of any experiment is the data around which it revolves. Every language consists of a set of sounds called phonemes which are used in combination to form words. Phonemes are the smallest sound units of any language which inspired us to record phonemes from speakers in order to explore our system's capability of identifying speakers from short utterances. Our database was built with the aid of 47 volunteers who uttered Bangla vowel phonemes. The distribution of male and female volunteers is presented in Fig. 2. Bangla was chosen because it is one of the most widely spoken languages in the world with approximately 261,862,630 speakers [15] which makes it the 6th most popular language in the world [15]. The vowel phonemes were recorded because of the fact that they are one of the most essential entities in the formation of words. Very few meaningful words can be found for various languages which do not have a vowel phoneme.

Distribution of male and female subjects

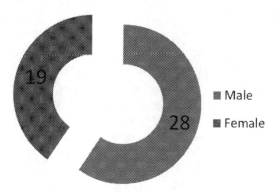

Fig. 2. Distribution of male and female speakers in the dataset.

The speakers pronounced the 7 vowel phonemes one after the other. This was repeated 10 times each. The uttered vowel phonemes along with a use for word formation is presented in Table 1.

Table 1. Symbolic and Bangla alphabetic representation of the Bangla vowel phonemes along with example of pronunciation.

IPA Symbol	ɔ	a	i	u	e	o	æ
Bangla Representation	অ	আ	ই, ঈ	উ, ঊ	এ	ও	অ্যা
Bangla Pronunciation as in	অনিল	আকা	বিষ	তুলো	বেল	রোজ	টেরা
Equivalent English Pronunciation	Dot	Meta	She	Rule	Gate	Moal	Cap

The recorded phoneme tracks were then separated semi automatically using an amplitude based approach which finally produced a Bangla Phoneme database of 3290 phonemes. The average clip length our database was found to be as low as 0.80 s. The phoneme wise average clip lengths are presented in Table 2.

Table 2. Average duration of the phonemes

Phonemes	Average Time (secs.)
ɔ	0.811879577
a	0.813524774
i	0.761695856
u	0.763069764
e	0.795970666
o	0.764227674
æ	0.874713466
Average	0.797868825

4   Proposed Method

4.1   Pre-processing

The spectral properties of an audio clip highly fluctuate throughout its entire length thereby posing difficulty in analysis. In order to reduce such fluctuations, the clips are divided into smaller frames having quasi stationary spectral characteristics. In our experiment, the audio clips were framed in overlapping mode as presented in [16]. The frame size was chosen to be of 256 sample points and the overlap factor was chosen to be 156 sample points as presented in [16].

Minute jitters often arise in the frames post framing which lead to spectral leakage during analysis of the clips in the frequency domain. In order to cope up with such issues, the frames are passed through a windowing function. In our experiment, Hamming window was chosen for this purpose whose utility is presented in [16]. The Hamming window ($H(n)$) is mathematically illustrated as under. where, n ranges from start to end of a frame of size N.

$$H(n) = 0.54 - 0.46 \cos\left(\frac{2\pi n}{N-1}\right), \tag{1}$$

4.2   Feature Extraction

Mel Frequency Cepstral Coefficient (MFCC) is widely used in speech based applications [17,18]. Every sound is composed of a set of frequencies which is termed as the frequency envelope whose shape determines what we actually perceive. MFCC is an artificial way of representing this envelope. The Mel filter bank (as presented in Fig. 3) was used to generate frame wise MFCC coefficients. We had extracted 19 standard MFCC coefficients whose utility for audio based applications is presented in [17,18].

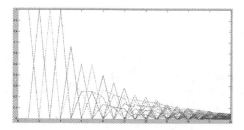

Fig. 3. Mel filter bank.

Since the clips were of disparate lengths so disparate number of frames were obtained for the clips. As we had extracted MFCC features for every frame, so features of different dimensions were obtained. In order to overcome this problem and obtain a feature whose dimension was static irrespective of the length of the clips, we computed the total energy in each of the bands. These values were used to grade the bands in ascending order. Along with these values, we computed the mean and standard deviation of each band as well. These values were also appended to the feature vector. It was observed that a clip of only 1 s produced 440 frames in accordance with the adopted framing strategy which yielded a feature of 8360 (19 * 440) dimension. However, using our proposed technique, a feature of 57 (19 grades + 19 means + 19 standard deviations) dimension was obtained.

We had further computed 15, 30 and 45 dimensional features to design a system with lower computational overhead whose details are presented in the subsequent paragraphs.

4.3   Classification

We had applied different popularly used classifiers on each of the feature sets. The selected classifiers are Random Forest (RF) [19], Naïve Bayes (NB) [20], Support Vector Machine (SVM) [21], Multi Layer Perceptron (MLP) [22] and LibLINEAR (Lib) [23]. These classifiers are briefly detailed as under:

Random Forest is an ensemble learning based classifier which works by combining the result of multiple decision tress built at the time of training. It is suitable both for classification as well as regression. It does not suffer from the problem of over fitting in terms of the training set which often occurs for decision trees.

Support Vector Machine abbreviated as SVM is a supervised learner which is suitable both for classification and regression. It generates an optimal hyperplane in accordance to its parameters from the training set which separates the instances according to their given class label.

Multi Layer Perceptron abbreviated as MLP is a neural network based classifier which uses backpropagation at the time of training. It consists of input, hidden and output layer. The number of neurons in the input layer correspond to the number of features while that of the output layer correspond to the number of classes. Neurons of different layers are connected by means of weight associated links.

LibLinear is a linear type of classifier which has the capability of handling large number of instances as well as high dimensional features. It can also be applied to regression problems. It also has the feature of model selection by means of cross validation.

Naïve Bayes based classifiers work are probabilistic classifiers which work in accordance with the bayes' theorem. It is highly scalable and assumes that the value of a feature is not dependent on any other given feature.

We used WEKA [24] in our classification tasks and a 5 fold cross validation technique for the purpose of evaluation.

5   Result and Discussion

Each of the 15, 30 45 and 57 dimensional feature sets were subjected to the classifiers whose results are presented in Table 3. It can be seen that Random Forest produced the best result for the 57 dimensional feature. Further experiments were carried out on this feature set with Random forest for obtaining better results.

Table 3. Performance of the classifiers on different feature dimensions.

	RF	SVM	MLP	LIB	NB
15	75.50	60.49	59.12	48.66	40.97
30	88.75	77.48	78.24	70.12	53.86
45	93.13	79.12	83.77	72.64	57.14
57	95.11	79.48	87.51	48.66	68.09

The number of cross validation folds were varied from 2 to 25 whose results are presented in Table 4. It is observed that the best accuracy was obtained for 20 fold cross validation. We also experimented by varying the bag size from 100 to 500. No change of accuracy was observed for this so the default bag size of 100 was used.

Table 4. Results of random forest on the 57 dimensional feature set for different folds of cross validation.

2	3	4	5	6
90.88	94.01	94.71	95.11	95.08
7	8	9	10	11
95.44	95.32	95.50	95.50	95.53
12	13	14	15	16
95.44	95.71	95.78	95.65	95.87
17	18	19	20	21
95.62	95.74	95.98	96.05	95.87
22	23	24	25	
95.99	95.84	95.38	95.71	

The number of training iterations were varied for 20 fold cross validation. The obtained results are presented in Table 5 where it can be seen that the highest accuracy was obtained for 1200 iterations which is the overall highest in our experiment.

Table 5. Results of random forest on the 57 dimensional feature set for different training epochs.

100	200	300	400	500
96.05	96.38	96.14	96.29	96.38
600	700	800	900	1000
96.47	96.54	96.44	96.44	96.47
1100	1200	1300	1400	1500
96.57	96.66	96.54	96.60	96.63

5.1   Statistical Significance Test

We carried out Friedman's test [25] on the 57 dimensional feature dataset for testing statistical significance. We divided the dataset into 5 parts and each of the parts were subjected to all 5 classifiers. The obtained ranks and accuracies for the different classifiers and different parts of the dataset is presented in Table 6. The value of (χ_F^2) [25] was calculated in accordance with the under mentioned formula where R_j is the mean rank of the jth classifier.

$$\chi_F^2 = \frac{12N}{k(k+1)} \left[\sum_j R_j^2 - \frac{k(k+1)^2}{4} \right]. \tag{2}$$

The standard critical value of (χ_F^2) was found to be 18.467 at a significance level of 0.001 for the afore mentioned setup. We obtained a value of 20 for (χ_F^2) thereby rejecting the null hypothesis.

Table 6. Distribution of ranks and accuracies for different classifiers on the 57 dimensional feature set.

Classifiers		Parts of the dataset					Mean rank
		1	2	3	4	5	
Random forest	A	56.54	70.52	67.78	70.97	70.52	1.0
	R	(1.0)	(1.0)	(1.0)	(1.0)	(1.0)	
SVM	A	15.5	15.96	15.05	12.61	13.07	5.0
	R	(5.0)	(5.0)	(5.0)	(5.0)	(5.0)	
MLP	A	46.66	50.91	52.28	47.26	51.52	2.0
	R	(2.0)	(2.0)	(2.0)	(2.0)	(2.0)	
Lib linear	A	38.45	38.91	37.69	38.45	38.15	4.0
	R	(4.0)	(4.0)	(4.0)	(4.0)	(4.0)	
Naive Bayes	A	45.14	46.2	46.5	44.68	44.68	3.0
	R	(3.0)	(3.0)	(3.0)	(3.0)	(3.0)	

6   Conclusion

In this paper, a system is presented for speaker identification from short utterances. The system has been tested on a phoneme database of 3290. The best result has been obtained for 57 dimensional MFCC based features and Random Forest based classification with a precision of 0.967. We plan to experiment with different machine learning techniques including clustering-based techniques like [26] and active learning-based approaches [27] as well as employ other audio features. In future, we will also employ different pre-processing techniques to remove header and trailer silence parts in order to obtain better identification accuracy. We also plan to test the system on a larger dataset in both even and uneven number of samples per speaker scenario.

References

1. Jain, A.K., Ross, A., Prabhakar, S.: An introduction to biometric recognition. IEEE Trans. Circuits Syst. Video Technol. **14**(1), 4–20 (2004)
2. Chakroun, R., Zouari, L.B., Frikha, M., Hamida, A.B.: A novel approach based on support vector machines for automatic speaker identification. In: AICCSA-2015. IEEE (2015)
3. Chaudhari, A., Rahulkar, A., Dhonde, S.B.: Combining dynamic features with MFCC for text-independent speaker identification. In: ICIP-2015, pp. 160–164. IEEE (2015)
4. Tsai, W.H., Lin, J.C., Ma, C.H., Liao, Y.F.: Speaker identification for personalized smart TVs. In: ICCE-TW-2016, pp. 1–2. IEEE (2016)
5. Indumathi, A., Chandra, E.: Speaker identification using bagging techniques. In: ICCCS-2015, pp. 223–229. IEEE (2015)
6. Chakroun, R., Zouari, L.B., Frikha, M., Hamida, A.B.: A hybrid system based on GMM-SVM for speaker identification. In: ISDA-2015, pp. 654–658. IEEE (2015)

7. Lei, L., She, K.: Speaker identification using wavelet Shannon entropy and probabilistic neural network. In: ICNC-FSKD-2016, pp. 566–571. IEEE (2016)
8. Sardar, V.M., Shrbahadurkar, S.D.: Speaker identification with whispered speech mode using MFCC: challenges to whispered speech identification. In: ICIP-2015, pp. 70–74. IEEE (2015)
9. Ma, Z., Yu, H., Tan, Z.H., Guo, J.: Text-independent speaker identification using the histogram transform model. IEEE Access **4**, 9733–9739 (2016)
10. Lin, W.: An improved GMM-based clustering algorithm for efficient speaker identification. In: ICCSNT-2015, vol. 1, pp. 1490–1493. IEEE (2015)
11. Biagetti, G., Crippa, P., Falaschetti, L., Orcioni, S., Turchetti, C.: An investigation on the accuracy of truncated DKLT representation for speaker identification with short sequences of speech frames. IEEE Trans. Cybern. **47**(12), 4235–4249 (2017)
12. Shafee, S., Anuradha, B.: Speaker identification and Spoken word recognition in noisy background using artificial neural networks. In: ICEEOT-2016, pp. 912–917. IEEE (2016)
13. Al-Kaltakchi, M.T., Woo, W.L., Dlay, S.S., Chambers, J.A.: Study of statistical robust closed set speaker identification with feature and score-based fusion. In: SSP-2016, pp. 1–5. IEEE (2016)
14. AboElenein, N.M., Amin, K.M., Ibrahim, M., Hadhoud, M.M.: Improved text-independent speaker identification system for real time applications. In: JEC-ECC-2016, pp. 58–62. IEEE (2016)
15. Lewis, M.P., Simons, G.F., Fennig, C.D.: Ethnologue: Languages of the World, vol. 16. SIL International, Dallas (2009)
16. Mukherjee, H., Halder, C., Phadikar, S., Roy, K.: READ—a Bangla phoneme recognition system. In: Satapathy, S., Bhateja, V., Udgata, S., Pattnaik, P. (eds.) AISC, vol. 515, pp. 599–607. Springer, Singapore (2017). https://doi.org/10.1007/978-981-10-3153-3_59
17. Mukherjee, H., Halder, C., Phadikar, S., Roy, K.: READ—a Bangla phoneme recognition system. In: Satapathy, S.C., Bhateja, V., Udgata, S.K., Pattnaik, P.K. (eds.) Proceedings of the 5th International Conference on Frontiers in Intelligent Computing: Theory and Applications. AISC, vol. 515, pp. 599–607. Springer, Singapore (2017). https://doi.org/10.1007/978-981-10-3153-3_59
18. Mukherjee, H., Dhar, A., Phadikar, S., Roy, K.: RECAL-a language identification system. In: ICSPC-2017, pp. 300–304. IEEE (2017)
19. Breiman, L.: Random forests. Mach. Learn. **45**(1), 5–32 (2001)
20. John, G.H., Langley, P.: Estimating continuous distributions in Bayesian classifiers. In: UAI-1995, pp. 338–345. Morgan Kaufmann Publishers Inc., August 1995
21. Cristianini, N., Shawe-Taylor, J.: An Introduction to Support Vector Machines and Other Kernel-Based Learning Methods. Cambridge University Press, Cambridge (2000)
22. Obaidullah, S.M., Mondal, A., Das, N., Roy, K.: Script identification from printed Indian document images and performance evaluation using different classifiers. Appl. Comput. Intell. Soft Comput. **2014**, 22 (2014)
23. Fan, R.E., Chang, K.W., Hsieh, C.J., Wang, X.R., Lin, C.J.: LIBLINEAR: a library for large linear classification. J. Mach. Learn. Res. **9**(Aug), 1871–1874 (2008)
24. Hall, M., Frank, E., Holmes, G., Pfahringer, B., Reutemann, P., Witten, I.H.: The WEKA data mining software: an update. ACM SIGKDD Explor. Newsl. **11**(1), 10–18 (2009)
25. Demšar, J.: Statistical comparisons of classifiers over multiple data sets. J. Mach. Learn. Res. **7**, 1–30 (2006)

26. Vajda, S., Santosh, K.C.: A fast k-nearest neighbor classifier using unsupervised clustering. In: Santosh, K.C., Hangarge, M., Bevilacqua, V., Negi, A. (eds.) RTIP2R 2016. CCIS, vol. 709, pp. 185–193. Springer, Singapore (2017). https://doi.org/10.1007/978-981-10-4859-3_17

27. Bouguelia, M.R., Nowaczyk, S., Santosh, K.C., Verikas, A.: Agreeing to disagree: active learning with noisy labels without crowdsourcing. Int. J. Mach. Learn. Cybern. **9**, 1–13 (2017)

Lazy Learning Based Segregation of Top-3 South Indian Languages with LSF-A Feature

Himadri Mukherjee[1]([☒]), Moumita Dutta[1], Sk. Md. Obaidullah[2],
K. C. Santosh[3]([☒]), Santanu Phadikar[4], and Kaushik Roy[1]

[1] Department of Computer Science, West Bengal State University, Kolkata, India
himadrim027@gmail.com, moumitadutta.email@gmail.com, kaushik.mrg@gmail.com
[2] Department of Computer Science and Engineering, Aliah University, Kolkata, India
sk.obaidullah@gmail.com
[3] Department of Computer Science, The University of South Dakota,
Vermillion, SD, USA
santosh.kc@ieee.org
[4] Department of Computer Science and Engineering,
Maulana Abul Kalam Azad University of Technology, Kolkata, India
sphadikar@yahoo.com

Abstract. Identification of language from voice signals is known as automatic language identification. It is very important for speech recognition in multi lingual countries like India where people use more than a single language while talking. Language identification for South Indian languages is difficult for a person without prior knowledge. In this paper, the top 3 most spoken languages of South India namely Telugu, Tamil and Kannada has been distinguished with the help of line spectral frequency based features namely LSF-A (Line spectral frequency-Approximation). Experiments have been performed on multiple datasets having as many as 21700 clips and a highest accuracy of 99.70% has been obtained with a lazy learning-based classifier.

Keywords: Language identification · Lazy learning ·
Line spectral frequency

1 Introduction

Speech recognition has developed significantly and people have benefited greatly from such advancements in the form of speech recognition enabled solutions. However, residents of different multilingual countries like India have not been able to take full advantage of the same. One reason for this is multilingual conversations as people are habituated in using keywords and phrases from multiple languages while talking. The complexity of Indic languages is also another issue for this. A speech recognizer first needs to understand the language of the input words prior to attempting recognition which demands for a language

© Springer Nature Singapore Pte Ltd. 2019
K. C. Santosh and R. S. Hegadi (Eds.): RTIP2R 2018, CCIS 1035, pp. 449–459, 2019.
https://doi.org/10.1007/978-981-13-9181-1_40

identification system. Such a system can help in invoking the language specific speech recognizers for different portions of the input thereby enabling multi lingual speakers to take advantage of the speech recognition based solutions. Multimedia contents like audio and video have also increased rapidly with the advent of technology. Most of these data are unstructured [1] which makes it difficult to retrieve required items. A language identifier can aid to this problem as well in most cases by narrowing down the search space based on the language of the searched audio or video content. Among different Indic languages it is particularly difficult to distinguish South Indian languages especially for a person with no prior knowledge of the same.

Manwani et al. [2] used Gaussian mixture model based features for language identification. They also used split and merge expectation maximization algorithm for training the system. They obtained improvements in the learning phase which thereby produced better performance. They experimented with 4 languages namely Hindi, Telugu, Gujarati and English with clip lengths in the range of 2–10 s and obtained an accuracy of 82.65% for all the languages. Gonzalez-Dominguez et al. [3] have experimented with multilingual speech recognition. They experimented with 8 languages in the thick of German, English, Spanish, French, Italian, Japanese, Russian and Chinese. They obtained an accuracy of 80% using only DNN which rose to 90% on using a weighted combination DNN based language identification and speech recognition confidence measures. Jin et al. [4] used language identification senones for classifying 23 languages from the NIST LRE 2009 dataset. They obtained a lowest equal error rate of 1.41 for 30 s clips using language identification network and i-vectors.

Aarti et al. [5] applied artificial neural network for language identification from Indian languages. They experimented with 75 h of data from 9 languages in the thick of Marathi, Hindi, Bangla, Gujarati, Tamil, Malayalam, Assamese, Kannada and Telugu. They used MFCC based features including deltas and double deltas and obtained accuracies as high as 44.61%. Bekker et al. [6] used intra cluster training technique for training a deep neural network for the task of language identification. They experimented with the NIST 2015 language recognition challenge dataset consisting of 50 languages. The deep neural network had two fully connected hidden layers with 200 and 100 neurons. They used a soft-max output layer and ReLU activation function coupled with mini batch stochastic gradient descent technique with momentum for optimization. Among different employed clustering techniques the best result was obtained for confusion matrix based clustering technique.

Revathi et al. [7] experimented with 7 Indian classical languages in the thick of Hindi, Kannada, Bangla, Malayalam, Marathi, Tamil and Telugu. Experiments were performed on a corpus composed of 1000 thousand sentences from each language which were recorded in studio environment and a highest accuracy of 99.4% was obtained. Lopez-Moreno et al. [8] used deep neural networks and short term acoustic features for language identification. They experimented with the Google 5M LID and NIST LRE 2009 datasets and obtained upto 70% performance improvement over the standard baseline system. A lowest average equal error rate 0f 9.58 was obtained for the NIST dataset.

In this paper, we have distinguished the top 3 South Indian languages namely Telugu, Tamil and Kannada. We have used line spectral frequency based features namely line spectral frequency-approximation (LSF-A) coupled with a lazy learning based classification. The system has been tested on over 30 h of data which are detailed in the subsequent paragraphs. A bird's eye illustration of our proposed system is presented in Fig. 1.

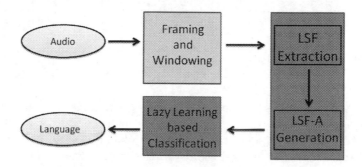

Fig. 1. Bird's eye view of the proposed methodology

In the rest of the paper, Sects. 2 and 3 presents the details of the used dataset and our proposed methodology respectively. The results are presented in Sect. 4 and the conclusion in Sect. 5.

2   Dataset

In the current experiment, the top 3 South Indian languages namely Telugu, Tamil and Kannada [9] were chosen. The audio clips were extracted from different news videos, interviews, talk shows available on YouTube [10]. More than 30 h of data for these languages were collected whose language wise distribution is presented in Table 1.

Table 1. Duration of data per language.

Language	Telugu	Tamil	Kannada
Duration (HH:MM:SS)	10:02:48	10:04:08	10:04:10

This data was used to engender 4 datasets D1, D2, D3 and D4 having clips of length 5, 10, 15 and 20 s respectively which detailed in Table 2.

The clips had multiple ambient backgrounds like studio condition, living room condition, outdoor condition etc. Moreover, there was presence of keywords from different languages within a single clip. It was ensured that the data had both the effect of multiple ambiances as well as multilingual speech in order to uphold real life scenario.

Table 2. Number of clips per language in the generated datasets.

Dataset (Clip length in seconds)	Number of clips			
	Telugu	Tamil	Kannada	Total
D1 (5)	7217	7242	7241	21700
D2 (10)	3604	3619	3618	10841
D3 (15)	2392	2410	2408	7210
D4 (20)	1792	1807	1804	5403

3 Proposed Method

3.1 Framing and Windowing

An audio signal consists of multiple frequency components which fluctuate throughout its entire length. Such fluctuations interfere with frequency based analysis of the signals. In order to tackle this problem, the signal is partitioned into smaller frames. The spectral characteristics within such frames tend to be pseudo stationary. Framing the signal in overlapping manner further ensures the continuity in between 2 successive frames. A signal consisting of x points can be subdivided into y frames of size z with o overlapping points. The mathematical expression for the same is demonstrated as under. We segmented the signals into 256 sample point wide frames with an inter frame overlap of 100 points due to its utility as demonstrated in [11].

$$y = \left\lceil \frac{x - z}{O} + 1 \right\rceil \tag{1}$$

It is very important to remove jitters from the frames which causes spectral leakage at the time of analysis. The frames are usually multiplied with a windowing function for doing the same. Here, we used Hamming Window as presented in [11]. The Hamming window (H(n)) is mathematically illustrated as under. where, n ranges from start to end of a frame of size N.

$$H(n) = 0.54 - 0.46 \cos\left(\frac{2\pi n}{N - 1}\right), \tag{2}$$

3.2 Feature Extraction

Line Spectral Frequency Extraction: Itakura et al. [12] devised a unique technique for representation of linear predictive coefficients termed as line spectral frequency (LSF). This technique ensures both high interpolation as well as effective quantization capability. Here, a signal is presented as the output of H(z) which is an all pole filter. The inverse of H(z) is presented as X(z) which is shown below, where $x_{1...T}$ are the are the predictive coefficients upto T^{th} order.

$$X(z) = 1 + x_1 z^{-1} + x_2 z^{-2} + x_3 z^{-3} + \ldots\ldots + x_T z^{-T} \tag{3}$$

The LSF representation is obtained by decomposing X(z) into $X_1(z)$ and $X_2(z)$ which are presented in the equations as under.

$$X_1(z) = X(z) + z^{-(T+1)}X(z^{-1}) \tag{4}$$

$$X_2(z) = X(z) - z^{-(T+1)}X(z^{-1}) \tag{5}$$

5, 10, 15 and 20 dimensional frame wise LSFs were extracted for the clips in our experiment.

Line Spectral Frequency-Approximation (LSF-A) Generation: In real life, audio clips have different durations which lead to disparate number of frames. Since, features were extracted for each frame, thus features of different dimensions were obtained. In order to make the feature dimension even, the feature values were analysed to obtain the overall highest and lowest energy values. These values were used to define 18 equally spaced classes. The occurrence of energy values in each of these classes for every band was computed. If 5 dimensional LSFs were extracted for a clip of just 1 s then a feature of 2200 (5×440) dimension was obtained. However, using LSF-A, the feature dimension was brought down to 90 $(18 * 5)$. On analysing the generated features, it was observed that there were some features which had the same value for all the instances. Such feature values were identified and discarded which further brought down the feature dimension. The obtained feature dimensions for the different datasets using LSFs of different dimensions before and after removal of the redundant features is presented in Table 3.

Table 3. Feature dimensions for the different datasets.

Dataset	LSF dimension	Feature dimension before reduction	Feature dimension after reduction
D1	5	90	57
	10	180	81
	15	270	98
	20	360	109
D2	5	90	58
	10	180	81
	15	270	98
	20	360	110
D3	5	90	58
	10	180	82
	15	270	99
	20	360	110
D4	5	90	57
	10	180	81
	15	270	98
	20	360	111

The trend of the feature values for the 20 dimensional LSF on D4 is presented in Fig. 2. This feature set was chosen for illustration because it produced the best result, which is detailed in the next Section.

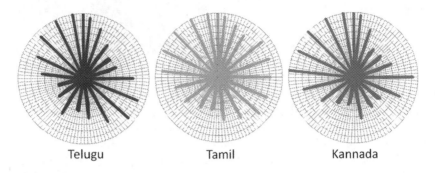

Telugu   Tamil   Kannada

Fig. 2. Trend of the 20 dimensional LSFs for the 3 languages on D4.

3.3 Classification

We used a lazy learning based classification technique in the present experiment. In the case of a single training set scenario and limited number of test case predictions at a stretch, lazy learners have a computation advantage [13]. This type of scenario is often observed in real life which motivated us to use lazy learning based algorithm for classification. Lazy learners are also suitable for such scenarios where the training data is often updated [13] as in the case of gradually learning systems. Lazy classifiers do not commit to a single hypothesis as because they generalize the data only when an instance is supplied for classification. In this technique, the approximation of target function for each query is done locally which enables it to solve multiple problems simultaneously thereby making it suitable for parallel processing systems.

K* classifier [14] is a lazy learner which was used in our experiment. It works based on entropic distance between instances for classification. It has the capability of handling real valued attributes, symbolic attributes and missing values consistently. In this technique, the distance between 2 instances is based on the complexity of transforming one instance to the other. The K* distance between 2 instances e and f is presented as under.

$$K^*(e|f) = -\log_2 P^*(e|f) \quad where, \tag{6}$$

$$P^*(e|f) = \sum_{\overline{r}\varepsilon P:\overline{r}(f)=e} p(\overline{r}) \tag{7}$$

Here, $0 \le P^*(e|f) \le 1$ $\overline{r}(f) = e$ refers to a transformation sequence or path for converting instance f to e.

$p(\overline{r})$ denotes the probability of the path where,

$$\overline{r}(f) = r_n(r_{n-1}(r_{n-2}(...r_1(f)))) \quad and \tag{8}$$

$\overline{r} = r_1, r_2, ..., r_n, r\varepsilon R$ (R is a finite set of transformations on I)
$\forall r\varepsilon R, r : I \rightarrow I$, where I is a set of instances.

5 fold cross validation scheme for the purpose of evaluation was applied for all the datasets due to its utility as demonstrated in [15,16].

4   Result and Discussion

Each of the datasets for all of the feature dimensions were fed to the K* classifier whose results are tabulated in Table 4.

Table 4. Obtained accuracies for the different LSF dimensions on the D1–D4.

	5	10	15	20
D1	98.37	99.25	99.40	99.40
D2	98.89	99.46	99.61	99.58
D3	99.02	99.53	99.61	99.61
D4	99.20	99.65	99.63	99.70

It can be observed from the Table, that the highest accuracy was obtained for the 20 s clip dataset with 20 dimensional LSFs. It was observed that different clips had silence portions, background noise only sections, intro and outro music. In the case of 20 s clips, the quantity of voiced and unvoiced data was close which led to the slightly higher accuracy than the rest. The language wise performance for the same is presented in Fig. 3 with the highest accuracy in green. It was found that Kannada had slightly lower noise content as compared to the other 2 languages which helped in obtaining the best performance. It can also be observed from Table 4 that the performance for D1 which is almost 4 times the size of D4 did not lack behind.

The percentages of confusion among the language pairs for the best result is presented in Table 5. It can be observed from the Table that the Tamil-Telugu language pair produced a highest confusion of 0.84%. This is primarily due to the fact that the different interviews in these 2 languages had keywords and phrases from each other as well as English phrases. Another reason for this confusion is the utterance of names of people and places common to both. We had also tested the performance of some other popular classifiers in the thick of LibSVM, LibLINEAR, Random Forest, Naïve Bayes and Multi layer perceptron using WEKA [17] on the 20 dimensional D4 (best result) whose accuracies are presented in Fig. 4. It can be seen in the Figure that MLP also produced similar accuracy to that of K* but the model building time is quite high of the former as compared to the later.

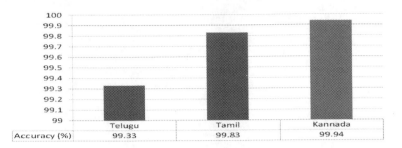

Fig. 3. Individual accuracies for the 3 languages for 20 dimensional LSF on D4.

Table 5. Percentages of confusion among the different language pairs for 20 dimensional LSF on D4.

	Telugu	Tamil	Kannada
Telugu	–	0.67	0.0
Tamil	0.17	–	0.0
Kannada	0.0	0.06	–

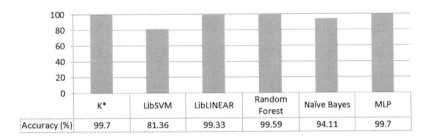

Fig. 4. Performance of different classifiers for 20 dimensional LSF on D4.

4.1   Statistical Significance Test

The robust non parametric Friedman's test was performed on the 20 dimensional D4 (best result) for testing statistical significance. The dataset was divided into 7 parts (N) and each of the parts were subjected to all the 6 (k) classifiers. The obtained ranks and accuracies of the classifiers along with their accuracies for the different parts of D4 is presented in Table 6 which aided in calculating the Friedman statistic (χ_F^2) [18] which is presented below.

$$\chi_F^2 = \frac{12N}{k(k+1)} \left[\sum_j R_j^2 - \frac{k(k+1)^2}{4} \right], \tag{9}$$

where, R_j is the mean rank of the jth classifier.

Table 6. Obtained ranks and accuracies of the classifiers for 20 dimensional LSF on D4.

Classifiers		Parts of D4							Mean rank
		1	2	3	4	5	6	7	
K*	A	99.74	99.61	99.48	99.74	99.35	99.48	99.87	2.64
	R	(3.0)	(2.0)	(2.0)	(3.0)	(4.0)	(3.0)	(1.5)	
Lib SVM	A	89.23	88.98	82.49	81.84	81.71	82.83	81.21	6.0
	R	(6.0)	(6.0)	(6.0)	(6.0)	(6.0)	(6.0)	(6.0)	
Lib LINEAR	A	99.87	99.61	99.48	100.0	99.74	99.61	99.87	1.64
	R	(1.5)	(2.0)	(2.0)	(1.0)	(2.5)	(1.0)	(1.5)	
Random forest	A	99.61	99.48	99.35	99.74	99.74	99.48	99.61	3.42
	R	(4.0)	(4.0)	(4.0)	(3.0)	(2.5)	(3.0)	(3.5)	
Naïve Bayes	A	98.18	97.8	97.67	97.15	97.54	97.15	99.61	4.79
	R	(5.0)	(5.0)	(5.0)	(5.0)	(5.0)	(5.0)	(3.5)	
MLP	A	99.87	99.61	99.48	99.74	99.87	99.48	99.49	2.5
	R	(1.5)	(2.0)	(2.0)	(3.0)	(1.0)	(3.0)	(5.0)	

The critical value of (χ_F^2) at a significance level of 0.001 was found to be 20.515 for the present setup. We obtained a value of 26.18, thereby successfully rejecting the null hypothesis.

5   Conclusion

In this paper, the top 3 South Indian languages are segregated with LSF-A features and lazy learning. Encouraging accuracies have been obtained for different clip lengths with a highest average precision of 0.997. In future, experiments will be carried out on a larger dataset and other languages will also be included in the study. We plan to use other speech parametrization techniques coupled with the newly evolving machine learning techniques like active learning [19] and clustering based approaches [20,21] for our experiments. We also plan to use different pre-processing mechanisms in the thick of noise removal and voice activity detection [22] to make the system more robust and obtain better performance.

References

1. Manjunath, T.N., Hegadi, R.S., Ravikumar, G.K.: A survey on multimedia data mining and its relevance today. IJCSNS **10**(11), 165–170 (2010)
2. Manwani, N., Mitra, S.K., Joshi, M.V.: Spoken language identification for indian languages using split and merge EM algorithm. In: Ghosh, A., De, R.K., Pal, S.K. (eds.) PReMI 2007. LNCS, vol. 4815, pp. 463–468. Springer, Heidelberg (2007)

3. Gonzalez-Dominguez, J., Eustis, D., Lopez-Moreno, I., Senior, A., Beaufays, F., Moreno, P.J.: A real-time end-to-end multilingual speech recognition architecture. IEEE J. Sel. Top. Sig. Process. **9**(4), 749–759 (2015)
4. Jin, M., et al.: LID-senones and their statistics for language identification. IEEE/ACM Trans. Audio Speech Lang. Process. (TASLP) **26**(1), 171–183 (2018)
5. Aarti, B., Kopparapu, S.K.: Spoken Indian language classification using artificial neural network–an experimental study. In: 2017 4th International Conference on Signal Processing and Integrated Networks (SPIN), pp. 424–430. IEEE (2017)
6. Bekker, A.J., Opher, I., Lapidot, I., Goldberger, J.: Intra-cluster training strategy for deep learning with applications to language identification. In: 2016 IEEE 26th International Workshop on Machine Learning for Signal Processing (MLSP), pp. 1–6. IEEE (2016)
7. Revathi, A., Jeyalakshmi, C., Muruganantham, T.: Perceptual features based rapid and robust language identification system for various indian classical languages. In: Hemanth, D.J., Smys, S. (eds.) Computational Vision and Bio Inspired Computing. LNCVB, vol. 28, pp. 291–305. Springer, Cham (2018). https://doi.org/10.1007/978-3-319-71767-8_25
8. Lopez-Moreno, I., Gonzalez-Dominguez, J., Plchot, O., Martinez, D., Gonzalez-Rodriguez, J., Moreno, P.: Automatic language identification using deep neural networks. In: 2014 IEEE International Conference on Acoustics, Speech and Signal Processing (ICASSP), pp. 5337–5341. IEEE (2014)
9. Lewis, M.P., Simons, G.F., Fennig, C.D.: Ethnologue: Languages of the world, vol. 16. SIL International, Dallas (2009)
10. https://www.youtube.com/ . Accessed 10 May 2018
11. Mukherjee, H., Phadikar, S., Roy, K.: An ensemble learning-based Bangla phoneme recognition system using LPCC-2 features. In: Bhateja, V., Coello Coello, C., Satapathy, S., Pattnaik, P. (eds.) Intelligent Engineering Informatics. AISC, vol. 695, pp. 61–69. Springer, Singapore (2018). https://doi.org/10.1007/978-981-10-7566-7_7
12. Itakura, F.: Line spectrum representation of linear predictor coefficients of speech signals. J. Acoust. Soc. Am. **57**(S1), S35–S35 (1975)
13. Webb, G.I.: Lazy Learning, pp. 571–572. Springer, Heidelberg (2010). https://doi.org/10.1007/978-0-387-30164-8_443
14. Cleary, J.G., Trigg, L.E.: K*: an instance-based learner using an entropic distance measure. In: Machine Learning Proceedings 1995, pp. 108–114 (1995)
15. Obaidullah, S.M., Halder, C., Santosh, K.C., Das, N., Roy, K.: PHDIndic_11: page-level handwritten document image dataset of 11 official Indic scripts for script identification. Multimedia Tools Appl. **77**(2), 1643–1678 (2018)
16. Obaidullah, S.M., Santosh, K.C., Halder, C., Das, N., Roy, K.: Automatic Indic script identification from handwritten documents: page, block, line and word-level approach. Int. J. Mach. Learn. Cybern. **10**, 1–20 (2017)
17. Hall, M., Frank, E., Holmes, G., Pfahringer, B., Reutemann, P., Witten, I.H.: The WEKA data mining software: an update. ACM SIGKDD Explor. Newsl. **11**(1), 10–18 (2009)
18. Demšar, J.: Statistical comparisons of classifiers over multiple data sets. J. Mach. Learn. Res. **7**, 1–30 (2006)
19. Bouguelia, M.R., Nowaczyk, S., Santosh, K.C., Verikas, A.: Agreeing to disagree: active learning with noisy labels without crowdsourcing. Int. J. Mach. Learn. Cybern. **9**, 1–13 (2017)
20. Vajda, S., Santosh, K.C.: A fast k-nearest neighbor classifier using unsupervised clustering. In: RTIP2R-2016, pp. 185–193 (2016)

21. Kulkarni, S.B., Kulkarni, R.B., Kulkarni, U.P., Hegadi, R.S.: GLCM-based multi-class iris recognition using FKNN and KNN. Int. J. Image Graph. **14**(03), 1450010 (2014)
22. Mukherjee, H., Obaidullah, S.M., Santosh, K.C., Phadikar, S., Roy, K.: Line spectral frequency-based features and extreme learning machine for voice activity detection from audio signal. Int. J. Speech Technol. **21**, 1–8 (2018)

Speech Based Interaction System Using DNN and i-vector

P. Shanmugapriya[✉], V. Mohan, S. Yogapriya, and Y. Venkataramani

Department of ECE, Saranathan College of Engineering, Trichy, Tamilnadu, India
priyavrs@gmail.com, mohanvrs@gmail.com, yogapriya@gmail.com

Abstract. In this paper, a speech based interaction system using Deep Neural Network (DNN) and i-vector based DNN approaches are proposed. In DNN based approach, Mel-frequency cepstral coefficients (MFCC) features are extracted from the speech signal and it is directly given to DNN. In i-vector based DNN approach, DNN is trained using i-vector which is formed from Gaussian Mixture Model-Universal Background Model (GMM-UBM). For both approaches, the performance of the system is obtained in the form of confusion matrix and compared. In addition to that, GMM-UBM based approach is also compared with the proposed work. MFCC is used for representing the characteristics of the speech and auto encoder is used for classification purpose. It uses stacked two auto encoder layers and one soft max layer. The proposed system achieves improvement in performance when increasing the number of hidden units and the input dimension of MFCC features. The proposed work is to develop ASR system for isolated words in Tamil language and the experiments are conducted for speaker independent case. The results demonstrated that i-vector based DNN approach provides 100% recognition rate for 17 classes with 20 hidden units in each of the 2 layers. The dimension of i-vector is 100.

Keywords: MFCC · Deep Neural Network · GMM-UBM · i-vector · Speech based interaction system

1 Introduction

The ability of the system to identify and understand words spoken out by the user is called Automatic Speech Recognition (ASR) system. The sound/speech signal uttered by the user which is obtained from either microphone or telephone conversation is converted into machine readable format i.e., textual words. The three important steps involved in speech recognition system are pre-processing, feature extraction and classification. In Pre-Processing, Pre-Emphasis of the speech signal is the first step. It is used for DC elimination or normalization of the frequency components of the signal. The second and third steps in pre-processing are Framing and windowing. Speech signal is quasi periodic in nature, so it is classified into number of frames each is of duration 20–30 ms. To maintain the continuity in the spectrum, hamming window is used.

© Springer Nature Singapore Pte Ltd. 2019
K. C. Santosh and R. S. Hegadi (Eds.): RTIP2R 2018, CCIS 1035, pp. 460–473, 2019.
https://doi.org/10.1007/978-981-13-9181-1_41

After pre-processing, features extraction [12, 16] is the next step involved in recognition system. In this step, the feature vectors are extracted from the speech signal. Classifiers are used to classify the data with the help of the input features and finally the speech signal is recognized [11]. Speech recognition system is classified into different categories based on the input speech [8]. They are grouped under various classes based on nature of utterances, number of speakers, spectral bandwidth and vocabulary size. Based on the utterances considered from speakers, the speech recognition system can be classified into speaker dependent, speaker independent and speaker adaptive. Based on nature of utterances, the system is classified into spontaneous word recognition, continuous word recognition, connected word recognition and isolated word recognition. Based on Vocabulary size, the recognition system is classified into small, medium, large and very large speech recognition system. Based on spectral Bandwidth, it is classified into narrow band speech and wide band speech recognition system.

In the proposed work, the objective is to develop isolated word recognition system for speaker independent case. Rehman et al. [1] developed the speaker independent recognition system for three languages namely Urdu, Persian and Pashto. The authors used Discrete Wavelet Transform (DWT) and Feed-Forward Artificial Neural Network (FFANN) for feature extraction and classification purpose. As a result, they achieved high accuracy for the classes of two and five. In Hinton et al. [2], the recognition system is modeled using DNN-HMM (Deep Neural Network-Hidden Markov Model), GMM-HMM (Gaussian Mixture Model-Hidden Markov Model). In addition to this, experiments are conducted on five different large vocabularies and their performances were compared. Ishwarya et al. [3] and Sigappi et al. [4] developed the speaker independent isolated speech recognition system for the language Tamil. Here they used three different classifiers such as Probabilistic Neural Network (PNN), Hidden Markov Model (HMM) and Support Vector Machines (SVM). Among the three, HMM is reported to have the better performance.

Vimala et al. [5] developed an isolated speech recognition system for Tamil using different techniques such as Dynamic Time Warping (DTW), Hidden Markov Model (HMM), Gaussian Mixture Model (GMM), Support Vector Machine (SVM) and Multi-Layer Perception (MLP). As a result, DTW and HMM provide better result for word level accuracy. For speaker independent case, MLP and SVM are found to provide better performance and also reduced time complexity. Patil et al. [6] developed the recognition system of isolated words for Hindi language using KNN as classifier and MFCC as feature extraction technique with the result of better accuracy. They have used Vector quantization (VQ) with Gaussian Mixture Model (GMM) and analyzed the performance. Manjutha et al. [7] implemented the recognition system for connected and continuous speech using MFCC and HMM. They got the accuracy of 69.22% for connected words and 50% for continuous words.

Harisha et al. [8] developed the isolated recognition system in Kannada language using MFCC and Artificial Neural Network (ANN) with satisfactory results. Dhanashri et al. [9] used HMM and DNN for developing the isolated word recognition system through which 86.06% of accuracy was achieved. They conducted the experiments on TI digit databases in which the features extracted used are MFCC.

2 Proposed Recognition System

In the proposed recognition system, MFCC [10] is used for representing the characteristics of the signal. Simply it is said to be feature extraction i.e., divide the sound waves into frames and characteristics are extracted and represented using some parameters.

2.1 DNN Based Approach

In Deep Neural Network, between input and output layer more number of hidden layers are present. In this approach, features from each input signal are extracted and given as an input. DNN based on auto encoder is used as a classifier. Auto encoders are the simplest form of Deep Belief Network which is used to reproduce its input at its output. It is one of the tools for making the DNN to learn. It is composed of an encoder and a decoder. In deep neural network, a neuron receives an input, processes it and generates an output. This output is either sent to other neurons for further processing or it is the final output. When input enters the neuron, it is multiplied by a weight. Consider the input to be a, and the weight associated to be w^1. When it is passed through the node, bias is added to the input obtained in the following form:

$$c = a \times w^1 + \text{bias} \tag{1}$$

where, c is the net input of the neuron.

After applying activation function, the net input obtained is given as

$$c = f(a \times w^1 + \text{bias}) \tag{2}$$

here, $f(\ )$ is the activation function. In the proposed work, for encoder logistic sigmoid and for decoder linear transfer function is used as activation function.

For simplicity, it is assumed that both encoder and decoder have one layer. Consider an auto encoder with the input vector x. The auto encoder maps the input vector x to the output vector z as

$$z^1 = h^1(w^1 x + b^1) \tag{3}$$

where, superscript '1' indicates first layer, w^1 and b^1 are the weight matrix and bias vector of the first hidden layer respectively and h^1 is the activation function of the encoder.

After that decoder maps the z (encoded representation) back into $\hat{x}$ (estimate of input vector x) and it is given as

$$\hat{x} = h^2(w^2 x + b^2) \tag{4}$$

where, superscript '2' indicates second layer, w^2 and b^2 are the weight matrix and bias vector of the second hidden layer respectively and h^2 is the activation function of the decoder.

The feature obtained from the auto encoder is used for training a soft max layer for classification. Then the deep network is formed by stacking two auto encoders and one soft max layer. Then the deep network is trained and the result is presented in the form of confusion matrix.

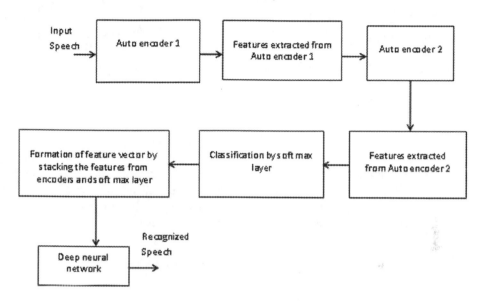

Fig. 1. Speech recognition using DNN

Figure 1 shows the illustration of speech recognition using DNN with auto encoder. Input block consists of MFCC features and Target class. With the help of the extracted features, the classification process can be done by creating soft max layer. It is a multi-class generalization of logistic sigmoid function and also called as normalized exponential [13]. Then deep network is formed by stacking encoders and the soft max layers. Finally deep network is trained and the performance of the system is obtained in the form of confusion matrix.

2.2 i-vector Based DNN Approach

It is the simplified version of Joint Factor Analysis (JFA) [14]. i-vector is adopted to train the DNN for the proposed recognition system. The speech signal of a person is slightly different in each time. These difference leads to increase in false rejection rate. In order to capture these differences i-vector creates a subspace called total variability subspace by using Expected Maximization (EM) algorithm. For this, factor analysis model which is given by

$$M = m + TX \tag{5}$$

where, M denotes adapted mean super vector, m denotes Universal Background Model mean super vector, T denotes total variability subspace or matrix with low rank and X denotes i-vector.

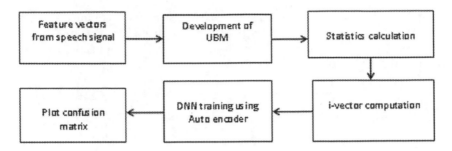

Fig. 2. Speech recognition using i-vector based DNN

Figure 2 shows the process involved in i-vector approach. Initially features are extracted from the speech signal and it is used for training the UBM model by Expected Maximization algorithm (EM). Then statistics are calculated using Baum Welch method [15]. Then total variability subspace is created in order to capture any variations which occur due to either channel or speaker/source. Finally, i-vectors are extracted and used to train the DNN.

3   Experimental Setup and Performance Analysis

For Speaker independent speech recognition, speech utterances are collected from different speakers with 8 kHz sampling rate and 16 bits/sample. Totally 675 utterances of 17 different words by 3 speakers are used for training the proposed system. The speech database has been developed by us in a noiseless room Cepstral Mean Variance Normalization (CMVN) is used to reduce the noise and non-linear channel effects. Out of 675 utterances, 450 utterances are used for training the proposed system and the remaining are meant for testing the system. From each frame, 12 MFCC values are estimated with this training data. In DNN, for classification problem, an auto encoder uses unsupervised learning algorithm. The parameters used for the training of DNN using auto encoder are listed in Table 1. The performance of the proposed system is analyzed with various techniques such as DNN approach, i-vector based approach, GMM-UBM approach and the results are compared.

3.1   MFCC Features-CMVN-DNN

The performance is analyzed by varying the number of classes 5, 10, and 17 and the results are obtained in the form of confusion matrix. Table 2 shows the recognition rate obtained for DNN based approach for different classes of 5, 10 and 17. From the Table 2, it is observed that when increasing the hidden units or number of neurons, the system achieves improved performance. The highest accuracy achieved for the proposed work of classes 5, 10 and 17 are 59.9%, 26.1% and 19.6% respectively.

Table 1. Parameters used for training DNN

Parameter	Value/functions
L2 weight regularizer	0.001
Sparsity regularizer	4
Sparsity proportion	0.05
Loss function	Mean Square Error (MSE) sparse
Transfer function of both encoder and decoder	Logistic sigmoid function, linear transfer function
Maximum iteration	1000
Techniques used to encode	Hamming, linear block, cyclic
Training algorithm	Scaled conjugate gradient descent algorithm

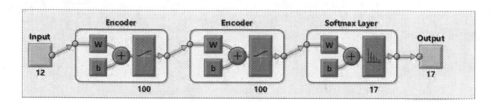

Fig. 3. Structure of deep neural network with auto encoder

Figure 3 shows the deep neural network stacking of two auto encoders and soft max layer. It is an example for DNN based approach for class 17. Here, 12 represent number of input given to the first auto encoder. Each auto encoder provides 100 hidden units. Each 12 input is processed in the first auto encoder and produces 100 outputs. These 100 outputs are given as an input to next auto encoder, processed and finally produce 17 outputs.

Table 2. Performance of speech recognition system using DNN for different number of hidden units

Number of words →	5	10	17
Number of neurons/hidden units	Recognition rate in %		
100	53.0	29.3	5.9
200	54.3	29.0	5.9
300	59.9	26.1	19.6

3.2   MFCC Features-CMVN-GMM-UBM

Similarly, the extracted MFCC features after normalization using CMVN is given as an input to the GMM-UBM based approach. In this GMM-UBM based approach, three phases are involved viz., training, enrollment and testing phase. In the first phase i.e., training phase, features extracted using MFCC are used for training the UBM by EM algorithm. In the second phase, speech models for speakers are derived from UBM using Maximum a Posterior (MAP) adaptation. In the final phase, the features of unknown speech utterances are compared against target speech model and UBM model. The Log-likelihood ratio (LLR) is calculated to take decision. Table 3 shows the performance of the GMM-UBM based approach. From the Table 3, it is observed that the performance of GMM-UBM approach is poor and the highest accuracy obtained is 48.78% for the 256 mixture components. Figure 4 shows the performance of GMM-UBM approach. In Fig. 4, the performance of GMM-UBM approach is given in the form of Detection Error Trade off (DET) curve which is compared between False Positive Rate (FPR) and False Negative Rate (FNR). Here the curve drawn for various mixture components.

Table 3. Performance of GMM-UBM based speech recognition system

Mixture component	Recognition rate in %
32	47.17
64	48.72
128	47.59
256	48.78

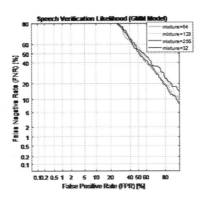

Fig. 4. DET curve for GMM-UBM approach for various number of mixture components

3.3 MFCC-GMM-UBM-i-vector

Figure 5 shows the process involved in i-vector approach. In i-vector approach, five steps are involved namely:

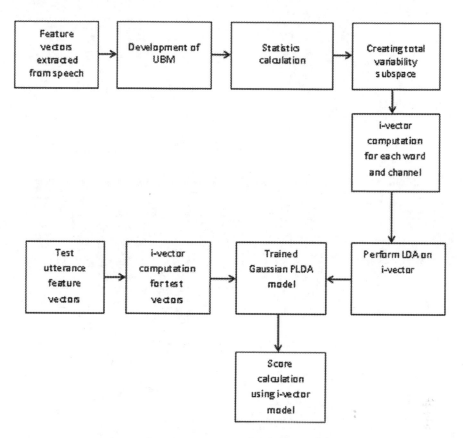

Fig. 5. i-vector based speech recognition system

Table 4. Performance of the proposed system using i-vector

i-vector dimension	Gaussian mixture components					
	32	64	128	256	512	1024
	Recognition rate in %					
40	58.65	61.58	60.09	61.54	62.03	61.24
50	59.25	60.38	61.62	60.84	62.24	63.77
60	58.82	62.04	61.09	61.15	63.30	63.38
70	59.10	59.80	59.67	61.03	61.11	61.52
80	59.04	60.30	59.28	59.69	51.16	61.20
90	57.49	59.68	58.85	50	62.16	61.00

Table 5. DET curve for i-vector approach for various dimensions

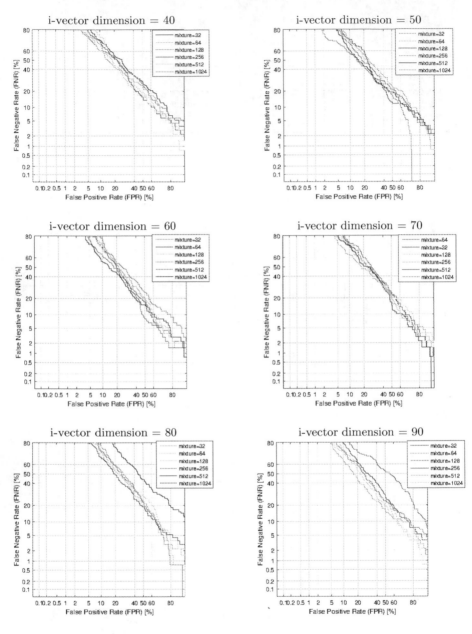

1. Train a Universal Background Model (UBM) from the training utterances.
2. Total variability subspace is learned from the statistics of training utterances.
3. With the help of developed i-vector, Gaussian Probabilistic Linear Discriminant Analysis (PLDA) model is developed.

4. Using the developed model and test i-vector, scoring is calculated and the performance measure is computed.

The recognition rate calculated for various mixture components and i-vector dimension is given in the Table 4 and the corresponding Detection Error Tradeoff (DET) curves are shown in Table 5. From the Table 4, it is observed that, training vectors are not sufficient. This approach achieves improved results when increase the training vectors. For the proposed work, this approach achieves the highest recognition rate of 63.77% for the i-vector dimension 50 and the mixture components 1024 which is calculated with the help of evaluation metrics such as True Positive rate (TP), False Positive rate (FP), True Negative rate (TN) and False Negative rate (FN). Figure 6 shows the DET curve for i-vector approach for i-vector dimension 40 to 80.

3.4   MFCC-CMVN-i-vector-DNN

In i-vector based DNN approach, instead of using MFCC features directly, i-vectors are extracted from MFCC features and applied to train the DNN. Table 6 shows the performance of i-vector based DNN approach. The dimension of i-vector is 100. From the Table 6, it is observed that when increasing number of hidden units will improve the performance of the system and for hidden units of 20, 100% of accuracy is achieved.

Table 6. Performance of speech recognition system using i-vector based DNN

Hidden size/ number of neurons	Recognition rate
10	5.9%
20	100%

3.5   MFCC-Delta Coefficients-DNN

In this approach, train the DNN by delta coefficients which is derived from the MFCC features. The input dimension is increased by taking first and second derivative from the MFCC features. Table 7 shows the performance of the recognition system which is modeled using delta coefficients. For the input vectors of dimension 60, the performance of the system achieves high accuracy. For the proposed recognition system, the highest accuracy for class 5 and 17 are 69.7% and 47.1%. Figure 7 shows the deep neural network trained using delta coefficients. Here the value 60 indicates number of inputs given to the first auto encoder. Each encoder has the hidden units of 400 and 17 shows the output class.

Upon comparison of the Table 2 with Table 6, the performance of the system is found to be improved for increased input dimensions. Table 8 shows the recognition rate for DNN based approach with the input dimension 60 for each word.

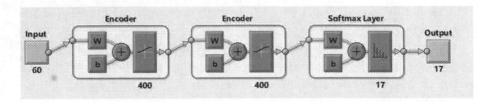

Fig. 6. Deep neural network architecture for 17 Classes

Table 7. Recognition rate of DNN trained using delta coefficients (input dimension 60)

Number of words $\longrightarrow$	5	17
Hidden units/number of neurons	Recognition rate	
100	62.9%	20.7%
200	67.9%	42.4%
400	69.7%	47.1%

This rate is obtained from the confusion matrix. The first column indicates that each word and second column indicates recognition rate. Table 9 shows the performance of five approaches where the first column represents type of the approach and the second column represents recognition rate for the relevant approach. On comparing the five approaches, it is observed that i-vector based DNN approach gives better results. Train the DNN using MFCC features and delta coefficients will give the better performance for more number of hidden units. Figure 7 shows the architecture of Speech Based Conversation (SBC) system used to perform an agricultural task domain. This SBC system is a mobile based conversation system built for farmers in semi urban and rural areas to obtain prices of agricultural commodities which are to be sold in the market across state of Tamil Nadu in India. It has two modules namely: automatic speech recognition system and Interactive Voice Response (IVR) module. IVR module is designed using Asterisk, an open source tool. It is developed for real time communication application. The call is initiated by the farmer or user. The computerized voice welcomes the user to the interaction system by interacting with the user in the language Tamil. It initiates the farmer to speak out the commodity name. Then it passes a sound/audio of spoken commodity name to Automatic Speech Recognition system. Here it decodes the sound/audio and return the corresponding text. Then the system reconfirms the text by playing it back to the farmer. In order to avoid the confusion among the system and user beep sound will be produced in between the conversation. In a proposed work, ASR module of Speech based Interaction system for enquiring about the prices of commodity is developed.

Table 8. Recognition rate for each word of input dimension 60 trained using DNN

Word	Recognition rate	Word	Recognition rate
1	44.62%	10	37.59%
2	39.16%	11	60.92%
3	55.83%	12	45.37%
4	33.88%	13	46.11%
5	59.81%	14	47.40%
6	57.96%	15	43.24%
7	46.57%	16	61.57%
8	51.38%	17	46.11%

Table 9. Comparison of system performance of different approaches

Approaches	Recognition rate for 17classes (in %)
MFCC + DNN	19.6%
MFCC + Delta Coefficients + DNN	47.1%
GMM-UBM	48.78%
MFCC + GMM-UBM + i-vector	63.77%
MFCC + i-vector + DNN	100%

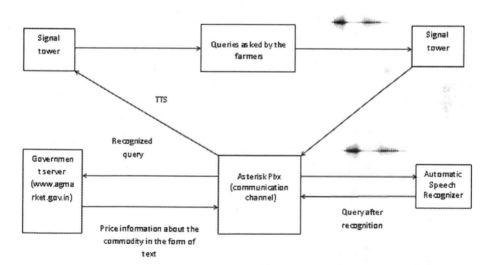

Fig. 7. Architecture of speech based interaction system

The dialogue function of proposed system is described below:

System: Welcome.

System: what is the commodity name?

(Beep sound)
User: tomato
System: did you say tomato?
(Beep sound)
User: yes
System: the price is ...
System: did you want to know another commodity price?
(Beep sound)
User: no
System: thank you

4 Conclusion

In order to obtain good accuracy for pattern recognition or classification problem, Deep neural network is adopted in the proposed work. As a result, it is observed that when the number of hidden units increases, the performance of the system also increases. Experiment is conducted using five different approaches namely DNN based approach (MFCC + DNN), i-vector based DNN approach (MFCC + i-vector + DNN), Delta coefficients based DNN approach (MFCC + delta coefficients + DNN), i-vector approach (MFCC + GMM-UBM + i-vector) and reference GMM-UBM (MFCC + GMM-UBM) based approach. When compared to other approaches, i-vector based DNN approach gives better performance.

The proposed i-vector based DNN approach (MFCC + i-vector + DNN) shows 100% accuracy and for DNN based approach (MFCC + DNN) shows 19.6% for 300 hidden units. If the system is implemented in high speed and high storage capability processors, DNN based approach achieves higher accuracy for larger hidden units. Also it is observed that when increasing number of input feature dimension will improve the performance of the system i.e. for input dimension 60, the system achieves an accuracy of 47.1% for 17 class and 69.7% with number of hidden units 400. i-vector approach (MFCC + GMM-UBM + i-vector) achieves better recognition rate of 63.77% when compared to GMM-UBM approach.

References

1. Rehmam, B., Halim, Z., Abbas, G., Muhammad, T.: Artificial neural network-based speech recognition using DWT analysis applied on isolated words from oriental languages. Malays. J. Comput. Sci. **28**(3), 242–262 (2015)
2. Hinton, G., et al.: Deep neural networks for acoustic modeling in speech recognition. IEEE Signal Process. Mag. **29**, 82–97 (2012)
3. Iswarya, P., Radha, V.: Speaker independent isolated Tamil words recognition system using different classifiers. Int. J. Comput. Sci. Eng. Technol. (IJCSET), **6** (2015)

4. Sigappi, A.N., Palanivel, S.: Spoken word recognition strategy for Tamil language. Int. J. Comput. Sci. **9**, 227–233 (2012)
5. Vimala, C., Radha, V.: Isolated speech recognition system for Tamil language using statistical pattern matching and machine learning techniques. J. Eng. Sci. Technol. **10**(5), 617–632 (2015)
6. Patil, U.G., Shirbahadurkar, S.D., Paithane, A.N.: Automatic speech recognition of isolated words in Hindi language using MFCC. In: International Conference on Computing, Analytics and Security Trends (CAST). IEEE, May 2017
7. Manjutha, M., Gracy, J., Subashini, P., Krishnaveni, M.: Automated speech recognition system–a literature review. Int. J. Eng. Trends Appl. (IJETA) **4**(2) (2017)
8. Harisha, S.B., Amarappa, S., Sathyanarayana, S.V.: Automatic speech recognition–a literature survey on Indian languages and ground work for isolated Kannada digit recognition using MFCC and ANN. Int. J. Electron. Comput. Sci. Eng. (IJCSE) **4**(1), 91–105 (2015)
9. Dhanashri, D., Dhonde, S.B.: Isolated word speech recognition system using deep neural networks. In: Satapathy, S., Bhateja, V., Joshi, A. (eds.) ICDECT, vol. 468, pp. 9–17. Springer, Singapore (2017). https://doi.org/10.1007/978-981-10-1675-2_2
10. Dhonde, S.B., Jagade, S.M.: Mel-frequency cepstral coefficients for speaker recognition: a review. Int. J. Adv. Eng. Res. Dev. **2** (2015)
11. Dhonde, S.B., Jagade, S.M.: Feature extraction techniques in speaker recognition: a review. Int. J. Recent Technol. Mech. Electr. Eng. (IJRMEE) **2**(5), 104–106 (2015)
12. Dave, N.: Feature extraction methods LPC, PLP and MFCC in speech recognition. Int. J. Adv. Res. Methods Based Percept. **1**, 1–4 (2013)
13. Bishop, C.M.: Pattern Recognition and Machine Learning. Springer, New York (2006)
14. Kenny, P.: Joint factor analysis of speaker and session variability: theory and algorithms. Technical report Crim-06/08-13 (2005). http://www.crim.ca/perso/patrick.kenny/
15. Dehak, N., Torres-Carrasquillo, P.A., Reynolds, D.A., Dehak, R.: Language recognition via i-vectors and dimensionality reduction. In: InterSpeech, pp. 857–860 (2011)
16. Mukherjee, H., Obaidullah, Sk.Md., Santosh, K.C., Phadikar, S., Roy, K.: Line spectral frequency-based features and extreme learning machine for voice activity detection from audio signal. Int. J. Speech Technol. 1–8 (2018)

Construction of Recognition Algorithms Based on the Two-Dimensional Functions

Shavkat Kh. Fazilov[1], Nomaz M. Mirzaev[1(✉)], Gulmira R. Mirzaeva[1,2], and Shakhzod E. Tashmetov[2]

[1] Scientific and Innovation Center of Information and Communication Technologies, Tashkent University of Information Technologies named after Muhammad al-Khwarizmi, Tashkent, Republic of Uzbekistan
nomazmirza@rambler.ru

[2] Tashkent University of Information Technologies named after Muhammad al-Khwarizmi, Tashkent, Republic of Uzbekistan

Abstract. The problem of pattern recognition is considered by defining in the space of interconnected features. A new approach to constructing a model of recognition algorithms is proposed, taking into account the interconnectedness of the features of the images under consideration. A distinctive feature of the proposed model of algorithms is the determination of a suitable set of two-dimensional threshold functions in the construction of an extreme recognition algorithm. The purpose of this article is to develop a model of modified RA based on the calculation of estimates. To test the efficiency of the proposed model of RA, the experimental studies were carried out to solve a number of model problems. The analysis of the obtained results shows that the considered models of algorithms are effectively used in those cases when there is certain dependence between the features of the objects.

Keywords: Pattern recognition · Model of recognition algorithms · Calculation of estimates · Feature dependence · Subset of strongly coupled characteristics · Representative feature · Preferred pair of characteristics

1 Introduction

Analysis of literary sources, in particular [1–10], shows that the development of pattern recognition (PR) is divided into two stages. At the beginning of the formation of the theory of PR, the most of its application were associated with poorly formalized areas - medicine, geology, sociology, chemistry, etc. Therefore, at the first stage, questions of development and investigation of image recognition algorithms (RA) oriented to solve specific applied problems were considered. The value of these algorithms was determined, first of all, by the achieved experimental results in solving specific problems [11].

As a result of acquiring certain experiences in solving a number of applied problems, a new stage in the development of the theory of PR has emerged,

© Springer Nature Singapore Pte Ltd. 2019
K. C. Santosh and R. S. Hegadi (Eds.): RTIP2R 2018, CCIS 1035, pp. 474–483, 2019.
https://doi.org/10.1007/978-981-13-9181-1_42

characterized by the transition from individual algorithms to the construction of models-families of algorithms for a unified description of methods for solving classification problems. The need for synthesizing patterns of PR algorithms was determined by the need to fix a class of algorithms when choosing the optimal or at least acceptable procedure for solving a particular problem [2,3,10].

At this stage of development, Zhuravlev has shown that an arbitrary recognition algorithm can be represented as a sequential execution of the operators B (the recognizing operator) and C (the decision rule) [2,3]:

$$A = B \circ C. \tag{1}$$

It follows from (1) that each algorithm for recognizing A can be divided into two consecutive stages. In the first step, the recognizing operator B translates the permissible object S_u into a numerical estimate represented by the vector $\tilde{\mathfrak{b}}_u$:

$$B(S_u) = \tilde{\mathfrak{b}}_u, \tag{2}$$

where $\tilde{\mathfrak{b}}_u = (\mathfrak{b}_{u1}, \ldots, \mathfrak{b}_{uv}, \ldots, \mathfrak{b}_{ul})$.

In the second stage, by using the numerical estimate $\mathfrak{b}_{uv}$, the decision rule C determines the belonging of the object S_u to the classes $K_1, \ldots, K_v, \ldots, K_l$:

$$C(\mathfrak{b}_{uv}) = \begin{cases} 0, & \text{if } \mathfrak{b}_{uv} < c_1; \\ \Delta, & \text{if } c_1 \leq \mathfrak{b}_{uv} \leq c_2; \\ 1, & \text{if } \mathfrak{b}_{uv} > c_2. \end{cases} \tag{3}$$

where c_1, c_2 - parameters of the decision rule. The estimate $\mathfrak{b}_{uv}$ is computed using the operator (2).

At the present time, a number of models of RA have been thoroughly developed and studied. We can divide them into groups such as [1–3,10]: (1) models based on the use of separating functions; (2) models based on the use of mathematical statistics and probability theory; (3) models based on the use of the apparatus of mathematical logic; (4) models based on the use of the principle of potentials; (5) models based on the use of algorithms for the calculation of estimates. However, the analysis of these models shows that at present, models of RA are mainly oriented to solve problems, where objects are described in the space of independent features (or the dependence between the signs is rather weak).

In practice, there frequently occur applied problems of PR, defined in the space of features of large dimension. When solving such problems, the assumption of the independence of signs is often not fulfilled. Consequently, questions remain about the creation of RA that can be used to solve applied recognition problems for large data dimensions. Therefore, the issues of improving, developing and researching models of RA oriented to solve problems of diagnosing, forecasting and classifying objects in conditions of large dimensionality of the feature space are relevant. This is evidenced by many publications in recent years, in which various approaches and algorithms are considered for problems of recognizing objects specified in the space of signs of large dimension, in particular [12–15]. It should be noted that the approach proposed in this paper is very close to the hierarchical approach considered in [12]. A distinctive feature of the proposed approach is that it relies on the evaluation of the interconnectedness of characteristics and the allocation of preferred models of elementary threshold rules for decision-making in the construction of RA.

The purpose of this work is to modify the model of evaluation algorithms, aimed at adapting this model to solve the problems of PR described in a character space of large dimension.

To solve the problem of PR in the conditions of a large dimensionality of feature space, an approach is proposed that relies on the results of research by scientific school of Zhuravlev and Zagoruiko. On the basis of this approach, a model of modified RA based on the calculation of estimates has been developed, the key point of which are: the formation of subsets of strongly-related features; the allocation of representative features and pair-wise recording of features. It should be noted that certain concepts and notation are borrowed from [1–3].

The results of this work represent an original solution of the problem associated with the construction of modified RA based on the calculation of estimates. A distinctive feature of the proposed model from existing algorithms for calculating estimates [1–3] is the construction of two-dimensional elementary threshold functions. The practical significance of the results obtained lies in the fact that the algorithms and programs developed can be applied to solve applied problems, where objects of recognition are defined in the space of features of large dimension.

2   Basic Concepts and Notation

Using [2], we introduce some terms and notation. Consider the set of admissible objects $\mathfrak{J}$, which consists of l disjoint subsets (classes) $K_1, \ldots, K_j, \ldots, K_l$:

$$\mathfrak{J} = \bigcup_{j=1}^{l} K_j, \quad K_i \cap K_j = \emptyset, \quad i \neq j, \quad i, j \in \{1, \ldots, l\}. \tag{4}$$

Moreover, the partition (4) is not completely defined, but only some initial information is given I_0 about classes $K_1, \ldots, K_j, \ldots, K_l$. To clarify the concept of initial information, we select m objects from the set of admissible objects $\mathfrak{J}$:

$$S_1, \ldots, S_u, \ldots, S_m \quad (\forall S_u \in \mathfrak{J}, u = \overline{1, m}) \tag{5}$$

To each selected object in the feature space X there corresponds the n-dimensional characteristic vector $(X = (x_1, \ldots, x_i, \ldots, x_n))$:

$$S_1 = (s_{11}, \ldots, s_{1i}, \ldots, s_{1n})$$
$$\cdots,$$
$$S_u = (s_{u1}, \ldots, s_{ui}, \ldots, s_{un}) \tag{6}$$
$$\cdots,$$
$$S_m = (s_{m1}, \ldots, s_{mi}, \ldots, s_{mn})$$

We introduce the following notation:

$$\tilde{S} = \{S_1, \ldots, S_u, \ldots, S_m\} \quad \tilde{K}_j = \tilde{S}^m \cap K_j \quad C\tilde{K}_j = \tilde{S}^m \setminus \tilde{K}_j \qquad (7)$$

where $C\tilde{K}_j$ - complement of the set $\tilde{K}_j$.

Then the initial information I_0 can be defined as a certain set whose elements are the pair $<S_u, \tilde{\alpha}(S_u)>$:

$$I_0 = \{<S_1, \tilde{\alpha}(S_1)>, \ldots, <S_u, \tilde{\alpha}(S_u)>, \ldots, <S_m, \tilde{\alpha}(S_m)\} \qquad (8)$$

where S_u - allowable object $(\forall S_u \in \mathfrak{I}, u = \overline{1,m})$, the $\tilde{\alpha}(S_u)$ - object information vector S_u.

Each component of the information vector $\tilde{\alpha}(S_u) = \{\alpha_{u1}, \ldots, \alpha_{uj}, \ldots, \alpha_{ul}\}$ is given in the form

$$\alpha_{uj} = \begin{cases} 1, & \text{if } S_u \in \tilde{K}_j; \\ 0, & \text{if } S_u \in C\tilde{K}_j. \end{cases} \qquad (9)$$

A set of information vectors corresponding to all objects $\tilde{S}^m$, forms an information matrix $\|\alpha_{uj}\|_{m \times l}$.

3   Statement of the Problem

Let $\tilde{S}^q \left(\tilde{S}^q = \{S_1', \ldots, S_u', \ldots, S_q'\}, \tilde{S}^q \subset \mathfrak{I}\right)$ be an arbitrary set of objects, described in the characteristic space X. For each object S $(S \in \mathfrak{I})$ in this space there corresponds a description (numerical characteristic) of the object $I(S) = (s_1, .., s_i, .., s_n)$. In this case, the dimension n of the space of the original features is sufficiently large. In these conditions, most of the features are interrelated, which makes it difficult to use many RA [10]. The task is to construct an algorithm A that, from the initial information (8), computes the predicate values $P_j(S_u') \left(P_j(S_u') = \text{"}S_u' \in K_j\text{"}\right)$:

$$A(I_0, \tilde{S}^q) = \|\beta_{uj}\|_{m \times l}, \quad \beta_{uj} = P_j(S_u') \qquad (10)$$

Here β_{uj} is interpreted as follows: if $\beta_{uj} \in \{1, 0, \Delta\}$ $(\beta_{uj} = 1$ - object S_u belongs to the class K_j, $\beta_{uj} = 0$ - object S_u do not belongs to the class $K_j)$, that is, the value of the characteristic function on an admissible object S_u, calculated by the operator B; if $\beta_{uj} = \Delta$, then it is considered that algorithm A could not determine the value of the predicate $P_j(S_u')$.

4   Proposed Approach

In this paper we consider an approach based on the evaluation of the interconnectedness of features, to the solution of the problem of constructing RA taking into account the large dimensionality of the feature space. Based on this approach, a model of modified RA based on two-dimensional threshold functions is proposed. The main idea of the proposed model is the formation of a space of independent representative features and preferred models of elementary threshold rules for decision-making with the subsequent calculation of the proximity estimate for object recognition. The task of these RA includes the following main steps.

The proposed model of recognition algorithm includes seven main stages. It should be noted that the first two stages were considered in detail in [16–19]. Therefore, for the sake of completeness, we will only give the names of these stages, focusing on the next five stages.

1. *Identification of subsets of strongly coupled features.*
2. *Formation of a set of representative characteristics.*
3. *Definition of the proximity function $d_u(S_p, S_q)$ between objects $S_p = S_q$ in the two-dimensional subspace of representative features.* At this stage, a function that characterizes the similarity of objects S_p and S_q in the two-dimensional subspace of representative features $\mathfrak{D}$ ($\mathfrak{D} = (\mathfrak{D}_1, \ldots, \mathfrak{D}_u, \ldots, \mathfrak{D}_n)$, $\mathfrak{D}_u = (x_{u_1}, x_{u_2})$, $x_{u_1}, x_{u_2} \in X'$) is defined. The distances between these objects in the subspace of representative features $\mathfrak{D}_u$ are defined as follows [20]:

$$d_u(S_p, S_q) = \sqrt{\sum_{i=1}^{2} (s_{p,u_i} - s_{q,v_i})^2} \tag{11}$$

In problems of PR as a measure of similarity $\mathfrak{D}_u$ we can take the square of the distance (11):

$$d_u^2(S_p, S_q) = \sum_{i=1}^{2} (s_{p,u_i} - s_{q,v_i})^2 \tag{12}$$

Then, by using (12), we introduce the notion of a first-level proximity function. The proximity function of the first level is the threshold function defined in the two-dimensional subspace of representative features $\mathfrak{D}_u$:

$$\mu_{1u} = \begin{cases} 1, & \text{if } d_u^2(S_p, S_q) \leq \varepsilon_{1u}^2; \\ 0, & \text{if } d_u^2(S_p, S_q) > \varepsilon_{1u}^2. \end{cases} \tag{13}$$

where ε_{1u} – parameter of the algorithm used in constructing the proximity function of the first level.

We denote the set of proximity functions of the first level by $\mathfrak{B}_1$.

The proximity function of the second level is the threshold function defined in the subspace of representative features $\mathfrak{D}_u$ and $\mathfrak{D}_v$:

$$\mu_{2u} = \begin{cases} 1, & \text{if } d_u^2(S_p, S_q) + d_v^2(S_p, S_q) \leq \varepsilon_{2u}^2; \\ 0, & \text{if } d_u^2(S_p, S_q) + d_v^2(S_p, S_q) > \varepsilon_{2u}^2. \end{cases} \tag{14}$$

where ε_{2u} – parameter of the algorithm used in constructing the proximity function of the second level.

The set of proximity functions of the second level is denoted by $\mathfrak{B}_2$.

The proximity function of the level is the threshold function given in the subspace of representative features $\mathfrak{D}_{u_1}, \ldots, \mathfrak{D}_{u_k}$:

$$\mu_{ku} = \begin{cases} 1, & \text{if } \sum_{v=1}^{k} d_{u_v}^2 (S_p, S_q) \leq \varepsilon_{ku}^2; \\ 0, & \text{if } \sum_{v=1}^{k} d_{u_v}^2 (S_p, S_q) > \varepsilon_{ku}^2. \end{cases} \tag{15}$$

where ε_{ku} – parameter of the algorithm used in constructing the proximity level function.

The set of proximity functions of the zth level is denoted by $\mathfrak{B}_k$.

4. *Selection of a set of preferred proximity functions.* At this stage, a selection of a set of preferred proximity functions is done, any of which is best in some sense at each level. Note that at this stage, the procedure for selecting the preferred proximity functions of the first level is considered. The selection of the preferred proximity functions of other levels is similar. Consider finding the preferred proximity functions constructed for each element of the set $\mathfrak{D}$.

We search the preferred proximity function in $\mathfrak{D}_u$ ($\mathfrak{D}_u \in \mathfrak{D}, u = \overline{1,n}$). It is based on an assessment of the dominance of the proximity functions under consideration for objects that belong to the set I_0:

$$\mathfrak{T}_u = \sum_{j=1}^{l} \left(\sum_{S_p, S_q \in \tilde{K}_j} \mu_{1u}(S_p, S_q) + \sum_{S_p, S_q \in C\tilde{K}_j} \left(1 - \mu_{1u}(S_p, S_q) \right) \right) \tag{16}$$

The larger the value of $\mathfrak{T}_u$, the greater the preference is given to the u-th proximity function, built on the features x_{u_1} and x_{u_2}. If several functions receive the same preference, then any one of them is selected.

Let $\tilde{\mathfrak{p}}$ be a boolean vector with n components. We select all the unit coordinates of the vector $\tilde{\mathfrak{p}}$, whose number is $\mathfrak{n}'$. Let these unit elements correspond to $i_1, .., i_u, .., i_{\mathfrak{n}'}$-th coordinates of a vector $\tilde{\mathfrak{p}}$. We remove from consideration all the proximity functions, except for $\mu_{1u_1}, \ldots, \mu_{1u_i}, \ldots, \mu_{1u_{\mathfrak{n}'}} (\mu_{1u_i} \in \mathfrak{B}_1)$ which correspond to unit vector coordinates $\mathfrak{p}$. The resulting part of the set (subset) of proximity functions is denoted by $\mathfrak{P}_1$.

Thus, each element of the set $\mathfrak{P}_1$ corresponds to a single boolean vector $\tilde{\mathfrak{p}}$ ($\tilde{\mathfrak{p}} = (\mathfrak{p}_1, .., \mathfrak{p}_{i_u}, .., \mathfrak{p}_{\mathfrak{n}'})$, where $\mathfrak{p}_{i_u} = 1$ ($u = \overline{1, \mathfrak{n}'}$), and the remaining components of this vector are zero). Next, only the preferred proximity functions are considered. At this stage, the vector parameter is given by the vector $\tilde{\mathfrak{p}}$.

5. *The estimation of the class from a set of preferred proximity functions of the same level.* Assessment of the object's ownership S to class K_j ($j = \overline{1,l}$) on a set of preferred proximity functions of one (v-th) level are calculated as follows ($v = 1, \ldots, k$):

$$\mathfrak{G}_j^v(S) = \sum_{S_p \in E_j} \sum_{u=1}^{\mathfrak{n}_v'} \gamma_u \mu_{vu}(S_p, S) \tag{17}$$

where γ_u - parameter of the algorithm ($u = 1, \ldots, \mathfrak{n}_v'$; $\mathfrak{n}_v' = |\mathfrak{P}_v|$).

In the formula (17), the calculation $\mathfrak{G}_j^v(S)$ is carried out on all $\mu_{vu}(S_p, S)$, where $\mu_{vu}(S_p, S) \in \mathfrak{P}_v$.

6. *Estimate for the object S by class K_j.* At this stage, the estimation of the belonging of the object S to the class K_j ($j = \overline{1, l}$) is done over all levels of the set of the preferred proximity functions:

$$\mathfrak{G}_j(S) = \sum_{v=1}^{k} \tau_v \mathfrak{G}_j^v(S) \tag{18}$$

where τ_v - parameter of the algorithm ($v = 1, \ldots, k$).

7. *The decision rule.* The decision is made element-wise [2,3], i.e. by the formula (3).

Thus, we defined a class of modified RA based on two-dimensional threshold functions. Any algorithm A from this model is completely determined by specifying a set of parameters π. We denote the set of all RA from the proposed model by $A(\pi, S)$. Search for the best algorithm is carried out in the parametric space π.

5   Experiments and Results

With a view of practical use and verification of the working capacity of the considered model of algorithms, functional schemes of recognition programs have been developed. Software implementation of the developed algorithms is implemented in C++. The working capacity of the developed program is verified on a practice.

5.1   Model Task

The initial data of recognized objects for the model problem is generated in the space of features of large dimension. The number of classes in this experiment is two, its attributes - 400. The number of subsets of strongly coupled characteristics is 6. The volume of the initial sample is 1000 implementations (500 implementations for objects of each class).

As test models of RA, the following model was chosen: the model of RA based on evaluation of estimates (A_1), and model (A_2), proposed in this paper. Comparative analysis of the above models of RA in the solution of the considered problem was carried out according to the following criteria: (1) accuracy of recognition of objects of the control sample; (2) time spent on training; (3) time spent on recognizing objects from the control sample.

To evaluate the algorithms A_1, A_2 according to these criteria in solving the considered problem, the cross-validation method is used [21].

As a result of the experiment, all subsets of strongly coupled characteristics were identified and a corresponding set of representative characteristics was formed. Further, the parameters of the proximity function between objects in a two-dimensional subspace of representative features are defined and an extreme recognition algorithm is constructed on their basis. The accuracy of recognition in the training process for A_1 is 96,4%, for A_2 – 99,1%. The results of solving the model problem under consideration with application of A_1 and A_2 in the process of control are given in Table 1.

Table 1. The results of solving the problem using various RA

Recognition algorithm	Training time (in sec.)	Recognition time (in sec.)	Accuracy of recognition (%)
A_1	8.69309	0.03766	83,7
A_2	11.72451	0.01715	96,2

The comparison of these results shows (see Table 1) that the proposed model of recognition A_2 algorithms allowed to increase the accuracy of object recognition by more than 10% relative to A_1. This is because the model A_1 does not take into account the interconnectedness of the characteristics. However, for model A_2, there is some increase in the training time due to the implementation of an additional procedure for the formation of independent subsets of interrelated features.

The analysis of the obtained results shows that the proposed model of RA allows to solve the problem of PR more accurately in conditions of interconnectedness of features. In this case, the time spent on recognizing objects is much less than the same index A_1 (see Table 1). This is due to the fact that in the proposed RA only the preferred proximity functions are used to recognize the object, which has caused an increase in the speed of object recognition. Therefore, this model can be used in the development of real-time recognition systems. At the same time, it is necessary to note the fact that the time expended on training the algorithm has increased. Because it is required to optimize a larger number of parameters than when using the traditional model of RA, in particular, A_1.

5.2   Practical Task

As a practical example, let us consider the problem of recognizing a person's identity from the image of a signature. A set of 400 signature images consisting of 5 disjoint subsets (classes) is given. In each class there are 80 different signature images of one person scanned at different times. In each experiment 320 images of the signature are treated as a training sample, and the remaining 80 as a control sample. Partitioning the original sample for training and a control sample was also carried out as in the model task (see Sect. 5.1) using a cross validation method [21].

As a result of this experimental study, the following recognition results were obtained using A_2: the error in the training process was 4.7%, the error in the control process was 12.1%. When recognizing with A_1, the same indicators were 6.0% and 17.8%, respectively.

The computational experiments carried out in solving the problem of recognizing the personality from the signature images showed a higher efficiency of the proposed algorithms in comparison with the traditional RA.

6   Conclusion

Today the solution of problems of PR, described in the space of signs of large dimension, is associated with significant computational difficulties. The considered model of RA improves accuracy and significantly reduces the number of computational operations when recognizing an unknown object specified in the space of interrelated features, and can be used to compile various software complexes oriented to solve applied recognition problems.

References

1. Zhuravlev, Yu.I., Kamilov, M.M., Tulyaganov, S.E.: Algorithms for calculating estimates and their application. Fan, Tashkent (1974)
2. Zhuravlev, Yu.I.: Selected scientific works. Master, Moscow (1998)
3. Zhuravlev, Yu.I., Ryazanov, V.V., Senko, O.V.: Recognition. Mathematical methods. Software system. Practical applications. Fazis, Moscow (2006)
4. Zagoruiko, N.G.: Applied methods of data and knowledge analysis. IM SB RAS, Novosibirsk (1999)
5. Schlesinger, M., Glavach, V.: Ten Lectures on Statistical and Structural Recognition. Naukova Dumka, Kiev (2004)
6. Lbov, G.S., Berikov, V.B.: Stability of decision functions in problems of pattern recognition and analysis of heterogeneous information. Publishing House of the Institute of Mathematics, Novosibirsk (2005)
7. Kudryavtsev, V.B., Andreev, A.E., Gasanov, E.E.: Theory of Test Recognition. Fizmatlit, Moscow (2007)
8. Fomin, Ya.A.: Pattern recognition: theory and application. PHASIS, Moscow (2012)
9. Ramakrishnan, S. (ed.): Pattern Recognition: Analysis and Applications. ITexLi, New York (2016)
10. Kamilov, M.M., Mirzaev, N.M., Radjabov, S.S.: The current state of the issues of constructing models of recognition algorithms. J. Chem. Technol. Control Manag. **2**, 67–72 (2009)
11. Kovalevsky, V.A.: Image Pattern Recognition. Springer, New York (1980). https://doi.org/10.1007/978-1-4612-6033-2
12. Santosh, K.C., Wendling, L.: Pattern recognition based on hierarchical description of decision rules using choquet integral. In: Santosh, K.C., Hangarge, M., Bevilacqua, V., Negi, A. (eds.) RTIP2R 2016. CCIS, vol. 709, pp. 146–158. Springer, Singapore (2017). https://doi.org/10.1007/978-981-10-4859-3_14
13. P.G., L., Mallappa, S.: Classification of summarized sensor data using sampling and clustering: a performance analysis. In: Santosh, K.C., Hangarge, M., Bevilacqua, V., Negi, A. (eds.) RTIP2R 2016. CCIS, vol. 709, pp. 159–172. Springer, Singapore (2017). https://doi.org/10.1007/978-981-10-4859-3_15

14. Hesabi, Z.R., Tari, Z., Goscinski, A., Fahad, A., Khalil, I., Queiroz, C.: Data summarization techniques for big data—a survey. In: Khan, S.U., Zomaya, A.Y. (eds.) Handbook on Data Centers, pp. 1109–1152. Springer, New York (2015). https://doi.org/10.1007/978-1-4939-2092-1_38

15. Kasun, L.L.C., Zhou, H., Huang, G.B., Vong, C.M.: Representational learning with extreme learning machine for big data. IEEE Intell. Syst. **28**(6), 31–34 (2013)

16. Kamilov, M.M., Fazilov, Sh.Kh., Mirzaev, N.M., Radjabov, S.S.: Estimates calculations algorithms in condition of huge dimensions of feartures' space. In: 4th International Conference on Problems of Cybernetics and Informatics (PCI 2012), vol. I, pp. 184–187. IEEE Press, Baku (2012)

17. Mirzaev, N., Saliev, E.: Recognition algorithms based on radial functions. In: 3nd Russian-Pacific Conference on Computer Technology and Applications (RPC-2018), pp. 1–6. FEFU, Vladivostok, Russia (2018)

18. Mirzaev, N.M.: About one model of image recognition. In: First Russia and Pacific Conference on Computer Technology and Applications, Vladivostok, pp. 394–398 (2010)

19. Fazilov, Sh., Mirzaev, N., Radjabov, S., Mirzaev, O.: Determining of parameters in the construction of recognition operators in conditions of features correlations. In: 7th International Conference on Optimization Problems and Their Applications (OPTA-2018), Omsk, Russia, pp. 118–133 (2018)

20. Tou, J., Gonzalez, R.: Pattern recognition principles. Mir, Moscow (1978)

21. Braga-Neto, U.M., Dougherty, E.R.: Error Estimation for Pattern Recognition. Springer, New York (2016)

Efficient GWR Solution by TR and CA

V. C. Mahavishnu[1], Y. Rajkumar[2(✉)], D. Ramya[3], and M. Preethi[4]

[1] PSG Institute of Technology and Applied Research, Coimbatore, Tamilnadu, India
[2] Vignan University, Guntur, Andhra Pradesh, India
rkrajdeveloper34@gmail.com
[3] Sri Krishna College of Engineering and Technology, Coimbatore, Tamilnadu, India
[4] AVS Engineering College, Salem, Tamilnadu, India

Abstract. One of the major source of global warming is the increasing use of automobiles which contributes to 30% in developed countries and 20% in developing countries. Globally, 15% of man made carbon dioxide comes from cars, trucks and other vehicles. Reducing transportation emissions is one of the most vital steps in fighting global warming and solutions to the transportation problem include usage of green vehicles and public transport modes. The traffic congestion and the delays in signals are the major causes for increasing pollution's. The solution to this problem is presented in this paper. The effective use of big data analytic to analyze the emission rate and the time delays and total difference of a vehicles alternate path distance is calculated and the emission difference for the alternate path is calculated using machine learning algorithms. The optimized route must be efficient in reducing the time to reach and reduction of pollution, which is calculated for a route from source to destination in soft real-time using the map reduce technique. The standard emissions of vehicles are used to calculate the idle emissions and the running emissions of the vehicles for the current path with the congestion and also the alternative path to analyze the emissions in total to determine the path with least emissions. This paper proposes techniques for regulating the traffic by a dynamic signaling system as well as a new personalized alternate route alert system form a source to the destination.

Keywords: Big data · Gaussian filtering · Machine learning · Markov fields · Vehicular adhoc Networks (VANETs) · Traffic Reduction (TR) · Congestion Avoidance (CA)

1 Introduction

India shows a prominent increase in terms of Automobile usage. During 2010 the number of vehicles on road hit a mark of hundred million and by 2016 the number of vehicles nearly doubled and hit a mark of 210 million and is expected to hit a mark of 225 million vehicles by the year 2018. The increasing number of vehicles pose a great threat to the environment due to the amount of emissions by the

K. C. Santosh and R. S. Hegadi (Eds.): RTIP2R 2018, CCIS 1035, pp. 484–492, 2019.
https://doi.org/10.1007/978-981-13-9181-1_43

automobiles. The increasing automobile population is major cause for the traffic congestions. Whenever there is a traffic congestion, the pollution increases and is a threat i.e. global warming. Traffic congestion in city will create pollutions leading to environmental problems and has a greater impact on the society. The drivers of the vehicle in traffic conditions are prone to stress and delayed arrival to their destinations. This stress may change into lack of concentration in driving and leads to problems like road raging and increases the probability of facing a road accident. The economic cost of traffic congestion is also very high. The average delay per person is approximately 30 h per year in traffic for normal cities and exceeds 70 h in the metropolitan cities. These congestions not only cause a loss of time, also include the wasted fossil fuels due to road congestion. The traffic congestion will also impact the environment by the emissions. The longer the time the vehicles are in congestions, the more fossil fuels are burnt, resulting in increased CO_2 emissions and acts as a high risk factor to the inhabitant's health while at congestions. In order to reduce the traffic congestion problem, engineers use the recent development of data collection and communication techniques to develop an intelligent transportation systems (ITS) using artificial intelligence techniques and help in the analysis of the traffic information to direct the traffic flow smoothly. The ITS have become more and more popular in the recent years due to the larger number of congestions. Intelligent transport system has two strategies in avoiding traffic congestion. One is to change the path of the vehicles moving towards areas which are prone to congestions and another method is to alter the traffic lights to efficiently make use of roads. The low emission vehicles are being introduced in the recent years to minimize the pollution rates. In cities like delhi, the pollution rate has gone extreme that the people are suffering severe lung disorders due to the pollution particles which is accumulated as a smog. One of the reason for these conditions is the heavy traffic congestions. The pollution by the road traffic can be controlled by environmental optimization of the Traffic signal timings and introduction of green vehicles [1]. There are several case studies for analyzing the consequences of traffic on CO_2 and Black carbon emissions. These studies [3] describe the amount of emissions caused due to the lack of the intelligent transport systems which are capable of sensing the traffic congestions and dynamic signalling systems.

2   Literature Review

A Unified Framework for Vehicle Rerouting and Traffic Light Control to Reduce Traffic Congestion was proposed in [2]. Digital pheromones of vehicles are constructed over the route of travel, while roadside agents are deployed to collect the data and will combine them to analyze the real-time traffic. These results are used to predict the road congestions that may develop. This analysis will help in the process of regulating the traffic by adjusting the signals for optimal movement of the vehicles. Once congestion is predicted, the vehicles are selected according to the distance to the road where congestion is identified and their driving destiny, and a probabilistic strategy is used and local pheromone is used to change the path of the vehicles. Based on the traffic conditions, two pheromone-based strategies are used to automatically control traffic lights to minimize the level of the traffic congestion. A multi-agent system for handling the unexpected urban traffic congestion using next road rerouting was developed in [4]. The system helps drivers in selecting the alternate choice of road to avoid congestions ahead. A heuristic re-routing decision is made based on a cost model that analyses the driver's destination and local traffic conditions. The positive rerouting is dependent on four factors, namely the vehicle density, the travel time, distance to the destination and the alternate path closeness. This system suffers a problem of clearing a certain level of congestion by the dynamic change of the signals. A guidance system combined with a personalized re-routing system for reducing travelling time of vehicles in cities was proposed in [7], which uses a rank based approach to rank the vehicles that are to be re-routed according to a criteria, effective link travel time to alternate route for each vehicle is computed. The system is updated whenever a vehicle is re-routed on same route to compute the impact of this vehicle on the following alternate paths. The system also has a high chance of reducing the travel time and also does not make the alternate path to become congested creating more delays. An adaptive and VANETS-based system for unexpected traffic congestion avoidance was proposed by [4]. This system has a vehicle re-routing strategy which can adapt to road traffic conditions. This involves a smart calibration of the system without any need for traffic constables. A coefficient of variation is used to calculate the weight values involved in the routing cost function and uses the k-means algorithm to choose the number of agents. This adaptive-NRR strategy is combined with the vehicular ad-hoc networks (VANETs) technology to provide a traffic aware system which can sense the traffic information at much faster rate and has larger coverage. A traffic prediction algorithm by comparing the current traffic data with historical data proposed in [10]. These traffic prediction results are used to create a routing technique which provides intelligent route services for dynamic routing. The algorithms were implemented for the complex urban areas and congested cities. The route selection algorithm gives the adaptive routes based on the traffic conditions, also based on the user's preferences. Wenbin Hu et al tested an actual urban traffic simulation model (AUTM) to predict the traffic and also reduce the traffic congestions. The model includes three key components, one to get the actual cellular spaces, an optimized spatial evolution rules that make simulation of vehicular dynamics better, and a congestion-avoidance algorithm to dynamically change the routes from the current locations to the destination. VANET based congestion avoidance systems use the current local traffic situation to the other vehicles to optimize the traffic. A wireless vehicle to vehicle communication used by the system to identify routes by avoiding the congestions proposed in [13]. Each vehicle transmits its average speed to other vehicles nearby. These nearby vehicles will recalculate the alternate routes based on the possible speed that the vehicle can move in the roads ahead. However the transmission of data by nearby vehicles can be disturbed by the buildings near the streets and also loss of data due to several data transfers. A multi-agent based approach, for avoiding Congestion and Alternate Route Allocation using Virtual Agent Negotiation (CARAVAN) developed in [14]. Vehicles communicate at decision points in their route and the route-allocation is done at the junctions. Inter-vehicular communication is used to transmit information to the other vehicles and also uses distributed processing. Vehicles exchange the route preference information to identify the initial routes. The identified routes are improved using virtual negotiation deals. No physical communication is made and hence communication latency is reduced. This system creates a fast and best route allocation and with less communication overhead. A multi-agent centralized technique for optimizing traffic for signal control system developed in [15]. They used evolutionary strategy and the total vehicle mean delay is reduced by using this strategy. The green signal time was optimized based on the algorithm and produce better results.

3   Proposed System

The proposed system has two modules namely prediction of vehicles movement and the alternate route determination based on the minimized CO_2 emissions. The input video is taken from the traffic cameras mounted at the signals on the road. The input video is preprocessed first to remove the noise and background and foreground sub-traction process is carried out. This approach uses the Gaussian filtering technique to enhance the input video streams that come from the traffic cameras. The Gaussian features are useful for the process of enhancing the video frames or the edge detection process once the enhancing process is completed. Video surveillance processing algorithm uses the Gaussian function to remove the noise in the video files. The noise reduction process using Gaussian function first filters in the x-direction and then it is filtered by a filter in a direction that is non-orthogonal. Now the images are free from the noises that can be a potential threat in the process of vehicle detection and prediction of the flow of the vehicles. The Markov Random Field (MRF) background subtraction method is used to separate a moving object as a foreground from the background. The segmentation of the foreground object such as a vehicle from a traffic scene from a traffic surveillance camera is to be done in order to complete the process of tracking a vehicle. The surveillance camera could be static or dynamic in case of a Pan Tilt and Zoom (PTZ) camera. Hence the background subtraction process has to detect the objects moving from the difference observed between the current frame and the reference frame using a pixel by pixel method or a block by block method. This reference frame is known to be the background image or background model. Indian traffic has a change in dynamic traffic scenes and requires a good background model and has to adapt to dynamic scenes. The background information update process is done in periodic intervals to update the background information whenever there is a change in the background. Foreground objects in a video stream are identified using the background subtraction method. The most important stage in surveillance application is to detect the vehicles accurately only after which the analysis can be done. A background algorithm like Markov Random Field (MRF) is used to enhance the performance of the objects classification and detection process. The proposed classification process has a feature extraction process and a scene classification process. The surveillance system uses the feature sets obtained by the convolution of the local mask patterns with the object from video file. These masks have been introduced for determining the position of the object in a video. A different number of samples in each scene is used to train scene-specific classifier in order to differentiate the foreground object from the background. With different distribution of training images, the system is capable of getting better results to track the objects. The probability values are calculated based on the movement of the vehicles. The density of the traffic is noted from the count of the vehicles at any particular time. These values are combined together to get the details of the congestion. Once a congestion is detected, the alternate path (AP) algorithm is initiated. The alternate path algorithm is a two phase algorithm where the alternate path to the congested path is detected first and then the second phase for the calculation of the emission of the vehicle in the current path and the alternate path. The standard emissions of vehicles are used to calculate the idle emissions and the running emissions of the vehicles for the current path with the congestion and also the alternative path to analyze the emissions in total to determine the path with least emissions. There are several techniques to calculate the emissions of CO_2 which include a gas tester which involves more cost and less feasibility for testing. The visual analysis of emissions by a camera involves less cost but it is an inaccurate solution. The proposed method uses the standard emissions values that are used to define the actual idle time emissions and the run-time emissions. The total duration of the travel along several paths will be calculated and the one with low emissions is likely to be taken by the user as it will be a less time consuming travel which also has less driver stress than the other routes. The alternate path for the destination is searched using the Google maps functionality. The map image of the route is now taken as the input and the areas of congestion are found using the colour codes. Now the system estimates the time to reach the destination using the current path and also the alternate paths. The time parameter is stored for the two paths. Using the distance of the current path and the alternate path, the difference in the distance to the destination is computed. The alternate path algorithm combines the results of the distance and the time to compute the vehicle idle time and the running time for the alternate path and the current path. When the computed values of the alternate path is less than the current path, the values are used to calculate the amount of the emission reduction and time saved. These values are displayed to the user to make the decisions. Whenever the emissions of the alternate path is more than the percentage of the emissions in the current path, the user is advised to continue in the same route. The system will compute the data for each and every place where the congestion are detected so that whenever there is a chance of taking an alternate path can be taken.

Experimental Results. The system is tested based on the sample videos available online and the implementations are done using the Matlab software. The results of the object detection process are shown in Figs. 1 and 2 depicts the prediction of movement of the vehicles based on the probability values. The object which is detected using the proposed algorithm is identified and a box is drawn to depict the vehicle identified. The numerical value on the figure below shows the probability value for the prediction of the movement of the vehicle. Table 1 shows the details of the moving vehicles. The vehicles are numbered and the vehicle speed detected with the prediction probability and direction of movement of the vehicles is tabulated. The predicted values are 86% accurate compared to the actual movement and speed of the vehicles.

Table 1. Details of moving vehicles in the input video.

Car	Direction	Prediction	Speed (Kmph)
1	'Left'	0.88889	55.019
2	'Left'	0.88889	74.904
3	'Straight'	0.77778	2.081
4	'Left'	0.88889	21.144
5	'Right'	0.66667	3.441
6	'Right'	0.55556	13.317
7	'Right'	0.66667	3.5572
8	'Straight'	0.77778	3.4731

Fig. 1. Object detection.

The alternate path algorithm is based on the congestion and hence only when the congestion are identified, the system computes the alternate paths to the

Fig. 2. Movement prediction result for the proposed methodology.

Fig. 3. Traffic found in a route.

destination based on the current values of the GPS coordinates. Figure 3 shows the route from the current position to the destination where traffic congestion is detected. The alternate path that is identified using the AP algorithm is shown in the Fig. 4. The alternate paths identified by the algorithm must be a lower emission path; only then the route will be suggested to the user.

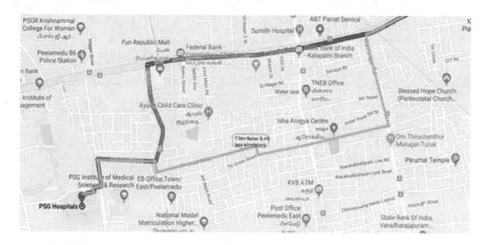

Fig. 4. Alternate path to the destination using AP algorithm.

4   Conclusion and Future Works

The paper proposed an intelligent traffic control system which helps the vehicles to avoid the traffic congestion and thereby reduce the CO_2 emissions by taking the alternate route and also utilizes the prediction of vehicles movement to predict the future traffic. The alternate paths are recommended based on the traffic and the amount of reduced emissions in the alternate path. Hence this system not only helps the drivers relieved from tensions over long waiting and pollution in traffic, but also reduces the total emissions by choosing the best alternate path. As a future work, the system can be integrated with the VANETs to communicate the information's about the speed and congestions ahead of start of the journey.

References

1. Stathopoulos, A., Argyrakos, G.: Control strategies for reducing environmental pollution from road traffic. Sci. Total Environ. **134**, 315–324 (1993)
2. Cao, Z., Jiang, S., Zhang, J., Guo, H.: A unified framework for vehicle rerouting and traffic light control to reduce traffic congestion. IEEE Trans. Intell. Transp. Syst. **18**(7), 1958–1973 (2017)
3. Kolbl, R., et al.: An assessment of VMS-rerouting and traffic signal planning with emission objectives in an urban network – a case study for the city of Graz. In: Models and Technologies for Intelligent Transportation Systems (MT-ITS), pp. 169–176 (2015)
4. Wang, S., Djahel, S., Zhang, Z., McManis, J.: Next road rerouting: a multi-agent system for mitigating unexpected urban traffic congestion. IEEE Trans. Intell. Transp. Syst. **17**(10), 2888–2899 (2016)
5. Pan, J., Popa, I., Borcea, C.: DIVERT: a distributed vehicular traffic re-routing system for congestion avoidance. IEEE Trans. Mob. Comput. **16**(1), 58–72 (2017)

6. Sanchez-Iborra, R., Cano, M.: On the similarities between urban traffic management and communication networks: application of the random early detection algorithm for self-regulating intersections. IEEE Intell. Transp. Syst. Mag. 9(4), 48–61 (2017)
7. Liang, Z., Wakahara, Y.: A route guidance system with personalized rerouting for reducing traveling time of vehicles in urban areas. In: IEEE 17th International Conference on Intelligent Transportation Systems (ITSC), pp. 1541–1548. IEEE Publishers (2014)
8. Wang, S., Djahel, S., McManis, J.: An adaptive and VANETs-based next road re-routing system for unexpected urban traffic congestion avoidance. In: IEEE Vehicular Networking Conference, pp. 196–203. IEEE Publishers (2016)
9. Maha Vishnu, V.C., Rajalakshmi, M.: Road side video surveillance in traffic scenes using map-reduce framework for accident analysis. Special Issue Biomed. Res., S257–S266 (2016). Special Section: Computational Life Science and Smarter Technological Advancement. ISSN 0970-938X
10. Kim, S., Kang, Y.: Congestion avoidance algorithm using extended Kalman filter. In: IEEE International Conference on Convergence Information Technology, pp. 913–918. IEEE Publishers (2007)
11. Hu, W., Wang, H., Yan, L.: An actual urban traffic simulation model for predicting and avoiding traffic congestion. In: IEEE 17th International Conference on Intelligent Transportation Systems (ITSC), pp. 2681–2686. IEEE Publishers (2014)
12. Kountras, A., Stathopoulos, Y.A.: Complementary diversion-sensitive route guidance systems. In: IEEE - IEE Vehicle Navigation and Information Systems Conference, VNIS 1993, Ottawa, pp. 363–366. IEEE Publishers (1993)
13. Wedel, W., Schunemann, B., Radusch, I.: V2X-based traffic congestion recognition and avoidance. In: 2009 IEEE 10th International Symposium on Pervasive Systems, Algorithms, and Networks (ISPAN), pp. 637–641. IEEE Publishers (2009)
14. Desai, P., Loke, W., Desai, A., Singh, J.: CARAVAN: congestion avoidance and route allocation using virtual agent negotiation. IEEE Trans. Intell. Transp. Syst. 14(3), 1197–1207 (2013)
15. Balaji, P.G., Sachdeva, G., Srinivasan, D., Tham, C.: Multi-agent system based urban traffic management. In: IEEE Congress on Evolutionary Computation, pp. 1740–1747 (2008)

An Experiment with Statistical Region Merging and Seeded Region Growing Image Segmentation Techniques

Anuja Deshpande[1](✉) ⓘ, Pradeep Dahikar[1] ⓘ,
and Pankaj Agrawal[2] ⓘ

[1] Department of Electronics, Kamla Nehru Mahavidyalaya,
Sakkardara, Nagpur 440024, Maharashtra, India
anuja_1978@yahoo.com, pbdahikarns@rediffmail.com
[2] Electronics and Communication Engineering Department,
G. H. Raisoni Academy of Engineering and Technology (GHRAET),
Nagpur 440028, Maharashtra, India
pankaz_agr@rediffmail.com

Abstract. This paper puts forth our observations from the experiments conducted on interactive segmentation techniques - Statistical Region Merging and Seeded Region Growing, both based on Region Growing methods, using Matlab software on selected natural images. Both these techniques meant to solve segmentation challenges posed by medical images and were effective as well; however, in this experiment, we have subjected natural images to these techniques to assess the effectiveness. We have chosen the images such that those have complexities and pose segmentation challenges. The objective of this experiment is to understand and assess the effectiveness of these techniques on select natural images, which have complex image composition in terms of intensity, color mix, indistinct object boundary, low contrast, etc. We have used Jaccard Index, Dice Coefficient and Hausdorff Distance as measures to assess the accuracy, besides visual assessment. We have compared the segmented images with ground truth using these accuracy measures. While both the techniques failed to give acceptable results on most of the images, relatively, we have found Statistical Region Merging to be slightly better than Seeded Region Growing method.

Keywords: Statistical Region Merging · Seeded Region Growing ·
Interactive segmentation · Effectiveness

1 Introduction

1.1 Background

Image segmentation is about extracting foreground or object of interest from background and image segmentation has been a challenge ever since the need came into existence. The purpose or application behind each segmentation need has been different and hence different algorithms; each suitable for the specific purpose. Since about last

© Springer Nature Singapore Pte Ltd. 2019
K. C. Santosh and R. S. Hegadi (Eds.): RTIP2R 2018, CCIS 1035, pp. 493–506, 2019.
https://doi.org/10.1007/978-981-13-9181-1_44

five decades hundreds of algorithms have been developed, but suitable for specific problem. Few decades back, as the advancements in medical engineering were beginning to take place, a lot of these were oriented to solve medical images; today however, Image Segmentation is actively in use in all forms of applications, which affect/influence our daily lives significantly. Image segmentation has direct influence and an important pivotal role in image analysis and computer vision applications. Successfully delineating area of interest and further extraction depends on the accuracy of the segmentation process and the outcome decides if the segmented image can be directly fed into next application or any additional processing is required. It appears that, Image Segmentation is still evolving although newer algorithms are improving the coverage for wider range of images, still it seems, we do not have one single algorithm, which can satisfy all segmentation problems.

As stated in [4], there are four main approaches [6, 7] for the segmentation of intensity images, viz. threshold-based, boundary-based, region-based, and hybrid techniques which combine boundary and region criteria. Threshold techniques [8] assume that adjacent pixels whose grey level or color value lie within a certain range belong to one class; either foreground or background and these methods discard spatial information of the image. In addition, Threshold techniques do not perform well if noise exists or the object boundary is blurred or has other complexities. The Boundary based methods [4] assume that the pixel values swiftly change at the boundary between two regions [9]. In this method, a gradient operator such as the Sobel or Roberts filter [4, 10] is employed and higher values of these filters yield pixels suitable for region boundaries. These need to be reformed, to yield closed curves, which represent the boundaries between the regions. It is difficult to convert edge pixels to boundaries of the regions of interest.

The counterpart of the boundary based [4] approach is the regions based approach [11]. In Region based methods, neighboring pixels falling within one region have similar values or attributes. This leads to creation of new family of algorithms known as region growing; "split and merge" technique [4, 12] is one of the best-known technique belonging to this class. In Region Growing method, one pixel is compared to its neighbor (4 or 8 connectivity) to evaluate homogeneity and if the condition is met, such pixels are grouped together to form the region. These methods are susceptible to noise and homogeneity criterion is extremely critical even to achieve moderate success [4, 13–15]. In the fourth type, i.e. hybrid approach [4], boundary and region criterion are combined. In this family, usually, morphological watershed segmentation [16] and variable-order surface fitting [6] is employed. As explained in [17], when the topography is flooded from the seed points, the region boundaries prevent water from different seed points from getting mixed up and yield the segmentation. Even if the transitions between regions are of variable strength or sharpness. The watershed algorithm is certain to yield closed boundaries. However, this technique is unable to be effective where regions are noisy and/or have blurred or indistinct boundaries. In the variable-order surface fitting method [6], a coarse segmentation of the image into several surface-curvature-sign primitives is performed and further refined using iterative region growing methods based on variable-order surface fitting.

In this experiment, we have studied and experimented on two techniques belonging to region growing and merging [1, 2], viz. Statistical Region Merging [3] and Seeded

Region Growing [4]. As stated in [3], in region merging, regions are grown iteratively by combining pixels which have similar properties to form region. Region growing/merging techniques usually employ statistical test to decide the merging of regions [1]. This test is used by a merging predicate and on the basis local decisions, builds the segmentation. This locality in decisions needs to preserve global properties, such as those responsible for the perceptual units of the image [2].

The key principle of Statistical Region Merging is to formulate image segmentation as an inference problem [5]. Statistical Region Merging algorithm is a method wherein values within a regional span are evaluated and based on the merging criteria and then grouped together. SRM has been used in wide range of image processing applications. In this method region merging is done following a particular order in the choice of regions.

The SRM algorithm with 4-connectivity can be described as, there are $N < 2|I|$ couples of adjacent pixels. Let S_I be the set of these couples. Let $f(P, P')$ be a real valued function, with p and p' pixels of I. At first the couples of S_I are sorted in increasing order of $f(.,.)$ and then traversed the order only once. The proposed algorithm makes for any current couple of pixels $(p, p') \in S_I$ for which $(R(p) \neq (R(p'),$ where, $R(p)$ stands for current region to which p belongs. The test $P(R(p), R(p'))$ and merge $(R(p)\,and\,R(p'))$ iff it returns true. The objective is to choose $f(.,.)$ so as to approximate A as best as possible. The merging predicate for SRM can be described as –

$$P(R, R') = \begin{cases} true & if\,|\bar{R}' - \bar{R}| \leq \sqrt{b^2(R) + b^2(R')} \\ false & otherwise \end{cases} \qquad (1)$$

Seeded Region Growing (SRG) [4] which is primarily oriented towards intensity images, is a region-based image segmentation method. Since it involves the selection of initial seed points, it is also known as pixel based image segmentation method. In this segmentation technique, neighboring pixels of initial seed points are examined to determine, if the pixels neighbor belong to the region and if so yes, are added to the region. This process iterates very similar to data clustering algorithms. Selection of initial Seed point is based upon user criterion such as pixels in a specific grayscale range, pixels evenly spread out on a grid, etc. The location of the seed leads to creation of initial region. Depending upon region membership criterion, such as pixel intensity, grayscale texture, color, etc., the region is then grown from this seed point to neighboring pixels until all pixels are grouped either belonging to the region of interest or outside. Seeded Region Growing can be expressed as –

$$\bigcup\nolimits_{i=1}^{n} R_i = R \qquad (2)$$

$$R_i\,is\,a\,connected\,region,\,i = 1,\,2,\,\ldots,\,n \qquad (3)$$

$$R_i \cap R_j = \emptyset\,for\,all\,i = 1,\,2,\,\ldots,\,n \qquad (4)$$

$$P(R_i) = TRUE \; for \; i = 1, 2, \ldots, n \tag{5}$$

$$P(R_i \cup R_j) = FALSE \; for \; any \; adjescent \; region \; R_i \; and \; R_j \tag{6}$$

The Eq. (2) states that every pixel belongs to a region and segmentation must be complete. Eq. (3) mandates that pixels in region are connected and those are disjoint as stated in Eq. (4). Equation (5) validates the properties which must be satisfied by pixels and Eq. (6) illustrates that region R_i and R_j are different in the context of predicate P. Logical predicate $P(R_i)$ is defined over the pixels in R_i and $\emptyset$ defines the null set.

Image information is important as the criterion used to group the pixels to form the region, e.g. for intensity threshold as criteria, knowledge of the histogram of the image would play an important role in grouping the pixels based on the suitable threshold value. Pixel adjacency relationship can employ 4-connected neighborhood or 8-connected neighborhood to grow from the seed point. The adjacency is assessed using iterative process until there is no change in two successive iterative stages and achieve the main goal of classifying the similarity of the image into regions.

Selection of initial seed point depends on the user and is crucial to achieve successful segmentation. For e.g. for grayscale image, using highest range from histogram may be helpful to achieve desired results. Minimum area threshold and similarity threshold values or homogeneity will determine adjacency of the pixels and thus regions.

2   Accuracy Measures

While there exist various methods to ascertain sensitivity and specificity, such as F1 score, True Positive Ratio (TPR), False Positive Ratio (FPR), Similarity Ratio (SIR), etc., these alone if used can lead to highly misleading results and additionally require worst-case for sensitivity and specificity to be calculated using methods like Average Hausdorff Error and Average Mean Error. Further, methods like Mean Squared Error have disadvantage that it weighs outliers heavily due to squaring function. ROC curve, is another measure for evaluation and uses TPR and FPR. Methods such as Jaccard Index, Dice Coefficient and Hausdorff Distance computationally inexpensive/faster, do not suffer from these shortcomings and yield conclusive results on similarity and diversity and hence used in this experiment to assess segmentation accuracy.

2.1   Jaccard Index

The Jaccard Index [18], also known as the Jaccard similarity coefficient, is a statistic used for comparing the similarity and diversity between the two sets. The Jaccard coefficient measures similarity between finite sample sets, and is defined as the size of the intersection divided by the size of the union of the sample sets:

$$J(A, B) = \frac{|A \cap B|}{|A \cup B|} = \frac{|A \cap B|}{|A| + |B| - |A \cap B|} \tag{7}$$

The Jaccard distance is obtained by subtracting the Jaccard coefficient from 1 and indicates dissimilarity between two sets. It is complementary to the Jaccard coefficient and is expressed by dividing the difference of the sizes of the union and the intersection of two sets by the size of the union:

$$d_J(A, B) = 1 - J(A, B) = \frac{|A \cup B| - |A \cap B|}{|A \cup B|} \tag{8}$$

2.2 Dice Coefficient

The Sørensen–Dice index [19], which was independently developed by the botanists Thorvald Sørensen and Lee Raymond Dice, is also an indicator used for comparing the similarity of two sets. Sorensen's formula was intended to be applied to presence/absence data, and is –

$$QS = \frac{2|A \cap B|}{|A| + |B|} \tag{9}$$

Where, |A| and |B| are the numbers of species in the two samples. QS is the quotient of similarity and ranges between 0 and 1. It can be viewed as a similarity measure over sets.

2.3 Hausdorff Distance

The Hausdorff distance [20], is also known as Hausdorff metric, and it measures how far two subsets of a metric space are from each other. Hausdorff distance is the greatest of all the distances from a point in one set to the closest point in the other set. Let X and Y be two non-empty subsets of a metric space (M, d). We define their Hausdorff distance dH (X, Y) as –

$$d_H(X, Y) = \inf\{\epsilon \geq 0; \ X \subseteq Y\epsilon \text{ and } Y \subseteq X\epsilon\} \tag{10}$$

Where

$$X \in \bigcup_{x \in X} \{z \in M; \ d(z, x) \leq \ \epsilon \tag{11}$$

3 The Experiment

In this experiment, we have studied and experimented on two techniques belonging to region growing and merging family [1, 2], viz. Statistical Region Merging [3] and Seeded Region Growing [4] and performed experiments using MATLAB software, to understand and study effectiveness of these techniques and accuracy of segmentation by assessing –

1. Visual confirmation
2. Jaccard Index
3. Dice Index
4. Hausdorff Distance

We have used the algorithms available at [28] for Seeded Region Growing and [29] for Statistical Region Merging techniques in this experiment. We have followed below process for this experimental study. The experiment involved performing segmentation, using varying initial seeds, study the impact on the output and such combination was chosen which had resulted in best output as final segmented image. For this experiment, we have considered select images from [26] and this segmentation evaluation dataset is free to use for research purposes. This image dataset consists of source image in RGB scale having sizes between 50 KB to 250 KB of varying dimensions. The image dataset also consists of ground truth for comparison. As stated in [26] the ground Truth has been constructed by doing manual segmentation by human subjects. We have used Grayscale images as an input to the segmentation process. The ground truth images were converted into binary using GIMP toolkit [27] for logical comparison with segmented image. We have performed following steps in this experiment (Fig. 1).

4   Observations

We have conducted this experiment on various natural images; however, have included only 10 such images, which we think are complex enough to pose a segmentation challenge to these techniques; intent being assessment of suitability. The original

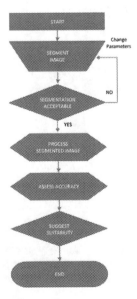

Fig. 1. Segmentation process

images are RGB images and we have converted those into grayscale image as an input to the segmentation process.

We have used Matlab 2017a on Windows PC to conduct this experiment and have observed that, relatively, Statistical Region Merging yields better output than Seeded Region Growing. We also observed that initial seed placement has significant impact on the segmentation output and we have chosen the best output based on visual confirmation for the comparison (Tables 1, 2, 3, 4, 5, 6, 7, 8, 9, and 10).

Visually, we can make out that Statistical Region Merging has been quite successful on the Segmentation Set I, II and III. All the three datasets have stark contrast between foreground object and background, even when converted into grayscale image. In this dataset, the boundaries of the foreground object are quite distinct and very sharp. Barring Segmentation Set I, Seeded Region Growing has failed to give acceptable results for Segmentation Set II and III.

Table 1. Segmentation Set I

Original Image	Ground Truth	Segmented Image (Seeded Region Growing)	Segmented Image (Statistical Region Merging)
Jaccard Index		0.810366427	0.960444028
Dice Coefficient		0.895251276	0.979822952
Hausdorrf Distance		6.08276253	3.464101615

Table 2. Segmentation Set II

Original Image	Ground Truth	Segmented Image (Seeded Region Growing)	Segmented Image (Statistical Region Merging)
Jaccard Index		0.705978409	0.965782565
Dice Coefficient		0.82765222	0.982593479
Hausdorrf Distance		10.63014581	3.605551275

Table 3. Segmentation Set III

Original Image	Ground Truth	Segmented Image (Seeded Region Growing)	Segmented Image (Statistical Region Merging)
Jaccard Index		0.893709614	0.903304475
Dice Coefficient		0.943871866	0.949195977
Hausdorrf Distance		4.582575695	7.280109889

Table 4. Segmentation Set IV

Original Image	Ground Truth	Segmented Image (Seeded Region Growing)	Segmented Image (Statistical Region Merging)
Jaccard Index		0.702536452	0.049034646
Dice Coefficient		0.825282127	0.093485275
Hausdorrf Distance		5.291502622	16.15549442

Table 5. Segmentation Set V

Original Image	Ground Truth	Segmented Image (Seeded Region Growing)	Segmented Image (Statistical Region Merging)
Jaccard Index		0.312908098	
Dice Coefficient		0.476664129	
Hausdorrf Distance		13.7113092	

Table 6. Segmentation Set VI

Original Image	Ground Truth	Segmented Image (Seeded Region Growing)	Segmented Image (Statistical Region Merging)
Jaccard Index		0.821411403	
Dice Coefficient		0.901950434	
Hausdorrf Distance		6.633249581	

Table 7. Segmentation Set VII

Original Image	Ground Truth	Segmented Image (Seeded Region Growing)	Segmented Image (Statistical Region Merging)
Jaccard Index		0.027366162	0.026435357
Dice Coefficient		0.053274407	0.051509054
Hausdorrf Distance		9.949874371	9.949874371

Table 8. Segmentation Set VIII

Original Image	Ground Truth	Segmented Image (Seeded Region Growing)	Segmented Image (Statistical Region Merging)
Jaccard Index		0.35723489	0.909278773
Dice Coefficient		0.526415719	0.952484033
Hausdorrf Distance		12.76714533	7.615773106

Table 9. Segmentation Set IX

Original Image	Ground Truth	Segmented Image (Seeded Region Growing)	Segmented Image (Statistical Region Merging)
Jaccard Index		0.061586124	0.05373217
Dice Coefficient		0.116026618	0.101984492
Hausdorrf Distance		14.35270009	15.49193338

Table 10. Segmentation Set X

Original Image	Ground Truth	Segmented Image (Seeded Region Growing)	Segmented Image (Statistical Region Merging)
Jaccard Index		0.123861027	0.441221163
Dice Coefficient		0.220420539	0.612287933
Hausdorrf Distance		14.24780685	9.591663047

In the Segmentation Set IV, both the techniques have failed to produce acceptable segmentation; the output is not complete. The high intensity line running along the vertical path in the foreground seems to have interfered with the Seeded Region Growing, resulting in incomplete object extraction. The similarity in foreground and background around this intensity line seems to have affected the output of the Statistical Region Merging technique as well.

Segmentation Set V and VI are a complete miss by Statistical Region Merging technique; however, Seeded Region Growing technique has yielded segmentation, though unacceptable. The complexity of the texture of the foreground object and similarity with certain background areas seem to have led to the failure for both the techniques.

Segmentation Set VII is a unique case where both the techniques have failed exactly same. The similarity of the foreground with background seems to have resulted in failed segmentation. Such an outcome is also due to localized approach employed by both the techniques with no clue about the global perception.

Segmentation Set VIII has complexities in unique ways, the background is visible through the transparent foreground object and a very high intensity spot at the base is adding to the segmentation challenges. Although both techniques have resulted in failed segmentations, Statistical Region Merging techniques still has handled these complexities quite well as compared with the Seeded Region Growing method. The only area where Statistical Region Merging could not handle well is where foreground and background have similarities in color/texture. Seeded Region Growing has resulted in failed segmentation completely.

Both the techniques have resulted in failed segmentation as is evident from the Segmentation Sets IX and X. Segmentation Set IX has complexities in terms of similarity in foreground and background color and texture, whereas in Segmentation Set X, both techniques have failed with a very similar output owing to darker areas in the foreground having similarity with background color.

5 Discussion

Both the techniques fall under category of Region Growing and Merging family and are matured and have been actively pursued by many researchers over last few decades. Seeded Region Growing and Statistical Region Merging are few of the variants belonging to this family, the others being Unseeded Region Growing [21] and its variants, λ-Connected segmentation [22, 25], Split-and-Merge (also called Quadtree) segmentation [23, 24], etc.

Placement of initial seeds is extremely important and directly influences the segmentation output; different choices of seeds leads to different output, almost in all the runs. These methods are localized and do not consider global view of the segmentation problem. In absence of the same, these methods when subjected to complex images are prone to segmentation failure. These methods and subsequent developments in this family of algorithms, some of which automatically place the seeds, largely have orientation towards solving segmentation problems in Medical imaging [30–35, 40] and not natural images. Recently, the authors of [36] have proposed for medical imaging, particularly for chest radiographs (CXR), newer method based on Edge-Map analysis for improving segmentation accuracy such that segmentation output can be directly fed to the next application for correct diagnosis. The authors of [37] for effective content-based image retrieval (CBIR) have proposed another significant approach in separation of subpanels from stitched multi-panel figures in biomedical images. The proposed technique also solves the problem which projection profile based methods cannot handle by performing line vectorization. In another recent development, for segmentation of complex images, the authors in [38] have proposed fuzzy binarization process to extract the regions using connected component principle [40] and have further proposed novel techniques for arrow detection [38, 39]; a key step towards region-of-interest (ROI) labeling for image content analysis. We have also seen that the subsequent developments have considered additional algorithms such as edge detection to complement the overall segmentation process and output.

6 Conclusion

For the region growing methods, placement of initial seed points is extremely important and can lead to success or failure of the segmentation process. These methods are effective where object to be separated has distinct edges with moderate to high contrast. Low contrast along the edges seems to affect the segmentation process adversely. Region Growing methods could not segment all such images successfully, where, edges were weak, had low contrast, or have similarity in foreground and background. In addition, these are computational expensive, sensitive to noise and are local with no global view of the problem. These methods usually employ threshold function. The experiment suggest that these algorithms are suitable to segment images with low complexities (Segmentation Set I to III) but are not suitable to segment images which have moderate to high complexity (Segmentation Set IV to X).

Acknowledgement. We acknowledge the great work done by the authors of Seeded Region Growing and Statistical Region Merging interactive image segmentation techniques belonging to Region Growing family. Both these techniques are quite popular and useful for fellow researchers to study various aspects of image segmentation.

References

1. Felzenszwalb, P., Huttenlocher, D.: Image segmentation using local variations. In: Proceedings of the IEEE International Conference, Computer Vision and Pattern Recognition, pp. 98–104 (1998)
2. Zhu, S., Yuille, A.: Region competition: unifying snakes, region growing, and Bayes/MDL for multiband image segmentation. IEEE Trans. Pattern Anal. Mach. Intell. **18**, 884–900 (1996)
3. Nock, R., Frank, N.: Statistical region merging. IEEE Trans. Pattern Anal. Mach. Intell. **26** (11), 1–7 (2004)
4. Adams, R., Bischof, L.: Seeded region growing. IEEE Trans. Pattern Anal. Mach. Intell. **16** (6), 641–647 (1994)
5. Forsyth, D., Ponce, J.: Computer Vision—A Modern Approach. Prentice-Hall, Upper Saddle River (2003)
6. Besl, P., Jain R.: Segmentation through variable-order surface fitting. IEEE Trans. Pattern Anal. Mach. Intell. **10**, 167–192 (1988)
7. Haralick, R., Shapiro, L.: Image segmentation techniques. Comput. Vis. Graph. Image Proc. **29**(1), 100–132 (1985)
8. Sahoo, P., Soltani, S., Wong, A.: A survey of thresholding techniques. Comput. Vis. Graph. Image Proc. **41**, 233–260 (1988)
9. Davis, L.: A survey of edge detection techniques. Comput. Vis. Graph. Image Proc. **4**, 248–270 (1975)
10. Ballard, D., Brown, C.: Computer Vision. Prentice-Hall, Englewood Cliffs (1982)
11. Zucker, S.: Region growing: childhood and adolescence. Comput. Vis. Graph. Image Proc. **5**, 382–399 (1976)
12. Horowitz, S., Pavlidis, T.: Picture segmentation by a directed split-and-merge procedure. In: Proceedings of the 2nd International Joint Conference on Pattern Recognition, pp. 424–433 (1974)

13. Cheevasuvit, F., Maitre, H., Vidal-Madjar, D.: A robust method for picture segmentation based on split-and-merge procedure. Comput. Vis. Graph. Image Proc. **34**, 268–281 (1986)
14. Chen, S., Lin, W., Chen, C.: Split-and-merge image segmentation based on localized feature analysis and statistical tests. CVGIP Graph. Models Image Proc. **53**(5), 457–475 (1991)
15. Pavlidis, T., Liow, Y.: Integrating region growing and edge detection. IEEE Trans. Pattern Anal. Mach. Intell. **12**, 225–233 (1990)
16. Meyer, F., Beucher, S.: Morphological segmentation. J. Vis. Commun. Image Represent. **1**, 21–46 (1990)
17. Vincent, L., Soille, P.: Watersheds in digital spaces: an efficient algorithm based on immersion simulations. IEEE Trans. Pattern Anal. Mach. Intell. **13**, 583–598 (1991)
18. Jaccard Index Web Page. https://en.wikipedia.org/wiki/Jaccard_index. Accessed 25 June 2016
19. Dice Coefficient Web Page. https://en.wikipedia.org/wiki/S%C3%B8rensen%E2%80%93Dice_coefficient. Accessed 25 June 2016
20. Hausdorff Distance Web Page. https://en.wikipedia.org/wiki/Hausdorff_distance. Accessed 25 June 2016
21. Shapiro, L., Stockman, G.: Computer Vision, pp. 279–325. Prentice-Hall, Englewood Cliffs (2001)
22. Chen, L., Cheng, H., Zhang, J.: Fuzzy subfiber and its application to seismic lithology classification. Inf. Sci. Appl. **1**(2), 77–95 (1994)
23. Horowitz, S., Pavlidis, T.: Picture segmentation by a directed split and merge procedure. In: Proceedings of the 2nd International Joint Conference on Pattern Recognition, pp. 424–433 (1974)
24. Horowitz, S., Pavlidis, T.: Picture segmentation by a tree traversal algorithm. J. ACM **23**(2), 368–388 (1976)
25. Chen, L.: The lambda-connected segmentation and the optimal algorithm for split-and-merge segmentation. Chin. J. Comput. **14**, 321–331 (1991)
26. Single object segmentation evaluation database, maintained by Sharon Alpert. Department of Computer Science and Applied Mathematics, Weizmann Institute of Science. http://www.wisdom.weizmann.ac.il/~vision/Seg_Evaluation_DB/index.html. Accessed 25 June 2016
27. GIMP image manipulation toolkit software. https://www.gimp.org. Accessed 25 June 2016
28. Region Growing Algorithm by Kirk-Jan Kroon. Segmentation by growing a region from seed point using intensity mean measure. https://in.mathworks.com/matlabcentral/fileexchange/19084-region-growing?s_tid=prof_contriblnk. Accessed 21 April 2018
29. Statistical Region Merging algorithm by Sylvain Boltz. Image segmentation using statistical region merging. https://in.mathworks.com/matlabcentral/fileexchange/25619-image-segmentation-using-statistical-region-merging. Accessed 21 April 2018
30. Poonguzhali, S., Ravindran, G.: A complete automatic region growing method for segmentation of masses on ultrasound images. In: 2006 International Conference on Biomedical and Pharmaceutical Engineering, pp. 88–92 (2006)
31. Malek, A., Rahman, W., Ibrahim, A., Mahmud, R., Yasiran, S., Jummat, A.: Region and boundary segmentation of microcalcifications using seed-based region growing and mathematical morphology. Procedia Soc. Behav. Sci. **8**, 634–639 (2010)
32. Oghli, M., Fallahi, A., Pooyan, M.: Automatic region growing method using GSmap and spatial information on ultrasound images. In: Proceedings of the 18th Iranian Conference on Electrical Engineering, pp. 35–38 (2010)
33. Jamil, N., Soh, H., Sembok, T., Bakar, Z.: A modified edge-based region growing segmentation of geometric objects. In: Proceedings of the Second International Conference on Visual Informatics: Sustaining Research and Innovations, Part I, pp. 99–112 (2011)

34. Shan, J., Cheng, H., Wang, Y.: Completely automated segmentation approach for breast ultrasound images using multiple-domain features. Ultrasound Med. Biol. **38**(2), 262–275 (2012)
35. Huang, Q., Yang, F., Liu, L., Li, X.: Automatic segmentation of breast lesions for interaction in ultrasonic computer-aided diagnosis. Inf. Sci. **314**, 293–310 (2015)
36. Santosh, K.C., Vajda, S., Antani, S., et al.: Edge map analysis in chest X-rays for automatic pulmonary abnormality screening. Int. J. Comput. Assist. Radiol. Surg. **11**(9), 1637–1646 (2016)
37. Santosh, K.C., Aafaque, A., Antani, S., et al.: Line segment-based stitched multipanel figure separation for effective biomedical CBIR. Int. J. Pattern Recogn. Artif. Intell. **31**(6), 1757003 (2017)
38. Santosh, K.C., Wendling, L., Antani, S., et al.: Overlaid arrow detection for labeling regions of interest in biomedical images regions. IEEE Intell. Syst. **31**(3), 66–75 (2016)
39. Santosh, K.C., Roy, P.: Arrow detection in biomedical images using sequential classifier. Int. J. Mach. Learn. Cybern. **9**(6), 993–1006 (2018)
40. Ruikar, D.D., Santosh, K.C., Hegadi, R.S.: Automated fractured bone segmentation and labeling from CT images. J. Med. Syst. **43**(3), 60 (2019). https://doi.org/10.1007/s10916-019-1176-x
41. Ruikar, D.D., Santosh, K.C., Hegadi, R.S.: Segmentation and analysis of CT images for bone fracture detection and labeling, Chap 7. In: Medical imaging: Artificial Intelligence, Image Recognition, and Machine Learning Techniques. CRC Press (2019). ISBN: 9780367139612

Machine Learning and Applications

Can We Understand Image Semantics from Conventional Neural Networks?

Thanh-Ha Do[1(✉)], Nguyen T. V. Anh[1(✉)], Nguyen T. Dat[2(✉)],
and K. C. Santosh[3(✉)]

[1] Department of Informatics, VNU University of Science, Hanoi, Vietnam
hadt_tct@vnu.edu.vn, vananhnt57@gmail.com
[2] FPT Technology Research Institute Hanoi, Hanoi, Vietnam
datnt18@fpt.com.vn
[3] Department of Computer Science, University of South Dakota, Vermillion, USA
santosh.kc@ieee.org

Abstract. The Convolutional Neural Networks (CNNs) have been employed successfully for object identification, behavior analysis, letters and digits recognition, etc. The researchers in computer vision committee have studied the capacity of this model in two directions. The first one is improving its performance by increasing layers of the network, using learned features, more data, or more computing (GPUs). The second one is theoretical understanding in architecture design, in optimization and in a generalization of deep networks. One of the first researches in limitation of CNNs in understudying the semantics of images has done by *Hosseini et al.* in 2017. This result puts the researchers in CNNs community to do more researches to keep up with proper understanding and continued advances in the fields. This paper also forces on analysis the CNNs capability in understanding semantics information in images by recognizing images of the same shape and semantics but opposite the intensity. Experimental results were done on MNIST and GTSRB dataset indicates the limitation of CNNs in understanding the image semantic.

Keywords: Drawback of CNN · Semantic image · Convolution

1 Introduction

In recent years, Convolutional Neural Networks (CNNs), one of the models of Deep Neural Networks, has had a lot of achievements in automatic feature extraction without human intervention and in an accurate prediction the labels of new data. In fields of computer vision, CNNs are leading the way in many computer vision tasks, such as object detection [4,16], word recognition [19,20], semantic segmentation [12]. Currently, CNNs is also considered as the best algorithm for

This research is funded by the Vietnam National University, Hanoi (VNU) under project number QG.18.04.

image classification since it analyzes information of images and then predicts labels for new images.

In the object recognition task, the performance of CNNs can be compared to the human capability. This success of CNNs has inspired researchers to exploit their abilities for understanding the semantics of images since human is incredible in recognizing objects without depending on brightness, scale, rotate, shape, color, etc. To the best of our knowledge, the first research about this capacity of CNNs is done by *Hosseini et al.* [6] and it quite surprised that following the authors CNNs do not recognize the semantics of the objects, but rather memorize the inputs. In [15] the authors also reported that CNNs cannot be an option when detecting pulmonary abnormalities over chest X-ray images.

In order to study and then continue advanced researches using CNNs in object recognition, this paper forces on analysis, find out the reasons why CNNs does not work well in understanding the semantics of images. To do that, we evaluate the performance of CNNs on recognition images have the same meaning (same object) but reversed in brightness. The original images are called the positive images and reversed version on brightness of positive images are named negative images.

The experiments have done on 4 types of CNNs and one full connected (FC) network with MNIST dataset, the variations on MNIST dataset, and grayscale version of German Traffic Sign Recognition Benchmark (GTSRB) dataset. During the first group of experiments, the training dataset is the positive images, and there are two test sets with the same number of images in which the first one includes positive images, and the second one is negative images. The results are presented that the negative set always achieved much lower accuracy than the positive set. This re-confirms the results in [6] about CNN does not understand the information in the image. The second group of experiments is done with the purpose of verifying the memorized capacity of CNNs: putting negative images in the training set will help increase the performance of CNN in recognition the negative examples.

By analyzing the experiment results, we found out the limitation of CNNs in understanding the semantics of objects is the using convolution operator. Because the convolution works directly on pixels using the kernel or the mask, therefore the change of grayscale value (the brightness) takes with to the change of the descriptor of images. In addition, the kernel is not good enough to keep the information of structure and the semantics of objects. Thus, to overcome the shortcomings of CNNs, adding more examples in training set is one direction, another direction is using classical methods in feature extract stage that can keep the structure and the semantics of images better than convolution filters.

The rest of this paper is organized as follows. Section 2 reviews definition of the Artificial Neural Network (ANN), it is the base to construct the CNN and Sect. 3 gives the basic concept of negative images and related works. Experimental results are provided in Sect. 4. Section 5 concludes the paper.

2   Convolutional Neural Networks

This section reviews the basic concepts of the ANN (Artificial Neural Networks) and then the CNNs (Convolutional Neural Networks). Artificial Neural Networks (ANNs), in general, are inspired from neural networks in the human brain. ANNs can be thought of as a robust approach to represent the dependence between vector x and label y of data. They are particularly effective for data with complex and hard to interpret and have had the great deal of success with handwriting recognition [1,11,13,14], object recognition, voice recognition [3,9], etc. However, in the field of computer vision, ANNs do not really give good results.

Images contain a lot of redundant information and the inputs, before putting into ANNs, have to be flattened. Thus, the data that ANNs learn from has a lot of noise. Moreover, the dimensions of the input is also a shortcoming of ANNs. In handwriting recognition that use MNIST dataset (ANNs achieve good results on this dataset), the images in this dataset have the size of 28×28 pixels, so the dimensions of the input vector for ANNs is $28 \times 28 = 784$. However, the images contain more complex information and larger size, for example, 128×128, the size of the input vector in the first layer is $128 \times 128 = 16384$. This leads to large calculations and easy overfitting. Resizing the images to smaller ones before vectorization is not feasible and thus inadvertently modifies the information that the network receives, even causing noise to the image. Furthermore, ANNs connect fully between layers and this is redundant for the images. Because the interdependence of two pixels that far apart is almost zero, the pixel only depends on the surrounding pixels. Consequently, Convolution Neural Networks (CNNs) are usually used to analyze information in images, reduce noise before putting to the network to train.

The CNNs analyze images through four main layers:

- Convolution layer: Uses different filters to highlight the features of the object in the image such as edges, line, colors, features in a region, etc.
- Pooling layer: Removes redundant information in images after convolution to reduce the spatial size of the representation, hence to not only reduce the amount of parameters and computation in the network, but also control overfitting. Simultaneously, this process does not loss any image properties.
- Rectified Linear Units layer (ReLU): This layer converts negative numbers to zero.
- Fully-connected layer: Designed as Neural Network with an input layer and an output layer, without the hidden layer. The input is the vectorization of the tensor on the previous layer. Since the input image has been adjusted, the input dimension of this layer is not too large.

Layers in CNNs can be repeated many times to get better representation data. Simultaneously, during training CNNs will adjust the weights and the filters.

3   Negative Images and Related Works

3.1   Negative Images

This paper evaluates the CNN's capability in understanding the semantics of images. To do this, CNNs will recognize two kinds of images, positive images, and negative images, but containing the same kind of information. In fact, positive images are the regular images provided by normal datasets, during the paper, the normal datasets are the basic MNIST, the variation of MNIST and the gray version of GTSRB dataset. The negative images are generated based on positive images with the same size and label. Both negative and positive images are easily identified by humans, but the a brightness of each pixel on the negative image is opposite the brightness of the corresponding pixel on the positive image. The brightest pixels on the positive image will be the darkest pixels on the negative image and vice versa, the darkest pixels on the positive image will be the brightest pixels on the negative image. More details of how to generating negative images from positive ones as following:

- If the positive image is binary image and the brightness at position n of column m of row is x, $x \in [0,1]$, the negative image at position n of column m of row is $1 - x$.
- If the positive image is grayscale image, the brightness at position n of column m of row is x, $0 \leq x \leq 255$, the corresponding negative image at position n of column m of row is $255 - x$.

For color images, do the same as grayscale images on each color channel. Figure 1 presents the positive images and their negative images corresponding.

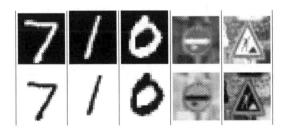

Fig. 1. Some examples of positive (first row) and negative images (second row)

3.2   Related Works

The effectiveness of CNNs depends on the training dataset and the structure of the network. Therefore, there are two research directions: the first one focus on enrich the dataset [2,5–7,21], and the second one improves the efficiency of convolution by developing other activation function or by improving feature extraction methods [10].

This first direction almost assumes that the larger of the training dataset, the more effective of CNNs. Therefore, the researches try to make a training set contains various forms of data. The images added to the training set are usually different in value of pixels but sometimes they are the same in structure or meaning. In addition, the number of distribution forms of data such as flip, rotate, color space transfer, etc is unlimited, so the generalization of the training set is almost impossible and unintentionally increases the noise for the data.

Besides that, the second direction is researches on the activation function, such as changing the ReLU function to cReLU [8,17], or using unsupervised feature learning [10]. In general, these methods of improving feature extraction of the image are more accurate and does not depend much on the forms of distribution data in the training set.

In this paper, besides improving the weakness of CNNs in understanding the semantics of images and its robustness in remembering the examples, we also compare the effectiveness of CNNs with different activation functions.

4   Experiment Results

The datasets are used in this paper is MNIST, the variations on MNIST digits, and the grayscale version of the German Traffic Signs Recognition Benchmark (GTSRB) datasets [18]. MNIST includes 10 classes representing handwritten digit from 0 to 9. Each example has the size of 28×28 pixels with a digit is centered, the background is black (pixel value equals 0) and the foreground introduced grayscale levels. In the experiment with the MNIST dataset, all images are normalized by divide each pixel by 255. In the experiment with MNIST, the size of the training set, testing set and validate set are 50.000, 10.000 and 10.000 respectively.

Variations on the MNIST dataset are more challenging than MNIST because they have fewer training samples and larger number of test samples. There are three kinds of variation databases used in this paper described as following and each variation has 10.000 training samples and 50.000 testing samples.

- $mnist - back - rand$: being digit images with uniformly distributed noise in back-ground
- $mnist - back - image$: being digit images with random image background
- $mnist - rot - back - image$: being digit images with random image background plus rotation.

The grayscale version of GTSRB is a dataset of traffic sign in real-world that consists of 43 classes. The images in this dataset have a lot of size with the smallest is 15×15 and the biggest is 250×250. Before put into CNNs, the images will be resized to the size of 32×32. The training set has 39.209 images, the test set has 12.630 images.

We conduct extensive experiments on 4 types of CNNs and one full connected (FC) network presented in Table 2. The difference between the CNNs is the number of convolution layer, we increase the number of convolution layer with the purpose of comparing the accuracy of CNNs when the convolution layer increase. In Table 1 conv $x \times x \times y$ denotes a convolutional layer with y filters of kernel size $x \times x$, pool $x \times x$ denotes a max pooling layer with $x \times x$ filters, FC x is a fully connected layer with x neurals/hidden layer, and $softmax$ is the softmax layer.

Table 1. The architectures used in the experiments.

Network 1	Network 2	Network 3	Network 4	Network 5
FC 100	conv $5 \times 5 \times 20$	conv $5 \times 5 \times 20$	conv $3 \times 3 \times 32$	conv $3 \times 3 \times 32$
softmax	pool 2×2	pool 2×2	conv $3 \times 3 \times 32$	conv $3 \times 3 \times 32$
	FC 100	conv $5 \times 5 \times 40$	pool 2×2	pool 2×2
	softmax	pool 2×2	conv $3 \times 3 \times 64$	conv $3 \times 3 \times 64$
		FC 100	pool 2×2	conv $3 \times 3 \times 64$
		softmax	conv $3 \times 3 \times 128$	pool 2×2
			pool 2×2	conv $3 \times 3 \times 128$
			FC 512	conv $3 \times 3 \times 128$
			softmax	pool 2×2
				FC 512
				softmax

To identify the power of CNNs, the precision rate is used. The higher the precision is, the high performance of recognition method.

$$precision = \frac{true\ positive}{true\ positive + false\ positive} \qquad (1)$$

In Eq. (1), true positive is the total number of images of which the true labels are similar with the predicted labels. The false positive is the total number of images of which the true labels are different from the predicted labels. The sum of true positive and false positive is the number of test set.

Table 2. Performance of CNNs in handwritten recognition with different activation functions

	Network 1	Network 2	Network 3
Sigmod	97.81%	98.86%	98.80%
ReLU	97.85%	98.58%	98.96%

The affect of activation functions is verified on MNIST dataset, and Table 2 indicates the performances of 3 networks for handwritten recognition using different activation functions. In general, two functions, the sigmod with the form f(t) $= 1/(1 + e^{-t})$ and ReLU with the form f(t) $= \max(0, t)$, give the quite similarity results, however the sigmod function involves expensive operation (exponentials) while ReLU can be implemented by simply thresholding a matrix of activations at zeros. Therefore, we decided to use ReLU function for the following experiments.

Table 3 presents the results since all images in training set are positive images and 2 types of test set, the first one is positive images (Positive results) and the second one is negative images (Negative results). These experimental results indicate the accuracy of the networks significantly change with negative data. With variations on the MNIST dataset, Network 1 gives the lowest results because it flattens the input image to a vector containing only information of grayscale levels. This vector does not reflect much of the interrelationships among the pixels in the image and the knowledge within the image. In addition, the negative images are images with reserved brightness, therefore the weight that network learned for the negative information storage area of negative images is destroyed while this does not happen to positive images. The recognition results are improved when using network 2 and 3 containing convolution layers to extract the information in the image before using full connected layer. The valuable properties of images including edges, lines, corners etc. used in FC layer instead of using only grayscale values, therefore the obtained results are better than network 1, but still not good enough. Particularly with Network 4 and Network 5, adding more layers reduces the performance of the network when working with the negative images (see Table 3(b)).

Table 3. Precision (%) when all images training is the positive and the test sets include the positive images (a), negative images (b).

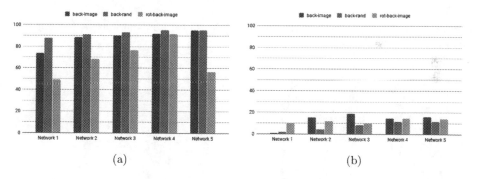

(a)   (b)

With GTSRB dataset consisting of a real-world images, the natural light makes both objects and backgrounds very bright or very dark. Thus there are still the big difference of performance of CNNs between the positive images and the negative images (see Table 4(a)).

The above results present the limitation of CNNs in understanding the images because even changing positive images to negative ones, the shape of objects over images does not change. One of the reason explains this drawback of CNNs are the limitation of convolution layers used to extract the descriptor of image.

Table 4. Performance of CNNs in handwritten recognition with different activation functions

Network	(a)		(b)	
	Positive result	Negative result	Positive result	Negative result
4	98.19%	13.26%	97.07%	96.12%
5	97.59%	12.01%	96.27%	94.15%

However, the recently good results on computer vision using CNNs is undeniable, this raise the question about what is the real robustness characteristic of CNNs: understanding or just memorizing?. In the next experiments, we will verify CNNs' capacity in memorize examples by adding some negative images into training set. More details, 1/3 images in training set now are negative images and the two test sets have no changes.

Tables 4(b) and 5 present the results obtained on GTSRB dataset as well as the variations on the MNIST dataset. In these table, the accuracy increased significantly and quite good, especially with the GTSRB. It confirms the robustness of CNNs in remembering the type of data. In addition, experimental results between Network 2 and 3; between Network 3 and Network 4 show a unstability of CNNs when the number of convolution layers increases. This proves that using more convolution layers sometimes is not good at extract properties of images, and sometimes it makes the noise. The number of convolution layers should match to the data type.

Table 5. Precision (%) for negative images with 1/3 training database is the negative images

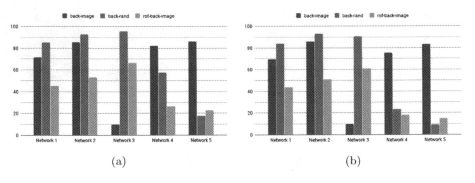

(a)   (b)

Figure 2 presents recognition results with 10 classes of MNIST dataset using Network 2 and 3 examples in GTSRB using Network 4. The mixed train refers to the training set having both positive and negative images and the positive train are the training set including only positive images.

Fig. 2. Illustration the recognition results of CNNs

5 Conclusion

The power of CNN is undeniable when it has succeeded on many visual applications, especially in the field of computer vision. However, CNNs have its own limits. In this paper, we confirm the limitation of CNNs in understanding the semantics of images by comparing the performance of CNNs on recognition two type of images having different value of pixels but presenting the same meaning. As the results, CNNs perform poorly when the test set does not have the same distribution as the training set. By changing the number of distribution data in the training set to make it more diversity, the CNNs work pretty well in this case. However, remembering but not understanding is not good for strong recognition model. Thus, in the future work, we will focus on the research of new descriptor network that allow to extract accurately the structure of the object and therefore can recognize the semantics of object.

Acknowledgements. This research is funded by the Vietnam National University, Hanoi (VNU) under project number QG.18.04.

References

1. Arnold, R., Miklos, P.: Character recognition using neural networks. In: 11th International Symposium on Computational Intelligence and Informatics (CINTI) (2010)
2. Chatfield, K., Simonyan, K., Vedaldi, A., Zisserman, A.: Return of the devil in the details: delving deep into convolutional nets. CoRR, abs/1405.3531 (2014)
3. Dede, G., Sazli, M.H.: Speech recognition with artificial neural networks **20**(3), 763–768 (2010)
4. Girshick, R.B., Donahue, J., Darrell, T., Malik, J.: Rich feature hierarchies for accurate object detection and semantic segmentation. CoRR, abs/1311.2524 (2013)
5. Hauberg, S., Freifeld, O., Larsen, A.B.L., Fisher III, J.W., Hansen, L.K.: Dreaming more data: class-dependent distributions over diffeomorphisms for learned data augmentation. CoRR, abs/1510.02795 (2015)
6. Hosseini, H., Xiao, B., Jaiswal, M., Poovendran, R.: On the limitation of convolutional neural networks in recognizing negative images. In: Computer Vision and Pattern Recognition (2017)
7. Krizhevsky, A., Sutskever, I., Hinton, G.E.: Imagenet classification with deep convolutional neural networks. In: Proceedings of the 25th International Conference on Neural Information Processing Systems, NIPS 2012, vol. 1, pp. 1097–1105. Curran Associates Inc., USA (2012)
8. Li, X., Jie, Z., Feng, J., Liu, C., Yan, S.: Learning with rethinking: recurrently improving convolutional neural networks through feedback. CoRR, abs/1708.04483 (2017)
9. Lim, C.P., Woo, S.C., Loh, A.S., Osman, R.: Speech recognition using artificial neural networks. In: Proceedings of the First International Conference on Web Information Systems Engineering. IEEE (2000)
10. Nguyen, K., Fookes, C., Sridharan, S.: Improving deep convolutional neural networks with unsupervised feature learning, pp. 3646–3653 (2015)
11. Perwej, Y., Chaturvedi, A.: Neural networks for handwritten english alphabet recognition. CoRR, abs/1205.3966 (2012)
12. Pinheiro, P., Collobert, R., Dollar, P.: Learning to segment object candidates. In: Advances in Neural Information Processing System 28 (2018)
13. Pradeep, J., Srinivasan, E., Himavathi, S.: Diagonal based feature extraction for handwritten alphabets recognition system using neural network. CoRR, abs/1103.0365 (2011)
14. Pradeep, J., Srinivasan, E., Himavathi, S.: Neural network based handwritten character recognition system without feature extraction. In: International Conference on Computer, Communication and Electrical Technology (ICCCET) (2011)
15. Santosh, K.C., Antani, S.: Automated chest x-ray screening: can lung region symmetry help detect pulmonary abnormalities? IEEE Trans. Med. Imaging **37**(5), 1168–1177 (2018)

16. Sermanet, P., Eigen, D., Zhang, X., Mathieu, M., Fergus, R., LeCun, Y.: OverFeat: integrated recognition, location and detection using convolutional networks. In: The International Conference on Learning Representations (2014)
17. Shang, W., Sohn, K., Almeida, D., Lee, H.: Understanding and improving convolutional neural networks via concatenated rectified linear units. CoRR, abs/1603.05201 (2016)
18. Stallkamp, J., Schlipsing, M., Salmen, J., Igel, C.: Man vs. computer: benchmarking machine learning algorithms for traffic sign recognition. Neural Netw. **32**, 323–332 (2012)
19. Suryani, D., Doetsch, P., Ney, H.: On the benefits of convolutional neural network combinations in offline handwriting recognition. In: The 15th International Conference on Frontiers in Handwriting Recognition (2016)
20. Ukil, S., Ghosh, S., Obaidullah, Sk.Md., Santosh, K.C., Roy, K., Das, N.: Deep learning for word-level handwritten indic script identification. CoRR, abs/1801.01627 (2018)
21. Wang, N., Li, S., Gupta, A., Yeung, D.: Transformation pursuit for image classification. CoRR, abs/1501.04587 (2015)

Semantic Memory Learning in Image Retrieval Using k Means Approach

Pushpa B. Patil[1(✉)] and M. B. Kokare[2]

[1] BLDEA's V. P. Dr. P.G. Halakatti College of Engineering and Technology,
Vijayapur 586103, Karnataka, India
cs.pushpa@bldeacet.ac.in
[2] SGGS IOT, Nanded, Maharashtra, India

Abstract. To reduce the conceptual gap in content-based image retrieval (CBIR) and small training problem in relevance feedback (RF), this paper attempts to focus on the semantic memory learning in image retrieval using proposed 2-means clustering. In this system, initial retrieval results of CBIR are obtained, and then user's opinion is given to the system as relevant/irrelevant to the user. With this user feedback, we can easily make the relevant image cluster and the irrelevant image cluster directly instead of random selection. Hence with initial known clusters and number of clusters, computational time is highly reduced for finding cluster center. We have also reduced the burden of clustering by considering only relevant cluster repeatedly for each feedback iteration. We experimented on two different data sets using proposed system. Results are found better compared to the earlier approaches.

Keywords: Image retrieval · k-means · Relevance feedback · Complex wavelets

1 Introduction

In this internet era, there is rapid enhancement and changes in digital technology. Hence there is a big collection of different variety of digitized images with respect to different applications like medical, entertainment, and biometric etc. So it is like galaxy with millions or billions of stars. With such huge information, user needs to search, browse, and retrieve relevant information. For fulfillment of the user, there is a need for efficient and effective retrieval systems. So in past, researchers introduced two kinds of retrieval systems namely based text and content of image. Initially, there was only image retrieval based text. The drawback of this system is manual labeling of huge image collection. It leads increase in labor cost and difficult to maintain user perception. To address these problems, researcher introduced Content Based Image Retrieval (CBIR) in the year 1990. It retrieves the images based on low level features like texture, color and shape etc. Therefore it is called as content based image retrieval. Earlier, a few marketable products and experimental models were developed, such as

© Springer Nature Singapore Pte Ltd. 2019
K. C. Santosh and R. S. Hegadi (Eds.): RTIP2R 2018, CCIS 1035, pp. 520–533, 2019.
https://doi.org/10.1007/978-981-13-9181-1_46

Virage, QBIC, SIMPLIcity, VisualSEEK, Netra and Photobook. Detailed surveys on CBIR presented in [2,4,17,18] In addition to these approaches, recently ontology based annotation tool used for image retrieval [13].

1.1 Related Work

Relevance feedback is a semantic classification approach. Here, user feeds both relevant and/or irrelevant data, and then it learns from that input to divide all data into appropriate and in appropriate groups with respect to query image. Hence many supervised machine learning algorithms are useful to design RF, namely Bayesian learning [19], decision tree learning [9], support vector machines and Gaussian mixture models [10], boosting, Re-weighting and, Query refinement [1] so on. The learning procedure is very hard job in RF, because of three causes, firstly training data set size is small, secondly imbalance in training data set images, finally RF takes more real time since both testing and training process has to be performed online for every feedback iteration.

Liu and Yu [8] used k-means to cluster images in the image database then similarity is applied to the clustered database instead of feature database in order to reduce retrieval time. With known number of image categories it works better. Murthy et al. [11] used hierarchical and the k-means clustering algorithms to group the images into clusters based on the color content. Initially images in the database are filtered using Hierarchical clustering and then applied the clustered images to k-means for better retrieval performance. Mishra et al. [12] used k-means to classify the coherent pixels and incoherent pixels for color images. With these observation of the above literature review in context to k-means clustering in CBIR, we found that k-means is applied for low level content in earlier approaches rather than semantic learning. Santosh et al. [21,22] proposed dynamic time warping for matching radon features. In 2018, Engin, and Cavusoglu proposed rotation invariant features using curvelet transform for retrieval of images [23].

The major goal of this paper is briefed out here, we have presented new semantic learning in image retrieval using 2-means clustering algorithm. With this we try to solve the small training data problem (number of training data is less than feature vector dimension) and real time problem (since RF is an online process). Relevance feedback works on two known image group namely relevant image group and irrelevant image group, this motivates us to use k-means algorithm to find the clusters centers directly instead of random computation. Hence we achieved better retrieval performance with less computational time. The practical results of anticipated method perform superior, compared to earlier method.

The remaining part of the paper is structured as follows. We discuss the image descriptors in brief in Sect. 2. The general k-means approach and proposed semantic memory learning in image retrieval using modified k-means algorithm called 2-means clustering are discussed in Sect. 3. Results are discussed in Sect. 4 and last section concludes.

2   Image Descriptors

We extracted the image features using combined "rotated complex wavelet filters (DT-RCWF)" and "complex wavelets (DT-CWT)". As a result, we will get information in twelve different directions. However results of depend on visual features [14] and similarity metrics [5]. Both the wavelets are discussed in the following section.

2.1   Complex Wavelet Transforms

DWT has drawbacks, namely it gives only four directional information with lack of shift invariance. To address these problems of DWT, We used dual tree complex wavelet transform (DT-CWT) [7]. It provides six directional information namely $(-15°, -45°, -75°, +15°, +45°$ and $+75°)$ shown in Fig. 1.

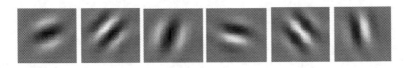

Fig. 1. Six orientations of the Wavelet Filters $(15°, 45°, 75°, -15°, -45°$ and $-75°)$ of Complex Wavelet.

2.2   Rotated Complex Wavelet Transforms

In 2005, authors [6] created 2D rotated complex wavelet filters(RCWF) which gives six different direction information's, which is 45° away from each other from decomposition of DT CWT. Hence we have another six different directional information oriented at $(30°, 0°, +30°, +60°, 90°$ and $120°)$. The six orientations associated with this are illustrated in Fig. 2. For similarity measure we used the Canberra distance measure. With these image features we developed the new relevance feedback framework using k means clustering in the following section.

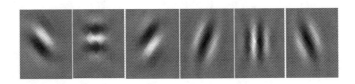

Fig. 2. Six orientations of Rotated Complex Wavelets $(-30°, 0°, +30°, +60°, 90°$ and $120°)$

3   Proposed Semantic Memory Learning Framework

The fundamental pace of k means is used to decide number of cluster k and then assume the centroid or center of these clusters. Since k is unknown for classification of objects. Therefore it considers any arbitrary objects as the initial centroids. An algorithm 1 will depicts the sequence of steps until convergence in general k-means clustering

Algorithm 1. *General k -means algorithm*

```
Inputs:o={o1,o2,...ok}   {objects to be clustered}
       k:number of clusters
Outputs: C={c1,c2,...ck} (cluster centroids)
         m:O->{1...k}(cluster membership)
1    Begin
2         Set  C to initial value (e.g. random selection of O )
3         For each oi belongs to O do
4              m(oi)=      argmin          dist(oi,cj)
                      j belongs to{1...k}
5         End
6         While m  has changed do
7              For each  i belongs to {1...k}  do
8                   Recompute the ci  as the centroid of {o|m(o)=i}
9                End
10             For each oi belongs O do
11                m(oi)=      argmin          dist(oi,cj)
                        j belongs to{1...k}
12             End
13        End
14   End
```

Here we presented novel RF approach using k means. The k-means plays an important role in relevance feedback in CBIR. However cost of computation of the initial cluster center is more using random objects as we have seen in the Algorithm 1. In this section we introduced the k-means algorithm for image retrieval, which takes least amount of computational time for generation of the cluster centers.

Figure 3 depicts the basic modules of the proposed semantic memory learning framework for interactive image retrieval. In order to reduce the conceptual gap between low level content and high level perception, the traditional CBIR system is enhanced by introducing relevance feedback (RF) loop in it. The relevance feedback is an online process, it takes the feedback (relevant/irrelevant) from the user and refines results using supervised/unsupervised [9,10,19,20] or query point movement or re-weighting approach [1]. It is continued till the user fulfillment or the output does not improve further.

In the proposed system, we used k-means clustering to retrieve the user perception information. However the k-means is unsupervised learning and cost of computation of the cluster center is more. If number of cluster centers k and dimension of vector d is constant, then the cluster center can be computed in

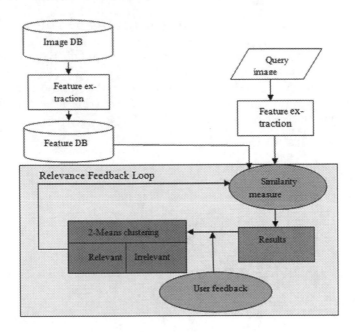

Fig. 3. Proposed system architecture

time $O(n^{dlogn})$, where n is the number of images to be clustered. Hence in this system k and d values are fixed and small values. That is $k = 2$ and $d = length$ of the feature vector. It motivates us to use k-means clustering for semantic learning with known number of cluster and hence it is easy to compute the cluster center in constant time(best case efficiency). In Sect. 3.1, the proposed semantic memory learning in image retrieval system is discussed in detail.

3.1   Proposed 2 Means Approach

The performance of the k means limits due to random selection of initial centroid by the user. It motivates to propose clustering algorithm which computes centroids appropriately with known relevant and irrelevant groups; As a results this, we will get the real and proper creation of the clusters. The proposed system uses the results obtained from CBIR as the initial training set. Then training set is annotated by user either relevant or irrelevant. Thus the training data set consists of N input vectors $(X_1, X_2, X_3, \ldots, X_N)$ with corresponding labels $(t_1, t_2, t_3, \ldots, t_N)$ and new data's are classified using k-means clustering. From user feedback, we have relevant data set $fr = \{fr_1, fr_2, \ldots, fr_p\} \subset X$ and irrelevant $fn = \{fn_1, fn_2, \ldots, fn_q\} \subset X$ such that $f_n \cap f_r = \phi$ (i.e null set). Where p and q are the number of related and unrelated images respectively. Hence the number of clusters $k = 2$. We determine the two cluster center for relevant image group $\overline{fr}$ and irrelevant image group $\overline{fn}$ using Eqs. (1) and (2) respectively.

$$\overline{fr} = \frac{1}{p} \sum_{i=1}^{p} fr_i \tag{1}$$

$$\overline{fn} = \frac{1}{q} \sum_{i=1}^{q} fn_i \tag{2}$$

We determine the similarity distance with the database images and relevant image group centriod $\overline{fr}$ and irrelevant image group centriod $\overline{fn}$ using Eqs. (3) and (4) respectively.

$$dr = \sum_{i=1}^{d} \frac{|x_i - \overline{fr}|}{|x_i| - |\overline{fr}|} \tag{3}$$

$$dn = \sum_{i=1}^{d} \frac{|x_i - \overline{fn}|}{|x_i| - |\overline{fn}|} \tag{4}$$

Hence it makes us to categories the relevant image group and irrelevant image group based on minimum distance. To speed up the testing time, here we concentrated on relevant image group and neglected the irrelevant group in every iteration of the feedback. We used the memory learning concepts to produce the results in feedback iteration.

4   Experimental Results

We conducted experiments with known number of category in the database and number of images in each category, we have designed RF framework to obtain the user feedback automatically. In this design, images belongs to the category of the query image are considered as relevant. In RF, we can carry out the number of rounds repetitively till there is no improvement in results/user satisfaction. Since, the numbers of rounds are directly proportional to the retrieval performance. A system tested for evaluation of retrieval performance by taking into account of top 20 images for each iteration. For performance evaluation the approach, we employed both Brodatz texture [6] and Corel color image dataset [3].

4.1   Image Data Set

We have used two standard image databases namely Brodatz texture data set and Corel Image Data Set. Brodatz texture data set comprises 116 variety textures. Size of image is 128×128. Database includes 1856 such images. Figure 4 shows the sample image of the each category from Brodatz texture database. Corel image set comprises 1000 color images of size 384×256 pixels, includes a various natural to artificial scenes [3]. The data set is divided into ten categories, each with 100 images. Ten categories are namely Dinosaurs, African people, Flowers, Beach, Building, Buses, Elephants, Horses, and Food. Figure 5 shows the example image of the each category from Corel natural color image database.

Fig. 4. Example Image of each category: Brodatz texture dataset-116 categories

Fig. 5. Example Image of each category: COREL image dataset-10 categories

4.2   Performance Parameters

For retrieval performance analysis, it is important to define a appropriate metric for performance evaluation. Therefore following performance measures are used.

$$recall = \frac{No. \quad of \quad relevant \quad images \quad retrieved}{Total \quad No. \quad of \quad relevant \quad images \quad in \quad the \quad Database} \tag{5}$$

$$precision = \frac{No. \quad of \quad relevant \quad images \quad retrieved}{Total \quad No. \quad of \quad relevant \quad images \quad retrieved} \tag{6}$$

A system performance is tested for 116 images from the texture database. The average accuracy is computed for all tested images. In each experiment, from each category randomly one image was selected as a query image. Thus, we have retrieved images. Then, the users has to identify images which are relevant from the retrieved images. This user selection image set is fed to the RF system for next round. Finally, average accuracy of all the categories in the database is computed. The number of iterations were performed up to 8 times for texture

Table 1. Average accuracy on each feedback iterations for texture data set

Approach	CBIR	1st iter	2nd iter	3rd iter	4th iter	5th iter
k-means (proposed)	78.50	89.83	91.41	92.27	92.60	92.82
SVMRF	78.50	89.27	91.75	92.18	92.29	92.29
ADABoostRF	78.50	88.52	91.32	91.70	91.70	91.70

database and 13 times for Corel database. Since the feedback process is repeated until result doesn't improve further.

Figure 6 depicts comparative retrieval results obtained using, AdaBoostRF, SVMRF and proposed k means RF on every feedback. The proposed k-means RF is compared with SVMRF [15] and AdaBoostRF [16]. From Fig. 6 we can observe that, the proposed k-means RF framework is better over AdaBoostRF and SVMRF However there is a quick boost in retrieval performance with each feedback of RF using both methods. Finally, the accuracy of k-mreansRF is also higher than that achieved by the SVMRF and AdaBoostRF, starting from the first iteration. Results are depicted in Table 1. Note that retrieval results of AdaBoostRF and SVMRF remain same after 3th and 4th iteration respectively, however results of the kmeansRF increases the retrieval performance from the previous iteration to the next iteration. It can be also observed that the performances achieved by Bordatz dataset are usually higher than those of the Corel data set. The reason of this performance is related to the different semantic of the images contained in the two datasets, and to their subdivision into categories. Similarly we computed results for Corel image data set, which consists of 10 categories of images and in each category 100 natural colour images. For testing we have selected randomly 5 images from each category as query images

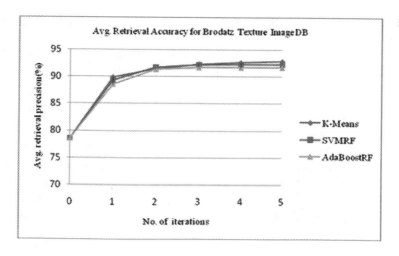

Fig. 6. Number of iteration versus average accuracy for texture images

(altogether 50 images). The reported results of average precision are obtained by taking an average over the 50 queries. Figure 7 depicts the complete assessment of average retrieval precision got from using SVMRF [15], AdaBoostRF [16] and proposed k-means RF on every feedback iteration for Corel Images. We can observe from the Fig. 7, the proposed approach produced superior retrieval performance than the Single_RBF and RBFGaussFunction anticipated by Ding et al. [3]. Results are listed in Table 2.

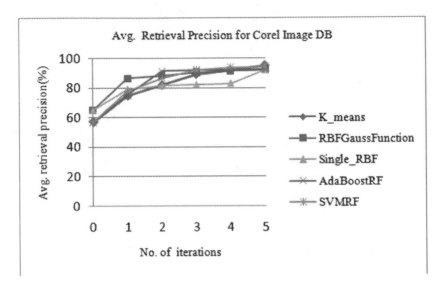

Fig. 7. Average precision versus iteration curves for Corel images

As stated before we have conducted experiments on five set of images, in each set we selected randomly an image from each category. In total there are ten categories in the database. Thus we tested 10 images from each image set. Hence, total number of testing images is fifty (5 × 10). For more clarity, Figs. 8(a)–(d) and 9 shows the precision versus the iterations curves of five testing image sets separately. For more clarity observe catg_2 (buildings image) graph in Fig. 8(b), where CBIR retrieval precision of catg_2 image is 20% and then it increases to 70% in the first iteration, 85% in the second iteration, 90% in the third iteration, 100% in the fourth iteration, and finally from the fifth iteration on words result remains same. For catg_5 (i.e Dinosaur image) in all five image sets (see Figs. 8(a)–(d) and 9) retrieval precision is 100% without relevance feedback. Furthermore, from all image sets in the Figs. 8(a)–(d) and 9, more than five categories images reached 100% precision at the fifth iteration of system.

Table 2. Average precision of each feedback iteration for Corel image database

Approach	CBIR	1st iter	2nd iter	3rd iter	4th iter	5th iter
RBFGaussFunction	65.2	86.5	88.4	90.4	91.5	92.3
SingleRBF	65.2	79.2	81.9	82.3	83.1	84.6
AdaBoostRF	57.2	75.4	91.32	91.70	91.70	92.5
SVMRF	57.2	78	86.9	92.2	94.0	94.6
k means (proposed)	57.2	74.9	81.96	89.35	91.89	95.07

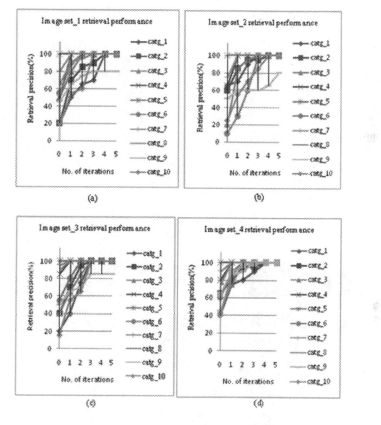

Fig. 8. Precision of all 10 categories images of Corel DB versus iteration curves five image sets: (a) Image set 1, (b) Image set 2, (c) Image set 3, (d) Image set 4

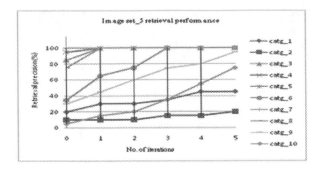

Fig. 9. Precision of all 10 categories images of Corel DB versus iteration curves five image sets: Image set 5

4.3 Image Retrieval Examples

Figures 10, 11 and 12 shows improvement of retrieval performance from the initial CBIR results to second feedback iteration. We can observe from Fig. 10, retrieval precision of initial CBIR is 55% and then retrieval precision is increased from 55% to 85% in the first round of the relevance feedback (see Fig. 11). Finally, we can observe from Fig. 12, improvement of retrieval precision reaches to the 100% in second iteration.

Fig. 10. Initial retrieval results of CBIR (11/20)

Fig. 11. Results after first feedback iteration (17/20)

Fig. 12. Results after second feedback iteration (20/20)

5   Conclusion

We have developed new semantic memory learning in image retrieval using k-means clustering. It is an interactive online RF process, hence the utilization of k-means become effective and efficient with known number clusters fed from the user in every round of feedback. In order to boost the retrieval time we considered only positive image group. It uses Canberra distance to classify the relevant and irrelevant image group. It is experimented on both e texture image database and natural image database. Proposed system gives very promising retrieval accuracy and precision. Proposed system can be extended to develop

RF for different unsupervised clustering algorithm Fuzzy C means, k-memoids, and to support the linear composition of the clustering as future work.

References

1. Chiang, C.C., Wu, J.Y., Yang, M.T.: Independent query refinement and feature re-weighting using positive and negative examples for content-based image re-trieval. Multimedia Tools Appl. **41**, 27–43 (2009)
2. Datta, R., Joshi, D., Li, J., Wang, J.Z.: Image retrieval: ideas, in-fluences, and trends of the new age. ACM Comput. Surv. **40**(2), 5:1–5:60 (2008). Article no. 5
3. Ding, R., Ji, X., Zhu, L.: Research on the relevance feedback based image retrieval in digital library. PWASET **25**, 48–53 (2007). ISSN 1307–6884
4. Kokare, M.B., Chatterji, B.N., Biswas, P.K.: A survey on current content-based image retrieval methods. IETE J. Res. **48**(3 and 4), 261–271 (2002)
5. Kokare, M.B., Chatterji, B.N., Biswas, P.K.: Comparison of similarity metrics for texture image retrieval. In: IEEE TENCON, pp. 571–575 (2003)
6. Kokare, M.B., Chatterji, B.N., Biswas, P.K.: Texture image retrieval using new rotated complex wavelet filters. IEEE Trans. Syst. Man Cybern. Part B: Cybern. **35**(6), 1168–1178 (2005)
7. Kingsbury, N.G.: Image processing with complex wavelet. Phil. Trans. Roy. Soc. London A **357**(1999), 2543–2560 (1999)
8. Liu, H., Yu, X.: Application research of k-means clustering algorithm in image retrieval system. In: Proceedings of the Second Symposium International Computer Science and Computational Technology (ISCSCT 2009), China, 26–28, pp. 274–277 (2009)
9. MacArthur, S.D., Brodley C.E., Shyu, C.R.: Relevance feedback decision trees in content-based image retrieval. In: Proceedings of the IEEE Work-Shop Content-Based Access of Image and Video Libraries, pp. 68–72 (2000)
10. Marakakis, A., Galatsanos, N., Likas, A., Stafylopatis, A.: Combining Gaussian mixture models and support vector machines for relevance feedback in content based image retrieval. In: Iliadis, Maglogiann, Tsoumakasis, Bramer, (eds.) IFIP International Federation for Information Processing, vol. 296, pp. 249–258. Springer, Boston (2009). https://doi.org/10.1007/978-1-4419-0221-4_30
11. Murthy, V.S., Vamsidhar, E., Swarup Kumar, J.N.V.R., Rao, P.S.: Content based image retrieval using hierarchical and k-means clustering techniques. Int. J. Eng. Sci. Technol. **2**(3), 209–212 (2010)
12. Mishra, J., Sharma, A., Chaturvedi, K.: An unsupervised cluster-based image retrieval algorithm using relevance feedback. Int. J. Manag. Inf. Technol. (IJMIT) **3**(2), 10–16 (2011)
13. Horvat, M., Grbin, A., Gledec, G.: Labeling and retrieval of emotionally annotated images using WordNet. Int. J. Knowl. Based Intell. Eng. **17**(2), 157–166 (2013)
14. Patil, P.B., Kokare, M.B.: Interactive content -based texture image retrieval. In: IEEE ICCCT2011, MNNIT, Allahabad, 15–17 September, pp. 71–76 (2011)
15. Patil, P.B., Kokare, M.B.: Relevance feedback in content-based image retrieval. In: Proceeding of 4th International Conference Computer Application in Electrical Engineering-Recent Advances, pp. 364–367. IIT Roorke (2010)
16. Patil, P.B., Kokare, M.: Semantic learning in interactive image retrieval. In: Nagamalai, D., Renault, E., Dhanuskodi, M. (eds.) DPPR 2011. CCIS, vol. 205, pp. 118–127. Springer, Heidelberg (2011). https://doi.org/10.1007/978-3-642-24055-3_12

17. Rui, Y., Huang, T.S., Chang, S.F.: Image retrieval: current techniques, promising di-rections and open issues. J. Vis. Commun. Image Represent. **10**, 39–62 (2011)
18. Smeulders, A.W.M., Worring, M., Santini, S., Gupta, A., Jain, R.: Content - based image retrieval at the end of the early years. IEEE Trans. Pattern Anal. Mach. Intell. **22**(12), 1349–1380 (2000)
19. Su, Z., Zhang, H., Li, S., Ma, S.: Relevance feedback in content-based image retrieval: Bayesian framework, feature subspaces, and progressive learning. IEEE Trans. Image Process. **12**(8), 924–936 (2003)
20. Tieu, K., Viola, P.: Boosting image retrieval. In: Proceedings of the IEEE Conference Computer Vision Pattern Recognition, pp. 228–235 (2003)
21. Zhou, X.S., Huang, T.S.: Relevance feedback in image retrieval: a comprehensive review. Multimedia Syst. **8**(6), 536–544 (2003)
22. Santosh, K.C., Lamiroy, B., Wendling, L.: DTW-radon-based shape descriptor for pattern recognition. Int. J. Pattern Recogn. Artif. Intell. (IJPRAI) **27**(3), 30 (2013)
23. Santosh, K.C., Lamiroy, B., Wendling, L.: DTW for matching radon features: a pattern recognition and retrieval method. In: Blanc-Talon, J., Kleihorst, R., Philips, W., Popescu, D., Scheunders, P. (eds.) ACIVS 2011. LNCS, vol. 6915, pp. 249–260. Springer, Heidelberg (2011). https://doi.org/10.1007/978-3-642-23687-7_23

Comparative Study and Analysis of Dimensionality Reduction Techniques for Hyperspectral Data

Hanumant R. Gite[✉], Mahesh M. Solankar, Rupali R. Surase, and K. V. Kale

Department of Computer Science and Information Technology,
Dr. Babasaheb Ambedkar Marathwada University, Aurangabad, MH, India
hanumantgitecsit@gmail.com, mmsolankar13@gmail.com,
rupalisurase13@gmail.com, kvkale91@gmail.com

Abstract. The enhanced capabilities of the remote sensing devices lead to capture more precise and accurate spatial and spectral information about surface materials. Increased spectral resolution results in more number of spectral bands and raises the challenge of data dimensionality. This high volume data holds plenty of redundant information. This redundancy affects both the time as well as space complexity of the system. To process and analyse the hyperspectral data with less computational cost with no information loss, data dimensionality needs to be reduced. The literature shows that the traditional image processing techniques with some modifications are applied for hyperspectral dimensionality reduction, but none of the methods give specific solution. This paper evaluates the performances and limitations of the state-of-the-art dimensionality reduction techniques. The algorithms studied and evaluated are Principal Components Analysis, Independent Component Analysis, Minimum Noise Fraction, Fisher Linear Discriminant Analysis, Factor Analysis and Linear Discriminant Analysis. The experiments are performed on the Indian Pines AVIRIS & Gulbarga Subset (AVIRIS-NG) hyperspectral datasets.

Keywords: Hyperspectral image · Dimensionality reduction ·
Principal component analysis · Minimum Noise Fraction ·
Independent Component Analysis

1 Introduction

The enhanced capabilities of the remote sensing devices lead to capture more precise and accurate spatial and spectral information about surface materials. Increased spectral resolution results in more number of spectral bands and raises the problem of data dimensionality. The hyperspectral data dimensionality reduction is very well known and essential problem to solve. It is not the case that the high volume hyperspectral imagery contains only significant information, it also contains the various noises and bands having no significant information. This portion of hyperspectral imagery leads to ill conditioned formulations

© Springer Nature Singapore Pte Ltd. 2019
K. C. Santosh and R. S. Hegadi (Eds.): RTIP2R 2018, CCIS 1035, pp. 534–546, 2019.
https://doi.org/10.1007/978-981-13-9181-1_47

and puts challenges (i.e. data storage, data transmission, data process and data visualization) to the hyperspectral image analysis. To process and evaluate the hyperspectral imagery simply with small computational cost, it is anticipated to diminish the sizes of the data while preserving the important information [1–4]. Figure 1 shows the sample view of higher and lower dimensional data. There are various techniques available in the literature to resolve issue of curse of dimensionality. This paper implements the four popular dimensionality reduction techniques and analyses their comparative outcomes.

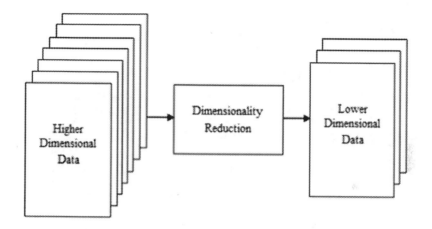

Fig. 1. Sample view of higher and lower dimensional data

The remaining part of the paper is categorized into six sections. Section 2 describes the dimensionality reduction algorithms implemented and evaluated. Section 3 describes the real hyperspectral data used for experimental analysis. Section 4 explains the methodology used for experimental analysis. Section 5 explores the detailed experimental outcomes. Section 6 performs the comparative analysis of experimental outcomes.

2 Dimensionality Reduction Techniques

Four popular dimensionality reduction techniques (PCA, MNF, ICA and LDA) are critically studied and analyzed. The theoretical and mathematical concept of these four dimensionality reduction techniques is highlighted below.

2.1 Principal Component Analysis (PCA)

The PCA is a second order statistics based dimensionality reduction approach. It transforms the data to remove high correlation between adjacent bands. PCA retains the maximum amount of information within first few principal components. The detailed step wise PCA approach is discussed below [5,6].

Steps

1. Take complete dataset containing of d-dimensional data samples ignoring the class labels. (PCA there is no need to class labels).
2. Calculate the mean vector with dimension 'd' of complete dataset.
3. Calculate the scatter matrix & covariance matrix of the entire data set.

The equation of scatter matrix

$$S = \sum_{\overline{k}=1}^{n} (x_k - m)(x_k - m)^T \tag{1}$$

Where m is represented as mean vector

$$m = \frac{1}{n} \sum_{k=1}^{n} x_k \tag{2}$$

The equation of Covariance Matrix

$$\Sigma_i = \begin{bmatrix} \sigma_{11}^2 & \sigma_{12}^2 & \sigma_{13}^2 \\ \sigma_{21}^2 & \sigma_{22}^2 & \sigma_{23}^2 \\ \sigma_{31}^2 & \sigma_{32}^2 & \sigma_{33}^2 \end{bmatrix}$$

Calculate eigenvectors $(e_1, e_2, \ldots \ldots e_d)$ and corresponding eigenvalues $(\lambda_1, \lambda_2, \ldots \ldots, \lambda_d)$ The equation for calculating eigenvector and eigenvalue $\Sigma \vartheta = \lambda \vartheta$ Where, $\sum$ is the covariance matrix, ϑ is eigenvector and λ is eigenvalue of the matrix Arrange the eigenvectors in descending and choose first k components with higher eigenvalue.

Use d * k eigenvector matrix to transform the samples on the new subspace. The subspace equation of data $y = W^T * x$.

2.2   Minimum Noise Fraction (MNF)

MNF is one of the most regularly applied unsupervised dimensional reduction techniques for the hyperspectral remote sensing data. The MNF transform is mostly developed as a linear revolution that increases the signal-to-noise ratio, thus resultant output images decreasing image feature in lower order parameter. The bases of the MNF transform were developed by Green et al. and Lee et al. [7].

Steps

1. X indicate complete n * n data matrix with $X_i, i = 1, \ldots, n$ with I spectrum as band. The sum of resultant signal to noise is given as,

$$X = (X_1, \ldots, X_n)^T \tag{3}$$

2. The MNF transform starts with hyperspectral data noise determination and calculation of noise covariance matrix of the hyperspectral image which is afterward followed by Eigen-value decomposition. If SNR ratio seems to be uncorrelated we can compute it as,

$$\sum_X^T = \sum_X^S + \sum_X^N \tag{4}$$

Where, covariance if

$$(x_i) - \sum_X^N \tag{5}$$

3. In the third step correction of image mean, noise decorrelation and lastly normalization process is called as noise whitening [8]. The MNF transform reduces the noise by covariance matrix with A as eigenvectors,

$$A \sum_x^s A^T = \Lambda, A \sum_x^r A^T - I \tag{6}$$

4. The covariance matrix is used to find $\sum_X^N$. The estimation of $\sum_X^N$ is calculated using,

$$A \sum_X^S A^T = \Lambda + I, A \sum_x^T A^T - I \tag{7}$$

5. The final covariance matrix is calculated in Eq. (8)

$$u_i = \lambda_i + 1, i - 1, ...d \tag{8}$$

After noise elimination data is decorrelated by applying a PCA transform which is the second step of MNF transform. The higher order images will have improved SNR which gradually decreases towards the lower order images [9].

2.3 Independent Component Analysis (ICA)

Independent component analysis (ICA) is a newly established technique for the purpose to detect a linear demonstration of non-Gaussian information to identify statistically independent component [10,11].

Steps

1. Here $X_1, ..., X_n$ are independent bands with X_j as a mixture of independent bands. The independent component with its mixture values gives zero mean without loss of information.

$$X_j = b_{j1}S_1 + b_{j2}S_2 + ... + b_{jn}S_n \tag{9}$$

$b_{j1}, ...to... b_{jn}$ are the hyperspectral bands contains information.

2. Suppose, A is the vector matrix with the elements b_{ij} and column matrix of A is denoted as, X = AS.
3. The estimated output of A is passed for transform in the form of W, the independent components are identified by, S = WX.

Now a days ICA is mostly used for dimensionality reduction with less loss of information.

2.4 Linear Discriminant Analysis (LDA)

The LDA is "Supervised" techniques to calculate the directions between numerous classes. LDA needs ground truth information for data transformation. As far the magnitude of information content is concerned, the substantial amount of information is present within initial few components and can be used efficiently for further hyperspectral data analysis and processing. The detailed step wise LDA approach is discussed below [6,12,13].

Steps

1. The various classes from different dataset are calculated using d-dimensional mean vectors.
2. The Scatter Matrix is calculated as ("intra-class and inter-class")
   (a) Within-class scatter matrix S_w computed by following equation

$$S_w = \sum_{i=1}^{c} s_i \tag{10}$$

Where

$$s_i = \sum_{x \varepsilon D_i}^{n} (x - m_i)(x - m_i)^T \tag{11}$$

Scatter matrix of every class and m_i is the mean vector

$$m_i = \frac{1}{n_i} \sum_{x \varepsilon Di}^{n} x_k \tag{12}$$

(2) Calculate the class covariance matrices by adding the scaling factor $1/(N-1)$ to the within scatter matrix class

$$\sum_i = \frac{1}{N_i - 1} \sum_{x \in D_i}^{n} (x - m_i)(x - m_i)^T \tag{13}$$

and

$$S_w = \sum_{i=1}^{c} (N_i - 1) \Sigma i \tag{14}$$

Where N_i is the sample size of the respective class

(c) Between-class scatter matrix S_B is computed by the following equation

$$S_B = \sum_{i=1}^{c} N_i \left(m_i - m\right) \left(m_i - m\right)^T \qquad (15)$$

where m is the overall mean, and m_i and N_i are the sample mean and sizes of the respective classes

3. Calculate eigenvectors $(e_1, e_2, \ldots\ldots, e_d)$ and eigenvalues $(\lambda_1, \lambda_2, \ldots\ldots, \lambda_d)$ for the scatter matrices.
4. Order the reduced eigenvalues and eigenvectors to choose k eigenvectors with the highest eigenvalues to form a d*k dimensional matrix W.
5. Refer d*k eigenvector matrix to transform the samples towards new subspace. It is summarized by the matrix multiplication: Y = X*W.

3 Dataset

In this research work, two real hyperspectral images are used. The detailed description of the data is given in Table 1.

Table 1. Hyperspectral images detailed description

Hyperspectral scene	Description	Ground truth
Indian Pines (AVIRIS) Fig. 2	Spatial Dimension: 145 × 145	Available
	Spectral Dimension: 220 Channels	
	Bad Bands: [104–108, 150–163, 220]	
Gulbarga Subset (AVIRIS-NG) Fig. 3	Spatial Dimension: 400 × 500	Not Available
	Spectral Dimension: 220 Channels	
	Spectral Resolution: 5 nm	
	Bad Bands: [1–20, 194–223, 281–333, 395–425]	

4 Methodology

The experimental work is decomposed into three steps including preprocessing, implementation of dimensionality algorithms and comparative result analysis (Fig. 4). In preprocessing, both the datasets are processed to remove the spectral bands with noise or no information. The bad bands (see Table 1) are removed and remaining spectral channels are taken for further experimental analysis. After preprocessing, above discussed dimensionality reduction algorithms are implemented and evaluated. The comparative outcomes of these dimensionality reduction evaluated in result analysis section.

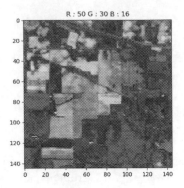

Fig. 2. Indian Pines (AVIRIS) data

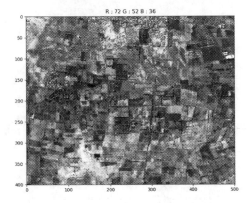

Fig. 3. Gulbarga Subset (AVIRIS-NG) data

5   Experiments

Every algorithm is evaluated separately using two real hyperspectral datasets (Table 1). The detailed experimental analysis for these four dimensionality reduction algorithms is given below.

5.1   Principal Component Analysis (PCA)

The principal component analysis removes the inter-band correlation of both the datasets. From both the datasets, maximum information containing eight principal components are preserved. The images given in Fig. 5 visualizes the eight PCA transformed principal components of Indian Pines dataset and Gulbarga Subset dataset respectively.

5.2   Minimum Noise Fraction (MNF)

The minimum noise fraction transformation is a two-step process. In first step, the Noise Whitening is performed on both the datasets. This noise whitened

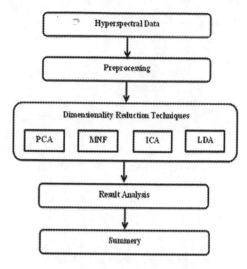

Fig. 4. Proposed methodology

scenes are then used to identify the principal component. From both the scenes datasets, maximum information containing eight principal components are preserved. The images given in Fig. 6 visualizes the eight MNF transformed principal components of Indian Pines dataset and Gulbarga Subset dataset respectively.

5.3   Independent Component Analysis (ICA)

The Independent Component Analysis transforms the set of mixed, random signal sources into mutually independent components. The ICA is performed on both the datasets, and first eight mutually independent components are preserved to contain maximum amount of significant information. These ICA transformed components of Indian Pines and Gulbarga Subset scene are visualized in Fig. 7.

5.4   Linear Discriminant Analysis (LDA)

The Linear Discriminant Analysis is supervised dimensionality reduction approach. It computes the directions also known as linear discriminants that represents the axes which maximizes the separation between multiple signal sources. As LDA is a supervised approach, the experiments are performed only on Indian Pines dataset. Figure 8 shows eight LDA transformed components of Indian Pines Dataset.

6   Result Analysis

This section explores the comparative experimental outcomes of above implemented dimensionality reduction algorithms. In case of PCA, the PCA finds the principal components directly from the original data. The maximum amount of information is contained within first five principal components. As the number of principal components increases, the information content get decreased. In case of MNF, the noise sensitivity of PCA is removed and original data is noise whitened before computing the principal components. In MNF transformed data, initial eight number of components retains maximum information and can be used efficiently for further processing. In case of ICA, first six statistically independent components are used to retain the significant information. In case of LDA, the data dimensionality is reduced using the ground truth reference information and

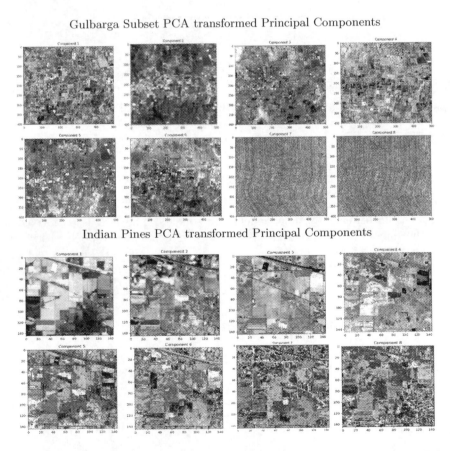

Fig. 5. PCA transformed Principal Components on Indian Pines & Gulbarga Subset data

Gulbarga Subset MNF transformed Principal Components

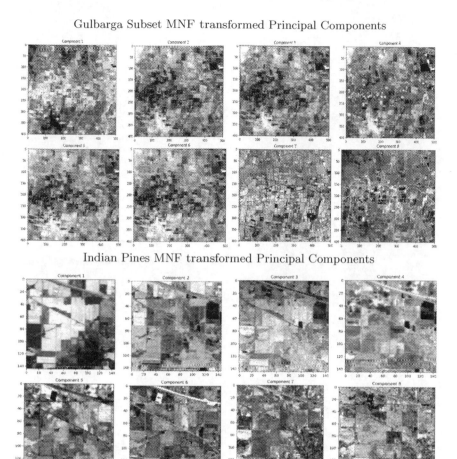

Indian Pines MNF transformed Principal Components

Fig. 6. MNF transformed Principal Components on Indian Pines & Gulbarga Subset data

resulting components are found inconsistent. First three dimensionality reductions namely PCA, MNF and ICA are unsupervised, and transforms the original data to conserve significant amount of information. The fourth dimensionality reduction called LDA is a supervised mechanism and needs ground truth information for data transformation. As far the magnitude of information content is concerned, the substantial amount of information is present within initial few components and can be used efficiently for further hyperspectral data analysis and processing.

Gulbarga Subset ICA transformed Principal Components

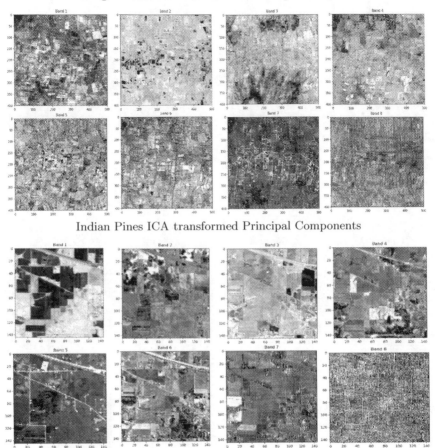

Indian Pines ICA transformed Principal Components

Fig. 7. ICA transformed Principal Components on Indian Pines & Gulbarga Subset data

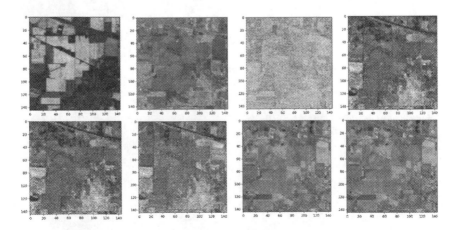

Fig. 8. LDA transformed Principal Components on Indian Pines data

7   Conclusion

The comparative experimental analysis drawn some key observations indicating some advantages and limitations of dimensionality reduction techniques. The major advantage of PCA is that, the large volume of information is wholly available in first few components which can be used for further analysis efficiently. The major limitation of PCA are, after PCA transformation, the original data is get transformed into new coordinate system with no consideration of factors like noise. The MNF transformation resolves the noise sensitivity of PCA algorithm and proceeds to transform data. ICA transformation can be efficiently used most significant band selection approach, but it fails in case of non-linear mixing models. The major issue of dimensionality reduction techniques, that is, how much number of principal component are supposed to be preserved is still unresolved. This issue can be solved by using efficient VD estimation techniques like HFC, NW-HFC or HySime.

Acknowledgement. The Authors acknowledge to UGC BSR Research Fellowship for financial support. The authors also extend sincere thanks to DST, GOI, for support under major research project (No. BDID/01/23/2014-HSRS/35 (ALG-V)) and for providing AVIRIS-NG data. And UGC SAP-II DRS Phase II for providing lab facilities to the Department of Comp. Science and IT, Dr. B. A. M. University, Aurangabad-(MS), India support.

References

1. Plaza, A., et al.: Recent advances in techniques for hyperspectral image processing. Remote Sens. Environ. **113**, S110–S122 (2009)
2. Dong, Y., Du, B., Zhang, L., Zhang, L.: Dimensionality reduction and classification of hyperspectral images using ensemble discriminative local metric learning. IEEE Trans. Geosci. Remote Sens. **55**(5), 2509–2524 (2017)
3. Qian, S.: Dimensionality reduction of multidimensional satellite imagery. SPIE Newsroom (2011). https://doi.org/10.1117/2.1201102.003560
4. Kale, K.V., Solankar, M.M., Nalawade, D.B., Dhumal, R.K., Gite, H.R.: A research review on hyperspectral data processing and analysis algorithms. Proc. Natl. Acad. Sci. India Sect. A **87**(4), 541–555 (2017)
5. Rodarmel, C., Shan, J.: Principal component analysis for hyperspectral image classification. Surv. Land Inf. Sci. **62**(2), 115 (2002)
6. Raschka, S.: Python Machine Learning. Packt Publishing Ltd., Birmingham (2015)
7. Green, A.A., Berman, M., Switzer, P., Craig, M.D.: A transformation for ordering multispectral data in terms of image quality with implications for noise removal. IEEE Trans. Geosci. Remote Sens. **26**(1), 65–74 (1988)
8. Mundt, J.T., Streutker, D.R., Glenn, N.F.: Partial unmixing of hyperspectral imagery: theory and methods. In: Proceedings of the American Society of Photogrammetry and Remote Sensing, vol. 2007, May 2007
9. Berman, M., Phatak, A., Traylen, A.: Some invariance properties of the minimum noise fraction transform. Chemometr. Intell. Lab. Syst. **117**, 189–199 (2012)
10. Hyvärinen, A., Oja, E.: Independent component analysis: algorithms and applications. Neural Netw. **13**(4–5), 411–430 (2000)

11. Wang, J., Chang, C.I.: Independent component analysis-based dimensionality reduction with applications in hyperspectral image analysis. IEEE Trans. Geosci. Remote Sens. **44**(6), 1586–1600 (2006)
12. Chang, C.I.: Hyperspectral Data Processing: Algorithm Design and Analysis. Wiley, Hoboken (2013)
13. Solankar, M.M., Gite, H.R., Dhumal, R.K., Surase, R.R., Nalawade, D., Kale, K.V.: Recent advances and challenges in automatic hyperspectral endmember extraction. In: Krishna, C.R., Dutta, M., Kumar, R. (eds.) Proceedings of 2nd International Conference on Communication, Computing and Networking. LNNS, vol. 46, pp. 445–455. Springer, Singapore (2019). https://doi.org/10.1007/978-981-13-1217-5_44

A Comparative Study of Different CNN Models in City Detection Using Landmark Images

Masum Shah Junayed, Afsana Ahsan Jeny[✉], Nafis Neehal,
Syeda Tanjila Atik, and Syed Akhter Hossain

Daffodil International University, Dhaka 1207, Bangladesh
{junayed15-5008,ahsan15-5278,nafis.cse,syeda.cse}@diu.edu.bd,
aktarhossain@daffodilvarsity.edu.bd

Abstract. Navigation assistance using different local Landmarks is an emerging research field now-a-days. Landmark images taken from different camera angles are being vividly used alongside the GPS (Global Positioning System) data to determine the location of the user and help user with navigation. However, determining the location of the user by recognizing the landmarks from different images, without the help of GPS, can be a worthy research trend to explore. Hence, in this paper, we have conducted a comparative study of 3 different popular CNN models, namely - Inception V3, MobileNet and ResNet50, and they have achieved an overall accuracy of 99.7%, 99.5% and 99.7% respectively while determining cities using landmark images.

Keywords: City detection · Landmark · Inception · ResNet50 · MobileNet · CNN

1 Introduction

A landmark is a recognizable physical or artificial characteristic used for navigation, a feature that stands out from its near circumstance and is often able to see from long distances. Landmarks are nationally momentous historic places denominated by the Secretary of the Interior because they occupy exceptional standard or quality in explaining or interpreting the tradition of the cities.

Landmark is an official determination that a possession is of significance to the people, the kingdom, or the topical community. To increase the community's wariness and pride in its past, it is this "learning of place" that motivates people to put down roots in a society. It supports to ennoble the ocular and aesthetic nature, beauty and rareness of the city. It also helps safeguard the city's generation and tradition, stabilize and raise possession values and enhance the city's fascination for occupants, the visitors, tourists, and expected residents. Historical and cultural travelers expend much more than other travelers do.

Actually, it is one of the main components that shape the picture and figure of historic cities. It is manifest that recent and improper developments have diluted

K. C. Santosh and R. S. Hegadi (Eds.): RTIP2R 2018, CCIS 1035, pp. 547–560, 2019.
https://doi.org/10.1007/978-981-13-9181-1_48

the precedence of landmarks. For landmarks recognition, the researcher already did so many works like topological navigation of mobile robots for landmark identification using the 2D pattern search engine [10], using Iconic Scene Graphs for recognizing landmark images [21].

The city's historical landmarks have always been exoteric among tourists because of its historical values and also observed as components of reference. Actually, we choose landmarks for city identification for the landmark's popularity. When people want to visit different countries to see landmark images, sometimes they can't detect these landmark places. And the other country's children have the same problem. That's why we select this idea for our paper so that we can solve this problem and remove the city identification problem without the help of GPS (Global Positioning System).

In this paper, we have used 3 different popular CNN [6] models. They are Inception-v3 [2], MobileNet [7] and Resnet50 [9]. These are pre-trained [3] models. We have used 6 different landmarks images of 6 different cities which are Taj Mahal for Agra, Burj Khalifa for Dubai, Pyramid for Giza, Statue of Liberty for NewYork, Eiffel Tower for Paris and finally Opera House for Sydney. By using a little training time we fulfilled a useful city detection model and obtain a higher accuracy from 3 different models. The remaining paper is arranged in the following manner: Details of Convolutional Neural Network (CNN) [6], Inception-v3 [2], MobileNet [7] and Restnet50 [9] model are discussed in Sect. 2. The comparison with other papers is discussed in Sect. 3. Data collection, model installation, and training are discussed in Sect. 4. Performance analysis is done in Sect. 5. Finally conclusion with some future work scopes is described in Sect. 6 and Sect. 7.

2   Background Study

Our paper is based on the Inception-v3 [2] model and MobileNet [7] of TensorFlow [4] platform and Resnet50 [9] model of Convolutional Neural Network [6].

TensorFlow [4] is an open-source software library for high-performance analytical calculations. Its flexible architecture allows easy deployment of various platforms (CPUs, GPUs), and desktop clusters from the desktop to mobile and end devices. Originally developed by Google's brain team of researchers and engineers in Google's AI organization, it is used across many other scientific domains for strong support and flexible numerical calculation for machine learning and deep education. It is malleable and has been used for amplifying machine learning sections of computer science which including recognition of speech, computer vision related works, natural language processing and so on.

Convolutional neural network (ConvNet or CNN) [6] is a class of deep artificial neural network that has been successfully implemented in visual image analysis. The following layers are used to create the ConvNet architectures:

Convolutional Layers: An example of the Convolutional Layer. Note that there are multiple neurons (5 in this example) with depth, all inputs are connected to the same local area. Convolutional layers CNN's [6] main part. Its output volume can be interpreted as descending neurons in a 3D volume. And its parameters are able to learn the filter set. Each filter is only connected to the input volume in a local area (width and height), but with full depth [6].

During the forward pass, each filter is applied to a small local area, computing dot production between filters and input. Then it iterates across the width of the input volume and height. The result of each filter is a 2-dimensional activation map. In this way, they start to learn some filters on the network when they show some local location of input with certain specifications.

Pooling Layers: Pooling layers another significant part of CNN [6]. It is a form of nonlinear sub-sampling. The input image outputs the pond partitions in a set of non-overlapping rectangles and outputs maximum for each sub-region. Insight is that once a feature is found, its exact position is not as important as its rough position compared to other features [6].

The layer of pooling significantly reduces input size and network parameters and counting numbers significantly. As a result, overfitting will not be a serious problem (Fig. 1).

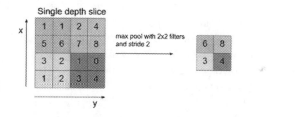

Fig. 1. An example of (max) pooling layer.

ReLU Layers: Rectified linear unit (ReLU) layers apply to non-saturating activation function $f(x) = maximum(0, x)$. The release layers increase the overall architecture's linearity, without affecting the acceptable areas of the coverage layer [6].

Other types of activation functions increase the linearity, such as the sigmoid function $f(x) = (1 + e^{-x})^{-1}$. However, RELU accuracy should be faster training without significant losses. So ReLU is used more on CNN [6].

Fully-connected layers: Fully-connected layers are usually the last layer of the overall architecture. They have a full connection to their previous layers, the same as the regular layers in the normal CNN [6] (Fig. 2).

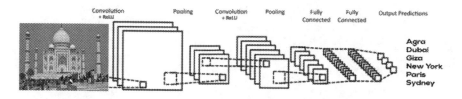

Fig. 2. Structure of Convolutional Neural Network (CNN).

Inception-v3 [2] is one of the TensorFlow [4] training models. This was followed by the re-review of the computer's start-up structure in 2015 after the Inception-v1, Inception-v2. Inception-v3 [2] model is trained in the ImageNet dataset, among which 1000 consist of two parts of the class Inception-v3 [2]: A convolutional neural network (CNN) [6] and the exhaustive parts of the properties with fully connected and softmax layers with classification parts [2,5].

Fig. 3. The architecture on Inception V3 of our dataset.

MobileNet [7] is a small effective convolutional neural network designed by researchers at Google. Limit two parameters in the MobileNets [7] network, which can tune to stop the trade/accuracy of the exact problem: a multiplier of width multiplier and resolution. Width multiplier allows slimming on the network, when the multiplier of the resolution changes the input level of the image, reducing the internal representation of each layer.

We have used 224 1.0 version for our code lab. Here 1.0 is the width multiplier and it can be 1.0, 0.75, 0.50 or 0.25. The 224 is the image resolution and it can be 224, 192, 160 or 128. Here the smallest version of MobileNet [7] is 128 0.25 and the biggest version is 224 1.0. Though 224 is the higher resolution image and takes more processing time but it provides better classification accuracy.

MobileNet [7] is based on a streamlined architecture that can be divided deeply to create a lightweight deep neural network. Here present two common global hyper-parameters that effectively control the latency and accuracy. These hyper-parameter models allow developers to select the right size model for their application based on the limit of the problem (Fig. 4).

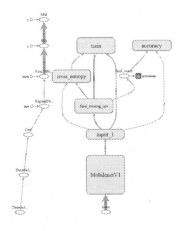

Fig. 4. The architecture on MobileNet of our dataset.

ResNet [9] is a short name of Residual Network which is a special type of neural network which helps us to handle more powerful deep learning tasks and models through a network with many layers. In 2012, the AlexNet had come which contain 8 layers and the error of 16.4%. In 2014 and 2015, the VGG16, VGG19, and GoogleNet model had come with 16 layers, 19 layers, and 22 layers respectively. And finally, the ResNet model has come with 152 layers which are also a top-5 classification error of 3.57%.

The main idea of Resnet [9] is introduced with a shortcut connection which is called identity shortcut connection or identity block that can skip one or more layers. Mathematically, A ResNet [9] layer approximately calculates $y = f(x) + id(x) = f(x) + x$. The gradients can easily be turned back and those shortcuts act like highways and the result can be found out so much faster with much more layers (Fig. 5).

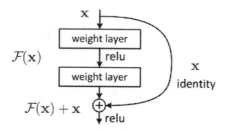

Fig. 5. A residual block of ResNet.

In our paper, we have used a deep CNN model based on the Residual Network architecture with 50 layers which termed as ResNet50 [9]. For implementing this model, we have used keras [1]. Keras [1] is a high-level neural network which is written in python and able to run on the top of TensorFlow [4]. ResNet50 [9] is much deeper than the VGG16 and VGG19. Though it has 50 layers but its size is small because of global average pooling and fully-connected layers. As a result of the model size down to 102 MB (Fig. 6).

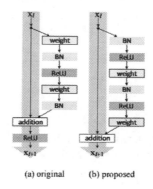

(a) original   (b) proposed

Fig. 6. (Left) the original residual module. (Right) The updated residual module using pre-activation.

3   Literature Review

The following tasks that were used by the Inception-v3 [2], MobileNet [7] and ResNet50 [9].

In 2015, He, Zhang, Ren, and Sun used deep Residual Learning for their image classification. They clearly described the different types of Resnet [9] model which is very important for all. They also discussed how the Resnet [9] had come with many layers and discussed these models accuracy [18].

In 2016, Elizalde, Chao, Zeng, Lane from Electrical and Computer Engineering Carnegie Mellon University Mountain View exposed a paper on City-Identification of Flickr Videos Using Semantic Acoustic Features. It was based on the UrbanSound8K set containing audio clips labeled by sound type. They showed to what extent the city-location of videos correlates with their acoustic information. But no CNN [6] models were used here [13].

In 2009, Li Crandall Huttenlocher expressed a paper on Landmark Classification in Large-scale Image Collections. In this paper, they study image classification on a much larger dataset of 30 million images and used a Support Vector Machine model and the accuracy was 53.58% [11].

In 2009, Zheng, Zhao, Song, Adam exposed a paper on Tour the World: building a web-scale landmark recognition engine. The resulting landmark recognition engine incorporates 5312 landmarks from 1259 cities in 144 countries and the accuracy was 80.8% [12].

In 2017, Gavai, Jakhade, Tribhuvan and Bhattad used MobileNets for Flower Classification using TensorFlow on the flower category datasets of Oxford-I7 and Oxford-102 for Flower Classification. The accuracy of 1.0 MobileNet-224 was 70.6% and 0.5 MobileNet-160 was 60.2% [14].

In 2017, Kim, Choi, Jang and Lim used Convolutional Neural Network [6] model such as Inception, ResNet, and MobileNet on Driver Distraction Detection which was pre-trained with the ILSVRC2012 dataset. Their accuracy was increased when they used MobileNet rather than Inception and ResNet [15].

Our experiment is also based on Inception-v3 [2], MobileNet [7] and ResNet50 [9] model of Convolutional Neural Network [6] for city detection using landmark images. City identification has not been done by using landmark images before. This is the first approach from us. And those model of CNN [6] has worked well in our experiment and also given a high accuracy.

4   Methodology

In this section, the list of items to be discussed are as follows: first of all we make a flowchart [16] which explains the process of our experiment; second, we provide a simple introduction to our dataset; third, we provide the data preprocessing of our experiment; then, we discuss the model installation; last of all, we introduce the train model.

A flowchart [16] is a type of diagram that represents an algorithm very easily. Here, the following flowchart Fig. 7 illustrates a solution model to our system.

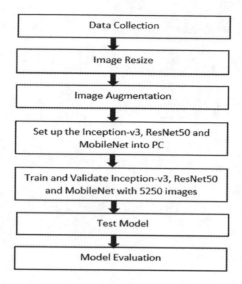

Fig. 7. Flowchart of our experiment.

4.1 Dataset

For our experiment, we have collected 900 images on six different landmarks of six different cities. The six landmarks are Taj Mahal for Agra, Burj Khalifa for Dubai, Pyramid for Giza, Statue of Liberty for New York, Eiffel Tower for Paris and finally Opera House for Sydney.

4.2 Data Preprocessing

In data preprocessing, we have artificially expanded the dataset for avoiding overfitting. This data will make a few variances that can happen when someone else takes refresh data from the web or in real life. After collecting data for each class we have augmented the dataset in 5 different methods. They are Rotate +30, Rotate -30, Translation, Shearing, and Flip.

Finally, we have found 5400 images for training from this augmentation. It is very difficult to display all data. So we display four images for each class in the following Fig. 8.

Fig. 8. The example of our dataset.

4.3 Model Installation

This experiment is based on the MobileNet [7] and Inception-v3 [3] model of TensorFlow [4] platform and ResNet50 [9] which is Keras [1] application. The processor is 2 GHz Intel i3, memory 4 GB 1600 MHz DDR3, System type: 64-bit Operating System, x-64 based processor.

First of all, we have downloaded TensorFlow [4]. Then we have also installed MobileNet [7] and Inception-v3 [2] model. Then we have used Keras [1] for ResNet50 [9].

4.4 Train Model

Inception-v3 [2], MobileNet [7] and Resnet50 [9] are deep neural network models that's why it is very difficult to train in a low-level configuration computer. Inception-v3 [2] takes one day, MobileNet [7] takes 6–8 h and Resnet50 [9] takes two days for training.

Tensorflow [4] offers a tutorial on how to rearrange the final layer of the installation of a new class using transfer learning. We use the transfer learning method that keeps the previous layer parameters and remove the last layer of the Inception-v3 [2] model, then try again at the end layer. The number of output nodes in the last layer is equal to the number of classes in the dataset. Fig. 3 is the Inception-v3 [2] architecture of our model.

Then the bottleneck files are generated. After finishing this, the original training begins of the final layer of the network. Our script has run 4000 training steps and each step have selected 10 images randomly from the training set and have found their bottlenecks from the cache. To get prediction images have fed into the final layer. That prediction is then compared against the actual label, and the results of this comparison are used to update the final layer weight through a backpropagation process. At the time of training the training accuracy, validation accuracy, and the cross-entropy graph are generated. After completing all the training steps, the script has run for the evaluation of final test accuracy. The finally the accuracy have been generated and have shown a value of accuracy. This number indicates the percentage of images in the standard test set that the model is labeled as perfect after being fully trained.

All of these things have happened in the time of Mobilenet [7].

Resnet50 [9] is the model of Residual Networks which using identity blocks for shortcut connection. This block names bottleneck blocks and it follows two rules. One if the map has the same output characteristics then the layers have the same number of filters and two if the map is half then the filters are doubled. Downsampling is composed directly by the convolution layer, which is an extension 2 and normalization of the batch takes place exactly before each convolution and RELU activation. When input and output levels are the same, identity shortcut is conducted. If the dimension is enhanced, then projection shortcut 1×1 is conducted to become level like convolutions. We have shifted the first 49 layers of ResNet-50 [9] by using the Transfer Learning Language. 1000 fully connected (fc) layer in the network ends with the softmax activation. Using bottleneck features of our passport cover images as input, we train 6 fully connected softmax, since we have 6 classes and our trained 6 fully connected software replaces 1,000 fully connected scams.

We have also made three Confusion Matrixes [8] for three different models. From Confusion Matrix [8], we have calculated Precision, Recall, Accuracy, and F1-Score [17]. And finally, we have calculated Macro Average Accuracy of three CNN [6] models for our experiment.

It is very difficult to give three Confusion Matrixes [8]. That's why we have given one Confusion Matrix [8] of ResNet50 [9] model. From the following Confusion matrix [8] of Table 1, we can say that our model has provided a very high number of True Positive values.

Table 1. Confusion matrix

	Agra	Dubai	Giza	Newyork	Paris	Sydney
Agra	25	0	0	0	0	0
Dubai	0	24	0	0	1	0
Giza	0	0	25	0	0	0
Newyork	0	0	0	25	0	0
Paris	0	0	0	0	25	0
Sydney	0	0	0	0	0	25

5   Result Analysis

The following figures are expressing the development of the model's accuracy and cross-entropy as it is trained. Figures 9 and 11 show the training progress (x-axis) as a process of the accuracy (y-axis). Again Figs. 10 and 12 show the training progress (x-axis) as a process of the cross-entropy (y-axis). Here the orange line represents the training set, and the blue line represents the validation set for Figs. 9, 10, 11 and 12.

Now overfitting happens when a model fits too well and when the training accuracy will be higher than the accuracy on the validation set. So we can say that little overfitting occurs among Figs. 9, 10, 11, 12, 13 and 14. Because among those figures, the training set is higher than the validation set.

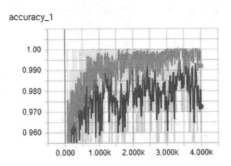

Fig. 9. The variation of accuracy on the training dataset of Inception-v3.

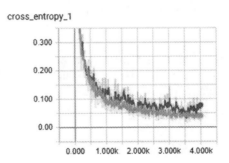

Fig. 10. The variation of cross entropy on the training dataset of Inception-v3.

Table 2. Description of the two figures.

	Index	Performance
Dataset	The training set accuracy	99.7%
	The validation set accuracy	99.1%-99.4%
	The training set cross-entropy	0.03
	The validation set cross-entropy	0.05

Table 2 shows the description of the two figures. For our dataset, the training accuracy can reach 99.7%, and the validation accuracy can be maintained at 99.1%–99.4%.

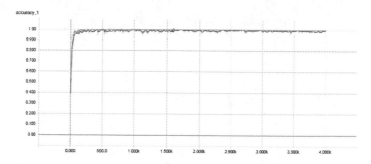

Fig. 11. Accuracy with respect to training and validation of MobileNet.

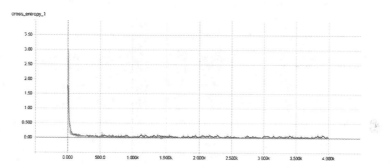

Fig. 12. Cross entropy with respect to training and validation of MobileNet.

Now Fig. 13 shows the number of epoch's progress (x-axis) as a process of the loss (y-axis). Again Fig. 14 shows the number of epoch's progress (x-axis) as a process of the accuracy (y-axis). Here the orange line represents the performance of the validation set and the blue line represents the performance of the training set in Fig. 13. On the other hand, the green line represents the performance of the validation set and the blue line represents the performance of the training set in Fig. 14 [19].

According to these figures, there shows a stability after the 8 epochs and the Resnet50 [9] model has given a high accuracy which is 99.7%.

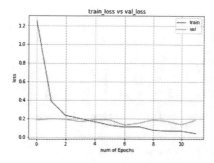

Fig. 13. Validation loss curve by using pre-trained model ResNet-50.

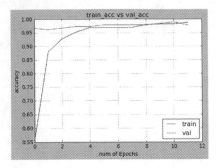

Fig. 14. Validation accuracy curve by using pre-trained model ResNet-50.

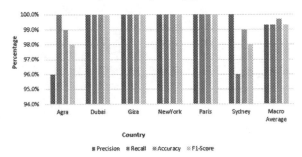

Fig. 15. Precision, Recall, Accuracy and F1-Score graph of Inception-v3.

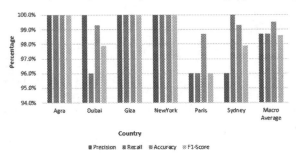

Fig. 16. Precision, Recall, Accuracy and F1-Score graph of MobileNet.

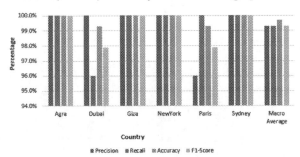

Fig. 17. Precision, Recall, Accuracy and F1-Score graph of ResNet50.

Figures 15, 16 and 17 show the precision, recall, accuracy and F1-Score [17] graph of Agra, Dubai, Giza, NewYork, Paris, and Sydney and also show the macro average [20].

Table 3. The accuracy of six classes and final accuracy of Inception-v3, MobileNet and ResNet50.

	Inception-v3	MobileNet	ResNet-50
City	Accuracy	Accuracy	Accuracy
Agra	99%	100%	100%
Dubai	100%	99.3%	99.3%
Giza	100%	100%	100%
Newyork	100%	100%	100%
Paris	100%	98.7%	99.3%
Sydney	99%	99.3%	100%
Macro Average	99.7%	99.5%	99.7%

Table 3 show the final accuracy of Inception-v3 [2] is 99.7%, MobileNet [7] is 99.5% and finally ResNet50 [9] is 99.7%.

6   Future Work

As we have overfitting problem in our models. In future for removing this overfitting, we want to add more data and regularization, use other augmentation methods and architectures and also reduce architecture complexity. The Inception-v3 [2], MobileNet [7], and ResNet50 [9] model of CNN [6] which is already generated and we have used it. So, our future work is also to study and make a new model so that we can use that model and can also obtain a high accuracy.

7   Conclusion

In our paper, we have represented three models of Convolutional Neural Network (CNN) [6] for city detection using landmark images. In Inception-v3 [2], we have used 21 million parameters, the loss and accuracy we have got from this model is 0.3% and 99.7% and the resulting model size was 96 MB. Then in MobileNet [7], we have used 4.24 million parameters, the loss and accuracy we have got from this model is 0.5% and 99.5% and the resulting model size was only 17 MB. And lastly in ResNet50 [9], we have used 23.5 million parameters, the loss and accuracy we have got from this model is 0.3% and 99.7% and the resulting model size was only 102 MB. Now we can say that MobileNet [7] has done better than the other two models because it is small in size and so much faster to run from others. We have tried to highlight the procedure and the performance of three models in a short time. Hopefully, our approach will be helped in the future.

References

1. https://en.wikipedia.org/wiki/Keras
2. https://arxiv.org/pdf/1512.00567.pdf
3. https://www.kaggle.com/keras/resnet50/home
4. https://arxiv.org/abs/1603.04467
5. Xia, X., Xu, C.: Inception-v3 for flower classification. In: 2017 2nd International Conference on Image, Vision and Computing (2017)
6. http://wiki.ubc.ca/Course:CPSC522/Convolutional_Neural_Networks#cite_note-wiki-3
7. https://arxiv.org/abs/1704.04861
8. https://en.wikipedia.org/wiki/Confusion_matrix
9. https://www.pyimagesearch.com/2017/03/20/imagenet-vggnet-resnet-inception-xception-keras/
10. Mata, M., Armingol, J.M., de la Escalera, A., Salichs, M.A.: A visual landmark recognition system for topological navigation of mobile robots. In: Proceedings 2001 ICRA. IEEE International Conference on Robotics and Automation (Cat. No. 01CH37164, 21–26 May 2001
11. Li, Y., Crandall, D.J., Huttenlocher, D.P.: Landmark classification in large-scale image collections. In: 2009 IEEE 12th International Conference on Computer Vision, 29 September 2009–2 October 2009
12. Zheng, Y.-T., Zhao, M., Song, Y., Adam, H.: Tour the world: building a web-scale landmark recognition engine. In: 2009 IEEE Conference on Computer Vision and Pattern Recognition, 20–25 June 2009
13. Elizalde, B., Chao, G.-L., Zeng, M., Lane, I.: City-identification of flickr videos using semantic acoustic features. arXiv: 1607.03257v1 [cs.MM], 12 July 2016
14. Gavai, N.R., Jakhade, Y.A., Tribhuvan, S.A., Bhattad, R.: MobileNets for flower classification using tensorflow. In: 2017 International Conference on Big Data, IoT and Data Science (BID), 20–22 December 2017. Vishwakarma Institute of Technology, Pune (2017)
15. Kim, W., Choi, H.-K., Jang, B.-T., Lim, J.: Driver distraction detection using single convolutional neural network. In: 2017 International Conference on Information and Communication Technology Convergence (ICTC), 18–20 October 2017
16. https://en.wikipedia.org/wiki/Flowchart
17. https://en.wikipedia.org/wiki/Precision_and_recall
18. He, K., Zhang, X., Ren, S., Sun, J: Deep residual learning for image recognition. arXiv: 1512.03385v1 [cs.CV], 10 December 2015
19. https://github.com/keras-team/keras/issues/3755
20. https://datascience.stackexchange.com/questions/15989/micro-average-vs-macro-average-performance-in-a-multiclass-classification
21. Li, X., Wu, C., Zach, C., Lazebnik, S., Frahm, J.-M.: Using iconic scene graphs for modeling and recognition of landmark images collections, 16 April 2011

Comparison of Deep Learning, Data Augmentation and Bag of-Visual-Words for Classification of Imbalanced Image Datasets

Manisha Saini[✉] and Seba Susan

Delhi Technological University, Delhi, India
manisha.saini44@gmail.com, seba_406@yahoo.in

Abstract. Image classification is a supervised machine learning task to classify images into different categories. As most real-world datasets are imbalanced in nature, instances are not equally distributed in all classes which often results in biased classification. So considering this objective, we are dealing with an imbalanced dataset. We have created a small size of an imbalanced dataset consisting of Ant and Plane Images from Caltech-101 dataset. This paper illustrates the comparison between Deep learning, Data Augmentation and the Bag-of-Visual Words (BOVW) for classification of imbalanced image datasets. According to the experimental results, it was found that deep learning results in higher accuracy in comparison to bag-of-visual-words (BOVW) and data augmentation.

Keywords: Deep learning · Bag-of-visual-words · Data augmentation · Image classification

1 Introduction

Image classification [1] is a supervised machine learning task, which can classify images into different categories based on the class label. Imbalanced dataset [2] is the dataset where data in different classes is imbalanced in proportion. Either some images in one class images are more in number in comparison to another, or we can say another class of images is under-represented in the training and testing image dataset. Dealing with the imbalanced dataset is a challenge in machine learning.

According to the researchers, deep learning technique generates better results using a large dataset. However, this doesn't directly imply that deep learning algorithm cannot extract information from "small" data. Lately, research is going in this direction of deep learning, when the samples are not sufficient to train the model [3, 4]. There are two significant challenges in training a deep learning model with less data: Overfitting and Outlier-related bias. In general, when using small data, preprocessing and cleaning of data is crucial to reduce these adverse effects [19].

This paper has been organized into following sections. In Sect. 2, literature survey is explained in detail. Section 3 discusses different techniques used for classification such as deep learning, data augmentation and BOVW (Bag-of-visual words). In

© Springer Nature Singapore Pte Ltd. 2019
K. C. Santosh and R. S. Hegadi (Eds.): RTIP2R 2018, CCIS 1035, pp. 561–571, 2019.
https://doi.org/10.1007/978-981-13-9181-1_49

Sect. 4, experiments and results are illustrated and analyzed. Finally, the conclusion is discussed in Sect. 5.

2 Literature Survey

Many researchers have worked on the effect of class-imbalanced data on classical machine learning algorithms. Extending the idea to CNNs, Buda et al. assessed the working of CNN and its applicability to the classification task using imbalanced data [23]. Authors subsample three popular datasets – MNIST, CIFAR-10, and ImageNet (ILSVRC-2012) to compare the different methods for the evaluation of oversampling and under-sampling. Based on the experimental results, it was found that the imbalanced dataset has an adverse effect on class performance. Moreover, oversampling emerged as the most dominant method to tackle class imbalances, whereas under-sampling can perform better when the imbalance is partially removed. Trivial deep learning methods are not tuned to handle the biases that occurs at the time of training on the imbalanced dataset. Dong et al. address this limitation by proposing the detailed class imbalanced deep learning technique incorporating a newly introduced Class Rectification Loss (CRL) function, which can be integrated easily within deep network architectures [24]. Authors carried out experiments on four benchmark datasets to examine the workability and scalability to design the model which can be used for the imbalanced dataset. Suh et al. [25] discussed about the classification of sugar beet and volunteer potato in natural and varying daylight conditions via Bag-of-Visual-Words (BoVW) model. The BOVW model is based on Scale-Invariant Feature Transform (SIFT) and Speeded Up Robust Feature (SURF) features with crop row information in the form of the Out-of-Row Regional Index (ORRI) which results in highest classification accuracy in case of SIFT and ORRI with Support Vector Machine.

Zhu et al. proposed a framework [26] for data augmentation using generative adversarial networks (GAN) to produce supplementary data in minority classes in an emotion detection task. They build a classical Convolutional Neural Network (CNN) classifier for emotion image classification and train the CycleGAN model to synthesize images for the minority classes of emotion from a related image source. To avoid gradient vanishing problem, they combine least-squared loss from LSGAN and adversarial loss in CycleGAN. The results indicate an increase in the classification accuracy after employing the GAN-based data augmentation techniques.

Harriet et al. have conducted a study on training Convolutional Neural Networks (CNNs) for image segmentation tasks [27] using BraTS Challenges 2013 imbalanced dataset. Authors had investigated the effect of various sampling techniques to deal with biased classification problem that occurs due to the unbalanced nature of the dataset. Wang et al. discussed about developing an ensemble method [28] for dealing with binary classification on imbalanced datasets. Authors had designed a synthetic minority oversampling technique that incorporates the borderline information called Bagging of Extrapolation Borderline-SMOTE SVM (BEBS). From the study it was found that the introduced algorithm 'BEBS' shows a lot of effectiveness in dealing with imbalanced learning.

3 Techniques Used

We have applied Deep learning, Data Augmentation, and Bag of Visual Words techniques on the imbalanced dataset problem. These are briefly described below.

3.1 Deep Learning

Deep learning is based on the artificial neural network [5, 6] which works upon three different layers (Input, Hidden, and Output layer). The number of hidden layers is increased for the automatic features extraction [5, 22] in deep learning. Tensor flow framework is used with Convolution Neural Networks (CNN) architecture [6] as shown in Fig. 1 for deep learning in image classification experiment. CNN architecture used in the experiment consisting of five Layers (each having Convolution, Pooling layer used repeatedly as a convolutional block) and two fully connected layers as shown in Fig. 2. Whereas Softmax and RELU are used as the Activation function. Dropout layer [17, 20] is also used in CNN architecture along with other layers to avoid overfitting which might occur while training the model with the threshold of 0.8 (i.e., 80% of the input units are dropped). This threshold value is kept high as the number of images is less, to generalize the model well [18] and not overfit. Table 1 shows model summary of CNN.

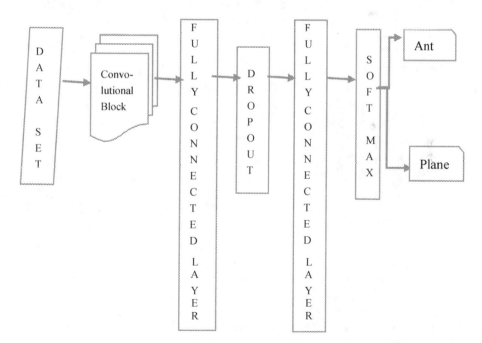

Fig. 1. Deep learning architecture

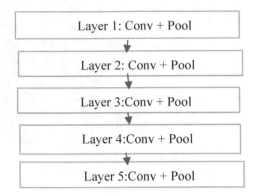

Fig. 2. Convolutional block architecture

Table 1. Model summary of CNN

Hyper parameters	
Layer activation	RELU, Softmax
Classifier design	Conv1 + Pooling→
	Conv2 + Pooling→
	Conv3 + Pooling→
	Conv4 + Pooling→
	Conv5 + Pooling→
	FC1 (fully connected) →
	FC2 (fully Connected)
Input image size	50 × 50
Other parameters	Optimizer → Adam
	Learning late → LR (1 e-3)
	Loss → Categorical_Cross entropy
Layer dropout	0.8

3.2   Data Augmentation

Data Augmentation [7, 13] is used to reduce the overfitting problem by increasing the number of observations in the datasets. Data Augmentation using keras library with Convolution Neural Networks (CNN) architecture [6] is implemented in Python to obtain transformed images from original images. In CNN architecture of data augmentation, dropout layer [17, 20] is used along with other layers to reduce the over fitting problem. Various transformation operations such as Zoom into Images, rotation, Shift images horizontally and vertically, Horizontal flip, and vertical flip were applied over ant and plane image dataset as shown in Fig. 3, to create a model to perform Ant and Plane images classification. Table 2 contains model summary of CNN with data augmentation.

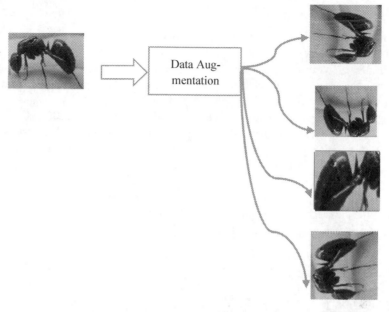

Fig. 3. Data Augmentation model

Table 2. Model summary of CNN with Data Augmentation

Model summary		
Layer (type)	Output_shape	Param #
Conv2d_1 (Conv2D)	(None, 50, 50, 2)	320
Conv2d_2 (Conv2D)	(None, 48, 48, 32)	9248
max_pooling2d_1 (Max Pooling)	(None, 24, 24, 32)	0
droupout_1 (Dropout)	(None, 24, 24, 32)	0
Conv2d_3 (Conv2D)	(None, 24, 24, 64)	18496
Conv2d_4 (Conv2D)	(None, 24, 24, 64)	36928
max_pooling2d_2 (Max Pooling)	(None, 11, 11, 64)	0
droupout_2 (Dropout)	(None, 11, 11, 64)	0
Conv2d_5 (Conv2D)	(None, 11, 11, 64)	36928
Conv2d_6 (Conv2D)	(None, 9, 9, 64)	36928
max_pooling2d_3 (Max Pooling)	(None, 4, 4, 64)	0
droupout_3 (Dropout)	(None, 4, 4, 64)	0
flatten_1 (Flatten)	(None, 1024)	0
dense_1 (Dense)	(None, 512)	524800
droupout_4 (Dropout)	(None, 512)	0
dense_2 (Dense)	(None, 2)	1026
Total params: 664,674		
Trainable params: 664,674		
Non-trainable params: 0		

3.3 Bag of Visual Words (BOVW)

The concept of Bag of Visual Words (BOVW) is derived from the Bag of Words (BOW) which is widely used in natural language processing. Bag of visual words approach [8, 9], constructs a codebook which comprises of a certain number of codewords. Susan et al. conducted the study that proved the significance of SIFT key points for face recognition [29], though the imbalanced dataset LFW results were not very high. Scale-invariant feature transform (SIFT) descriptor [10] and K-Means clustering [12, 21] have been used to compute clusters which further results in the formation of the histogram to assess the frequency of occurrence of a particular visual word as shown in Fig. 4 [30]. Finally, SVM classifier in [11] has been trained with the features derived from the histogram along with the train labels obtained for each image present in the training dataset consisting of both classes (Ant and Plane). From trained classifier, the class label can be predicted of the unknown image from the test dataset. Table 3 shows various parameters used in BOVW.

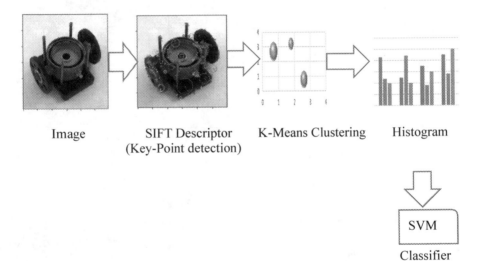

Image   SIFT Descriptor   K-Means Clustering   Histogram
               (Key-Point detection)

SVM
Classifier

Fig. 4. Bag-of-visual-words model

Table 3. Various parameters used in BOVW

BOVW parameters	
Feature extraction	SIFT (128 D)
Clustering technique	K Means-Clustering (No of Clusters = 100)
Classifier	SVM (RBF Kernel)

4 Experiments and Results

A study was conducted to compare the results of deep learning, data augmentation, and BOVW techniques which were applied to the similar dataset consisting of images of Ant and Plane. Experimental work was conducted using Python 3.6 version. For the implementation of deep learning using CNN architecture, we have used Tensor flow framework 1.5.1. Whereas in case of data augmentation, using CNN architecture Keras library 2.1.3 version is used and BOVW is implemented using sci-kit-learn library 0.19.1 version.

4.1 Dataset

The dataset contains 421 images each used for the training and testing purpose as shown in Table 4. Out of the 421 images of both training and testing, 21 images of Ants and 400 images of Plane are obtained from Caltech-101 Dataset to create imbalanced dataset [14, 15] consisting of majority (Plane) and minority (Ant) classes. Figures 5 and 6 shows some of the examples of training and testing images respectively.

Table 4. Dataset

	Ant	Plane
Training	21	400
Testing	21	400

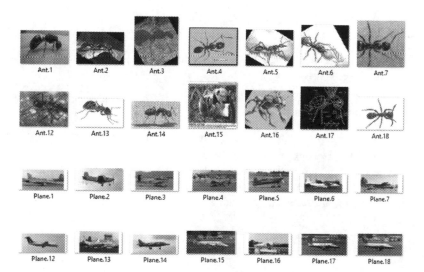

Fig. 5. Examples from the Training dataset consisting of Ant and Plane images sampled from Caltech 101 dataset

Fig. 6. Examples from the Testing dataset consisting of Ant and Plane images sampled from Caltech 101 dataset

4.2   Performance Evaluation

A comparison was done on the basis of accuracy for image classification task with the help of confusion matrix [16, 18]. Accuracy of classifier denotes how proficiently classifier is capable to do classification task. Accuracy can be computed with the help of a Confusion Matrix. Where Confusion Matrix shows the number of correct and incorrect predictions made by the classification model compared to the actual outcomes or target value in the data.

$$Accuracy = \frac{TN + TP}{TN + TP + FN + FP} \tag{1}$$

Where, TP denotes true positive, TN denotes true negative, FN denotes false negative and FP is the false positive.

4.3   Results and Discussion

Results show that deep learning has the highest accuracy in comparison to data augmentation and BOVW (Bag of visual words) techniques. Deep learning demonstrates 98% accuracy for image classification whereas 94% and 95.72% accuracy were obtained using data augmentation and BOVW techniques respectively as shown in Fig. 7 in case of the imbalanced dataset.

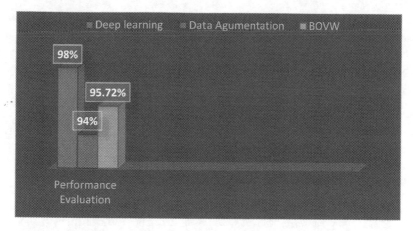

Fig. 7. Comparison of performance of Deep learning, Data Augmentation, and BOVW in terms of accuracy obtained

The Confusion Matrix of deep Learning technique is illustrated in Table 5. Where 20 denotes TP (true positive), 1 denotes FN (False Negative), and 9 denotes FP (False Positive), and 391 denotes TN (True Negative).

Table 5. Confusion Matrix in the case of Deep learning

	Predicted Ant	Predicted Plane
Ant	20	1
Plane	9	391

Results obtained from Deep learning have higher accuracy in comparison to data augmentation and BOVW (Bag of visual words) techniques in case of imbalanced dataset because of the self-learning abilities of deep neural networks to automatically extract features from data which makes them different from conventional machine learning approaches. Moreover, deep learning scheme also optimizes the extracted features before performing the classification due to which it results in higher accuracy in comparison to other techniques.

5   Conclusion

This paper illustrates the comparison between three different image classification techniques (Deep learning, BOVW and Data Augmentation) on the imbalanced dataset. Imbalanced dataset consists of Ant and Plane Images from Caltech-101 dataset. Imbalanced dataset reflects the real-world scenario which is imbalanced in nature and results in the biased classification towards the majority class. According to the experimental results it was found that deep learning produces higher accuracy in comparison with BOVW and Data Augmentation for the imbalanced dataset. Results indicate that deep learning technique can be used to identify real-world imbalanced classification problems accurately such as fraud detection, health diagnostics, etc. Future work will involve creating hybrid CNN with BOVW and compare the results of the imbalanced and balanced dataset in terms of accuracy.

References

1. Frome, A., Singer, Y., Malik, J.: Image retrieval and classification using local distance functions. NIPS (2006)
2. Villar, P., Fernandez, A., Carrasco, R.A., Herrera, F.: Feature selection and granularity learning in genetic fuzzy rule-based classification systems for highly imbalanced data-sets. Int. J. Uncertainty Fuzziness Knowl. Based Syst. **20**(3), 369–397 (2012)
3. https://beamandrew.github.io/deeplearning/2017/06/04/deep_learning_works.html
4. Zhao, W.: Research on the deep learning of the small sample data based on transfer learning. AIP Conf. Proc. **1864**, 020018 (2017)
5. Krizhevsky, A., Sutskever, I., Hinton, G.E.: Imagenet classification with deep convolutional neural networks. In: Advances in Neural Information Processing Systems, pp. 1097–1105 (2012)
6. Jia, Y., et al.: Caffe: convolutional architecture for fast feature embedding. In: Proceedings of the 22nd ACM International Conference on Multimedia, pp. 675–678. ACM (2014)
7. Bjerrum, E.J.: SMILES enumeration as data augmentation for neural network modeling of molecules. ArXiv e-prints, March (2017)
8. Yang, J., Jiang, Y.-G., Hauptmann, A.G., Ngo, C.-W.: Evaluating bag-of-visual-words representations in scene classification. In: Proceedings of the International Workshop on Multimedia Information Retrieval, pp. 197–206. ACM (2007)
9. Csurka, G., Dance, C., Fan, L., Willamowski, J., Bray, C.: Visual categorization with bags of keypoints. In: Workshop on Statistical Learning in Computer Vision, ECCV, Prague (2004)
10. Lowe, D.G.: Distinctive image features from scale-invariant keypoints. Int. J. Comput. Vision **60**(2), 91–110 (2004)
11. Platt, J.: Sequential minimal optimization: a fast algorith for training support vector machines. Microsoft Research Tech Rep MSR-TR-98-14 (1998)
12. Bunkhumpornpat, C., Sinapiromsaran, K., Lursinsap, C.: DBSMOTE: density-based synthetic minority over-sampling technique. Appl. Intell. **36**(3), 664–684 (2012)
13. LeCun, Y., Kavukcuoglu, K., Farabet, C.: Convolutional networks and applications in vision. In: Proceedings of 2010 IEEE International Symposium on Circuits and Systems (ISCAS), pp. 253–256. IEEE (2010)
14. Xie, L., Tian, Q., Wang, M., Zhang, B.: Spatial pooling of heterogeneous features for image classification. IEEE Trans. Image Process. **23**(5), 1994–2008 (2014)
15. http://www.vision.caltech.edu/Image_Datasets/Caltech101/
16. Szegedy, C., et al.: Going deeper with convolutions. In: Proceedings of the IEEE Conference on Computer Vision and Pattern Recognition, pp. 1–12 (2015)
17. Lin, D., Shen, X., Lu, C., Jia, J.: Deep LAC: deep localization, alignment and classification for fine-grained recognition. In: The IEEE Conference on Computer Vision and Pattern Recognition (CVPR) (2015)
18. Reed, S., Lee, H., Anguelov, D., Szegedy, C., Erhan, D., Rabinovich, A.: Training deep neural networks on noisy labels with bootstrapping. arXiv preprint arXiv:1412.6596 (2014)

19. Zhou, B., Lapedriza, A., Xiao, J., Torralba, A., Oliva, A.: Learning deep features for scene recognition using places database. In: Advances in Neural Information Processing Systems, pp. 487–495 (2014)
20. Yosinski, J., Clune, J., Bengio, Y., Lipson, H.: How transferable are features in deep neural networks? In: Advances in Neural Information Processing Systems, pp. 3320–3328 (2014)
21. Vajda, S., Santosh, K.C.: A fast k-nearest neighbor classifier using unsupervised clustering. In: Santosh, K.C., Hangarge, M., Bevilacqua, V., Negi, A. (eds.) RTIP2R 2016. CCIS, vol. 709, pp. 185–193. Springer, Singapore (2017). https://doi.org/10.1007/978-981-10-4859-3_17
22. Ukil, S., Ghosh, S., Md-Obaidullah, S.K., Santosh, K.C., Roy, K., Das, N.: Deep learning for word-level handwritten Indic script identification. arXiv:1801.01627 (2018)
23. Buda, M., Maki, A., Mazurowski, M.A.: A systematic study of the class imbalance problem in convolutional neural networks. arXivpreprint arXiv:1710.05381 (2017)
24. Dong, Q., Gong, S., Zhu, X.: Imbalanced deep learning by minority class incremental rectification. IEEE Trans. Pattern Anal. Mach. Intell. 1–1 (2018)
25. Suh, H.K., Hofstee, J.W., IJsselmuiden, J.M.M., van Henten, E.J.: Sugar beet volunteer potato classification using Bag-of-Visual-words model, scale-invariant feature transform, or speeded up robust feature descriptors and crop row information. Bio Systems Engineering. Elsevier (2017)
26. Zhu, X., Liu, Y., Li, J., Wan, T., Qin, Z.: Emotion classification with data augmentation using generative adversarial networks. In: Phung, D., Tseng, V.S., Webb, G.I., Ho, B., Ganji, M., Rashidi, L. (eds.) PAKDD 2018. LNCS (LNAI), vol. 10939, pp. 349–360. Springer, Cham (2018). https://doi.org/10.1007/978-3-319-93040-4_28
27. Harriet, S., Jonathan, V.: Handling unbalanced data in deep image segmentation (2017)
28. Wang, Q., Luo, Z.H., Huang, J.C., Feng, Y.H., Liu, Z.: A novel ensemble method for imbalanced data learning: bagging of extrapolation-SMOTE SVM. Hindawi Publishing Corporation Computational Intelligence and Neuroscience (2017)
29. Susan, S., Jain, A., Sharma, A., Verma, S., Jain, S.: Fuzzy match index for scale-invariant feature transform (SIFT) features with application to face recognition with weak supervision. IET Image Proc. 9(11), 951–958 (2015)
30. Suh, H.K., Hofstee, J.W., Jsselmuiden, J.I., van Henten, E.J.: Sugar beet volunteer potato classification using Bag-of-Visual-words model, scale-invariant feature transform, or speeded up robust feature descriptors and crop row information. Bio Syst. Eng. 166, 210–226 (2018)

A Survey on Extreme Learning Machine and Evolution of Its Variants

Subhasmita Ghosh[1], Himadri Mukherjee[2(✉)], Sk Md. Obaidullah[1],
K. C. Santosh[3], Nibaran Das[4], and Kaushik Roy[2]

[1] Department of Computer Science and Engineering, Aliah University,
Kolkata, India
I.subhasmitaghosh@gmail.com, sk.obaidullah@gmail.com
[2] Department of Computer Science, West Bengal State University,
Kolkata, India
himadrim027@gmail.com, kaushik.mrg@gmail.com
[3] Department of Computer Science, The University of South Dakota,
Vermillion, SD, USA
santosh.kc@ieee.org
[4] Department of Computer Science and Engineering, Jadavpur University,
Kolkata, India
nibaranju@gmail.com

Abstract. Extreme Learning Machine (ELM) is most popular emerging learning algorithm that modify classical 'Generalized' single hidden layer feed forward network. Though some traditional gradient based learning algorithm like variant Levenberg-Marguardt (LM) and Back propagation (BP) are widely utilized for training in multi layer FFNN but some drawbacks of this mechanism are the most prime issue to promote ELM. It imparts efficient learning solutions for different practices of classification and regression under supervise learning. ELM sharply deals with the messes arise from the gradient based learning algorithm like stopping criteria, learning rate, learning epoch, local minimum etc. But due to some fallibility the different concepts of variants of ELM are presented. This paper clarifies about Extreme Learning Machine along with different types of variants.

Keywords: Single-hidden layer FFNN · ELM · Classification · Activation functions

1 Introduction

Feed forward Neural Network (FFNN), a biologically inspired model is vividly used in past decades due to its simplicity and learning ability of handling complex problems. But the learning speed of FFNN is quite unsatisfactory and all parameters of FFNN are tuned manually. To defeat this downside of FFNN the key idea of ELM are instigating. Basically ELM [1,2] is Single Layered Feed Forward Neural Network for classification and regression. Input weights of the

© Springer Nature Singapore Pte Ltd. 2019
K. C. Santosh and R. S. Hegadi (Eds.): RTIP2R 2018, CCIS 1035, pp. 572–583, 2019.
https://doi.org/10.1007/978-981-13-9181-1_50

ELM, connected input to hidden layer are selected randomly i.e. random projection. The output Weight of ELM layer is resolute by Moore-Prone generalize (MP) inversed. Although ELM has strength to overcome problems in Neural Network it also has some boundaries. For the deduction of input weights and bias ELM highly demands of maximum numbers of hidden neurons. It can't give any superlative solution for the hidden node's learning parameters that are arbitrarily assigned while they remain constant throughout training so some data near to classification boundary may misclassify. To deal with these issues some variants and applications of ELM is discussed. Rong et al. [3] proposed an idea that deals with the classification problems accurse in ELM. An optimization method for classification is enhanced by Huang et al. [4]. A technique for regression and multiclass classification in ELM is discussed by Huang et al. [5]. ELM that deals with sample data set with noise for both input and output values is proposed by Zhao et al. [6]. An enhanced ELM called Polyharmonic ELM is that rebuild a smoother surface with a high accuracy is proposed by Zhou et al. [7]. ELM leaves an important foot step in medical system.

2   Contributions

This paper fully focused on the ELM as well as the application of ELM and the variants of ELM. Especially the pitfalls and the boundaries of Extreme Learning Machine are the prime issue to establish an idea of variants. The main intention of this paper is to drive the paramount implementation of ELM in many research fields and many enhanced form of ELM those are use to overcome the limitations of ELM.

3   Synopsis of ELM

A dataset with N number of neurons in hidden layer with the activation function G the ELM can be representing as follows.

$$f(x) = \sum_{i=1}^{N} \beta_i G(a_i, b_i, x_i) = \beta.h(x) \tag{1}$$

β_i represent the output weight of the i th hidden layer node, a_i is the input weight.

$$h(x) = G(a_1, b_1, x_1), \dots G(a_N, b_N, x_N) \tag{2}$$

The output weights β_i can be acquired by resolving the least-squares solutions of linear equation.

$$min \| \sum_{i=1}^{N} \beta_i.h(x) - y_i \| \tag{3}$$

The least square solution is following.

$$HB = yY // \beta = H^{-1}Y \tag{4}$$

4   Brief Discussion About the Variants of ELM

4.1   Incremental ELM (I-ELM)

It clearly perceives for most of the neural network that the complications occur during learning and training due to the tuning of parameters and weights. To get a grip on this situation Huang et al. [8] established an extension form of ELM called I-ELM or Incremental ELM. The hidden nodes of I-ELM are randomly assigned to the hidden layer one after another and harden the output weights of the existing hidden neurons. I-ELM is one of the most powerful extensions of ELM which is sufficient for SLFN where the activation function is continuous. As the activation function is continuous ELM can fix any desire function in complex domain.

Extensions. The complexity of the network of I-ELM is increased due to the arbitrarily generation of hidden nodes. To eschew this problem an extension of I-ELM called EI-ELM [9] is proposed. EI-ELM nominates the appropriate hidden nodes to reduce the error minimally at every learning step and gain faster convergence rate. Due to the slow rate of convergence of ELM another enhanced form is proposed called CI-ELM [10]. In which the network architecture as well as the convergence rate is more compact and high as compared with traditional ELM.

4.2   Error Minimized ELM (EM-ELM)

Another boosted method of ELM called EM-ELM or Error-Minimized ELM is proposed by Feng et al. [11]. EM-ELM is quite similar with I-ELM. In Error Minimized ELM the nodes in hidden layers are assigned either one after another or group by group. And all the forgoing output weights are modernized consistently at each step, which almost decrease computational complexity. EM-ELM archive better generalization performance compared with I-ELM.

4.3   Pruning ELM (P-ELM)

ELM is the most well liked practices in machine learning for classification and regression problem. But for a large architecture in ELM some complications occur due to a huge amount of hidden nodes. As there exists a massive number of hidden nodes over fitting problem may occur. To defend this issue Rong et al. [3] a system with automatic approach i.e. Pruning ELM (P-ELM). P-ELM firstly justify which nodes are relevant to the network, and then irrelevant nodes are pruned from network. So the network becomes more compact and automated. P-ELM is used to handle the mainly benchmark problem of classification and it gives fast response and satisfactory precision on unseen data.

Extensions. As the movement of P-ELM is restricted only in classification problem, an enhanced version of P-ELM called OP-ELM or Optimally Pruned ELM is established by Miche et al. [12]. OP-ELM applies a leave-one-out (LOO) criterion to select appropriate numbers of relevant neurons.

4.4 Two Stage ELM (TS-ELM)

As the procedure that regulate network architecture of ELM is monotonous and may not give a miser solution Lan et al. [13] proposed an algorithm to solve this problem namely Two Stage ELM (TS-EM). In the primary stage an iterative forward algorithm is engaged in each step to select the hidden node from randomly produced candidates and append them to the network until it gain it's minimum stopping criteria. And in the next step the substance of each node in hidden layer is appraised. After this the insignificance nodes are eliminate from network which reduce network complexity.

4.5 Voting Based ELM (V-ELM)

For traditional ELM there is no optimal solution due to random deduction of input weight and bias while they prevail unchanged throughout training. Thus the data near to classification border may miss classify. To reduce this issue Cao et al. [14] proposed Voting Based ELM (V-ELM). In V-ELM multiple training are made instead of solitary training and then take ultimate decision based on major voting method. V-ELM not only deals with classification problem but also reduce misclassified data.

Extension. Shukla et al. [15] proposed V-ELM with Gain based ensemble Pruning (VELMGP) that amplifies both the pruning method and voting based ELM. VELMGP technique diminish the complexity by reducing the pruning set size by eliminating training instants that are adjacent and abstracted from the decision boundary. These instances are classified correctly majority of classification.

4.6 Online Sequential ELM (OS-ELM)

Liang et al. [16] recommend a consecutive learning algorithm called Online Sequential ELM (OS-ELM) that may fix or vary the dataset size and then learn the data either one after another or set by set. It is perceive that OS-ELM can deals with additive including RBF nodes. In OS-ELM the weights of input neurons to hidden neurons are randomly produced and output weights are determined well organized manner. It is observed that OS-ELM is faster and generate better generalization implementation than traditional learning algorithm.

Extension. For further improvement of OS-ELM Lan et al. [17] an integrated network architecture called EOS-ELM or Ensemble of Online Sequential ELM. It is an integrated design of multiple number of OS-ELM. EOS-ELM calculates the average values of output of each and every OS-ELM in the ensemble and quantifies the network performance. Another extension version of OS-ELM is proposed by Zhao et al. [18]. Zhao et al. proposed Online Sequential ELM including forgetting mechanism [FOS-ELM]. FOS-ELM not only modifies the learning effort of OS-ELM but also modify the learning effort of EOS-ELM by promptly tossing out the backdated data. So the bad patch of those outdated data cannot hamper the learning procedure.

4.7   Evolutionary ELM (E-ELM)

For the traditional ELM due to the huge numbers of hidden neurons and indiscriminate determination of input weight with hidden bias the generalization performance of network is quite unsatisfied. To overlook this problem Zhu et al. [19] proposed Evolutionary ELM, which makes application of the advantage of both Differential Evolutionary (DE) algorithm and ELM. The preference of E-ELM is to regulate the output weight instead of tuning by using minimum least square scheme. E-ELM attains greater generalization performance than traditional learning algorithm and does not require the activation to differentiate.

Extension. To refine the performance of E-ELM Cao et al. [20] establish a modified learning algorithm called SaE-ELM or Self Adaptive Evolutionary ELM. The hidden neurons of SaE-ELM are boosted by the self adaptive differential evolution algorithm. SaE-ELM can cleverly handle the parameters and generalization strategies involved in Differential Evolutionary (DE).

4.8   Fully Complex ELM (C-ELM)

For the comfortable movement in complex domain of traditional ELM and non linear channel equalization application Li et al. [21] propose further enhanced version called Fully Complex ELM (C-ELM). C-ELM not only avoids the local minimum problem but also avoids the tuning parameters problem. C-ELM completes the learning phase in significantly high speed and acquire lower symbol error rate (SER).

4.9   Ordinal ELM (O-ELM)

For further application of ELM for ordinal regression problem Ordinal ELM (O-ELM) is proposed by Deng et al. [22]. This method consists of three different steps. At the prime stage three encoding scheme are used. Single multi output classifier, collective binary classifiers with OAA or One-Against-All dissection method and OAO or One-Against-One methods are proposed for encoding based framework. Then based on the proposed framework SLFN is rebuilt for ordinal regression problem and input weight are assigned randomly as well as output weight are chosen analytically in the time of training. At the end a wide range of dataset is appended to this algorithm.

4.10   Symmetric ELM (S-ELM)

To gain better generalized performance with high learning speed and compact network Liu et al. [23] a variant of ELM named S-ELM or Symmetric ELM. In S-ELM the initial particulars are directly integrated into ELM by modifying the activation function of the hidden neurons into a symmetric one. For N unpredictable distinct samples S-ELM has the strength to store by approximating with zero error.

4.11   TLS ELM

Most of the ELM handles the problems for sample dataset with output noise not the Error in Variable (EIV) model. In EIV model there exists noise in sample data for both input and output values. An algorithm proposed by Zhou et al. [6] called TLS-ELM that fix the least square error. TLS-ELM gives better precision and shorter training time compared with others.

4.12   Fuzzy ELM (F-ELM)

It is observed in real applications some imbalanced problems and weighted classification problems occur. As the conventional ELM is not potential to handle these problem Zhang et al. [24] discuss about Fuzzy ELM (F-ELM). Fuzzy ELM establishes a fuzzy membership to the conventional ELM. To learn output weight, the inputs with different fuzzy matrices play an important role. F-ELM delivers more logical results for weighted classification problems.

4.13   PCA ELM

To train any types of SLFN with hidden nodes and linear activation function Castano et al. [25] presents PCA-ELM. By resolving the information from PCA on given training dataset, PCA evaluates the hidden node parameters. And by utilizing Moore-Penrose generalized inverse the output node parameters are regulated rationally.

4.14   Parallel ELM

ELM can attain superior generalization performance at faster learning speed for regression problem. But for a wide range of data set it is very challenging task. He et al. [26] recommended Parallel ELM to face mentioned problem. For regression Parallel ELM is established and also executed based on Map Reduce Framework, which is not simple only but powerful program technique also.

4.15   Robust ELM

Conventional ELM has two major problems one is computational encounter problem and other is robustness while computing of output weights. To deals with these problem Horata et al. [27] present Robust ELM. This kind of ELM is robust to noise level close to class borders and far from the class boundaries which can result from error in labeling in measuring input feature.

4.16   Regularized ELM

For most of the cases the data that one near to classification boundary are missing in ELM. To solve this problem Yu et al. [28] nominate Regularized ELM. This method uses two tools for missing data problem. One is cascade of L1 penalty (LARS) and L2 penalty (Tikhonov regularization). And hence the MSE computation becomes more definitive. It calculates presume pair wise gap between samples on incomplete data. Thus the missing data problem is solved.

4.17   Weighted Extreme Learning Machine (W-ELM)

Zong et al. [29] projected an extended version if ELM called weighted Extreme Learning Machine (W-ELM). W-ELM has the strength to cover data set with imbalance class distribution. It can be derived to cost sensitive learning approach by applying different weights.

The variants of ELM are briefly summarised in Table 1.

5   Applications of ELM

Not only ELM but the variants of ELM may serve in many extents. Consider the classification problem ELM is applied in different purpose. Elm plays a big cast in medical domain. It classifies Electro Cardio Signals to diagnose heart disease. ELM also assists the task of Thyroid diagnosis. To adapt the changes in territory ELM also reveal mobile object index by classifying the region. Considering uni-label and multi-label situation ELM is used to categorize texts. ELM also plays a significant role for regression problem. For very large scale dataset that can solve regression problem ELM as well as extensions of ELM are vividly used. ELM also works for framework based regression problems. Not only that ELM significant for pattern recognition. ELM sharply entertains multilevel face as well as human face detection problems. ELM is served in various aspects such as text categorizations, gender identifications, finger print matching, and re-establishment of surface, 3D object recognition in the terms of regression problems. Some applications of ELM are discussed briefly in the following Table 2.

Table 1. Summary of the variants of ELM.

Variants name	Proposed by	Explanations	Extension of variants	Proposed by	Remarks
Incremental ELM (I-ELM)	Huang et al. [8]	It handles the complication occur during learning and training by assigning hidden nodes randomly	EI-ELM	Huang et al. [9]	Optimally hidden nodes are chosen to reduce the errors minimally
			CI-ELM	Huang et al. [10]	It is implemented to achieve a compact convergence rate
Error Minimized ELM (EM-ELM)	Feng et al. [11]	By modernizing previous output EM-ELM decrease the computational complexity	Not extended	-	-
Pruning ELM (P-ELM)	Rong et al. [3]	By pruned irrelevant nodes P-ELM handle the benchmark problem of classification	OP-ELM	Miche et al. [12]	By using LOO select relevant nodes
Two Stage ELM (TS-ELM)	Lan et al. [13]	A two stage algorithm is applied to adjust the hidden node to achieve compact network	Not extended	-	-
Voting-based ELM (V-ELM)	Cao et al. [14]	To reduce misclassified data problem, multiple training is done	VELMGP	Shukla et al. [15]	Combination of P-ELM and V-ELM ELM, pruning instance are classified correctly

Table 2. Applications of ELM.

Application domain	Proposed by	Remarks
Technology (Mobile object)	Wang et al. [30]	ELM is employed to classify the mobile objects
Text Categorization	Zheng et al. [31]	Regularized ELM is used for classification of text where the situation is both uni-level and multi-level
Regression	He et al. [26]	Parallel ELM is established to solve regression on very large scale data
	Li et al. [32]	To suppress the effects of perturbation Ridge Regression is proposed
	Balasundaram [33]	It deals with E-insensitive regression
Pattern Recognition	Zong et al. [34]	Multi label face reorganization ELM is used
	Mohammed et al. [35]	Human face reorganization for bidirectional 2D components
	Nian et al. [36]	ELM is applied for 3D object reorganization
	Yang et al. [37]	By applying ELM and ternary pattern, gender face reorganization is used
Pattern Recognition	Yang et al. [38]	Fingerprint matching is possible using Extreme Learning Machine
Retail Industry	Chen et al. [39]	Grey Extreme Learning Machine is proposed to build a forecasting replica in the retail industry
Power System	Xu et al. [40]	For the evolution of real time, frequency stability ELM based predictor is used
Wavelet Transformation	Malathi et al. [41]	For classification, fault part discrimination WT-ELM is proposed
Indic Scripts identification	Obaidullah et al. [42]	Different Indic Scripts identification, including writer identification, word spotting are made by using ELM
Voice Activity detection	Mukherjee et al. [43]	By implementing VAD technique ELM classification is proposed

6   Open Problems of ELM

Though the ELM has shown sensible presentation in many areas but there are some open problems that draw the attention of researchers. The issues are as follows. • Elm cannot give any optimal solution while the quantities of hidden neurons are wide in range. • For different dataset ELM cannot regulate the vague number of neurons in hidden layer. • ELM cannot calculate generalization problem for the swinging bound. • The applications of ELM are still open for parallel and distributed computing. • The effectiveness of ELM for generalization problem is quite unsatisfactory and unstable compared with conventional learning algorithm. • The ELM algorithm needs to be tested more and more for big data to resolve classification problems.

7 Conclusion

With the intension to present significance of ELM in various aspects and research section this paper reveal a concept of ELM with the challenges. Many authors establish various version of ELM to challenge various complications. It is observed that ELM and it's variants not only deals with the issues occur in classification and regression problem but it is proved that ELM is well define application in the field of pattern recognition, medical diagnosis and forecasting areas. The prime job of this paper is to give a metaphysical view of ELM and variants of ELM, approach of ELM in distinct fields and open problems that one can compass the further approaches of ELM.

References

1. Huang, G.B., Zhu, Q.Y., Siew, C.K.: Extreme learning machine: a new learning scheme of feedforward neural networks. In: Proceedings of 2004 IEEE International Joint Conference on Neural Networks, vol. 2, pp. 985–990. IEEE, July 2004
2. Huang, G.B., Zhu, Q.Y., Siew, C.K.: Extreme learning machine: theory and applications. Neurocomputing 70(1–3), 489–501 (2006)
3. Rong, H.J., Ong, Y.S., Tan, A.H., Zhu, Z.: A fast pruned-extreme learning machine for classification problem. Neurocomputing 72(1–3), 359–366 (2008)
4. Huang, G.B., Ding, X., Zhou, H.: Optimization method based extreme learning machine for classification. Neurocomputing 74(1–3), 155–163 (2010)
5. Huang, G.B., Zhou, H., Ding, X., Zhang, R.: Extreme learning machine for regression and multiclass classification. IEEE Trans. Syst. Man Cybern. Part B (Cybern.) 42(2), 513–529 (2012)
6. Zhao, J., Wang, Z., Cao, F.: Extreme learning machine with errors in variables. World Wide Web 17(5), 1205–1216 (2014)
7. Zhou, Z.H., Zhao, J.W., Cao, F.L.: Surface reconstruction based on extreme learning machine. Neural Comput. Appl. 23(2), 283–292 (2013)
8. Huang, G.B., Chen, L., Siew, C.K.: Universal approximation using incremental constructive feedforward networks with random hidden nodes. IEEE Trans. Neural Netw. 17(4), 879–892 (2006)
9. Huang, G.B., Chen, L.: Enhanced random search based incremental extreme learning machine. Neurocomputing 71(16–18), 3460–3468 (2008)
10. Huang, G.B., Chen, L.: Convex incremental extreme learning machine. Neurocomputing 70(16–18), 3056–3062 (2007)
11. Feng, G., Huang, G.B., Lin, Q., Gay, R.K.L.: Error minimized extreme learning machine with growth of hidden nodes and incremental learning. IEEE Trans. Neural Netw. 20(8), 1352–1357 (2009)

12. Miche, Y., Sorjamaa, A., Bas, P., Simula, O., Jutten, C., Lendasse, A.: OP-ELM: optimally pruned extreme learning machine. IEEE Trans. Neural Netw. **21**(1), 158–162 (2010)

13. Lan, Y., Soh, Y.C., Huang, G.B.: Two-stage extreme learning machine for regression. Neurocomputing **73**(16–18), 3028–3038 (2010)

14. Cao, J., Lin, Z., Huang, G.B., Liu, N.: Voting based extreme learning machine. Inf. Sci. **185**(1), 66–77 (2012)

15. Shukla, S., Wadhvani, R., Bharti, J., Gyanchandani, M.: Voting based extreme learning machine with search based ensemble pruning. IJCSNS **17**(3), 223 (2017)

16. Liang, N.Y., Huang, G.B., Saratchandran, P., Sundararajan, N.: A fast and accurate online sequential learning algorithm for feedforward networks. IEEE Trans. Neural Netw. **17**(6), 1411–1423 (2006)

17. Lan, Y., Soh, Y.C., Huang, G.B.: Ensemble of online sequential extreme learning machine. Neurocomputing **72**(13–15), 3391–3395 (2009)

18. Zhao, J., Wang, Z., Park, D.S.: Online sequential extreme learning machine with forgetting mechanism. Neurocomputing **87**, 79–89 (2012)

19. Zhu, Q.Y., Qin, A.K., Suganthan, P.N., Huang, G.B.: Evolutionary extreme learning machine. Pattern Recogn. **38**(10), 1759–1763 (2005)

20. Cao, J., Lin, Z., Huang, G.B.: Self-adaptive evolutionary extreme learning machine. Neural Process. Lett. **36**(3), 285–305 (2012)

21. Li, M.B., Huang, G.B., Saratchandran, P., Sundararajan, N.: Fully complex extreme learning machine. Neurocomputing **68**, 306–314 (2005)

22. Deng, W.Y., Zheng, Q.H., Lian, S., Chen, L., Wang, X.: Ordinal extreme learning machine. Neurocomputing **74**(1–3), 447–456 (2010)

23. Liu, X., Li, P., Gao, C.: Symmetric extreme learning machine. Neural Comput. Appl. **22**(3–4), 551–558 (2013)

24. Zhang, W.B., Ji, H.B.: Fuzzy extreme learning machine for classification. Electron. Lett. **49**(7), 448–450 (2013)

25. Castano, A., Fernandez-Navarro, F., Hervás-Martínez, C.: PCA-ELM: a robust and pruned extreme learning machine approach based on principal component analysis. Neural Process. Lett. **37**(3), 377–392 (2013)

26. He, Q., Shang, T., Zhuang, F., Shi, Z.: Parallel extreme learning machine for regression based on MapReduce. Neurocomputing **102**, 52–58 (2013)

27. Horata, P., Chiewchanwattana, S., Sunat, K.: Robust extreme learning machine. Neurocomputing **102**, 31–44 (2013)

28. Yu, Q., Miche, Y., Eirola, E., Van Heeswijk, M., SéVerin, E., Lendasse, A.: Regularized extreme learning machine for regression with missing data. Neurocomputing **102**, 45–51 (2013)

29. Zong, W., Huang, G.B., Chen, Y.: Weighted extreme learning machine for imbalance learning. Neurocomputing **101**, 229–242 (2013)

30. Wang, B., Wang, G., Li, J., Wang, B.: Update strategy based on region classification using ELM for mobile object index. Soft Comput. **16**(9), 1607–1615 (2012)

31. Zheng, W., Qian, Y., Lu, H.: Text categorization based on regularization extreme learning machine. Neural Comput. Appl. **22**(3–4), 447–456 (2013)

32. Li, G., Niu, P.: An enhanced extreme learning machine based on ridge regression for regression. Neural Comput. Appl. **22**(3–4), 803–810 (2013)

33. Balasundaram, S.: On extreme learning machine for E-insensitive regression in the primal by Newton method. Neural Comput. Appl. **22**(3–4), 559–567 (2013)

34. Zong, W., Huang, G.B.: Face recognition based on extreme learning machine. Neurocomputing **74**(16), 2541–2551 (2011)

35. Mohammed, A.A., Minhas, R., Wu, Q.J., Sid-Ahmed, M.A.: Human face recognition based on multidimensional PCA and extreme learning machine. Pattern Recogn. **44**(10–11), 2588–2597 (2011)
36. Nian, R., He, B., Lendasse, A.: 3D object recognition based on a geometrical topology model and extreme learning machine. Neural Comput. Appl. **22**(3–4), 427–433 (2013)
37. Yang, J., Jiao, Y., Xiong, N., Park, D.: Fast face gender recognition by using local ternary pattern and extreme learning machine. KSII Trans. Internet Inf. Syst. (TIIS) **7**(7), 1705–1720 (2013)
38. Yang, J., Xie, S., Yoon, S., Park, D., Fang, Z., Yang, S.: Fingerprint matching based on extreme learning machine. Neural Comput. Appl. **22**(3–4), 435–445 (2013)
39. Chen, F.L., Ou, T.Y.: Sales forecasting system based on Gray extreme learning machine with Taguchi method in retail industry. Expert Syst. Appl. **38**(3), 1336–1345 (2011)
40. Xu, Y., Dai, Y., Dong, Z.Y., Zhang, R., Meng, K.: Extreme learning machine-based predictor for real-time frequency stability assessment of electric power systems. Neural Comput. Appl. **22**(3–4), 501–508 (2013)
41. Malathi, V., Marimuthu, N.S., Baskar, S., Ramar, K.: Application of extreme learning machine for series compensated transmission line protection. Eng. Appl. Artif. Intell. **24**(5), 880–887 (2011)
42. Obaidullah, S.M., Halder, C., Santosh, K.C., Das, N., Roy, K.: PHDIndic_11: page-level handwritten document image dataset of 11 official Indic scripts for script identification. Multimedia Tools Appl. **77**(2), 1643–1678 (2018)
43. Mukherjee, H., Obaidullah, S.M., Santosh, K.C., Phadikar, S., Roy, K.: Line spectral frequency-based features and extreme learning machine for voice activity detection from audio signal. Int. J. Speech Technol. **21**, 753–760 (2018)

Performance and Evaluation of Support Vector Machine and Artificial Neural Network over Heterogeneous Data

Ashish Kumar Mourya$^{(\boxtimes)}$

Jamia Hamdard, Hamdard Nagar, New Delhi, India
ashishkumarmourya@gmail.com

Abstract. The objective of this research is to evaluate the pursuance of Support Vector Machine, Neural Network over heterogeneous data. Heterogeneous data refers to data containing a mix of real, ordinal, and categorical data, possibly with missing values. This data is very common in the real world. Support Vector Machine is a powerful learning classifier which currently used for classifying the multisource as well as mono source remotely and heterogeneous conceived data in various implementaion research and outperforms other discoveries in various comparable studies. In this study, ourselves found that neural networks endure thesir theoretical weaknesses. The support vector machine achieved higher overall accuracy for the uninterrupted span of training typifying sizes as estimated to neural network. Support vector machine systematization performance exhibited nominal variability in reciprocation to different training data.

Keywords: Support Vector Machine (SVM) · Neural Network (NN) · Classification and Regression Tree (CART) · Kernel · Receiver Operating Characteristic (ROCR)

1 Introduction

In the domain of Feature engineering and Learning classifiers, SVM has proven to be an effective method for classification cause. SVM classifier is also known to be very strong in term of achieving best output on the statistical (nominal) figures [1], thanks to its straightforward endeavour to make best use of the margin of misclassification along the limits among the classes of statistics [2–6]. Traditional Support Vector Machine is quadratic ally complex O (n^2), yet there are booming attempts to cunningly decrease its complexity to linear complexity [7]. It is widely used in many research areas such as gene Categorization [8,9], time series classification [10,11], image retrieval [12–14,44] and handwriting recognition [15,16,45,46]. SVM is currently used in different assortment works that use statistical inputs or heterogeneous data. But the goal of training support vector machine, neural network and Classification and Regression tree with heterogeneous data has not been tested yet. On the other hand, Artificial Neural

© Springer Nature Singapore Pte Ltd. 2019
K. C. Santosh and R. S. Hegadi (Eds.): RTIP2R 2018, CCIS 1035, pp. 584–595, 2019.
https://doi.org/10.1007/978-981-13-9181-1_51

Network (ANN) is another classifier which is flexible and vigorous predictor for both of regression and classification issues [17–21]. Its basic formation allows learning practically any function lucratively, with ample hidden layers of processing nodes with training data. Both of these classifiers are typically O (n^3), or at finest quadratically complex with more examples. Convoluted structures added broaden computational demands of learning artificial neural network.

In the supervised learning classifiers, SVM has learned through one to one or one to many classes of data. Within bioinformatic and computational biotechnology, SVMs have been used in various problems, including proteins, genes remote protein homology detection, various types of gene expression analyses, splice site, and tandem mass spectrometry analysis, alternative splicing detection, etc. [22] proposed support vector classifier as a novel approach to learning classifier which totally rely on the statistic principle (structural risk minimization). Support vector classifiers find the hypothesis space h of a learning system, which roughly minimizes the bound of the existing error by controlling the VC (Vapnik–Chervonenkis) dimension of H [23].

It was firstly proposed as a binary classifier [24]. Support vector classifier uses two different positive and negative classes for learning samples within different dimensional feature space to fit an optimal separating hyperplane (in each dimension, vector component is a biophysical variable). In this direction, support vectors tries to maximize the margin, that is, the distance between the closest training samples, or support vectors, and the hyperplane itself. Support vector consists in projecting vectors into a high dimension feature space by means of a kernel method. For a basic motif x, the reciprocal predicted label is given by (1)

$$\hat{z} = sign[f(x)] = sign(\sum_{i=1}^{n} a_i y_i \ K(x_i, x + C)) \tag{1}$$

Where n is the number of training points, the label of the ith sample is y_i, c is a bias parameter, $K(x_i, x)$ is the chosen kernel function and a_i denotes the Lagrangian multipliers [25–27]. Because the input vectors come in the binate form of dot products only, the classifierlearner can be comprehensive to non-linear classification by mapping the inputs into a high dimensional vector space through an apriori selected non-linear mapping function Φ. So by erecting a distinguishing hyperplane in the given vector space leads to a non-linear determination boundary in the input space. $a_i y_i$ is also constant that we used in linear support vector machine equation. When we applying an Support vector machine to a categorization problem, it consist of 2 parts: training and testing. During first phase, the support vector machine takes datasets as an input with fixed vector length example. Moreover, each sample must have an analogous binary classifier description. We apply '+1' label for indicating the positive class and '−' for denoting the negative data points. The support vector machine algorithms find the hyperplane in the high diamensional vector that distinguish the positive (+1) from the negative class.

Neural Network Classifier for classification technology has worn significant attentiveness in previous years. Neural Network Classifier, as compared with statistical methods, has some important advantages. On the one hand, statistical classifiers frequently need initial facts about the pattern dispensation, while on the other hand, neural network learners work excellently without any comprehension distribution. They have capability to achieved excellently on composite patterns resulting from unstructured data and are useful for tasks requiring information fusion. Neural networks are more useful for function and classification estimate problems, typically when rules such as those that might be used in heterogeneity and expert system cannot easily be applied [28]. We have explained neural network classifier in next section.

2   Related Works

Before comparing our heterogeneous datasets, we have reviewed few facts and figure associated to support vector machine and neural networks on accounts of some critical concepts and key ideas based on which our result has been established. Recently, Several scientists and Data Analysts have implemented and recommended MKL method with Support vector machine [35,36]. They codify an individual optimization measure method which simultaneously finds the Support Vector Machine assortment solution with weights on single attribute types in a mixed value.

2.1   Support Vector Machine

Within learning classifiers, for binary classification tasks, support vector machine is an effective method. It builds an optimally dividing hyperplane in a vector space. Consider a simple example with two classes $y = 1, -1$ (Figs. 1 and 2), then a hyperplane that separates all data $\rightarrow W^T \mathrm{X} + B = 0_{+1}^{-1}$. through a method (higher dimensional) Φ, we map an input vector y into an higher diamensional space. For example g samples $\{(x_i, y_i)\}_i^g = 1$, support vectors look for a linear decision function $[\mathrm{f}(\mathrm{x}) = \mathrm{sgn}(W^T X + B]$, x: test sample data) from input space to feature space with a highest margin between other classes. The values of W and b are taken by clarify the following quadratic equation dilemma [29].

$$\min_{w,b,\xi} \frac{1}{2} ||W^T||^2 + C \sum_{i=1}^{n} \xi \tag{2}$$

subject to $y_i [\mathrm{w}, \Phi, (x_i) + \mathrm{b}] \geq 1 - \xi_i, \xi_i \geq 0, \mathrm{i} = 1, 2, 3$
where w is infinite variable, ξ denote to slack variable, and constant variable is denoted by C that penalizes for training error.

In the non-linear separation, Support vector machine map the input training data into a feature space $\Phi(X_i) = Z_i$, we find the optimal decision function in the feature space. The non-linear support vector machine is alike to the optimization.

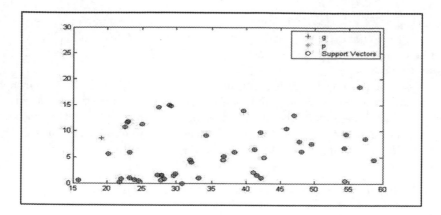

Fig. 1. Scatter data representation of Support Vector Machine

The main difference is that W & Z_i are defined in the feature space. The nonlinear version of support vector machine solves the optimization problem as follows

$$\min \tag{3}$$

$$\text{Fulfill to: } y_i\Big((w, z_i) + b\Big) \geq 1 - \xi_i \text{ where } \xi_i > 0$$

Kernel methods give an ethical means to constitute and, hence, sketch inferences from assorted sets of information. Most of the kernel methods represent a group of illogically composite data objects by using a so-called kernel tricks which defines the resemblance between any given set of objects. For example, the group of various objects can be adequately denoted through m * n matrix of pairwise kernel methods.

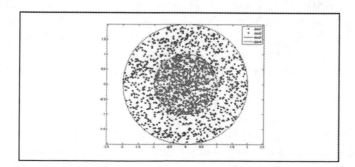

Fig. 2. Binary classifier representation of Support Vector Machine

When applying support vector classifier to the unstructured dataset, kernel tricks must be distinct for all information and grids must be associated numerically [30,31]. Used this approach in their work to combine heterogeneous gene expression and phylo-genetic profiles in an un-weighted mode [32]. An un-weighted sum of kernels has also been used successfully in the forecasting of protein relations.

A few years ago, researchers proposed MKL (Multiple Kernel Learning) approaches that associate different kernels within the support vector classifier itself [33]. These methods put together an individual optimization measure which simultaneously finds the Support Vector Machine classification solution and weights on the single data types in the unstructured set.

2.2   Trained Neural Network with Heterogeneous Data

The neural network is a popular effective classification tool to map any nonlinear function [34]. It is a complex network system which connects with the vast simple artificial neuron in order to emulate the human brain. The initial values of weight of the connection links can be affected by the performance of neural network learning algorithms. Consider a set of weights (population of heterogeneous data sample). To balance the weights on links we proportionally divide the population into S disjoint subsets. Now each neural network has m synaptic connections $[W_i...W_n]$ populated by a sample from the subset $[a_1...a_s]$ and repeats it to distribute the sample on the connection links. Now, applying random sampling technique to select the proportional number of samples from each S to populate every m, we get S_m. Let us take an example by assuming different weight $[W_1...W_n]$ with stratum $A_1 = 0.5, 0$ and $A_2 = 0, 0.5$, with trained neural network $T = S_n$. The error rate is closer to zero, that is considering the best set of first weight.

3   Feature Abstraction

Feature Abstraction is an essential step in heterogeneous data mining, especially for heterogeneous and homogeneous datasets. Feature selection is a process commonly used in data selection and preparation for heterogeneous data mining. Feature or variable selection is the process of identifying and removing redundant and irrelevant information as much as possible before collecting data. The problem of feature selection has been addressed in various research areas, especially in data mining, medical diagnosis, machine learning. The next section we have presented an overview of feature selection. There are various prospective benefits of an attributes and feature abstraction: data understanding and facilitating data visualization, tumbling the computation and data warehouse requirements, minimizing training, disregarding the curse of linearity to refine prediction and performance. Many feature selection classifiers encompass variable ranking as a prime or reserve selection system due to its scalability, lucidity and good factual triumph.

3.1   Feature Selection Background

Lets the dataset of n attributes $\{k_1, k_2, k_3...k_n\}$ the major approach of attributes selection is to eliminates a lots of irrelevent and unneeded variables as it may & find an attribute subset $\{k_{x_1}, k_{x_2}, k_{x_3}...k_{x_r}\}$ where $(r < n)$ such that with dimensionally condensed data, a learning classifier can attain better or similar performance. The aforesaid process has been applied on a wide scale in bioinformatics [35,36], text mining [37,38], image processing [39]. But conventional feature abstraction classifiers work on mono source only. The question is how to invent powerful feature abstraction classifiers for heterogeneous data sources, called "multi-source feature selection".

3.2   Wrapper for Feature Abstraction Subset

In the feature selection subset problem, The wrapper technique has been applied to determine feature weights that measure the performance of attributes by using the classification model. To accomplish the most excellent desirable achievement and accuracy with a distinct learning classifier on an appropriate training sample, a feature abstraction subsets function should acknowledge how training set and the algorithm collaborate. The inductive algorithm is used by wrapper method as the assessment method [40,41]. This method takes a binary classifier for assessment of subsets of test data by their anticipating accuracy cross-validation of datasets. Moreover, the wrapper techniques achieve better performance rates than a filter approach. Further, wrappers methods have techniques to avoid over fitting, since usually cross-validation method measures of anticipating accuracy had used by [42,43].

3.3   Predicting Data Sets Using Feature Eradication

Here, we have performed feature abstraction and finds predictors among data sets. The outer re-sampling method is cross-validating (10 folds). This method provides top two variables out of data sets (Fig. 9).

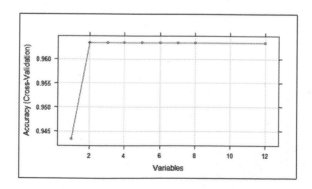

Fig. 3. Feature selection representation

4   Experiments

This segment has two portion. We have described here about the data, content, and tools used in processing heterogeneity in data. We have used Heterogeneous Data Repository of AIM Laboratory. We have used real or synthetic data, and Meta that are collected or created for heterogeneous data in semantics and/or in structure. There are at least two heterogeneous data [Meta data] sets. We have used R studio for processing these heterogeneous data. All the algorithms and graphs are mostly generated from these processing tools. In this section, we have performed various experiments to compare the performance of SVM

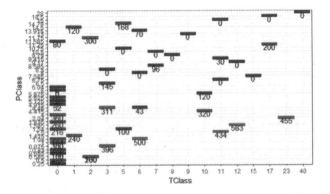

Fig. 4. Confusion matrix

Fig. 5. Representation of dataset (histogram)

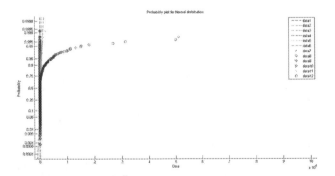

Fig. 6. Probability of normal distribution

over NN. First, we have checked the cross- validation with the heterogeneous dataset. We got Root node error: $3.387e+10/74 = 457697174$ $n = 74$ (denoted by total number of rows used in cross-validation in Fig. 7) (Figs. 4, 5 and 6).

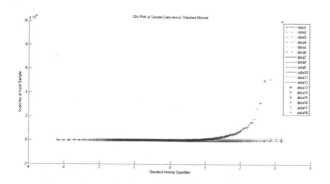

Fig. 7. Quantile data plot diagram

4.1 Evaluation and Prediction of Support Vector Machine Using ROC

In this section, we have evaluated the performance of SVM through prediction using the radial kernel to plot the ROC Curve.

Parameters:

SVM-Type: eps-regression
SVM-Kernel: radial,
Cost: 100,
gamma: 0.01,
epsilon: 0.1,
Sigma: 0.4131442
Number of Support Vectors: 535
5-fold cross-validation on training data:
Total Mean Squared Error: 14.89463
Squared Correlation Coefficient: 0.3759034
Mean Squared Errors: 15.65744 7.593007 6.966136 37.47904 6.783069 (Fig. 8).

4.2 Prediction Using Heterogeneous Data Through Neural Network

Now we have created an object using available heterogeneous data for Neural Net function (Table 1). We have also used decay variable to ensure that our model does not get over trained. Performance variables and their data values have been shown in Table 1.

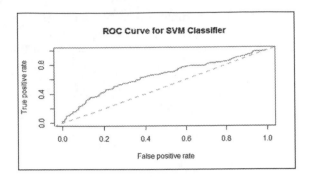

Fig. 8. ROC Curve for SVM classifier to predict heterogeneity using binary classifier data set

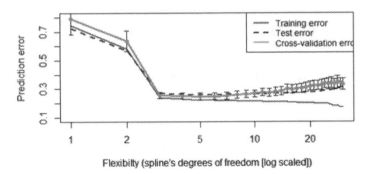

Fig. 9. Prediction of data using 10-fold cross-validation

Table 1. Performance variable for neural network

Error	8780.849327420618
Reached threshold	0.009943102786
Steps	16080.000000000000
Intercept.to.1layhid1	−48.276181549523
mydata$X0.1 to.1layhid1	0.069007175597
mydata$X1.25.to.1layhid1	18.475568853558
mydata$X0.to.1layhid1	9.265457887122
Intercept.to.1layhid2	57.971082341961
mydata$X0.1.to.1layhid2	−10.761068961874
mydata$X1.25.to.1layhid2	−64.418659697550
mydata$X0.to.1layhid2	4.059651025810
Intercept.to.mydata$X01	10.695965010828
1layhid.1.to.mydata$X01	115.393147262166
1layhid.2.to.mydata$X01	−12.163619246007

5   Conclusion

Currently classification problems have been solved through different machine learning classifiers. Support vector classifier has been compared with the neural network over heterogeneous datasets to predict the performance here. CARTS are habitually narrated by numerical and nominal features in various real world medical problems. The classification experiments for performance and prediction were executed with respect to the impacts of training feature sizes, dissimilarity, and the characteristics of allusions data points. In the training process support vector classifiers have achieved overall highest accuracies for the entire range of instruction sample sizes in comparison to the Neural networks. Support Vector Machine classifier performance exhibited minimal variability in response to different training data. The main dissimilarities were especially outsized for least training data points.

References

1. http://aimlab.cs.uoregon.edu/benchmark
2. Mitchell, T.M.: Machine Learning. McGraw-Hill, New York (1997)
3. Duda, R.O., Hart, P.E., Stork, D.G.: Pattern Classification. Wiley, New York (2001)
4. Bishop, C.M.: Pattern Recognition and Machine Learning. Springer, New York (2006)
5. Marsland, S.: Machine Learning, An Algorithmic Perspective. Chapman and Hall, CRC Press, Boca Raton (2009)
6. Mohri, A., Rostamizadeh, A., Talwalker, A.: Foundations of Machine Learning. The MIT Press, Cambridge (2012)
7. Joachims, T.: Training linear SVMs in linear time. In: Proceedings of the 12th ACM SIGKDD International Conference on Knowledge Discovery and Data Mining (KDD 2006), pp: 217–226 (2006)
8. Tapia, E., Bulacio, P., Angelone, L.: Sparse and stable gene selection with consensus SVMRFE. Pattern Recognit. Lett. **33**(2), 164–172 (2012)
9. Ruiz, R., Riquelme, J.C., Aguilar-Ruiz, J.S.: Incremental wrapper-based gene selection from microarray data for cancer classification. Pattern Recogn. **39**(12), 2383–2392 (2006)
10. Huerta, R., Vembu, S., Muezzinoglu, M.K., Vergara, A.: Dynamical SVM for time series classification. In: Pinz, A., Pock, T., Bischof, H., Leberl, F. (eds.) DAGM/OAGM 2012. LNCS, vol. 7476, pp. 216–225. Springer, Heidelberg (2012). https://doi.org/10.1007/978-3-642-32717-9_22
11. Liao, T.W.: Clustering of time series data a survey. Pattern Recogn. **38**(11), 1857–1874 (2005)
12. Santosh, K.C., Lamiroy, B., Wendling, L.: DTW-radon-based shape descriptor for pattern recognition. Int. J. Pattern Recogn. Artif. Intell. **27**(03), 1350008 (2013)
13. K.C., S., Lamiroy, B., Wendling, L.: DTW for matching radon features: a pattern recognition and retrieval method. In: Blanc-Talon, J., Kleihorst, R., Philips, W., Popescu, D., Scheunders, P. (eds.) ACIVS 2011. LNCS, vol. 6915, pp. 249–260. Springer, Heidelberg (2011). https://doi.org/10.1007/978-3-642-23687-7_23

14. Kachouri, R., Djemal, K., Maaref, H.: Multi-model classification method in heterogeneous image databases. Pattern Recogn. **43**(12), 4077–4088 (2010)
15. Niu, X.-X., Suen, C.Y.: A novel hybrid CNN-SVM classifier for recognizing handwritten digits. Pattern Recogn. **45**(4), 1318–1325 (2012)
16. Liu, C.-L., Nakashima, K., Sako, H., Fujisawa, H.: Handwritten digit recognition: benchmarking of state-of-the-art techniques. Pattern Recogn. **36**(10), 2271–2285 (2003)
17. Osborne, H., Bridge, D.: Models of similarity for case-based reasoning. In: Interdisciplinary Workshop on Similarity and Categorization, pp. 173–179 (1997)
18. Baeza-Yates, R., Ribeiro-Neto, B.: Modern Information Retrieval. ACM Press, New York (1999)
19. Laurini, R. (ed.): VISUAL 2000. LNCS, vol. 1929. Springer, Heidelberg (2000). https://doi.org/10.1007/3-540-40053-2
20. Tversky, A.: Features of similarity. Psychol. Rev. **84**(4), 327–352 (1977)
21. Santini, S., Jain, R.: Similarity measures. IEEE Trans. Pattern Anal. Mach. Intell. **21**, 871–83 (1999)
22. Cortes, C., Vapnik, V.: Support vector networks. Mach. Learn. **20**(3), 273–297 (1995)
23. Joachims, T.: Making large-scale SVM Learning Practical. In: Advances in Kernel Methods Support Vector Learning. MIT Press, Cambridge (1999)
24. Vapnik, V., Chervonenkis, A.: Statistical learning theory. In: Support Vector Machines for Pattern Recognition. Wiley, New York (1998)
25. Mourya, A.K., Tyagi, P., Bhatnagar, A.: Genetic algorithm and their applicability in medical diagnostic: a survey. **7**(12), 1143–1145 (2016)
26. Schölkopf, B., Smola, A.: Learning with Kernels. MIT Press, Cambridge (2002)
27. Hsu, C.W., Chang, C.C., Lin, C.J.: A practical guide to support vector classification. Technical Note, Department of Computer Science and Information Engineering, National Taiwan University, Taiwan (2009)
28. Hepner, G.F.: Artificial neural network classification using a minimal training set. Comparison to conventional supervised classification. Photogram. Eng. Remote Sens. **56**(4), 469–473 (1990)
29. Boser, E., Guyon, I., Vapnik, V.: A training algorithm for optimal margin classifiers. In: Proceedings of the Fifth Annual Workshop on Computational Learning Theory, pp. 144–152. ACM Press (1992)
30. Scholkopf, B., Burges, C.J.C., Smola, A.J. (eds.): Advances in Kernel Methods: Support Vector Learning. MIT Press, Cambridge (1999)
31. Pavlidis, P., Westen, P., Cai, J., Grundy, W.N.: Gene functional classification from heterogeneous data. In: Proceedings of the Fifth Annual International Conference on Computational Molecular Biology, pp. 242–248. ACM Press, New York (2001)
32. Pavlidis, P.: Learning gene functional classifications from multiple data types. J. Comput. Biol. **90**, 401–411 (2002)
33. Lanckriet, G.R.G., et al.: Kernel-based data fusion and its application to protein function prediction in yeast. In: Altman, R.B., Dunker, A.K., Hunter, L., Jung, T.A., Klein, T.E. (eds.) Proceedings of the Pacific Symposium on Biocomputing, pp. 300–311. World Scientific, Hawaii (2004)
34. Zhang, G.P.: Neural networks for classification: a survey. IEEE Trans. Syst. Man Cybern. Part C (Appl. Rev.) **30**(4), 451–462 (2000)
35. Li, T., Zhang, C., Ogihara, M.: A comparative study of feature selection and multiclass classification methods for tissue classification based on gene expression. Bioinformatics **20**, 2429–2437 (2004)

36. Li, Y., Campbell, C., Tipping, M.: Bayesian automatic relevance determination algorithms for classifying gene expression data. Bioinformatics **18**, 1332–1339 (2002)
37. Forman, G.: An extensive empirical study of feature selection metrics for text classification. J. Mach. Learn. Res. **3**, 1289–1305 (2003)
38. Keerthi, S.S.: Generalized LARs as an effective feature selection tool for text classification with SVMs (2005)
39. Fung, G., Stoeckel, J.: Svm feature selection for classification of spect images of Alzheimer's disease using spatial information. Knowl. Inf. Syst. **11**, 243–258 (2007)
40. Pervez, M.S., Farid, D.M.: Literature review of feature selection for mining tasks. Int. J. Comput. Appl. **116**, 30–33 (2015)
41. Beniwal, S., Arora, J.: Classification and feature selection techniques in data mining. Int. J. Eng. Res. Technol. (IJERT) **1**, 1–6 (2012)
42. Chandrashekar, G., Sahin, F.: A survey of feature selection methods. Comput. Electr. Eng. **40**, 16–28 (2014)
43. Naseriparsa, M., Bidgoli, A.M., Varaee, T.: A hybrid feature selection method to improve performance of a group of classification algorithms. Int. J. Comput. Appl. **69**(17), 28–35 (2013)
44. Bouguelia, M.R., Nowaczyk, S., Santosh, K.C., Verikas, A.: Agreeing to disagree: active learning with noisy labels without crowdsourcing. Int. J. Mach. Learn. Cybern. **9**(8), 1307–1319 (2018)
45. Santosh, K.C.: Character recognition based on DTW-radon. In: 2011 International Conference on Document Analysis and Recognition, Beijing, pp. 264–268 (2011). https://doi.org/10.1109/ICDAR.2011.61
46. Santosh, K.C., Wendling, L.: Character recognition based on non-linear multi-projection profiles measure. Front. Comput. Sci. **9**(5), 678–690 (2015)

Training Dataset Extension Through Multiclass Generative Adversarial Networks and K-nearest Neighbor Classifier

Hubert Cecotti[(✉)] and Ganesh Jha

Department of Computer Science, College of Science and Mathematics,
Fresno State, Fresno, CA, USA
hcecotti@csufresno.edu

Abstract. The performance of deep learning architectures, where all the feature extraction stages are learned within the artificial neural network, requires a large number of labeled examples to model the variability of the different possible inputs. This issue is also present in other classification tasks with a large number of features where the number of examples can limit the number of possible input features, involving the creation of handcraft feature sets. Typical solutions in computer vision and document analysis and recognition increase the size of the database with additional geometric transformations (e.g. shift and rotation) and random elastic deformations of the original training examples. In this paper, we propose to evaluate the impact of additional images created through generative adversarial networks (GANs), which are deep neural network architectures. We study the addition of images created through a multiclass GAN in different databases of handwritten numerals from different scripts (Latin, Devanagari, and Oriya). The contributions of this paper are related to the use of multiclass GANs to extend the size of the training database after filtering the images with a k-nearest neighbor classifier where the k nearest neighbors must all agree on the decision to validate a GAN generated image. The accuracy is evaluated with the original training dataset, the GAN generated images, and the combination of the original training images and the GAN generated images. The results support the conclusion that GAN generated images through a multiclass paradigm can provide a robust and fully data driven solution for enlarging the size of the training database for improving the accuracy on the test dataset.

Keywords: Generative adversarial networks (GAN) ·
Artificial neural networks · Document analysis and recognition

1 Introduction

Pattern recognition and artificial intelligence systems are now able to compete with human performance on a large number of tasks, such as in computer vision

© Springer Nature Singapore Pte Ltd. 2019
K. C. Santosh and R. S. Hegadi (Eds.): RTIP2R 2018, CCIS 1035, pp. 596–610, 2019.
https://doi.org/10.1007/978-981-13-9181-1_52

for the classification of images. Despite the recent progresses in artificial neural networks, and in particular in the field of deep learning, some research issues remain such as the need to obtain a large number of labeled examples to train classifiers. A key issue is to model the variability across examples from the original data distribution to model the manifold on which the data is laying. The more labeled data is available, the easier it will be for the classifier to learn the underlying structure of the data distribution, in particular for examples described in a high dimensional space. In addition to the progresses due to key techniques such as dropout and the family of rectifier activation functions, typical techniques for improving the performance of a classifier include the addition of deformed examples into the existing training dataset. Because problems change fast, and it is needed to train models in a rapid fashion to develop applications, it can become time consuming to label new examples. In such a case, strategies such as transfer learning and semi-supervised learning [6,24] are often considered, where layers of an existing pre-trained neural network can be exploited for features extraction. Furthermore, active learning approaches involving experts for labeling key instances can provide an alternative solution [5].

The choice of a good architecture in deep learning and classifiers such as convolutional neural networks (CNNs) that require some specific knowledge of the problem to determine the architecture can be an obstacle for designing high performance classifiers. Due to the lack of labeled examples, a large number of approaches have been considered in the literature to increase the number of labeled images [1,22]. These approaches include the addition of images that have been translated and/or rotated, or where local elastic deformations have been applied on the images [21]. In these cases with images, the knowledge of the type of signal and the type of deformations that can be allowed without changing the class of an example are key assets for the use of such techniques. Elastic deformation techniques typically require tuning some hyperparameters, such as the strength of the deformations and the size of the Gaussian kernel for smoothing the random fields of deformations. These parameters need to be validated through cross validation or to be empirically set in relation to some prior information related to the images, e.g. size, content.

In this paper, we propose to investigate the use of generative adversarial networks (GAN) for the generation of multiclass images. Given a training dataset of images from different classes, we wish to evaluate the extent to which the generated images will come from all the classes, and if they will respect the original distribution. Because the artificial images don't have a label, we propose to estimate their labels with a constrained k-nearest neighbor approach that rejects unreliable images. This approach allows to estimate the quality of the generated images from the GAN. In addition to the discriminator classifier that deals with real versus artificial images, we propose to add a multiclass classifier that rejects unreliable images. If a high number of images are rejected then the generated images are probably too confusing and/or of low quality. This multiclass classifier aims at estimating the overall quality of the GAN generated outputs. Moreover, we wish to estimate if the addition of these artificial images and their estimated labels to the original training database can improve the accuracy on the test database. The GAN is typically used to generate new examples in relation to images given during training. In the present study, we consider three databases of handwritten digits, each database contains images from a given script (Latin, Devanagari, and Oriya). These scripts possess different features in terms of noise and variability across images within a same class. It is unknown whether a GAN can provide images from multiple classes that can help to discriminate other new images by considering a dataset containing examples from multiple classes. The system must not only create images from random noise, but it must create images from multiple classes of images that may have some high structural similarities (e.g. the shape of digits '5' and '2'). The remainder of the paper is organized as follows. First, the GAN architecture and the method to extract the label of the GAN generated images are presented in Sect. 2. The accuracy of the different approaches and the analysis of the class distribution are then detailed in Sect. 3. Finally, the impact of the results are discussed in Sect. 4.

2   Methods

2.1   Generative Adversarial Networks

Generative Adversarial Networks (GANs) represent a type of unsupervised machine learning architecture involving two main classifiers: a generator and a discriminator, which are competing against each other during the training phase [10], with the concept of adversarial training being presented in the early 90s [20]. The generator creates artificial data that are then given as an input to the discriminator, which tries to determine if the example from the generator was provided by the generator or real data. In addition, the discriminator gets as inputs real data and predicts if the data it has received is real or artificial, i.e. from the generator. With both data from the generator (class 1) and data from the original training dataset (class 2), the discriminator is a binary classifier (class 1 vs. class 2). The generator is trained to fool the discriminator. Its goal is to create data that look as close as possible to the original training data. The discriminator is trained to determine which data is real and which is artificial, i.e., from the generator. Finally, the generator learns how to make data that is indistinguishable from real data to the discriminator without accessing directly to the original training datasets.

The latent sample corresponding to the input of the generator is a random vector the generator uses to construct its artificial images. As the generator learns through training how to generate images, it determines how to map these random vectors to images that can fool the discriminator, i.e., that can lower the error rate of the discriminator. The output layer of the discriminator function corresponds to the measure of confidence related to the presence of a real image given as an input, e.g. 0 indicates an artificial image and 1 indicates a real image from the original data distribution. An overview of a GAN system is depicted in Fig. 1. For the application to images, the generator is based on a deconvolution neural network (from the features to the image), while the discriminator is built on a convolutional neural network (from the image to the features). GANs have been used in multiple applications in recent years, such as text generation [25], image generation [16], and image restoration [19]. A large number of GAN algorithms have been proposed to improve the learning process stability [11]. Despite some improvements, it has been shown that there is no evidence to support these claims [14]. In the subsequent sections, we will consider the original GAN learning process.

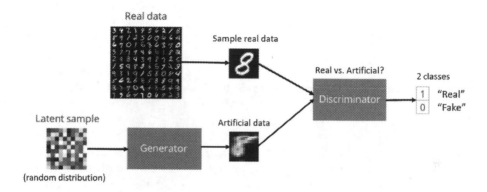

Fig. 1. General structure of GAN networks.

Discriminator Architecture. The discriminator classifier is based on a CNN that takes as an input a tensor of size $28 \times 28 \times 1$ and returns a single scalar number that represents whether or not the input image is "real" or "artificial", i.e. whether it's drawn from the set of original images or created by the generator. The architecture of the discriminator is presented as follows:

- Layer 0: Input layer (image): 28×28 units.
- Layer 1: Hidden layer 1: Convolution from Layer 0 to Layer 1 (Mask size: 5×5) 8 feature maps (stride $= 1$).
- Layer 2: Hidden layer 2: Convolution from Layer 1 to Layer 2 (Mask size: 5×5) 16 feature maps (stride $= 1$).
- Layer 3: Hidden layer 3: 128 units - Fully connected from Layer 2 to Layer 3.
- Layer 4: Output layer (1 unit) - Fully connected from Layer 3 to Layer 4.

Generator Architecture. The generator classifier is based on a deconvolutional neural network with three deconvolutional layers along with interpolation until a 28×28 image is formed. At the output layer, we add a sigmoid activation function, which maintains the range of the pixel values within a predefined range. The architecture of the generator is defined as follows:

- Layer 0: Input layer: (noise vector as input) 100 units.
- Layer 1: Hidden layer 1: Deconvolution from Layer 0 to Layer 1: 32×32 units with 50 feature maps.
- Layer 2: Hidden layer 2: Deconvolution from Layer 1 to Layer 2: 16×16 units with 25 feature maps.
- Layer 3: Output layer of 28×28 units: Deconvolution from Layer 2 to Layer 3.

2.2   K-nearest Neighbor

For the analysis of the GAN generated images, we consider a k-nn classifier. k-nn has been widely studied and can be used in different settings [23] with appropriate distance that can model variability such as dynamic time warping [7, 17,18]. In this study, the k-nn classifier has two purposes. First, it is used as a baseline to determine how easily the GAN generated images can be classified. Second, it is used to label the GAN generated images in relation to the original training dataset. It is worth mentioning that in the present case, the goal of the classifier is more to determine if the images can be properly classified, and not to directly get the best performance. If the performance of the classifier is too high and can grasp a high variability across the examples, then it is more difficult to estimate which images are properly generated from other images. In addition, we exploit the neighborhood of test examples in the training set to draw a decision based on voting techniques. In the regular k-nn, the label is chosen in relation to the maximum number of examples sharing the same label. We consider two approaches: the 50% and 100% agreement rules. With 50%, the number of neighbors sharing the same label must be superior to half of the neighbors in order to assign a label to the test example. With 100%, there must be a consensus among the different neighbors in order to assign a label to the test example. In both cases, if a decision cannot be reached, then no label is assigned to the test example: the example is rejected. This approach puts a strong constraint on the labeling process of the artificial images generated by the GAN.

2.3   Performance Evaluation

We denote the couple (X_{train}, Y_{train}) the set of N_{train} images and its corresponding groundtruth for the training database. (X_{test}, Y_{test}) represents the couple of N_{test} images and its groundtruth, respectively. The first step consists of generating artificial images, X_{artif} based on the GAN described before. A key issue for increasing the size of the training database with such an approach is the absence of groundtruth for the images that are produced. Therefore, we propose to estimate the label of the X_{artif} by considering the k-nn classifier where the decision to assign a class to an example is based on a voting scheme described previously. We denote by Y_{artif} the labels of all the images from X_{artif}.

The purpose of this estimation is twofold. First, its goal is to estimate the label of the produced images, and to evaluate the extent to which it is possible to retrieve a similar distribution across classes between the real and artificial examples. Second, we wish to estimate if the addition of the artificial examples and their estimated labels to the training dataset can lead to an improvement of the accuracy on the test dataset. Three experimental conditions are therefore evaluated with a regular k-nn classifier. These conditions represent variations of the considered training dataset: the original dataset only (case 1: default case (C1)), the artificial images (case 2 (C2)), the combination of the artificial images and the original training dataset (case 3 (C3)). For the evaluation on the test, we consider the regular k-nn (reg), and the methods with 50% and 100% agreement that we denote by 50% and 100%.

2.4   Datasets

In this study, we consider three datasets of handwritten numerals. Each dataset corresponds to a unique script. Examples from each dataset are depicted in Fig. 2. The MNIST database is a benchmark in supervised classifiers containing a training and test database [13,21]. In this dataset, quasi human performance is obtained with an accuracy of 99.77% with decisions obtained from the combination of 35 CNNs [9]. With k-nn classifiers, the best error rate is 99.48%, and was obtained with a Pseudo 2D Hidden Markov Models [12]. The Image Deformation Model provides an error rate of 99.46%, and 99.37% is obtained with shape matching using shape contexts [2]. Two databases of Indian numerals containing Devanagari and Oriya numerals were provided by the Indian Statistical Institute, Kolkata, India [3,4,8,15].

(a) Western Arabic (Latin script)   (b) Devanagari

(c) Oriya

Fig. 2. Examples of handwritten numerals for the three scripts.

3   Results

Given the current problem where the GAN generated images come from a multiclass dataset, a key research question was first to estimate the type of images that can be generated by the GAN. In particular, we wish to estimate the distribution of the examples in the classes of the problem (i.e., 10 for the numerals) and how they change in relation to k in k-nn. The ratio between the number of examples estimated through k-nn for a particular class and the number of

Table 1. Distribution of the examples in the training dataset and the labeled GAN images.

Class	MNIST		Devanagari		Oriya	
	Original	GAN	Original	GAN	Original	GAN
0	5923	733	1842	301	502	3748
1	6742	3383	1892	1334	498	298
2	5958	6217	1892	332	496	45
3	6131	4271	1883	70	498	103
4	5842	460	1877	74	498	25
5	5421	747	1890	668	490	55
6	5918	1828	1870	409	500	33
7	6265	2617	1870	721	498	31
8	5851	260	1888	130	498	22
9	5949	736	1890	380	492	802
Mean	6000	2125	1879	442	497	516
sd	340	1980	16	385	4	1161

examples in the original datasets is depicted in Figs. 4, 5, and 6. These figures highlight the variations that occur between classes and how some classes can be significantly underrepresented, or overrepresented, in the GAN images. The distribution of the examples across classes in the original training dataset and the labeled GAN images after k-nn with consensus voting is given in Table 1. The table shows a substantial decrease in terms of labeled images compared to the generated GAN images. For MNIST, only about a third of the generated images were labeled. It is worth noting the low number of examples labeled as belonging to the class '8' for MNIST, '3' and '4' for Devanagari, and '4' and '8' for Oriya. For Oriya, most of the examples were labeled as belonging to the class 0.

Examples of images produced by the GAN are depicted in Fig. 3. Each column represents an estimated class (0 to 9) after using k-nn on the training dataset and a consensus decision among the neighbors. The images highlight how some examples in some classes are poorly represented and how the images have erroneous labels.

The accuracy for the 10 classes, the total accuracy, and the rejection rate, are given in Tables 2, 3, and 4. The results are typically lower with the second condition that considers only the examples produced through the GAN and labeled with the consensus voting approach. With the addition of the GAN generated images and their estimated labels to the original training dataset, the accuracy for MNIST increases from 96.50% to 96.87%. The quality of the estimated labels and the generated GAN images suggest a poor quality of the images as the accuracy with the regular k-nn is only 58.73%. In all cases, the voting approach

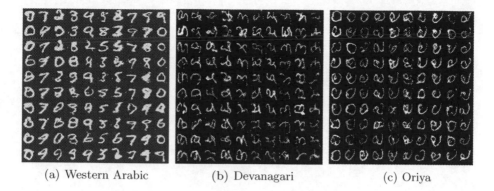

(a) Western Arabic   (b) Devanagari   (c) Oriya

Fig. 3. Examples of GAN generated images for the three scripts.

Table 2. Accuracy (in %) for MNIST with training only (C1), multiclass GAN (C2), and training + multiclass GAN (C3).

Class	C1			C2			C3		
	Reg.	50%	100%	Reg.	50%	100%	Reg.	50%	100%
0	99.39	99.59	99.69	59.49	62.36	85.61	99.39	99.39	99.69
1	99.65	99.91	100.00	92.16	92.40	99.73	99.82	99.82	100.00
2	95.74	96.80	98.59	62.98	64.42	77.85	96.03	96.39	98.80
3	96.83	97.85	99.10	64.36	68.43	83.00	96.63	97.00	99.21
4	96.54	97.03	98.50	29.23	26.39	27.50	96.13	96.52	98.95
5	96.19	98.13	99.22	43.27	48.51	65.92	96.64	97.27	99.48
6	98.12	99.05	99.57	76.93	83.75	91.40	98.64	98.75	99.57
7	95.82	96.91	98.42	96.40	96.87	98.80	96.11	96.38	98.94
8	91.89	96.37	98.74	6.37	6.23	5.30	93.63	95.38	99.11
9	94.45	97.53	99.22	47.67	50.37	54.64	95.34	96.59	99.44
Total	96.50	97.95	99.13	58.73	62.48	80.62	96.87	97.38	99.34
Rejection	-	2.91	8.95	—	11.13	58.30	-	0.80	9.57

provides an improvement of the accuracy with the cost of some rejected examples. The accuracy reaches 99.13% with 8.95% of rejected images. We observe the same pattern of performance for the Devanagari and Oriya datasets. The accuracy increases from 93.81% to 95.19% thanks to the addition of the GAN generated images for the Devanagari test dataset, while the accuracy increases from 91.30% to 92.70% thanks to the addition of the GAN generated images for the Oriya test dataset. For Devanagari and Oriya, it is worth mentioning the difficulty of the GAN to classify properly some classes alone as some classes are probably easier to generate than others.

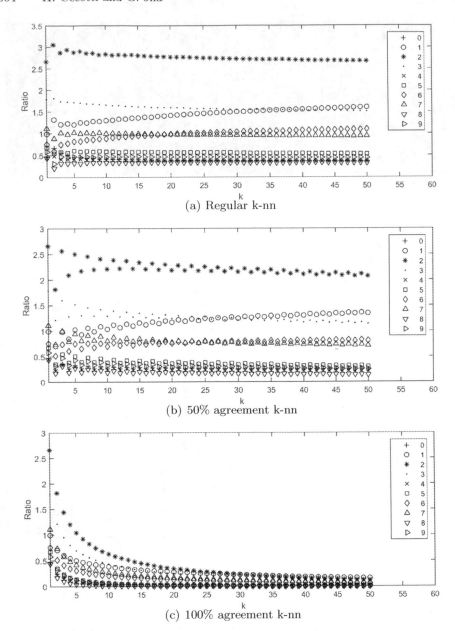

Fig. 4. MNIST - ratio between the original distribution of the classes in the training dataset and the GAN images after k-nn labeling in relation to k.

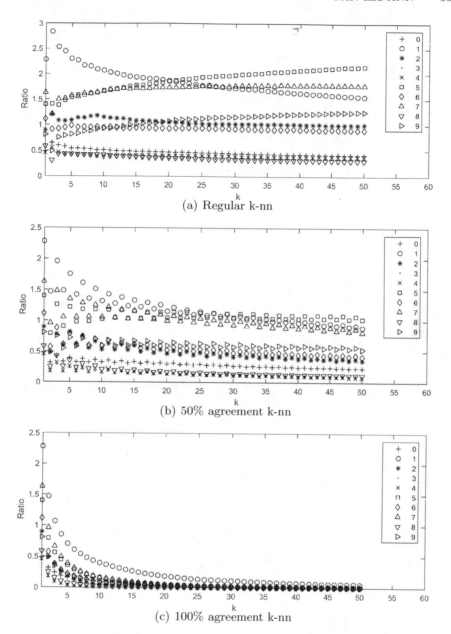

Fig. 5. Devanagari - ratio between the original distribution of the classes in the training dataset and the GAN images after k-nn labeling in relation to k.

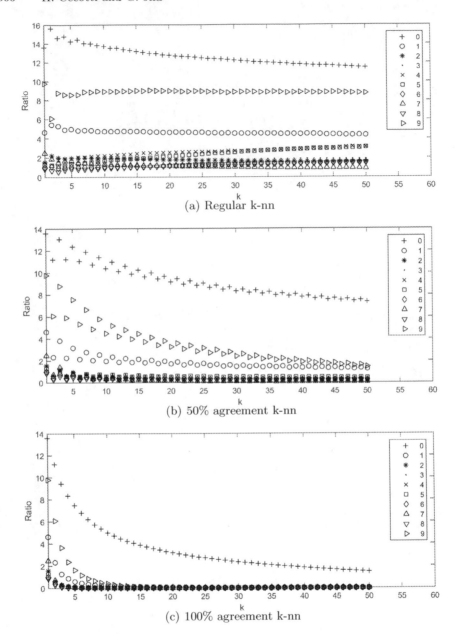

(a) Regular k-nn

(b) 50% agreement k-nn

(c) 100% agreement k-nn

Fig. 6. Oriya - ratio between the original distribution of the classes in the training dataset and the GAN images after k-nn labeling in relation to k.

Table 3. Accuracy (in %) for Devanagari with training only (C1), multiclass GAN (C2), and training + multiclass GAN (C3).

Class	C1			C2			C3		
	Reg.	50%	100%	Reg.	50%	100%	Reg.	50%	100%
0	98.64	98.90	99.16	75.88	79.34	94.52	98.92	98.91	99.15
1	97.35	98.35	100.00	71.43	75.44	94.92	97.62	97.86	100.00
2	91.53	94.44	96.82	29.89	24.49	32.26	92.33	93.17	97.47
3	86.74	92.73	96.90	6.90	4.98	2.56	90.45	91.94	97.25
4	96.00	98.32	99.39	16.00	12.36	2.94	96.53	97.55	99.39
5	87.83	94.97	97.52	73.28	79.68	92.52	91.01	93.41	98.18
6	93.58	96.56	98.68	40.11	39.86	38.46	95.19	96.17	99.33
7	94.71	97.27	98.82	67.46	71.12	88.37	96.30	97.33	99.41
8	94.96	97.77	99.10	40.58	45.36	62.03	95.76	97.30	99.70
9	96.83	98.65	100.00	94.97	98.07	100.00	97.88	97.88	100.00
Total	93.81	96.86	98.74	51.65	56.01	76.48	95.19	96.17	99.08
Rejection	-	5.95	15.34	–	19.88	71.64	-	2.05	16.19

Table 4. Accuracy (in %) for Oriya with training only (C1), multiclass GAN (C2), and training + multiclass GAN (C3).

Class	C1			C2			C3		
	Reg.	50%	100%	Reg.	50%	100%	Reg.	50%	100%
0	97.00	97.98	98.96	98.00	98.00	100.00	97.00	98.98	100.00
1	93.00	96.63	98.75	64.00	67.44	72.97	94.00	95.83	98.72
2	100.00	100.00	100.00	82.00	82.95	84.21	98.00	98.00	100.00
3	97.00	96.97	97.83	25.00	29.58	33.33	96.00	96.97	97.83
4	99.00	98.98	100.00	81.00	91.78	100.00	99.00	99.00	100.00
5	95.00	98.94	100.00	39.00	44.62	100.00	99.00	99.00	100.00
6	80.00	88.24	95.08	15.00	12.28	0.00	79.00	80.41	94.92
7	66.00	83.12	91.11	1.00	1.64	0.00	76.00	79.17	95.12
8	98.00	98.00	98.96	79.00	89.41	97.22	98.00	98.00	98.96
9	88.00	96.67	98.81	51.00	57.65	79.31	91.00	95.79	98.72
Total	91.30	95.89	98.37	53.50	62.13	80.07	92.70	94.19	98.71
Rejection	–	7.60	20.40	–	22.90	70.40	-	1.90	22.40

4   Discussion and Conclusion

Generative adversarial networks are a new type of architecture to generate artificial inputs based on an original dataset. This type of architecture is difficult to train as it embeds two classifiers: the generator and the discriminator, with their respective loss function. A key issue is to balance these two classifiers in such a way that they can learn from each other and the overall training procedure can progress over time, without having the generator or the discriminator completely leading the other one. In the case of a dataset containing examples from multiple classes, a key problem is to create images that can keep the approximate distribution across classes to avoid under-represented classes.

In this paper, we investigated the outputs of GAN based artificial images in three datasets of handwritten numerals. We have analyzed the produced examples in terms of distribution across classes and the overall rejection rate through the use of k-nn for the classification. We have estimated the label of the GAN images by using k-nn and a consensus voting scheme. It is possible to enrich the original training dataset and increase the overall accuracy. After visual inspection of the generated GAN images, it seemed that they would disturb the original training database more than enrich it, however, the experimental results suggest that it can increase the robustness of the classification with k-nn. K-nn being a density based classifier, it is probably more robust to complete outliers once combined with the original training dataset. Despite the improvement allowed by this technique, the number of examples for each class varies significantly and can be a drawback for the creation of examples for a particular class, which is the source of high confusion with other classes. Moreover, the choice of the classifier for both the estimation of the labels and the evaluation of the results could be changed to a convolutional neural network. The choice of the architecture for the generator and the discriminator can be enhanced with the addition of more feature maps. Overall, the system includes four key components: the generator, the discriminator, the classifier for the estimation of the GAN labels, and the multiclass classifier for the estimation of the labels of test examples. The GAN part is unsupervised but may include parameters related to the label of the images while the classifier for the estimation of the GAN labels and the test examples are supervised.

The results support the conclusion that GAN generated images can be beneficial as a data augmentation technique in the multiclass condition, i.e., when the generated images can belong to multiple classes that need to be trained. Future work will include GAN class-specific generated examples and the addition of criteria based on the class distribution for estimating the GAN images for improving the quality of the images, in particular for classes with a low prior probability or that can be easily confused with other classes.

References

1. Baird, H.: Document image defect models. In: Proceedings of the IAPR Workshop on Syntactic and Structural Pattern Recognition, pp. 38–46 (1990)
2. Belongie, S., Malik, J., Puzicha, J.: Shape matching and object recognition using shape contexts. IEEE Trans. Pattern Anal. Mach. Intell. **24**(4), 509–522 (2002)
3. Bhattacharya, U., Chaudhuri, B.: Databases for research on recognition of handwritten characters of Indian scripts. In: Proceedings of the 8th Intetnational Conference on Document Analysis and Recognition (ICDAR 2005), pp. 789–793 (2005)

4. Bhowmick, T., Parui, S., Bhattacharya, U., Shaw, B.: An HMM based recognition scheme for handwritten Oriya numerals. In: Proceedings of the 9th International Conference on Information Technology (ICIT 2006), pp. 105–110 (2006)
5. Bouguelia, M.R., Nowaczyk, S., Santosh, K.C., Verikas, A.: Agreeing to disagree: active learning with noisy labels without crowdsourcing. Int. J. Mach. Learn. Cybern. **9**, 1307–1319 (2018)
6. Cecotti, H.: Active graph based semi-supervised learning using image matching: application to handwritten digit recognition. Pattern Recogn. Lett. **73**, 76–82 (2016)
7. Cecotti, H.: Hierarchical k-nearest neighbor with GPUS and high performance cluster: application to handwritten character recognition. Int. J. Pattern Recogn. Artif. Intell. **31**(2), 1–24 (2017)
8. Chaudhuri, B.B., Pal, U.: A complete printed Bangla OCR system. Pattern Recogn. **31**, 531–549 (1998)
9. Cireşan, D., Meier, U., Schmidhuber, J.: Multi-column deep neural networks for image classification. In: Computer Vision and Pattern Recognition (CVPR), pp. 3642–3649 (2012)
10. Goodfellow, I., et al.: Generative adversarial nets. In: Proceedings of the 2014 Conference on Advances in Neural Information Processing Systems, vol. 27. pp. 2672–2680 (2014)
11. Gulrajani, I., Ahmed, F., Arjovsky, M., Dumoulin, V., Courville, A.C.: Improved training of Wasserstein GANs. In: Advances in Neural Information Processing Systems, pp. 5767–5777 (2017)
12. Keysers, D., Desclaers, T., Gollan, C., Ney, H.: Deformation models for image recognition. IEEE Trans. Pattern Anal. Mach. Intell. **29**(8), 1422–1435 (2007)
13. LeCun, Y., Bottou, L., Bengio, Y., Haffner, P.: Gradient-based learning applied to document recognition. Proc. IEEE **86**(11), 2278–2324 (1998)
14. Lucic, M., Kurach, K., Michalski, M., Gelly, S., Bousquet, O.: Are GANs created equal? a large-scale study. arXiv preprint arXiv:1711.10337 (2017)
15. Pal, U., Chaudhuri, B.B.: Indian script character recognition: a survey. Pattern Recogn. **37**(9), 1887–1899 (2004)
16. Reed, S., Akata, Z., Yan, X.C., Logeswaran, L., Lee, H., Schiele, B.: Generative adversarial text to image synthesis. In: Proceedings of the 33rd International Conference on Machine Learning (ICML) (2016)
17. Santosh, K.C.: Character recognition based on DTW-radon. In: Interntional Conference on Document Analysis and Recognition (ICDAR), pp. 264–268 (2011)
18. Santosh, K.C., Wending, L.: Character recognition based on non-linear multi-projection profiles measure. Front. Comput. Sci. **9**(5), 678–690 (2015)
19. Schawinski, K., Zhang, C., Zhang, H., Fowler, L., Santhanam, G.K.: Generative adversarial networks recover features in astrophysical images of galaxies beyond the deconvolution limit. Mon. Not. Roy. Astron. Soc. Lett. **467**(1), L110–L114 (2017)
20. Schmidhuber, J.: Learning factorial codes by predictability minimization. Neural Comput. **4**(6), 863–879 (1992)
21. Simard, P., Steinkraus, D., Platt, J.: Best practices for convolutional neural networks applied to visual document analysis. In: Proceedings of the 7th International Conference on Document Analysis and Recognition (ICDAR), pp. 958–962, August 2003

22. Simard, P., Victorri, B., LeCun, Y., Denker, J.: Tangent prop - a formalism for specifying selected in variances in an adaptive network. In: Moody, J.E., Hanson, S.J., Lippmann, R.P. (ed.) Advances in Neural Information Processing Systems, pp. 895–903 (1991)
23. Vajda, S., Santosh, K.C.: A fast k-nearest neighbor classifier using unsupervised clustering. In: Santosh, K.C., Hangarge, M., Bevilacqua, V., Negi, A. (eds.) RTIP2R 2016. CCIS, vol. 709, pp. 185–193. Springer, Singapore (2017). https://doi.org/10.1007/978-981-10-4859-3_17
24. Vajda, S., Rangoni, Y., Cecotti, H.: Semi-automatic ground truth generation using unsupervised clustering and limited manual labeling: application to handwritten character recognition. Pattern Recogn. Lett. **58**, 23–28 (2015)
25. Zhang, Y.Z., Gan, Z., Carin, L.: Generating text via adversarial training. In: Proceedings of the 2016 Conference on Advances in Neural Information Processing Systems, p. 29 (2016)

StackDroid: Evaluation of a Multi-level Approach for Detecting the Malware on Android Using Stacked Generalization

Sheikh Shah Mohammad Motiur Rahman[1,2(✉)] and Sanjit Kumar Saha[1]

[1] Department of Computer Science and Engineering, Jahangirnagar University,
Savar, Dhaka, Bangladesh
`motiur.ion@gmail.com`, `sanjit@juniv.edu`
[2] Department of Software Engineering, Daffodil International University,
Dhaka, Bangladesh

Abstract. Attackers or cyber criminals are getting encouraged to develop android malware because of the rapidly growing rate of android users. To detect android malware, researchers and security specialist have been started to contribute on android malware analysis and detection related tasks using machine learning algorithms. In this paper, Stacked Generalization has been used to minimize the error rate and a multi-level architecture based approach named StackDroid has been presented and evaluated. In this experiment, Extremely Randomized Tree (ET), Random Forest (RF), Multi-Layer Perceptron (MLP) and Stochastic Gradient Descent (SGD) classifiers have been used as base classifiers in level 1 and Extreme Gradient Boosting (EGB) has been used as final predictor in level 2. It's been found that StackDroid provides 99% of Area Under Curve (AUC), 1.67% of False Positive Rate (FPR) and 97% detection accuracy on DREBIN dataset which provides a strong basement to the development of android malware scanner.

Keywords: Android malware · Machine learning ·
Multi-level approach · Stacked generalization ·
Android malware detection

1 Introduction

Android is a mobile based and open source operating system built on the Linux kernel. Today, smartphones that running android operating system are increasing rapidly. Unfortunately, attackers whose aims are to obtain users personal information illegally and to be benefited financially, target the mobile devices [1]. Attackers are targeted the android devices and infected the android devices with malicious application. Application installation from unverified and unknown sources can be allowed in android rather than other platforms. Installing android apps from third party sources makes easy for attackers to distribute malware with android application [2]. Malicious applications (malware) hide the malicious code

© Springer Nature Singapore Pte Ltd. 2019
K. C. Santosh and R. S. Hegadi (Eds.): RTIP2R 2018, CCIS 1035, pp. 611–623, 2019.
https://doi.org/10.1007/978-981-13-9181-1_53

which performs as a background services which threatens the user's privacy and sensitive information. Stealing user's contacts, text messages, subscribing users to premium services, login credentials are the common activities performed by malicious applications. Without the notifying the users all these activities are performed by android malware [3]. Researchers have been proposed various solutions to detect android malware along with the increase of android malware [4], for enforcing the security of data by applying security policies [5,6]. However, they basically focus on attack specific and try to defend specific security attack such as privacy specific [7], privilege escalation [8,9]. For that there are several drawbacks still exist in those solutions. Because of the rapid growing of the variability of modern attacks [10], in security related tasks the application of machine learning algorithms has increased [11]. There are two major categories of android malware detection mechanisms [12] such as static analysis [13] and dynamic analysis [14]. Static analysis refers to inspect the source code or the binaries of applications to identify the suspicious patterns. Maximum antivirus companies are used static analysis. And, dynamic analysis refers to behavior based detection. It is done by running a sample in controlled environment and tracing the behavior or execution to further analyze [15].

In this paper, a multi-level approach has been proposed and investigated to increase the rate of predictive power of machine learning algorithms. The approach is designed by constructing an android malware detection model by preprocessing the datasets and extract features from android apks at the lower level. Even also create a dictionary from extracted features. For training the base classifiers, splitting the features from dictionary has been performed at the lower level. The presented approach named StackDroid, the static analysis technique has been performed by applying stacked generalization concepts. Stacked generalization provides the minimum error rate of generalizers. It works to deduce the biases of the classifiers with respect to a provided learning set [16]. Stack-Droid performed n-fold cross validation with base classifiers at level 1. A mean of temporary predictions are obtained and select stacking features to build final model at level 2. A meta estimator then retrain from stacking features and performed to provide final prediction of classification. StackDroid can perform not only just with the traditional machine learning algorithms but also the ensemble and neural network based learning algorithms for the betterment of the classification accuracy. Experiments are performed by extracting the features from widely used publicly available malware dataset DREBIN. The contributions of this paper can be summarized as follows:

– A multi-level classifier approach (StackDroid) has been presented and evaluated the approach in the context of android malware detection on a real publicly used dataset.
– StackDroid can be performed not only individually with traditional machine learning techniques respectively ensemble and neural networks but also the combination of all as base classifiers.
– StackDroid creates a features dictionary from dataset which represents a set of benign and malware features.

- StackDroid constructs based on stacked generalization to minimize the error rate of generalizers which improve the accuracy of the android malware detection.
- The result are presented by applying the combination of ensemble and multi-level perceptron learning algorithms. And evaluated the effectiveness of Stack-Droid in Android Malware Detection.

The structure of this paper is organized as follows. The related works based on the android malware detection held recently are described at Sect. 2. Proposed model architecture is illustrated and research methodology is described at Sect. 3. Section 4 is presented the evaluation metrics of proposed approach. Section 5 presents the result analysis and evaluates the performance of Stack-Droid. Section 6 concludes the paper with future work.

2   Related Works

Sahs and Khan [17] proposed a technique to detect android malware using supervised machine learning technique. They used Support Vector Machine to classify and 'Androguard' to extract information from the APKs and the Scikit-learn framework to experiment [18]. Yeima [19] proposed a framework using supervised machine learning method where a binary variables being generated by analyzing APKs to characterize the application as suspicious or benign from the data with constructing a class. They have obtained 90.6% TPR (True Positive Rate), 0.094% FNR (False Negative Rate), 93.5% accuracy and 97.22% AUC (Area Under Curve) for a total of 20 features. A dynamic analysis framework using machine learning named DroidDolphin [20] to detect android malware has been proposed. This framework starts with the analysis of API calls by extracting APKs. They obtained 86.1% precision and 0.875 F-score by running the application on virtual environments and look at 13 activities. They used supervised machine learning algorithm SVM and the LIBSVM library [21]. Another model using dynamic analysis was proposed by Feizollah [22]. They have applied five supervised machine algorithms and got the highest TPR of 99.94% with an FPR (False Positive Rate) result of 0.06% for KNN. 'APK Auditor' is a permission based android malware detection tools proposed by Talha [23] to classify the Android apps as benign or malicious. They used total 8762 applications where 1853 were benign and 6909 were malicious applications. They have obtained 88% of accuracy. A static analysis framework is proposed by Urcuqui and Cadavid [24]. To detect Android malware, they have used Naïve Bayes, Bagging, K-Neighbors, Support Vector Machines (SVM), Stochastic Gradient Descent (SGD) and Decision Tree.K-Neighbors algorithm provides highest accuracy with 94% with their experiment. Xiao [25] proposed a deep learning based detection model which consider system call sequences and construct a classifier based on the LSTM - Long Short-Term Memory. They achieved recall of 96.6% with false positive rate of 9.3%. Wang [26] proposed an approach using permission patterns from Android. To extract the requested and used permissions from android, they have used Andrubis [13]. They obtained that UUP pattern has the highest accuracy and have achieved 94% accuracy, 5% false positive, and 1% false negative. Rana [40] evaluate tree based machine learning algorithms with 97.24% accuracy and proposed a substring based approach.

3 Methodology

In order to detect android malware using machine learning algorithms we categorize our proposed StackDroid malware detection architecture into six functionalities illustrated on Fig. 1.

3.1 StackDroid: Architecture of Presented Approach

Pre-processing. Dataset balancing has been considered at this pre-processing part. It is done by randomly selecting the same number of malware and the benign apps from the dataset.

Feature Extraction. In this stage, reverse engineering of the android application is performed and extract the features from the manifest an XML file and the disassembled (.DEX) code. Eight features set are focused during extraction as we use DREBIN dataset from two sources:

Features set from the Manifest.XML file:

– Hardware components (HC): HC represents a set of hardware components such as camera, touchscreen, GPS and so on.
– Requested permissions (RP): During installation of android application, it throws a window for allowing a set of permissions. Android permission system has dangerous permissions by which sensitive informations can be accessed by malicious application.
– App components (AC): There are 4 types of app components such as services, activities, broadcast receivers and content providers.
– Filtered intents (FI): During inter process and intra process communication in android, intents are performed. Most of the malicious application or malware trigger malicious activities after rebooting the android phone using BOOT_COMPLETED.

Feature sets from disassembled code (classes.dex file):

– Restricted API calls (RAC): Based on the allowed android permissions during the installation, RAC is performed. Without requesting the permission in manifest.xml file, the usage of RAC indicate malicious activities (root exploits).
– Used permissions (UP): From UP and RAC, we can identify whether it's directed to malicious activities or not.
– Suspicious API calls (SAC): Malwares sometimes use the API functions such as Cipher.getInstance(), Runtime.exec(), getDeviceId() and so on to get access sensitive information about device and some of those are used for obfuscation.

– Network addresses (NA): To pass data from user device or to execute malicious scripts or commands, NA or URLs are used by malware.

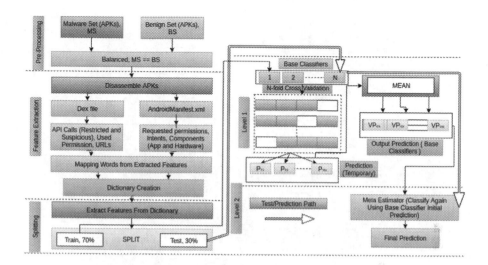

Fig. 1. Architecture of StackDroid.

Dictionary Creation. For dictionary creation, we count the last word of permissions, services, intents, activities which are a sequence of words as a feature. For example, from android.hardware.camera, android.permission.SEND_SMS and android.permission.WRITE_EXTERNAL_STORAGE, we count camera, SEND_SMS and WRITE_EXTERNAL_STORAGE respectively as a representative of these features and make a dictionary of those features. But for API calls, URLs are counted as a single word because those are meaningful as whole. Word Cloud of generated dictionary is illustrated on Fig. 2.

Pre-level Stage. To classify using machine learning, it's mandatory to train the classifiers. The preliminary stage before starting the level 1 training phase, loading the dictionary of features and splitting the features as train:test ratio has been performed. In our experiment, we splits the whole features with the ratio of 70:30 where 70% for training and 30% for test.

Level 1 Training and Temporary Prediction - (Base Classifiers). In level 1, N-fold cross validation [31] is performed where P_{T1}, P_{T2}, ..., P_{TN} are the temporary predictions according with the base classifiers. And from base classifiers, the probability predictions or crisps predictions are found as output which are expressed by VP_{O1}, VP_{O2}, VP_{O3}, ..., VP_{ON}.

Level 2 Training and Final Prediction - (Meta Estimator). In Level 2, the temporary predictions and crisp predictions are utilized and train the meta estimator for computation and final prediction during the construction of proposed model.

Fig. 2. Word Cloud of generated dictionary

The summary of the concept [27] applied in StackDroid are:

- After Preprocessing, Feature Extraction, Dictionary Creation and Pre-Level Stage as data pre-preparation in Level 1, to predict android malware or benign train and test set used along with base classifiers and obtained some predictions which are used on Level 2 as features named stacked features.
- Any classifiers or combination of classifiers can be used on Level 1 or Level 2.
- To avoid overfitting N-Fold cross-validation is used in proposed model for training data and out-of-fold (OOF) part of train portion has been predicted in every fold.
- Most commonly 3-10 folds are used and on our experiment 5-fold is used.
- Prediction stage on test set has two steps:
  - Step 1: Test set of data will be predicted after training from test set. After that, mean operation will be performed on all of the temporary predictions P_{T1}, P_{T2}, ... P_{TN} from each fold.

- Step 2: Initially from base classifiers, final prediction won't be done for test set. Because the features obtained during n-fold cross validation will be used on Level 2 as train set to fit meta-estimator as additional classifier and test set will be evaluated by performing classification to obtain final predictions. As, the model performs additional fitting, the approach may take more time rather than others.
- Stacking concept has been applied after some initial stages such as Preprocessing, Feature Extraction, Dictionary Creation and Pre-Level.
- To get more features for next Level, level 1 can be repeated as it a cycle.

3.2 Dataset Used

The most popular publicly available 'DREBIN' dataset is used for experiments that contains of 123,453 real android applications. From those applications, 5,560 applications contain malware of 179 different malware families and rests are benign applications. The samples contains the dataset were collected from August 2010 to October 2012. The top 15 malware families are illustrated in Fig. 3.

3.3 Experimental Environment

The configuration of the machine used in experiment is Processor: Intel(R) Core(TM) i5-6500 CPU 3.20 GHz, 64-bit PC with 16 GB RAM. The operating system is Linux Mint 18.3 Sylvia. Python is used as a programming language. And scikit-learn, panda and numpy packages of python are used for the experiments.

4 Evaluation Parameters

As this study focus on binary decision which classifies the data as either malware or benign like negative or positive labels. Using a structure, the classifiers decision can be expressed which is called confusion matrix [28]. Confusion matrix has four attributes: True positives (TP), False positives (FP), True negatives (TN) and False Negative (FN). Correctly identified the positives as positives is called True positives (TP). Identified a negative value as positive is defined by False positives (FP). True negatives (TN) defined to identify negative as negative correctly. When the positive one is identified as negative then it is called False negatives (FN) [29]. Precision, Recall, F1-Score, ROC curve, Confusion Matrix, Precision-Recall Curve, AUC and False Positive Rate [30,31] are used to evaluate the performance of StackDroid.

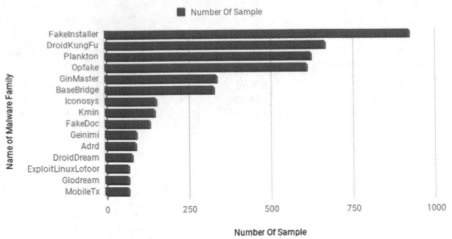

Fig. 3. Top 15 malware families in used dataset

4.1   ROC Curve

ROC represents a curve where two plots exist one is on the x-axis named False Positive Rate (FPR) and another is on the y-axis named True Positive Rate (TPR). FPR is defined as the ratio or the fraction of negative values those are classified as positive. TPR is defined as the ratio or the fraction of positive values that are correctly classified.

4.2   Precision-Recall Curve

Precision-Recall is a curve where two plots exist such as the plot named recall is on the x-axis and the precision plot is on the y-axis. TPR and Recall both are same. The measures of that rate of correctly identified values which are truly positive is referred to precision.

4.3   Accuracy

Accuracy refers to the ratio of correctly classified data to total number of data.

$$Accuracy = (TP + TN)/(TP + TN + FP + FN) \qquad (1)$$

5   Result Analysis and Performance Analysis

Table 1 represents the accuracy obtained from base classifiers along with 5-Fold cross validation in Level 1 of StackDroid. Extremely Randomized Tree [32] (ET),

Random Forest [33] (RF), Multi-Layer Perceptron [34] (MLP) and Stochastic Gradient Descent [35] (SGD) classifiers are used in this experiment as base classifiers. In level 1, base classifiers are applied with 5-fold cross validation and obtain the accuracy in each fold. After that, obtain mean accuracy of each fold in total and also obtain standard deviation [36] (STD) which means the measures of the dispersion of a group or dataset (be calculated by square root of the variance in a group or dataset) relative to its mean [37]. Mean accuracy and STD along with the accuracy obtained from each fold are outlined in Table 1. And in Table 2, the confusion matrix, precision, recall, f1-score, overall accuracy and False positive rate are shown. StackDroid provides 97% accuracy of detection along with 1.67 FPR. The ROC curve of StackDroid with 99% AUC area and the Precision-Recall curve of StackDroid with 98% average area are illustrated in Figs. 4 and 5 accordingly. In level 2, Extreme Gradient Boosting [38] (EGB) has been used as a meta estimator and as a final predictor.

Table 1. Accuracy comparison from base classifiers with 5-fold cross validation in Level 1.

Classifiers	1-Fold	2-Fold	3-Fold	4-Fold	5-Fold	Mean	STD
ET	96.47%	95.89%	95.57%	96.72%	95.57%	96.04%	0.47%
RF	95.96%	95.70%	94.61%	96.34%	95.95%	95.57%	0.59%
MLP	83.25%	87.15%	81.18%	82.58%	80.21%	82.87%	2.39%
SGD	81.00%	80.28%	80.92%	82.01%	85.60%	81.96%	1.90%

Table 2. Evaluation parameters after final prediction of StackDroid in Level 2.

Confusion matrix			Evaluation parameters			Accuracy	FPR
Actual data	Correct label		Precision	Recall	F1-Score		
	0	1					
0	1649	28	0.95	0.98	0.97	97%	1.67%
1	86	1573	0.98	0.95	0.97		
TP = 1573, FP = 28, FN = 86, TN = 1649			0.97	0.97	0.97		

It's been observed that StackDroid almost producing better results with 97% accuracy and 1.67% FPR. Also, it's been found during our dictionary creation phase that the most important words of any activities, permissions, services, intents are the last words of them rather than the combination of other words. Dictionary created using the last 2 and 3 words provides irrelevant information to classifiers and it was observed during experiment. So that, during dictionary creation, only the last word has been considered. The performance is obtained by StackDroid using the features of Filtered Intents, Requested Permissions, Hardware Components, App Components, Restricted API Calls, Used Permissions, Suspicious API Calls, and Network Address. This produced 98% of the average Precision-Recall area and 99% of AUC.

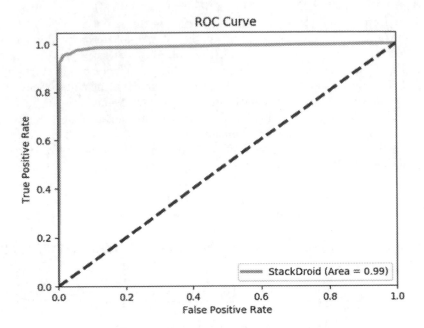

Fig. 4. ROC curve of StackDroid with AUC area

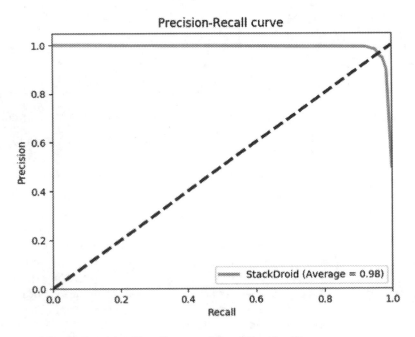

Fig. 5. Precision-Recall curve of StackDroid with average area

6   Conclusion

Due to the rapid increase of android mobile devices, detecting the android malware has become a popular problem to researcher and anti-malware developers. Recently, for android malware research and analysis, there are multiple datasets and online communities have been created. Support Vector Machine provides the best detection result with respect to the DREBIN dataset which has shown in previous research. In this paper, a multi-level approach stacked generalizer has been applied and evaluated on the same dataset using Extremely Randomized Tree (ET), Random Forest (RF), Multi-Layer Perceptron (MLP) and Stochastic Gradient Descent (SGD) as base classifiers and XGBoost as final predictor. StackDroid provides a detection framework where machine learning, ensemble learning even neural networks can be used as individually as well as combined. Android permission, API function call and System function call were used in most of the previous research to detect android malware. To evaluate StackDroid in our investigation, 8 feature sets are used and experimented. StackDroid provide 97% of accuracy, 1.67% FPR along with 99% AUC on the DREBIN dataset. It provides a strong basement for developing an effective malware detection tools. For future work, it's been proposed to study and experiment DanKu protocol [39] for android malware detection using a consortium blockchain and the deep neural network in real time manner.

References

1. Sen, S., Aysan, A.I., Clark, J.A.: SAFEDroid: using structural features for detecting android malwares. In: Lin, X., Ghorbani, A., Ren, K., Zhu, S., Zhang, A. (eds.) SecureComm 2017. LNICSSITE, vol. 239, pp. 255–270. Springer, Cham (2018). https://doi.org/10.1007/978-3-319-78816-6_18
2. Arp, D., Spreitzenbarth, M., Hubner, M., Gascon, H., Rieck, K., Siemens, C.E.R.T.: DREBIN: effective and explainable detection of android malware in your pocket. NDSS **14**, 23–26 (2014)
3. Saracino, A., Sgandurra, D., Dini, G., Martinelli, F.: MADAM: effective and efficient behavior-based android malware detection and prevention. IEEE Trans. Depend. Secure Comput. **15**, 83–97 (2016)
4. Reina, A., Fattori, A., Cavallaro, L.: A system call-centric analysis and stimulation technique to automatically reconstruct android malware behaviors. In: EuroSec, April 2013
5. Backes, M., Gerling, S., Hammer, C., Maffei, M., von Styp-Rekowsky, P.: AppGuard – fine-grained policy enforcement for untrusted android applications. In: Garcia-Alfaro, J., Lioudakis, G., Cuppens-Boulahia, N., Foley, S., Fitzgerald, W.M. (eds.) DPM/SETOP -2013. LNCS, vol. 8247, pp. 213–231. Springer, Heidelberg (2014). https://doi.org/10.1007/978-3-642-54568-9_14
6. Bugiel, S., Davi, L., Dmitrienko, A., Fischer, T., Sadeghi, A.R., Shastry, B.: Towards taming privilege-escalation attacks on android. NDSS **17**, 19 (2012)
7. Gibler, C., Crussell, J., Erickson, J., Chen, H.: AndroidLeaks: automatically detecting potential privacy leaks in android applications on a large scale. In: Katzenbeisser, S., Weippl, E., Camp, L.J., Volkamer, M., Reiter, M., Zhang, X. (eds.)

Trust 2012. LNCS, vol. 7344, pp. 291–307. Springer, Heidelberg (2012). https://doi.org/10.1007/978-3-642-30921-2_17

8. Viswanath, H., Mehtre, B.M.: U.S. Patent No. 9,959,406, U.S. Patent and Trademark Office, Washington, DC (2018)

9. Zhong, X., Zeng, F., Cheng, Z., Xie, N., Qin, X., Guo, S.: Privilege escalation detecting in android applications. In: 2017 3rd International Conference on Big Data Computing and Communications (BIGCOM), pp. 9–44. IEEE (2017)

10. Aafer, Y., Du, W., Yin, H.: DroidAPIMiner: mining API-level features for robust malware detection in android. In: Zia, T., Zomaya, A., Varadharajan, V., Mao, M. (eds.) SecureComm 2013. LNICST, vol. 127, pp. 86–103. Springer, Cham (2013). https://doi.org/10.1007/978-3-319-04283-1_6

11. Demontis, A., et al.: Yes, machine learning can be more secure! a case study on Android malware detection. IEEE Trans. Depend. Secure Comput. (2017)

12. Papadopoulos, H., Georgiou, N., Eliades, C., Konstantinidis, A.: Android malware detection with unbiased confidence guarantees. Neurocomputing. **280**, 312 (2018)

13. Shabtai, A., Moskovitch, R., Elovici, Y., Glezer, C.: Detection of malicious code by applying machine learning classifiers on static features: a state-of-the-art survey. Inf. Secur. Tech. Rep. **14**(1), 16–29 (2009)

14. Egele, M., Scholte, T., Kirda, E., Kruegel, C.: A survey on automated dynamic malware-analysis techniques and tools. ACM Comput. Surv. (CSUR) **44**(2), 6 (2012)

15. Burguera, I., Zurutuza, U., Nadjm-Tehrani, S.: Crowdroid: behavior-based malware detection system for android. In: Proceedings of the 1st ACM Workshop on Security and Privacy in Smartphones and Mobile Devices, pp. 15–26. ACM (2011)

16. Wolpert, D.H.: Stacked generalization. Neural Netw. **5**(2), 241–259 (1992)

17. Sahs, J., Khan, L.: A machine learning approach to android malware detection. In: Intelligence and Security Informatics Conference (EISIC), pp. 141–147. IEEE (2012)

18. Scikit-learn: machine learning in Python Scikit-learn 0.19.1 documentation. http://scikit-learn.org/stable/

19. Yerima, S.Y., Sezer, S., McWilliams, G., Muttik, I.: A new android malware detection approach using Bayesian classification. In: IEEE 27th International Conference on Advanced Information Networking and Applications (AINA), pp. 121–128 (2013)

20. Wu, W.C., Hung, S.H.: DroidDolphin: a dynamic Android malware detection framework using big data and machine learning. In: 2014 Conference on Research in Adaptive and Convergent Systems, pp. 247–252. ACM (2014)

21. Chang, C.C., Lin, C.J.: LIBSVM: a library for support vector machines. ACM Trans. Intell. Syst. Technol. (TIST) **2**(3), 27 (2011)

22. Feizollah, A., Anuar, N.B., Salleh, R., Amalina, F., Ma'arof, R.U.R., Shamshirband, S.: A study of machine learning classifiers for anomaly-based mobile botnet detection. Malays. J. Comput. Sci. **26**(4), 251–265 (2014). (in Malaysian)

23. Talha, K.A., Alper, D.I., Aydin, C.: APK auditor: permission-based Android malware detection system. Digit. Invest. **13**, 1–14 (2015)

24. Urcuqui, C., Navarro, A.: Machine learning classifiers for android malware analysis. In: IEEE Colombian Conference on Communications and Computing (COLCOM), pp. 1–6 (2016)

25. Xiao, X., Zhang, S., Mercaldo, F., Hu, G., Sangaiah, A.K.: Android malware detection based on system call sequences and LSTM. Multimedia Tools Appl. **78**, 3979–3999 (2019)

26. Wang, C., Xu, Q., Lin, X., Liu, S.: Research on data mining of permissions mode for Android malware detection. Clust. Comput. 1–14 (2018)
27. Python package for stacking (machine learning technique). https://github.com/vecxoz/vecstack
28. Townsend, J.T.: Theoretical analysis of an alphabetic confusion matrix. Percept. Psychophys. **9**(1), 40–50 (1971)
29. Davis, J., Goadrich, M.: The relationship between precision-recall and ROC curves. In: Proceedings of the 23rd International Conference on Machine Learning, pp. 233–240. ACM (2006)
30. Sokolova, M., Japkowicz, N., Szpakowicz, S.: Beyond accuracy, F-score and ROC: a family of discriminant measures for performance evaluation. In: Sattar, A., Kang, B. (eds.) AI 2006. LNCS (LNAI), vol. 4304, pp. 1015–1021. Springer, Heidelberg (2006). https://doi.org/10.1007/11941439_114
31. Boyd, K., Eng, K.H., Page, C.D.: Area under the precision-recall curve: point estimates and confidence intervals. In: Blockeel, H., Kersting, K., Nijssen, S., Železný, F. (eds.) ECML PKDD 2013. LNCS (LNAI), vol. 8190, pp. 451–466. Springer, Heidelberg (2013). https://doi.org/10.1007/978-3-642-40994-3_29
32. Geurts, P., Ernst, D., Wehenkel, L.: Extremely randomized trees. Mach. Learn. **63**(1), 3–42 (2006)
33. Breiman, L.: Random forests. Mach. Learn. **45**(1), 5–32 (2001)
34. Taud, H., Mas, J.F.: Multilayer perceptron (MLP). In: Camacho Olmedo, M.T., Paegelow, M., Mas, J.-F., Escobar, F. (eds.) Geomatic Approaches for Modeling Land Change Scenarios. LNGC, pp. 451–455. Springer, Cham (2018). https://doi.org/10.1007/978-3-319-60801-3_27
35. Bottou, L.: Large-scale machine learning with stochastic gradient descent. In: Lechevallier, Y., Saporta, G. (eds.) Proceedings of COMPSTAT 2010, pp. 177–186. Physica-Verlag HD, Heidelberg (2010)
36. Tsiang, S.C.: The rationale of the mean-standard deviation analysis, skewness preference, and the demand for money. In: Finance Constraints and the Theory of Money, pp. 221–248 (1989)
37. Leys, C., Ley, C., Klein, O., Bernard, P., Licata, L.: Detecting outliers: do not use standard deviation around the mean, use absolute deviation around the median. J. Exp. Soc. Psychol. **49**(4), 764–766 (2013)
38. Chen, T., He, T., Benesty, M.: Xgboost: extreme gradient boosting. R package version 0.4-2, pp. 1-4 (2015)
39. Kurtulmus, A.B., Daniel, K.: Trustless Machine Learning Contracts; Evaluating and Exchanging Machine Learning Models on the Ethereum Blockchain. Algorithmia Res. (2018)
40. Rana, M.S., Rahman, S.S.M.M., Sung, A.H.: Evaluation of tree based machine learning classifiers for android malware detection. In: Nguyen, N.T., Pimenidis, E., Khan, Z., Trawiński, B. (eds.) ICCCI 2018. LNCS (LNAI), vol. 11056, pp. 377–385. Springer, Cham (2018). https://doi.org/10.1007/978-3-319-98446-9_35

An Adaptive and Dynamic Dimensionality Reduction Method for Efficient Retrieval of Videos

Praveen M. Dhulavvagol$^{(\boxtimes)}$, S. G. Totad$^{(\boxtimes)}$, Anand S. Meti$^{(\boxtimes)}$, and V. Shashidhara$^{(\boxtimes)}$

School of Computer Science Enginering, KLE Technological University, Hubli, Karnataka, India
{praveen.md,totad,anandsmeti,shashidhara.v}@kletech.ac.in

Abstract. In today's multimedia age, Content Based Video Retrieval (CBVR) is a trending area and lot of research is being carried out in Video Surveillance, Big Data analysis and multimedia applications. Usage of multimedia data is becoming very common in day today life, content based video retrieval provides an effective mechanism for maintaining, managing and retrieving large number of videos efficiently as per user's interest. The advancement in the technology is evolving and multimedia applications are gaining more importance so the performance of the CBVR system need to be high and accurate to fulfill user demands. The proposed paper focuses on surveying the different techniques for feature extraction and similarity computation for retrieving relevant videos. Feature extraction can be done using different techniques such as shot boundary detection, based on histogram, PCA Shift, Gist and SURF (Speeded up Robust Features) and Quadratic Equation are used for feature extraction and similarity computation. In CBVR technique the videos are retrieved from the large databases based on the given Input Query as an image, on processing this query the features from videos and the query image are extracted mainly the color, texture and shape. Once these features are extracted then a similarity between query and the videos is computed, ranking will be done based on the similarity score. The results interpret that SURF technique provides better results as compared to other techniques and the system has a retrieval performance of more than 70%.

Keywords: SURF · PCA · PCA-SIFT · LDA · Precision · Recall

1 Introduction

In recent days, advancements in progress of multimedia technologies and usage of multimedia applications is the main source for information exchange in various applications, a huge volume of digital multimedia data is available publicly with

© Springer Nature Singapore Pte Ltd. 2019
K. C. Santosh and R. S. Hegadi (Eds.): RTIP2R 2018, CCIS 1035, pp. 624–639, 2019.
https://doi.org/10.1007/978-981-13-9181-1_54

an increased speed. So an efficient video retrieval mechanism is required to access the relevant videos fulfilling the user requirements. As huge volume of data is available publically, as it becomes difficult to users for process of retrieval relevant videos based on person's interest matching to the given query [6]. Considering the above facts it is necessary to build a system which can retrieve user interest relevant videos within a shorter span of time.

The proposed system is an effective and efficient mechanism for retrieving videos from large databases. The CBVR system provides efficient techniques for storing the video in database, indexing, feature extraction and retrieval of videos. The main goal of CBVR systems is to retrieve user interested relevant videos from database storage matching to the given input query image. In CBVR system the main focus is on retrieving relevant videos based on the feature vectors. Generally the features are classified as global features or local features. In CBVR system given a query image as input we need to retrieve the relevant videos matching to the given user query in an efficient manner. CBVR systems analyze the video content and extract the local features required to compute the similarity [8]. One of the major challenges for a CBVR system is its high computational cost in terms retrieval time and efficiency [12,13]. Generally the videos will have the following characteristics:

- Rich source content compared to each of the images.
- Large volume of raw data.
- Very less amount of prior structure.

Indexing and retrieval mechanism is tedious and complex due the characteristics listed above [7]. Earlier text based techniques were used for indexing and retrieval of videos due to small database size, but today text based techniques are not so efficient because of the large sized database, as it mainly effects the performance of the application. Due to this reason content based video indexing and retrieval are in huge demand.

CBVR techniques which are discussed in the literature survey are based on local feature descriptors [3]. However, a local descriptor feature extraction technique assumes to be costly in terms of processing time and storage space [5]. A CBVR technique typically converts an image into a feature vector representation. For computing a local descriptor features many different techniques are available such as SIFT, SURF and GIST. In this article, comparative study of SIFT, PCA-SIFT and SURF feature extraction techniques is done in order to find which feature extraction technique is better in terms of computational and storage cost factors [9]. A sequence of videos usually consists of thousands, millions of frames; processing of these frames to find the relevant videos matching to the given query is very expensive so appropriate and efficient technique need to be used to lower down the computational cost this is the major challenge for any video retrieval system.

Generally in the video retrieval process parameters like precision, recall and accuracy are used to measure the performance of the system. Relevance plays a vital role because given a input query in this case an image is considered as input query the system should retrieve relevant video similar to the input query based on the similarity measures, once the relevant videos are retrieved the next process is to rank the videos based on the similarity score which ever video has highest similarity score that video will be ranked at the top of the list and will be retrieved.

In CBVR system, the main features which are considered are shape, texture and color of the video. In CBVR system focuses on retrieval of pertinent videos related to input image passed as query for computing the similarity score [10,11]. CBVR system comprises of different processes and subsystem as shown in the Fig. 1. Initial step is to build the index of videos in the collection. The next process is feature extraction and content analysis prior to these key frames is extracted from the videos using key frame extraction techniques such as shot boundary detection. Next step is low level feature extraction which is done using these techniques PCA, PCA-SIFT, GLOH, SURF any one of these techniques is used to extract the feature depending on the dataset. Next step is to retrieve the videos computing the similarity for the query image and the stored database videos.

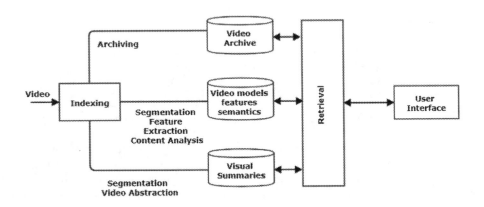

Fig. 1. Generic block diagram of video retrieval system

2   Related Work

Survey is carried out in identifying the dimensionality reduction and feature extraction techniques. There are different challenges in CBVR system. Based on the user's interest relevant videos need to be retrieved efficiently. Generally in retrieving any video, video frame's modeled data is compared to the stored database image frame with the help of key frame extraction and similarity computation techniques, Based on computed similarity score ranking of the videos is done.

Shot Boundary Refinement for Long Transitioning Digital Video [1], in this paper the author discusses on the shot boundary detection or scene change detection. The main purpose of using shot boundary technique is to extract the features of the video frames and process those frames to identify the shot type depending on the features extracted from those video frames. Basically there are two different methods to detect the shots: shot abrupt change and shot gradual change, In case of shot abrupt the two shot or frames are connected directly without any delay but in case of gradual change method some spatial and temporal effects will be added to the frame so there might be certain delay in connecting these frames, so shot abrupt method is able to provide efficient results as compared to the gradual. The different methods which are available to detect abrupt shots are: method based on pixel or histogram or based on clustering.

In the first method we try to estimate the shot boundary by comparing the gray scale difference between the two adjacent frames [2]. This can be achieved using the below equation.

$$Fd(x, y) = fi(x, y) - fj(x, y)$$

Where, $fi(x, y)$ and $fj(x, y)$ represents the pixel(x, y) value in ith and jth frame, the total difference between the frames can be calculated using the equation:

$$FD = \frac{1}{MN} \sum_x \sum_y fd(x, y)$$

The second method is based on histogram, which is commonly used for shot boundary detection. Using this method the color, shape and texture can be extracted to compute the similarity and to identify weather there is any shot changes in the frames or no. In this method initially we extract the histograms of the frames and then we compute the distance between the histograms. If the computed distance value is more than the threshold value then it is considered as abrupt shot. The drawback of this method is, it doesn't consider the pixel position values so may result in wrong values, Fig. 2 shows the difference between abrupt shot.

A Stable local feature detection and representation [3], In this paper the authors discuss on different feature extraction techniques Such as SIFT and PCA-SIFT. The identified SIFT algorithm is nearly resistant to common image deformations. Principal Component Analysis (PCA) to the normalized gradient patch is used over SIFT's smoothed weighted histograms. The experimental results states that PCA based local descriptors are very much robust to image deformations, distinctive and more compact than standard SIFT representation.

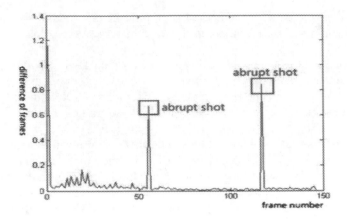

Fig. 2. Difference between abrupt shot

Scaling up top-K cosine similarity search [4], in this paper, the author discuss on methods to find top-K firmly correlated pairs of objects as measured by the cosine similarity.

3   Proposed Work

The CBVR system mainly consists of 4 modules i.e. Key frame extraction, Feature extraction and Similarity computation and Ranking as shown in the Fig. 3.

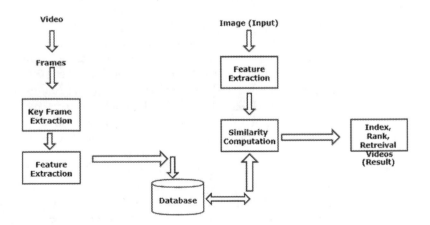

Fig. 3. CBVR system architecture

In the first step, extraction of frames from the given video samples and identify and locate the key frames using appropriate key frame extraction technique, Next step is to extract the features using feature extraction technique SIFT, GIST, PCA-SIFT and SURF the extracted key feature vectors will be maintained in the local repository. At the other end a test query image is used as input image to retrieve the relevant videos matching to the input query image, the input query image features are extracted and mapped with the features extracted from the video samples, this mapping is carried out by computing similarity score between both the feature vectors, if there is a match then relevant video will be retrieved and ranked at the top subsequently all the other matching videos will be ranked as shown in Fig. 4.

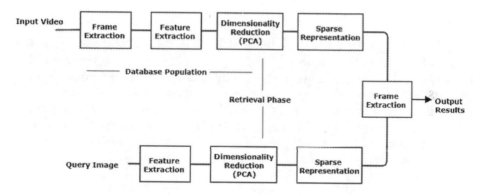

Fig. 4. Dimensionality reduction for Video search and retrieval

3.1   Frame Extraction

The frames are extracted from the videos using Normalized histogram technique in which frame differencing method is used, this method uses pixel-based difference to determine the moving objects. Here we compute the difference between the reference frame and the existing frame, if the pixels have changed, then apparently two frames are different. If suppose In is the value of Kth frame in a sequence of images then In+1 is the value of $(i+1)^{th}$ frame in a sequence of images, the difference between k^{th} frame and $(i+1)^{th}$ frame is calculated by:

$$Id(K, K + 1) = |Ik + 1 - Ik|$$

3.2   Feature Extraction

The features considered are color and shape. In case of color feature extraction a histogram based technique is used to compute the color features, with shape feature extraction, points where image brightness changes sharply are organized into a set of curved line segments termed edges shown in Fig. 5.

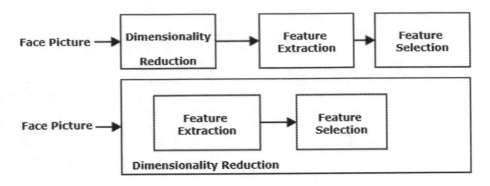

Fig. 5. Feature extraction process

PCA-SIFT algorithm is basically used for dimensionality reduction and is derived from the Eigen vectors, these Eigen vectors encompasses the major features of any given images, PCA applies linear transformation technique for mapping higher dimensional space data to lower dimensional space eliminating the minor components of an image. PCA determines the direction based on maximum variance of data, in face recognition these directions or the Eigen vectors will be orthogonal. Mathematically, the transformation is defined by a set of p-dimensional vectors of weights.

$$W (k) = (W1....Wp) (k) \text{ that map each row vector}$$
$$X (i) \text{ of X to a new vector of principle component scores}$$
$$T (i) = (T1...Tk) (i), \text{ and is given by } Tk (i) = X (i).W (k)$$

This consists of sensor nodes deployed on the field for collecting environmental data such as temperature and pressure. This forms sensing station where all the sensors regularly transmit data to the gateway nodes.

4   Implementation

Implementation is shown by considering different algorithms, the flow of the algorithms is explained in further sections.

4.1   Data Preprocessing

The steps followed are shown below. M vectors of size N representing a set of sample dataset of images. The Covariance of matrix is calculated by multiplying matrix A with its transposing matrix of A.

$$C = A * A^t$$

Algorithm 1. Data Preprocessing

1: **procedure** DATA PREPROCESSING
2:     Represent image as 1 dimensional vector of NxN size
3:     Calculate the mean intensity of each pixel values and subtract it from the corresponding image
4:     Mean is subtracted from the original image
5:     Calculate the co variance matrix of order N2xN2 represented as C=AAT
6:     Compute Eigenvectors and Eigen values of co variance matrix and then select principle component values
7:     Determine Eigen values of covariance matrix C using equation: $(C\lambda - I) = 0$
8:     Sort the Eigen vectors in the descending order
9:     Select the first K Eigen vectors and Eigen values
10: **end procedure**

4.2 PCA-SIFT Algorithm

PCA-SIFT algorithm is used to extract feature descriptors of video or images. These descriptors will have scale invariant and can easily identify the feature points on the given image, to detect the feature points of an image the following steps need to be carried out.

Algorithm 2. PCA-SIFT Algorithm

1: **procedure** PCA-SIFT ALGORITHM
2:     Identify the extreme points and determine the scale invariant by Scale-space peak selection
3:     Compare the sample points with all its adjacent points
4:     Consider sample points greater or smaller than the adjacent points of image scale domain   ▷ such points are considered as feature points
5:     Delete feature points with low contrast, unreliable and edge response from the future point set
6:     Establish gradient direction histogram for Orientation assignment
7:     Construct the keypoints descriptor by determining the gradient value
8:     Gradient value is rotated to move upto the orientation of keypoints
9:     Weighted by a Gaussian with variance of 1.5 * keypoints scale to get description of 128 D points
10:     PCA algorithm is applied to make 128 D descriptor down to 20 D or less
11: **end procedure**

Through Scale-space peak selection, animage is represented as:

$$L(x, y, \sigma) = G(x, y, \sigma) * I(x, y)$$

G is a scale variable Gaussian Function.

Orientation assignment is used to establish gradient direction histogram; hence the direction of future point is calculated using the formula:

$$q(x,\ y) = \tan - 1((L(x,\ y+1) - L(x,\ y-1))/L(x+1, y) - L(x-1, y)))$$

Where M(x, y) is the model value of future point and q (x, y) is direction value.

$$dist = \sqrt{L(x+1,y) - L(x-1,y))^2 + (L(x,y+1) - L(x,y-1))^2}$$

4.3 SURF Descriptors

Speeded up Robust Features (SURF) technique basically explores the rotation-invariant and scale interest points of a given image. However SURF algorithm is similar to SIFT, but SURF is simple and more efficient in performing computation and similarity measure operations. Basically SURF algorithm uses Hassian matrix to determine the keypoints or interest point's i.e.

Consider a point p(x, y) from a given image I, then the determinant of hessian at point p and scale σ is given by:

$$H(p, \sigma) = L_{XX}(p, \sigma) L_{YY}(p, \sigma) - L_{XY}^2(p, \sigma)$$

$L_{XX}(p, \sigma)$ represents convolution of Gaussian second order derivative with image I on point p:

$$L_{XX}(p, \sigma) = \delta 2 / \delta x 2 \ G(I, \sigma) \otimes I$$

Here $\otimes$ indicates convolution operation, σ is scale factor and G (I, σ) are same which are defined in SIFT descriptors.

Next it uses integral image and box filters to approximate Hassian determinant interest points.

Consider D_{XX}, D_{YY} & D_{XY} be convolution results of the filters and image on which the Hassian Matrix is simplified and is given as:

$$\Delta H = D_{XX} D_{YY} - (0.9 \ D_{XY})^2$$

4.4 Similarity Computation

There are different measures used to compute the similarity score between the given query and database videos.

Distance Measures

Similarity computation plays a vital role in retrieving the relevant videos, Given a query image the system need to retrieve the relevant videos matching to the given query, distance metric is used to compute the similarity between the given query image and the stored database videos. There are different methods for similarity computation such as Euclidean distance, Manhattan, Quadratic Distance.

Euclidean Distance

This method is used for similarity computation, if the computed distance is smaller then the query image is having more relevance to the stored database videos, so based on the distance factor relevant videos were retrieved.

$$d_{(x,y)} = \sqrt{\sum_{j=1}^{j} (x_j - y_j)^2}$$

Manhattan Distance

For two dimensions, the distance is computed as follows:

If $A = (x1, y1)$ & $B = (x2, y2)$ are two points, Then distance between A and B is:

$$MH\ (A, B) = |x1 - x2| + |y1 - y2|$$

If the points have "n"-dimensions,

$$X = (x1, x2, ..., xn)\ \text{and}\ Y = (y1, y2, ..., yn)$$

Then the above equation can be rewritten as

$$MH\ (X, Y) = |x1 - y1| + |x2 - y2| + .\ |xn - yn| = \sum |xi - yi|\ \text{for i} = 1, 2..., n.$$

Quadratic Distance

This method is used to describe the distance between two Images based on similarity.

$$D2\ (Q, I) = (HQ - HI)\ tA\ (HQ - HI)$$

In quadratic distance method we consider color histogram for retrieving relevant images. The above equation denotes three terms, the $(HQ - HI)$ indicates the difference value among the two color histograms. The $(HQ - HI)$ t denotes the Vector transpose, and the similarity matrix (A) is defined by middle term. D represents the color distance between the two images.

4.5   Indexing, Ranking and Retrieval

Once dimensionality reduction is performed the projections of the reduced subspaces need to be indexed efficiently, for ease of maintenance we index all the projections in a single structure instead of using index for each subspace, here we have chosen iDistance as the base index because of its B+ tree data structure. Finally the top ranked relevant videos are retrieved and displayed to the user. The top ranked videos are displayed to the user. If no matching frames found in the database then appropriate message will be displayed to the user. The above process is done by matching a frame along with a video so that we will get to know about the video which is having maximum similarity has been matched or not based on the frames which are extracted.

5   Results and Discussions

The experimental results and analysis are discussed in this section. The proposed system is evaluated considering 3 different scenarios.

Firstly, the system performance is measured considering precision and recall measures.

$$P(\text{relevant} \mid \text{retrieved}) = tp/(tp + fp) = P$$

$$Precisionrate : \frac{Number\ of\ relevant\ videos\ selected}{Total\ number\ of\ retrieved\ videos}$$

$$P(\text{retrieved} \mid \text{relevant}) = tp/(tp + fn) = R$$

$$Recallrate : \frac{Number\ of\ relevant\ videos\ selected}{Total\ number\ of\ similar\ videos\ in\ the\ dataset}$$

Second, the performance evaluation of video retrieval is done comparing different similarity computation algorithms like Euclidean distance, Manhattan distance algorithms as shown in Fig. 9.

In our experiments we have considered a sample dataset of 100 videos as a reference dataset, the size of each video ranges from 200 KB to 5000 KB each consisting of more than 600 key frames. The reference dataset consists of different video clippings which belong to different categories like animals, nature, sports and movies. From the reference dataset videos a test set clips are constructed, the test set consists of 40 video clippings which belongs to all the different categories. The Fig. 9. shows the performance analysis for randomly picked 6 query images for which the relevant videos are retrieved from the dataset. In our experiments we have taken sample videos in each set consisting of 4 different sets of videos which are incrementally increased.

The Fig. 8 shows the average performance evaluation carried out using Euclidean and Manhattan distance metrics, from the graph we can interpret that both the similarity computation measures gives the proportional retrieval rates, however the proposed system gives better statistical results using Euclidean distance metric for the given test data.

Fig. 6. Sample input query images

Fig. 7. Sample key frame extracted

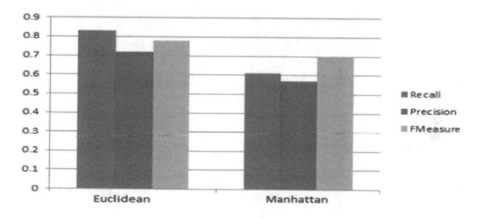

Fig. 8. Average performance analysis

Total numbers of videos considered for experimentation purpose are 120 i.e. 35 videos of Lion, 12 videos of Zebra, 28 videos Elephant, 22 videos of Bear, 21 videos of Giraffe and 2 other videos. Experimentation is conducted by considering Surf, Gist and PCA-SIFT algorithms. The results obtained from 3 different graphs are discussed here.

1. Surf. The graph shown in Fig. 10. Depicts the accuracy of identifying the particular animal out of the different animal from the datasets. For Lion, Surf

Video Data set	Distance metric	Precision	Recall	F-Measure
Video 1	Euclidean Method	0.6	0.83	0.6
	Manhattan Method	0.62	0.84	0.7
Video 2	Euclidean Method	0.7	0.82	0.8
	Manhattan Method	0.6	0.9	0.78
Video 3	Euclidean Method	1	0.9	1
	Manhattan Method	0.5	0.9	0.6
Video 4	Euclidean Method	1	0.9	0.9
	Manhattan Method	0.8	1	0.9
Video 5	Euclidean Method	0.6	0.7	0.6
	Manhattan Method	0.2	1	0.5
Video 6	Euclidean Method	0.8	1	0.92
	Manhattan Method	0.8	1	0.85

Fig. 9. Similarity measures performance analysis

algorithm is able to identify the given image/video is of Lion with an accuracy of 97% and with error rate of 3%. Similarly for other animals accuracy is Zebra-99.1%, Elephant-96.3%, Bear-97.7%, Giraffe-98.4%.

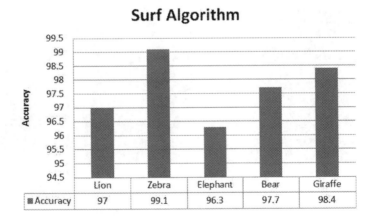

Fig. 10. SURF algorithm

2. Gist. The graph shown in Fig. 11. shows accuracy of identifying the particular animal out of the different animal from the datasets. For Lion, Gist algorithm is able to identify the given image/video is of Lion with an accuracy of 95.1% and with error rate of 4.9%. Similarly for other animals accuracy is Zebra-92.3%, Elephant-96.1%, Bear-95.3%, Giraffe-93.9%.

Gist Algorithm

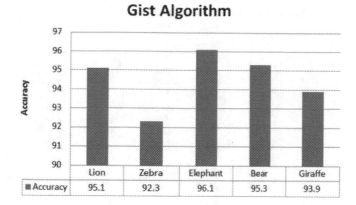

	Lion	Zebra	Elephant	Bear	Giraffe
■ Accuracy	95.1	92.3	96.1	95.3	93.9

Fig. 11. Gist algorithm

3. PCA-SIFT. The graph shown in Fig. 12. shows accuracy of identifying the particular animal out of the different animal from the datasets. For Lion, PCA-SIFT algorithm is able to identify the given image/video is of Lion with an accuracy of 88.9% and with error rate of 11.1%. Similarly for other animals accuracy is Zebra-91.3%, Elephant-90%, Bear-89.3%, Giraffe-88.4%.

PCA-SIFT Algorithm

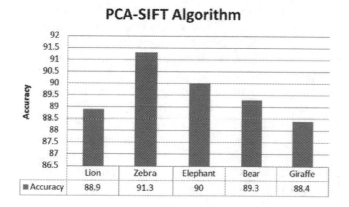

	Lion	Zebra	Elephant	Bear	Giraffe
■ Accuracy	88.9	91.3	90	89.3	88.4

Fig. 12. PCA-SIFT

From the Fig. 13 it can be inferred that SURF algorithm has more accuracy compared to Gist and PCA-SIFT algorithms in retrieving the particular video from a given dataset of images. SURF algorithm has the minimum error rate compared to the other algorithms.

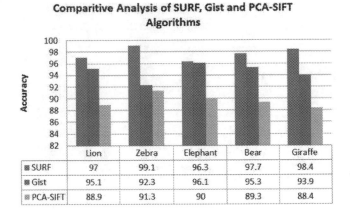

Fig. 13. Comparative analysis of SURF, Gist and PCA-SIFT algorithms

6 Conclusion

In any video retrieval application performance depends on the size and type of the video which is used for processing, so a dimensionality reduction technique plays an important role in video processing of large size data, many different techniques are being proposed for dimensionality reduction such as PCA, LDA, and PCA-SIFT. In this paper we have evaluated three feature detection methods for dimensionality reduction. SIFT technique is not good at illumination changes and is bit slow, while it is invariant to rotation and scale changes, PCA-SIFT is the good choice. In the proposed system we try to speed up the retrieval process by applying dimensionality reduction techniques, for feature extraction SURF algorithm gives the efficient results compared to other. The experimental results interpret the average precision is 80% with 90% of recall.

It is inferred from the results, continuous monitoring helps in reduction of energy consumption. As, complete interval energy consumption's data makes it bit inefficient. The future scope of application is to use it in agricultural field for analyzing varying electricity usage pattern and also providing predictive analysis of energy consumption using Bigdata Analytics in distributed environment.

References

1. Perry, S.W., Yap, K.-H., Guan, L., Wong, H.-S.: Top-k computational intelligence prospective. Adapt. Image Process. **2**(6), 15–200 (2009)
2. Kankanhalli, M.S., Zhu, Y., Angot, F., Sun, X., Wu, J.: Top-k1 content based representative frame extraction, p. 2 (2011)
3. Oliva, A., Torralba, A.: Top-k1 Modelling the shape of the sea. Holistic Representation of the Spatial Envelope (2001)
4. Dhulavvagol, P.M., Kundur, N.C.: Human action detection and recognition using SIFT and SVM. In: Nagabhushan, T.N., Aradhya, V.N.M., Jagadeesh, P., Shukla, S., M. L., C. (eds.) CCIP 2017. CCIS, vol. 801, pp. 475–491. Springer, Singapore (2018). https://doi.org/10.1007/978-981-10-9059-2_42

5. Sunderhauf, N., Bauer, J., Protzel, P.: Comparing several implementations of two recently published feature detectors. In: International Conference on Intelligent and Autonomous Systems (2002)
6. Dhulavvagol, P.M.: Recommendation system based on content filtering for specific commodity. Int. J. Latest Technol. Eng. Manag. Appl. Sci. (IJLTEMAS) **V**(VII) (2016). ISSN 2278–2540
7. Sreeraj, M., Asha, S.: Content based video retrieval using PCA SIFT. In: Third International Conference on Advances in Computing and Communications (2013)
8. Hu, W., Xie, N., Li, L., Zeng, X., Maybank, S.: A survey on visual content-based video indexing and retrieval. IEEE Trans. Syst. Man Cybern. Parts C: Appl. Rev. 41(6), 797-819, 2011
9. Nianhuaxie, L., Li, X., Maybank, S.: A survey on visual content-based video indexing and retrieval. IEEE Trans. Syst. Man Cybern.-Part C: Appl. Rev. **41**(6), 797–819 (2011)
10. Huang, S., Cai, C., Zhao, F.: An efficient wood image retrieval using surf descriptor. In: Proceedings of International Conference on Test and Measurement, pp. 55–58 (2009). ISBN 978-1-4244-4700-8/09
11. Pradeep, C., Sadafale, K., Thakare, K.: A survey on content based video retrieval using different feature extraction. In: National Conference on Technical Revolution (NCTR-2015), p. 127, 9–10 January 2015
12. Beatty, M., Manjunath, B.S.: Dimensionality reduction using multidimensional scaling for image search. In: Proceedings of IEEE KIP, Santa Barbara, CA, vol. 11, pp. 835–838 (1997)
13. Mu, K., Akki, M.M., Praveen, M., Meti, A.S., Patil, M.S., Sunil, V.G.: An ontological approach towards retrieval of video semantically. Asian J. Convergence Technol. (AJCT) **3** (2017). http://www.asianssr.org/index.php/ajct/article/view/268

A Machine Learning Algorithm for Solving Hidden Object-Ranking Problems

Gaël Mondonneix[✉], Sébastien Chabrier, Jean Martial Mari,
and Alban Gabillon

University of French Polynesia, Géopôle du Pacifique Sud EA4238,
LABEX CORAIL, Punaauia, France
gael.mondonneix@upf.pf

Abstract. Hidden object-ranking problems (HORPs) are object-ranking problems stated in instance-ranking terms. To our knowledge, there is no algorithm able to process these problems with the appropriate bias. This lack is not significant as long as the size of the dataset makes it possible to capture enough information by mining more data; however, when the data are scarce, any information lying in the data is worth exploiting and such an algorithm would become useful. We explicit the appropriate bias for object-ranking problems and propose an algorithm able to apply this bias to cases where these problems arise in an instance-ranking form. The theoretical foundations of the algorithm are discussed and the algorithm is tested on scarce real data, yielding better results (94.4% accuracy) than traditional algorithms (92.6% accuracy for the best case).

Keywords: Object-ranking · Instance-ranking · Learning bias · Support vector machine

1 Introduction

1.1 Context

Supervised learning is usually split into two different types of tasks: classification tasks and regression tasks. However, a third type of supervised learning, borrowing to both classification (the labels to predict take on discrete values) and regression (the labels to predict convey order-related information), is getting more attention as recommender systems play an increasing role on the Web: ranking tasks.

Ranking Tasks. Fürnkranz and Hüllermeier [1] distinguish three subtypes of ranking tasks depending on the problem to solve: object-ranking, instance-ranking and label-ranking problems. In an object-ranking problem, we have to

© Springer Nature Singapore Pte Ltd. 2019
K. C. Santosh and R. S. Hegadi (Eds.): RTIP2R 2018, CCIS 1035, pp. 640–652, 2019.
https://doi.org/10.1007/978-981-13-9181-1_55

infer a total order from a set of partially ordered items (see [2]). In an instance-ranking problem, we are given a set of items belonging to ordered classes and have to infer for any new item the class it belongs to (see [3]). In a label-ranking problem, we are given a set of labels as well as a set of items, each one associated with a partial order on the set of labels; the task consists of inferring a total order on the set of labels for any new item (see [3,4]).

Hidden Object-Ranking Problems (HORPs). We call "hidden object-ranking problem" (HORP) an object-ranking problem expressed in a form of an instance-ranking problem. A HORP has the appearance of an instance-ranking problem: the training data consist of a set of items distributed in some ordered classes and the task consists of distributing new items in these classes on a way that is consistent with the training data. However a HORP is not an instance-ranking problem in the sense that if two items are in a same class, it does not mean that they are tied (i.e. ordinally equal); it does only mean that we have no explicit information about their ordinal relation. In a HORP, the classes have no intrinsic meaning; they are external constraints meant to capture the trend of a total order by expressing it in a compact way, but the number of classes, as well as their boundaries, can change arbitrarily without having any impact on the ordinal information: ordinal relations between objects stay the same.

HORPs often arise in machine learning but they seem to get no particular attention and are solved as if they were simple instance-ranking problems. A typical example of HORP is when someone is asked to rate something by giving it from 1 to, say, 5 stars: if we ask this person to rate six items, then at least two of them will be given the same number of stars; the reason yet has less to do with preference than with external constraints we imposed on the way to express preference; this problem is not a true instance-ranking problem but a HORP.

Learning Bias. The bias is crucial in a learning process for being able to generalize to unseen data [5, p. 42], and the less the data, the most the predictions have to rely on the bias.

In a context of big data, losing some information on some data is not a problem because more information will be extracted from more data. The challenge is not to exploit all the information contained in a given piece of data but to process all the available data.

On the contrary, in a context of scarce data, if we do not exploit all the information lying in the available data, notably the possible ordinal information, there is no opportunity of recovering it through additional data. The choice of the bias becomes then a critical point (see Fig. 2. for an illustration): it has to be properly decided whether a problem stated in an instance-ranking form is a true instance-ranking problem (that is, there exists no ordinal difference between two items lying in a same class) or a HORP (ordinal differences exist between items inside a same class, even though they are unknown).

1.2 Related Work

Instance-Ranking Approach. Traditional classification algorithms do not take into account the possible ordinal information lying in the data. In multiclass classification, the problem comes from an undifferentiated cost function: if we have ordered classes C_i, $C_i \prec_p C_{i+1}$ for a given preference p, then a misclassification between C_i and C_{i+2} should be somehow more penalized than a misclassification between C_i and C_{i+1}.

Several methods have been proposed to address instance-ranking problems by extending or adapting traditional algorithms. For example, some authors propose a multiclass classification by SVM (support vector machine) with multiple parallel hyperplanes [6]. The set of hyperplanes is chosen in such a way that it maximizes the margin of the hyperplane with the thinnest margin. Since the hyperplanes are parallel, they preserve the ordinal information conveyed by the classes. Another method, called the data replication method [7], [8], is a setting that allows using binary classifiers to solve instance-ranking problems. The principle consists of learning a discrete cumulative distribution function: for all classes C_k but the last one, a binary classifier is trained to decide whether an item belongs to $\bigcup_{i=1}^{k} C_i$. At the prediction stage, an item is considered to belong to a class C_k if the classifiers put it in $\bigcup_{i=1}^{k} C_i$ but not in $\bigcup_{i=1}^{k-1} C_i$.

These methods however solve the true instance-ranking problem: they do not treat two items lying in a same class as two different objects but as two ordinally equal instances of the class; therefore their inductive bias seems not to be the most adapted for solving HORPs.

Object-Ranking Approach. Object-ranking consists of predicting a total order given only a set of sorted pairs. Solving object-ranking problems is usually done by learning a binary relation from the set of ordered pairs and choosing the closest total order [2]. Because this choice implies to solve the slater's problem [9], which is NP-equivalent [10], a way to approximate the right order is needed [2,11].

Even though this method is tailored for object-ranking, the fact that it goes through a binary relation that is not necessarily a total order, as well as an approximation process, makes it tricky to have a control on the learning bias. Nonetheless, the pairwise approach is interesting in the perspective of solving HORPs since the training set of ordered pairs of the object-ranking problem can be derived from the interclass relations of the instance-ranking setting in which the object-ranking problem is stated.

1.3 Guideline

The two following sections present a machine learning algorithm for solving HORPs. The presentation follows the distinction between search space and search strategy [5]: in Sect. 2 we describe the search space and prove its expressive power; in Sect. 3 we discuss candidate algorithms with respect to their generalization power and their learning bias. The proper bias of object-ranking learning is explicited in Subsect. 3.2 and a setting is proposed in Subsect. 3.3 for enabling SVM solvers to deal with HORPs. In Sect. 4, an experiment is reported, where the algorithm is tested on a real dataset.

2 Search Space

2.1 Definitions

Ordinal Equivalence. Let x and y be two sequences of n elements $(x_1, ..., x_n)$ and $(y_1, ..., y_n)$, $x_i \in X$, $y_i \in Y$, with order relations $\prec_x$ and $\prec_y$ on X and Y respectively. We define the ordinal equivalence between x and y, and we write $x \Leftrightarrow_{ord} y$, the property that $\forall i \leq n, \forall j \leq n, x_i \prec_x x_j \Leftrightarrow y_i \prec_y y_j$. By extension, we say that two derivations are ordinally equivalent if their left-hand members are ordinally equivalent *and* their right-hand members are ordinally equivalent.

For example, $\begin{pmatrix} 0 \\ 1 \\ 3 \end{pmatrix} \rightarrow \begin{pmatrix} 3 \\ 0 \\ 1 \end{pmatrix} \Leftrightarrow_{ord} \begin{pmatrix} 1 \\ 2 \\ 3 \end{pmatrix} \rightarrow \begin{pmatrix} 3 \\ 1 \\ 2 \end{pmatrix}$ since $\begin{pmatrix} 0 \\ 1 \\ 3 \end{pmatrix} \Leftrightarrow_{ord} \begin{pmatrix} 1 \\ 2 \\ 3 \end{pmatrix}$ and

$\begin{pmatrix} 3 \\ 0 \\ 1 \end{pmatrix} \Leftrightarrow_{ord} \begin{pmatrix} 3 \\ 1 \\ 2 \end{pmatrix}$.

Ordinal equivalence is just a convenient way of ignoring scales: an ordinal equivalence between two sequences is the same as a Kendall tau of 1 between two statistical ordinal variables.

Dimensionality Extension. The rank of a matrix can be increased by adding rows or columns that are linearly independent of the rows and columns of the original matrix. Under the hypothesis that no row of X be null, we define the basis function φ_r such that $\varphi_r(X)$ extends X to rank r by adding columns that are nonlinear combinations of its original columns.

As an illustration, if $X = \begin{bmatrix} x_{1,1} & x_{1,2} \\ x_{2,1} & x_{2,2} \\ x_{3,1} & x_{3,2} \end{bmatrix}$ with $rank(X) = 2$, we can have for

example $\varphi_3(X) = \begin{bmatrix} x_{1,1} & x_{1,2} & (x_{1,1} + x_{1,2})^2 \\ x_{2,1} & x_{2,2} & (x_{2,1} + x_{2,2})^2 \\ x_{3,1} & x_{3,2} & (x_{3,1} + x_{3,2})^2 \end{bmatrix}$.

2.2 Formalization

Description of the Search Space. Let X be a set of n items represented by vectors x_i, $1 \leq i \leq n$. Let y be a permutation of the first n positive integers indicating an order between the items ($y_i = k$ means that the item represented by the vector x_i is in the kth position in the sequence of items).

Without loss of generality, we suppose that any two items are distinct and that the mapping from the items to their representing vectors is injective ($i \neq j \Rightarrow x_i \neq x_j$). We search a vector w such that $\varphi_r(X)w \Leftrightarrow_{ord} y$.

Expressivity of the Search Space. Let write $\varphi_r(X)|y$ the matrix X extended to rank r, itself augmented with the column vector y.

If $rank(\varphi_r(X)|y) = rank(\varphi_r(X))$, then there necessarily exists a vector w such that $\varphi_r(X)w = y$; yet $y \Leftrightarrow_{ord} y$, so there necessarily exists a vector such that $\varphi_r(X)w \Leftrightarrow_{ord} y$. In other terms, the search space is expressive enough to contain any object-ranking target concept.

3   Search Strategy

3.1   Search by Extension

Derivation of a Greedy Algorithm. We can derive from the formalization of the search space an algorithm consisting of greedily computing w by iteratively increasing r until being able to solve $\varphi_r(X)w = y$.

Algorithm 1. Greedy Approach

$r \leftarrow rank(X)$
while $r < rank(\varphi_r(X)|y)$ **do**
    $r \leftarrow r + 1$
end while
return w s.t. $\varphi_r(X)w = y$

For n items, $rank(\varphi_r(X)|y) \leq n$. Since n is finite, the algorithm is guaranteed to terminate (there are at most $n - 1$ iterations).

Limitations of the Greedy Algorithm. We can learn an order on a dataset as soon as we find a vector w such that $\varphi_r(X)w \Leftrightarrow_{ord} y$, and it is shown in the previous section that such a w exists in the search space for any X provided that r be high enough. Nonetheless, even though the greedy algorithm is guaranteed to find a vector w such that $\varphi_r(X)w \Leftrightarrow_{ord} y$, it is not guaranteed to find the one for which r is minimal.

We can illustrate this point with the following example: when we run the algorithm, we notice that it needs to go up to $r = 4$ for learning $\begin{pmatrix} 1 \\ 2 \\ 3 \\ 4 \end{pmatrix} \rightarrow \begin{pmatrix} 1 \\ 2 \\ 4 \\ 3 \end{pmatrix}$

but needs only to go up to $r = 2$ for learning $\begin{pmatrix} 1 \\ 2 \\ 3 \\ 4 \end{pmatrix} \rightarrow \begin{pmatrix} 27 \\ 44 \\ 51 \\ 48 \end{pmatrix}$; yet, $\begin{pmatrix} 1 \\ 2 \\ 3 \\ 4 \end{pmatrix} \Leftrightarrow_{ord}$

$\begin{pmatrix} 27 \\ 44 \\ 51 \\ 48 \end{pmatrix}$.

In order to generalize well to unseen examples, the algorithm has to find the solution with the lowest r. The search for the lowest r seems justified from the information theory point of view: the lowest the rank r, the highest the exploitation of patterns lying in the training set; if the training set is representative of the data on which predictions are made (which is a reasonable assumption), then these data contain the same regularities as the test set and in the same proportion; therefore, predictions based on this information will be correct with a probability equal to this proportion.

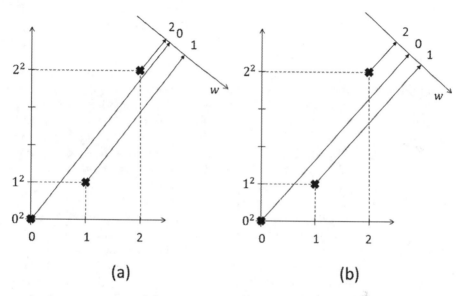

Fig. 1. Resolution of $\varphi_r \left(\begin{bmatrix} 0 \\ 1 \\ 2 \end{bmatrix} \right) w \Leftrightarrow_{ord} \begin{bmatrix} 2 \\ 0 \\ 1 \end{bmatrix}$ with the extension/adaptation algorithm. This algorithm ensures to find w with a minimal r (here $r = 2$) but does not ensure to find the most relevant solution for this value of r. (a) A candidate solution. (b) A relevant solution.

3.2   Search by Extension/Adaptation

Refinement of the Algorithm. The greedy algorithm takes a determined y and iterates on the dimensionality until it can solve the equation: it is able to extend the dimensionality of the search space but it does not adapt the target y.

We then modify the algorithm by adding an adapting phase at each stage.

The extension/adaptation algorithm retains the properties of the greedy algorithm but ensures a minimal r (see Fig. 1.). Everything now depends on how to search $argmin_\gamma \{rank(\varphi_r(X)|\gamma)\}$ such that $\gamma \Leftrightarrow_{ord} y$.

Algorithm 2. Extension/Adaptation Approach

$r \leftarrow rank(X)$
while $r < rank(\varphi_r(X)|z), z = argmin_\gamma\{rank(\varphi_r(X)|\gamma)\}s.t.\gamma \Leftrightarrow_{ord} y$ **do**
    $r \leftarrow r + 1$
end while
return w s.t. $\varphi_r(X)w = z$

Choice of the Appropriate Vector. The improved algorithm allows expressing all the possible orders with the lowest r. The problem remaining now is that to each of these orders can correspond an infinity of sequences (due to the fact that the sequences are real valued). The right bias has to be found in order to select the most appropriate solution (see Fig. 1).

In the case of SVM classification, it has been statistically proven that the most appropriate solution is the one that corresponds to the hyperplane with maximal margin [12]; In the case of instance-ranking, it has been proven that the most appropriate solution is the one that corresponds to a set of parallel hyperplanes among which the hyperplane lying between the closest classes has maximal margin [6]. Building on the existence of the latter proof, we can state that in the case of object-ranking, *the most appropriate solution is the vector on which the projection of all points results in a sequence in which the distance between the two closest points is maximal* (see Fig. 2c).

Indeed, we can consider object-ranking as a specific case of instance-ranking where there is only one instance per class. Then the most appropriate solution corresponds to the set of parallel hyperplanes among which the hyperplane lying between the closest classes, hence the closest points, has maximal margin. Since these hyperplanes are parallel, we can pass a vector through them at a normal angle: the intersections between the vector and the hyperplanes correspond to the projections of the points onto this vector, thus the distances between the hyperplanes correspond to the distances between the points of the resulting sequence.

3.3 Optimization Method

Herbrich et al. [6] extend the idea of large margin to ordinal learning and propose to solve instance-ranking problems by finding the hyperplane maximizing the margin between the two closest consecutive classes.

At first glance, it could be applied to object-ranking problems by setting each vector as a single instance of a class, as we did in the previous subsection for deriving the bias from instance-ranking problems to object-ranking problems. However, this method only allows finding hyperplanes with maximal margin between points that are explicitly defined as ordered pairs in the training set, whereas for solving our problem, we would need to find the hyperplane with maximal margin between the two closest points of the dataset even if the information about the order between them is not explicitly contained in the training data. The solution we are looking for would then imply to consider every permutation of the intra-class elements to discover the permutation allowing finding a vector on which the distance between the two closest projected elements is maximized.

On the one hand, extending the idea of large margin to hidden object-ranking allows finding the appropriate solution but implies an exponential complexity with respect to the size of the biggest class due to the need for considering every permutation; on the other hand, considering only inter-class information is tractable but puts emphasis on the differences between classes, solving then the instance-ranking problem, not the object-ranking one. Instead, we look for a way to put emphasis on the order between elements, that is, to find the vector that lies at maximal distance from the closest vector yielding a wrong order.

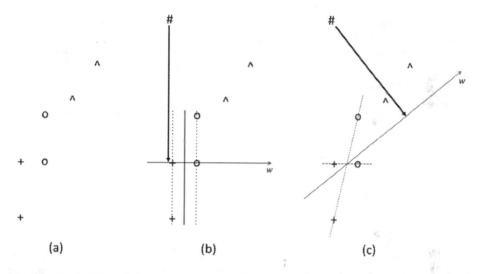

Fig. 2. Illustration of the importance of identifying a HORP for solving it with the right bias. (a) The training data. (b) The solution obeying the instance-ranking bias (traditional way of solving HORPs); '#' is predicted as the first element of the sequence and put in the class of '+'. (c) The solution obeying the object-ranking bias; '#' is predicted as the sixth element of the sequence and put in the class of '^'.

Resolution by Elimination. We derive a new training set from the original one by taking as new training examples the ordered pairs made explicit by the hinges between classes: let C_k and C_l be two different classes with $C_k \prec_p C_l$ for a given preference p; then for any $x_i \in C_k$ and any $x_j \in C_l$, our new training set will contain the vector $x_{ij} = \varphi_r(x_j) - \varphi_r(x_i)$.

In the case of a noise-free dataset, there exists a set of vectors whose dot product with any vector x_{ij} is positive. This set of possible solutions can be found by elimination: each vector x_{ij} determines the direction of a hyperplane going through the origin and splitting the space into two half spaces; the possible solutions lie necessarily in the half space where the vector lies. As long as we suppose the dataset consistent, we can let each vector x_{ij} reduce the space of possible solutions: this space will never be empty.

Most of the vectors x_{ij} won't have any impact on the final space. Only vectors on the edges will. The goal is to find them so that the appropriate solution can be computed: it is the vector maximizing the angle with the hyperplanes normal to the edge vectors, or equivalently, minimizing the angle with these edge vectors (see Fig. 3b).

Setting for an SVM Solver. The resolution by elimination could be carried out analytically. However, it would be cumbersome as soon as the number of dimension increases. Moreover, it would need to be adapted in order to deal with noisy datasets.

Since solving a HORP boils down to finding the vector that minimizes the maximal angle, or, equivalently, that maximizes the minimal cosine, we propose to use SVM solvers instead. Indeed, the optimization problems implied by HORPs and SVMs are very close, and a HORP can be set in such way that an SVM solver can process it. Equations 1 and 2 express the HORP and SVM optimization problems respectively ('$*$' denotes the optimal arguments and y_n is the label associated to the training example x_n; $y_n \in \{-1, 1\}$).

$$w^*_{HORP} = argmax_w \{min_{i,j} \frac{w^t}{||w||} \frac{x_{ij}}{||x_{ij}||}\} \tag{1}$$

$$(w_{SVM}, w_0)^* = argmax_{w,w_0} \{min_n \frac{y_n(w^t x_n + w_0)}{||w||}\} \tag{2}$$

The setting is as follows: we normalize the size of any vector x_{ij}, label it as positive and add its opposite vector, normalized and negatively labelled, in the training set. Since the vectors have all the same magnitude and the positive and negative examples are symmetrical, the support vectors will coincide with the vectors lying on the edges, that is, the only vectors that have an impact on the final space. It follows that the weight vector yielded by the SVM solver will be w^*_{HORP} (Fig. 3c). Moreover, this setting allows taking advantage of the soft margin of the SVM to deal with noisy datasets. As well, as for the SVM, the basis functions can be replaced by properly designed kernel functions.

Time Complexity. The time complexity for solving an SVM optimization problem is $O(n^3)$ [13] with respect to the size of the input. In our setting, the size of the SVM input is $O(n^2)$ with respect to the size of the HORP input since it consists of pairs of training examples. Our method needs then $O(n^6)$ time for solving a HORP. This represents a serious drawback from a scalability point of view and has to be addressed in a future work.

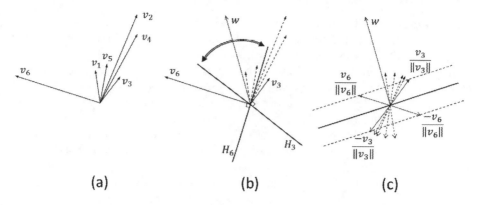

Fig. 3. (a) Six vectors v_h representing interclass relations $x_{ij} = \varphi_r(x_j) - \varphi_r(x_i)$ in a two-dimensional space. (b) Resolution by elimination: v_3 and v_6 are the edge vectors; the hyperplanes going through the origin and normal to them completely determine the set of possible solutions (shown by the double arrow); the appropriate solution, w, maximizes the angle to these hyperplanes, or equivalently, minimizes the angle with the edge vectors v_3 and v_6. (c) Resolution with an SVM solver; once normalized and symmetrized, the edge vectors correspond to support vectors.

4   Experiment

We conduct an experiment in order to test the extension/adaptation algorithm with an SVM solver for the adaptation step.

4.1   Methods

Dataset. The dataset consists of 54 instances, each describing a Tahitian pearl by 10 features corresponding to visual properties of their luster.

A description of these visual properties can be found in [14] and the way corresponding features are extracted from photographs of pearls is detailed in [15]. Briefly, three features quantify the appearance of specular reflectance and five features account for appearance of contrast between specular and diffuse reflectance, distinctness of reflected image, appearance of haze around the specular reflectance area, appearance of multiple reflectance on the successive layers of nacre the pearl is made of, and iridescence on the surface of the pearl. Two additional features, that do not *a priori* correspond to perceptual aspects of luster but are meant to test the impact of diffuse reflectance on luster determination, are mean saturation and chromaticity variance of the color on the surface of the pearl.

The instances are labeled by a human expert in 3 levels of luster quality. The classes are equally balanced.

Performance Evaluation. We use a 9-fold cross-validation method.

We run the experiment with 3 different settings. The first one is a traditional SVM multiclass classification; the second one implements the extension/adaptation algorithm with a genetic algorithm (population: 100; mutation rate: 0.2) for the adaptation step; the third one implements the extension/adaptation algorithm with a resolution by elimination carried out by an SVM solver for the adaptation step.

In all the settings, the experiment is run with and without feature selection. Feature selection is operated by picking the best combinations of features over the $2^{10} - 1$ possible non empty combinations for each setting. All the selected combinations turn out to involve specular reflectance, haze, deep reflectance, and chromaticity variance; none of them involves contrast or distinctness of reflected image (see [15] for a specification of the selected combinations).

Since the dataset is small, we test the statistical significance of the result; under the null hypothesis, the result would follow a binomial distribution of parameters $n = 54$ and $p = \frac{1}{3}$.

4.2   Results

Results are given in Table 1. The traditional multiclass classification reaches an accuracy of 77.7% with all features and 87% with selected features. The extension/adaptation algorithm with genetic algorithm reaches an accuracy of 90.7% with all features and 92.6% with selected features. The extension/adaptation algorithm with resolution by elimination reaches an accuracy of 94.4% with both all and selected features.

Let $Z \sim B(54, \frac{1}{3})$ under the null hypothesis; the p-value corresponding to an accuracy of 94.4%, which amounts to 51 correct predictions over 54, is equal to $Pr(Z \geq 51) < 10^{-19}$.

Table 1. Accuracy and 95% confidence interval estimate of different learners solving a HORP on a dataset of Tahitian pearls.

	All features	Selected features
SVM multiclass classification	77.7% ± 11.1%	87% ± 9%
Extension/adaptation with a genetic algorithm	90.7% ± 7.7%	92.6% ± 6.7%
Extension/adaptation with resolution by elimination	94.4% ± 6.1%	94.4% ± 6.1%

4.3   Discussion

The extension/adaptation algorithm with resolution by elimination reaches the highest accuracy. It confirms the theoretical insights. Moreover, with a p-value lower than 10^{-19}, this result is statistically significant, notwithstanding the small size of the dataset.

The extension/adaptation algorithm with genetic algorithm reaches a higher accuracy than the traditional multiclass algorithm even though the genetic algorithm returns the first solution it finds, which is not necessarily the best adapted; that is not surprising since the extension/adaptation makes it still ensure a minimal r.

Both SVM traditional multiclass classification and extension/adaptation with a genetic algorithm yield better results with selected features, while extension/adaptation with resolution by elimination makes no difference. Feature selection can be thought of as a way of experimentally finding the appropriate bias by letting the solution rely on the most relevant features, that is, on the features whose information they convey is the most representative of the information to capture for generalizing. From this point of view, we can interpret the results as a sign that the bias contained in our algorithm is better adapted to HORPs and makes therefore feature selection become less necessary.

5 Conclusion

Sum Up. In this paper, we propose an algorithm able to solve hidden object-ranking problems. The learning bias of object-ranking is explicited and the theoretical aspects of the algorithm are discussed. The algorithm is tested on scarce real data, yielding better results (94.4% of correct predictions) than traditional algorithms (92.6% of correct predictions for the best case) and suggesting that a feature selection step can be skipped without prejudicing accuracy.

Future Work. Even though the proposed algorithm is useful for scarce data because it allows exploiting the most information contained in object-ranking data, the optimization method we use makes it very sensitive to the size of the dataset. It would be worth finding an optimization method allowing the algorithm to scale.

References

1. Fürnkranz, J., Hüllermeier, E.: Preference learning: an introduction. [16], pp. 1–17
2. Cohen, W.W., Schapire, R.E., Singer, Y.: Learning to order things. J. Artif. Intell. Res. **10**, 243–270 (1999)
3. Fürnkranz, J., Hüllermeier, E.: Preference learning and ranking by pairwise comparison. [16], pp. 65–82
4. Fürnkranz, J., Hüllermeier, E.: Pairwise preference learning and ranking. In: Lavrač, N., Gamberger, D., Blockeel, H., Todorovski, L. (eds.) ECML 2003. LNCS (LNAI), vol. 2837, pp. 145–156. Springer, Heidelberg (2003). https://doi.org/10.1007/978-3-540-39857-8_15
5. Mitchell, T.M.: Machine Learning. McGraw-Hill Series in Computer Science, International edn. McGraw-Hill, New York (1997)
6. Herbrich, R., Graepel, T., Obermayer, K.: Support vector learning for ordinal regression. In: International Conference on Artificial Neural Networks, pp. 97–102 (1999)

7. Frank, E., Hall, M.: A simple approach to ordinal classification. In: De Raedt, L., Flach, P. (eds.) ECML 2001. LNCS (LNAI), vol. 2167, pp. 145–156. Springer, Heidelberg (2001). https://doi.org/10.1007/3-540-44795-4_13

8. Cardoso, J.S., da Costa, J.F.P.: Learning to classify ordinal data: the data replication method. J. Mach. Learn. Res. **8**, 1393–1429 (2007)

9. Slater, P.: Inconsistencies in a schedule of paired comparisons. Biometrika **48**(3/4), 303–312 (1961)

10. Hudry, O.: On the complexity of Slater's problems. Eur. J. Oper. Res. **203**(1), 216–221 (2010)

11. Shmoys, D.B.: Approximation Algorithms for NP-Hard Problems, pp. 192–235. PWS Publishing Co., Boston (1997)

12. Vapnik, V.N.: Statistical Learning Theory. Wiley, Hoboken (1998)

13. Abdiansah, A., Wardoyo, R.: Time complexity analysis of support vector machines (SVM) in LIBSVM. Int. J. Comput. Appl. **128**(3), 28–34 (2015). Published by Foundation of Computer Science (FCS), NY, USA

14. Mondonneix, G., Chabrier, S., Mari, J.M., Gabillon, A., Barriot, J.P.: Tahitian pearls' luster assessment. In: McDonald, J., Markham, C., Winstanley, A. (eds.) Proceedings of the 19th Irish Machine Vision and Image Processing Conference, Irish Pattern Recognition & Classification Society, pp. 186–193 (2017)

15. Mondonneix, G., Chabrier, S., Mari, J.M., Gabillon, A.: Tahitian pearls' luster assessment automation. In: Proceedings of the IEEE Applied Imagery Pattern Recognition Workshop: Big Data, Analytics, and Beyond (2017)

16. Fürnkranz, J., Hüllermeier, E. (eds.): Preference Learning. Springer, Heidelberg (2010). https://doi.org/10.1007/978-3-642-14125-6

Image Processing

Feature Fusion Approach for Differently Exposed Images with Weighted Guided Filter

Aparna Vijayan[✉] and V. R. Bindu

M. G. University, Kottayam, Kerala, India
aparnavijayan22@gmail.com, binduvr@mgu.ac.in

Abstract. Multi-exposure image fusion methodologies collect image information from multiple images and convey to a single image. Fusion with the aid of edge aware smoothing filters is a new treanding area. The difficultes of multi-scale processing and low level fusion operations are the main problems of the existing algoritms. In this paper we propose a novel multi-exposure image fusion method which uses a feature fusion method based on an edge aware weighted guided filter. Three important image features accounting for the quality of an image viz. contrast, sharpness and exposedness are extracted from the differently exposed input images and fused together to form a single saliency map which holds all the important information. A decision map is constructed for the fused feature and an efficient edge aware filtering technique called weighted guided filter is used for optimizing the obtained decision map. A two scale decomposition of input images is done in parallel with the initial feature extraction procedure. This decomposed image representation is fused with the optimized decision map to get the final result. The proposed method encompasses the advantages of simple two scale decomposition, optimization with edge weighting and simplicity of using a single fused feature. The experimental results and objective evaluations demonstrate that the proposed method can produce more accurate results with very good visual quality.

Keywords: Multi-exposure image fusion · Two scale decomposition · Feature fusion · Weighted guided filter

1 Introduction

The increasing popularity of digital images and image editing tools has brought a wide variety of image enhancement operations within a mouse click of the creative consumer. While considering image enhancement operations, apart from existing techniques there is still room for improvement. Under different classes of enhancement approaches there are different methods for enhancing different kinds of images. Coupled with the ever growing image fusion area, research area

© Springer Nature Singapore Pte Ltd. 2019
K. C. Santosh and R. S. Hegadi (Eds.): RTIP2R 2018, CCIS 1035, pp. 655–666, 2019.
https://doi.org/10.1007/978-981-13-9181-1_56

of image enhancement is one of the most vibrant sectors of digital image processing. The information captured by a single imaging sensor is usually insufficient to describe a scene in a comprehensive manner.

In computer vision, image fusion employs gathering all the important information from multiple images and combining relevant information to form an enhanced fused resultant image. The final fused image will be more appropriate and understandable for the human and machine perception. There exists a wide variety of image fusion algorithms such as referred in [7–9,15,16,18,20,22] etc and fusion of shapes [27]. In this paper we are concentrating on images which are differently exposed to light. Several situations in image processing require images with high quality in different aspects, however the instruments being used are not capable of providing such information due to their design. One best solution for such situations is image fusion. Creative applications of image fusion include pan-sharpening, remote sensing and satellite imagery and medical diagnosis and treatment.

Image filtering is another technique used for modifying or enhancing digital images. Most basic forms of image filters are meant to emphasize certain features or remove certain features of input image. The wide variety of filtering applications include noise reduction, edge enhancement etc. Many of the recent researches anticipated that image filtering based image fusion will be useful for developing new methods and to spark new ideas within the image enhancement domain.

2   Related Works

Exposure fusion is a very interesting area within image fusion. There exists a large number of multi-exposure fusion algorithms like mentioned in [12,13,17,25] etc. Edge preserving smoothing technique play a vital role in image fusion, image detail enhancement, image haze removal etc. The guided image filter (GIF) [14] is a well known edge aware smoothing filter which is derived from a local linear model. The guided filter performs filtering by considering an image as guidance image, which can be the input image i.e. image to be filtered itself or a different image. The problem with GIF is that it suffers from halo artifacts. A Weighted Guided Filter (WGF) is introduced in [26] to overcome the halo artifact problem in GIF by incorporating a weighting scheme to achieve more intelligent results near edges. Weighted framework used here imposes more weights on edges and less over the smooth regions. The detailed algorithm of this weighted guided filter is provided in [26].

Recently the fusion with edge preserving filter became very popular in the area of image processing. Many image fusion strategies like [19,23,24] and [5] were proposed which are based on edge aware filtering techniques. The algorithm in [23] is mainly concentrated on remote sensing applications. GFF [19] and GD-GFF [24]is two successful methods among the existing literatures. But the GFF [19] algorithm is limited to pixel level fusion operation; which is the lowest fusion level in the DFD (Data/pixel level - Feature level - Decision level) fusion schema. While moving from GFF [19] to GD-GFF [24] the performance is increased by adopting a feature level fusion strategy. But the problem with [24] is its time complexity for performing the complex feature extraction procedures. The method in [5] introduces another flavor of feature extraction with improved performance. However it suffers from difficulties in handling multi-scale representations of images. In this paper we introduce a novel fusion method especially for multi-exposed images, which overcomes the limitations of the existing algorithms. The main contribution of the proposed image fusion technique is which encompases all the advantages of two-scale decomposition strategy, enhanced feature extraction, feature level fusion methodology and a novel entropy weighted fusion rule.

3   Proposed Method

In this paper a fast and effective image fusion method is proposed for performing fusion on differently exposed input images for creating a highly informative fused result. A detailed methodology and sample fused results are provided in the following section. The basic architecture of the proposed method is shown in Fig. 1. Decomposition with Gaussian filtering, feature extraction, feature fusion, creating refined decision map with weighted guided filter, entropy weighted fusion

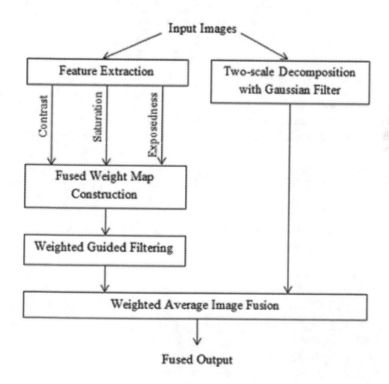

Fig. 1. Architecture of proposed method

are the major steps involved. The major features of this proposed method are:
(1) Simplicity with a spatial filter based two-scale decomposition (2) Extraction
of important image features and performing a feature level fusion strategy (3)
Application of an edge aware weighted image filtering and (4) Fusing the pixels
by using an entropy weighted fusion rule.

3.1   Two Scale Image Decomposition with Gaussian Image Filtering

Here the Gaussian low pass filter is used for describing the input images in two
representations [24]. The two scales produced are called base or approximation
layer and detail layer. Each source image is filtered by Gaussian image filter to
get the approximation layer A_n.

$$A_n = I_n * G \qquad (1)$$

Here G is Gaussian filter and the parameters radius r and variance σ are set to
11 and 5 respectively. Then the detail layer D_n is obtained by simply subtracting
the base layer from input image.

$$D_n = I_n - A_n \qquad (2)$$

The above mentioned decomposition step splits each input image into an
approximate or base component containing the large scale variations in intensity
and a detail component containing the other detail information.

3.2   Feature Extraction

Contrast, saturation and exposedness [21] are the three important image features accounting for the quality of the fused image, where inputs are differently
exposed to light. Hence our proposed method is designed to extract these three
features

Contrast: Our human visual system is less sensitive to intensity values in
each single pixel but it rely heavily on local contrast or contrast changes in
image regions. Hence we extract the contrast feature of each input image to
transfer the contrast saliency features to fused output. We measure the contrast
by using a sliding window laplacian filter with size 3×3 and obtain the absolute
value of filtered result. The contrast measure is defined by the following equation:

$$C = |G_I * L| \qquad (3)$$

Here, L is laplacian filter, G_I is the gray scale input and C represents the contrast
feature map. This contrast map provides a good description of saliency levels of
image details.

Saturation: In image processing the concept saturation is the strength or
purity of the color and represents the amount of gray in proportion to the hue.
A saturated color is pure and an unsaturated color has a large percentage of

gray. Here the saturation is measured as the standard deviation of R, G and B colour channels. The expression for computing saturation is

$$\mu = \frac{R + G + B}{3} \tag{4}$$

$$S = \sqrt{\frac{(R - \mu)^2 + (G - \mu)^2 + (B - \mu)^2}{3}} \tag{5}$$

Exposedness measure: This measure is yielded by multiplying the well-exposedness of each colour channel obtained by applying a Gaussian curve to each channel separately.

$$R = e^{-0.5*\frac{(I_r - 0.5)^2}{\sigma^2}} \tag{6}$$

$$G = e^{-0.5*\frac{(I_g - 0.5)^2}{\sigma^2}} \tag{7}$$

$$B = e^{-0.5*\frac{(I_b - 0.5)^2}{\sigma^2}} \tag{8}$$

$$E = R * G * B \tag{9}$$

Here I_r, I_g and I_b represent the red, green and blue channels respectively of our rgb colour input image. R, G and B are the corresponding exposedness maps for R, G and B channels. These three measures are fused to form the total exposedness E measure of each image.

3.3   Feature Fusion

The decision map is constructed by combining the previously obtained feature measures of three features. Contrast, saturation and exposedness maps are fused together using simple multiplication operator to get the decision map. This should be done for each input image taken; C_n, S_n and E_n are the corresponding contrast, saturation and exposedness maps for input I_n. Initial decision maps corresponding to each input image is obtained and this obtained initial decision map ID_n globally handles each image and it also depends on local information within each source image.

$$ID_n = C_n * S_n * E_n \tag{10}$$

Initial decision maps are compared to get the final decision maps DM

$$DM_n^k = |1, if ID_n^k = max(ID_1^k, ID_2^k, ...)| \cap$$
$$|0, otherwise| \tag{11}$$

Here k represents the pixel position.

3.4   Refined Weight Maps with Weighted Guided Filter

The initial weight map constructed in previous step should be followed by refinement process. Most of the conventional methods used optimization based methods. However, the optimization based methods are often relatively inefficient. The literature in [19] proposed an interesting alternative to optimization based methods in which a guided filtering process is used to get refined weight maps. The Weighted Guided Filter (WGF) [26] proposed an enhanced version of guided filter [14] by incorporating an explicit edge-aware weight constraint and this makes edges to be preserved better. In addition, as the WGF is less sensitive to the blur degree parameter selection, it can enhance the versatility for practical applications. The WGF avoids halo artifacts like all other global smoothing filters and is applicable to many vibrant applications of image processing like single image detail enhancement, single image de-hazing and fusion of differently exposed images. Even though the WGF increases the execution time slightly than GIF, it provides significantly greater impact on visual quality of final fused results. Hence, in this method we propose to apply the weighted guided filtering for refining decision map.

$$W_n^A = WGF_{r1}(DM_n, I_n) \tag{12}$$

$$W_n^D = WGF_{r2}(DM_n, I_n) \tag{13}$$

where WGF is the weighted guided filter and W_n^A and W_n^D are the approximation and detail layers of weight map. r1 and r2 are the size of WGF which are set to 45 and 7 in this implementation. Finally, all the N weight maps are normalized such that the summation at each corresponding pixel k of all N weight maps give result one. The refined weight maps obtained are passed to next step for final fusion. The base layers look spatially smooth and thus the corresponding weights also should be spatially smooth. Otherwise, artificial edges may be produced. In contrast, sharp and edge-aligned weights are preferred for fusing the detail layers since details may be lost when the weights are over-smoothed. Therefore, a large filter size and a large blur degree are preferred for fusing the base layers, while a small filter size and a small blur degree are preferred for the detail layers.

3.5   Entropy Weighted Image Fusion

Here we introduce a novel entropy weighted average scheme for fusion. The approximate and detail components of different source images are fused together by entropy based weighted averaging scheme.

$$E = \sum_{n=1}^{N} Entropy(I_n) \tag{14}$$

$$E_n = Entropy(I_n)/E \tag{15}$$

E represents the total entropy measure of all input images and E_n indicates the contribution of each input n.

$$A_F = \sum_{n=1}^{N}(W_n^A * (A_n * E_n))$$ (16)

$$D_F = \sum_{n=1}^{N}(W_n^D * (D_n * E_n))$$ (17)

A_n and D_n represents the base and detail layers respectively of input image n. Then, the fused image F is obtained by combining the fused base layer A_F and the fused detail layer D_F.

$$F = A_F + D_F$$ (18)

4   Experiments and Discussions

We performed experiments to verify the feasibility of our proposed image fusion method for multi-exposure images. Different image quality metrics measure the visual quality of images from different aspects, but none of them can directly measure the quality. So inorder to assess the fusion performance we have considered three performance metrics. The Execution Time (ET) measures the time required to perform fusion. Mutual Information (MI) [6] measures how much information the fused image conveys about the source images. Finally here a new Non Reference Image Quality Assessment (NR-IQA) [11] is used to evaluate the quality of final fused image.

Table 1. Source input image specification

Input	Size
Belgium House-Dani Lischinski (a)	$384 \times 512 \times 9$
Cadik Lamp-Martin Cadik (b)	$384 \times 512 \times 15$
Cave-Bartlomiej Okonek (c)	$384 \times 512 \times 4$
Farmhouse-hdr-project.com (d)	$341 \times 512 \times 3$
Balloons-Erik Reinhard (e)	$339 \times 512 \times 9$
House-Tom Mertens09 (f)	$340 \times 512 \times 4$
Kluki-Bartlomiej Okonek (g)	$341 \times 512 \times 3$
MadisonCapitol-Chaman Singh Verma (h)	$384 \times 512 \times 30$
Memorial-Debevec97 (i)	$512 \times 381 \times 16$
Office-Matlab (j)	$340 \times 512 \times 6$

The experiment was conducted on different sets of multi-exposed inputs. Here results obtained for a sample of 10 input sets (denoted as a to j) from

Waterloo IVC multi-exposure fusion image database (see [11] and [10]) are shown in Tables 2, 3 and 4. The specification of sample data is given in Table 1. The proposed fusion method is compared with two other image fusion algorithms GFF [19] and GD-GFF [24] which also used edge preserving smoothing filters for fusion.

Fig. 2. Input sequence (i, ii, iii and iv) of House-Tom Mertens09 and Fused result (v)

Sample input sequence of 'House-Tom Mertens09' (f) and the corresponding fused result is shown in Fig. 2. The fused result images for all the 10 sample inputs from Table 1 are shown in Fig. 3.

It is evident from the performance measures that the results of our proposed method are better than [24] and [19] for all input sequences. Obviously, we can observe the increase in MI values which indicates the information retained in fused result. Compared with those existing methods, the proposed algorithm transfers almost all of the useful information of the source images to the fused images. From Table 2 it is clear that the fusion results of the proposed fusion method are superior to other fusion methods in [19] and [24] in terms of MI values for all sample images considered. Also in connection to IQA score it is clear that the proposed method outperformed the other fusion methods. The key feature with our proposed methods is that they offer a satisfactory IQA score for all categories of input image sequences. The proposed method successfully operates

Table 2. Mutual Information

Input	GFF [19]	GD-GFF [24]	Proposed method
Belgium House-Dani Lischinski (a)	1.11	0.99	**1.38**
Cadik Lamp-Martin Cadik (b)	0.61	0.54	**0.65**
Cave-Bartlomiej Okonek (c)	1.78	1.69	**1.80**
Farmhouse-hdr-project.com (d)	2.55	2.57	**2.86**
Balloons-Erik Reinhard (e)	1.13	1.20	**1.29**
House-Tom Mertens09 (f)	0.73	0.66	**0.79**
Kluki-Bartlomiej Okonek (g)	1.53	1.41	**1.56**
Madison-Capitol (h)	0.84	0.65	**1.03**
Memorial-Debevec97 (i)	0.96	0.93	**1.01**
Office-Matlab (j)	1.02	1.21	**1.30**

its feature fusion model within less amount of time than other feature extraction models. The method in [19] is not used any feature extraction procedures but [24] employs a separate feature extraction model. Our proposed model outperforms both [19] and [24]. Even with the feature extraction step involved, the proposed method gives better results in terms of execution time; result of the same is shown in Table 4.

Fig. 3. Fused results of sample (a) to (j)

Table 3. NR-IQA

Input	GFF [19]	GD-GFF [24]	Proposed method
Belgium House-Dani Lischinski (a)	0.96395	0.99987	**0.99998**
Cadik Lamp-Martin Cadik (b)	0.92849	0.99988	**0.99997**
Cave-Bartlomiej Okonek (c)	0.97797	0.99991	**0.99999**
Farmhouse-hdr-project.com (d)	0.98469	0.99994	**0.99998**
Balloons-Erik Reinhard (e)	0.94755	0.99994	**0.99999**
House-Tom Mertens09 (f)	0.95676	0.99986	**0.99998**
Kluki-Bartlomiej Okonek (g)	0.96823	0.99993	**0.99999**
Madison-Capitol (h)	0.96788	0.99970	**0.99998**
Memorial-Debevec97 (i)	0.96833	0.99983	**0.99998**
Office-Matlab (j)	0.96742	0.99993	**0.99999**

Table 4. Execution time (in seconds)

Input & (without feature extraction) & (with feature extraction) & (with feature extraction)	GFF [19]	GD-GFF [24]	Proposed method
Belgium House-Dani Lischinski (a)	10.47	31.11	**9.96**
Cadik Lamp-Martin Cadik (b)	17.63	40.97	**16.69**
Cave-Bartlomiej Okonek (c)	4.66	20.81	**4.48**
Farmhouse-hdr-project.com (d)	3.21	16.95	**2.98**
Balloons-Erik Reinhard (e)	9.55	26.90	**9.02**
House-Tom Mertens09 (f)	4.13	19.30	**3.92**
Kluki-Bartlomiej Okonek (g)	3.20	17.96	**3.05**
Madison-Capitol (h)	34.48	67.82	**32.86**
Memorial-Debevec97 (i)	16.22	42.83	**15.42**
Office-Matlab (j)	6.07	24.26	**5.79**

5   Conclusion

In this paper we proposed a novel multi-exposure image fusion method which extracts multiple features and obtained the fused result by weighted guided filter. A decision map construction method is presented which uses contrast, saturation and exposedness as three key feature measures. This decision map construction improves the results with greater accuracy and execution efficiency. A feature level fusion approach is used in this method to obtain a higher level of decision making. The weighted guided filter is used for optimizing the decision maps for obtaining more accurate results all over the image, especially near edges. Finally an advanced entropy based weighted average fusion scheme generates outputs by allocating priority levels for different inputs based on their information content. Experimental results clearly demonstrate that the proposed algorithm can preserve the original and complementary information of multiple source images which are differently exposed better than other fusion methods. Despite this, we also found that different types of source images like multi-modal, multi-focus etc. adapt to different parameters. Thus, how to better choose the parameters according to different types of source images can be researched in future works.

Acknowledgement. The authors acknowledge DST - Promotion of University Research and Scientific Excellence (PURSE), Government of India.

References

1. Dogra, A., Goyal, B., Agrawal, S.: From multi-scale decomposition to non-multi-scale decomposition methods: a comprehensive survey of image fusion techniques and its applications. IEEE Access **5**, 16040–16067 (2017)
2. Moorthy, A.K., Mittal, A., Bovik, A.C.: Referenceless image spatial quality evaluation engine. In: 45th Asilomar Conference on Signals, Systems and Computers, November 2011
3. Mittal, A., Moorthy, A.K., Bovik, A.C.: No-reference image quality assessment in the spatial domain. IEEE Trans. Image Process. **21**, 4695–4708 (2012)
4. Yang, B., Li, S.: Multifocus image fusion and restoration with sparse representation. IEEE Trans. Instrum. Meas. **59**, 884–892 (2010)
5. Kou, F., Li, Z., Wen, C.: Multi-scale exposure fusion via gradient domain guided image filtering. In: IEEE International Conference on Multimedia and Expo (ICME), July 2017
6. Qu, G., Zhang, D., Yan, P.: Information measure for performance of image fusion. Electron. Lett. **38**(7), 313–315 (2002)
7. Li, H., Manjunath, B.S., Mitra, S.K.: Multisensor image fusion using the wavelet transform. Graph. Models Image Process. **57**(3), 235–245 (1995)
8. Zhao, H., Shang, Z., Tang, Y.Y., Fang, B.: Multi-focus image fusion based on the neighbor distance. Pattern Recogn. **46**, 1002–1011 (2013)
9. Liang, J., He, Y., Liu, D., Zeng, X.: Image fusion using higher order singular value decomposition. IEEE Trans. Image Process. **21**(5), 2898–2909 (2012)
10. Zeng, K., Ma, K., Hassen, R., Wang, Z.: Perceptual evaluation of multi-exposure image fusion algorithms. In: The 6th International Workshop on Quality of Multimedia Experience (QoMEX) (2014)
11. Ma, K., Zeng, K., Wang, Z.: Perceptual quality assessment for multi-exposure image fusion. IEEE Trans. Image Process. (TIP) **24**, 3345–3356 (2015)
12. Ma, K.D., Wang, Z.: Multi-exposure image fusion: a patch-wise approach. In: 2015 IEEE International Conference on Image Processing (ICIP), pp. 1717–1721 (2015)
13. Ma, K.D., Zeng, K., Wang, Z.: Perceptual quality assessment for multiexposure image fusion. IEEE Trans. Image Process. **24**(11), 3345–3356 (2015)
14. He, K., Sun, J., Tang, X.: Guided image filtering. IEEE Trans. Pattern Anal. Mach. Intell. **35**(6), 1397–1409 (2013)
15. Nejati, M., Samavi, S., Shirani, S.: Multi-focus image fusion using dictionary-based sparse representation. Inf. Fusion **25**, 72–84 (2015)
16. Miao, Q.G., Shi, C., Xu, P.-F., Yang, M., Shi, Y.-B.: A novel algorithm of image fusion using shearlets. Opt. Commun. **284**(6), 1540–1547 (2011)

17. Shen, R., Cheng, I., Shi, J., Basu, A.: Generalized random walks for fusion of multi-exposure images. IEEE Trans. Image Process. **20**, 3634–3646 (2011)

18. Li, S., Yang, B.: Multifocus image fusion using region segmentation and spatial frequency. Image Vis. Comput. **26**(7), 971–979 (2008)

19. Li, S., Kang, X., Hu, J.: Image fusion with guided filtering. IEEE Trans. Image Process. **22**(7), 2864–2875 (2013). https://doi.org/10.1109/TIP.2013.2244222

20. Yang, S., Wang, M., Jiao, L., Wu, R., Wang, Z.: Image fusion based on a new contourlet packet. Inf. Fusion **11**(2), 78–84 (2010)

21. Mertens, T., Kautz, J., Reeth, F.V.: Exposure fusion: a simple and practical alternative to high dynamic range photography. Comput. Graph. Forum **28**, 161–171 (2009)

22. Liu, Y., Liu, S., Wang, Z.: A general framework for image fusion based on multiscale transform and sparse representation. Inf. Fusion **24**, 147–164 (2015)

23. Yang, Y., Wan, W., Huang, S., Yuan, F., Que, Y.: Remote sensing image fusion based on adaptive IHS and multiscale guided filter. IEEE Access **4**, 4573–4582 (2016)

24. Yang, Y., Que, Y., Huang, S., Lin, P.: Multiple visual features measurement with gradient domain guided filtering for multisensor image fusion. IEEE Trans. Instrum. Meas. **66**(4), 691–703 (2017). https://doi.org/10.1109/TIM.2017.2658098

25. Li, Z.G., Zheng, J.H., Rahardja, S.: Detail-enhanced exposure fusion. IEEE Trans. Image Process. **21**(11), 4672–4676 (2012)

26. Li, Z., Zheng, J., Zhu, Z., Yao, W., Wu, S.: Weighted guided image filtering. IEEE Trans. Image Process. **24**(1), 120–129 (2015). https://doi.org/10.1109/TIP.2014.2371234

27. Jagtap, A.B., Hegadi, R.S.: Offline handwritten signature recognition based on upper and lower envelope using eigen values. In: World Congress on Computing and Communication Technologies (WCCCT), pp. 223–226. IEEE (2017)

Multi-frame Super Resolution Using Enhanced Papoulis-Gerchberg Method

K. Joseph Abraham Sundar[1]($\boxtimes$) (iD) and R. Sekar[2]

[1] School of Computing, SASTRA Deemed University,
Thanjavur 613401, Tamil Nadu, India
kjoseph_88@yahoo.com
[2] Department of Electronics and Communication Engineering,
Koneru Lakshmaiah Education Foundation, Vaddeshwaram,
Guntur 522502, Andhra Pradesh, India
shekharmohith09@kluniversity.in

Abstract. The research work, discusses the Papoulis-Gerchberg method with re-spect to image restoration procedure called super resolution image reconstruction. This underlined work also demonstrates that Papoulis-Gerchberg performs well only in certain conditions. Modifications are proposed to the Papoulis-Gerchberg method to obtain better super resolution results. The proposed modifications overcome the restrictions of Papoulis-Gerchberg method making it possible on a wide range of images. The suggested modification not only improves the quality of the image but also reduces the computation complexity. The proposed method has greater advantage and high computation speed which is most needed for most of the applications in the real world. The results for the modified Papoulis-Gerchberg are presented to demonstrate its performance.

Keywords: Super resolution · Image registration ·
Image reconstruction · Back projection

1 Introduction

Super resolution is defined as the process of obtaining a high-resolution (HR) image from a group of low resolution (LR) images which are sub-pixel shifted from one another. In the process of Super Resolution Image Reconstruction (SRIR) we try to create high frequency components and reduce the error due to noise, aliasing and blur. Various researches have been proposed and carried out to generate high super resolution images.

Contemporary research work [1] used multiple aperture camera system to enhance the image resolution. The research work [2] proposed frequency domain technique, a predominant method for SRIR. In this technique, the low frequency image is accounted as aliased signal in frequency domain and to predict the de-aliased signal which is high resolution frame. A drawback noticed in the frequency domain technique is the numerous restrictions lay over the observation

© Springer Nature Singapore Pte Ltd. 2019
K. C. Santosh and R. S. Hegadi (Eds.): RTIP2R 2018, CCIS 1035, pp. 667–677, 2019.
https://doi.org/10.1007/978-981-13-9181-1_57

model. More over construction needs advance knowledge about the data and a highly computational process because data is inter-correlated in frequency domain. The recent research work [2] has proposed a technique called projection on to convex sets. In this technique, the HR frame is obtained by including a cost function that depends on the linear model which explains the relation between the HR and LR frames. But the use of linear model produces a trivial solution and computation process is also very high. The statistical method for SRIR stands on Bayesian method [3] uses greatest probability to predict the solution. This technique neglects the high frequency of the edge information and henceforth minimizing the quality of HR frame. Recent years have given many reconstruction methods in spatial domain which are [4–9]. The SRIR is also proposed using singular value decomposition [10,11] were the singular values from the decomposed matrix is chosen using maximum operator to reconstruct a HR frame. These spatial domain methods can incorporate spatial domain early information in the formulation. Moreover, they are not limited by non-global translational motion as spatial domain methods are not much sensitive to it. But in general, the computational cost of the spatial domain methods is high. The latest advances around SR image are the introduction of wavelet transformation [12]. Initially the image analysis was the first path to which wavelets was introduced called as multi-resolution theory. In this the images analysis was carried on in different resolutions as the name rightly indicated. It uses the reverse wavelet transform for joining the LR frames that are introduced into different level of decomposition to give out a HR frame. The tight frames with perfect reconstruction condition and the symmetric property of the framelet have made framelet more advantageous than wavelets as proposed by [13,14]. Contemporary research work [15] proposed an adaptive block matching filtering technique where modifications are done in the observation models of super-resolution. In this method, the reconstruction algorithm of wavelets is also modified into general scaling transform. But the algorithm totally depends on the prior knowledge of the blurring model. Kernel regression method for super resolution has been proposed by [16]. This technique make use of the Taylor series in the process of defining of every pixel values in the image which plays a major role in defining the behavior of the neighborhood pixels. The preliminary advantage of this technique is that it requires no information about the motion estimation as a preprocessing stage. In case we extract different image layers by using fuzzy binarization, we will be able to extract more information [17,18]. The research [19,20] has proposed a method for signal reconstruction. This method has some drawbacks which we overcome by proposed modifications. The proposed modifications overcome the restrictions of Papoulis-Gerchberg method making it possible on a wide range of images. The suggested modification not only improves the quality of the image but also reduces the computation complexity. In Sect. 2 we present the Papoulis-Gerchberg method with respect to super resolution reconstruction application. Modifications to Papoulis-Gerchberg are given in Sect. 3. The results are presented in Sect. 4 in order to show the performance improvement.

2   Papoulis-Gerchberg Method

The Papoulis-Gerchberg method has evolved as a result of two independent works by Papoulis and Gerchberg. The idea of Gerchberg [20] work is to perform signal reconstruction given a part of spectrum and also the diffraction limit of a signal. The idea of Papoulis [19] is to determine the transform

$$P(\sigma) = \int_{-\infty}^{+\infty} p(t)e^{-j\sigma t}\, dt \tag{1}$$

of a signal $p(t)$ given a finite segment [19]

$$r(t) = p(t)s_T(t) \tag{2}$$

where

$$s_T(t) = \begin{cases} 1, & |t| \leq T \\ 0, & |t| > T \end{cases}$$

The signal $r(t)$ is low pass filter having cut off frequency ω. It is also considered ω is the signal bandwidth of $p(t)$. For nth iteration, this is given as [16]

$$P_n(\sigma) = G_{n-1}(\sigma)s_\sigma(\sigma), \quad s_\sigma(\sigma) = \begin{cases} 1, & |\sigma| \leq \omega \\ 0, & |\sigma| > \omega \end{cases} \tag{3}$$

The inverse of $P_1(\sigma)$ is calculated as $p1(t)$. Obviously the signal $p1(t)$ is not similar to the detected signal $r(t)$ in the region $[-T, T]$. This portion of the signal is then back projected to the original segment creating the function $r_1(t)$ for the next iteration. After each iteration, the MSE is reduced and the signal approaches the desired signal $p(t)$. But to achieve this infinite number of iterations are required.

2.1   SRIR Using Papoulis-Gerchberg Method

The Papoulis-Gerchberg [19, 20] method can be applied with only one LR frame. Here the LR frame is considered on a high dimensional grid having and unknown values of pixel. Zero has been assigned to the unknown pixel values. Then the low pass filter with standardized cut off frequency of ω is applied on the image. During this process of filtering the unknown pixels get new values. But there are changes in the known pixel values also causing blur in the image. Finally, in order to recover the values of known pixels high frequency components are created. The entire procedure is repeated.

The method seems to be fast but it has several drawbacks. Ringing artifacts appears near the edges when the cut of frequency is steep. Here the images need to be free from blur and noise since the reconstruction process is carried out without any filtering process. With such restrictions and drawbacks, the Papoulis-Gerchberg method cannot be considered for good reconstruction.

3   Enhanced Papoulis-Gerchberg Method

In this section, we first talk about the proposed modifications done to the Papoulis-Gerchberg method followed by the entire algorithm for enhanced Papoulis-Gerchberg method.

Initially the group of LR frames are registered by the method proposed by Vanderwalle in [21]. So, unlike the Papoulis-Gerchberg method the low resolution image need not be a single image. In enhanced Papoulis-Gerchberg method we see to that after every iteration the resolved image adapts to the LR frame. In order to do this the [4] is used in the Papoulis-Gerchberg method. In order to incorporate the iterative back projection we estimate the error between LR frames and simulated LR frames. The expression for error E_i is given by

$$E_i = \chi - DBf_i \qquad (4)$$

where χ is the LR frame, D is the down sample operator, B is the blur operator and f_i is the estimated super resolution image that we get after i iterations. To overcome this error we update the image by adding the error to the respective pixels in the obtained super resolution image. The expression for the image update is given by the expression below

$$f_i = f_i + H(E_i) \qquad (5)$$

where H projects the error in LR space to HR space. H is also a matrix operator. The ideal condition for H should be $H = (DB)^{-1}$. Practically it is not possible to find the inverse of blur and sampling operators. So in the experiments carried out we have added the error E_i back to every pixel in the respective high resolution block. The help of point spread function has been used in deciding the size of block. Due to this adjustment, some blocking artifacts appear in the super resolution image. These blocking artifacts are greatly reduced as it enters into the next iteration with the help of low pass filter. The image approaches the desired high resolution image after every iteration. So as the number of iteration increases the original high resolution image may be obtained, but practically increasing the iterations increases the computation intensity for the algorithm. To avoid this we introduce a terminating condition. This terminating condition is based on the threshold value we fix for the error given by Eq. (4). This terminating condition reduces the number of iteration which obviously reduces the computation power required for the algorithm. The image becomes more resolved when the threshold value is small. The usage of back projection of error and the low pass filtering at every iteration make the image smoother.

The pseudo-code for enhanced Papoulis-Gerchberg method is as follows

$x \rightarrow$ Low resolution image which is the input

$f \rightarrow$ High resolution grid

$D \rightarrow$ Down sample operator

$H \rightarrow$ Back projection operator

$B \rightarrow$ Blur operator

loop

$F \rightarrow FFT(f)$

$\hat{F} \rightarrow$ Lowpass filter with cut $-$ off frequency ω

$f \rightarrow IFFT(\hat{F})$

//Error Calculation//

$E \rightarrow \chi - DBf$

if $|E| \leq threshold$ then

terminate loop

else

$f \rightarrow f + H(E)$

endif

end loop

4   Results and Discussions

In this section, the data used for the experiments followed by the experimental results obtained with comparison with various existing methods and finally the discussion over these results are discussed.

4.1   Experimental Setting

To experiment the capability of the enhanced Papoulis-Gerchberg method, five data sets are used. In these, the first three data sets (image sets) are simulated images and we call it as simulated experiments. The remaining two data sets are real time data and we call it as real time experiments.

In each of the experiments Vanderwalle technique [21] of image registration is considered for the registration process. To assess the reconstruction results, PSNR and sharpness index [22] are applied for simulated experiments. The HR frame is needed for calculation of PSNR which is unknown in the samples of real data experiment.

So, for the real data experiments performance measure of the quality of the image was performed on the basis of quality index BIQI [23] and sharpness index. For the simulated and real time experiments the greater the value of the quality indices higher will be the image quality. The merits of the proposed model are compared with basic Papoulis-Gerchberg method, Projection onto convex set method, Adaptive block-matching filtering method, Kernel regression method.

4.2   Experimental Results

The simulated data sets involved for the simulated experiments are taken from MSPRG [24]. For minimizing the computational complexity, the immediate four frames from are selected. Figs. 1, 2 and 3 shows the results of these three data sets. In this Figs. (a) LR frame; (b) Papoulis-Gerchberg method; (c) Projection onto convex set method; (d) Adaptive block-matching filtering method (e) is enhanced Papoulis-Gerchberg method.

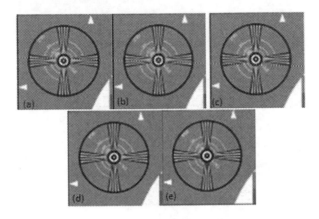

Fig. 1. "EIA" image sequence. (a) LR frame (b) Projection onto convex set method (c) Papoulis-Gerchberg method (d) Adaptive block-matching filtering method (e) Enhanced Papoulis-Gerchberg method

The performance measure results are tabulated in Table 1. This proves that the proposed enhanced Papoulis-Gerchberg method has the maximum values of Peak Signal to Noise Ratio and Sharpness index which is in line with the results presented in Figs. 1, 2 and 3.

Table 1. Performance measure of different reconstruction methods in simulated

LR sequence	Assessment index	Papoulis Gerchberg method	Projection onto convex set method	Adaptive block-matching filtering method	Enhanced Papoulis-Gerchberg method
EIA	PSNR	26.09	27.66	28.35	29.00
	Sharpness index	19.92	19.98	20.68	21.90
Alpaca	PSNR	29.08	30.12	30.44	31.00
	Sharpness index	20.99	21.09	21.16	22.12
Disk	PSNR	28.87	29.35	30.20	34.01
	Sharpness index	17.49	18.22	19.11	20.36

Fig. 2. "Alpaca" image sequence. (a) LR frame (b) Projection onto convex set method (c) Papoulis-Gerchberg method (d) Adaptive block-matching filtering method (e) Enhanced Papoulis-Gerchberg method

In experiments carried on using the real data, two videos captured by an aerial vehicle are used. The first one namely "Aerial 1" has 297 frames. Second one namely "Aerial 2" has 438 frames. Figures 4 and 5 show the results of the two real data. In these figures, (a) LR frame; (b) is the re-construction result of Papoulis-Gerchberg method; (c) is the reconstruction result of Projection onto convex set method; (d) is Adaptive block-matching filtering method reconstruction result; and (e) is enhanced Papoulis-Gerchberg method reconstruction result.

The achievement of the proposed enhanced Papoulis-Gerchberg method is also shown by the Blind Image Quality Index and sharpness index tabulated in Table 2. The table proves that enhanced Papoulis-Gerchberg method has the greatest values of BIQI and sharpness index, which illustrates that the proposed enhanced Papoulis-Gerchberg method produces a better reconstruction result.

Fig. 3. "Disk" image sequence. (a) LR frame (b) Projection onto convex set method (c) Papoulis-Gerchberg method (d) Adaptive block-matching filtering method (e) Enhanced Papoulis-Gerchberg method

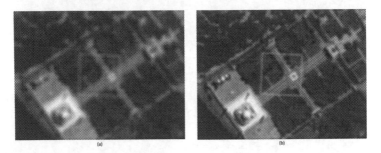

Fig. 4. "Aerial1" image sequence. (a) LR frame (b) Projection onto convex set method

4.3 Discussion

Using Super Resolution technique the resolution of the frame has improved which is highly evident from the figures and tables presented above. The results can be

Fig. 5. (c) Papoulis-Gerchberg method (d) Adaptive block-matching filtering method (e) En-hanced Papoulis-Gerchberg method

Fig. 6. "Aerial2" image sequence. (a) LR frame (b) Projection onto convex set method

Table 2. Performance measure of different reconstruction methods in real data

LR sequence	Assessment index	Papoulis Gerchberg method	Projection onto convex set method	Adaptive block-matching filtering method	Enhanced Papoulis-Gerchberg method
Aerial 1	BIQI	40.44	41.58	43.67	56.18
	Sharpness index	5.45	5.48	5.62	5.75
Aerial 2	BIQI	18.83	20.69	23.39	31.50
	Sharpness index	4.94	5.02	5.20	5.51

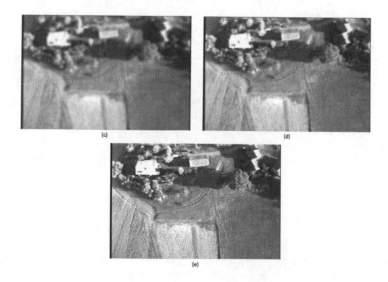

Fig. 7. (c) Papoulis-Gerchberg method (d) Adaptive block-matching filtering method (e) En-hanced Papoulis-Gerchberg method

interpreted very clearly in the case of the real time experiments. The numbers in Fig. 1(e) appear much clear that the numbers in any other figures. In Fig. 2(e) the artifacts along the edges is not seen and appears to be smooth, but in Fig. 2(a–d) the artifacts are clearly visible along the edges. In the disk image shown in Fig. 3(e), the word "color makes" could be clearly identified in the case of enhanced Papoulis-Gerchberg method. In the case of real time data Fig. 5(e) shows that the blurring effect has reduced to greater extent compared to Fig. 5(a) to (d) (Figs. 6 and 7).

5   Conclusion

In this paper we proposed an enhanced Papoulis-Gerchberg method of super resolution reconstruction. The inclusion of back projection of error has reduced the blurring effect in the enhanced Papoulis Gerchberg method. The enhanced Papoulis Gerchberg method has also reduced the number of iteration by inducing a threshold for the error. This reduces the computational power greatly. Thus the suggested modification in the PG technique is fast and simple. The results and analysis of the experiments illustrates that suggested modification in the PG technique is greatly advantageous and provides better performance improvement than other methods.

References

1. Komatsu, T., Igarashi, T., Aizawa, K., Saito, T.: Very high resolution imaging scheme with multiple different-aperture cameras. Sig. Process. Image Commun. **5**(93), 511–526 (1993). https://doi.org/10.1016/0923-5965(93)90014-K
2. Hardeep, P., Prashant, B., Joshi, S.M.: A survey on techniques and challenges in image super resolution reconstruction. Int. J. Comput. Sci. Mobile Comput. **2**(4), 317–325 (2013)
3. Babacan, S.D., Molina, R., Katsaggelos, A.K.: Variational Bayesian super resolution. IEEE Trans. Image Process. **20**(4), 984–999 (2011). https://doi.org/10.1109/TIP.2010.2080278
4. Tom, B.C., Katsaggelos, A.K.: Reconstruction of a high-resolution image by simultaneous registration, restoration, and interpolation of low-resolution images. In: Proceedings of Interntional Conference on Image Process, pp. 539–542. IEEE, Washington, DC, USA, February 1995
5. Schultz, R.R., Stevenson, R.L.: Extraction of high-resolution frames from video sequences. IEEE Trans. Image Process. **5**(6), 996–1011 (1996). https://doi.org/10.1109/83.503915
6. Belekos, S.P., Galatsanos, N.P., Katsaggelos, A.K.: Maximum a posteriori video super-resolution using a new multichannel image prior. IEEE Trans. Image Process. **19**(6), 1451–1464 (2010). https://doi.org/10.1109/TIP.2010.2042115
7. Elad, M., Feuer, A.: Restoration of a single superresolution image from several blurred, noisy, and under sampled measured images. IEEE Trans. Image Process. **6**(12), 1646–1658 (1997). https://doi.org/10.1109/83.650118
8. Nguyen, N., Milanfar, P.: A wavelet-based interpolation-restoration method for super resolution (wavelet super resolution). Circuits Syst. Signal Process. **19**(4), 321–338 (2000). https://doi.org/10.1007/BF01200891

9. Sundar, K.J.A., Divyalakhsmi, K., Ahmed, M.I., Sivagami, R., Sangeetha, V., Vaithiyanathan, V.: Super resolution image reconstruction using frequency spectrum. Indian J. Sci. Technol. **8**(35), 1–5 (2015)

10. Sundar, K.J.A., Vaithiyanathan, V., Manickavasagam, M., Sarkar, A.K.: Enhanced singular value decomposition based fusion for super resolution image reconstruction. Defence Sci. J. **65**(6), 459–465 (2015). https://doi.org/10.14429/dsj.65.8336

11. Sundar, K.J.A., Vaithiyanathan, V.: Multi-frame super-resolution using adaptive normalized convolution. Sig. Image Video Process. **11**(2), 357–362 (2017)

12. Fermüller, C.: Robust wavelet-based super-resolution reconstruction: theory and algorithm. IEEE Trans. Pattern Anal. Mach. Intell. **31**(4), 649–660 (2009). https://doi.org/10.1109/TPAMI.2008.103

13. Sundar, K.J.A., Vaithiyanathan, V., Thangadurai, G.R.S., Namdeo, N.: Design and analysis of fusion algorithm for multi-frame super-resolution image reconstruction using framelet. Defence Sci. J. **65**(4), 292–299 (2015)

14. Sundar, KJ.A., Jahnavi, M., Lakshmisaritha, K.: Multi-sensor image fusion based on empirical wavelet transform. In: International Conference on Electrical, Electronics, Communication Computer Technologies and Optimization Techniques, ICEECCOT, Mysuru, India, pp. 93–97 (2017)

15. Danielyan, A., Foi, A., Katkovnik, V., Egiazarian, K.: Image and video super-resolution via spatially adaptive block-matching filtering. In: Proceedings of International Workshop on Local and Non-local Approximation in Image Process, pp. 1–8 (2008)

16. Takeda, H., Milanfar, P., Protter, M., Elad, M.: Super-resolution without explicit subpixel motion estimation. IEEE Trans. Image Process. **18**(9), 1958–1975 (2009). https://doi.org/10.1109/TIP.2009.2023703

17. Santosh, K.C., Wendling, L., Antani, S., Thoma, G.R.: Overlaid arrow detection for labeling regions of interest in biomedical images. IEEE Intell. Syst. **31**(3), 66–75 (2016)

18. Santosh, K.C., Roy, P.P.: Arrow detection in biomedical images using sequential classifier. Int. J. Mach. Learn. Cybern. **9**(6), 993–1006 (2018)

19. Papoulis, A.: A new algorithm in spectral analysis and band-limited extrapolation. IEEE Trans. Circ. Syst. **22**(9), 735–742 (1975). https://doi.org/10.1109/TCS.1975.1084118

20. Gerchberg, R.W.: Super-resolution through error energy reduction. Opt. Acta Int. J. Opt. **21**(9), 709–720 (1974). https://doi.org/10.1080/713818946

21. Vandewalle, P., Susstrunk, S.: Super resolution images reconstructed from aliased images. In: Proceedings of SPIE/IS&T Visual Communications and Image Processing Conference, Lugano, Switzerland, pp. 1398–1405 (2003). https://doi.org/10.1117/12.506874

22. Feichtenhofer, C., Fassold, H., Schallauer, P.: A perceptual image sharpness metric based on local edge gradient analysis. IEEE Sig. Process. Lett. **20**(12), 379–382 (2013)

23. Moorthy, A.K., Bovik, A.C.: A two-step framework for constructing blind image quality indices. IEEE Sig. Process. Lett. **17**(5), 513–516 (2010). https://doi.org/10.1109/LSP.2010.2043888

24. Milanfar, P: MDSP super-resolution and demosaicing datasets [Online]. http://users.soe.ucsc.edu/~milanfar/software/srdatasets.html. Accessed Sept 2018

Bit-Plane Specific Selective Histogram Equalization for Image Enhancement and Representation

Arvind[1] and Ram Ratan[2(✉)]

[1] Hansraj College, University of Delhi, Delhi, India
arvind_ashu12@rediffmail.com
[2] Scientific Analysis Group, Defence Research and Development Organization,
Delhi, India
ramratan_sag@hotmail.com

Abstract. Images acquired in poor acquisition conditions which are unavoidable and cannot be ignored in many visual applications require enhancement to achieve high contrast for better representation and interpretation of image objects. For efficient image storage and communications, compression and preserving of image details is required apart from contrast enhancement. A popular histogram equalization approach leaves undesirable artefacts in enhanced images and increases its data size due to excessive contrast enhancement. In this paper, we present a bit-plane specific selective histogram equalization technique which narrows the range of enhanced image than original image and keeps image details intact without unnoticeable artefacts with reduced image data size. The qualitative and quantitative measures as visual perception, histogram, edge details, entropy, data storage size, mean intensity and mean square error obtained for different images demonstrate the effectiveness of the selective bit-plane specific histogram equalization over to other methods of histogram equalization.

Keywords: Digital image · Edges detection · Entropy ·
Histogram equalization · Image enhancement · Image compression ·
Image measures

1 Introduction

In modern era of computer and multimedia technology, most of the information is accesses in visual form as images in various applications such as whether forecasting, medical imaging object tracking, combating terrorism, urban planning, biometric access control and even entertainment. In these applications the good quality of images is required to understand and interpret image contents accurately. In many situations, the acquisition conditions are not favourable to acquire image with reasonable good quality due to scanning errors and environmental disturbances. Poor image acquisition conditions are often unavoidable

© Springer Nature Singapore Pte Ltd. 2019
K. C. Santosh and R. S. Hegadi (Eds.): RTIP2R 2018, CCIS 1035, pp. 678–687, 2019.
https://doi.org/10.1007/978-981-13-9181-1_58

but these can be compensated in various vision based applications through image enhancement. Image enhancement techniques improve the quality of poor contrast images by rescaling gray labels or suppressing noise from noisy images by gray label interpolation for better appearance [1]. Contrast enhancement of an image can be taken as the slope of the mapping function which modifies the gray labels of input image to give enhanced output image. Higher the slope of mapping function gives higher enhancement. Contrast of an image can be enhanced by stretching its gray labels within the available dynamic range or equalizing its histogram [2]. In histogram equalization (HE) method, slope of mapping function is driven by the cumulative histogram where contrast enhancement is proportional to the height of histogram at gray labels. In the histogram of an image, high peaks are appeared due to nearly uniform regions of an image. Poor contrast images have certain characteristics such as the occurrences at some places on the gray scale are very high and very small in the rest of the gray scale in histograms which makes it difficult to improve the contrast of such images.

This paper is related to the image enhancement based on HE which can be performed locally or globally to enhance the contrast of images. Various image enhancement techniques based on histogram modification such as histogram stretching, specification and histogram equalization have been reported. The HE method is widely used in almost all kinds of images to enhance the contrast of images [1–3]. The HE method maps narrow range of input gray labels to a wide range of gray labels within the available dynamic range. It enhances the appearance of image content but leaves undesirable artefacts and information loss in enhanced image due to excessive contrast enhancement [4]. Another version of HE is the Contrast Limited Adaptive Histogram Equalization (CLAHE) in which histogram of an image is clipped for some gray values of histogram prior to apply HE method [5]. There are some other versions of HE such as Adaptive Histogram Equalization (AHE) which divide given image into non-overlapping blocks and each block is processed by HE [6–8] and Dynamic Histogram Equalization (DHE) which performs HE for specified values of histogram [9,10]. In case of block based histogram equalization, a blocking effect may appears near the block boundaries. In sub-image based histogram equalization, a given image is segmented into sub regions and each region is histogram equalized. In bi-histogram equalization, a histogram of given image is segmented into sub-regions and each sub-region is equalized individually [11,12]. The comparative study and survey on some histogram equalization methods are reported in some of the paper [13–16]. A bit planes based histogram equalization for high contrast images is also reported in a paper [17]. For image enhancement, some soft computing based histogram equalization methods are also reported [18,19]. Achieving good quality of enhanced images, preserving image details intact and compressing image data high are very much required in efficient image information management for image communication or storage during transition or at rest. Conventional histogram equalization approaches increase image data size. The compressibility is attained by reducing the dynamic range of gray levels. The reduction of dynamic range of enhanced image is also helpful to display and view such high contrast images on low resolution display devices with lesser degradation of image quality.

We present a Selective Bit-plane Histogram Equalization (SBPHE) method, in this paper, which keeps image details intact without unnoticeable artefacts with edge preserving capability and reduced image data size. The qualitative and quantitative measures such as visual perception, histogram, edge details, entropy, data storage size, mean intensity and mean square error measured for different images demonstrate the effectiveness of the presented SBPHE method over to other histogram equalization methods. Various qualitative and quantitative measures for assessing the quality of images are reported in the literature and one can see [20–23] for detail on such measures.

The rest of the paper is organized as follows. Section 2 presents the SBPHE method. The performance of SBPHE method is demonstrated in Sect. 3 by presenting resulting images and measuring various qualitative and quantitative measures. Paper is concluded in Sect. 4 followed by the references.

2   Methodology of Selective Bit-Plane Histogram Equalization (SBPHE)

Image enhancement methodology consists of the following steps:

2.1   Image Decomposition in Bit-Planes

Digital images known as Gray level images are represented normally with 8 bit per pixel. An image can be decomposed in bit-planes as BP_1 to BP_8, where BP_1 is known as least significant bit (LSB) plane and BP_8 is known as most significant bit (MSB) plane. After processing bit-planes, these can be combined together in their order to get the processed image. As an example, Fig. 1 shows an image of Monalisa and its bit-planes.

2.2   Histogram Equalization (HE)

For an image, $I(x,y)$, $0 \leq I(x,y) \leq 255$, $1 \leq x \leq M$, $1 \leq y \leq N$, $M \times N$ is the size of $I(x,y)$.

The Probability Density Function (PDF) is given as $P(G) = n_g/(M \times N)$, where, n_g is the occurrence of gary level g and $(M \times N)$ is the number of pixels in an image.

For performing HE, a transformation function based on Cumulative Density Function (CDF) is used which is given as

$$s_k = T(r_k) = \sum_{i=0}^{k} p(r_i), 0 \leq k \leq 255.$$

Transfer function is a monotonically increasing single valued function, $0 \leq T(r_k) \leq 1$ for $0 \leq r_k \leq 1$. The s_k maps uniformly over the range of intensities 0 to 255 to get an enhanced image.

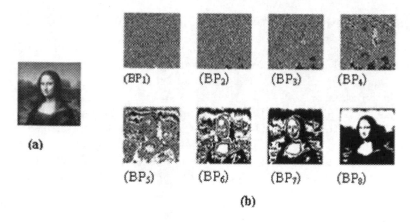

(a)

(BP₁)   (BP₂)   (BP₃)   (BP₄)

(BP₅)   (BP₆)   (BP₇)   (BP₈)

(b)

Fig. 1. Image and its Bit-planes: (a) Monalisa (b) Bit-planes

HE also known as Global Histogram Equalization (GHE) considers overall histogram of an image as its transformation function. It cannot adopt local conditions of an image and results deterioration of background and small objects.

2.3 Bit-Plane Histogram Equalization (BPHE)

We extract bit-planes of an image and perform HE on each bit-planes. The histogram equalized bit-planes are combined together [17] to get enhanced image. The bit-planes of Monalisa image obtained after histogram equalization on bit-planes are shown in Fig. 2.

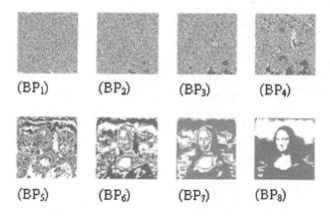

(BP₁)   (BP₂)   (BP₃)   (BP₄)

(BP₅)   (BP₆)   (BP₇)   (BP₈)

Fig. 2. Histogram equalization of individual bit-planes of Monalisa image

The bit-planes of histogram equalized image look smooth as compared to bit-planes of original image.

2.4   Selective Bit-Planes Histogram Equalization (SBPHE)

It is seen from Fig. 1 that LSB planes of an image look random and unintelligible and Performing their histogram equalization is not giving any advantage to attain enhancement. So, it is not necessary to perform histogram equalization for all the bit-planes.

We consider only five MSB planes for performing histogram equalization. Five MSB planes are sufficient to get enhanced image with reasonable contrast, edge details and compression with reduced dynamic range.

As we discarded three LSB planes, histogram equalization of selected bit-planes takes less processing time compared to histogram equalization of all bit-planes.

The processed images for Monalisa after applying HE, BPHE and SBPHE are shown in Fig. 3.

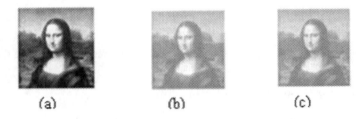

(a)   (b)   (c)

Fig. 3. Image of Monalisa after (a) HE, (b) BPHE, (c) SBPHE

3   Results and Discussions

The HE, BPHE and SBPHE methods are applied on a number of images to study their performance. We consider the images of size 256×256 and 512×512 as shown in Fig. 4. The images in first row of Fig. 4, each of size 256×256, are taken from MATLAB, Google etc. And the images in second row of Fig. 4, each of size 512×521, are taken from a standard image database [24]. The MATLAB platform is used to obtain the results.

We consider visual perception, edge detail and histogram as qualitative measures and entropy, data size required for storing, mean intensity value and mean square error (MSE) as quantitative measures to see the performance of HE, BPHE and SBPHE methods. We apply Canny edge detector [25,26] for finding edge details and JPEG image format [27] for finding data size needed for storing original and processed images. The Canny edge detection performs better than other gradient based edge detectors as it is less sensitive to the noise. The JPEG image file format is the most common format for storing and transmitting images on the World Wide Web.

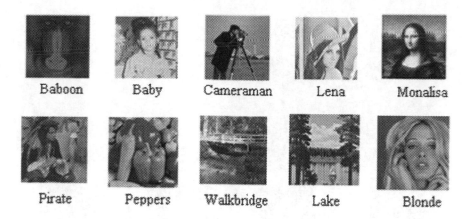

Baboon   Baby   Cameraman   Lena   Monalisa

Pirate   Peppers   Walkbridge   Lake   Blonde

Fig. 4. Input Images for evaluating performance of SBPHE

The resulting image obtained by HE, BPHE and SBPHE methods for Baby and Monalisa images are shown in Fig. 5 which shows the visual perception, histogram and edge details.

The values of entropy and data size requirement measured for original and processed images are shown in Table 1.

Table 1. Entropy and data size values for original and processed images

Image	Original		HE		BPHE		SBPHE	
	Entropy	Byte	Entropy	Byte	Entropy	Byte	Entropy	Byte
Baboon	6.6962	12867	5.9379	24223	5.6121	07813	5.6920	07943
Baby	7.1482	11781	5.8550	16318	5.8626	10945	6.1337	11004
Cameraman	7.0097	10717	5.9106	14868	5.7259	09834	5.9249	10107
Lena	7.2486	09953	5.9684	13288	6.1626	09179	6.2735	09323
Monalisa	7.6916	10363	5.9777	10799	6.2483	05669	6.3482	06004
Pirate	7.2367	43098	5.9258	57382	5.8566	25859	5.9687	26607
Peppers	6.7624	35489	5.8674	48102	6.0021	19824	6.0166	20495
Walkbridge	7.6830	61325	5.9865	75346	6.2024	39175	6.2686	39186
Lake	7.4826	44108	5.9726	57090	6.0554	30176	6.1487	30921
Blonde	6.9542	41037	5.9587	61830	5.8838	33210	5.9355	34170

We observe from Fig. 5 that the SBPHE method provides nearly same results as of the BPHE method and preserves edge details intact with reduced dynamic range of output image. Some additional edges appeared in enhanced images obtained by HE which are not appeared in given images or images obtained by the BPHE and BPHE methods. The histograms for images obtained by the

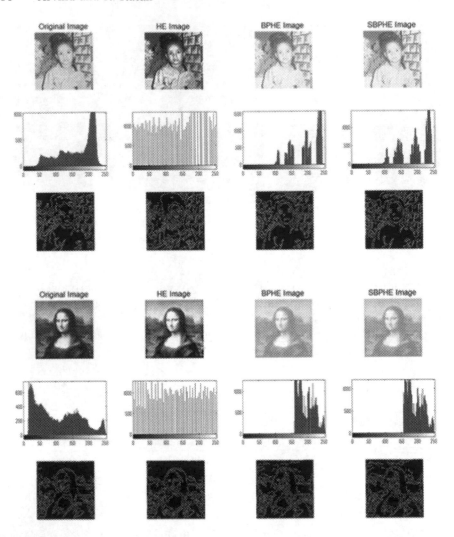

Fig. 5. Visual perception, histogram and edge details of original image and processed images by HE, BPHE and SBPHE for Baby and Monalisa images

SBPHE and BPHE methods appeared same whereas it appear flattened and uniformly distributed for images obtained by HE method. The edge details found in images obtained by the BPHE and SBPHE methods are comparatively good that in images obtained by the HE method. It is clear from Table 1 that the processed images by the HE method take larger data size than the original images. Resulting images by the SBPHE and BPHE methods take same data size approximately. The values of entropy measured for images obtained by the SBPHE method is slightly higher than measured for images obtained by the BPHE method.

The values of mean intensity for original and processed images and the MSE between original and processed images are shown in Tables 2 and 3.

Table 2. Mean intensity values for original and processed images

Image	Original	HE	BPHE	SBPHE
Baboon	066.6278	127.4662	223.3040	221.5587
Baby	169.1812	127.4660	203.3236	201.5480
Cameraman	118.7245	127.4200	199.1344	197.4670
Lena	180.2305	127.6774	205.8501	204.1484
Monalisa	102.7847	127.6060	194.5338	192.6862
Pirate	111.6399	127.3836	193.2141	191.4787
Peppers	116.9074	127.4743	192.4297	190.7725
Walkbridge	114.1323	127.4023	193.8137	192.0716
Lake	124.3706	127.4743	192.3709	190.6800
Blonde	135.0839	127.5041	194.8452	193.0790

Table 3. MSE values for original and processed images

Image	Original and HE images	Original and BPHE images	Original and SBPHE images	BPHE and SBPHE images
Baboon	5968.7000	24732.0000	24190.0000	4.4890
Baby	2647.1000	01323.8000	01207.4000	4.4546
Cameraman	0800.5393	07252.7000	06987.1000	4.2682
Lena	3716.3000	00780.4803	00695.6649	4.2904
Monalisa	0845.5431	10115.0000	09773.8000	4.9100
Pirate	1018.1000	07420.8000	07148.0000	4.5179
Peppers	0610.7802	06544.3000	06299.0000	4.0313
Walkbridge	0759.5806	07545.8000	07276.1000	4.4942
Lake	0237.9578	05825.0000	05604.9000	4.3002
Blonde	1305.8000	03774.9000	03566.5000	4.6249

We can see from Table 2 that the mean intensity values of processed images by BPHE and SBPHE are higher to the mean intensity values of original and processed images by HE. The mean intensity values for images obtained through HE are approximately to 127. We can also see from Table 3 that the values of MSE between images obtained through BPHE and SBPHE is not very significant and these images visually look similar.

4   Conclusion

A selective bit-plane histogram equalization (SBPHE) method has been presented for image enhancement and representation. The performance of SBPHE method has been demonstrated by presenting qualitative measures as visual perception, histogram and edge details and quantitative measures as average intensity, entropy, data storage size and mean square error. The SBPHE method provides enhanced images efficiently with better results compared to histogram equalization (HE) method and similar to bit-plane histogram equalization (BPHE) method with less image data size and reduced dynamic range. The SBPHE preserves the image details intact and it can be applied to process poor contrast images for acceptable representation to display these on low resolution display devices. Moreover, SBPHE can be applied for getting lesser data size to transmit and store images as required in various image processing and pattern recognition applications for efficient image information management.

References

1. Jain, A.K.: Fundamentals of Digital Image Processing. Prentice Hall, Upper Saddle River (1989)
2. Russ, J.C.: The Image Processing Handbook, 6th edn. CRC Press, Boca Raton (2011)
3. Ting, C.-C., Wu, B.-F., Chung, M.-L., Chiu, C.-C., Wu, Y.-C.: Visual contrast enhancement algorithm based on histogram equalization. Sensors 15(7), 16981–16999 (2015)
4. Yoon, H., Han, Y., Hahn, H.: Image contrast enhancement based sub-histogram equalization technique without over-equalization noise. Int. J. Electr. Comput. Eng. 3(2), 189–195 (2009)
5. Pizer, S.M., et al.: Adaptive histogram equalization and its variations. Comput. Vis. Graph. Image Process. 39, 355–368 (1987)
6. Ooi, C.H., Isa, N.A.M.: Adaptive contrast enhancement methods with brightness preserving. IEEE Trans. Consum. Electron. 56(4), 2543–2551 (2010)
7. Zhu, Y., Huang, C.: An adaptive histogram equalization algorithm on the image gray level mapping. Phys. Procedia 25, 601–608 (2012)
8. Stark, J.A.: Adaptive image contrast enhancement using generalizations of histogram equalization. IEEE Trans. Image Process. 9(5), 889–896 (2000)
9. Jordanski, M., Arsic, A., Tuba, M.: Dynamic recursive subimage histogram equalization algorithm for image contrast enhancement. In: Telecommunications Forum Telfor (TELFOR), pp. 819–822 (2015)
10. Sun, C.C., Ruan, S.J., Shie, M.C., Pai, T.W.: Dynamic contrast enhancement based on histogram specification. IEEE Trans. Consum. Electron. 51(4), 1300–13005 (2005)
11. Kim, Y.T.: Contrast enhancement using brightness preserving bi-histogram equalization. IEEE Trans. Consum. Electron. 43(1), 1–8 (1997)
12. Chen, S.D., Ramli, A.R.: Minimum mean brightness error bi-histogram equalization in contrast enhancement. IEEE Trans. Consum. Electron. 49(4), 1310–1318 (2003)

13. Zhai, D., Wu, C., Zeng, Q.: Brightness preserving multipeak histogram equalization. Comput. Simul. **26**(1), 222–224 (2009)
14. Patel, O.P., Marvai, Y.P.S., Sharma, S.: A comparative study of histogram equalization based image enhancement techniques for brightness preservation and contrast enhancement. Sig. Image Process. J. (SIPIJ) **4**(5), 11–25 (2013)
15. Kaur, M., Kaur, J., Kaur, J.: Survey of contrast enhancement techniques based on histogram equalization. Int. J. Adv. Comput. Sci. Appl. (IJACSA) **2**(7), 137–141 (2011)
16. Raju, A., Dwarakish, G.S., Reddy, D.V.: A Comparative analysis of histogram equalization based techniques for contrast enhancement and brightness preserving. Int. J. Sig. Process. Image Process. Pattern Recogn. **6**(5), 353–366 (2013)
17. Agarwal, R.: Bit planes histogram equalization for tone mapping of high contrast images. In: IEEE Proceedings of the Eighth International Conference on Computer Graphics, Imaging and Visualization, pp. 13–18 (2011)
18. Magudeeswaran, V., Ravichandran, C.G.: Fuzzy logic-based histogram equalization for image contrast enhancement. In: Mathematical Problems in Engineering (2013)
19. Tuba, M., Jordanski, M., Arsic, A.: Improved weighted thresholded histogram equalization algorithm for digital image contrast enhancement using the bat algorithm. In: Bio-Inspired Computation and Applications in Image Processing, pp. 61–86 (2017)
20. Sheikh, H.R., Bovik, A.C.: Image information and visual quality. IEEE Trans. Image Process. **15**(2), 430–444 (2006)
21. Janssen, T.J.W.M., Blommaert, F.J.: Computational approach to image quality. Displays **21**(4), 129–142 (2000)
22. Avcibas, I., Sankur, B., Sayood, K.: Statistical evaluation of image quality measures. J. Electron. Imag. **11**(2), 206–223 (2002)
23. Ratan, R., Arvind: Bit-plane specific measures and its applications in analysis of image ciphers. In: Thampi, S.M., Marques, O., Krishnan, S., Li, K.C., Ciuonzo, D., Kolekar, M. (eds.) SIRS 2018. CCIS, vol. 968, pp. 282–297. Springer, Singapore. https://doi.org/10.1007/978-981-13-5758-9_24
24. Standard test images. Image Databaes. www.imageprocessingplace.com
25. Canny, J.: A computational approach to edge detection. IEEE Trans. Pattern Analys. Mach. Intell. **8**(6), 679–698 (1986)
26. Gonzalez, R.C., Woods, R.E.: Digital Image Processing. Addison-Wesley, Boston (1992)
27. Miano, J.M.: Compressed Image File Formats JPEG, PNG, GIF, XBM, BMP. Addison Wesley, Boston (1999)

Edge Preserved Satellite Image Denoising Using Median and Bilateral Filtering

Anju Asokan and J. Anitha[✉]

Department of Electronics and Communication Engineering,
Karunya Institute of Technology and Sciences, Coimbatore 641114, India
anju.asok@yahoo.com, anithaj@karunya.edu

Abstract. The satellite images acquired from long distances are affected by different atmospheric disturbances such as noise and the image quality is degraded. The images thus require pre-processing to preserve the image quality for use in classification, fusion, segmentation etc. In the domain of image processing, analyzing the different noise types which affect the satellite images and also design the filter according to the affected noise is important. The existing filtering methods are capable of removing the noise in the image but is not much effective in preserving the image information such as edges, lines etc. This paper proposes a hybrid filtering technique for impulse noise removal. The hybrid filter comprises of a median filter which removes the impulse noise followed by a bilateral filter for edge preservation. The performance is studied based on the Peak Signal-to-Noise Ratio (PSNR), Mean Square Error (MSE), Feature Simillarity Index (FSIM), Structural Similarity Index (SSIM), Entropy and CPU time by comparing the results with existing denoising filters.

Keywords: Satellite images · Remote sensing · Image denoising · Median filter · Bilateral filter

1 Introduction

Remote sensing data find wide applications in the field of agriculture, navigation, disaster management and so on. These images are acquired over long distances from satellites and conveyed to the ground station. When these images are acquired, noise interferences can affect the image quality. Hence image pre-processing is taken up as the first stage in any image processing application to sharpen the image features perceived by humans [25, 26]. The most important noises which affects the satellite images are the additive noise, also called the Gaussian noise, salt and pepper noise and the speckle noise [1]. The filtering technique comprises of following procedures: detecting the noise and removing the noise. It is also essential that the information in the image such as edges, shapes etc. be kept unchanged. Hence the design of the filter is essential such that it can remove the unwanted noise components while maintaining the image features, finding wide use when trying to remove the cloud covers in an image [2] and extracting features from an image. Both these applications involve the use of morphological filtering [3].

© Springer Nature Singapore Pte Ltd. 2019
K. C. Santosh and R. S. Hegadi (Eds.): RTIP2R 2018, CCIS 1035, pp. 688–699, 2019.
https://doi.org/10.1007/978-981-13-9181-1_59

Considering the Gaussian noise, each pixel value is changed slightly from its existing value. The Gaussian model is thus good to model this kind of noise [4]. Speckle noise is much difficult to remove since the noise intensity sharply increases with the intensity of signal. In salt and pepper noise, the image pixels are distinct from their neighbors in terms of color and intensity and affects only less number of pixels. It appears as black or white dots and hence called salt and pepper noise. Currently, different denoising techniques are being used namely wavelet based approach, Bayesian approach, principal component analysis, soft thresholding and hard thresholding. These methods are effective in removing the noise from the image and preserving the quality of the image to some extent. But they suffer from the disadvantage of computational efficiency and image quality.

Impulse noise is another type of noise introduced in the image during the transmission from the satellite to the ground station. Here, some pixels in the image get replaced by random values. Median filter is the most commonly used filter for suppressing salt and pepper noise [5, 6]. But the outcome of the filter is not satisfactory since it creates a smooth and blurred image. This is so because in the median filter, the noise affected pixel values are replaced by a median value without taking into consideration what type of feature lies adjacent to the noisy pixels. Due to the smoothing of the image, the edge details also get blurred. To overcome this, a bilateral filter can be used. A hybrid filter combining median filter and bilateral filter is proposed in [7]. A bilateral filter is a non-linear filter which is capable of preserving the edges in the image [8]. The filter output will be such that intensity of each pixel will be replaced with the weighted average of the intensity values of the pixels in the neighborhood. But the bilateral filter suffers from the disadvantage of gradient reversal which appears due to the introduction of false edges in the image. Also the calculation of weighted average can be highly unstable for a pixel on the edge of the image. To overcome these limitations in the bilateral filter, guided filter, wiener filer was introduced [9, 10, 27] respectively. The filtered image is simply a linear transform of the guidance image. It can preserve edges like a bilateral filter and avoids the introduction of false edges. It is one of the most widely used filters for image dehazing. Reduction of speckle noise was yet another challenge faced in image processing. Various filters such as like Kalman, geometric, Oddy and Adaptive Filter on Surfaces (AFS) were used to reduce the speckle noise but suffered from complexity in the algorithm. The above drawbacks were overcome using an adaptive filter which used a homomorphic technique involving multiplicative noise log changed to additive noise. This method in turn estimates the input image using an exponential operation but resulted in poor image reconstruction due to loss of information. In recent times, frequency domain based techniques involving wavelets and curvelets are being widely used for speckle noise reduction [11]. A useful method for image denoising is the wavelet transform based threshold neural network (WT-TNN). Even though this method is seen to outperform soft and hard thresholding methods, it suffers from the drawback of high computational cost. To overcome the limitation of WT-TNN [12], this paper describes an adaptive threshold function based denoising (using JADE) while preserving the quality of the edges by not over-blurring them. The adaptive threshold function decides a threshold value beforehand using which the noise can be separated from the source image maintaining the data in the image. But this method has some drawbacks. It cannot give the threshold value and threshold function together. The edge preserving problem is not addressed here. In this method, wavelet thresholding of the image which is corrupted by noise is obtained. Using the thresholding function, wavelet coefficients are modified. The inverse wavelet thresholding is performed to form the reconstructed image. Differential evolution (DE) algorithm finds wide use in image processing and multi-level thresholding applications [13]. JADE is an improved version of differential evolution algorithm. JADE uses a new mutation technique to be used in combination with DE. An individual is randomly picked to find the best possible solution among the population using this method. JADE, compared to DE, has the capability to use a stored set of parent solutions which gets substituted with successful offsprings which it utilizes during mutation. Histogram based image correction is yet another prevalent method being used today [14, 15].

Edge detection is an important application in image processing. Currently various edge detection techniques such as PSO Preweitt, Laplacian and Laplacian of Gaussian is being used. The disadvantage of this technique is that the edge thickness is fixed and implementation of threshold is difficult. Another method is using the linear time invariant filters which consider edge as a change in the intensity of the grey scale pixel. This is a computationally effective technique. Various approaches to image segmentation in medical field involve segmentation on the basis of active contours or snakes which are controlled using gradient vectors [16]. Applying bilateral filter to such vectors can enhance the edges thus helping in better image segmentation. There is another prominent edge detection technique involving edge map to extract the variations in pixels [17–19]. Changes in edge maps can also be analyzed utilizing histogram of orientation gradients [20, 21]. Line segment detection and line vectorization also finds wide use in medical imaging [22]. Analyzing Region of Interest by selecting candidates using the principle of connected components on a binary image is also extensively used in medical images [23]. Widely used object recognition techniques involve extraction of features. Some descriptors may not enable proper matching. So Rotation- and Scale-Invariant, Line-based Color-aware descriptor (RSILC) can be of use in such instances which can effectively combine both global and local information [24].

In the proposed work, a hybrid filtering technique is adopted by combining median filter with a bilateral filter and comparing the results with the traditional median filter and Weiner filter in terms of the PSNR, MSE, SSIM, FSIM, Entropy and CPU time. Further the same method is repeated on the JPEG compressed satellite images and compared in terms of the computation time taken.

The remaining part of the paper is organized as follows. Section 2 gives the proposed algorithm for image filtering technique. Section 3 includes comparison of the results and discussions of various techniques. Section 4 highlights the advantages of the proposed algorithm.

2   Proposed Methodology

In the proposed method, the LANDSAT image of an area is acquired and subjected to filtering, with and without compressing the image. The data was taken from earth explorer site (http://earthexplorer.usgs.gov/) and from global land survey (http://changematters.esri.com/). A total of 70 images are available out of which 10 image sets are used for carrying out the analysis. The block diagram of the method is represented in Fig. 1.

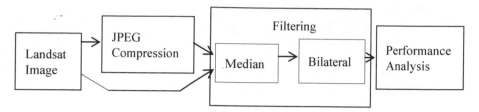

Fig. 1. Proposed block diagram

The dataset used for the method are LANDSAT images of different regions of size 648 × 1462. The images considered are affected by noise. The most important noises which affect the satellite images are the additive noise also called the Gaussian noise, salt and pepper noise, also called impulse noise and the multiplicative noise also called the speckle noise. The images taken are affected by impulse noise. The best known filter which can remove the impulse noise is the median filter. The median filter smoothen the image and the high intensity regions such as edges get blurred. So there is a need for an edge preserving filter to be used in combination with the median filter. Hence a hybrid filtering technique involving the median and the bilateral filter is used in the proposed method.

2.1 JPEG Compression of Input Image

JPEG compression is a lossy compression technique which can describe the data in the images such that minimum memory is utilized with the data appearing to be identical, but at reduced quality. JPEG takes into account the fact that humans cannot perceive colors at high frequencies and these are the points which are eliminated as part of compression. The level of compression can be modified by allowing a tradeoff between storage size and image quality.

JPEG utilizes transform coding. It is developed taking into account the observation that low frequency components contain useful information when compared to the higher frequency components and humans cannot perceive high frequency components and are not affected by the loss of higher frequency components. JPEG uses DCT based quantization. Since humans cannot perceive high frequencies, these are treated as inessential data. To separate the raw data based on frequency, it should be converted to frequency domain which primarily is a function of DCT.JPEG compression is seen to be suitable for both gray scale and color images.

In the proposed method, the images acquired are very large in size and there is a need to compress these images before filtering is applied. The results obtained are then compared with those obtained by filtering without compressing the image.

2.2 Noise Removal Using Hybrid Filtering

The impulse noise affected satellite image is subjected to hybrid filtering which involves a combination of two filters namely median filter and bilateral filter. Impulse noise is removed using the median filter by smoothing the image which also leads to the smoothing of the edges. The edges which are the sharp transitions in the image are detected by the bilateral filter and are preserved. Here the noise in the rest of the image is eliminated to get the denoised output.

The median filter moves through the image pixel by pixel. Each pixel value is then replaced with the median value of neighboring pixels.

The output of the median filter can be formulated as

$$Y[m, n] = \text{median}\{x[i, j], (i, j) \in w\} \tag{1}$$

where w is the neighborhood centered around (i, j).

The Wiener filtering provides a tradeoff between inverse filtering and noise smoothing. It can remove the noise and inverts the effect of blurring simultaneously. To apply Wiener filter, the power spectra of the source image and the noise are estimated.

The bilateral filter is a non-linear and smoothing filter. The pixel intensity is replaced with the weighted average of pixel intensity values. Mathematically, the output of the bilateral function at any pixel location x is given by Eq. (2)

$$\hat{I}(x) = \frac{1}{C} \sum_{y \in N(x)} e^{\frac{-||y-x||^2}{2\sigma_d^2}} e^{\frac{-||I(y)-I(x)||^2}{2\sigma_r^2}} I(y) \tag{2}$$

Where σ is the control parameter and $N(x)$ is the neighbor of pixel $I(x)$ and C is the normalization constant.

$$C = \sum_{y \in N(x)} e^{\frac{-||y-x||^2}{2\sigma_d^2}} e^{\frac{-||I(y)-I(x)||^2}{2\sigma_r^2}} \tag{3}$$

The selection of window size in a bilateral filter is an important factor. It is related to the spatial Gaussian parameter. Depending on the property of the Gaussian distribution, the window size is selected such that it is 2 or 3 times the standard deviation of Gaussian. This is so because if the selected window size is more than 3 times Gaussian, the output of Gaussian almost converges to zero.

The output of the bilateral filter will be such that it will be free from impulse noise with the edges in the image well preserved.

3   Results and Discussion

The image dataset considered is LANDSAT 7 images of size 648×1462. The proposed hybrid filter denoises the input image. Further the input image is compressed and the same hybrid filtering is applied. The results are compared in terms of PSNR, MSE, SSIM, FSIM, Entropy and CPU time.

The PSNR depends on the intensity values of the image and is a measure of the accuracy of the final image. It is calculated using Eq. (4) as

$$PSNR = \log_{10}\left(\frac{255 * 255}{MSE}\right) \tag{4}$$

where MSE is the Mean Square Error, sum of the square of error between the source image and the noise affected image. Lower the MSE, lower is the error. The PSNR values of the proposed method and the traditional filtering methods are compared with and without the presence of compression method as shown in Table 1.

Table 1. PSNR values for proposed method with and without compression.

Input dataset	PSNR (without compression) (dB)			PSNR (with JPEG compression) (dB)		
	Median filter	Weiner filter	Median + Bilateral filter	Median filter	Weiner filter	Median + Bilateral filter
Image 1	37.3801	37.3993	38.7709	36.5249	36.8251	39.3866
Image 2	34.4512	35.0338	37.5040	33.8213	34.0851	37.1773
Image 3	36.9425	37.9650	39.5183	36.7505	38.2224	39.1491
Image 4	34.1913	34.9622	37.6943	33.4635	34.0768	37.2648
Image 5	34.9998	36.4190	38.4327	34.2960	35.4271	37.9790
Image 6	37.6877	38.0061	42.1443	35.8895	36.1097	38.1124
Image 7	39.1176	39.5353	47.8199	36.0680	36.7203	42.7707
Image 8	38.1123	38.6171	44.2716	37.6088	37.9910	41.9218
Image 9	39.4517	39.7710	52.8780	38.5117	38.9636	49.6986
Image 10	39.3122	39.3675	42.6318	37.5877	37.7553	40.1858

The PSNR increases on applying hybrid filtering on the input image since along with image smoothing to remove noise contents in the image, the bilateral filter preserves the edges in the image. As a result, compared to median filter, the hybrid filter performs better in terms of the PSNR. But when the input image is compressed before the hybrid filter is done, image quality gets affected. Hence the PSNR reduces. On an average, the PSNR has increased from 37.1646 dB in the case of a median filter to 40.666 dB in the case of hybrid filter with a percentage increase of 9.422 without compression. Also there is an increase of PSNR from 33.0527 dB in the case of median filter to 39.2646 dB in the case of hybrid filter with a percentage increase of 18.793 with compression.

The MSE values of the proposed method and the traditional filtering methods are compared with and without the presence of compression method as shown in Table 2.

Table 2. MSE values for proposed method with and without compression.

Input dataset	MSE (without compression)			MSE (with JPEG compression)		
	Median filter	Weiner filter	Median + Bilateral filter	Median filter	Weiner filter	Median + Bilateral filter
Image 1	11.98	10.70	10.97	14.59	12.16	10.27
Image 2	23.52	22.65	11.64	27.19	25.05	12.55
Image 3	13.25	13.04	10.32	13.85	13.46	10.55
Image 4	24.96	22.51	11.14	29.52	25.67	12.30
Image 5	20.73	20.27	10.40	24.37	22.52	11.04
Image 6	18.53	18.05	15.71	21.16	20.44	18.33
Image 7	19.31	18.94	17.50	23.95	21.52	20.40
Image 8	22.68	21.85	20.96	24.51	23.53	22.68
Image 9	21.31	20.88	20.25	23.32	23.21	22.51
Image 10	18.53	17.97	16.47	21.42	20.60	19.05

The MSE values are inversely related to PSNR. Hence when median filter and bilateral filter are combined, the PSNR increases but MSE decreases. Also when input dataset is compressed, the PSNR decreases and MSE increases. On an average, the MSE has decreased from 19.48 in the case of a median filter to 14.53 in the case of hybrid filter with a percentage decrease of 25.41 without compression. Also there is a decrease in MSE from 22.38 in the case of median filter to 15.96 in the case of hybrid filter with a percentage decrease of 28.68 with compression.

The entropy H is calculated using Eq. (5). Here P is the normalized histogram value of image i. The H values of the proposed method and the traditional filtering methods are compared with and without the presence of compression method as shown in Table 3.

$$H = -\sum_{i=0}^{L} P(i) \log_2 P(i) \tag{5}$$

H measures the information content in the image.

When the hybrid filtering is done, the edge details in the image which were smoothened using the median filter are enhanced and the entropy improves. When the image is compressed, the quality of the image gets reduced and the entropy value decreases. On an average, the entropy has increased from 4.4837 in the case of a median filter to 5.7302 in the case of hybrid filter with a percentage increase of 27.80 without compression. Also there is an increase of entropy from 4.3619 in the case of median filter to 5.6306 in the case of hybrid filter with a percentage increase of 29.08 with compression.

Table 3. Entropy values for proposed method with and without compression.

Input dataset	H (without compression)			H (with JPEG compression)		
	Median filter	Weiner filter	Median + Bilateral filter	Median filter	Weiner filter	Median + Bilateral filter
Image 1	4.2556	4.2642	5.2418	4.2492	4.2606	5.2267
Image 2	4.0276	4.1829	5.9896	4.0025	4.1176	5.9537
Image 3	4.3019	4.3445	5.4871	4.2888	4.2925	5.4636
Image 4	4.0929	4.2761	6.0262	4.0872	4.2126	5.9880
Image 5	4.0929	4.1988	6.0354	4.0894	4.1543	6.0108
Image 6	4.6807	4.7123	5.4801	4.5949	4.6722	5.2209
Image 7	4.8799	4.9177	5.9910	4.7655	4.8976	5.8863
Image 8	4.9094	4.9122	5.6267	4.5622	4.7128	5.4432
Image 9	4.9653	4.9823	5.9380	4.7572	4.7909	5.8786
Image 10	4.6318	4.7223	5.4870	4.2229	4.3787	5.2343

The proposed hybrid filtering is implemented and executed on a personal computer equipped with an Intel i3-4005U 1.70 GHz processor. The computation time required for the method is tabulated in Table 4.

Table 4. CPU time (in sec) for the proposed method with and without JPEG compression.

Input dataset	Without compression	With JPEG compression
Image 1	0.99993	0.99520
Image 2	1.00695	0.99829
Image 3	1.00489	0.99503
Image 4	1.00709	0.99233
Image 5	0.99588	0.99404
Image 6	0.99703	0.97760
Image 7	0.99419	0.97682
Image 8	1.00066	0.97233
Image 9	0.99650	0.97734
Image 10	0.99431	0.98772

From the Table 4, it is evident that the hybrid filtering on compressed input image reduces the CPU time when compared to applying the filtering on uncompressed input image. FSIM is a measure of the feature similarity between the source image and the processed image. It is calculated using Eq. (6) as

$$FSIM = \frac{\sum\limits_{x \in X} S_L(x)PC_m(x)}{\sum\limits_{x \in X} PC_m(x)} \tag{6}$$

where X represents the whole image, $S_L(x)$ denotes the similarity in the two images and PC_m is the phase congruency map. Table 5 shows the FSIM values for median, Weiner and hybrid filter.

Table 5. FSIM values for median, Weiner and hybrid filter.

Input dataset	Median filter	Weiner filter	Median + Bilateral filter
Image 1	0.868777	0.878910	0.879013
Image 2	0.870293	0.874552	0.880547
Image 3	0.852603	0.857756	0.874353
Image 4	0.880599	0.884054	0.913883
Image 5	0.874561	0.875422	0.884824
Image 6	0.876005	0.881575	0.886470
Image 7	0.782556	0.795928	0.845822
Image 8	0.780266	0.785829	0.840783
Image 9	0.880601	0.886559	0.892952
Image 10	0.876123	0.881339	0.886453

On an average, the FSIM has increased from 0.854242 in the case of a median filter to 0.872654 in the case of hybrid filter with a percentage increase of 2.155.

SSIM is a measure of the Structural Similarity. It is computed using Eq. (7) as

$$SSIM = \frac{(2\mu_x\mu_y + C_1)(2\sigma_{xy} + C_2)}{(\mu_x^2 + \mu_y^2 + C_1)(\sigma_x^2 + \sigma_y^2 + C_2)} \quad (7)$$

Table 6 shows the SSIM values for median, Weiner and hybrid filter.

Table 6. SSIM values for median, Weiner and hybrid filter

Input dataset	Median filter	Weiner filter	Median + Bilateral filter
Image 1	0.872090	0.858527	0.888217
Image 2	0.982392	0.980562	0.993836
Image 3	0.980101	0.980023	0.983111
Image 4	0.986911	0.984657	0.990047
Image 5	0.980467	0.978646	0.989684
Image 6	0.867233	0.862213	0.877293
Image 7	0.974551	0.971225	0.988406
Image 8	0.902968	0.901104	0.927861
Image 9	0.978052	0.971901	0.981375
Image 10	0.964738	0.962689	0.978691

On an average, the SSIM has increased from 0.948950 in the case of a median filter to 0.959852 in the case of hybrid filter with a percentage increase of 1.148.

Figure 2 represents the input and output images after hybrid filtering method.

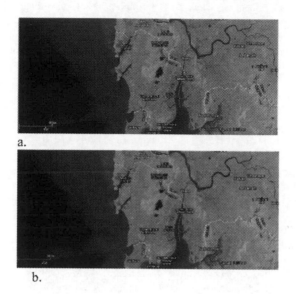

a.

b.

Fig. 2. (a) Input image of size 648 × 1462 (b) Image after hybrid filtering

4 Conclusion

In this paper, hybrid filtering for image denoising is presented. Here a combination of median filter and bilateral filter is used to eliminate the impulse noise in the image and preserve the edge details in the image. The results obtained are then compared with those obtained after compressing the input image. It is observed that the proposed method gives superior performance in terms of PSNR, MSE and H values and outperforms the traditional median filter and Weiner filter. As a future step, the proposed method could be expanded to incorporate optimization techniques along with filtering for greater efficiency.

References

1. Bhosle, N., Manza, R., Kale, K.V.: Analysis of effect of gaussian, salt and pepper noise. In: Proceedings of the Second International Conference on Emerging Research in Computing, Information, Communication and Application. Elsevier (2014)
2. Siravenha, A.C., Sousa, D., Bispo, A., Pelaes, E.: The use of high-pass filters and the inpainting method to clouds removal and their impact on satellite images classification. In: Maino, G., Foresti, G.L. (eds.) ICIAP 2011. LNCS, vol. 6979, pp. 333–342. Springer, Heidelberg (2011). https://doi.org/10.1007/978-3-642-24088-1_35

3. Courtrai, L., Lefevre, S.: Morphological path filtering at region scale for efficient and robust road network extraction from satellite imagery. Pattern Recogn. Lett. **83**, 195–204 (2016)
4. Varghese, J.: Adaptive threshold based frequency domain filter for periodic noise reduction. Int. J. Electron. Commun. **70**, 1692–1701 (2016)
5. Wang, Y., Wu, G., Chen, G., Chai, T.: Data mining based noise diagnosis and fuzzy filter design for image processing. Comput. Electr. Eng. **40**, 2038–2049 (2014)
6. Josselin, D., Mora, J.R., Ulmer, A.: MeAdian robust spatial filtering on satellite images. In: International Conference on Spatial Thinking and Geographic Information Sciences, vol. 21, pp. 222–229. Elsevier (2011)
7. Sankaran, K.S., Nagappan, N.V.: Noise free image restoration using hybrid filter with adaptive genetic algorithm. Comput. Electr. Eng. **54**, 382–392 (2016)
8. Renza, D., Martinez, E., Arquero, A., Sanchez, J.: Pansharpening of high and medium resolution satellite images using bilateral filtering. In: Bloch, I., Cesar, R.M. (eds.) CIARP 2010. LNCS, vol. 6419, pp. 311–318. Springer, Heidelberg (2010). https://doi.org/10.1007/978-3-642-16687-7_43
9. Guo, Y., Han, S., Li, Y., Zhang, C., Bai, Y.: K-nearest neighbor combined with guided filter for hyper spectral image classification. In: International Conference on Identification, Information and Knowledge in the Internet of Things, vol. 129, pp. 159–165. Elsevier (2018)
10. Dong, W., Xiao, S., Li, Y.: Hyper spectral pan sharpening based guided filter and Gaussian filter. J. Vis. Commun. Image Represent. **53**, 171–179 (2018)
11. Jadhav, B.D., Patil, P.M.: Satellite image resolution enhancement using dyadic-integer coefficients based on bi-orthogonal wavelet filters. Procedia Comput. Sci. **49**, 17–23 (2015)
12. Bhandari, A.K., Kumar, D., Kumar, A., Singh, G.K.: Optimal sub-band adaptive thresholding based edge preserved satellite image denoising using adaptive differential evolution algorithm. Neurocomputing **174**, 698–721 (2016)
13. Suresh, S., Lal, S.: Modified differential algorithm for contrast and brightness enhancement. Appl. Soft Comput. **61**, 622–641 (2017)
14. Singh, H., Kumar, A., Balyan, L.K., Singh, G.K.: A novel optimally weighted framework of piecewise gamma corrected fractional order masking for satellite image enhancement. Comput. Electr. Eng. 1–7 (2017)
15. Gupta, S., Kaur, Y.: Review of different local and global contrast enhancement techniques for digital image. Int. J. Comput. Appl. **100**(18), 18–23 (2014)
16. Hegadi, R.S., Pediredla, A.K., Seelamantula, C.S.: Bilateral smoothing of gradient vector field and application to image segmentation. In: 19th IEEE International Conference on Image Processing, pp. 317–320. IEEE (2012)
17. Aafaque, A., Santosh, K.C.: Automatic compound figure separation in scientific articles: a study of edge map and its role for stitched panel boundary detection. In: Santosh, K.C., Hangarge, M., Bevilacqua, V., Negi, A. (eds.) RTIP2R 2016. CCIS, vol. 709, pp. 319–332. Springer, Singapore (2017). https://doi.org/10.1007/978-981-10-4859-3_29
18. Zohora, F.T., Antani, S., Santosh, K.C.: Circle-like foreign element detection in chest x-rays using normalized cross-correlation and unsupervised clustering. In: Proceedings of the SPIE: Medical Imaging, vol. 10574 (2018)
19. Zohora, F.T., Santosh, K.C.: Foreign circular element detection in chest X-rays for effective automated pulmonary abnormality screening. Int. J. Comput. Vis. Image Process. **7**(2), 36–49 (2017)
20. Santosh, K.C., Vajda, S., Antani, S., Thoma, G.R.: Edge map analysis in chest X-rays for automatic pulmonary abnormality screening. Int. J. Comput. Assist. Radiol. Surg. **11**(9), 1637–1646 (2016)

21. Santosh, K.C., Vajda, S., Antani, S., Thoma, G.: Automatic pulmonary abnormality screening using thoracic edge map. In: IEEE 28th International Symposium on Computer-Based Medical Systems (CBMS). IEEE (2016)
22. Santosh, K.C., Aafaque, A.: Line segment-based stitched multipanel figure separation for effective biomedical CBIR. Int J. Pattern Recogn. Artif. Intell. **31**(6), 1757003(1–18) (2017)
23. Santosh, K.C., Wendling, L., Antani, S., Thoma, G.: Overlaid arrow detection for labeling biomedical image regions. IEEE Intell. Syst. **31**(3), 66–75 (2015)
24. Candemir, S., Borovikov, E., Santosh, K.C., Antani, S., Thoma, G.: RSILC: rotation- and scale-invariant, line-based color-aware descriptor. Image Vis. Comput. **42**, 1–12 (2015)
25. Ruikar, D.D., Santosh, K.C., Hegadi, R.S.: Automated fractured bone segmentation and labeling from CT images. J. Med. Syst. **43**(3), 60 (2019). https://doi.org/10.1007/s10916-019-1176-x
26. Ruikar, D.D., Santosh, K.C., Hegadi, R.S.: Segmentation and analysis of CT images for bone fracture detection and labeling, Chap 7. In: Medical imaging: Artificial Intelligence, Image Recognition, and Machine Learning Techniques. CRC Press (2019). ISBN: 9780367139612
27. Hegadi, R.S., Navale, D.I., Pawar, T.D., Ruikar, D.D.: Multi feature-based classification of osteoarthritis in knee joint X-ray images, Chap 5. In: Medical imaging: Artificial Intelligence, Image Recognition, and Machine Learning Techniques. CRC Press (2019). ISBN: 9780367139612

Image Fusion Technique Using Gaussian Pyramid

B. Sujatha[1]([⊠]), B. Vanajakshi[2], and Nitta Gnaneswara Rao[3]

[1] Godavari Institute of Engineering and Technology, Rajahmundry, AP, India
bsujatha@giet.ac.in
[2] SRK Institute of Technology, Vijayawada, AP, India
vanaja2birudu@gmail.com
[3] Vignan University, Vadlamudi, AP, India
gnani.nitta@gmail.com

Abstract. The aim of image fusion is to combine similar information from multiple images into a single image. The methods which are based on discrete cosine transform (DCT) of image fusion are more competent and time-saving in real-time systems using DCT based standards of still Image. The existing DCT based methods are suffering from some side effects like blurring which can reduce the quality of the output image. To address this issue, the paper proposing new method for image fusion using Gaussian pyramid in DCT domain. The pyramid fusion provides better fusion quality. The execution time is extremely reduced, compare with existing methods. This method can be used for multi model image fusion as well as fusion of complementary images. The algorithm given in proposed system is simple and easy to implement. Also, it could be used for real time applications. The performance of our method is analyzed and compared with other image fusion methods. Experimental results show that there is no difference between the result of our method and water-based image fusion result. But our algorithm is carried out in DCT domain; it is efficient in processing time and simple.

Keywords: Image fusion · DCT · Wavelet transform · Gaussian pyramid

1 Introduction

THE image multi sensor data fusion found to play a vital role in defense as well as in civilian applications because of the availability of diversity of sensors and these are working in various spectral bands. Image fusion, is defined like combine the images to increase the information content. It is a promising area of research. Numerous image fusion algorithms such as multi-resolution [1, 2], statistical signal processing [3, 4] and multi scale [5] based techniques are evaluated. In this paper, a novel technique "image fusion using DCT based Gaussian pyramid" is presented and its performance is evaluated. In all sensor networks, every sensor can observe the environment and transfer data by production. Visual sensor networks (VSN) is the term used in the literature to refer to a system with a large number of cameras geographically spread at monitoring points [6]. A distinguished feature of visual sensors or cameras is the great

© Springer Nature Singapore Pte Ltd. 2019
K. C. Santosh and R. S. Hegadi (Eds.): RTIP2R 2018, CCIS 1035, pp. 700–711, 2019.
https://doi.org/10.1007/978-981-13-9181-1_60

amount of generated data. To deliver only the useful information represented in a conceptualized level, this characteristic feature is necessary for more local processing resources [7]. The goal of image fusion, besides reducing the amount of data in network transmissions, is to create new images that are suitable for both visual perception and further computer processing as well as more informative [8]. So far, several researches have been focused on image fusion which are performed on the images in the spatial domain [9–13]. The algorithms based on multi-scale decompositions are more popular.

The activity level determines the quality of each source image. The integration can be carried out either by a weighted average of the coefficients or by choosing the larger activity level coefficients. The fused image is finally reconstructed by performing the inverse multi-scale transform. Examples for this approach include gradient, Laplacian, discrete wavelet transform (DWT), morphological pyramids, and the superior ones [14] and shift invariant discrete wavelet transform (SIDWT) [10]. For image fusion in the literature, the two later methods are considered as standard methods. A professional survey on these methods may be found in [15–19]. Recently, Tang [20] has considered the above mentioned issue of complexity reduction and proposed two image fusion techniques in DCT domain, namely, DCT + Average and DCT + Contrast. As defined in JPEG standard, Tang has implemented his proposed methods on 8 × 8 DCT blocks. DCT + Average obtain the DCT representation of the fused image by simply taking the mean (average) of all the DCT coefficients of all the images which we give at the input. This simple and easy method of averaging leads to some undesirable side effects including blurring.

This paper is organized as follows: Sect. 2 explains the basic concepts of DCT domain, Sect. 3 presents our proposed method of image fusion. The simulation results are analyzed in Sect. 4 and finally, the conclusion provides in Sect. 5.

2 DCT in Compression Standards

Variance in DCT Domain as a Contrast Criterion
Two- dimensional DCT transform of an N * N block image x (m, n) is defined as:

$$d(k,l) = 2\alpha(k)\alpha(l) \div N \times \sum_{m=0}^{N=1}\sum_{n=0}^{N-1} x(m,n) \times cos[(2m+1)\pi k \div 2 \div N]$$
$$\times\ cos[(2n+1)\pi k \div 2N] \tag{1}$$

Where k, l = 0, 1, 2 ⋯ N − 1 and

$$\alpha(k) = \{1/\sqrt{2},\ if\ k = 0,\ else\ 1. \tag{2}$$

The inverse DCT (IDCT) is defined as:

$$x(m,n) = \sum_{k=0}^{N-1} \sum_{l=0}^{N-1} 2\alpha(k)\,\alpha(l) \div N \times d(k,l) \times \cos[(2n+1)\pi k]$$

$$\div 2N \times \sum_{m=0}^{N-1} \sum_{n=0}^{N-1} x(m,n) \times \cos[(2m+1)\pi k \div 2N] \tag{3}$$

Where m, n = 0, 1, 2 … N − 1.

d (0, 0) is the DC coefficient and the other d (k, l)'s are the AC coefficients of the block. The normalized transform coefficients d (k, l) are defined as below:

$$d(k,l) = d(k,l) \div N \tag{4}$$

Mean value, μ and variance, σ of an N × N block in the spatial domain are calculated as:

$$\mu = 1 \div N \sum_{m=0}^{N-1} \sum_{n=0}^{N-1} x(m,n) \tag{5}$$

$$\sigma = 1 \div N \sum_{m=0}^{N-1} \sum_{n=0}^{N-1} x(m,n) - \mu. \tag{6}$$

As we know the mean value, μ of the N × N block is given by d (0, 0). With a little mathematical calculation, we can also provide the variance of the block from DCT coefficients. We have:

$$\sum_{m=0}^{N-1} \sum_{n=0}^{N-1} x(m,n) = \sum_{m=0}^{N-1} \sum_{n=0}^{N-1} x(m,n).x(m,n) = \sum_{m=0}^{N-1} \sum_{n=0}^{N-1} x(m,n)$$

$$\times \left(\sum_{m=0}^{N-1} \sum_{n=0}^{N-1} 2\alpha(k)\alpha(l) \div N.d(k,l).\cos[(2m+1)\pi k \div 2N] \right). \tag{7}$$
$$\times \cos[(2n+1)\pi k \div 2N]$$

By interchanging the positions of the summations, we will have:

$$= \sum_{k=0}^{N-1} \sum_{l=0}^{N-1} 2\alpha(k)\,\alpha(l) \div N \times d(k.l) \times \sum_{m=0}^{N-1} \sum_{n=0}^{N-1} x(m,n)$$
$$\times \cos[(2m+1)\pi k \div 2N] \times \cos[(2n+1)\pi k \div 2N] \tag{8}$$

$$= \sum_{k=0}^{N-1} \sum_{l=0}^{N-1} 2\alpha(k)\,\alpha(l) \div N \times d(k,l) \times N \times d(k.l) \div 2\alpha(k)\,\alpha(l) \tag{9}$$

$$= \sum_{k=0}^{N-1} \sum_{l=0}^{N-1} d(k,l).d(k,l) \tag{10}$$

$$\Rightarrow \sum_{m=0}^{N-1} \sum_{n=0}^{N-1} x(m,n) = \sum_{k=0}^{N-1} \sum_{l=0}^{N-1} d(k,l) \tag{11}$$

Then from the above equations:

$$\sigma = 1 \div N \sum_{m=0}^{N-1} \sum_{n=0}^{N-1} x(m,n) - \mu \tag{12}$$

$$\Rightarrow \sigma = \sum_{k=0}^{N-1} \sum_{l=0}^{N-1} d(k,l) \div N - d(0,0) \tag{13}$$

In conclusion, the variance of an N × N block of pixels can be exactly calculated from its DCT.

3 Proposed Method

The proposed method is corresponding to the high variance. Generally, in image processing applications, variance value is presumed as a contrast measure. It was shown in Sect. 2 that the calculation of the variance value in DCT domain is so easy. Hence, we are able to use the variance value as the activity level measure of the 7 × 7 blocks of the source images. The following Fig. 1 represents the proposed method of the paper.

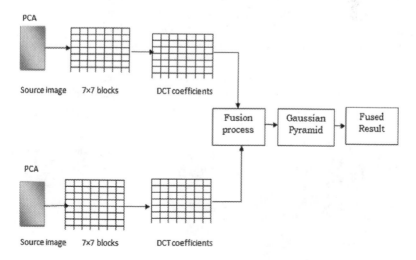

Fig. 1. Proposed fusion method using PCA, DCT and Gaussian pyramid.

The image fusion methods using discrete cosine transform (DCT) are considered to be more suitable and in real-time systems, it makes time-saving also. A methodical method for multi-focus images fusion is proposed. The proposed algorithm will integrate PCA, DCT and Gaussian pyramid to attain the fusion process. Histogram equalization is used on the output image in order to enhance the results.

The overall objective of this paper is to improve the visibility of fused images. Figure 8 depicts the flowchart for proposed algorithm. This proposed algorithm includes the following below steps:

1. Initially two images, which are partially blurred are passed to the system.
2. Apply RGB2PCA to convert given image in PCA plane.
3. For PCA(:,:,1) of Figs. 1 and 2 will be passed for fusion using DCT by considering 7×7 block and PCA(:,:,2) & PCA(:,:,3) of Figs. 1 and 2 will determine new components by taking their averages respectively.
4. Now concatenation of each output of step 3 will be done.
5. Consider the Gaussian pyramid levels in fusion process.

4   Simulation Results

In this section, experimental results of the presented image fusion method are given and evaluated by comparing with the results obtained by four other prominent techniques as shown in Table 1. Initially, the algorithms were performed on five couples of artificially created source images by blurring six standard original images shown in Figs. 2, 3, 4, 5 and 6. The images are balanced in means that the blurring occurs at the left as well as at the right halves of the images. The proposed algorithm has been implemented in MATLAB using image processing toolbox. We have conducted some experiments by taking different partially blurred images by using existing PCA and DCT based fusion and proposed algorithm. It is found that the integrated approach of DCT based fusion with adaptive Gaussian pyramid produce quite better results than existing DCT based fusion. Figures 2, 3, 4, 5 and 6(a) and (b) showing the input images which are partially blurred (left and right). Both images are of the same size and of the same scene and also as per the assumptions they are of the same scene.

Figures 2, 3, 4, 5 and 6(c) clearly shown the output image is fused. It is clearly shown from the figure that the output image is fused as well as there exists no artifact as well as no random noise as both problems are presented in the output image of DCT based fusion.

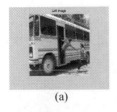  

(a)   (b)   (c)

Fig. 2. (a) Left Blur Image (b) Right Blur Image (c) Fused Image of proposed method.

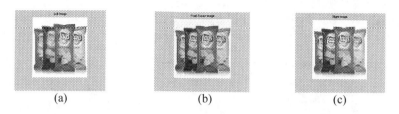

(a)   (b)   (c)

Fig. 3. (a) Left Blur Image (b) Right Blur Image (c) Fused Image of proposed method.

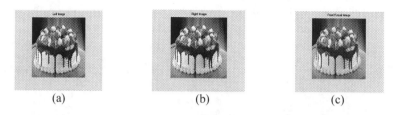

(a)   (b)   (c)

Fig. 4. (a) Left Blur Image (b) Right Blur Image (c) Fused Image of proposed method.

(a)   (b)   (c)

Fig. 5. (a) Left Blur Image (b) Right Blur Image (c) Fused Image of proposed method.

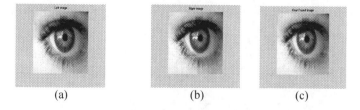

(a)   (b)   (c)

Fig. 6. (a) Left Blur Image (b) Right Blur Image (c) Fused Image of proposed method.

Quality Metrics for the Proposed Method

1. *Mean Squared Error (MSE):* MSE is used to measure the difference between a processed image and reference image. MSE with a size of a (i × j) is expressed as,

$$MSE = \frac{1}{m \times n} \sum_{i=0}^{m-1} \sum_{j=0}^{n-1} (r_{ij} - x_{ij})^2 \tag{14}$$

Where r_{ij} and x_{ij} are the image pixel value of reference image and processed image respectively. m and n are the number of rows and columns in the input images, respectively. The smaller value of the MSE represents the better result.

2. *Peak signal to Noise Ratio (PSNR):* It represents a measure of the peak error. It describes the ratio of the maximum possible power of a signal to the power of corrupting noise and is normally represented in decibel scale. PSNR can be expressed as follows:

$$PSNR = 10 \log_{10} \left(\frac{255^2}{MSE} \right) \tag{15}$$

A higher value of PSNR provides the reconstruction of higher quality.

3. *Maximum Difference (MD):* It provides the maximum of the error signal. MD is defined as follows:

$$MD = Max(|r_{ij} - x_{ij}|) \tag{16}$$

Where, i = 1, 2... ... ..., m, and j = 1, 2 ... ..., . n.
The higher the value of the maximum difference, the poorer the quality of the image.

4. *Normalized Absolute Error (NAE):* It measures the quality of processed image.

$$NAE = \frac{\sum_{i=1}^{m} \sum_{j=1}^{n} (|r_{ij} - x_{ij}|)}{\sum_{i=1}^{m} \sum_{j=1}^{n} (r_{ij})} \tag{17}$$

A higher value of NAE describes that image is of poor quality.

5. *Normalized Cross Correlation (NCC):* It shows the comparison of the processed image and reference image.

$$NCC = \sum_{i=1}^{m} \sum_{j=1}^{n} \frac{x_{ij} \times r_{ij}}{x_{ij}^2} \tag{18}$$

6. *Entropy*: The entropy of a system as defined by Shannon [1, 2] gives a measure of uncertainty about its actual structure and it is calculated as,

$$H = -\sum_{i=1}^{n} p_i \times \log_2 p_i \qquad (19)$$

Where, H is Entropy of an image
P_i is the probability of the occurrence of symbol i (Figs. 7, 9, 10, 11, 12 and 13).

7. *Gradient*: An image gradient is a measure of directional change in the intensity of an image. To get the full range of direction, gradient images in the x and y directions are computed as,

$$\nabla f = \left(\frac{df}{dx}, \frac{df}{dr} \right) \qquad (20)$$

Table 1. Quantitative comparison results for the image i.e. Couple with bus (outdoor).

	PSNR	MSE	MD	NAE	Correlation	Entropy	Gradient
Wavelet transformation [21]	45.67	3.54	34	0.005	75.12	3.5	4.68
Sparse representation (SRF) [22]	46.68	3.41	30	0.004	78.45	4.56	5.64
Cross bi-lateral filtering (CBF) [23]	51.64	2.84	28	0.002	79.36	4.89	5.72
Image matting (IFM) [24]	52.34	2.56	24	0.002	80.13	5.62	5.73
Proposed GP-DCT	60.35	1.32	21	0.002	81.45	5.97	6.01

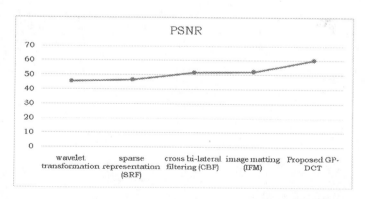

Fig. 7. PSNR comparison graph of proposed and existing methods.

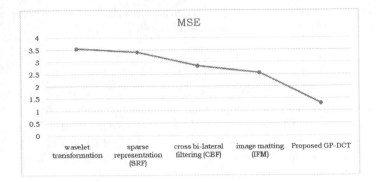

Fig. 8. MSE comparison graph of proposed and existing methods.

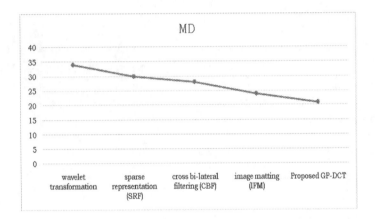

Fig. 9. MD comparison graph of proposed and existing methods.

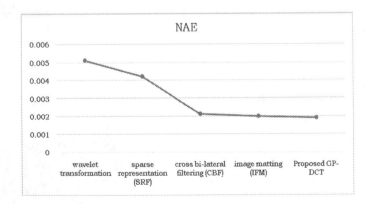

Fig. 10. NAE comparison graph of proposed and existing methods.

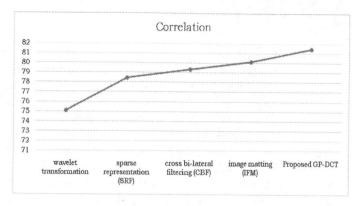

Fig. 11. Correlation comparison graph of proposed and existing methods.

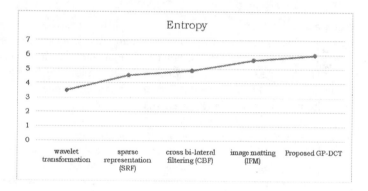

Fig. 12. Entropy comparison graph of proposed and existing methods.

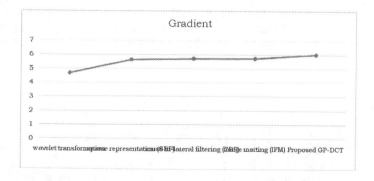

Fig. 13. Gradient comparison graph of proposed and existing methods.

5   Conclusion

In this paper, a new DCT based fusion technique for multi-focus images was proposed. The method is proposed based on definition of the variance in discrete cosine transform domain. The proposed method leads to it appropriate for real-time applications. Furthermore, in the proposed algorithm, utilization of variance as an appropriate contrast measure in multi-focus images which leads to better quality in the fused image. Numerous experiments on evaluating the fusion performance were conducted and the results depicts that the proposed method give better performance when compared to the previous DCT based methods regarding both in complexity reduction as well as in quality. Moreover, it is more efficient than the other methods when the fused image is saved or transmitted in JPEG format or the source images are in JPEG format, particularly in visual sensor networks. A shortcoming of our method without consistency. The process of combining two or more images information into a single image but which can retain all important features of the all original images is termed as Image fusion. It is found that DCT based image fusion give results with less PSNR value, lesser clarity and also with more Mean square error (MSR). It is found that most of researchers have neglected image filtering and restoration and it must need the image fusion. Hence to give better results than the older techniques, the given proposed work incorporate the adaptive histogram equalization with DCT based technique. This is clear from the various experimental results. The integrated techniques have successfully reduced the limitations of the DCT based fusion technique.

Acknowledgments. Dr. B. Sujatha received the Doctorate degree from JNT University, Kakinada in 1997 and received her M. Tech. (Computer Science & Engineering) from Andhra University in 2002. She is having 10 years of teaching experience. Presently she is working as an Assoc. Professor in GIET, Rajahmundary. She has published 1 research publications in Inter National Journal. She is a member of SRRF-GIET, Rajahmundry. She is pursuing her Ph.D from Mysore University in Computer Science under the guidance of Dr. V. Vijaya Kumar. Her research interest includes Image Processing and Pattern Recognition. She is a Life member of ISCA.

B. Vanajakshi received the Doctorate degree from JNTUH, Hyderabad Presently she is working as Professor in SRK Institute of Technology, Vijayawada. She has published more than 20 research publications in various National, Inter National conferences, proceedings and Journals. She is a Life member of IETE.

References

1. Manjunath, L., Mitra, S.K.: Multisensor image fusion using wavelet transform. Graph. Models Image Process 57(3), 235–245 (1995)
2. Naidu, V.P.S., Raol, J.R.: Pixel-level image fusion using wavelets and principal component analysis – a comparative analysis. Defence Sci. J. **58**(3), 338–352 (2008)
3. Blum, R.S.: Robust image fusion using a statistical signal processing approaches. Image Fusion **6**, 119–128 (2005)
4. Naidu, V.P.S.: Discrete cosine transform-based image fusion, special issue on mobile intelligent autonomous system. Defence Sci. J. **60**(1), 48–54 (2010)

5. Toet, L., Van Ruyven, J., Valeton, J.M.: Merging thermal and visual images by a contrast pyramid. Opt. Eng. **28**(7), 789–792 (1989)
6. Perez, O., Patricio, M.A., Garcia, J., Carbo, J., Molina, J.M.: Fusion of surveillance information for visual sensor networks. In: Proceedings of the IEEE Ninth International Conference on Information Fusion (ICIF), pp. 1–8
7. Garcia, F.J., Patricio, M.A., Molina, J.M.: Analysis of distributed fusion alternatives in coordinated vision agents. In: Proceedings of the IEEE Eleventh International Conference on Information Fusion (ICIF), pp. 1–6
8. Drajic, D., Cvejic, N.: Adaptive fusion of multimodal surveillance image sequences in visual sensor networks. IEEE Trans. Consum. Electron. **53**(4), 1456–1462 (2007)
9. Lewis, J.J., O'Callaghan, R.J., Nikolov, S.G., Bull, D.R., Canagarajah, N.: Pixel- and region-based image fusion with complex wavelets. Inf. Fusion **8**(2), 119–130 (2007)
10. Li, S., Yang, B.: Multifocus image fusion using region segmentation and spatial frequency. Image Vis. Comput. **26**(7), 971–979 (2008)
11. Xu, L., Roux, M., Mingyi, H., Schmitt, F.: A new method of image fusion based on redundant wavelet transforms. In: Proceedings of the IEEE Fifth International Conference on Visual Information Engineering, pp. 12–17
12. Zaveri, T., Zaveri, M., Shah, V., Patel, N.: A novel region based multi focus image fusion method. In: Proceedings of IEEE International Conference on Digital Image Processing (ICDIP), pp. 50–54
13. Arif, M.H., Shah, S.S.: Block level multi-focus image fusion using wavelet transform. In: Proceedings of IEEE International Conference on Signal Acquisition and Processing (ICSAP), pp. 213–216
14. Li, H., Manjunath, B., Mitra, S.: Multisensor image fusion using the wavelet transform. Graph. Models Image Process. **57**(3), 235–245 (1995)
15. Rockinger, O.: Image sequence fusion using a shift-invariant wavelet transforms. In: Proceedings of IEEE International Conference on Image Processing, vol. 3, pp. 288–291
16. Blum, R.S., Liu, Z.: Multi-sensor Image Fusion and Its Applications. CRC Press/Taylor & Francis Group, Boca Raton (2006)
17. Goshtasby, A., Nikolov, S.: Image fusion: advances in the state of the art. Inf. Fusion **8**(2), 114–118 (2007)
18. Aizawa, K., Kodama, K., Kubota, A.: Producing objected-based special effects by fusing multiple differently focused images. IEEE Trans. Circ. Syst. Video Technol. **10**(2), 323–330 (2000)
19. Hill, D., Edwards, P., Hawkes, D.: Fusing medical images. Image Process. **6**(2), 22–24 (1994)
20. Li, H., Manjunath, B.S., Mitra, S.K.: Multisensor image fusion using the wavelet transformation. Graph. Models: Image Process. **57**, 235–245 (1995)
21. Shirai, K., Nomura, K., Ikehara, M.: All-in-focus photo image creation by wavelet transforms. Electron. Commun. Jpn. (Part III: Fund. Electron. Sci.) **90**(3), 57–66 (2007)
22. Yang, B., Li, S.: Multifocus image fusion and restoration with sparse representation. IEEE Trans. Instrum. Meas. **59**(4), 884–892 (2010)
23. Kumar, B.S.: Image fusion based on pixel significance using cross bilateral filter. Sign. Image Video Process. **9**, 1–12 (2013)
24. Li, S., Kang, X., Hu, J., Yang, B.: Image matting for fusion of multi-focus images in dynamic scenes. Inf. Fusion **14**(2), 147–162 (2013)

Author Index

Printed in the United States
By Bookmasters